Therapeutic Psychology

Psychology

Fundamentals of Counseling and Psychotherapy

Lawrence M. Brammer, Ph. D.

Associate Dean of Students and Associate Professor of Psychology, Sacramento State College; Diplomate in Counseling, American Board of Examiners in Professional Psychology

Therapeutic

Fundamentals of

Englewood Cliffs, N. J.

Everett L. Shostrom, Ph. D.

Clinical Psychologist, Affiliated Psychological Consultants, Downey and Newport Beach, California; Training Staff, Institute of Industrial Relations, University of California at Los Angeles

Psychology

Counseling and Psychotherapy

PRENTICE-HALL, INC.

PRENTICE-HALL PSYCHOLOGY SERIES
Paul E. Meehl, Editor

THERAPEUTIC PSYCHOLOGY:
FUNDAMENTALS OF COUNSELING AND
PSYCHOTHERAPY

Lawrence M. Brammer and Everett L. Shostrom

Library of Congress Catalog Card No.: 60–12703

First printing .... June, 1960
Second printing .... July, 1961
Third printing .... January, 1963
Fourth printing .... January, 1964

Printed in the United States of America
91465–C

To our children,
Connie, Karin, Kristen, Dean and Dale
who taught us so much about people.

Preface

This book is based upon the assumption that the ultimate goals of scientific psychotherapy are human betterment, fulfillment, and happiness. This condition of psychological maturity and health can be reached largely through the *proper use* of the psychological process of counseling and psychotherapy. The great social need for counseling and psychotherapy makes it necessary for the counselor to avail himself of all the techniques and knowledge currently available in order to help the many neurotic and marginally adjusted individuals, who could profit from even a brief period of counseling and psychotherapy. We feel that counseling and psychotherapy are often practiced too soon by the counselor without enough understanding either of the fundamentals, historical or practical, or the special adaptations necessary for counseling different types of clients.

Therapeutic psychology is an endeavor to delineate the fundamentals necessary for the achievement of therapeutic growth as envisioned by specialists in both counseling and psychotherapy. Therapeutic psychology has solid roots in the empirical sciences and is now supplementing this history with constructs developed through clinical experience. In this book, much attention is given to the problems of "normal" "neurotic" or "borderline" individuals, because little has been written on the problems of such people compared to the vast literature on pathological behavior.

This book describes the methods of personal counseling and clinical psychology. It includes excerpts from case histories which illustrate how techniques, developed from a study of nonpathological clients, facilitate the therapeutic process. We feel that current techniques present intriguing challenges for further validation research. Furthermore, our many positive assertions are to be construed only as hypotheses in various stages of being tested. Until these hypotheses have been tested, trust must be placed in the "creative insight" of the counselor in that he sees human events in relationship.

This book is written for the upper division and graduate student who wants a thorough introduction to the field of counseling and psychotherapy. It is written also for the practitioner, whether he be a clinical psychologist, counseling psychologist, school counselor, psychiatrist, social worker, industrial counselor, pastoral counselor, marriage counselor, or any specialist who feels a need for re-examining the fundamental processes of helping human beings grow to maturity.

We are indebted to many individuals for ideas derived from their conversations and writings. Some material has become so much a part of the common domain that it hardly needs citation. We have been as careful as possible, however, to document statements and research conclusions from the many articles and books surveyed. Naturally, all research reports in a field cannot be used; and due to oversight some important work may have been excluded. Since we have leaned heavily on the published and unpublished research of leaders at such universities as Ohio State, Columbia, Oregon, Michigan, Minnesota, UCLA, Missouri, Stanford, and Chicago, we wish to acknowledge our special indebtedness to them.

Our colleagues in the Affiliated Psychological Consultants have helped us with various aspects of the book. Long association with Dr. Richard Hogan stimulated ideas which are incorporated in this volume. We are grateful for Dr. David Eitzen's valuable ideas for Chapter 15 and for Dr. Maurice Riseling's helpful criticisms of the whole book.

We wish to express our appreciation to Dr. Thomas Gordon for his material and advice for the Chapter entitled "Human Relations Counseling in Industry and Government." Particular appreciation is expressed to Mrs. Lucille Colby, Dr. Theodore Newcomb, and Dr. James Bugental for complete readings of the manuscript and for their many fruitful suggestions. Special thanks are given also to Mrs. Edna K. Upton and Mrs. Roberta Lovell for their contributions to the chapters on children and marriage. Our typists, Mrs. Betty McGregor, Mrs. Phyllis Munson, and Miss Nancy Wolters, deserve much credit for the final appearance of this book. To the many other individuals, organizations, and publishers who made this work possible, we offer our most sincere thanks.

LAWRENCE M. BRAMMER
EVERETT L. SHOSTROM

Contents

PART I.   FOUNDATIONS

PART II.   TECHNIQUES

PART III. SPECIAL AREAS OF APPLICATION

Introduction

According to Webster, an "eclectic" is one who selects what is thought best from various doctrines or systems. Taken literally, this definition would seem to place the eclectic in a rather favorable light, assuming that a composite of what is best from many sources might reasonably be expected to turn out well. One has the distinct impression, however, that within the field of contemporary counseling and psychotherapy, eclecticism has somewhat unfavorable connotations. Most of us, if we hear a psychotherapist described as being eclectic, tend immediately to think of someone who has not been trained to do anything particularly well, and whose cognitive activity with respect to the technology he practices is either muddled or nonexistent. The authors point out that this (usually meant) type of eclecticism is a "transitional stop-gap approach to meet current practical problems until theory is further developed." One suspects that there is a considerably larger number of eclectics engaged today in the professional activity of helping troubled individuals with their problems than would willingly so describe themselves. It is a truly remarkable social phenomenon, which the scientific psychotherapy of future years will, no doubt, look back upon with amazement, that practitioners who have been thoroughly trained either in the biological or the social sciences in preparing themselves for the psychological-helping function, nevertheless find themselves strongly impelled to identify with the "party line" of a particular therapeutic club. In his recent *Psychoanalysis and Psychotherapy* (Englewood Cliffs, N.J.: Prentice-Hall, Inc., 1959), Dr. Robert A. Harper found it no strain at all to marshal a list of thirty-six distinguishable orientations or systems! Dr. Albert Ellis, in a monograph published in 1956, came up with a sizeable list of contradictory statements regarding theoretical and technical problems in therapy simply by collating what reputable therapists of different persuasions had to say about their clinical experience. In a recent questionnaire study (as yet unpublished) of the "tactical" views held by 168 medical and nonmedical therapists of several persuasions, I was unable to find a single item among 132 which elicited unanimity. It is a refreshing experience to read the comments made by leading proponents of several orientations on the dynamics and handling of concrete episodes, presented in Standal and Corsini, *Critical Incidents in Psychotherapy* (Englewood Cliffs, N.J.: Prentice-Hall, Inc., 1959). From observations of the kinds cited, it is evident that the combination of academic training and experience as a psychological helper does not guarantee that a professional person will decide in favor of any particular one of the existing schools, nor opt for a specific therapeutic attitude, aim, or tactic.

This situation leaves those of us who are responsible for the education of psychotherapists in an uncomfortable pedagogical situation. What shall we teach our students? Some have held that, both from the cognitive and motivational points of view, it is better for the fledgling therapist to identify with and think in terms of *some* fairly close-knit system of concepts and principles, even if it is not the best one and, at best, is one which must be presumed to involve an unknown proportion of error. Personally, after several years of supervising trainees in psychotherapy, I am rather inclined to agree with this method, although it makes the "scientific psychologist" in me quite nervous at times. Another approach is to see that students are exposed to a diversity of orientations, both didactically and in supervision, hoping, presumably, that the best students will achieve some kind of "higher synthesis," and the others will pick the one that appeals the most to them individually. A third approach represents eclecticism in what I would consider the respectable sense. Although we recognize that any "system" either of personality theory or of the therapeutic technology deriving therefrom will, in the present state of knowledge, necessarily be characterized by vagueness, sketchiness, and incompleteness, but that there is a significant difference between an incomplete sketch and a random assortment of scribbles, the true eclectic ventures boldly forth in an attempt to approach the ideal specified by Webster. He recognizes that the axiomatic tightness of any of the available systems is very feeble, so that it is easy, without generating internal contradictions, to modify the basic principles of a system or to drop some of them entirely. The selection might conceivably be carried out solely on the basis of accumulated clinical experience, utilizing the same kind of "evidence" that the various systematists present in defense of their own orientations. But a more powerful procedure might be, after scanning the available offerings in the light of such clinical experience, to ask whether suitable reformulations of principles from various systems can bring about a more satisfactory conceptual unification and, thereby, a theoretical underpinning for the diverse collection of tactical generalizations which are available and tentatively admitted to the therapeutic armamentarium by the eclectic.

I think that the authors of this book have produced a notable achievement in striving for this latter type of eclecticism. No fair-minded reader will say that they have created yet *another* "system" to add to the already excessive list. They have approached the problem of counseling and psychotherapy with a rare combination: they have genuinely entered into the frame of reference of this or that school when trying to understand and explain the strategy and tactics associated with it, and they have been fair-minded in shifting from one to another. They operate within the framework of a conceptualization of human personality and its development (Chapters 2, 3) and of the therapeutic interaction (Chapter 4) which is sufficiently broad (without being empty!) to be capable of assimilating a diversity of technical emphases. The student who is beginning to learn about the counseling process will have available, after study of this book, a set of concepts which he can use directly in thinking about his clients. Except, perhaps, for the most doctrinaire, those who are strongly identified with a particular position will find it possible to agree with much of what is said about technical maneuvers and will, I should think, find that much of the theory is also assimilable to their preferred frame of reference with only slight changes.

The distinction between "counseling" and "psychotherapy," if there is one, presents a knotty problem for our profession. Approximately one-half of APA-approved graduate programs make no curricular distinction between their clinical and counseling candidates. Protocols submitted by counseling and clinical candidates for the ABEPP diploma are remarkably similar, at least in the editor's experience as a board member. Whatever may be the final educational and administrative resolution of the various puzzles involved, the authors—one a "clinical" and the other a "counseling" psychologist—have made a careful, fair attempt to treat the problem in terms of a continuum involving several components (Chapter 1); throughout the book this continuum is kept in mind as the more specific situations and the procedures for handling them are considered.

One of the commonest complaints of fledgling therapists about books, articles, and lectures on the therapeutic process is their relative lack of "concreteness." The student dutifully may have acquired a set of general principles about personality and about treatment, but he has the feeling of not being told enough about what specifically he should *listen for,* when he *should talk* or *be silent,* what he *should say,* and *how* he should say it. Part of this is unrealistic expectation and dependent behavior, to be sure, and it must be combated in one way or another by the supervisor. In addition, I have the impression that a great deal more is believed by therapists (I almost said "known") than usually finds its way into beginning textbooks. The authors have done an excellent job of spelling out many such concrete matters. For example, psychotherapists constantly are warned to "be alert to signs of your own countertransference feelings," and perhaps two or three examples are given by a writer or lecturer of what such signs look like. It seems unfortunate that therapists should spend many years of their professional activity painfully engaged in building up a list of signs when they are, after all, not terribly difficult to spell out in some detail. Drs. Brammer and Shostrom, in Chapter 8 on "Special Relationship Problems," list nineteen concrete indicators which should alert the counselor to the possibility that he is responding on a countertransference basis. Most therapists will experience immediate feelings of familiarity with all or nearly all the items on this list; but I suspect that very few teachers or supervisors of therapy have ever bothered to collect them in one place or to present them systematically so that the beginning student might be saved months or years of making mistakes because he was never alerted properly to one of these simple indicators.

Because of the authors' excellent integrative efforts, their frequent reliance upon concrete examples of therapist and client remarks in illustrating a principle, and their masterful interweaving of published research with their personal clinical experience, this book is suitable for use both by the beginner and the experienced counselor or therapist. It would be admirably suited for use as the staple text in a first course in counseling or therapy; yet a seasoned worker can also study it with profit.

The third part of the book, on special areas of application, makes available to the beginning or intermediate student material on problems and techniques for which he would ordinarily have to rely upon the lecturer or upon supplementary reading. It was particularly gratifying to me to read the final chapter on problems of values, in which the authors present a forthright treatment of a topic which is cropping up with ever greater insistence in our field but about which many counselors and psychotherapists appear to feel very skittish. With the increased dissemination of psychological knowledge and the heightened awareness of the availability of professional helpers which has taken place in our culture, practitioners of all forms of psychotherapy have become aware of a shift over the years in the composition of their clientele. Recently, a New York analyst who has been in practice since the early 1920's was quoted to me as having said, "In the old days we used to analyze sick people; now we analyze people who are merely unhappy." It is too early to say what will be the impact of this change upon theory and technique. But, whatever course the profession may take in response to this sociological development, it would seem that *one* necessary prerequisite must be the explicit recognition that our clients do, at times, suffer psychologically from the consequences of what have been variously described as "attitudinal pathoses" (Thorne), "postulates" (Ellis), and the like. It is becoming increasingly difficult to shunt these aside as problems to be referred, for example, to the client's pastor or rabbi (especially when he doesn't have one!), or to construe them in every instance as derivatives whose "real origin" is of a totally different character than would be suggested by their manifest content. The authors are to be commended for their inclusion of a sophisticated and fair-minded discussion of this question.

I think that this is an excellent book, and that it can well be put into the hands of students in counseling and clinical psychology with the expectation that their study of it will leave them informed about what is available today to practitioners of the art of psychological helping. The perspective gained will, I should think, be broad without being superficial, and the student should be able either to grow upon this foundation into a primary identification with one of the orientations included or, if he has the personality for it, to mature with experience into an eclectic in the best sense of that word.

PAUL E. MEEHL

Therapeutic Psychology

Psychology

Fundamentals of Counseling and Psychotherapy

I.

Foundations

I.

Professional Counseling and Psychotherapy

INTRODUCTION

As the fields of counseling and psychotherapy become of age, it is apparent that professional competence requires more than knowledge of pat techniques. The counselor may be highly skilled, but lack the broad understandings and professional sophistication which come from thorough background knowledge. In this book, we shall try to cover both of these vital areas of professional development. In addition to describing the fundamental techniques of counseling and psychotherapy, this volume presents significant historical foundations, personality theory, and special adaptations necessary for the practice of counseling and psychotherapy in various settings: schools, colleges, agencies, churches, industries, and clinical practice.

This chapter covers the origins of the counseling and psychotherapeutic emphases in psychology, the present status and trends, and some pressing professional problems.

Since counselors and psychotherapists are concerned with facilitating personality changes in their clients, an introductory discussion of the significance of theory, varied approaches, and brief descriptions of views on the nature and functioning of personality are included in Chapter 2. Principles of personality growth with the special problems of each stage from birth to old age are discussed in Chapter 3, whereas an overview of the nature of the counseling and psychotherapeutic processes is presented in Chapter 4.

The principal purposes of Part I are to promote broad understandings of the practitioner's professional problems and to prepare the reader with personality theory and concepts about the development of the human personality for the technique discussions in Parts II and III.

Part II includes the "how to do it" aspect of counseling and psychotherapy. Beginning with Chapter 5 on preparing the client for his counseling experience, the important points of the technique description are made in Chapters 6 through 8, which are concerned with the nature of the counseling relationship, how it is established and maintained, and which factors create problems for the counselor. In Chapters 9 through 11, important techniques of interpretation, appraisal, information-giving, and group methods are described and illustrated. A basic assumption underlying Part II is that psychotherapeutic attitudes and techniques are learned, not endowed. Hence, with conscientious study and assiduous practice and evaluation, effective counseling methods can be acquired.

It is anticipated that the reader, whatever his professional setting, may be able to choose from the techniques which follow those which have particular application to his specialty and institutional role.

Part III covers applications of the foregoing techniques to human problems concerned with marriage, family life, philosophy and religion, intellectual functioning, educational and vocational choice, discipline and industrial management. The purpose of this part is to present some of the problems and methods in each area, unique materials needed, and the adaptations of general theory and technique which are required. An additional purpose is to acquaint the student with the multitudinous applications of applied psychology to intimate human problems.

The overview of this volume will help the reader to understand the title of the book, *Therapeutic Psychology*. Much material has been included which is not technique, but rather knowledge which is considered to be necessary to the professional background of the counselor or psychotherapist. Although we do not assume that this material represents *all* that should be known for competence in this field, we hope that the student in training and the practitioner already at work will find this volume a useful attempt to define more precisely what is needed for counseling skill.

THERAPEUTIC PSYCHOLOGY

Therapeutic Psychology represents a body of knowledge which gathers its data from a number of related professions all of which embody the "helping function." In psychology, the clinical psychology specialty, with its traditional emphasis on diagnostic evaluation, is concentrating now on psychotherapy and counseling. Counseling psychology is another aspect of psychology which incorporates traditional counseling and newer clinical emphases. School psychology is a third division of the broad field of psychology where counseling and psychotherapy are beginning to be utilized. Psychiatry, of course, has contributed in great measure to the concepts and techniques currently employed in the helping process. The field of social work also gave us a rich heritage of counseling and interviewing skills. Pastoral counseling by clergymen is one of the professional areas which incorporates much of therapeutic psychology. Industrial employee counseling is a growing field which also applies counseling and psychotherapy methods.

The present trend toward the establishment of a formal discipline of therapeutic psychology is a natural phenomenon. Psychology has for many years collaborated with other professions in contributing its unique approaches to understanding human behavior. In order to succeed in counseling and psychotherapeutic efforts, it seems necessary that psychologists recognize and utilize the understandings of all the established helping professions in addition to capitalizing on the unique findings of their own science. Figure 1 illustrates the interrelationship among disciplines which contribute to and utilize the material in this volume.

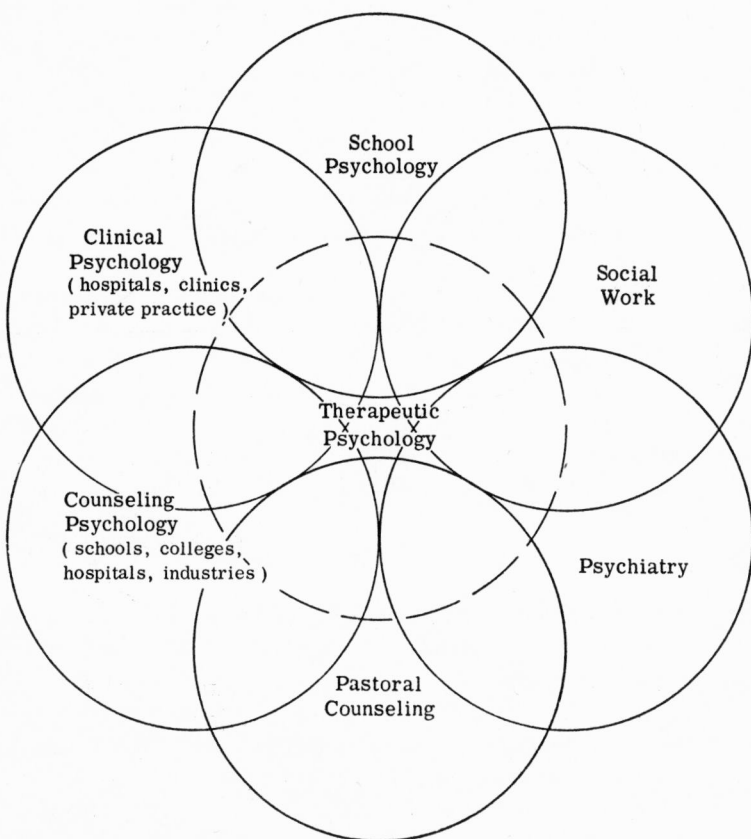

FIG. 1. Relationship of Therapeutic Psychology to Selected Helping Professions.

Therapeutic psychology embraces both counseling and psychotherapy. Before this chapter is complete it is necessary to comment on differences concerning these forms of helping people.

The writers of this book are a counseling psychologist in a college setting and a clinical psychologist in a private-practice setting. Here we bring together viewpoints which embrace our respective areas of experience to create a body of knowledge which overlaps and contributes to both counseling and psychotherapy. The result, which is entitled *Therapeutic Psychology,* may be defined as that body of understandings, appreciations, and skills common to both processes of counseling and psychotherapy.

In Figure 1a the scope of therapeutic psychology is illustrated. Coun-

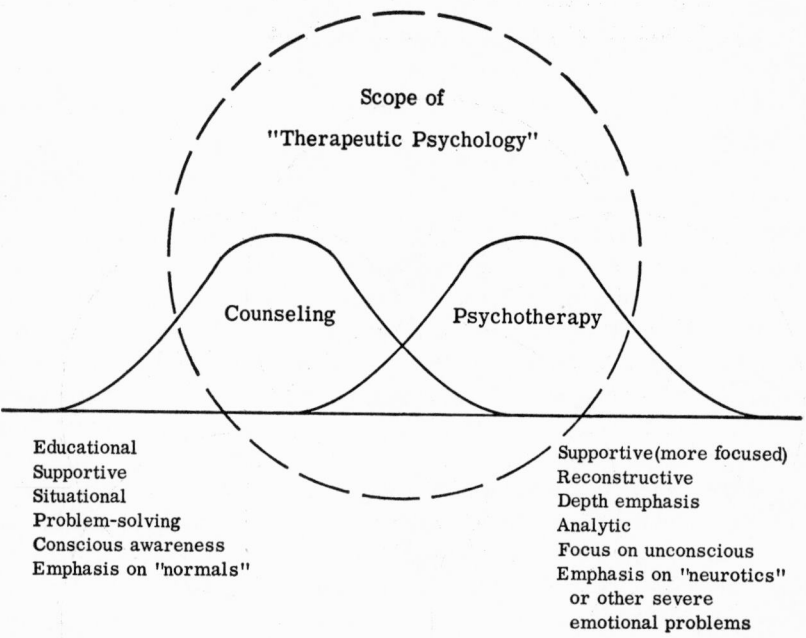

Fig. 1A. The Scope of Counseling and Psychotherapy Within the Framework of Therapeutic Psychology.

seling and psychotherapy are viewed as overlapping areas of professional competence. Counseling is characterized by the following words: educational, supportive, situational, problem-solving, conscious awareness, emphasis on "normals," and short term. Psychotherapy is characterized by: supportive (in a more particular sense), reconstructive, depth emphasis, analytical, focus on the unconscious, emphasis on "neurotics" or other severe emotional problems, and long term.

We believe that one could hardly quarrel with the two lists in Figure 1a which characterize the ends of the counseling-psychotherapeutic continuum. The principal exception might be the fact that a sizeable amount of time is currently spent in essentially supportive treatment of ambulatory schizo-phrenics on an out-patient basis. Many therapists in Veterans Adminis-tration Clinics, for example, would call this psychotherapy; but they would also emphasize its supportive rather than personality-changing features. Most people probably would not call this type of activity counseling, how-ever.

The study of therapeutic psychology, then, has three broad purposes: (1) to create an appreciation of the scope and magnitude of the learnings necessary for competency as a skilled counselor and psychotherapist; (2) to develop an understanding of the fundamental knowledge which must be studied in detail before techniques of counseling or psychotherapy can be utilized; and (3) to assist in developing an appreciation of the refinements of technique necessary for the various specialties which have arisen within both of these fields.

Blos (36) and Pepinsky (228) state that counseling deals with relatively nonimbedded problem cases, that is, with those persons who have not developed rigid neurotic patterns, but who are primarily victims of pres-sures from the outside environment. Thorne (298), however, who is both a psychologist and a psychiatrist, describes counseling as a type of psycho-therapy adaptable to problems of normal people. Robinson (243) con-tributed a useful concept to the definition of counseling which he describes as aiding normal people to achieve higher level adjustment skills which manifest themselves as increased maturity, independence, personal inte-gration, and responsibility.

Although attempts to formulate precise inclusive definitions of *counseling* have been difficult, Gustad (133) marshalled the published definitions into three categories: *participants,* generally two in number and with specified professional roles or affiliations, such as teachers, ministers, or psycholo-gists; *goals,* in terms of improved adjustment, higher functioning, and greater happiness; definitions stressing the *learning* emphases in counseling.

Gustad, from his survey, suggests a composite definition of *counseling* which includes three key elements:

> Counseling is a learning-oriented process, carried on in a simple, one-to-one social environment, in which a counselor, professionally competent in rele-vant psychological skills and knowledge, seeks to assist the client by meth-ods appropriate to the latter's needs and within the context of the total personnel program, to learn more about himself, to learn how to put such understanding into effect in relation to more clearly perceived, realistically defined goals to the end that the client may become a happier and more productive member of his society (133, pg. 17).

Psychotherapy, in contrast, is defined as a more inclusive re-education of the individual at both the conscious and unconscious levels. The basic aims of psychotherapy are to assist the client to gain perceptual reorganization, to integrate the consequent insights into his personality structure, and to work out methods of handling feelings originating deep within his personality. His existing defenses are usually modified to such a degree that readjustment is obtained. Thus, psychotherapy emphasizes *depth* of involvement in the personality and is more concerned with alleviating pathological conditions, whereas counseling is not so deep. Counseling also stresses more rational planning, problem-solving, and support for situational pressures arising in the everyday lives of normal people. Counseling, consequently, is shorter in duration than psychotherapy. Therapeutic psychology has a broad connotation, blending on the one hand with educational or teaching functions, and on the other hand with intensive psychotherapy.

To many clinicians the distinctions between psychotherapy and counseling appear to be primarily quantitative rather than qualitative in nature. We have chosen for purposes of this book to use the terms counselor, psychotherapist, clinician, psychological counselor, psychotherapeutic counselor, and psychologist interchangeably in the broad areas of overlap. Yet, we recognize that there are some differences in usage of the terms. Wherever possible distinctions will be made throughout this book in those areas which are judged to be primarily the concern of either counseling or psychotherapy.

Another approach to differentiating forms of therapeutic help and distinguishing medical from psychological responsibilities is illustrated in Figure 2. This figure shows the great overlap that exists between psychology and psychiatry, as well as some of the unique functions of medical therapists on the extreme left and of psychologists and counselors on the extreme right. The re-educative or psychotherapeutic functions shared by both groups are listed in the middle with factors to be considered in determining responsibility for psychotherapy.

There are psychiatrists who claim that all psychotherapy is medicine and would crowd counselors and clinical psychologists to the extreme right of Figure 2. Some psychologists and educators would do the same for physicians. We feel there are logical and practical reasons for sharing psychotherapy responsibility. The answer, in our opinion, lies in making carefully defined distinctions around the middle transitional area of Figure 2. The criteria of depth, training, experience, responsibility, and institutional setting should determine who does psychotherapy and in what degree.

This introductory chapter deals with six trends leading to the professionalization of therapeutic psychology: (1) Insistence on responsible service; (2) Professionalization along many dimensions; (3) Concentration on the personal relationship between the client and counselor rather than on problems or techniques; (4) Use of data and research methods in the solution of human problems; (5) The emergence of unifying constructs to reconcile conflicting viewpoints and to explain the process of change in the client; (6) Broadening goals and applications of counseling.

Psychiatry and Neurology (Medicine)		Counseling-Clinical (Psychology)
Treatment of Severe Neuroses or Psychoses, involving, for example	Psychotherapy or Re-education	Planning and Problem Solution, involving, for example
Psychosurgery Electro-shock Narcosynthesis Tranquilizers Sedatives Hormones Insulin shock Vitamins	(Criteria applied to determine the locus of responsibility in a medical or psychological therapist) Therapist Factors: Amount of training in psycho- therapy Experience in psychotherapy Diagnostic skill and know- ledge of psychotherapy Amount of therapeutic respon- sibility delegated by the institution Type of institutional setting (hospital or school) Legal restrictions Patient or Client Factors: Depth of involvement in the personality Rigidity of defense structure Strength of the ego and other personality resources Somatic involvement Incapacitating nature of the symptoms Nature of the therapeutic goal	Diagnostic and predictive psychological tests Informational resources Interpretation of data Learning Difficulties involving: Remedial techniques Diagnostic psychological tests Feeling Problems, including: Working through situational anxiety, hostility, ambivalence, and their nonincapacitating, non- imbedded symptoms Case studies and descrip- tions of personality functioning through use of psychometric tests

FIG. 2. Therapy Continuum Between Medicine and Psychology.

TREND I: A DISCRETE AND RESPONSIBLE SERVICE

Therapeutic psychology has its roots in the many disciplines mentioned in the introduction. The following historical sketch covers the development of therapeutic psychology as a responsible service and illustrates how each field is related to therapeutic psychology.

Counseling Psychology

Counseling psychology is a synthesis of the many related trends found in the guidance, mental hygiene, psychometrics, social casework, and psycho-therapy movements. A counseling psychologist assumes that it is *people* who need help through counseling—not problems. The fractionation of the personality into vocational, marital, reading, or other problems needing solution is largely a phenomenon of past, narrow interests, although the counselor recognizes that human difficulties tend to focus in specific problem areas.

Counseling psychology is just beyond the point in its history which was comparable to the position of medicine at the turn of the century. Sir

William Osler, at that time, took the medical "tower of Babel" and formulated an eclectic system of scientific medical practice from the many diffuse and conflicting therapies.

Counseling Psychologists and Psychological Counselors

"Counseling psychologist" has been incorporated in occupational titles (Super 298) which the Veterans Administration, for example, uses (Moore and Bouthilet, 211). Many private and collegiate counseling centers, having psychologically trained counselors at a professional level on their staffs, are beginning to call them "counseling psychologists."

Other occupational designations for counselors have been made. It is quite apparent that the term "counselor" must be preceded by an adjective to be meaningful, since so many persons with differing skill levels claim to do "counseling." Other terms have been suggested to describe the psychological counseling function—general clinical counselor (Hahn 136), psychological counselor (Bordin 40, Tyler 306), and psychotherapeutic counselor (Porter 237).

Largely as a result of a conference of psychologists at Northwestern University in 1951, the American Psychological Association has changed the designation of Division 17 from Counseling and Guidance to Counseling Psychology in recognition of the growing discreteness of the counseling branch of psychology (Super 298). Similarly, the American Board of Examiners in Professional Psychology conducts certification proceedings for counseling psychologists as one of its three areas. Hence, a growing body of terminology underwrites further the contention that counseling psychology is a full professional endeavor.

Clinical Psychology

Clinical psychology grew largely out of intelligence testing efforts during the period from 1912 to 1930. Clinical psychology and counseling psychology have much in common, since both use case study methods, evaluation instruments, and psychotherapeutic interviewing techniques. There are, nevertheless, significant historical and functional distinctions. After studying differentiations between counseling and clinical psychology at length, Gustad (132) concluded that counseling and clinical psychology are essentially the same general endeavor, but that they have differing emphases. This is substantially the same conclusion reached by Watson:

> The characteristic educational setting and the fact that counseling psychologists work primarily with normal people probably are the chief lines of demarcation, not training or breadth of responsibilities . . . Counseling psychologists and clinical psychologists are *not* engaged in a struggle of opposing camps, but rather, are seriously, and without undue heat, attempting to work through their intra-professional problems to a mutually satisfactory solution (314, pp. 9–10).

The clinical psychologist's skill in assisting with diagnostic evaluation of the mentally ill and his consequent unique role of a clinical or hospital team is another major distinction. As Super (298) has pointed out, counseling is more concerned with the "hygiology" than the "psychopathology" of behavior. Hygiology is the study of problems in normal people and the prevention of serious emotional difficulties. Clinical psychologists, on the other hand, are often found in hospitals and clinics where pathological behavior is treated.

Institutional settings for counseling or therapy determine other distinctions between counselors and clinicians. As Williamson (319) has suggested, therapeutic counseling takes its place naturally in the educational setting where the school assumes its societal function of learning and personality development. Clinical psychologists, however, are found in hospitals, clinics, and increasingly, in private practice. Some counseling psychologists are found in hospitals and private practice (211). The educational setting for counseling invites a selective factor in that counselors deal primarily with maturational problems of school-age youth. On the other hand, clinical psychologists in private or nonschool institutional practice deal with marital, rehabilitation, geriatric, and other largely nonschool-age problems.

Psychiatry

Psychiatry, a third psychotherapeutic counseling specialty, is difficult to distinguish functionally from other counseling specialties. The obvious distinction is one of differential training—the psychiatrist having an M.D. degree and the psychologist generally having a Ph.D. Medical therapies used in the treatment of severe emotional illnesses contribute other clear distinctions.

Counselors and psychotherapists cannot escape the reality of the societal concept of medical responsibility. The physician has legal responsibility for care, having life or death implications for the individual. From one point of view, this concept embraces all of life's activities. From another view, the psychiatrically trained physician's responsibility covers psychotherapy mainly to the point where the problem becomes one of ignorance or learning rather than one of illness. Mowrer, for example, offers a useful distinction between the psychologist's and the psychiatrist's view of psychotherapy:

> Personality disorders are from one point of view no more disease than ignorance is a disease. Both prominently involve the phenomenon of *learning*. And if, as educators, we have any business working with the ignorant mind, we also have a right and an obligation to be interested in the confused, disordered mind (216, pg. 21).

Fine distinctions between ignorance and illness, however, become very vague in practice.

Psychotherapeutic counseling, according to Mowrer, involves helping the individual whose learning is incomplete or who has more or less conscious conflicts which have as their accompaniment so-called "normal" anxiety. This, of course, places a severe burden on the counselor to distinguish "normal" from "pathological"; but this recognition of pathology and therapeutic limitations has become part of the psychologist's professional training. It is important for any professional group to realize that it cannot be all things to all people.

Psychiatric Social Work

Psychiatric social work, a fourth counseling specialty, also is difficult to distinguish from psychology in terms of psychotherapeutic function. Many practitioners of this professional group feel they are doing psychotherapy in the formal sense. One principal difference, however, is the training route. Social workers generally complete a two-year graduate program leading to a masters degree in social work. The social worker functions, as does the clinical psychologist, on a psychiatric team. In clinics he specializes in the intake process, deals with other agencies, and collects psychiatric histories. Often he has an assigned therapeutic role, as in the Family Service Agency system where family counseling is conducted almost entirely by the social worker.

School Psychology and School Counseling

A fifth counseling specialty, educational counseling, differs from other specialties largely on the basis of breadth of training and experience required. The school psychologist or counselor deals with a wide variety of educational problems close to the areas of teaching and administration, in addition to working with the personal counseling problems of children and adolescents.

A significant concept in school counseling is that of levels of service. Three general counseling levels are identifiable on the basis of differences in training, competence, and counseling time. These are functional levels, not status differentials. On the first level is the educational counselor whose professional roots are mostly in teaching and who may be doing part-time counseling largely of the educational planning type. They give information and suggestions primarily. The counselors on this level are frequently called "advisers."

At the second level is the counselor whose professional affiliation is primarily in education and who generally has a masters degree or special training in guidance. This counselor deals with the majority of school counseling problems ranging from giving simple information on college requirements, through vocational planning and social conduct, to dealing with the more emotionally involved problems concerned with maturation.

The counselor on the third level is the counseling or clinical psychologist, described earlier in this chapter. The school or college counselor, on this level, generally has experience in educational positions; but his primary graduate professional education has been psychology, psychiatric social work, or medicine.

Pastoral Psychology

Clergymen have been counseling for years. Not until recently, however, has there been a real emphasis on professional preparation for clergymen to do psychological counseling. In Chapter 15 we describe more completely some of the specialized concerns with which all secular and religious counselors must come to grips as they deal with clients on moral and spiritual value problems.

TREND II: PROFESSIONALIZATION

The assertion that therapeutic psychology is a professional specialty must be substantiated. As indicated earlier, many professional groups use counseling and psychotherapeutic techniques. Conflicts tend to grow among psychologists when they view themselves as *either* scientists *or* professional practitioners. Hughes (151) emphasizes the danger of "hardening an endeavor prematurely," before the techniques used by a "profession" are validated. Pepinsky (232) faces this problem neatly in his concept of the "scientist-practitioner," in which the counselor or psychotherapist is a scientist primarily, using the methods of hypothetico-deductive thinking, and a practitioner secondarily. This view is stressed because of the undeveloped state of psychological knowledge.

These important characteristics of a profession are discussed below: (1) socially useful services which individuals cannot render to themselves; (2) skills and procedures; (3) definite sequences and standards of training (including selection procedures); (4) professional societies and journals dedicated to advancement of the profession and its basic scientific foundations; (5) a planned research program; (6) certification and licensing; (7) a code of ethics; (8) working relationships with other professions, and (9) professional freedom.

The development of the characteristics mentioned above is made from the viewpoint of the psychological practitioner. Variations will be found in the psychotherapeutic training of psychiatrists, social workers, and clergymen. The following material on training, certification, publications, and organizations is cited to illustrate the broad developments in the psychological fields. These developments are included also as a sobering reminder that reading this book will not make a psychotherapist or counselor out of the reader. Extensive background is needed for such a complex human service.

Socially Useful Services

The first and most important value of psychotherapeutic counseling is its usefulness in helping *individuals* with problems. During the last three decades, a climate has existed in America which not only enables acceptance of, but increases the need for, counseling services. The military forces utilized psychological personnel extensively during World War II. The vast postwar program of the Veterans Administration is testimony to public acceptance of counseling. The flourishing public marriage and mental-hygiene clinics, as well as school and college counseling programs, are further evidence that not only are such services requested, but also that clients are satisfied that the services are effective in helping them achieve their goals.

Another socially useful service which psychotherapeutic counseling performs is that of *conserving human talent*. There is talent in all segments of our social structure. Finding the talented, and appraising educational need and opportunity have been special functions of counselors. Likewise, the efforts of counselors to conserve human talent and to prevent emotional breakdowns have been extended to the emotional and social areas at all age levels. Their efforts have not been limited to the potential delinquents and the social "wallflowers" alone. Many leaders in the helping professions are asking why a youth must break down emotionally before he receives help. These preventive and personal development services need more attention now that the focus seems to be moving away from the pathological.

The third value of psychotherapeutic counseling, and another value of the concept for conserving human talent, is that of *national survival*. The recent political and economic crises throughout the world make it imperative that we find the talented youth of the free world, encourage them to make the most of their potentialities, and help them over the rough spots in achieving high-level productive and personal adjustment skills without sacrificing values of freedom of choice and responsibility.

Assisting the individual in the American dream of *social advancement* is a fourth value of psychotherapeutic counseling. Although many persons find themselves hemmed in by circumstances of birth, such as race or poverty, still, our American democratic social organization and expanding economy provide means for social mobility. Psychotherapeutic counseling services are ideally suited to help the individual acquire a knowledge of his needs and goals as well as to plan for the opportunities facing him.

Skills and Procedures

One of our assumptions is that there is an identifiable body of fairly valid techniques and procedures for counseling and psychotherapy. The major portion of this book is devoted to substantiating this assertion, and to describing these techniques and procedures.

Training Sequences and Standards

Two organizations which are interested deeply in counselor and psychotherapist training are the American Psychological Association and the American Personnel and Guidance Association. The American Psychological Association Committee on Counselor Training (11) and the National Vocational Guidance Associations (222) have published recommended training standards and areas for counseling psychology and clinical psychology. Recent descriptions of training programs have appeared (134, 135) and are presented here as examples.

Training programs are superimposed generally on a basic background of physical, biological, and social sciences as well as mathematics and the humanities. Early graduate years contain further basic training in general psychology, experimental methods, statistics, measurement, developmental and physiological and social psychology, personality theory, and behavior pathology. The advanced training leading to the doctoral degree contains, according to the APA Subcommittee on Ph.D. Training Programs (11), the following:

(1) Personality organization and development.
(2) Knowledge of social environment.
(3) Appraisal of the individual.
(4) Counseling.
(5) Professional orientation.
(6) Practicum.
(7) Research.

The APA Committee stresses the need for practicum training to give supervised experience in counseling and clinical psychology as well as to enable the student to synthesize many fragments of information from previous graduate work. Internships, generally half-time, are becoming increasingly more common in training programs.

The National Vocational Guidance Association, in cooperation with seven other groups interested in counseling, has published *Counselor Preparation* (222). This manual contains the following recommended competencies and areas of training for counselors, particularly those in school environments:

(1) A philosophy of guidance.
(2) Growth and development of the individual.
(3) Study of the individual.
(4) Collection evaluation and use of occupational, educational, and related information.

(5)   Administrative and community relationships.
(6)   Techniques used in counseling.
(7)   Supervised experience in counseling.
(8)   Group methods in guidance.

Selection of candidates for counseling and therapy functions is still in a rudimentary stage. Prediction research has not been as fruitful as desired, but there are reasons for optimism in discovering more about the characteristics of the practitioners of therapeutic psychology and in developing criterion measures of counseling and clinical skills.

Professional Societies and Publications

Another criterion of a profession is the existence of societies and publications dedicated to improving the science and practice of the profession. In psychology, for example, the American Psychological Association is one group the object of which is "to advance psychology as a science, as a profession, and as a means of promoting human welfare" (8). The American Personnel and Guidance Association is another professional association dedicated to the improvement of counseling services, particularly in educational institutions.

The vigor of professional journals is a further criterion of a profession's growth. Some of the representative publications of help to counselors and psychotherapists are the *Journal of Counseling Psychology, Journal of Clinical Psychology, Journal of Consulting Psychology, Educational and Psychological Measurement, Personnel and Guidance Journal,* and the *American Psychologist.*

Research Orientation

In a profession as young as psychology, research plays a significant part in discovering new procedures, validating current techniques, and resolving contradictions and theoretical confusion. A large portion of the graduate program is directed to research techniques so that the practitioner has a research orientation in whatever professional activity he performs. In addition, there is a strong social obligation to validate constantly the psychological services offered to the public.

It should be emphasized that the frontiers of knowledge in the field of psychological services are pushed back through an interaction of both practice and pure research in human sciences. One endeavor helps the other in reciprocal fashion.

Certification and Licensing

With the prevalence of quacks in the field of counseling and psychotherapy, it is imperative that the public be protected as well as the profession. Steiner's (288) survey revealed astounding findings on disreputable help for troubled people. Although a certificate or license does not guarantee competence, it informs the public that the practitioner has been exposed to several years of training in the techniques he espouses.

A certificate is a document granted by a public or private group. It is solicited voluntarily by the individual. An example is the postdoctoral certificate or diploma granted by the American Board of Examiners in Professional Psychology (6). Diplomas are issued by this Board in three areas: clinical, industrial, and counseling. The written examination covers basic professional knowledge in the candidate's specialty. The oral examination includes questions on client relationships, professional relationships, and a field situation where the candidate under observation performs services in his specialty.

Many state boards of education maintain counselor certification as part of their credentialling programs. California, for example, has a "Pupil Personnel Services Credential" (53) which grants permission to render services in five basic areas: counseling, social work, attendance, psychometry, or school psychology.

Actual licensing of psychologists poses a somewhat different problem from certification. A license gives a psychologist a legal right to engage in psychological practice. A licensing law forbids certain practices, generally defines what a psychologist is, and describes psychological practice. Certification laws generally restrict the use of the title "psychologist" only. Licensing and certification are further marks of a profession.

Code of Ethics

The opening statement in the APA *Summary of Ethical Principles* is, "The worth of a profession is measured by its contribution to the welfare of man." (9, pg. 1). Psychotherapeutic counseling, being a welfare service, is faced with ethical practice problems. Until codes were formulated, there were few concrete guides for determining unethical practices. The presence of a well-defined code and tradition of ethical practice is a distinguishing mark of a profession.

Section 2 of the APA Ethical Code (9) pertains to client relationships and covers questions of confidentiality, responsibility, competence, and client welfare. The ethical behavior of the counselor or therapist is such an important topic that further material is given in Chapter 6 of this book.

The influence of values on the perception of people and the value context of psychology itself are important ethical topics (182, 130, 284, 155, 96). The papers just cited contain provocative discussions on the problems of goals (such as "adjustment"), value conflicts, social forces, parochialism, and professional vanity. We feel strongly that both the professional counselor and psychotherapist need to give much serious thought to these problems. Therefore, the problems mentioned above are covered at several points in this book.

Working Relationships with Other Professions

Each profession must recognize its limitations and the role of other professional groups in rounding out its knowledge and skills. One mark of the psychology profession is its willingness to collaborate with other professional disciplines in working for the client's best interests.

Professional Freedom

The American Psychological Association (10) lists as one of the characteristics of a "good" profession the freedom to accept its responsibilities and to carry them out in ways dictated by its own wisdom. The profession willingly faces all evidence of social need for services and its own competence to fulfill these needs. The profession must not be swayed by attempts to restrict its activities which demonstrably fulfill its social function and advance human values. We feel that counseling and psychotherapy are well along in attempts to fulfill this professional principle.

TREND III: EMPHASIS ON PERSONALITY FACTORS OF THE COUNSELOR OR THERAPIST

Since counseling is much concerned with prediction, considerable effort has been expended in sharpening the effectiveness of its instruments and techniques along these lines. Consequently, attitudes and personality, as variables in the counseling equation, have been less emphasized by most researchers and writers. Although the area of counselor personality is difficult to assay with present research techniques, it is receiving at the time of this writing increasing attention in the research and speculative literature.

Chapter 6 contains a detailed discussion of the desirable counselor personality. The question of counselor personality is mentioned here to emphasize the great increase in attention it has been given during the past decade. There is a danger in ignoring technique through a preoccupation with attitudes; yet, as the student of psychotherapeutic counseling peruses the literature, he is impressed by the plethora of writing on techniques— tests, records, surveys, sociometrics—as if these were central. Shoben estimates that the amount of space in counseling texts devoted to the "modification of client behavior through face-to-face contacts" (pg. 259) is only 8 per cent of the total. One explanatory hypothesis regarding this deficit would be that so little is known about this important face-to-face relationship and the related personality factors that writers fall back on the traditional test and records approach to counseling and psychotherapeutic problems.

TREND IV: USE OF DATA IN THE SOLUTION OF HUMAN PROBLEMS

Although interest in personality factors in counseling has mushroomed, it has not appeared to overshadow or diminish the studies on the use of data in counseling. Efforts to develop new predictive and diagnostic tests, as well as to improve old instruments, have increased at a rapid rate (290). The interest in using projective techniques is a newly developing facet of this work. More detailed results in the area of testing and its counseling implications are summarized in Chapter 10.

Information from the fields of anthropology, developmental psychology, gerontology, economics, rehabilitation, and sociology is appearing in forms useful to counselors and psychotherapists. An example is the Kinsey series on sexual behavior. The vast resources of the Federal Bureau of Labor Statistics are producing more useful materials to aid the counselor with vocational planning problems. Comparative culture studies on sexual behaviors, child-rearing methods, and personality determinants are further examples.

TREND V: UNIFIED THEORETICAL CONSTRUCTS

Out of concern for the divorce of science from practice during the last five years, much thought has been devoted to integrating psychotherapeutic counseling practice with personality and learning. Instead of thinking of the counseling process as a collection of cookbook recipes or miscellaneous techniques culled from experience, psychotherapeutic counseling may be viewed as the application of systematic and unified theory and principles to specialized learning situations in the interview. Some of the current and historical views on personality development, structure, and function and their applications to counseling and psychotherapy are presented in Chapters 2 and 3.

Throughout this book, we have attempted to bridge the gap between systematic theory and loose practice. This ideal is difficult to realize, however. Part of the problem lies in terminology and translation of phenomena such as transference and resistance into a meaningful theoretical framework. The counselor must strive constantly, nevertheless, to analyze what he is doing and to know what is happening in his counseling interviews. Theory often supplies the needed conceptual tools, though it is recognized that the need for technique often surpasses available verified knowledge and conceptual developments.

The psychotherapeutic counselor's awareness of his social responsibility and the welfare of his clients forces him to maintain a healthy balance between skepticism and confidence in his methods. As Shoben so aptly said, "When the chips are down, as they generally are in professional practice, skepticism about one's own resources is a luxury that few can afford" (277, pg. 252). Hahn and McLean comment in pointed language also:

> The Counselor's humility of self-recognized ignorance is therefore of continuing importance. It must be a rational humility, however, an objective admission of limitation in the face of infinite complexity. It must never develop into an emotional sense of inferiority which leads to self-recrimination, depression, over-timidity, about undertaking responsibility for new cases. When this happens, the counselor himself is ready for psychotherapy (136, pg. 37).

Rogers (254) has neatly stated the mixed feelings of the psychotherapeutic counselor when he perceives himself as the subjective sensitive therapist and toughminded scientist combined.

Psychotherapy and counseling practice offer rich opportunities for formulating hypotheses and elaborating theory through applications to practical events in counseling. The Pepinskys (232) stress the role, mentioned earlier, of the counselor as a "scientist-practitioner." In this dual role, the counselor and psychotherapist continuously utilize a process of observation, inference, and assessment of behavior changes during and after counseling.

Rotter (260) summarizes the principal values of theories in clinical work as follows: as bases for construction of new instruments and methods and of testing old ones, as tools for evaluating counseling techniques where experimental evidence is lacking, as encouragement for consistency of terminology and assumption, as evaluation devices for new ideas or unusual problems in practice, and as aids to help clinicians recognize and resolve apparent contradictions and inconsistencies in experiments, concepts, or practice.

Attempts to unify constructs have served to diminish the "school" emphasis in psychotherapeutic counseling. Wherever a parochial or segmental approach to counseling is promulgated, a "school" of counseling tends to spring up. This is not to discourage individual practitioner-scientists from launching into creative thinking or theory. Rogers (253) comments that one of the critical problems of practicing psychologists today is the climate in the profession which discourages theory construction. Rogers goes on to postulate that this lack of theorizing rests in a "real fear of grappling with the new and unconventional" (253, pg. 247).

TREND VI: CONCERN WITH GOALS

Another prominent trend discernible in psychotherapeutic counseling discussions is that of increasing clarification of the goals and purposes of counseling. This trend naturally takes a tack into the realm of values. This topic of goals and values is treated at several points in this volume—under ethical problems in Chapter 6, within the context of goals of psychotherapeutic counseling in Chapter 4, under relationship problems in Chapter 6, and in the discussion of values in Chapter 15.

The change in emphasis from the solution of immediate manifest problems the client may have, such as choosing a vocational goal, or relieving momentary situational anxiety, to more long-range goals is quite apparent. An example of a long-range, generalized goal is the reinforcement of the self-directive capacities of the client which make him better able to solve his problems in the future without help.

SUMMARY

This introductory statement has included a survey of the trends contributing to the recent professionalization of therapeutic psychology. The field of therapeutic psychology has many historical antecedents in clinical psychology, counseling psychology, psychiatry, social work, school psychology, and pastoral psychology. With this rich background, the profession is facing and mastering many problems of responsibility, interprofessional relationships, training, selection, scientific societies, research, certification, licensing, ethics, and freedom. Points of overlap and uniqueness were indicated between counseling and psychotherapy. Psychotherapists generally aim at personality reorganization at relatively deep levels of personality, whereas the counselor is more concerned with the denouement of incomplete maturing or learning processes.

2.

Theoretical Foundations of
Therapeutic Psychology

To give precision, coherence, and promise to counseling and psychotherapy techniques, it is necessary to become familiar with certain aspects of personality theory. One of our basic assumptions is that counseling or therapy becomes an impulsive application of "cookbook" recipes to human problems unless the clinician has a firm foundation in the current thinking and research of other practitioners and has a consistent set of assumptions about personality structure and function. The psychological counselor must know his medium just as the mechanic must know the intricacies of a vehicle, or as the surgeon must know anatomy and physiology.

This chapter contains, therefore, a discussion of the significance of theory, an overview of various approaches to counseling from the standpoint of personality and learning theory, and an attempted integration of various historical and contemporary theories as a basis for the consistent application of techniques. The principal purpose in presenting the following material is to provide the student with some of the concepts from various personality theories which have useful implications for counseling.

THE SIGNIFICANCE OF THEORY

The model of a psychotherapeutic counselor as a scientist-practitioner was proposed in Chapter 1. The premise of this model is that the counselor can be both subject and object, that is, he can be an objective observer, hence critical, of what goes on; yet he can be a participant in the counseling process at the same time. The essences of scientific method used by this model counselor are observation, inference, and verification. Therapeutic practice involves the application of principles deduced from generalizations, or theories, developed through scientific method. The foundation of the scientific practice of psychotherapy and counseling, therefore, is theory. By counseling theory we mean a structure of hypotheses and generalizations based on counseling experience and experimental studies.

When speaking of the counselor as a scientist, two related meanings should be distinguished. The first is the scientific attitude which the counselor assumes so that he can verify his rough hypotheses and improve his services. The second view of the counselor as a scientist is his application of the scientific process to his work. He is required, typically, to control extraneous variables and manipulate the experimental variables according to the established rules of scientific practice. This is rarely possible in a counseling situation unless a deliberate study is designed to test certain hypotheses about counseling. Therefore, the scientific approach to counseling in the latter sense remains, admittedly, an ideal.

Although the therapist or counselor is interested in the applications of scientific attitudes and methods to improve his practice, he is interested also in behavioral science *qua* science. That is, he is interested broadly in the greater understanding of human behavior, whether or not it leads to any practical results in his counseling.

The Values of Theory

Theory helps to explain what happens in the counseling relationship and assists the counselor in predicting, evaluating, and improving results. Theory provides a framework for making systematic observations about counseling. Theorizing encourages the coherence of ideas about counseling and the production of new ideas. Hence, counseling theory can be very practical.

The Scientific Attitude

What behaviors exemplify the scientific attitude? A counselor or psychotherapist who proceeds through his daily tasks without asking himself the following questions is not likely to progress in developing his therapeutic effectiveness, nor is he likely to contribute new ideas to the profession. What is happening here? What is my model? What are my assumptions? What accounts for this event? What will happen if I try this? The "unscientific" counselor, who does not ask himself these vital questions, is likely to develop a dangerous feeling of smugness and certainty about his counseling methods.

The clinician, as a scientist, starts with a question or problem; then he *observes* what happens in the interaction between himself and his client. He formulates hypotheses about what is happening. These hypotheses are the *inferences* based on his observations. Sets of refined hypotheses are generally referred to as theories. Then, from his theories the counselor attempts to explain or predict further events in counseling. He must check constantly the validity of his new theories against the reality of his observations so as to bring the two closer together. The refined theories are then used to make more precise explanations and predictions of counseling events.

To illustrate this process, let us take a simplified example of the phenomenon of defense. A counselor observes that when he "pushes" a client too hard with questions or interpretations he gets angry, stops talking, or even leaves counseling. He observes the various conditions under which the client behaves in the negativistic fashion and speculates as to why he might do so. The clinician observes other similar cases and notes a pattern and a consistency. He hypothesizes that clients become negativistic or "defensive" when they are threatened, or perceive the counselor as a source of frustration and even psychological danger. The counselor may postulate an "unconscious" or a "self" in his client with feelings or attitudes which are inconsistent with the client's conscious feelings or attitudes. The client perceives the inconsistency between his own behavior and deeper attitudes as well as the discrepancy between his attitudes and the counselor's attitudes. The therapist or counselor, perhaps, may be "pushing" the client too fast, so of course he checks his hypothesis about threat and defense with further observations until he has refined the concepts and generalizations to the point where they are useful in predicting what will happen to a client under threat. The counselor is then in a better position to evaluate both his hypotheses and his techniques.

The "miniature" theories, or confirmed hypotheses, are combined with much other data and hypotheses into more consistent and larger theories about personality structure and function in general. The broader theory is then used in a deductive fashion to produce more hypotheses to be tested experimentally or through counseling experience.

Although the preceding section expresses the ideal of the scientific clinician's approach, the novelty of the scientific approach for many practicing counselors makes it difficult to use in practice. In addition, there is still no compelling evidence that counseling effectiveness depends definitely upon the extent and explicitness of one's theoretical foundations, nor that one particular theory of personality or psychotherapy is superior to another.

Much work has been done in the last few years in the area of systematic theory construction by psychologists having the temperament and ability to do so. A really satisfactory general counseling and psychotherapeutic theory, however, is not yet available. Each counselor attempts to explain what he sees with his unique and limited perception. Hence, there are still a number of "schools" of counseling or therapy. This multiplicity of theories is a healthy state of affairs in a young profession; but, ultimately, it is expected that a unified theory of behavior and of counseling practice will evolve. In the meantime, each clinician must examine the thinking of others as well as work on the formulation of his own hypotheses about the structure and function of the human personality and the counseling process. Even though most counselors cannot be creative theoreticians they can develop an attitude of careful critical observation of everyday practice and an understanding of formal experimental approaches to counseling problems.

One further point in reference to differential theoretical approaches should be made. Black (34) has pointed out in his comparative study of psychotherapeutic approaches that follow-up research data indicate that all "schools" get positive results. Black thinks that the ultimate resolution to theoretical differences will come about through critical analysis of the process itself rather than through the promotion of a parochial or "school" point of view. Although differing in emphasis, all approaches stress the significance of adequate rapport, acceptance of the client, need for support, professional status of the counselor, and some type of limits.

In light of the foregoing points, we would like to counter the tendency of counselors and psychotherapists to explain the events of the interview by means of a single theoretical view of personality. No theory has been found so far to explain the process completely. Furthermore, clients respond differently to various approaches. Sometimes one approach works well in the initial phases when the need for support overshadows all other therapeutic efforts, whereas another client takes well to a highly interpretive approach immediately. Also of significance is the fact that the counselor's theory must match his style of counseling. In other words, the psychotherapist must use a point of view and a psychotherapeutic style with which he feels comfortable and effective.

The views expressed above might be summarized as follows: The student of counseling and psychotherapy must not only have a tentative theory, he must also have an open view toward the possibility of altering his theoretical foundations. Therefore, he must study the various views with the aim of familiarizing himself with their distinguishing features as well as the technical and programmatic aspects of the various theories. Then he should be able to make a reasonable estimate of his own tendencies and seek further intensive training there. When he has developed competence in a particular area, then he can return to the rigorous eclectic task with a new integrative capacity.

Each counselor and psychotherapist, furthermore, must ultimately develop a point of view which is uniquely his own. Freud was not a Freudian, Jung not a Jungian, and Rogers not a Rogerian. Each of them was himself most fully and completely, while building upon the wisdom of the past. Each practitioner must feel that his counseling practice reflects such individuality. This is the reason why no one text or school is fully adequate for any counselor or therapist.

Evolving Eclecticism

There are many practitioners who decline to identify themselves with a current theoretical system or "school," and who use the identifying label "eclectic" since they either de-emphasize theory or feel that it is too premature to identify too closely with a current position. Some eclectics take their position out of a feeling of defeatism or inertia so as to avoid the rigorous exercise of scientific thinking. Their views are based on a process of picking and choosing between the many theories, relying on a superficial knowledge of them, to suit their needs and fancies of the moment.

Other eclectic counselors realize fully the current limitations of systematic theory, so they struggle to integrate and rationalize the elements and conflicts among several theories of personality. They try assiduously to organize their observations and hypotheses into a flexible but workable and consistent position. They prefer to keep their opinions open and to struggle creatively and honestly toward a more highly developed theory. This view represents our position and is most descriptive of therapeutic psychology.

We believe that no counselor or therapist at this early stage of our science can afford to be too parochial in his views. From the latest research and theories he must continue to evolve new positions which have meaning for him. Furthermore, he must be willing to revise his present practices in light of the new data. We have come to call this position "evolving eclecticism."

We feel that even though a counselor or therapist claims to be eclectic or perhaps non-theoretically based, he has implicit assumptions about the structure and function of personality, though he may not be able to verbalize them. One task of the scientific counselor is to make his implicit assumptions explicit and then to test and criticize them. We feel, also, that the eclectic position, as an approach to meeting current practical problems, at best, is a transitional one, taken until theory is further developed. To illustrate, there are analogies in other fields, from dog training to politics, where practice is ahead of theory. Ultimate development, however, must depend upon the laborious, yet in our opinion more dependable, results of scientific method and theory construction. Present developments indicate that it is very probable that personality theory and counseling practice will develop simultaneously.

The following section contains a summary of the major theories of personality with implications for counseling theory and practice.

History of Psychological Counseling Theory

Two historical bases for psychological counseling theory can be traced. One, the behavioristic approach, stresses relearning more adaptive problem-solving modes of response to life's demands through use of rewards, punishments, and information. Logic, information, and problem-solving methods are components of the behavioristic approach. Consider, for example, a client who has difficulty concentrating on his studies. The counselor makes rational diagnosis to determine if his client is in the right field, if his study skills are adequate, if he possesses sufficient ability to do the work, and so on. Learning conditions are created wherein the client can acquire better work habits, more information, further appraisal of the realism of his goals, or more counseling on personal problems.

The other, depending largely on psychoanalytic principles, stresses the more emotional, so-called "dynamic," aspects of personality. Hence, although not overlooking the rational attack, the dynamic approach stresses attempts to elicit feelings about the problem and to understand the unconscious bases for behaving. Thus, through removing emotional obstacles to learning or "lifting of repression," the client is enabled to use more rational approaches to problem-solving. For example, if a client has difficulty concentrating on his studies and also appears to resent his parents forcing him to go to school, it may be hypothesized that he unconsciously resists his parents by "inability" to study.

The following variations on theory may be fitted into one or the other of the two historical categories. First, some of the dominant dynamic approaches will be described and secondly, some of the behavioral approaches.

DYNAMICALLY ORIENTED THEORIES

Psychoanalytic Approaches

The psychoanalytic approach stresses the importance of the client's life history (psychosexual development), the influence of genetic impulses (instincts), a life energy (libido), the influence of early experiences on later personality of the individual, and the irrationality and unconscious sources of much of human behavior. The psychoanalytic concepts of levels of awareness are significant contributions. The conscious level consists of those ideas of which the individual is aware at the moment. The preconscious contains those ideas of which the individual is not aware at the moment but which can be recalled. The unconscious level consists of those memories and ideas which the individual has forgotten and cannot remember. Freud conceived the unconscious as making up the bulk of the personality and of having a powerful influence on behavior.

A significant psychotherapeutic issue raised by the psychoanalytic approach is this: Do we need a "depth" approach which postulates that the origin and solution of human problems lie deep within the personality, or do the explanation and solution lie more within the perceptual organization of the individual? The psychoanalytic counselors emphasize the importance of having a concept of depth in personality and postulate a series of structural elements known as Freud's "iceberg" concept, which are illustrated in Figure 3. The largest element is the *id,* which has the character-

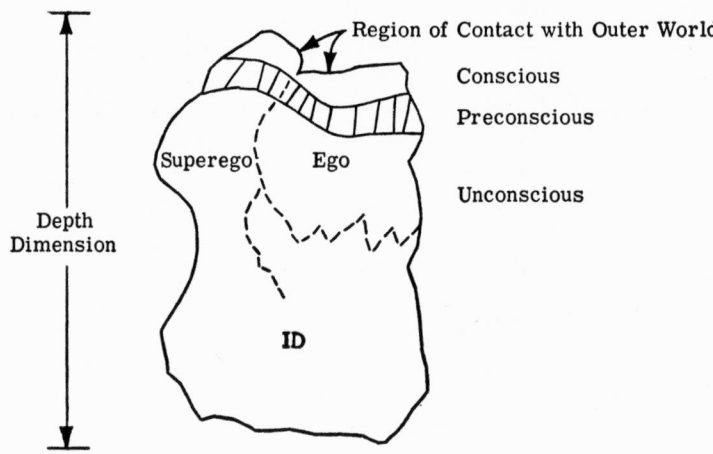

FIG. 3. Psychoanalytic Conception of Personality Structure. J. F. Brown, *Psychodynamics of Abnormal Behavior* (New York: McGraw, 1940), adapted from W. Healy, A. Bronner, and A. Bowers, *The Structure and Meaning of Psychoanalysis* (New York: Knopf, 1930).

istics of being unconscious, irrational, unorganized, pleasure-oriented, primitive, the source of "libido" or life force and energy, and the source of drives and basic wishes for life and death.

Another element of structure is the *ego* which functions as a controlling, reality-oriented, mastery mechanism. The ego functions also as a mediating element between superego, id, and reality demands. One of the principal functions of the ego is that of controlling the id and keeping impulses and feelings, such as anxiety, out of consciousness. Ego control is accomplished through the mechanism of "defense," of which the main type is "repression." The id impulse, thwarted in direct expression, penetrates the ego barrier in a disguised and usually safer derivative form.

Although the early psychoanalytic theorists placed great emphasis upon repression of anxiety and the consequent symptoms, more recent classical or "orthodox" psychoanalytic therapists have been giving greater attention to ego psychology which emphasizes the adaptive mastery functions of personality.

The superego is another Freudian concept which functions as a controlling agent in the personality. It is conceived generally as parental moral attitudes and social mores learned in early years, and which become an important structural and functional part of personality in later years. In many ways, the concept is similar to the popular term "conscience."

Later students of Freud, such as Adler, Jung, and Rank, not only modified, but also abandoned many of his basic postulates. *Adler* emphasized the goal-directedness or purposiveness of human beings more than did Freud, who saw clients more as blind victims of their impulses operating in a rather mechanical deterministic fashion. Adler felt that power and status motives were more significant for behavior than the broadly sexual motives of Freud. Adler saw superiority attitudes as compensations for perceived weakness or the "inferiority complex." Related to Adler's drive for mastery is the "masculine protest" of women who envy the status and power of men.

Adler emphasized also the "social interest" or current "life style," as well as the biological determinants of behavior. One of the Adlerian therapist's devices to gain clues to his life style is to ask the client for his "first recollection." This approach gives the therapist an idea on what experiences the client's style of life is based.

Adler is well known for his concept of the "ego ideal" or the person's model of the kind of person he would like to be, a prelude to the now popular concept of "self-image." Helping the client become more aware of his unique life style, ideals, and self-images is one of the major goals of counseling.

Jung stressed the uniqueness of human motives and the striving toward individuation. Jung postulated a broad "collective unconscious," consisting of inherited "archetypes" which are collections of primordial universal motives and human images. His second structural element is the "personal unconscious" which contains forgotten and repressed material. The "conscious" is the external awareness level concerned with problems of everyday living. The "persona" is a type of mask hiding the deeper personality characteristics from others. Jung felt that the persona was an important and healthy element of personality except where it tended to dominate the "real" personality, or to blind the person to what Jung called his "shadow." The shadow part of the personal unconscious is considered to be impulsive and generally not consciously nor socially acceptable. In addition to the "persona" and "shadow" there are other examples of archetypes—"animus" (masculine aspect of women), "anima" (feminine element in men), and "self" (the achievement of oneness and unity).

Jung emphasized that the psychotherapist must help the individual get something in place of his neuroses and "build" an individual self. Hence, he placed high value on religion and the integration of religion and psychology. Jung's descriptions of the paradoxes in human personality, such as the mixed feminine and masculine components, are often useful concepts in the interpretation phase of psychotherapy. Both Jung and Adler stressed the value of the direct, face-to-face contact of the psychotherapist with the client, as contrasted with the less direct, couch-centered treatment of the Freudians.

Rank contributed much to psychoanalytic theory by his emphasis upon the traumatic events of birth and separation from the mother. These ideas were expanded to include the security-seeking efforts of people. Rank pointed out many implications from the growth and development as a child for development of independence and security as an adult, thus offering counseling theory a significant and meaningful developmental point of view. One implication, for example, is the importance of "limits." According to this concept, the client is helped to gain a feeling of security by setting limits to his behavior, such as making him stay within the time and place of the interview. With children, especially, this is a significant part of the therapeutic process.

Rank's central concept is the "will," which is a guiding, integrating, and instinct-inhibiting force. He views resistance as the operation of the will in maintaining the integrity of the personality. Rank's a-historical views placed considerable emphasis upon the positive motivations of the client and his present feelings rather than upon the therapist and his interpretations of the past.

Rank's major contributions to counseling were his insistence on viewing the client as a person, and his casting of the psychotherapist into a more personalized role. Rank believed strongly in "ethical self-determination," implying that the counselor should be careful not to force values on the client. Rank's view sharpens another significant issue in counseling: Where should the content of the process come from, primarily—the client's field of awareness or the counselor's?

Rank's theories have influenced several American psychotherapeutic writers. In addition to Carl Rogers in the adult psychotherapy field, Jesse Taft in social work and F. H. Allen in child psychotherapy have extended Rank's special adaptations of psychoanalytic theory. Rank's will is interpreted as a positive growth force. The conflict between dependence and independence needs is seen as a tendency to regress to earlier dependent relationships when the demands of life become too overpowering. Allen perceives that the basic adjustment difficulties of clients result from excessive demands being made upon them before they have the resources to cope with them. Rank's insistence upon the therapeutic power of the relationship itself has led naturally to a strong emphasis being placed on the attitudes held by the counselor and the importance of having the client assume his own psychotherapeutic responsibility.

Implications of Classical Psychoanalytic Positions for Counseling and Psychotherapy

A significant implication for counseling is Freud's theory of defense mechanisms. Psychoanalysis has made us more aware of the unconscious bases of behavior, with the result that counselors are less concerned with the symptoms (defenses) and are more concerned with the origins of the defensive behaviors. One therapeutic task is to help the client become more aware of his style of handling unconscious wishes and anxieties and to find more socially approved, as well as personally satisfying, ways of resolving tensions. The analytic counselor, furthermore, sees his task as one of making the "unconscious more conscious," that is, of helping the client to know and utilize in a mature way his psychic energies, and of becoming more aware of distorted behaviors that result from threatening unconscious impulses. Helping the client to become more aware of his unconscious feelings tends to result in more spontaneity, rationality, and other values implicit in the mature personality.

Psychoanalytic therapists use techniques such as abreaction, free association, and interpretation of resistance, dreams, and transference material. The assumptions, style, and length (usually two to five years) of psychoanalytic therapy make it of limited utility in psychotherapeutic counseling. A prominent feature of psychoanalytic technique is to encourage regression in the client through persistent frustration. The aim of this technique is to promote exploration of early experiences and to enable the therapist to help the client work through experiences which might otherwise have been beyond his awareness.

Counseling and brief psychotherapy, in contrast, are not as concerned with attempting *major* personality transformations through detailed interpretation of early and persistent unconscious conflicts as is psychoanalysis. Psychotherapy is concerned more with conflicts and feelings which are already in, or dimly in, awareness and with helping the client to develop resources for handling them. In other words, the psychotherapist concentrates more on the "here and now," whereas the psychoanalyst is concerned with lifting repressions of deeply unconscious material. The relevance of analytic techniques to psychotherapeutic counseling is treated in later chapters on relationship techniques.

One key implication of a deterministic system like Freud's, in which one has a blocked urge, then repression, then the neurotic symptom, is that individual responsibility tends to be de-emphasized: "It is not I who is at fault; it is my frustrated id impulses which are causing me trouble." For example, "My hunger stole the fruit, not I." Psychotherapeutic counselors operate on the assumption that the client must, sooner or later, accept personal responsibility for his behavior. Existential therapists, for example, place great stress on the client feeling a sense of "ownership" of himself.

Jung's and Adler's amplification of psychoanalytic theory includes more of the social determinants, such as cooperativeness, and the purposive character of behavior. Rank, as well, stresses the person's integrating powers and the necessity for understanding the client's feelings and potentialities. This concept paved the way for later therapists such as Sullivan, Horney, Taft, Allen, and Rogers to develop theoretical positions of even greater value to psychological counselors.

Recent Positions Evolving from Psychoanalytic Theory

Sullivan is known for his theory of interpersonal relationships, including the interaction between personality development and culture. According to the "interpersonal theory," the individual appears quite different, both to himself and to others, depending upon the particular personalities with whom he is interacting at the moment. The practical import of this view is that the individual can be understood only within the context of his family, friendships (real or imaginary), and broader social groups.

Sullivan postulates two basic goals of human behavior—physical satisfactions (food, drink, rest, sex), and security (defined as a state of pleasantness or euphoria resulting from fulfilled social expectations). The child, in the process of acculturation, finds himself in frequent conflict between need satisfaction and security. As parents use prohibitions and disapprovals in the acculturation process, he begins to feel anxiety as a result of his inability to fulfill these expectations. The child develops increased muscle tension. He excludes from his consciousness selected phases of his experience which have proved anxiety-provoking. His attempts to resolve the tensions through activity do not result in complete relief since anxiety-reduction does not tend to follow release patterns of other physiological tensions.

If the child can obtain both satisfaction and security, he gains a sense of mastery or power; hence, he begins to experience a higher evaluation of himself. This self-regarding attitude is thus determined by the attitude of others toward him. Self-attitudes, in addition, seem to determine the attitudes which he has toward others.

It is important to realize, therefore, that much anxiety originates in an interpersonal context. If considerable anxiety has been generated during the acculturation process, then useful learning, awareness, and capacity for insight will be greatly reduced. Sullivan speaks of this process as "selective inattention." When other persons in the interpersonal situation mention words or feelings which provoke anxiety in one's self, the evaluation of others tends to change in a negative direction; hence, individuals are alienated from one another. It helps, therefore, to understand that an aggressive client responds in this manner largely because he has been rebuffed in his bids for affection and understanding. Through his inability to receive as well as to give affection, he maintains hostile attitudes even toward those who attempt to satisfy his needs.

Sullivan traces self-development through a series of stages from preverbal infancy through adult maturity. The principal implications for counselors are the necessity to provide security relationships, to accept emotional outbursts which are indicative of tension build-ups, and to organize learning situations which result in enhancement of self-regarding attitudes of worth and confidence. Therapists and counselors must realize that affectional growth may be poorly developed due to disturbances in interpersonal relationships; and, as a result, the client needs a treatment environment where he can develop self-esteem and confidence adequate to any situation. He needs an opportunity to develop the ability to love another person whose welfare is as significant as his own.

The counselor must be cautious, however, in interpreting the explanations of personality dynamics to the individual. He must recognize also that he too has developed through the same social processes as his client and that the present counseling relationship is changing him further through what Sullivan describes as his "participant-observer" status. This topic will be treated in Chapter 8 under "countertransference."

In summary, the principal implication of Sullivan's theory for therapists and counselors is that the individual can be understood mainly in light of his interpersonal history. The quality of the client's interpersonal relationships must be examined, in particular, as a key to the client's understanding of his attitudes. The counselor must realize that the client's responses to the counselor are affected by these past relationships and that feelings expressed are displacements of feelings from previous personal relationships. Sullivan's ideas are related to the current emphasis in counseling known as the "communications approach."

Karen Horney (148), who may be classified among the so-called neo-Freudians, differs from the earlier psychoanalysts in that she too stresses the cultural determinants of behavior and emphasizes that maladaptive behaviors arise largely from disturbances in human relationships. Horney, while remaining in the general framework of psychoanalytic theory, shifted the stress from early childhood experiences and repression of biological drives to presently existing character structure and conflicts. She does this, however, without negating the significance of early experience in personality formation. Horney feels that the totality of early childhood experiences and conflicts form an unique character structure which predisposes the person to later neurotic difficulties. This view differs somewhat from the earlier Freudian idea that adult conflicts and neuroses are essentially repetitions of isolated childhood experiences.

An example of the cultural origin of personal problems is the American emphasis on competition, which appears to produce considerable frustration and hostility. Our hostilities are projected to others who are then viewed as competitors. This creates anxiety about the potential danger of others and fear of retaliation for having hostilities of our own. This situation results in a need for security which is satisfied partially through love relationships. Since deeply satisfying affectional relationships are infrequent for many persons in our society, we are subjected to further frustration.

Horney stresses the competing and contradictory demands of our culture upon the person as one source of tensions. Examples are the conflicts between stimulation of demand for material goods and the limited means for satisfying them, independence and free choice as opposed to the limitations imposed by birth and social circumstances, brotherhood and love for your neighbor against competition and an "eye for an eye and a tooth for a tooth."

The conflicts in the culture are often internalized and express themselves in various forms of aggressiveness and yielding, personal power and helplessness, self-aggrandizement and self-sacrifice, trust of people and fear of them. An implication here for psychological counseling is that these conflicts, faced by all people in our society, become accentuated or reappear as unintegrated childhood conflicts, causing feelings of distress. The individual may then develop defense mechanisms annoying to himself or others. The awareness of these conflicts, or the associated anxiety, drives the person to seek psychological counseling. An example is the person with a self-effacement defense, so common in our middle-class culture. He feels it is important to "be nice to everyone, so they will be nice to me and will love me." He finds, however, that other people often dislike him anyway; so he is baffled and concludes that he is fighting a losing battle.

Another useful distinction that Horney makes is between "normal" anxiety, which is fear of concrete events such as accident and death, and "neurotic" or "basic" anxiety, which is fear that arises in early relationships when the person faces a potentially hostile world and which leads to neurotic defenses. One of the psychological counselor's jobs is to help the individual to recognize his basic anxieties and to help him build more satisfying ways of handling them.

Closely related to her concept of basic anxiety is "basic hostility." Horney postulates that much neurotic anxiety stems from the presence of repressed hostility which has been projected to others. The perception of the world as a hostile place generates anxiety and further repression of hostility, and so begins the "vicious circle."

Of further interest to counselors is Horney's concept of the "basic conflict," which exists largely at an unconscious level. This conflict concerns the feelings of dependence and affection which one has for a parent versus feelings of hostility toward them for having to be dependent. The conflict may not be recognized at the conscious level because one cannot easily alienate himself from those on whom he depends. The more normal individual moves freely between the opposing tendencies of independence and dependence, whereas the more neurotic person is more compulsive about his behavior and experiences his independence-dependence feelings as being in direct conflict with one another. This condition has the effect of limiting spontaneity and of giving the victim a feeling of helplessness, indecision, and fatigue. One of the therapist's tasks, according to Horney, is to make the client aware of his basic conflicts and his attempts to solve the conflict by moving toward, against, or away from people.

One of Horney's (147) formulations of interest to therapists is her description of the basic types of personalities which come for psychotherapy. The "expansive type" gives an impression of glorified self-regard, exhibits an arrogant and contemptuous demeanor, and seems to feel that he can impress and fool others into believing he is someone he is not. This type of client is difficult to involve in a therapeutic relationship initially, but later when his defenses are reduced he becomes involved quite easily.

The "self-effacing type" tends to subordinate himself to others, to be dependent upon them, and to seek protection and affection. He is characterized by a strong feeling of failure, inferiority, and self-hate. He exhibits a demeanor of passivity and obsequiousness. He generally becomes involved easily in a counseling relationship.

The "resigned" type puts on an air of disinterest, reflecting his retreat from his inner feelings and from the rigors of life. He takes on more of a detached observer role in life's activities. He lacks a strong achievement drive and avoids serious effort. This type of client maintains an emotional distance from others and avoids pressures to get involved in any kind of close human relationship. This avoidance behavior makes involvement in a counseling relationship very difficult.

Additional utilitarian concepts for counselors are Horney's "alienation from self" and the "tyranny of the shoulds" (147). The former term refers to common client conditions involving fear of losing identity, hazy thoughts and feelings, and feelings of remoteness from one's thoughts and feelings. Horney's "tyranny of the shoulds" refers to the strong tendency in many clients to strive compulsively to be their ideal selves without due regard for reality conditions in their lives. Such a client, for example, operates on the assumption that nothing is or should be impossible for himself.

Erich Fromm (114, 115), like Sullivan and Horney, is concerned with the social influences on behavior. He, too, stresses the individuality of the client, his goal-directedness and productive possibilities.

Fromm was one of the first to use the term "self-realization" in a therapeutic context, viewing growth as an unfolding process of man's psychological powers. He places the responsibility for many personal conflicts on the economic structure and guilt formation. More broadly, Fromm conceives that the main problems of modern man center around ethical conflicts and relatedness, particularly in regard to loving and being loved. An example would be the social emphasis upon unselfishness versus social competitiveness and self-interest, both of which involve problems of relatedness and ethics. The relatedness of man to his world, particularly to people, is an unending human problem. The counselor helps his client on these matters through improving his ability to lead a creative life and to relate to his world. The unifying "glue" in Fromm's discussion of human relationships is mature love which will be elaborated upon in later chapters of this book.

Alexander and French (2), though adhering closely to more classical Freudian assumptions and techniques, have modified the practice of psychoanalytic therapy so as to reduce the time required to achieve results.

The amount of time that should be spent on a client is one of the key issues of professional counseling. Alexander and French have reduced the time required for therapy by selecting carefully therapists to match the clients' particular needs, by keeping techniques flexible in order to suit individual styles, and by varying the time between interviews. They emphasize that psychotherapy is a "corrective emotional experience" achieved through forced insight and liberal use of supportive techniques. This latter approach highlights another counseling issue concerning the effectiveness of very direct therapist activity and liberal use of support.

Summary of Recent Psychoanalytic Positions

In summary, the current directions and implications of neo-psychoanalytic theory are as follows: (1) greater recognition of the cultural determinants of behavior; (2) more concern with the client's present circumstances, especially people close to him, and less preoccupation with infantile development and traumata; (3) more emphasis upon the quality of the therapeutic relationship and how the client perceives it; (4) a de-emphasis of sexual needs and aberrations, and increasing stress on other needs and feelings such as love, hostility, and ambivalence.

Self-Theory Approaches

Self-theories are relatively new in counseling and psychotherapy. Although the concept of a "self" was postulated many years ago by Jung, McDougall, and others, a counseling approach based upon this basic concept was not specifically offered until Rogers' controversial volume, *Counseling and Psychotherapy,* appeared in 1942 (250). Rogers' position became known as "nondirective" because it was counter to the traditional counselor-centered methods of solving client problems. Rogers emphasized the client's creative responsibility for reperceiving his problem and enhancing his "self."

The reader who is familiar with the problems of classifying counseling and psychotherapy theories may note the painful difficulties in systematizing them. In the present classification, the writers recognize that some theorists would not like some of the others they are classified with. Others can be classified in several places. Self-theorists, for example, cover a wide range of persons who classify themselves as psychoanalysts. Horney is a conspicuous example with her frequent use of the concept of self.

The Pepinskys (232) have written a succinct history and have woven together the many little threads which form the current trend and which are variously called "nondirective," "phenomenological," "self-theory," and "client-centered." The reader is referred to the Pepinskys for a summary of the contributions of numerous authors who, with many others, have contributed the vast volume of research and theoretical writings which form the bulk of counseling literature at the present time.

Carl Rogers (249) is generally recognized for having collected the most systematic set of assumptions and constructs on self-theory as well as for applying the theory to counseling and psychotherapy. His "client-centered therapy" highlights an issue in counseling; namely, how much responsibility can be placed on the client for his own problem-solving or psychotherapy? Many of the following summaries are taken from Rogers' thinking.

The nature of the self. The "self" is a construct rooted in Gestalt and phenomenological psychology. It is typically defined as "the individual's dynamic organization of concepts, values, goals, and ideals which determine the ways in which he should behave" (277, pg. 8). It is the individual's consistent picture of himself and is best represented by what he calls "I" or "me." Various terms such as "concept of self," "self-image," "self-concept," and "self-structure" are used to describe this personality construct. The main source of these personal evaluations are direct experience and the values and concepts of parents which are incorporated as if directly experienced.

As with all constructs of this type, there is great danger in thinking of the "self" as a type of homunculus, or "man within a man" having personal qualities. The next temptation is to use the concept as a universal explanation for motivation and action problems. Rogers (249) used "self" in the sense of awareness of being or functioning, not as a synonym for organism or a "place where."

The concept of self is a learned attribute, a progressive concept starting from birth and differentiating steadily through childhood and adolescence like an unfolding spiral. For example, one of the earliest manifestations of the self is the negativistic attitude of the two-year-old child when he begins to realize that he has an individuality of his own with pressing and distinctive needs and powers. This growing awareness of himself as an unique person is his concept of self. This self takes on various subjective attributes in the form of "I am" (his nature), "I can" (his capacities), "I should or should not" (his values), and "I want to be" (his aspirations) (277).

When the individual perceives himself as behaving in a manner consistent with his picture of himself, he generally experiences feelings of adequacy, security, and worth. If he acts in a manner different from the way he defines himself, he experiences what is known as "threat" and feels insecure, inadequate, or worthless. The individual, if he perceives no other alternative, may then defend himself against this threat or inconsistency via one of the commonly described "defense mechanisms."

An example of this phenomenon is the client who comes for counseling in an anxious state. His first attempts at handling the feelings of anxiety have been to deny or distort them. The client describes his mixed feelings about going to college and continues: "My parents keep telling me I can make it; my aptitude test scores indicate I can do it; I would like to do it; but I am somehow convinced I can't. I feel caught between, so I freeze when I take exams. I would like to junk the whole idea." The client continues to describe his discomfort and other symptoms.

The client's *self-definitions,* capacity concepts, and aspirations run partially along these lines: "I am a young adult; I respect my parents' opinions, I do not have the ability to do college work; I want a college degree; I want to be liked and admired." Yet, the client experiences the fact that he is in college now; his parents have expressed themselves and he values their judgment; the tests indicate that he has the ability to do the work. He is very much *aware* of the anxiety which results and is aware that this anxiety expresses itself in "exam panic." He does not yet perceive, however, that he is experiencing *threat* because his self-concepts are so incongruent with the data. The *symptom* is anxiety which is experienced when threat occurs. He is tempted to *deny* (defense mechanism) the conflict by running away from the situation. This evasive action may reduce his awareness of the threat, but not the threat itself. Unless counseling or other life experience breaks this defensive chain reaction, the defensive behavior (exam troubles, running away) will very likely increase susceptibility to further threat and guilt, thereby creating more distortion and more mechanisms. The preceding sequence is the self-theorist's threat and defense theory in a nutshell. The theoretical points on defense, mentioned above, are modelled after those of Hogan (146).

Another common example of the threat-anxiety-defense sequence is that of the young woman who feels a conflict between career and marriage. If she falls in love she would satisfy the need for marriage; but it would threaten her career. However, if she does well in her grades in school and spends much time on training instead of social activities, it would support her career needs but it would seriously threaten her marriage goal. The preceding analysis of threat-defense sequences could be applied to this situation where there are two seemingly opposing self-concepts. In this case, the counselor tries to help the client recognize and accept both desires.

When a person is not acting in accord with his self-concept we might say he is maladjusted in the sense that his awareness of threat and anxiety, and his consequent defensiveness, are high. His concept of self and his experience as perceived by himself are dissimilar, as indicated in Diagram A of Figure 4. The student in the former illustration who feels deeply that he cannot do college work, yet denies the significance of parental judgments and test data, fits this paradigm.

Conversely, when the person's concept of self is in relative harmony with his perceived experience and he feels that he is acting in accordance with his values, ideals, and past experiences, we might say he has good adjustment. Our student illustration recast in hypothetical terms to match Diagram B of Figure 4 would say, "I'm convinced I can make it. My parents expect it; my grades and test scores all point to the fact that my plans are realistic."

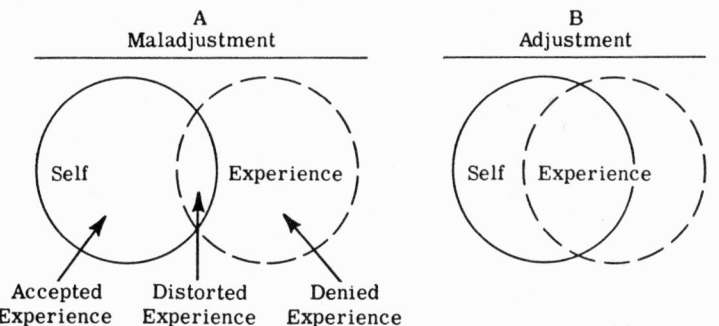

FIG. 4. Maladjustment and Adjustment from the Self-Theorist's Viewpoint. Adapted from Rogers (246, pg. 526).

Congruence is a significant term used by self-theorists, particularly Rogers (249). It means the close matching of awareness and experience. If a client is aware of communicating a feeling which he is genuinely experiencing, his behavior is said to be congruent or integrated. If a client is *aware* of trying to *communicate* a feeling of love to another person, for example, yet he *experiences* hostility toward that person, the recipient of his feelings may experience an awareness of phony communication. The recipient is often aware, furthermore, of the unconsciously motivated defensiveness underlying the client's inaccurate communication. This illustration points up the clear incongruence between experience and awareness, because what the client is aware of and what he is genuinely experiencing are two different phenomena. This condition is also an illustration of the nature of defense from a self-theorist's viewpoint.

A further example of incongruence is the bored guest who insists he is having a wonderful time. Here the guest is aware of the incongruence between his real feeling of boredom and his desire to be polite. Rogers would say this is a type of incongruent behavior which is deceptive rather than defensive because he is aware that his communication is incongruent with his genuine experience of boredom.

The principal counseling implication of this theory of congruence, it would seem, is that the counselor's problem is how to help the client to face courageously the incongruence between his awareness and his experience so that his communication of his real experiences is in full awareness and not defensively distorted.

Further characteristics and assumptions. Although the "self" is the key structural construct, the principal assumption or central hypothesis of the self-theory group is that the individual has a self-actualizing growth tendency or need. The organism not only strives to maintain itself but also to enhance itself in the direction of wholeness, integration, completeness, and autonomy. Hence, the client is believed to have the capacity and the motivation to solve his own problems. The main implication of this view is that the counselor's role is to create an interview "climate" and to use techniques which allow these natural growth forces to emerge in the direction of mentally healthy and creative behaviors.

Although the "self-actualizing tendency" is postulated as being biologically determined, the direction of the growth tendencies is assumed to be culturally determined by parents, peers, teachers, and other persons significant to the child. Since the individual tends to deny perceptions which conflict with his self-concept, these growth forces often become distorted in the developmental process. This condition often gives the picture of a person devoid of positive growth motives. There seems to be a strong belief on the part of the self-theorists that the positive growth forces will ultimately triumph. For example, independence will supersede dependence; integration will overcome disintegration; social behavior will replace anti-social behavior.

A third assumption, based on the point of view called "phenomenology," is that the individual's "reality" is that which he perceives. External events are significant for the individual only insofar as he experiences them as meaningful. The phenomenologists say that the way to understand the individual is to infer his "phenomenological field" from his behavior. In other words, to really know a person, the observer, or counselor, must know how the individual views his environment and himself. Thus, the term "internal frame of reference" has come into common use in counseling with the implication that the counselor must try to perceive the client's perceptual world as closely as he can. This intimate understanding is a necessary prelude to "acceptance" of the client's feelings. This viewpoint explains why the client-centered counseling group focuses on deep understanding and acceptance of client attitudes. Thus, the phenomenological approach places a premium upon the empathic skill of the psychotherapist.

Rogers (249) has developed a tentative system of fourteen postulates which go beyond the basic assumptions summarized above. Much current effort is being expended to clarify his propositions and to submit them to rigid experimental tests. The exploration centers on how the conscious and unconscious states of the organism are organized and altered. It is a difficult problem, however, to relate the changes which are observed in client-centered counseling to the self-theory postulates, particularly the basic one of self-actualization. Examples of research efforts toward this goal are collected in Rogers' and Dymond's report (258).

A related group of personality theorists is the "need"-centered group. Maslow (197), for instance, combines the self-theorist's basic postulates, such as the self-actualization principle, with basic human needs. He views the human being as an integrated holistic organism with a series of basic needs organized into a hierarchy of importance dictated largely by the culture in which he is raised. The psychotherapeutic process becomes a systematic need gratification through a very special type of interpersonal relationship. Maslow feels that his need gratification theory explains why so many people are helped by persons who are well-meaning but who are untrained in counseling technique and theory.

General implications of self-theories. One of the basic contributions of this view for counseling and psychotherapy is that the experiencing individual becomes the center of focus in the counseling process. Since the client holds the power of growth and meaningful perception within himself, the responsibility for change and the "locus of evaluation" of his experience must be within the client. His internal frame of reference is generally close enough to "objective reality" so that the counselor can follow meaningfully what the client is saying. The counselor, nevertheless, constantly must ask himself, "What is he trying to say; and what does this mean to him?" His understanding of the perceptual world of the client is then communicated to the client in fresh language. This condition facilitates further elaboration and clarification of feelings, which leads to insight, and in turn results in positive planning and action.

Another implication of the growth principle is that the counselor's attitudes in the interview must be so permissive and accepting that the threat to the self is reduced to a minimum. Reduction of threat allows the client to accept hitherto unaccepted parts of himself and to express feelings never before admitted. Since he accepts more of his previously denied and distorted experiences into his self-organization, he is in a better position to accept others and to achieve the characteristics of the fully functioning person as described by Rogers (252).

A third implication is that the emotional quality of the relationship is the most significant therapeutic element. Wealth of information, diagnostic accuracy, and historical understanding, which are primary in some theories of psychotherapy, are secondary to the "climate" created by the counselor's sincerity, warmth, acceptance, and sensitive empathic understanding. There is less concern about the *direction* in which the client will move and more concern about providing a *relationship* where he can freely and safely move in exploring his own feelings. When a "delinquent," for example, is given this type of relationship, the expectancy is that he will move in a socializing direction because he sees this as the most rewarding way to go. Thus, there is little emphasis upon changing basic motivations or habits. The self-theorist claims that these behaviors automatically change in a socially desired direction when the client's perception is more finely differentiated and when he discovers for himself more satisfying ways of meeting his own and society's needs.

Summary of self-theory approaches. The principal mark of the self-theory group is their postulation of a self-concept. A second distinguishing characteristic is the belief in the innate positive growth potential or self-actualizing power of the organism. The main focus in therapy is on the relationship of counselor to client. In this relationship, the counselor's attitudes of acceptance and permissiveness are crucial. A main difference from other dynamic approaches appears to be in the effort to build and maintain a nonthreatening, anxiety-reducing relationship from the very beginning. Another difference from other approaches is the increased amount of responsibility placed upon the client compared to that ascribed to the counselor.

BEHAVIORAL APPROACHES

Although the dynamically oriented theorists seek to understand conscious and unconscious conditions through inference, the behavioral group concentrates on the objective study of client behavior and the learning process in particular as the source of hypotheses about counseling. Since the emphasis of this group is on behavior, their primary concern is to discover how the behavior was acquired and how it can be changed.

The Gestalt or field theorists are a rather independent group. They are included with the broad behaviorist group since they, too, stress learning and systematic behavior observation. The differences, however, between Gestalt approaches and behaviorism are more striking than their similarities. In many ways, the Gestalt views, with their emphasis upon perception, are significant sources for the self-theory group's views.

Learning-Theory Contributions

Historically, this group evolved from the Pavlovian conditioned-response approach to learning and the Watsonian behaviorism of the 1920's. Their objective orientation resulted in a heavy emphasis upon studying behavior in its most simple forms through the medium of animal experiments. Although there are few direct applications of formal learning theory to counseling and psychotherapy problems, there have been several speculative books and articles the past few years which have attempted to explain the events of counseling in learning-theory terms. Mowrer (217), Dollard and Miller (83), Shoben (274), and Shaw (270), for example, made such integrative efforts.

Characteristics and assumptions. The learning theorist assumes, first of all, that most of human behavior is learned. He assumes also that behavior can be modified and that client behavior and its relationship to antecedent conditions in the client can be described by hypotheses derived from a model of the personality. Some of the terms and the rationale used by the various learning theorists are discussed below.

The strictly behavioristic explanations of client behavior are based largely upon the works of Thorndike, Hull, Guthrie, Skinner, and Tolman. Mowrer and Miller, Shaw, Rotter, and Shoben have attempted to apply these principles to counseling. All these investigators start with the assumption that the person has *drives*. These drives are primarily physiological, but through social learning a vast hierarchy of secondary *motives* is acquired. These drives and motives propel the individual toward goals. From past learning, the individual acquires *expectancies* (excluded by some reinforcement theorists) that, if he seeks a goal in a certain way, he will achieve it. A *stimulus* or *cue* sets off the *response* which propels the client toward his goals. This sequence is described as an S-R model (stimulus-response). The individual *discriminates* among various stimuli according to past *conditioning*.

A key concept of the behavior approach is that of *reinforcement*. This is a rewarding condition which occurs when a stimulus-response sequence has been completed. The S-R pattern then tends to be repeated under similar circumstances and *generalizes* to other types of responses which are similar to the learned pattern. Also, response patterns which are not repeated and reinforced periodically tend to be *extinguished,* that is, disappear. The process of substituting one stimulus for another to get the same response, or of getting a different response for the same stimulus is called "reconditioning," or in psychotherapeutic terms, *re-education*. The concept of anxiety for the learning theorists is a type of nonspecific fear in which one is unaware of the source as well as the object of his fears.

An example of a learning-theory approach to counseling is Phillips' (235) "interference theory." Phillips stresses the contemporary assertive and choice-making behaviors of a person and leaves out concepts involving "depth" and "defense" in the personality. To change behavior in psychotherapy, then, the counselor sets up conditions which interfere with present behaviors and which teach the client new ways of responding to his environment. Phillips hits directly on one of the major issues of psychotherapy; namely, is it necessary to postulate a depth dimension of personality invoking assumptions about an unconscious and defense mechanisms such as repression?

Another issue faced squarely by the learning-theory advocates is that of experimental validation. The learning theorist strives valiantly to state his concepts, postulates, and hypotheses in forms which have behavioral correlates and which can be observed and studied in laboratory situations. Learning theorists criticize other theory-making efforts severely because the concepts, postulates, and hypotheses are "slippery," vague, and difficult to correlate with behavioral referents. However, learning theory does not offer utilitarian substitute concepts for some of the inferred structural and functional concepts of personality propounded in the dynamic and self-theories.

Implications and limitations of learning theory for counseling and psychotherapy. Experimental psychologists make few attempts to draw parallels between laboratory conditions and the interview. A few hardy clinicians, however, have made attempts to define counseling variables in learning-theory terms. They reason along the following lines: An almost universal condition of clients, from those who have superficial counseling problems to those who need deep psychotherapy, is some form of *anxiety;* the counseling relationship as experienced by most clients is *anxiety-reducing;* many defense mechanisms are anxiety-reducing also and have been reinforced so many times that they become fixed; although a defense mechanism, such as sarcasm, may reduce tensions, it is paradoxically self-defeating or socially maladaptive; hence, the defensive measure itself creates more anxiety.

Learning theory may some day shed light on why counselor acceptance and permissiveness enable clients to feel secure and to learn more personally rewarding behavior in place of the maladaptive defenses. Pleasure experienced from smoother interpersonal relationships appears to have a reinforcing effect on the new behavior.

We need to know why some clients fail to learn more satisfying behaviors under the same conditions. Why do some clients persist in their maladaptive defenses even when they are very much aware of their source and of the pain they cause themselves and others? Many clients can label the dynamisms and symptoms with great aplomb; yet they do not seem able to act upon this knowledge.

How impulses can be inhibited in clients with immature characteristics and so-called "character disorders" is another problem which may someday be explained by learning theory. How can responses considered undesirable by the client himself be extinguished so that they do not recur? How can this inhibition of undesirable responses be accomplished without resorting to conscious suppression or unconscious repression?

Learning theory has stimulated the idea that the client should be encouraged to experiment with new behaviors for the purpose of enlarging his repertoire of behavior in social situations.

How can the client be helped, furthermore, to *generalize* or *transfer* from *response sets* (138) discovered as rewarding in the counseling relationship to situations outside of counseling? This question often plagues counselors.

Rotter (260) emphasizes that one psychotherapeutic task is to increase the *freedom of movement* of the client so that he is aware of, and can engage in, more activities which lead to satisfaction. After loosening up the client's rigid perceptions of his situation, *expectancies* are built up which anticipate reward instead of punishment. Then, when the client tries out a new expectation of himself, such as speaking before a group, his feelings of success about himself are reinforced, for example, through people telling him he did a good job. The counselor's attitude of acceptance alone seems to be helpful in supplying positive reinforcements and positive expectancies. The client may come expecting criticism for his exploits; but he finds the counselor understanding and relaxed about the matter. This feeling of being understood and liked is a type of positive reinforcement which may lead to more generalized feelings of being liked by others outside the psychotherapeutic interview.

Although there is a fair amount of agreement among clinicians interested in learning theory as to what learning labels can be applied to client behavior, they differ greatly as to how active the counselor should be in promoting new learning. Some think the counselor is obliged to have the client spell out his problem so that he can perceive and redefine it accurately; then the counselor helps the client through suggestion and interpretation to build expectancies for more satisfying outcomes. Then, the counselor tries to get the desired behavior and, then, reinforces it.

Other counselors with a learning orientation feel that the first chore is to prevent the client's anxiety from generalizing to other stimuli and to allow expectation principles to operate. Next, the counselor attempts to help him recognize his distorted expectancies without using argument or pressure. Meanwhile, the counselor's accepting attitude conveys the idea that the client's difficulties are due to his confusion and lack of understanding rather than to "weak will power, orneriness, laziness, or perverseness." New behaviors are then elicited as tryout suggestions from the client rather than through direct suggestion or approval rewards from the counselor.

In some cases, the counselor may decide to intervene more actively, to teach the client *skills* which he may use to achieve the expected rewards. For example, the failing student may need improved study methods before he can experience the rewards of achieving his new expectancy of being the "successful student," which he will very likely generalize to being the "successful person."

The principle of expectancy has another implication in the phenomenon of transference. Transference, which will be described in Chapter 8, can be explained in learning terms as a series of learned client expectancies. Examples of such expectancies are that the counselor will be like other persons the client has known who are feared or disliked, loved, or depended upon.

Summary of learning approaches. In summary, the learning approach to counseling and psychotherapy has great promise even though the application is highly limited at the present time. The participants in the Kentucky Symposium on learning theory, personality theory, and clinical research (1), for example, concluded that current learning theory, which is based on controlled and highly artificial experimental situations, has limited applicability to practical problems at the present time. They agreed also that personality and clinical theories which are based on clinical case observation do not have suitable forms for experimental testability. The Kentucky Symposium participants suggest that one way to mesh the two is to strive for more generality of learning theory and to be more concerned with finding means whereby results of psychotherapy can be measured with laboratory methods. There was full agreement that theory is in such a primitive stage that there is great need for clear statements of the dividing issues and honest skepticism and criticism of present theories.

Critics of the learning approach to counseling feel that emphasis on objectivity and denial of unconscious manifestations leads to sterile, mechanistic, atomistic approaches, and that the personality is too complex to study with the present methods which are designed to study lower organisms. The next criticism logically following is that theories based upon simple models have little applicability to complex human processes. Learning theorists aim to understand behavior in small, highly controlled samples and argue strongly against premature attempts to explain higher processes until methods for study of these processes are developed. The self-theory group is generally skeptical of the learning-theory approach because it tends to stress the process of learning rather than to focus on the client who is doing the learning.

It is concluded, therefore, that the learning approach to counseling and psychotherapy has promise for the future; but at present it offers the therapeutic psychologist some vocabulary and a few hypotheses and models for making some sense out of the puzzling phenomena he observes in his interviews.

Field Theories and Counseling

Field theorists are often classed with the behavioristic group because of their emphasis on learning as change of perception and their stress upon systematic behavior observation. They differ, however, in several ways, and particularly with respect to their phenomenological approach to perception. Among field theories, Gestalt psychology has the more formalized approach and is represented by such familiar names as Koffka, Kohler, Wertheimer, and Lewin.

The Gestalt approach was introduced to the United States from Europe about the same time Behaviorism reached full flower. The Gestalt movement was radically different from Behavioristic movements in that it tended to de-emphasize minute analysis of behavior into mechanistic stimulus-response bonds and stressed, instead, the dynamic organization of whole units of behavior.

Perls, Goodman, and Hefferline (233) have developed a therapeutic approach called Gestalt Therapy which stresses the applications of Gestalt psychology to psychotherapy. They emphasize problems of awareness, the whole self in creative contact with the environment, and the reshaping of one's sensory capacities. Perls' system of therapy claims a reintegration of Gestalt principles, Freudian structures, Reichian viewpoints, and the principles of general semantics.

Two principal contributions to counseling theory have been made by the Gestalt psychology group. These are principles of perceptual organization and the phenomenon of insightful learning. The Gestalt group postulate that psychological organization of the person tends to move in the direction of wholes or the "good gestalt." This means that the person tends to organize his perceptions simply and completely in order to reduce tensions arising from a state of disorganization. For example, when we see an incomplete drawing of a familiar object we tend to complete the details to make it a meaningful figure. The Gestalt group stresses the influence of the "field," that is, surrounding forces in the environment, on the organism.

Lewin, although not thinking necessarily of applications to psychological counseling, formulated some concepts of particular value to counselors. Lewin calls his theory a "topological theory" of personality because he used a mathematical model to account for the psychological field of the person (183). He pictured the personality in his psychological field with field theory terms such as *vector* (direction) and *valence* (attraction power). He conceives a dynamic system of interdependent subsystems of personality which offer a considerable contrast to Freud's more historical deterministic system.

Lewin describes the person as "differentiated life-space" organized into energy systems. In this framework, the child begins life as a relatively simple organism; and, as he grows, the processes of differentiation and integration become more rapid. Along with growth comes more rigidity of boundaries within the personality. The tensions, or needs, developing from internal conflicts and from frustrations in goal-seeking act as motivating forces. These forces impel the personality toward actions to alleviate the tensions or reduce the needs.

One implication of Lewin's theory for counseling is the importance of helping the individual to make the barriers within his personality more permeable so that he does not suffer from the dissociating effects of rigidity. Another counselor task is to help the individual keep goals within reasonable grasp in order to reduce the frustration concomitant with goal barriers, that is, develop a realistic "level of aspiration." A consequence of frustration, for example, is to force the personality to make fantasy solutions. In severe cases, the individual so displaces reality with fantasy that the latter is perceived as reality.

The principal goals of the counselor, summarizing implications from

Lewin, are to increase the life-space of the client so that he has more flexibility in living, to help the client reduce the rigidity of the barriers which prevent him from reaching his goals (such as achieving better reading skills so as to obtain success in his job or in school), and finally to reduce the rigidity within his own personality to allow an experience of freedom and spontaneity.

Values of Gestalt Principles

Perception. The first significant contribution of field theory was the influence of perception in behavior. The main principles of perception theory are summarized as follows by Combs (67): First, the physical state of the organism determines the nature of what is perceived. Therefore, how the person behaves is a function of the state of his perceptual field at the moment. Second, perception is a function of time since the exposure must be long enough to allow sensory organs to function adequately. Third, perception cannot occur unless there is an experience, either concrete or symbolic. Fourth, the client's values and goals influence perception. In general, people perceive what they want to perceive, or are trained to perceive. Fifth, the ego and the self-systems selectively determine what is perceived. Sixth, experiencing threat (as previously defined) affects the range and quality of perception. Threat seems to narrow the perceptual field as well as to force the individual to maintain the integrity of his personality organization by various defenses.

The perceptual learning group, then, begins with the basic postulate that behavior is a primary function of the person's perceptual field at the moment. Snygg and Combs (285), for example, emphasize the importance of understanding a person in terms of his unique perceptual or "phenomenal field." This phenomenological view is a considerable contrast to the psychoanalytic view that behavior is influenced by deeply repressed historical events in the personality. The psychoanalytic theorist is inclined to say that how the person behaves now is a function of the meaning automatically given to an event in terms of his unique past history of repressions and "libido," or life energy, uses. The behaviorist, in contrast, would stress the importance of past learning.

Kelly (165) has devised a system which he calls "constructive alternatism." This view is a perception theory wherein the client construes his world in a variety of ways; hence, the client is not bound to a particular set of constructs about his world. Kelly's fundamental postulate is that "a person's processes are psychologically channelized by the ways in which he anticipates events" (165, pg. 46). There are many corollaries and definitions in his "psychology of personal constructs"; but it reduces to a perceptual learning viewpoint incorporating the personal history of the client as a basis for understanding the perceptions of the moment. There are many implications for counseling in Kelly's formulations, including the strategy of assisting the individual to change his role constructs, or pictures of himself, as a basis for planned changes in his behavior. Kelly's view differs from Rogers' and the self-theory group in the important respect that Kelly does not postulate a "growth principle" impelling the client toward a "mature self."

Self-theory leans heavily on principles of perception. For instance, a significant part of the rationale of the self-theory group is that the counselor attempts to get within the perceptual frame of reference of the client so that he can see the world in somewhat the same way the client sees it. Since the client's reality is that which he perceives, it is quite important that the counselor get a good look at the client's reality.

Related to the idea above is the client's need to "free his perception," which means making it less rigid and less subject to distortion. The counselor does this by allowing himself to be used as a screen upon which the client can project his perceptions. The counselor reflects these back in ways which help the client to see that there are other ways of looking at his problem. The counselor encourages the client to explore feelings and ideas which heretofore had been outside of his awareness. This verbalizing process helps the individual to alter and extend his perceptual world so that he has more flexibility of choice.

A significant contribution of the perception researchers to psychotherapeutic counseling has been the development of projective techniques. Although they were instigated primarily as diagnostic personality instruments, they are important aids to counseling, as indicated later in Chapter 10. Rorschach, Murray, Beck, and Klopfer not only pioneered the projective instruments but they added much to the perception theory of personality.

Insight. The second important contribution of the Gestalt group to counseling is that of insight-learning. Here, a process of searching for solutions leads to a "restructuring of the field," or reshuffling of relationships, which, in turn, often results in a sudden solution. Past experiences are seen in a different manner and events stand in a different relationship to one another. Insight accounts for the, "Oh yes, why didn't I realize this before," type of response heard so frequently in counseling.

Insight is achieved in counseling by helping the client to review his past experiences, to arrange them for clear observation, to search actively for new solutions, and then to wait for the perceptual reorganization to take place. In an actual counseling situation, the client usually has some form of hypothesis about causes and some tentative solutions he anticipated trying. The counselor's job is to help him loosen his rigid ways of thinking so that perceptual reorganization resulting in insight can take place. This is done through a thorough discussion by the client of his feelings and ideas about the relevant aspects of the problem. It is through the process of verbalizing that he actually relives or re-experiences his past or present perceptions. Something happens within the perceptual organization of the individual when superficial knowledge about himself and others is translated into deep understanding and the increased awareness which we label "insight."

The importance of an "incubation" period must be stressed here. The counselor and client may discuss many relevant aspects of the client's problem without a satisfactory solution being presented. Then, after a period of time, the client comes back with a fresh "set" to attack the problem, or he may have a solution which he wishes to discuss in the interview. Insight often cannot be rushed. It seems to be spontaneous and sudden when it comes; but the surest way to bring it about seems to be through the counselor's success in creating an interview climate where the client can explore many of his relevant past experiences and present feelings with a sense of freedom and deep personal intensity. Insight is more likely to come when the client is "involved" with his problem; that is, when he lets his feelings have full sway in the deep re-experiencing of those feelings he has tended to deny, distort, or project. There also must be an intense desire to find a solution to his discomfort.

Limitations of Gestalt views for counseling or psychotherapy. The principal limitations of Gestalt views for counseling are their incompleteness. Perception theories aid considerably in hypothesizing how attitudes are learned and changed. Insight theory gives further enlightenment to these matters. The therapist or counselor is still in the dark, however, when it comes to setting conditions whereby perceptual changes and insight are accomplished. How intellectual understanding of one's feelings and thought processes can be translated into the deep awareness which is labelled insight is still unclear.

Trait and Factor Approaches

Other theories have been constructed which do not claim to have the inclusiveness or systematization of some of the other approaches; yet, they help to explain the events observed in counseling. The trait theorists see personality as a system of interdependent traits or factors such as abilities (verbal, numerical, memory, spatial, and so on), interests and values, attitudes, and temperament. Social traits and adjustment types are included also. The trait approach has a long history of attempts to classify people into dominant character types, and to describe them in terms of test scores along various trait dimensions.

The trait and factor approaches have been used widely by the non-psychotherapeutic counselor, the counselor most concerned with educational and vocational problems. His problem has been one of prediction where an all-around appraisal of factors having (more or less) validity for prediction of school and job success have been dominant. On the other hand, the psychotherapeutic counselor, concerned with deep attitudes and debilitating feelings, has looked more to the dynamic and perception theories.

The trait and factor group was influenced greatly by the early measurement movement in psychology. Psychometrics was concerned with measuring the various dimensions of personality in order to make accurate diagnoses and predictions of probable success. Paterson, Bingham, Darley, and Williamson were pioneers in the early attempts to make counseling an objective measurement-centered process. Thorne and Symonds did the same for psychotherapeutic counseling. They have written profusely about integrating the procedures of testing, case study, observation, diagnosis, prediction, planning of action, and follow-up, making this a formal process which has become known as professional counseling.

Other theorists are contributing side lights to counseling. Factorial methods of statistical analysis are being utilized to gather data on the organization of personality. Cattell (60), for example, has amassed considerable data on "trait clusters." Several major developments on aptitude factors have emerged in research centers. A number of test batteries based on factorial studies are available to the counselor and have influenced his theoretical model of personality organization and function. These developments will be explained further in Chapter 10 on testing.

Allport (4) has strongly influenced counseling groups with his views on the independent unitary trait. A large group of personality tests have been based upon the general premise that personality can be broken down into quite consistent generalized response units called "traits." Tests of traits such as social introversion, honesty, aggressiveness, cheerfulness, and self-confidence, for example, attest to the widespread infiltration of this view into counseling language.

Implications and limitations of trait and factor theory for counseling and psychotherapy. The trait and factor people are devoted to an empirical study of the counseling relationship with only modest attempts at conceptualizing these observations into broad theories. Their pragmatic concerns seem to have led them to focus on the minute-by-minute study of the interview, factors or traits which can be measured and incorporated into prediction formulas, and upon the total counseling process as a series of steps to rather specific counseling goals.

One important problem arising from this practical concern with specific goals is how to establish criteria of success in counseling and psychotherapy. How to relate events in counseling, meaningfully, to measurable criteria of success in counseling is the subject of much current research effort. For example, what is the relationship between the degree of lead assumed by the counselor and the client's subsequent ability to assume responsibility for his own life and to seek a job, raise his grades, get along more amicably with his family, or just feel happier? In this empirical method, there is little interest in the client's past except as it seems relevant in the counselor's opinion through the systematic case study.

The emphasis on objectivity, diagnosis, and prediction by this group of researchers on counseling led to some reaction and alarm. They were labelled "directivists," with the implication that this method of counseling was: "Find out what's wrong with 'em and tell 'em." Misapplication of the diagnostic and predictive techniques and avoidance of more dynamic views led to abuses and extremes which stimulated much of the vitriolic writing on the directive-nondirective "controversy" during the forties. One of the more naive followers of the trait school of thought believed that if one collected enough facts about the client's various traits his behavior would make sense. We know now that mere cataloging of facts has limited value.

Process Research

Later research men continued to study counseling by the analytic approach. The process researcher focuses on the counseling process from the standpoint of procedures which work best for accomplishing the particular goal with the particular type of client in the particular institutional setting. The process approach is more empirical than eclectic. Theorists in this area have studied the interview searching for elements which retard or accelerate interview progress and for factors which improve communication between counselor and client. Robinson (246), for example, has developed a "communications approach" which delineates the verbal dimensions of the interview. Problems are studied by means of recordings along dimensions such as "responsibility," "leading," "talk ratios," "planning statements," and "discussion units." Robinson is concerned with the effect of counselor attitude and technique on the client without special regard to a particular systematic personality or learning theory.

A MULTIDIMENSIONAL APPROACH

Introduction

Counseling theories and personality models are not yet sufficiently comprehensive or systematic to guide the counselor through the multitudinous problems he meets in everyday practice. However, the conscientious therapist or counselor in his professional role as scientist-practitioner, must examine critically the variety of theories for ideas which will broaden his scope and enhance his proficiency.

As counseling theory progresses, the intuitive dynamic theories may become integrated with the more objective tough-minded approaches of the laboratory. The historical depth model of personality, which stresses inner drives and impulses to action, may become reconciled with theories that emphasize the individual's present perceptual matrix.

Awaiting future development is clarification of the goals of psychotherapy. The bases of the goals in a model of personality which clarifies man's slavery to inner predispositions and defensive measures versus his adaptability, freedom of choice, and growth potential need clarification also.

Even though there is no one theoretical key to solve all problems, numerous theories have limited application. Thoughtful counselors struggle with theories, trying to stretch them to fit broad problems of counseling as they observe them in the complexity of counseling relationships. Every professional counselor and clinician has an obligation to work continuously toward the improvement of his conceptual models.

The problem of devising a parsimonious, multidimensional approach to counseling involves selection of concepts which hold up in practice, or which are workable for the majority of clients. The selection of a personality model which has consistency for the universe in which the counselor works, and the selection of techniques which fit the counselor's personality, add to his own behavioral repertoire and give him a vocabulary and a frame of reference within which he can verbalize, communicate, and test his observations about the counseling relationship.

The following concepts are an attempt to make the events of counseling and psychotherapy more understandable to us, and we hope more understandable to the reader. The ideas are offered not as "another theory," but more as an illustration of an attempt to weave together assumptions about the structure and function of human beings in order to make their counseling and psychotherapy more understandable. The reader will note considerable "borrowing" from other theories which have made their unique and rich contributions. Figure 5 illustrates the process by which a counselor formulates and applies his model from the many available theories. It should be noted that while the therapeutic psychologist formulates his model from his observations and theories, he must keep in the foreground the unique nature of each individual client.

A Descriptive Model

In considering applications of current and historical theories of personality to counseling, several dimensions must be considered. As seen earlier in this chapter, there is considerable disagreement on the necessity to include a depth approach in one's conceptual framework, but we feel that the inclusion of a time dimension is very important to explain the events observed in counseling.

An historical depth approach is necessary at present because of the understanding of the present which the counselor and client obtain from the client's history. Each developmental stage has its unique problems which form the seeds of future problems. Furthermore, the psychothera-

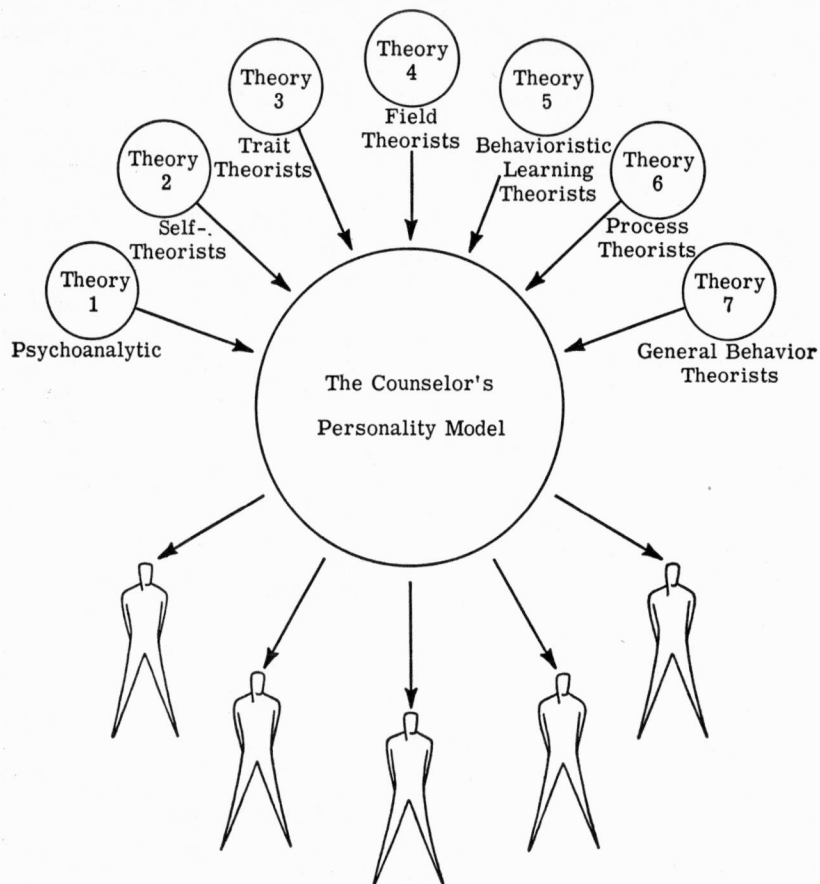

Unique Variations and Applications of the Model

FIG. 5. A Multidimensional Approach to a Personality Model.

peutic counselor begins working with the client at a particular level of personality development. The changes or behavior which take place in the process at any particular time are a function of the client's total developmental history as well as his current perception of the outside world.

A further reason for incorporating a depth dimension in our model is that it appears to make diagnostic statements more meaningful. The rationale underlying our approach to the diagnostic issue in Chapter 5 is predicated upon an historical view. Even the goals of the psychotherapeutic process itself hinge upon the ongoing growth processes established earlier in the client's developmental history. If we view the psychotherapeutic process as a continuation and facilitation of normal growth, and as a mutual therapist-client endeavor, it is important that the counselor as well as the client be aware of the developmental dimension.

The historical-depth approach does not do violence to the current stress upon contemporary perception theories since the client's present perception of his reality is a vital clinical datum also. One cannot really get to know what a house is like, for example, until one has lived in it. We can measure it, photograph it, and know its history; but we still do not know it well. Similarly, a client is not understood until we know how he views his present environment.

The following ideas are an attempt to integrate the historical and contemporary emphases into a multidimensional time approach to understanding clients. Figure 6 contains a schematic illustration of personality

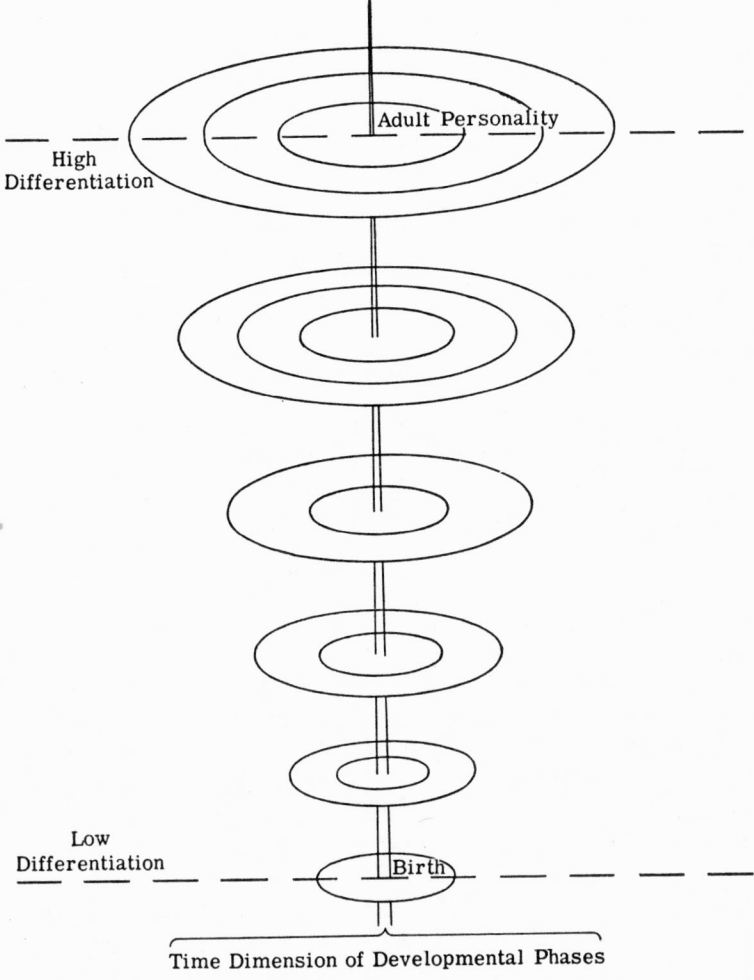

Time Dimension of Developmental Phases

FIG. 6. A Model of Personality Development,

development emphasizing differentiation with growth. The personality is conceptualized as a series of ever-widening rings. The culture within which the personality develops is represented by three-dimensional space surrounding the growing personality.

The Individual Personality

The writers have chosen a conceptual scheme to represent a personality which is analogous to the growth of a tree from sapling to maturity. To view the personality at particular points in time, then, would make it look like a group of concentric rings expanding outward. Figure 7 contains an illustration of the adult model.

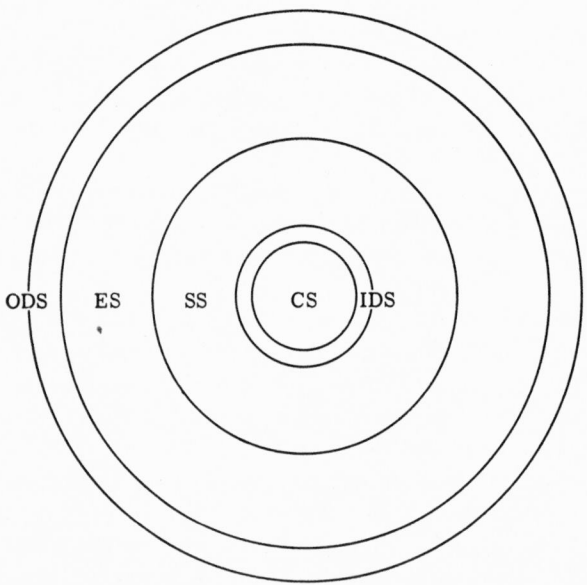

ODS - Outer-Defense System
ES - Ego System   CS - Core System
SS - Self-System   IDS - Inner-Defense System

FIG. 7. The Individual Personality. A Unitary Organization of Interacting Energy Systems.

The outer-defense system hypothesis. In Figure 7 the outermost ring is a protective "bark" designed to protect the softer, more vulnerable inner rings from damage resulting from threatening interpersonal transactions. This bark may be a tough, relatively impermeable shell; or it may be a soft, spongy, and easily penetrated covering which offers little protection to the personality.

The term "system" is used to denote a dynamic interactive characteristic among levels in the personality, rather than a static, rigidly structured hierarchy of functions. These systems are not topographical in the structural sense; but they refer to postulated interacting energy systems with rather definitive characteristics.

Another useful analogy is to consider the defensive system as being similar to the walls of a fort which can defend the personality against onslaughts from without as well as to a smoke screen which can hide defensive maneuvering of the personality from others. Thus, the defense system not only protects, but "hides" the inner elements of personality from outside scrutiny.

A third function of the defense system is what might be called counterattack. The defense mechanisms are analogous to soldiers who can counterattack as well as defend. An example of a defense-system mechanism is projection which is an attempt to attribute to a present but false source, material which really exists at a deeper level within the personality. The personality is unable to "tolerate" the painful experience of seeing that which is within itself. Therefore, the feeling is projected outward to another object.

It should be kept in mind that a defense system is being discussed here. Albeit, the writers do not wish to convey the idea that the world is construed necessarily as a basically hostile place and that the personality reacts in a naturally aggressive and hostile manner. The writers tend to agree with Montague's interpretations (209) of much biological and anthropological research which indicates that organic life is basically social, cooperative, and constructive. The ego system, to be described shortly, has a major task of reconciling the paradox of hostility-aggression with lovecooperation tendencies in humans.

The defenses are learned in the process of development and become quite automatic, even though partially under the control of other personality elements. One objective of psychotherapeutic counseling is to make the defenses less "blind" and more serviceable to the whole personality.

Another characteristic of the "healthy" defense system is to have an element of permeability. The defensive wall can be so thick and rigid as to restrict the personality within, thus preventing open contact with the culture outside the personality. Without a flexible defense system, the personality seems to develop a series of stereotyped and rigid responses or roles to meet specific life demands. On the other hand, the personality elements within should not be, in our opinion, too easily influenced as will be seen later in the model of the psychopath.

The ideal model of an outer defense system, then, is one in which there is a balance between the loose structured chameleon-like system which changes with every new social demand or whim, and the rigid, impermeable shell which makes the personality unable to change defenses to meet life's variable demands.

The reader will note that the description of defense systems is modeled after the Freudian "ego defense" mechanisms and the Jungian "persona" which is the mask-like, role-playing shell of the personality. It should be emphasized that the personality defense system described above is more of a discrete functional entity rather than a characteristic of the ego.

The ego-system hypothesis. The second ring of Figure 7, labelled *ES,* is the ego system which encompasses a considerable range of Figure 7 and of personality functions. The concept is comparable to the Freudian ego or Jungian ego-consciousness. It is equivalent to the "I" or "me" of everyday language.

One of the characteristics of the ego system is awareness of events happening within and without the personality. It is a common idea in personality theory that the individual's self-awareness is a reflection of the perceptions we think other people have of us. Hence, the principal origin of the ego system is interpersonal relationships.

A further characteristic of the ego system is the locus of trait characteristics and habit hierarchies in terms of trait and learning theory. In addition, the aptitudes, abilities, and adaptation or mastery mechanisms (as opposed to automatic defense mechanisms) have their loci here. As in the Freudian ego, this ego system contains the mastery mechanisms for dealing rationally with reality demands and for controlling the outer defense system.

Because the ego system is beneath the more apparent defensive wall, or role, it is more private. The ego system is uncovered generally only after fairly prolonged and intimate association with the person.

As implied above, the ego system has the capacity to be both subject and object. That is, it can be perceived from within the personality as the "I" or the "me"; yet, it can be the conscious experiencing element of the personality also. This capacity to be objective enables the ego system to distinguish between "external reality" (or what is outside the personality) and what is sensation from deeper subsystems in the personality.

Through its intellectualizing functions, the ego system is a type of filter device for selecting stimuli to which the organism will attend. The ego symbolizes and assists in projecting outward, or externalizing, much of the material which comes from the deeper, nonrational, noncognitive levels within. As a symbolizing agent, the ego system helps the personality to rationalize conflict by attempts to reduce apparent inconsistencies; hence, the ego system is the major integrating force within the personality.

One of the important functions of the ego system is construing the world in a manner so as to make perceptions "fit." Following the above-mentioned symbolizing and filtering functions, the ego system organizes and attaches meanings to current sensations. The ego system also compares perceptions with past experiences and data from the deeper systems. The ego directs certain defensive operations such as: (1) rejecting or projecting outward; (2) rationalizing or incorporating the perceptions into the ego and self-systems; or (3) repressing the "unassimilated" perceptions to a deeper core-system level.

When the ego system is functioning in the ways described above, which are effective and satisfying for the whole person, it is said that he has a "strong" ego system. The person is perceiving events as accurately as he is able with his unique experience background. He is aware of a feeling of competence to master both internal and external pressures. He is also aware of a feeling of value and individuality which permeates from the next deeper level of his personality, the self-system, to be discussed below.

When we spoke of differences between counseling and psychotherapy in Chapter 1, it was noted that counseling dealt more with surface-level problems. More specifically, ordinary counseling deals more with ego-system functioning and with methods of improving ego function; psychotherapeutic counseling is more specifically a concern of the next two levels of personality to be discussed. The counseling-level goal, therefore, is to increase the client's understanding of his ego capacities. Examples are his relationship skills, and his awareness of traits, aptitudes or abilities. The goals of psychotherapy, in contrast, are to understand the defensive processes and unconscious core drives in addition to helping the client to understand his ego capacities and to develop a mature self-system. The implications of ego-functioning for counseling and psychotherapy will be treated in Chapter 9 on interpretation.

The self-system hypothesis. The third ring in the present conceptualization of Figure 7 is labeled the *SS,* or self-system. This system is primarily a vague undifferentiated semi-conscious (and often unconscious) element of the personality. This system is close to what Jung and Sullivan describe as the "self" or what the man-in-the-street calls the "real me" or the "real self." In this sense, it is an achievement rather than a biological inheritance, although it is assumed that each person has enormous potential for developing a basic individuality of uniqueness and depth. Few people, in our opinion, achieve an awareness of the possibilities of self-development and the use of their basic individuality, or self-system.

The achievement of a mature self-system is one of the principal goals of psychotherapeutic counseling. Its ultimate achievement is best described by Maslow's and Goldstein's concept of "self-actualization" or Rogers' "fully functioning person" to be described in Chapter 4. Religious experiences, broadly conceived, seem to take place at this creative level of the personality where a sense of unity or oneness with the universe is achieved.

In the immature personality (by our definition) the surface (or conscious) and the deep (or unconscious) elements of the personality are kept discrete and unrelated. The mature personality has a self-system which becomes the focal point of personal growth. The self-system, rather than the ego system or the defense system, becomes this focal point in personal growth. The immature person tends to focus on ego-system development.

Concern for the development of the self-system becomes manifest in the late teens, for example, when the young adult looks within and shows more concern for social ideals and internal values. It seems that this concern is quickly diminished by the problems of young adulthood where he must look outside himself for assistance, as in selecting an occupation and becoming established in a career. Then, in middle age, when the person has achieved at least a modicum of mastery over his external environment, he tends to look for an internal type of mastery represented by an integration of his ego system and his self-system, as well as an awareness of unique individuality. It seems that no person ever fully realizes his unique basic individuality; nevertheless, this Jungian idea is offered as a partially attainable personal and psychotherapeutic goal.

The self-system, as implied above, is the locus of the person's value system. The life hopes, goals, and values of the person appear to be generated and refined at this level. Since the characteristics of a personality, just described, are relatively stable and consistent in adult life they are strong motivating forces in the personality. One goal of the psychotherapist is to help the person make his value system more explicit through more thorough knowledge of his implicit values.

The inner-defense system hypothesis. The *IDS,* or inner defense system, illustrated in Figure 7, is similar to the outer defense system in that it is a protective ring between the self-system and the core of the personality.

The principal function of this inner defense system is to contain the core dynamisms and to keep them from consciousness. An analogy might be that of a potentially troublesome prisoner who must be kept from the larger society by prison walls. As in the case of the outer defense system, the inner defenses form a natural protective ring to prevent disintegration of the personality by inner inconsistencies and pressures. Again, one of the functions of deep psychotherapy is to transform this rigid, impermeable fortress into a type of protection which is constructive and useful for maintaining internal peace and consistency.

It is postulated that dreams are a manifestation of the temporary loosening of the inner defense system, which allows hitherto unsymbolized material to come to the ego-system level in rich symbolic form.

As in the outer defense system, there are mechanisms which enable the personality to maintain its integrity and consistency. One of the principal defense mechanisms of the inner defense system, for example, is repression. This term is used in the Freudian sense where the energy system of the core is held in check, and the process whereby psychic material not easily handled by the ego or self-systems is relegated to the core.

Whereas the inner defense system restrains the repressed nonsocial impulses, it has a checking effect on the positive social and creative impulses from the core also. One of the functions of deep psychotherapy is to help the person to learn to be more selective regarding which impulses to allow to become conscious. Therefore, the deep loving, social, creative impulses can be utilized by the ego system, whereas the later learned, socially destructive impulses can be controlled more effectively or removed altogether.

The core-system hypothesis. This system is similar in many respects to the Freudian "id" or the Jungian "shadow" and "collective unconscious." It is close to what the man in the street calls "human nature." The core is represented in Figure 7 as *CS,* the innermost ring in the personality "tree."

The core system contains the basic fundamental needs and drives common to all human beings. In this sense, the core system is the common denominator of humans, and of many living creatures; whereas the self-system is the unique element of the personality. Examples of some of the characteristics of the core system are the basic drives such as sexuality and security. Basic aggressiveness needs are a part of this pattern also. These core needs and drives may be dominating forces in the personality, particularly in times of great threat or crisis, and may show in many behavioral derivatives.

Evidence on the hereditary characteristics of the core system is fragmentary and conflicting. It is postulated from anthropological and biological evidence that the human being comes into this world with a basically out-reaching, loving, cooperating, security-seeking need system. In the process of satisfying his security needs, and in the give-and-take of family life, he experiences frustrations. These frustrations lead to defensive behaviors, which combine with particular social learnings within the culture, and often give an appearance of deep-seated aggressive needs and a very hostile antisocial human nature. It is postulated, therefore, that the anti-human characteristics of the core system are learned rather than being a part of the hereditary behavior matrix.

The behavioral expressions of core drives and needs which permeate through the defense systems may be in opposition to more conscious and rationally planned behaviors. According to Jung's hypothesis, the exaggeration of any particular conscious behavior will develop its antithesis at an unconscious level. For example, an extreme conscious emphasis on virtue should create a similar degree of emphasis upon its opposite—

licentiousness at the core-system level. Generally, the defensive means of handling this conflict is to project the conflict on others in the form of criticism.

The writers view the core system as being neither positive nor negative, but as incorporating elements of both types of feelings. This view of the core is very much like Fromm's description of the unconscious which he describes as follows:

> In Freud's thinking the unconscious is esentially that in us which is bad, the repressed, that which is incompatible with the demands of our culture and of our higher self. In Jung's system the unconscious becomes a source of revelation, a symbol for that which in religious language is God Himself. In his view the fact that we are subject to the dictates of our unconscious is in itself a religious phenomenon. I believe that both of these concepts of the unconscious are one-sided distortions of the truth. Our unconscious—that is, that part of our self which is excluded from the organized ego—*contains both the lowest and the highest, the worst and the best* [italics ours]. We must approach the unconscious not as if it were a god whom we must worship or a dragon we must slay but in humility, with a profound sense of humor, in which we see that other part of ourselves as it is, neither with horror nor with awe. We discover in ourselves desires, fears, ideas, insights which have been excluded from our conscious organization and which we have seen in others but not in ourselves (117, pg. 97).

One of the principal problems of living, in general, and of deep psychotherapy, in particular, is how to reconcile conscious needs and desires with the drives of the core system, thus reducing internal conflict. Even though counselors dealing with ego and self-system problems do not perhaps tackle the matters mentioned above, nevertheless, it is significant to know some of the hypotheses about the presence and functions of the core system.

SUMMARY

This chapter maintains the view that counselors and psychotherapists should have a consistent and explicit theory of personality to guide their practice as scientists-practitioners in therapeutic psychology. Although there is no one theory of personality which is suitable to frame the practice of counseling and psychotherapy, each position has unique implications for practice. The various dynamic and behavioral models of personality can be drawn upon to help understand this particular unique client. Our multidimensional approach is presented to serve as a framework on which conceptions about the counseling relationship and process may be built.

3.

The Development of Personality

The process of psychotherapy has different goals according to the orientation of the therapist. A significant general goal is to assist the individual to develop a creative and expansive personality. The accomplishment of this goal requires an understanding of the client's past, his present stage of development, and his future goals. In this chapter, significant events in the life of man are traced in order to place the process and goals, described in Chapter 4, in developmental perspective. This survey is not intended to be a comprehensive digest of growth and development literature. Rather, for the purposes of counseling and psychotherapy, the viewpoint is taken that psychological growth takes place through the medium of human interaction and that many human problems come about through inhibition of the capacity to love in the sense of relating closely to people. Thus, in the discussion which follows, the different meanings and significance of love at the various stages of development will be stressed.

HUMAN GROWTH AND HUMAN PROBLEMS

General Periods of Growth

The growth curve of man may be viewed either physiologically or psychologically. Physiologically, but with wide variation, there is a decrease in strength and a gradual physical deterioration following the period of maximum growth between the ages of eighteen and twenty-one. Psychological growth, in general, increases throughout life, although certain functions reach a peak and then decline.

Psychological growth occurs in two general stages: from birth to about thirty-five years, and from age thirty-five to death. The first mastery stage is one in which the individual has broad capacities for learning and adapting to his external environment and his internal needs and drives. His unfolding intelligence and his physical and emotional maturation are in his service to pursue countless goals which are both created and limited by his physical and cultural environment. In this stage, the individual first must develop habits to cope with parental demands; he must develop rational skills; acquire a formal education; enter and progress on a job; marry and start a family.

At the end of this first stage, the individual's intellectual, physical, and emotional potentials have taken direction; habits have been formed; choices have been made; both mastery skills and a way of life have been developed. Following this stage of activity, the person begins to think of ways to consolidate his gains. He has in some fashion mastered his economic and social environment. His learning capacities and physical strength, if not his creative powers, begin to diminish. The goals of youth begin to be replaced by the goals of maturity and old age. He finds himself beginning to scrutinize his values and to look for a way of life that will support and reward him and those he loves until the end of life.

Basic Principles of Growth

Psychological growth has several general, underlying principles. Growth is *progressive* and *cumulative;* that is, it moves by steps and through stages. The analogy of the tree rings, developed in Chapter 2, is appropriate here. The rings become thicker and more numerous as life progresses. Growth is *integrative* and *disintegrative;* that is, growth is a building- and fitting-together process as well as a tearing-down process. For example, childhood patterns must be disrupted before adult patterns can become operative. Psychological growth depends upon the twin principles of *maturation* and *learning.* Maturation implies a potential for development which unfolds under the proper stimulating conditions when the organism is ready to respond. Restrictive environments and restrictive adaptations of the individual, such as overly intense psychological threat and consequent defensiveness, inhibit psychological growth. Finally, psychological growth is dependent upon contact with people. It is believed that one reason why the psychotherapeutic relationship provides a powerful growth medium is because of the special optimum human-relationship qualities it offers. The general view of life and growth, given here, is the basic framework for this chapter.

The principle that growth takes place through intimate human contact is highly significant for psychotherapy. All the relationship techniques discussed in Chapter 7 are for the purpose of establishing a warm and accepting environment between the therapist and the troubled client to provide a maximum climate for growth. Within the context of this principle, to which the relationship techniques apply, the capacity to love is perhaps the most important growth ingredient. Fromm, who has written extensively on the topic of love, asserts that, "Analytic therapy is essentially an attempt to help the patient gain or regain his capacity for love" (117, pg. 87). He defines love as, ". . . the active concern for the life and growth of that which we love" (113, pg. 26). In a similar vein, Sullivan says, "Love begins when a person feels another person's needs to be as important as one's own" (294, pg. 246).

A principal quality of mature love is deep concern about the other person's welfare. We postulate that the experiencing of this kind of love from parents or their surrogates is necessary for normal growth. As will be seen in the following discussion of personality development, the experiencing and the expressing of love have special meaning for the psychological growth and health of the individual at every stage from infancy through old age. Paralleling this theme, an effort is made to show how psychological privation and frustration have differing consequences at different age levels.

One may say that man becomes ill when the conditions for growth are not fulfilled. But the problems with which the counselor and client struggle are not so much "mental illness" as they are problems of inhibition of normal growth processes. In an individual client, these growth problems may take one or both of two general forms. On the one hand, the person may be experiencing difficulties which are endemic to his particular age level. On the other hand, his problems may be those which, considering his age and capacity, he should have mastered already. Such a person may be trapped at a developmental stage which is incommensurate with his age and experience and, hence, be ill-prepared to cope with the problems of his chronological age. In brief, the kinds of problems possessed by individuals may be related either to their present age level or to an earlier stage which has not been mastered.

Implicit in the above is the further postulate that the individual is the product of all those experiences which he has had until the time he receives counseling or therapy. Moreover, the experience to which he has been subjected in his early formative years determines, in large part, the type of adjustment that he will make at any later level of development. All individuals have "problems" in growing up. When these are solved successfully and successively, the person is well equipped to progress in his psychological development. When the problems have been too threatening or too difficult for him to resolve, he falters in his growth or develops a shield of defensive mechanisms which inhibits or distorts his creative potentials.

Considering the foregoing viewpoint, there are several reasons why the psychotherapist should have a broad knowledge of the stages in personality development. Since he may work with individuals of varying ages, he needs to be familiar with the problems common to particular age levels as well as variations in techniques. Although the greater part of this book pertains to working with adolescents and adults, in Chapter 13 some of the modifications in techniques that are necessary and useful when working with children and parents are reviewed.

When the therapist is working with adults, it is desirable for him to assess frequently the maturity level of the individual client. The therapist, for instance, may assist the individual more readily when he knows whether the client's problems are typical of his age and experience or whether he has carried unresolved mastery problems of the past into the present. Many individuals are better able to understand and resolve their present problems by working back through their life experiences to the major frustrating issues which blocked or distorted their growth.

The following discussion of the early phases of life will be heavily laden with classical psychoanalytic concepts since this seems to us to be the only comprehensive, historically centered theory of child development extant.

STAGES OF DEVELOPMENT

The Dependency Stage (Birth to Two Years)

During the first stage of life, the child is helpless and must depend solely on his parents for the gratification of his needs. Much of what he first learns about human relationships is derived from the manner in which his needs are met. It is largely through the feeding process that he interprets the nature of his environment. This is why Freud (111) called the first year of life the "oral period." If the mother's attitude is one of warm acceptance combined with prompt alleviation of the child's hunger, he experiences pleasurable feelings with his food. If he feels rejection or distance in his feeding relationships, he experiences anxiety and displeasure.

The eating-sucking functions thus become closely allied to feelings of security. In this period the child develops a concept of what happens to people who are dependent. These may be lessons in security and love—or in the lack of them. When he is fed regularly and with accompanying warmth and affection, and is weaned gradually, he learns to tolerate frustration without excessive tension. It has become axiomatic in child-development theory that privations should not be too many, too early, or too sudden. When the dependency needs of this period are met and handled properly, the way is paved for natural development in the next stage.

For the child who experiences excessive frustration, deprivation or inconsistency in this early oral period, there may be significant outcomes for personality development. The tense, orally frustrated child sucks his thumb; in adult life he may smoke, chew gum, crave candy, or drink coffee, tea, or alcoholic beverages excessively. Disturbances in eating, both compulsive overeating and anorexia, may reflect oral frustrations. Freud (109) has suggested that people who pass this stage successfully will tend to be optimistic, whereas frequent oral deprivation will predispose them toward pessimism. Erikson (93) suggests that significant infant learnings of "trust" and "mistrust" grow out of early oral experiences. Buhler (47) refers to the period from birth to eight months as the stage of *mastery* in which the child learns the control of the body and its functions. Oral mastery would be one of these functions. The mastery of the dependency relationship to parents is another form of mastery.

Love at this stage is a primitive, relatively undifferentiated *dependency* love which is largely a matter of *receiving* from others. Thus, the feelings which the child experiences at the time when he is the recipient of food and other need fulfillments are crucial in the development of his personality. The lack of capacity to express affection, so often noted in the neurotic adult, probably has its roots in this stage. The child who has *received* love generously and unconditionally, seems to be able to *give* love later in life with less effort. Children who experience inconsistency and rejection in their early love relationships may be unduly demanding of love, attention, and dependency in later years. Others, fearing rejection of their tender feelings, may ward off dependency and intimacy with others to avoid repetition of unpleasant experiences. Such efforts are frequently unsuccessful and likely to reflect impaired capacity both to receive and to give love.

Thus, for the future growth of the child, it is essential that there be a close, warm, loving relationship between mother and child. In psychotherapy of adults, the recollection of early childhood memories or, more commonly, the childhood data as related by parents or friends, may give valuable insights into the origins and purposes of a client's unhealthy attitudes toward dependency and love.

One final word of caution. Although dependency gratifications do and should predominate at this early oral stage, the seeds of unhealthy fixations can be sown if the stage is prolonged. The child must realize even at this early age that is is gradually growing away from the parent. The so-called "reality principle" needs to be introduced to the child early, in the form of weaning activities. Therefore, the optimum rhythmic balance between physical maturation and personal-social evolution can be maintained.

The Independence Stage (Two to Three Years)

Between the ages of two and three, the child is still helpless in many respects. He has, however, a gradually increasing physical autonomy and begins to develop independence as he learns to walk and to manipulate things with his hands. Not only is he learning control of his movements, he is also beginning to differentiate more of the elements of his environment that are specific to his needs and pleasures; he becomes an explorer to satisfy his growing curiosity. As he senses his power he begins to rebel more directly against restrictions and wants to make up his own mind about things.

The year from two and one-half to three and one-half is sometimes referred to as the "negative stage"—the "first adolescence." The child feels a growing sense of independence; his concept of self-hood is becoming apparent; adults seem to thwart him at every turn. Aggression and its management become a paramount problem.

Buhler sees the negativistic period as one in which the child "sits up" and tests other people's love. She describes the period from eight months to four years as the period of *relationships,* in which the child experiments or tries out one thing with another. In this period of independence, he tries out his self-determination needs and experiments with independence from mother. The child's first social achievement is to be able to let mother out of sight and to trust in her ability to return.

Freud has called this period the "anal" stage, since the first real clash between the child's need to be autonomous and parental discipline is associated with adult efforts to encourage the child's control of elimination processes. The first lessons in bladder- and bowel-training affect the child's relationships with his parents. He soon learns that he can give pleasure or create anxiety by either giving or holding back feces or urine. Thus, in addition to food resistance, the elimination process becomes one of the child's first weapons in dealing with parents.

Freud suggested that the superego or conscience (concepts of right and wrong) develop out of this early period. Psychoanalysts suggest that harsh bowel- or bladder-training may predispose the child toward a rigid or strict conscience (95). Lack of parental assistance in learning these important values may predispose the child to a dearth of "conscience." "Compulsive-giving" in an adult is often traced back to the necessity of conforming during the anal period when the parent makes control of elimination equivalent to loving (95). "Overcontrol" in adulthood often can be traced to premature teaching of bowel and bladder control. The overcontrolled person is frequently afraid of natural impulses, with this fear often spreading to other areas of the personality. He feels he always must conform, thus reducing his spontaneity.

Compulsive habits about cleanliness, neatness, time, or organization also appear to have roots in severe bowel- or bladder-training (95). Persons in whom such habits are entrenched are said to be "overresponsible," having learned early to worry about a function which is "dirty" or which must adhere to a "schedule." There are personalities who are overly independent, who cannot delay pleasures, suggesting that training in this period was without control, the parents feeling that any delay would be harmful. The tensions of people concerning elimination processes are evident when one considers the number of efforts at humor about them. Underlying this humor are feelings of shame and anxiety. The ability of the average child to label his anatomy, excepting the eliminative organs, also illustrates the inhibitions and avoidance tendencies which have been learned from the parents.

The management of aggression becomes a paramount problem at this stage. Fenichel compares this to the management of sexual tensions:

> If they cannot find gratification in their original form, they have the capacity to change, to alter their objects or aims, or to submit to repression by the ego and then to make themselves apparent again in various ways and in different disguises (95, pp. 55–57).

The parental problem at this stage, therefore, is one of channeling the child's aggression so that it is not unduly postponed, disguised, or displaced. Since it is as harmful to give the child unlimited freedom as it is to overly restrict him, it is well to remember, as Horney (149) points out, that it is not the frustrations and deprivations which are crucial in the development of the child, but rather the manner in which they are imposed. Actually, the child is able to endure much of both if they are backed with love and otherwise considerate attitudes.

Rosensweig (259) suggests that there are three possible ways to manage aroused aggression: (1) *Extrapunitive:* Here the hostility is directed outward to other people or objects. When this becomes the primary method, the person may be a "chronic criticiser." (2) *Intropunitive:* In this case, direct blame and anger are directed toward oneself in a punishing manner through self-criticism or self-accusation. They may be overly apologetic and accepting of blame. (3) *Impunitive:* The aggressive elements in a situation are minimized. When this method becomes primary, the person may so minimize his aggressive feelings and actions that he fails to estimate their effects on himself and on others.

The preceding viewpoint on the relationship between anal-stage developmental problems and later aggression and frustration difficulties are in line with classical Freudian hypotheses. Newer psychoanalytic emphases introduce more social-learning principles in accounting for aggressive behavior. Freud used biological terms to describe the consequences of the mishandling of eliminative functions; but he recognized that the social microcosm of the family during these early years provided the bases for later behaviors. The child, for example, during the dependency period learns how to feel safe even though helpless and weak. Similarly, during the anal period the child is concerned with testing the social climate in the family where eliminative processes are the principal visible aspect of this developmental problem.

Each of the ways of dealing with aggression, just described, may be appropriate in certain situations. The parental role is to help the child learn that sometimes others are at fault, sometimes he himself is at fault, and sometimes his feelings are exaggerated. The child is then given opportunity to channel his aggressive or angry feelings in constructive ways.

Erikson refers to this independent period as the "stage of autonomy"

(93). The child develops a need to be independent, yet continues to need dependency and support. In terms of the development of the individual's capacity to love, the child needs to learn at this stage that he is loved for his own "dirty little ornery" self. He needs to learn that he is respected for his independence as well as for his dependence.

Many adults in counseling and psychotherapy have problems in the management of their aggressive feelings because of improper handling by the parents at this early stage of development. For them, psychotherapy provides an outlet for *verbal* expression of hostility without the serious consequences of hurting others. The chronically intrapunitive individual is given opportunity to re-evaluate his feelings of unworthiness or self-hate. His psychosomatic reactions to bottled up anger may be alleviated, too. Psychotherapy also may permit the unhappily submissive or dependent person to discover his privilege of owning aggressive feelings and independence.

A goal of psychotherapy is to assist the adult to manage his aggressions wisely. Through psychotherapy he can learn that it may be appropriate to express aggressive feelings in selected circumstances. He also can learn to perceive frustration in appropriate proportions. With major annoyances, where his basic individuality is threatened, he may learn to channel his aggression into constructive action.

The Role-Taking Stage (Four to Six Years)

Between the ages of four to six the child experiences a need for even greater freedom to match his increased motility and mastery of his environment. His curiosity and exploratory activities expand in many directions and he begins to develop a conscience whose nature is in many crucial respects determined by the manner in which the parents relate to him. The child's curiosity about his sexual organs and about differences in sexual roles reaches a peak. The natural outcomes of this curiosity are the discovery of pleasurable excitement through masturbation and the playing of masculine and feminine roles for which the parents are the models.

How the parents react to the child's curiosity about sex and masturbation has important outcomes for the child's self-regard and later feelings about sexual impulses and activities. Parents and teachers should neither over- nor underemphasize the sexual activities of the child. Many fears of punishment and castration which the psychotherapist has to help clients overcome in later years can be related back to being shamed, scolded, or threatened with dire punishment for early innocent sexual activities. If parents understand the natural development of the child's interests and do not themselves relate to the child in either a highly sexualized or overly prudish, intolerant fashion, the child is better assisted to develop healthy attitudes toward sex and sexual roles.

An important development of the role-taking stage is that the child normally accepts his own sex through a process of identification with the sexually similar parent. Parents form the models from which children develop notions of "masculinity" and "femininity." It is natural for boys to develop attachments to the mother and girls to the father. Freud referred to this stage of love as the "oedipal period." If the child fails to outgrow this initial attachment he is said to have an "Oedipal complex," or, in the case of a girl, an "Electra complex." In this period, which psychoanalysts have called the "family love affair," the parent of the same sex as the child is often viewed as a competitor for the affection of the other parent.

It is important for the parents, through their understanding attitudes, to help the child "work through" this stage to avoid future problems. The average child learns to compromise and share the loved parent with the parent of his same sex. Through this, the child develops identification love for the parent of his own sex. This identification is made manifest by boys' interest in what dad does and girls' interest in the activities of mother.

The important result of this developmental period is that the child emerges with a feeling of value toward, and acceptance of, his own sex. This is most optimally accomplished if the parent of the same sex is a model worthy of imitation. If father is comfortable in his masculine role, the son will want to be a man like his father and will not be afraid of this role. If mother is happy in her feminine role, the little girl can respect, admire, and desire to be like her.

Erickson (93) refers to this early childhood period as the "stage of initiative." By this he means that the child is moving into the future. In growing up, he needs to take the parent of the same sex with him. If the Oedipal situation has been resolved, the boy identifies with the father, thinking of himself as aggressive and masterful in his approach to life. The girl, following her mother's example, becomes endearing, attractive, and indirect in her mode of approach.

Desirable heterosexual relationships tend to result if, during the role-taking period, the child's affections are received naturally by the parents of the opposite sex. In adolescence, when it is important to establish good heterosexual relationships, the foundations for "liking" of members of the opposite sex which began in early childhood will have their effect.

During this stage of role-playing and extension of initiative, the parents have to exert practical controls which in turn assist the child in the development of a conscience. The kind and quality of these parental controls which are external to the child have important consequences both for the inner controls or conscience which the child develops and for the directions his initiative will take.

Fromm (115, pg. 157) feels that the conflict of this period is not brought about primarily by sexual rivalry but is the result of the child's negative reaction to parental authority. It is a battle between the child's freedom or spontaneity, on the one hand, and the expectations, and sometimes irrational authority, of the parents on the other.

As has been said in Chapter 2, spontaneity and independence are characteristics of the mature person; and if the child is defeated at this early stage in his struggle for freedom, he will very likely have laid the foundations for neurotic submissiveness later in life. As in other areas of life, over-protectiveness and rejective attitudes can complicate the child's progression through this childhood stage. Parents can assist in the development of conscience by a combination of praise and punishment given with understanding. At this stage the child may learn that love is not always expressed by warmth and loving attention but by punishment as well. Parents can encourage curiosity, open-mindedness, willingness to try new things, and readiness to see new solutions. They can give the child a positive conscience wherein the child is assured that within limits his impulses can be trusted and followed. However, parents can stifle curiosity, kill initiative, and create a punitive conscience that prevents trusting of impulses. The development of conscience is more readily accomplished by subtlety and indirection than by force. It seems to be most readily facilitated by example, by the kinds of behaviors which the parents demonstrate to the child and the way in which they deal with him in everyday family relationships.

Buhler (47) sees the period from five to eight years as the *task phase,* in which the child learns to enjoy making things. When there are healthy parental concern and interest, the child develops "task consciousness"— a sense of responsibility to his task. It is for this reason that kindergarten becomes meaningful. Children can create and feel an ethical obligation to their creations as well as for their other activities.

Some Conclusions about Early Childhood Development

In counseling and psychotherapy there appear to be three major developmental problems with which the individual must deal: (1) the expression of affection and dependency, (2) the handling of hostility and aggression, and (3) the management of sexual tensions. Each of these has its roots in the first six years of life. Affection has its roots in the dependency stage wherein the child is given love and security and learns that he must rely on others. In this stage it appears that he learns to give affection in kind. In the independence stage the child learns both that he has power and that he can handle his first frustrations. When the parent deals wisely with tantrums and aggressions, the child is given the means of managing acceptably his aggressive tendencies later in life. Finally, in the role-taking stage, patterns are established for effective relationships with the opposite sex so that satisfying heterosexual relationships are possible in later years. Sexual identity and role seem to develop most effectively if the mother and father represent appropriate models of masculinity and femininity.

The Conformity Stage (Six to Ten Years)

Between the years of six and twelve there is an important consolidation of the three early stages which Freud referred to as the "latency period" because the sexual drives appear to be dormant until their emergence in a later stage. Gesell (120) often has likened development to an ever-widening spiral. In the mid-child stage, the spiral of life widens remarkably. In the words of Havighurst there are three great outward pushes:

> There is the thrust of the child out of the home and into the peer group, the physical thrust into the world of games and work requiring neuro-muscular skills, and the mental thrust into the world of adult concepts, logic, symbolism, and communication" (140, pg. 25).

The child enters for the first time a world which is not completely dominated by parents and siblings and is "on his own" for many hours. He is responsible to authorities other than his parents, a fact which may create more problems for the parents than for the child. The youngster is suddenly catapulted by the necessity of going to school into a peer group to which he must learn to conform and with which he must cooperate and share. The selection of friends is no longer restricted to the child's immediate neighborhood and his intellectual and cultural interests widen as well. A typical nine-year-old's interests are multiple: dolls, bugs, dramatics, crafts, sports, games, and other group activities.

In the realm of social activities, boys appear to have an advantage over girls because of the formation of close knit "gangs" which teach many lessons. During the seventh and eighth years, the natural "homosexual stage" occurs in which boys are interested in the YMCA, the Cub Scouts, or the Indian Guides. Girls are generally not encouraged to have gangs in our culture, although the peer group influences them markedly on the conformity-nonconformity dimension. They may take interest in Brownie or Bluebird activities, for example.

Children of both sexes continue their role-playing and tend to be more interested in the activities of their own sex than in the opposite sex. The differences in sexual roles become more apparent to them, and they strongly emulate the behavior of their friends in this and other areas. In many respects, this is a time in which many more and varied behaviors relative to their sexual role are being explored and learned.

In this conformity stage, the child continues to need love, understanding, and judicious discipline combined with freedom of initiative. As in earlier stages, the parents can provide a rich environment in which the child may learn and experiment with a wide variety of things and human relationships, as well as have a sense of belonging to a wider group than the family. Or the parents, through undue restriction, disinterest, or privation, may force the child into a narrow frustrating orbit in which he senses his difference from others. Hence, his expanding potentialities may be stifled or fixed at this developmental stage.

The Transition Stage (Nine to Thirteen Years, Pre-Adolescence)

During the pre-adolescent years from ten to thirteen, which Buhler (47) aptly calls the *transition* period, the child's world is shaken up. Two major developments which occur are efforts to break away from family domination and the maturing of sexual functions. The youngster's behavior is often characterized by irritability, restlessness, moodiness, back-talk, and other defiances which try the patience of those around him. He will often talk of running away—a symptom of his efforts to break away from the family. He also begins to experience an increase in heterosexual interests. His capacity to love, which hitherto has been qualified by dependency, identification, and narcissism, begins to change in the direction of mature love as defined earlier in this chapter. Fromm (113) described this period as a basic change from narcissism to mature love manifested by a concern for the needs of others.

Another important characteristic of this transition period is the remarkable feeling of separateness and individuality which is felt by the typical pre-adolescent. They become more aware of themselves as persons separate from their parents. Parental love at this stage is best expressed by a willingness to give up the child to himself and to respect him for his growing individuality. The fears and guilts which the parents retain from their own pre-adolescent years make them fearful for their own children, and so hinder the parents from loosening the cord of emotional control and permitting the child to have his individuality.

The Synthesis Stage (Thirteen to Twenty Years, Adolescence)

With the beginning of sexual maturity in the early teens, childhood comes to an end and youth begins. Because of rapid body growth and genital maturation, the youth is faced with physiological and psychological revolution within. Since he is chronologically approaching the age of adult responsibility, he becomes subject to increasing pressures and restrictions from without. Within this framework, the youth relives his early conflicts and experiences new conflicts in his struggle to find himself and his role in life.

Physical growth in adolescence is asynchronous, meaning that there are intra-individual differences in growth rates for various aspects of the body such as height, weight, circumference, hands, feet, and neck. Furthermore, sex differences in growth create special problems. The findings of Shuttleworth (279) reveal almost a two-year difference between the maximum physical growth rates of boys and girls. The mean age for maximum growth of girls is 12.6 years, whereas for boys it is 14.8 years. He finds that at about age thirteen, girls are both heavier and taller than boys. Moreover, differential growth peaks are found within each sex. Some boys, for example, reach their peak physical growth as early as twelve years, whereas others may not reach their peak until seventeen years.

These individual and widely variant growth patterns create and complicate many problems. Erikson (93) refers to early adolescence as the "stage of identity" wherein the problem appears to be one of doubt as to one's sexual identity. Intra-individual asynchronous growth of body parts, differential growth peaks within each sex, and sex differences in rates of growth contribute to feelings of uncertainty regarding one's sexual identity. The feelings of inadequacy resulting from the "clumsiness" of uneven growth are well known. Many youngsters are subject to joking remarks from adults as well as from peers. They view their mirror images with alarm as they note any unexpected deviation in growth pattern or complexion. They become fussy and preoccupied with dress and behaviors which help them to identify with their peers. The youngsters who are late developers often resist public showers or other activities involving physical display because of feelings of physical unfitness. Those who cannot compete, or who perform awkwardly in sports often wonder if they are sissies.

Sex differences in rate of growth tend to drive the sexes apart from their own age groups. Junior high school girls, for example, usually desire the companionship of high school or older boys, because the boys of their same age are still "boys," whereas they in the meantime have developed into young women. Successful heterosexual "dates" between the ages of twelve and fifteen seem to be the best insurance for assisting youth to cross the channel of doubt to a stable heterosexual relationship, but this is better done through indirect environmental manipulation than by force. In our experience, youngsters have been thrown into homosexual panics where they have felt a tremendous threat to their sexual security. This happens especially in situations where they have been rejected by the opposite sex.

Klopfer (173) estimates that about one-half of all male clients have anxieties about homosexuality. Kinsey's findings (168) suggest that about one out of three males have had a homosexual experience. The homosexual panic which some adolescents experience between the ages of twelve and fifteen are related to several factors: (1) anxieties about heterosexuality which often develop at this time, (2) the need to exhibit male prowess, to show off through masturbatory activities, and (3) the opportunities for homosexual exploration which come in gangs.

Psychotherapy can reduce the usual homosexual anxieties of the adolescent through verbalizing them and helping the youth to realize that they are part of normal development at this period. For example, the problem may be traced to its source to determine in what way masculinity has not been made attractive, or it may relate back to developmental problems of middle childhood or the Oedipal period. If the mother relationship has not been satisfying because she was cold or smothering, the child may withdraw from her. If, at the same time, the father shows much affection, the child may then withdraw from normal Oedipal rivalry with the father to the reverse. In this situation the youth may try to get the mother to take the father's role and to get the father to love him like a mother. The roots of this problem seem to develop between the ages of four and six and then appear to be re-activated during pubescence.

As the adolescent approaches the age of adult responsibility, there are numerous and increasing demands and restrictions from without which complicate his struggle to find himself and his role in life. Our Western culture places serious demands on youth. Some of these pressures and their alleviations are:

(1) He must select his life work. Counselors can assist youth by being well prepared in vocational guidance.

(2) He must choose and secure an education. This is complicated by his dependence on parents during the years of education.

(3) He must break emotional ties with the family. Wise parents encourage a gradual emancipation since it assists maturity. Mark Twain is alleged to have said that when he was thirteen he discovered his father was utterly stupid; but when he was twenty he felt his father had grown and learned a great deal.

(4) He must choose a life mate. In our culture, the basis for selecting a mate is "romantic love," an experience of strong elation in which the individual feels that "this is it." In reality, romantic love is a delusional type of experience with a strong element of projection. The ideal image of a mate is projected to the other person which distorts the true character of that person. Eventually, married couples must realize the neurotic nature of romantic love or their marriage is probably doomed to failure.

In addition to the above demands, our culture also places certain difficult restrictions on the adolescent:

(1) Parents have various forms of legal authority over the adolescent until he reaches the age of twenty-one. Because parents feel a sense of responsibility for the behavior of the adolescent, many tribulations ensue. The adolescent is thus in continual conflict; he wants to be dependent, to have his needs cared for, and yet he wants all the privileges which come with independence.

(2) The adolescent is dependent on parents for economic support and requires help to get an education, a process which is getting longer and more costly. In late adolescence (eighteen to twenty) the boy and girl are physically ready for marriage, but are financially unable to marry.

(3) Prohibitions against sexual gratification are a source of conflict. Boys of eighteen have reached a peak of sexual interest, but society does not allow gratification until marriage. Young people desperately want to know the solutions; but they are difficult to give. Masturbation serves as an

avenue of tension release for some, the only known adverse effect of which is the feeling of guilt that develops as a result of real or imagined parental punishment, scolding, or disapproval.

With such demands and restrictions, adolescence becomes a natural period of rebellion. Psychoanalysts postulate that the youth relives his early psychosexual problems once again. He has a need to be dependent and to be orally occupied, as witnessed in the need to chew gum, smoke and chatter, for example. He needs to be independent; he is often obstinate, a hoarder, and interested in "dirty stories." He has strong genital interests; he masturbates, pets, and is narcissistic and exhibitionistic. It seems that the adolescent must declare himself autonomous even though it causes himself and others pain. Both parents and youth need reassurance that the development of autonomy must take place if he is to mature to adulthood. The process can be made much less painful to all concerned if insight is acquired before misunderstandings develop.

Later adolescence begins the period of adult responsibility with incomplete knowledge for handling that responsibility; consequently, it is a period of "collision" of retrospect and prospect. Buhler (47) describes this period as one of *synthesis* of the first four stages of life. The youth settles down to relating himself to the larger system of society. He has needs to establish his role in religion, to go beyond the family outlook to a universe outlook, and to realize his own potential in the world.

Buhler, perhaps more than any other psychologist, has been concerned with adolescence as a period in which one first raises the question, "What is life about, anyway?" For the first time the teenager sees his life as a unit from birth to death. He looks backward as well as forward in an autobiographical fashion as a means to give him perspective.

If the question "What for?" makes this time of life so difficult, intense, and perplexing, it is the answers youth finds which carry meaning into the periods of life which follow. Counseling and psychotherapy relationships along with institutional relationships in churches and youth organizations offer ideal opportunities for the youth to work out tentative answers to perplexing questions of life.

Adolescence brings closer to fruition a mature capacity to love in those young people who successfully replace their idealized parental images. The adolescent learns to accept the idea that he can both love and hate the same person, that people have faults as well as assets. If dependency and independency needs assume healthy proportions, a youth is in a position to look for a mate with whom he can share his life on a realistic and satisfying give-and-take basis. Bibliotherapy can be beneficial both in helping young people to help themselves and in assisting parents to help their children. Baruch's book on teenagers (21) is one of the many which can give assistance.

The Experimentation Stage (Twenty to Thirty-five Years)

Buhler sees the ages from twenty-one to thirty as a "second try-out" period, similar to that which occurs between eight months and four years. For the first time, the young adult is completely on his own, testing out the areas of love and work. Since the selection of a mate and of one's life work are two of the most important decisions one makes, one needs an accumulation of experience to choose wisely. There is often a tendency to settle down too quickly in both of these areas. Parents and counselors can counteract impulsive decisions by assisting young people to experience many friendships and to try out many job opportunities.

During this experimental, or young-adult, period of life, young people go through many significant experiences and life crises which Havighurst describes as follows:

> Early adulthood . . . usually contains marriage, the first pregnancy, the first serious full-time job, the first illness of children . . . and the first venturing of the child off to school. If ever people are motivated to learn and to learn quickly, it is at times such as these (140, pg. 257).

The interesting thing about such experiences is that formal education does little to prepare the adult for these significant developmental tasks. Havighurst describes these tasks as goals toward which earlier education has been aiming. The final examinations are met later in life. That many fail these examinations is indicated by the great demand for re-educative experiences in psychotherapy.

Havighurst suggests also that early adulthood is a period of stress because it is the time of life which marks a transition from an age-graded to a social-status-graded society. "In adult society prestige and power depend not so much on age as on skill and strength and wisdom, and family connections. . . ." (140, pg. 258).

Selecting a marriage partner is one of the most disquieting tasks in the early part of this period. It seems that little help can be given by parents or teachers. However, some assistance is given through courses in marriage and family life and through pre-marital counseling. Unmarried persons must cope with tremendous social pressure. They are the objects of unnecessary attention and subtle ridicule, as well as of clumsy attempts at match-making. Unless young people have been able to find the right mate in school or college a problem exists of where to meet potential mates. The local cocktail lounge often becomes such a place; but it is fraught with obvious dangers. Lonely-heart clubs flourish in metropolitan areas, but these agencies are often unreliable. Furthermore, there are the serious problems of dating behavior. Shall one kiss or pet on the first date, for example? Shall one have pre-marital intercourse? What are the methods of contraception? Group therapy often helps young people share such mutual problems. Under the leadership of a wise teacher or psychotherapist, such groups often arrive at individually, socially, and spiritually satisfactory answers and tension release.

A healthy marital relationship should be one in which there is a fusion of erotic love and mature love. A healthy sexual relationship, climaxing in an orgasm, causes a convulsion-like discharge of tension which, according to Erikson, "breaks the point off the hostilities and potential rages caused by the oppositeness of male and female . . ." (93, pg. 230). "Satisfactory sex relations thus make sex less obsessive, overcompensation less necessary, sadistic controls superfluous" (93, pg. 231). Erikson, furthermore, puts sex into a larger framework of love and describes it as follows: "(1) Mutuality of orgasm; (2) With a loved partner; (3) Of the other sex; (4) With whom one is able and willing to have a mutual trust; (5) And with whom one is able and willing to regulate the cycles of work, procreation and recreation; (6) So as to secure for the offspring, too, a satisfactory development" (93, pp. 230–231).

Preserving a healthy marital relationship is a complex problem. An important aspect of this problem is that the marital partners need to recognize that marriage is not a fusion of two lives; each should accept the need for the other to maintain a healthy independence. The philosopher Gibran in *The Prophet* likens a healthy marriage to the pillars of a temple. They are fused at the top; but they maintain their independence (122).

Pregnancy and childbearing are problems not to be taken lightly. Children often come by chance rather than by choice, often creating psychological problems for the young adult. There is the question then of acceptance or rejection of the pregnancy. Self-induced abortion is a frequent topic in psychotherapy. There are many anxieties during pregnancy such as worry over possible failure to have a normal child, breast-feeding issues, and the anticipated reactions of relatives and friends to the pregnancy.

The culture of today has created another problem by providing conflicting roles for the young wife, that of housewife and career woman. If she desires both roles, she has a most complex challenge to do each task well.

Divorce threats often plague the lives of young people during this stage. Often it is not a solution and simply treats the symptoms of personal maladjustment. The divorcee has most of the problems of the unmarried person plus many more. Financial insecurity is a major one, such as how to budget two households on one salary. Divorced women generally must accept the necessity of work. Furthermore, there is the task of meeting social opprobrium. The divorcee is still looked upon as a type of social mis-fit. Sex is an additional problem since the divorced woman is generally considered "fair game." Organizations such as Divorcees Anonymous are helpful; but they do not meet the great need for help in this problem area.

The age of twenty-nine has particular relevance for women in our culture. There is much joking about the fact that women are allowed to stay twenty-nine for ten years. Signs of physical decline have much to do with this concern. Overweight often becomes a problem to which the success of slenderizing organizations bears witness. Yet, according to Kinsey's data, the peak of interest in sexuality comes about this time (167). Men, furthermore, are often in the maximum years of vocational productivity and are not giving the attention to women which characterized their earlier courtship years.

The emphasis in our culture on productivity and achievement creates a dangerous competitive concern about masculinity in men. Men of this age take pride in their ability to "take it" and will frequently push themselves to the limit to prove that they are not "weaklings." The following conditions are common damaging patterns of health abuse in men which Crampton discusses:

> (1) He hides illnesses. When a man's wife contracts a nasty head cold he will insist that she stay home, keep warm, rest, give her doctor a ring and let her housework go. Yet when he himself is really sick and wretchedly uncomfortable he takes pride in working harder than ever. He props himself up with coffee, aspirin and alcohol. He grouchily insists he is not ill. Then afterward, he boasts he never spent a day in bed.
>
> (2) He denies fatigue. He is just too proud to admit that a "real man" ever gets tired. . . . There are thousands like him. He enjoys people saying "Jim puts in a twelve-hour day at his desk." Later when you see him at parties where he forces himself to be gay he should be home in bed.
>
> (3) He conceals emotion. The ability to choke back tears, to deny fear, to conceal humiliation, disappointment and embarrassment is another of the extreme burdens these men load upon themselves. . . . It is impossible to estimate what enormous damage to nervous and emotional stability is caused by so much grimly repressed feeling.
>
> (4) He ignores injury. So many men who are invalided at 55 with heart or circulatory disturbances admit that they felt the first warning flutters 20 years before. There was shortness of breath, pain, dizziness. "I was scared all right but I made myself forget about it. I figured if there was anything wrong with me, I didn't want to know about it" (71, pp. 8–12).

The problems of young adulthood are largely neglected in the literature. The age period from twenty-five to thirty-five, however, has many problems. Havighurst (140) calls it the loneliest period because the most important tasks of life must be accomplished with little attention and support. Because of their intense awareness of problems, and because their general education and language development provides the ability to express their ideas cogently, this age group seems able to benefit more than others from counseling and psychotherapy.

The Consolidation Stage (Thirty-five to Fifty Years)

About the age of thirty-five, a man enters the second major phase of life, described in the beginning of this chapter. In the first half of life, his energies, interests, and values have taken direction within his own personal and cultural milieu. The average man has accomplished his vocational goal by the time he reaches his middle-thirties and is beginning to be comfortable financially. The woman experiences new freedom as the children begin to reach adolescence, since she no longer has to cope with them so diligently.

When one considers the many demands made on the middle-aged adult, who often has restricted creative potentials with which to meet them, it is no wonder that some unhappy individuals develop the pattern described by O'Kelly and Muckler:

> That paranoid ideas of infidelity and discrimination by superiors are so prevalent and that the disorder occurs primarily from age 35 on suggests the validity of ascribing paranoid delusions to this mechanism. It is at middle age that the individual first starts to experience competition, sexually and in his work, with younger people. To face the fact that age brings with it a reduction in some types of adjustmental potential is too bitter a fact for many individuals to face; the easier way is to seek for the causes of inadequacy in circumstances exterior to himself (225, pp. 299–300).

As a man enters the second phase of life, it appears basic to his mental health that he recast his energies and values in directions which will reward him and his family to the end of life. He must, as in his early youth, turn inward and ask "What for?" Jung, perhaps more than other writers, expresses the need for re-evaluation to preserve and enhance mental health for the years to come:

> We see that in this phase of life—between thirty-five and forty—a significant change in the human psyche is in preparation. . . . Just as the childish person shrinks back from the unknown in the world and in human existence, so the grown man shrinks back from the second half of life.
>
> In order to characterize it I must take for comparison the daily course of the sun. In the morning . . . the sun pursues its unforeseen course of the zenith. . . . At the stroke of noon the descent begins. And the descent means the reversal of all the ideals and values that were cherished in the morning.
>
> . . . We cannot live the afternoon of life according to the programme of life's morning—for what was great in the morning will be little at evening, and what in the morning was true will at evening become a lie.
>
> For a young person it is almost a sin—and certainly a danger—to be too much occupied with himself; for the aging person it is a duty and a necessity to give serious attention to himself. After having lavished its light upon the world, the sun withdraws its rays in order to illumine itself. Instead of doing likewise, many old people prefer to be hypochondriacs, niggards, doctrinaires, applauders of the past or eternal adolescents—all lamentable substitutes for the illumination of the self, but inevitable consequences of the delusion that the second half of life must be governed by the principles of the first (161, pp. 120–125).

The dread with which man anticipates his latter years is exemplified in the phenomenal success of Jack Benny's joking about his being "thirty-nine." The age of thirty-nine for men seems to be as critical as twenty-nine is for women. Men and women at forty feel that they have "crossed the bridge" and are no longer young. Many men and women cannot accept this fact and go through a phase of intensive sexual experimentation and frantic efforts to look and act youthful. Jung suggests that the forties create special problems for the counselor and psychotherapist:

> Let us take, for example, the most ordinary and frequent of questions: What is the meaning of my life, or of life in general? Men today believe that they know only too well what the clergyman will say—or rather, must say—to this. They smile at the very thought of the philosopher's answer, and in general do not expect much of the physician. But the psychotherapist who analyzes the unconscious—from him one might doubtless learn something. He has perhaps dug up from the depths of his mind, among other things, a meaning for life which could be bought for a fee! It must be a relief to every serious-minded person to hear that the psychotherapist also does not know what to say. Such a confession is often the beginning of the patient's confidence in him (161, pg. 267).

But this problem does not let the counselor or therapist off the hook. As Jung says, "That is why we psychotherapists must occupy ourselves with problems which, strictly speaking, belong to the theologian" (161, pg. 278). Thus, although the psychotherapist does not know or give answers, he must know the questions people are asking themselves and some of the answers they usually discover.

The processes of counseling and psychotherapy described in the chapter which follows are not different for people of this age. But Jung's outstanding work with people in the second half of life suggests how important it is that this process assist the individual to find a workable philosophy of life. Creative self-hood, one goal of psychotherapy, does not come easily. Jung comments on this as follows: "It is no easy matter to live a life that is modeled on Christ's, but it is unspeakably harder to live one's own life as truly as Christ lived his" (161, pg. 273). This could be a significant goal of psychotherapy.

Love during the early phases of the second half of life seems to be described best by the word "respect." By this is meant the ability to accept fully and completely the individuality of the other person. In marriage, particularly, it means respecting the uniqueness of the marriage partner. It means that each partner is so secure individually that each has his own individuality, his own center, his own life; yet, each is able to relate to the other without dominance or exploitation.

The Involutional Stage (Forty-five to Sixty Years)

Between the ages of forty and fifty in women, and forty-five to sixty in men, a type of depression sometimes develops which is called involutional melancholia. It occurs around the menopause or change-of-life in women. Men often experience depression when they are aware of a decline in virility. Research findings suggest that this reaction is not caused by endocrine dysfunction or other organic changes, but rather by psychological problems associated with the time of life (95).

Buhler (47) likens the menopause period to the period of adolescence. In both stages there is a physical and a psychological metamorphosis of the individual, his code of life, and a consequent period of intense self-evaluation.

At the involutional stage of life, one may feel that he has passed his most productive period and that many ambitions, ideals, and goals will never be attained. Women, especially, feel that their beauty is fading fast, and their inability to bear children makes them feel that their life is spent. Old conflicts, successfully repressed during maturity, often are felt again.

Bergler (28) refers to this middle-adult period in men as their "second adolescence." A man begins to feel that he is forgotten, that he is taken for granted as a family provider, and that his business security is threatened by younger competitors. At home, his children have grown to maturity and his wife has moved into the menopause. He worries about health, sexual adequacy, and "success." He defends himself in these situations by projecting to his wife the reasons for his dissatisfaction. She is blamed for his troubles. He believes she never did love or understand him. Often the next step is to find a "girl-friend" who will provide for his fancied need for understanding and love.

Bergler (28) suggests that the extent of the revolt is determined by the rebel's degree of "psychic masochism" or the need he seems to have for pleasure in self-damage. Inevitably, the revolt is abortive and leads either to the realization that it is self-induced or to feelings of bitterness and reproach that may end in divorce. Divorce, however, generally is not the cure, for it deals only with the symptoms and not the real problem.

In addition to family problems, the middle-aged man is concerned about job success. As part of the accelerated process of looking inward that occurs in the late thirties, he begins to evaluate himself as having been a "success" or "failure." Counseling and psychotherapy can help people to see the bases for their evaluations, and to realize that perhaps there are gradations or degrees of what is termed "success."

The middle years in our modern times are much different from those in past generations. Medical science has added about twenty years to the average life span. In order to avoid spending these years in empty diversion and to use post-family freedom constructively, mothers might be encouraged to return to work or perform some community service. The number of mothers who go back to work when their children reach secondary school age is increasing. "Since 1947 there has been an increase of 76% in the number of working married women between the ages of 35 and 44 and an increase of 123% between the ages of 46 to 64" (193, pg. 29).

Erikson refers to this stage of life as "the stage of generativity" (93). By this, Erikson means that the adult can meet the many problems he must face by developing an interest in the leadership of young people and thereby satisfy a need for a parental type of responsibility. Buhler suggests that life can be thought of as increasing in significance and interest if the parent can identify himself "both with his own existence and with that of his offspring" (47, pg. 184). This is one of the reasons why having children is so important for mental health. For those who have not been so fortunate, it is important to suggest that people in this stage accept a kind of parent-surrogate role.

For one thing, love at this stage of life means being able to *give,* particularly to one's children. One form of giving, however, which should be avoided is that of projection. Parents during this stage often project the problems which they are re-living from their own adolescence onto their children. The psychotherapist often has opportunities to interpret these ideas to clients.

For the woman in this middle period of life, it is often suggested that she resume actively the role of *wife,* a role which has been of secondary significance during the years of childbearing. She can give new attention to her husband as a man, meet his needs for affection, understanding, and solitude. She may need to be more concerned about maintaining her own personal attractiveness and charm. The husband also needs to understand the special concerns of his wife as she goes through the menopause. Her condition should increase his genuine courtesy, attentiveness, and regard.

Love at this crucial involutional stage of life can be expressed in a unique way. It is becoming well known that masculine and feminine components exist within each man and each woman. As Fromm says, "Just as physiologically man and woman each have hormones of the opposite sex, they are bisexual also in the psychological sense" (113, pg. 33). Fromm continues later in this same vein:

> There is masculinity and femininity in *character* as well as in *sexual function.* The masculine character can be defined as having the qualities of penetration, guidance, activity, discipline and adventurousness; the feminine character by the qualities of productive receptiveness, protection, realism, endurance, motherliness. (It must always be kept in mind that in each individual both characteristics are blended, but with the preponderance of those appertaining to "his" or "her" sex) (113, pp. 36–37).

Jung made an interesting hypothesis that in the first half of life, unequal use is made of the masculine and feminine components within each sex. "A man consumes his large supply of masculine substance and has left over only the smaller amount of feminine substance, which he must now put to use. It is the other way round with a woman; she allows her unused supply of masculinity to become active" (161, pg. 123).

When man and woman reach the ages of forty to fifty, a crucial psychological change occurs: Jung describes this change vividly as follows:

> How often it happens that a man of forty or fifty years winds up his business, and that his wife then dons the trousers and opens up a little shop where he sometimes performs the duties of a handy man. There are many women who only awake to social responsibility and to social consciousness after their fortieth year. In modern business life—especially in the United States—nervous breakdown in the forties or after is a very common occurrence. If one studies the victims a little closely one sees that the thing which has broken down is the masculine style of life which held the field up to now; what is left is an effeminate man. Contrariwise, one can observe women in these self-same business spheres who have developed in the second half of life an uncommon masculinity and an incisiveness which push the feelings and the heart aside. Very often the reversal is accompanied by all sorts of catastrophes in marriage; for it is not hard to imagine what may happen when the husband discovers his tender feelings, and the wife her sharpness of mind (161, pg. 124).

It would seem, therefore, that one phase of love in marriage at this stage of life can be expressed best by each partner understanding and encouraging the development of neglected sex potentials in the other. This would mean the development of respect for the feminine principle as well as for the masculine principle. As Fromm (113) points out, Freud's extreme patriarchalism led to the assumption that sexuality per se is masculine; and thus he ignored the values of feminine character components.

Immature love in the involutional phase, therefore, would be criticized in the same way that Freud is criticized by Fromm: "My criticism of Freud's theory is not that he overemphasized sex, but his failure to understand sex deeply enough" (113, pg. 37). The middle-aged revolter often can be helped to regain his love for his spouse when sex is translated and deepened into a characterological and psychological dimension.

A final developmental task of this age is that of adjusting to aging parents. During this middle-life period, the individual finds himself at the center of a three-generation family. As the children grow to maturity and leave home, the grandparents become older and a charge of the home. They may need financial help or physical care. In general, neither generation wants to live with the other, and unresolved parent-child conflicts generally are re-activated whenever two generations are forced to live together. One architectural solution is to build "three-generation houses" with privacy for grandparents living with their children. The limitation here, however, is a financial one.

The Evaluation Stage (Sixty Years to the End of Life)

Buhler again compares the period from sixty to seventy-five to adolescence in which there is preoccupation with the past and the future. The individual is evaluating his life and is also preoccupied with death.

Havighurst (140) suggests that the developmental task of later maturity (from sixty onward) differs in one major respect from other ages in that it involves a "defensive strategy"—of holding on to life rather than seizing it.

At the age of 65, now widely recognized to be the age of retirement, the chances are that the individual will still live another ten years. During this time of life, a man and wife usually experience the following: decreased income, the loss of spouse by death, or the illnesses of old age. The last item—illness—is a stark reality, since a considerable number of older people must adjust to a period of invalidism or degenerative disease.

Retirement today usually means a marked reduction in income since retirement plans established twenty to thirty years ago, when inflation was not present, are now inadequate to provide for comfortable living. This means that the luxuries of leisure, such as membership in fraternal organizations, can no longer be kept up at a time when they are most needed.

According to Adler, a major problem of old age is that of not knowing what to do with leisure time. The elderly feel futile and useless, and try to prove their worth again, just as adolescents do. "They interfere and want to show in many different ways that they are not old and will not be overlooked, or else they become disappointed or depressed" (14, pg. 443).

Since most women outlive men, Havighurst (140) claims that by the late sixties there are in the average community as many widows as there are women living with their husbands. Learning to live alone again, to attend to business matters after forty years, is a difficult task to undertake. The various solutions to this problem generally involve moving into an old folks home, living with children, remarriage, or moving in with relatives.

According to Erikson, the period of later maturity is one of "ego integrity" or of despair, depending on the individual's adaptation to life. He claims that the possessor of integrity is ready to defend the dignity of his own life style. On the other hand, it is a period of despair if there is fear of death and the feeling that life was spent unwisely. He relates the period of adult integrity to the first stage of infantile trust by saying that "healthy children will not fear life if their parents have integrity enough not to fear death" (93, pg. 233).

Buhler's (48) concept of "productivity" is important for the period of adult maturity. She maintains that even though there is biological decline, the personality can continue to grow and mature as long as the individual can continue to be productive. Productivity is established in these latter years through identifying with the achievements of offspring, and by evident results of work, play, and community service. It seems, therefore, that old age is enriched by a healthy, retrospective view of life.

Gilbert (123) suggests that older people can maintain psychic health if they will "develop neglected potentials." Areas for development would include service, travel, music, arts and crafts, and gardening, as well as developing one's professional competence further.

There are many examples of people who have forged successful new careers for themselves in their late middle years when they could devote time to things they "really wanted to do." Others have remained active in their chosen profession far past the usual age of retirement. There are many conspicuous examples of outstanding achievement in old age—Titian in art, Lamarck in biology, and Humboldt in philosophy. Fisher, a practicing psychiatrist in his later years, wrote vividly of his feelings about growing old:

> If it is a sad thing to be a psychiatrist because you become uncomfortably aware of your own neurotic tendencies, then, I have discovered in recent years, it is a doubly sad thing to be an aged psychiatrist. For you may sit and watch the encroachment of senility with an abstract and almost professional attitude—like a surgeon watching the mirrored reflection of his own appendectomy.
>
> At least once to every man, I'd imagine, must come the sudden and disconcerting discovery that the corporate cells of his physical body are rapidly approaching insolvency. The sand is running low in the hourglass of time. And the option has already lapsed on a thousand youthful dreams which were never brought to pass. . . .
>
> Youth rides in the cab of the locomotive and jubilantly surveys the track ahead. Age rides in the observation car and gazes back with sweet sorrow, upon the fading scenes of the past. And it requires a certain amount of readjustment.
>
> In my struggle to avoid melancholia and to keep interested in the game, rather than bowing gracefully to Father Time who holds all the trumps, I have striven particularly hard in recent years to keep alive a fading curiosity and hold an open mind capable of admitting new ideas. This, in fact, is why I felt impelled to go traipsing off to Lima, Peru, at eighty-two years of age to study the progress of psychosomatic medicine.
>
> And thus, in my eighty-seventh year, I find myself planning, not a trip back to Boston or Vienna, or Zurich, or Paris, or Chicago, or any of the places I have known in the past. Rather, my plans include a visit to Jackson Hole, Wyoming, and after that a trip up the Inside Passage to Alaska—two places where I have never been and both of them which have been described in glowing terms by others.
>
> And these things, I am afraid I would have to recommend to others who might come to me, as a psychiatrist, and ask how best to postpone the eventual encroachment of advancing senility. Don't sit in the observation car, with folded hands, gazing back upon the fading scenes of the past. Force yourself to seek new experiences and to turn your eyes to the track ahead. Spend at least a share of your time peering into the future (103, pp. 254–256).

Viewing the sunset years from the viewpoint of love, it may be that love between husband and wife during these years can best be expressed by the dimension of *knowledge*. To love a person completely means partly to *know* him, knowledge from the very core of his personality. To make this acquaintance a developmental task of later maturity would seem to be a way in which the internal mastery principle may be completed. Man, therefore, before death can discover, partially at least, the "secret of life." Man's personality is an unfathomable secret; but the penetration into the depth of being a person whom we love can satisfy this need in a very real way. Fromm illustrates this idea of more complete knowledge as follows:

> I may know, for instance, that a person is angry, even if he does not show it overtly; but I may know him more deeply than that; then I know that he is anxious, and worried; that he feels lonely, that he feels guilty. Then I know that his anger is only the manifestation of something deeper, and I see him as anxious and embarrassed, that is, as the suffering person rather than as the angry one (113, pg. 29).

In our therapeutic experience, couples in the later phases of life who have a healthful approach to living seem to have mastered the problem of really knowing one another in a way similar to that described above. And this mastery seems to give them a certain peace not discernable in others. Finally, the *communication* of this knowledge freely to one another makes them a team in the business of living.

SUMMARY

In this chapter we have sketchily traced the life history of man. Much has been left out. An attempt has been made, however, to describe some of the significant activities and events in each of these stages which seem to have pronounced psychological effect upon the individual as he travels through life. It is hoped that students of therapeutic psychology will utilize this chapter as a beginning in the collection of normative data. These data can be useful in helping him to understand his clients better as he meets them in various stages of life.

The "golden thread" running through this chapter is that the life of man may be understood psychologically by relating it to dimensions of love as it is expressed in various phases.

4.

The Process of Counseling
and Psychotherapy

The term "process," as used in everyday and psychological parlance, has the implication of continuous change. This chapter describes the steps and changes which take place and delineates some problems in promoting personality changes through the process. The reader is reminded of the distinctions between counseling and psychotherapy established in Chapter 1. In this chapter on process stages, attempts will be made to distinguish between the two models. Most of the chapter, however, will deal with problems which tend toward the psychotherapy end of the continuum of helping relationships. The emphasis, in keeping with the general tenor of this book, will be on short-term, light- and medium-depth psychotherapy rather than on long-term deep psychotherapy.

The focus of therapeutic psychology is on understanding, that is, on seeing relationships among one's ideas, feelings, and acts. Clients come to psychotherapists, for example, wanting to know what to do about their misery. Counseling or psychotherapy is not just a negative or manipulative process of releasing impulsive feelings, curbing desires, removing fears, persuading on a predetermined course of action, or changing basic value systems of the client. Therapeutic psychology applied through counseling and psychotherapy is primarily a process of building understanding, integrating disparate elements of the personality, and enabling the client to utilize his good judgment, social skills, problem-solving capacities, and planning abilities.

Psychological counselors and therapists are not concerned, in a professional sense, with specific values (such as *kinds* of behavior), or the meaning of existence and life. Although they recognize the significance of these values for the client's complete and effective living, they are more the concern and responsibility of others—religious counselors, teachers, and parents. Psychological counseling and psychotherapy are concerned primarily with the *process* by which a person perceives and achieves his goals; the goals themselves generally come from sources other than the counseling relationship itself.

Though we hold closely to the preceding philosophy about goals in our client relationships, we are concerned about general types of therapeutic outcomes which come within the purview of values. These goals will be discussed in the latter half of this chapter.

NATURE OF THE PROCESS

General Models

Although the process is roughly the same for all types of problems, there are some differences in steps of development depending upon the degree of emphasis upon facts and feelings. For example, in problems of planning vocational or educational futures there is a heavy emphasis upon collection of factual information; whereas for feeling problems, in which the person is trying to work out a desperate interpersonal problem, there is little emphasis upon information as such and heavy stress is placed upon understandings of self and others' feelings.

Educational-vocational counseling model. In counseling problems focusing on information such as vocational planning, the counseling model generally includes the following steps:

(1) Establishment of the relationship.

(2) Statement and elaboration of the problem(s).

(3) General structuring of the nature of the counseling process.

(4) Discussion of the problem and collection of data (via interview, case history, tests, inventories, checklists).

(5) Individual appraisal (if tests are utilized).

(6) Occupational and educational study by the client.

(7) Discussion of data from the appraisal and from the client's individual study.

(8) Synthesis of the data into a meaningful plan.

(9) Discussion of steps necessary to carry out the plan.

(10) Follow-up procedures including possible re-assessment and change of plans.

The changes which take place in such an intellectual process are largely ego-system changes; although the self-system becomes involved in substantial choices of vocation. The self-system covers aspirations and self-regarding attitudes which are present in most educational-vocational counseling. These steps will be illustrated and applied in Chapter 14.

A psychotherapeutic model. Although the information-laden and planning problems have a clearcut and compelling logic to them, the primarily feeling-laden problems are not so sequentially clear. Because of individual differences in clients, and in light of variations in philosophy and technique of psychotherapy, the combination of steps in the psychotherapeutic process take myriads of forms. From these various styles, however, a rough sequence of events can be extracted which are typical of the psychotherapeutic process. The steps in this sequence are selected quite arbitrarily for didactic purposes and are not as discrete as the numbered steps might imply.

The psychotherapeutic model has the following general outline of stages:

(1) Realizing that there is a complaint, problem, or symptom, and that there is a need for help.
(2) Establishing the relationship.
(3) Expressing feeling and clarifying and elaborating upon the problem(s).
(4) Exploring feelings (depth depending on type and structure of the psychotherapy).
(5) Expressing deep feelings and exploring symbolisms (if deeper psychotherapy is being attempted).
(6) Working through feelings.
(7) Developing insight and planning action.
(8) Externalizing and terminating the relationship.

In terms of the multidimensional theory developed in Chapter 2, the psychotherapeutic model would appear as a series of hypotheses in Figure 8. Stage 1 is the presentation of the complaint, problem, or symptom which is projected outward into the relationship as "object" or "it." The psychotherapist responds to the presentation largely with silence and other relationship techniques so that the client can gradually "take his projection back" to make it more "subject" or part of "me."

The start of making the problem subjective is indicated by Stage 2 in Figure 8 in the outer-defense system. Here, the main therapeutic problem is handling "resistance," the protective and defensive function of personality (Chapter 8). Also, the main techniques are those of relationship-building and support (Chapters 6 and 7).

The personality structure of the client at the beginning of the process is indicated in Figure 9. The client has a strong defensive wall which often makes it difficult for him to react spontaneously to the psychotherapist. His anxiety about the process is often so strong that his defense systems are mobilized to prevent the tapping of deeper feelings too soon.

Stage 3 is reached in the ego system when the problem is more intellectualized and elaborated through clarification and interpretive techniques (Chapter 9). At this point the counseling process shades into the psychotherapeutic process, since the next stage, Stage 4, is working in the self-system with deeper feelings, values, and unconscious material. Here again, psychotherapeutic counseling shades into deep psychotherapy since Stage 5 involves the core system and inner-defense system with their more rigid

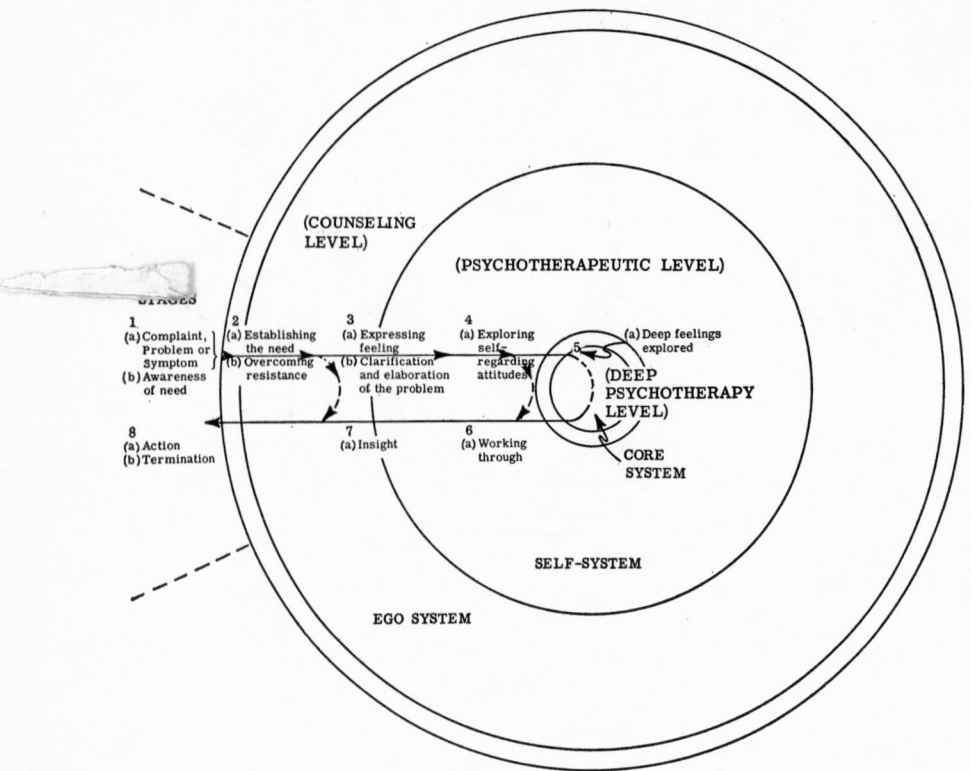

FIG. 8. Stages in the Counseling and Psychotherapeutic Processes.

defenses and more intense feelings. In addition to the usual relationship and interpretive techniques, deep psychotherapy specialists use such methods as psychoanalysis, depth interpretation, dream interpretation, hypno-analysis, and narco-analysis.

Stage 6 is the "working-through" step toward insight which will be described later in this chapter. Here, the real work of the process takes place in the form of changing attitudes, toward self and others. Stage 7 is a further working through at the ego-system level where insight and understanding are consolidated and translated into plans of action. Here is where the bulk of the usual run of so-called personal counseling or moderate psychotherapy takes place. During Stages 6 and 7 there is an increasing awareness of both the subjective and objective nature of the personal material in such a way that some can be projected as "nonself" and some retained as part of the "self."

For the material to be externalized further as "nonself" there is Stage 8 in which the externalization process is complete. An example of an externalized feeling would be inferiority. At the end of the therapeutic process

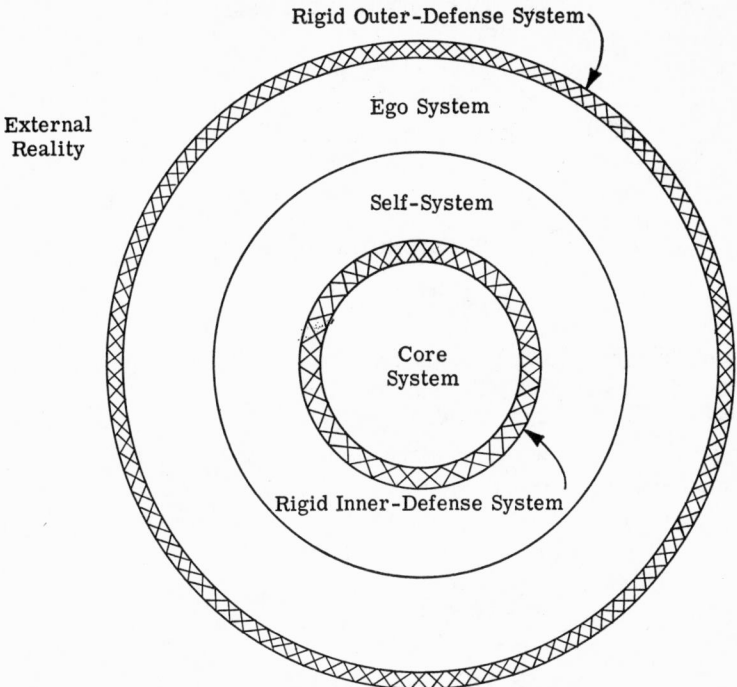

FIG. 9. The Personality at the Beginning of Counseling or Psychotherapy.

the client sees himslf as a confident person and projects outward as "it" or "nonself" his former self-regarding characteristic of inferiority.

The process described here in schematic form is never a continuous straight-line development. More typically there are various levels of the process involved at any one time. Stages may be skipped too, as in cases where clients plunge immediately into deep core-system feelings.

Rogers (255) views the psychotherapeutic counseling process as a series of on-going attitudinal changes. His opinion on the manner in which study of the process of psychotherapy should proceed is: First, observe the behavior of the client with as few preconceived notions as possible, or as Rogers states it, ". . . to steep oneself in the *events* . . ." (255, pg. 142). Then, from these observations come low-order abstractions and hypotheses which can be tested empirically. Rogers tries to grasp characteristics of the changes in the therapeutic process without thinking of them as fixed or static stages. The seven dynamic stages which he perceives in the process range from an early client condition of threat, resistance to change, and little communication, through a gradual loosing of feelings, assumption of greater personal responsibility for feelings, greater clarity and accuracy of perceiving feelings. Finally, the client experiences his feelings as part of himself. He no longer views himself or his feelings as "objects" or as "problems."

The next section is a further elaboration of the practical aspects of the process hypotheses, a description of the conditions necessary for changes, and some of the difficulties encountered in dealing with problems at various stages in the process.

STEPS IN THE PSYCHOTHERAPEUTIC PROCESS

Stage 1—Awareness of Need for Help

Clients characteristically come for psychological assistance because of feelings of distress. They feel that they lack sufficient information or competence to deal with a life problem. Often their feelings of difference from other people and their desire to be someone different from their present self create a condition of tension and a vague gnawing fear that something is wrong. Others come for counseling out of a feeling of curiosity or to satisfy the obligation to someone else who feels they have a problem.

As you will note in the next chapter on readiness for counseling, certain conditions must be satisfied before psychological counseling can be effective. Briefly, the client must:

(1) Be aware of the feelings of distress cited above.

(2) Desire and expect change in his personality or life-problem situation.

(3) Accept the emotional character of his problem.

(4) Accept the possibilities and limitations of psychological counseling as a vehicle for helping him to help himself.

(5) Voluntarily arrange to see the counselor.

Each stage in the process has certain objectives, called process goals, to be accomplished. The goals for this first stage are listed above under preliminary conditions which must be satisfied before a relationship can be built.

Stage 2—Development of the Relationship and Overcoming Resistance

The relationship bridge. We know of no disagreement to, or contrary evidence on the assertion that the development of an emotionally warm, permissive, understanding relationship is a first step in the counseling process. The development of such a working relationship characterized by mutual liking, trust, and respect is one of the first tasks of the counselor. It is as if the counselor must build a bridge or pipeline through which the client perceives the counselor as a powerful ally in his struggle with himself and his world. This task is illustrated in Figure 10.

The various techniques with which this process of communication is accomplished are described in a later chapter. Here, it is only necessary to point out that the pipeline widens as the attitudes of the counselor and the client become more mutually effective in communicating feelings and ideas. This pipeline becomes the "lifeline" of psychological counseling because by it the client can "use" the more mature, strong, constructive counselor ally in his struggle with himself and his environment. It is hypothesized that the counselor "lends" part of his own ego to the client. A first step in establishing the relationship bridge and penetrating the client's outer defense system is the opening of the counselor's own outer defense system as indicated in Figure 10.

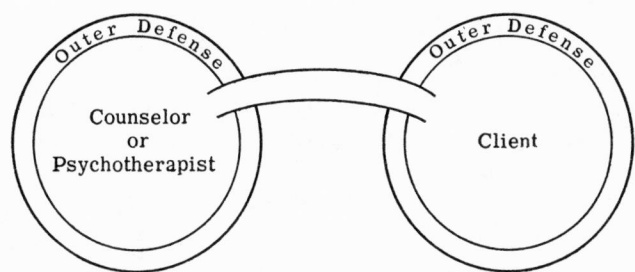

FIG. 10. The Relationship and the Opening of the Outer-Defense System.

Process goals of relationship. The "pipeline" analogy and the idea of outside help may give the impression that counseling is merely a supportive device which might build a dangerous and lingering dependency. Although this difficulty is ever present, there is the need to build a feeling of confidence in the counselor and his capacity to provide the necessary temporary support. This relationship-building feature does not deny the strong growth potential within each personality as postulated in Chapter 2. The psychotherapeutic relationship is, again, a bridging element to be relied upon until the inner growth forces of the personality are able to function adequately.

Another goal of the relationship bridge is to assist the client to experience trust in the real self of the therapist so that the client will come to feel that it is safe to investigate defensive patterns, ego capacities, and core drives about which he had been only vaguely aware.

Stage 3—The Expression of Feeling and Clarification of the Problem(s)

This phase of the process known as "catharsis" generally takes place early in counseling. It is characterized by a release of feelings mainly through the medium of language although it may come in direct forms such as weeping. Often the counseling relationship offers the first opportunity such a client has had to express his deepest feelings openly and freely.

Values of catharsis or ventilation. This "ventilation of feelings," as it is sometimes called, has several benefits and limitations. The first value of emotional catharsis is the feeling of relief it gives from strong physiological tension. A second benefit is the awareness of relief from emotional pressure it gives the client which comes from verbalizing the material he has controlled by resistance or has long avoided facing directly. A feeling of satisfaction and courage often follows because the client finally could come to admit having the feelings which he heretofore had declared so alien to himself. In addition, he feels a sense of security and freedom from the continuing and often onerous task of defending his feelings. This awareness of security often gives him the courage to attack the problems confronting him. Thus, new creative energy is released. Previous emotional energy was so tied up with defending himself that the client had little energy available to use constructively. For example, if a client has discussed a fight he had with his father he often will be more ready to discuss other things, such as his own aggressive feelings. A final value of verbalizing feelings is that it prevents "acting out," that is, instead of directing aggression towards others, the client is encouraged to use symbolic means through language.

Limitations of catharsis. Catharsis has several distinct limitations. If allowed to "ventilate" excessively, the client may feel so good afterward that he will feel it is unnecessary to go on to the causes of his difficulties and the steps necessary to change his attitudes and acts. He leaves counseling for the time being with a condition described as a "flight into health." He will stay away then until his anxiety builds up to an intolerable point again. Some anxiety is necessary, however. The optimal amount of anxiety necessary for good working motivation is discussed in Chapter 7 under relationship techniques.

Allowing the client to have continuous palliative relief without working into the insight phase of counseling may serve to reinforce his repetitive neurotic patterns. It is as if he has an emotional tranquilizer each week without moving further toward self-understanding. There is little evidence available to us which might indicate that periodic, emotionally cathartic sessions have much psychotherapeutic value other than the temporary supportive effect of draining off excess tension. Some life experiences, such as confessionals in religious settings, relieve guilt but tend not to produce the type of insight necessary for personality changes.

Clarifying the problems. Characteristically, clients with emotional problems express them only after feeling it is safe to do so with the counselor. Although expressing feelings, stating problems, or giving reasons for coming often blend together, there is an early point in the process when the counselor helps the client to verbalize the nature of his problem. Often clients come in with vague complaints or dissatisfactions which they feel should be satisfied. Examples are: difficulty concentrating, deteriorating family relationships, lack of a vocational goal, feelings of inadequacy, general inefficiency, or complaints about some condition in life over which they have no control. So often these complaints are symptoms of the "real" or "deeper" problem. Counselors soon realize that problems exist at various personality levels. The counselor must, at first, accept the client's *prima facie* statement of what he thinks is the problem. Then, as the material unfolds, the counselor helps the client to see that the problem has manifold aspects and depths.

If counseling, as opposed to re-educative therapy is the focus, then the counselor should discuss quite frankly with each client the problem as both the client and the counselor see it through the words and feelings of the client. Clients with "loose" thinking frequently talk "in circles" and, as a result, become more confused unless the counselor asks a clarifying question: "Now, just what is the problem?" Problems stated in the form of questions have an incisive quality which force the client to get down to work on the hidden as well as the manifest problems confronting him. For example, the client says that his problem is over doing better school work, although, more basically, it is over deciding why he is in school at all and facing up to the unconscious feelings that he does not really want to be there.

Process goals of Stage 3 are necessary principally to maintain expression of feelings and to help the client clarify his problem. The counselor thus can begin to formulate his diagnostic hypotheses on the basis of the cognitive and connotive aspects of the client's communication. This diagnostic process is described in the next chapter.

Stages 4 and 5—Deeper Exploration of Feelings

During Stages 4 and 5, further explorations of feelings are made, although many types of counseling problems are worked out at the ego-system level. This is especially true concerning the general run of educational-vocational problems which are handled at a rationalistic level.

Psychotherapeutic counseling often proceeds to Stage 4 which involves exploration of the deeper self-regarding attitudes in the self-system. As indicated in Figure 8 Stage 4 may move then to the working-through aspects of Stage 5.

Generally, the counseling process does not include work at Stage 5 which involves deep psychotherapy at the inner-defense and core-system levels. Most psychological counselors are neither personally nor educationally equipped to deal with the intense feelings and intricate problems of the basic character structure of the personality. Furthermore, psychological counselors generally practice in such agencies as schools and colleges in which agency policy and time limitations prevent work at Stage 5.

Criteria for depth-of-feeling exploration. To help the psychotherapist determine the degree of personality depth he should allow the client to explore, the following criteria are suggested:

(1) The nature and severity of the client's symptoms. For example, delusional thinking is almost always a sign of mental illness. Hysterical outbursts in which uncontrolled anxiety or hostility is poured forth is another example of a situation which is outside the purview of psychological counseling and in most cases is restricted to intensive psychotherapy.

(2) Length and persistence of symptoms. If a behavior, such as stealing, for example, is persistent and difficult to explain with data at hand, there is a high probability that one is dealing with a pathological process.

(3) The nature of the predisposing and precipitating experiences. Some clients, for example, have had a series of severe traumas falling within a short period of time. Deaths in the family, divorces, desertions plus many small crisis-producing experiences are examples. These experiences often mobilize more feeling than the client can handle in the interview.

(4) Past stability and defensive functioning. A client who desires to express strong feelings and who has a history of stability and adequate defenses generally can be allowed to express his emotions more deeply than the client who has a spotty psychological history.

(5) Resistance to psychotherapy. Resistance to further exploration and probing by the counselor is a fairly reliable indicator of the sensitivity of the client's feelings and the rigidity of his defenses.

(6) Extent and adequacy of the counselor's or therapist's training. Generally speaking, there is a direct relationship between amount of training and experience in psychotherapy or counseling and the depth at which the process may be pitched.

(7) The problems of the counselor or therapist. Often the counselor is unable to handle feelings because the client's feelings touch upon sore spots of his own. This condition should discourage the counselor from delving into similar client feelings.

(8) The amount of time available. Time for the counseling or therapy series is significant in that the deeper the involvement in feelings, the more time to work the feelings through must be budgeted. This may mean a hundred or more hours.

(9) Institutional policy on doing psychotherapy. Policymakers often dictate to the therapist in general terms how far he can go in probing for feelings and allowing the client to express himself. This is especially true in public school settings where so-called personal counselors have consideration of parental and administrator attitudes as well as numerous technical problems to face.

Stage 6—The Working-Through Process

A significant concept in developing understanding is a process often called "working through."[1] In the present context the term refers to becoming aware of the meaning of past experiences and feelings as well as present feelings to the final point of understanding of one's self—which we shall define broadly as insight. In the working-through stage, the client gains a rational type of understanding of his problems and feelings which lead to the deep creative type of understanding of Stage 7. The principal technique to accomplish this step is interpretation which is described in Chapter 9.

Along with the rational understanding is a process called "desensitization" which is the reduction of the emotional intensity which once surrounded the experience. Through re-experiencing via language, the anxiety or psychic pain is reduced. The client, therefore, is able to bring the old experience into his present perceptual organization to see it as part of himself. By means of the working-through process the client moves psychic material from deep within his personality to the ego system.

The "working through" stage is occasionally characterized by a combination of individual and group psychotherapy. The group experience serves as a laboratory to point out to the client his characteristic defensive maneuverings, his inadequate ego capacities and relationship skills, and his inefficient management of unconscious core drives. The result is, often, a breakthrough in the form of heightened awareness of real self-system feelings which the client now can use in a more effective relationship with others.

We have developed the following diagrammatic representation of some critical points in the middle stages of the process, particularly the "working-through" stage. From Figure 11 it may be seen that psychotherapy is analogous to the experience of going deeply into a pit. The vertical dimension represents depth of involvement in the process. The horizontal dimension represents temporal stages in the process.

It will be noted in Figure 11 that after the client states his problem and feels at ease in the relationship, he reaches critical Point Number 1, generally in Stage 3. This is the point where he plunges into more detailed exploration of feelings which may not be a pleasant experience. At this point he feels insecure, uncomfortable, and doubtful whether the results will merit the psychic pain which he is beginning to experience. This point is labelled a "critical point" because many clients drop out here. Experienced therapists view critical Point Number 1 as the place where the client seems to get worse before he gets better. If this phenomenon can be interpreted to the client and if he can persist through this period, he generally can weather Critical Point Number 1. It is at this point, furthermore, that support and

---

[1] The origin of the term "working through" is credited to Freud. Originally it meant the progressive attrition of the network of resistance.

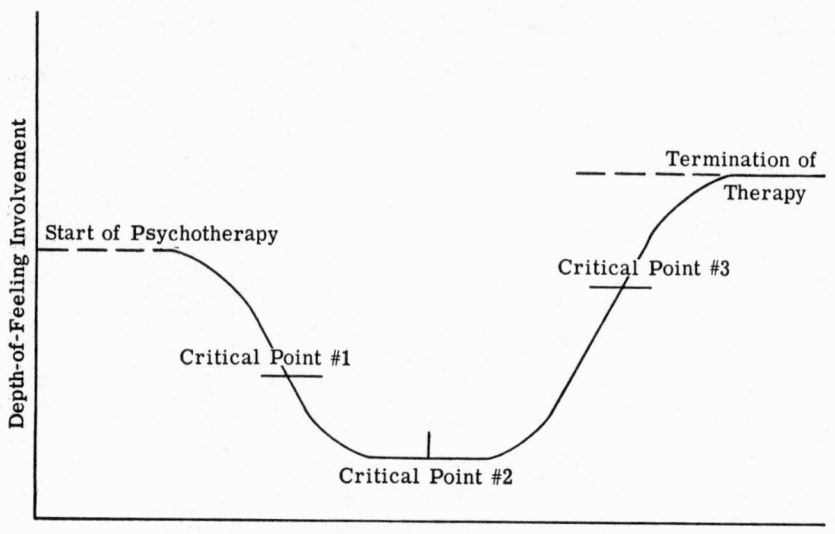

Fig. 11. Critical Points in the Process of Psychotherapy.

process interpretation techniques to be described in later chapters relax his defenses and make him feel more comfortable so he can proceed with courage on his psychic journey. White, speaking of a similar phenomenon in psychoanalysis, said:

> To the extent that the patient is dominated by anxieties he may be likened to a frightened child. Alone he cannot face the threats, but in the company of the analyst he dares to peek at them and finally approach them. The patient becomes a little more daring because he is not alone in the enterprise. This increase of daring is at the heart of his corrective emotional experience (316, pg. 333).

White continues to compare this painful emotional exploration to the condition of mourning.

> Facing the fact of bereavement, the person may attempt to perform an all-inclusive act of renunciation; but his attempt is bound to fail. Each vivid reminder of the lost person will at first cause a renewal of pain and call up another renunciation. As Linderman has pointed out, there is a "grief-work" that has to be accomplished, and it takes time. Similarly, in the analysis of a neurosis, each fresh reminder of the pathogenic conflict sets it going again, calling for a new relaxation of defenses. Fortunately each new experience makes the work a little easier (316, pg. 333).

Critical Point Number 2, in Figure 11, is reached in Stage 4 when the client has expressed considerable feeling. Often he becomes aware of the inadequacy of his defenses suddenly. They no longer give him comfortable protection against the onslaughts of his deepest feelings of guilt, hatred, and fear. In addition, the previous verbalizations opened the door to more feelings which heretofore had been well suppressed. On this point Shneidman, conversing with one of the writers, suggested that the unconscious is like a basement full of cats waiting to spring out. Uncovering or experiencing too many of the unconscious desires, impulses, inhibitions, or thoughts of the past would be like opening the cellar door and letting all the cats out. It would be quite traumatic or even physically catastrophic. The therapist must control the relationship to enable the client to open the cellar door just enough to allow one cat at a time out to be examined and tamed. The succeeding sessions would be occupied with "taming more cats."

It should be pointed out that the short-term therapist must be alert to the possibility that a psychotic process already underway can blossom forth at this stage. This is a critical point where such incipient psychoses are likely to become apparent. However, it should be emphasized that the vast majority of clients have defenses which protect them quite adequately from various types of psychotic deterioration.

Process goals of Stage 6. What actually goes on in this "pit bottom" phase of the working-through process of Stage 6 is: (1) clarifying and accepting *present* emotional difficulties; (2) rationally understanding the *historical* roots of the problems and feelings; (3) working out the problem in terms of the *relationship* of past and present events and in terms of the relationship between client and therapist. Experiences must be worked through in all three areas before the experience can be said to be "assimilated," or, in terms of our previous analogy with mourning, through the "grief work." In this sense there is no "old" material in psychotherapy; material is there waiting to be worked through again—in fresh ways. To illustrate what is meant by the means of working through emotional content, the story of the blind men and the elephant is cited. In this fable, the blind men each attempt to describe the elephant from his own particular vantage point—from the part each could touch. They did not get the total picture of what an elephant was like until they compared notes. Likewise, conflicts must be worked through from many vantage points and by describing them in different words.

After a thorough exploration of past experiences and present feelings during Stage 6, the client often reaches a point of well-being and elation. He may even have tried out some new behaviors with fair success as part of the "working through" of his problem. All this takes place at Critical Point Number 3. It is here that the client often wishes to terminate psychotherapy prematurely, feeling that all is well and thinking that he doesn't "need" the therapist any more. Although there is some logic to the claim that the process properly should be ended when this feeling comes, the therapist must use his best judgment to determine whether this is an appropriate stopping point, or whether it is only a point characterized by the client's desire to leave. The therapist may have to interpret this situation frankly so that the client does not leave just when the greatest gains are about to be made and consolidated in Stage 7, insight development.

Clients, in general, should not be kept in psychotherapy longer than they desire; but the greatest gains often are missed by the premature optimism gained from the client's first flush of success. Clients generally will tolerate psychotherapy to the point where they must aggressively *do something* about their problem.

The "working through" phase of the process shades into the insight and action stages. Little good is accomplished if the client gets considerable relief from his feelings and an intellectual understanding of his problems. The critical questions are: Does he act on the basis of his new feelings, perceptions, and understandings? Does he try out new methods of behaving?

Stage 7—Development of Insight

As stated earlier in this Chapter, counseling or psychotherapy without insight is of dubious value. The test of effectiveness is the acquisition of insight or understanding of self and others as well as the consequent positive action which is based upon that insight.

The concept of "insight" has a varied history. Literally it means to "see into" or understand. In Gestalt psychology the term is used to describe the sudden perceptual reorganization leading to discovery or solution of a problem. An example is Kohler's experiment (176) in which a chimpanzee suddenly discovered how to put various sticks together and pile boxes to reach a much-coveted banana. Insight in counseling and therapy has some of this sudden "aha" or "so that's the way it is" quality to it, in which significant detail stands out from the background.

We prefer to restrict the use of the term insight, however, to the deep understanding and changed perception of relationships among scattered elements in one's personality in such a way that one can act more positively in terms of an integrated self-system. There is a deepened awareness of what is going on objectively and subjectively within and without the personality at the ego- and self-system levels. The client sees relationships he never saw before. This "seeing into" process may be a slow imperceptible one or it may be sudden as in the Gestalt sense of rapid reorganizing of the perceptual field. There is a rich all-inclusive experiencing in this type of insight which involves many modalities of feeling and cognition.

To achieve insight of the type just described often involves as complete an understanding of one's life events as possible. In the preceding chapter we traced the life history of the individual through his various developmental stages and tasks. We suggested that in all of these stages of life everyone has experiences which are assimilated and integrated into the personality. At the earlier stages of life, ages five to seven for example, certain emotional experiences are very intense. The experiences are of such nature that they are deeply repressed and often not assimilated into the personality. The working-through stage opens these experiences to awareness.

The psychotherapeutic process is designed to achieve insight into these early experiences by the process known as "re-experiencing" of past events. These events are reinterpreted, or seen in a different light, so as to diminish their anxiety or "psychic pain." The understanding of formerly defensive patterns leads to a new awareness of freedom and expressive self-confidence.

As the client examines his life happenings a more basic process is going on. Through the insight process, he comes to a more accurate and explicit definition of his "self" as described in Chapter 2. Out of all his everyday interactive and therapeutic experiences he comes to abstract his "real self." Thus, insight is not only a process of understanding the past and tying together the heretofore scattered elements, but insight is also a process of constructing from the self-system a current view of his "real self" as it has developed through the years and is evolving in present life processes.

Process goals of the Stage 7 insight. To illustrate the preceding insight development process, we have abstracted from Rogers (249, pg. 135) some descriptive statements about changes in the client's thinking and feeling: Symptoms to self, environment to self, others to self, unconscious to conscious, past to present, negative to positive feeling about self and others, many defenses to decreased defensiveness and greater awareness of one's defensiveness.

Symonds (300) also gives some illustrations of some types of general insights which clients achieve in counseling and therapy. Examples are, the realization that one is doing his best under the circumstances, that he cannot control all the forces working on him, that happiness comes from within rather than from without, that people are basically friendly rather than hostile, and that one must be lovable in order to receive love.

Stage 8—Experience Outside Psychotherapy

It has been our experience that the most significant integrative work in psychotherapy comes from encouraging the client to go into the world to live his "therapeutic insights," thereby proving to himself that he is no longer acting in a self-defeating manner.

Well-ordered life experiences offer the best therapeutic medium, once the client has sufficient relief from crippling feelings and symptoms and has achieved some insight. Maslow points this idea out very succinctly:

> . . . major life experiences can be therapeutic in the fullest sense of the word. A good marriage, success in a suitable job, developing good friendships, having children, facing emergencies, and overcoming difficulties—I have occasionally seen all of these produce deep character changes, get rid of symptoms, *etc.,* without the help of a technical therapist. As a matter of fact, a case could be made for the thesis that good life circumstances

are among the *ultimate* therapeutic agents and that technical psychotherapy often has the task only of enabling the individual to take advantage of them (197, pg. 311).

It appears from Maslow's thinking above that everything which has been described in the process thus far has been an attempt to prepare the client for therapeutic life experiences. Thus, the counselor or therapist makes himself more and more dispensable through the client's ability to utilize successfully his new skills. Robinson (246) stresses a further point that people can be taught new and higher level adjustment skills much in the same way that dog paddlers can be taught the more efficient Australian Crawl.

The Personality at the Termination of Successful Psychotherapy

The conceptualization of the personality at the beginning of psychotherapy was presented in Figure 9. It was noted that the principal structural

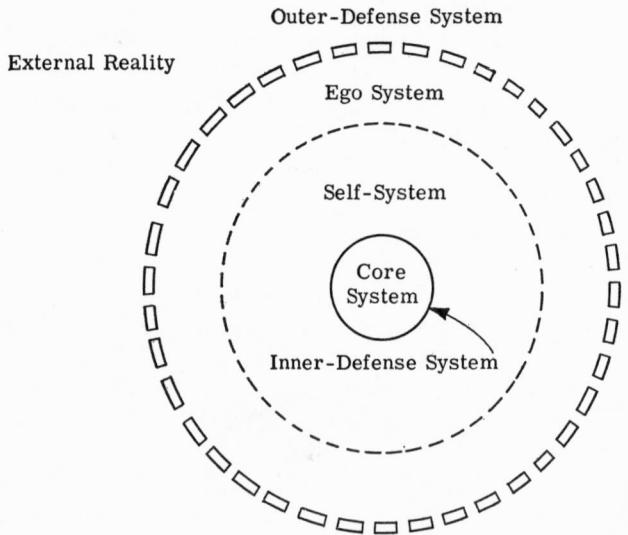

FIG. 12. The Personality at the End of Psychotherapy.

characteristic was an inner and outer rigidity. In Figure 12 the personality at the end of successful psychotherapy is presented showing the increased permeability of the inner and outer defensive wall, the expansion of the self-system and its greater accessibility to the ego-system. The decreased area of the core system is another characteristic, since in the deep psychotherapy process, the core is more fully integrated into the ego and self-systems.

The preceding changes will be made more explicit in the following criteria of successful psychotherapy. These characteristics may be construed as descriptive terms for a mentally healthy personality also. Earlier in this chapter cautions were raised about the psychotherapist setting himself up as a type of "cultural high priest" in deciding values for the client. Though the psychotherapist or counselor strives to allow the client to select his own values, there are some general social and individual values for which the counselor or therapist is striving in the psychotherapeutic process. These goals are presented in the following section.

GOALS OF PSYCHOLOGICAL COUNSELING AND PSYCHOTHERAPY

What is the psychological counselor or therapist trying to do? If pressed, he would probably answer that he has several short-range and long-range goals. The short-range goals can be classed into process and client goals. Process goals, described earlier in this chapter, are objectives, such as free verbalization, keeping the client working on the problem, and maintaining an optimum anxiety level. Client goals, in contrast, are solutions to immediate problems—desire for information, reduction of worries, removal of annoying symptoms, or easing of situational pressures.

Some of the more specific process objectives are to find answers to questions such as: (1) What brought this client to the counselor? (2) What meaning does this relationship have for the client? (3) What is the significance of the stated problem for the client? (4) What is the history of this problem and the various kinds of rewards that were experienced to reinforce and rigidify this behavior or conflict? (5) How does the client perceive the goals of the process? (6) What is the potential for developing mature behavior in this particular client in light of the questions above? (7) What seem to be the most likely paths to the general goals of the process? (8) How can the client be helped to gain a consistent, meaningful frame of reference by which he can think about his problem and through which he can gain insight and solutions?

Long-range general goals are tied in closely with social values and the kinds of behaviors required to live effectively in American culture. In another sense, these goals are characteristics of a theoretical model personality which would seem to "fit" in Western cultural settings. This statement does not imply that psychological counseling or therapy leads necessarily to passive adjustment or to conformity. The principal emphasis is upon developing the individuality of the client, at the same time helping him to see his social responsibilities for contributing to, and possibly changing, the culture about him.

The general goals to be described in the functional model of the mature personality need the following qualifying statements: (1) While counseling and psychotherapy processes aim for the same general goals, counseling does not press for the same degree of reorganization as psychotherapy. (2) Psychotherapy and counseling can be regarded as quite successful without achieving all of the following goals. (3) Finally, even the most successful counseling and psychotherapy do not produce a person who lives according to the following criteria at all times and under all circumstances.

Spontaneity

Earlier in this chapter, as part of Figure 12, a personality model was presented in which spontaneity was illustrated as a marked decrease in rigid defensive walls. Spontaneity may be construed as the polar opposite of defensiveness. Rogers (248) describes this characteristic as "increasing openness to experience." The world of experience for the client is no longer threatening. His picture of himself is more congruent with the way he is seen by others; therefore, he need not defend himself as strenuously as he did before counseling.

There are objective indices of such a characteristic as spontaneity on psychological instruments. Rorschach protocols, for example, show how spontaneity follows as the constrictive control indices decline. Flexibility takes its place.

As a result of the decrease in defensiveness the client is better able to perceive reality as defined by others. There is less rigidity of perception and less need to distort or narrow perceptions in the direction of delusions. As Rogers says:

> He sees that not all trees are green, not all men are stern fathers, not all women are rejecting, not all failure experiences prove that he is no good, and the like. He is able to take in the evidence in a new situation, *as it is,* rather than distorting it to fit a pattern which he already holds (248, pg. 16).

A close relative of spontaneity is a concept called "tolerance for ambiguity." He can live comfortably with value and factual conflicts or unclear situations. He can hold beliefs in a tentative fashion while sifting conflicting evidence. He is not compulsively bound to seek definiteness in all things.

Another related term used by Rogers is "getting behind the mask." Successful counseling results in dropping the false front, the mask, or the role. The client becomes more genuinely his true self. In Jungian terms the "persona" decreased. As one of Rogers' clients put it, "I haven't been really honestly myself, or actually known what my real self is, and I have been just playing a sort of false role" (248, pg. 11). It should be emphasized that the individual retains some of his defenses and roles. Counselors, are not trying to "standardize" personalities in psychological counseling. Counselors strive to help the individual appreciate his uniqueness providing the unique qualities are not maintained at too high a price. It seems, however, that there would be some value if the client realized that people are basically alike in many ways. They have similar hopes, feelings, and thoughts, though their various roles and "persona" characteristics often make them appear to be vastly different.

Living Here and Now

By this phrase is meant an increasing tendency to live each moment fully. The client tries to live so as to extract the richness of every moment. He does not try to anticipate life with too many ready-made answers. Rather, each moment is new; what he will do with that moment is something creative, hence, unpredictable. His value structure, which is part of his basic individuality, will assist him to act appropriately. As Rogers says in his reflective paper on the *Fully Functioning Personality,* the individual is "dependable but not predictable" (252, pg. 11).

The client, in terminating psychological counseling or psychotherapy, feels as if the job is not done, but just beginning. It is as if he were on the right train, not exactly knowing where he was going, but yet feeling that he is moving in the right direction. He is in closer contact with his own feelings and goals, and is more aware of social values and goals. He does not, however, approach a new situation with a rigidly preformed structure. His personality is flexible and his defensive walls permeable. He can, thereby, make possible modifications of inner structures from each new experience. The client is satisfied in the feeling that he never quite "arrives."

Rogers (252) points out in his discussion of the "fully functioning person" that he enjoys an activity for the pleasure of doing it, not necessarily because it is a means to an end. Our American culture puts great stress on the value of *means* toward ends, and not enough stress, in our opinion, on the *ends* themselves. So many people, for example, feel it is necessary to rationalize golfing because it is good for their health—they get sunshine and air—and do not admit that the act of golfing itself is pleasurable.

Trust in Self

The client terminating successful psychotherapy has certain attitudes toward himself which may be characterized as "self-confidence" or "self-worth"—belief in what we call his "real self." He trusts himself and his judgment. In deciding what course of action to follow in any question, he does not necessarily rely on rules, common-sense aphorisms, or mandates laid down by institutions or "Emily Post." Rather, he trusts his judgment and does what he feels is right or appropriate—all things considered.

The last phrase, "all things considered," should be emphasized. The confident, self-directive individual does not just act impulsively or whimsically. As Adler points out he considers consequences. He thinks, for example, of his social responsibility. He trusts his own inner promptings rather than depending exclusively upon external motivation to behave. He believes in himself, as well as in other persons and institutions.

The stringent controls of the self-system are relaxed so as to make their modification more possible. The writers incorporate the concept of "conscience" or the Freudian "superego" as part of the self-system. The earlier learnings from parents regarding social values are more amenable to critical examination and alteration after a course of successful psychotherapy.

The writers are indebted to Rogers (257, pg. 8) for an illustration of how the process of achieving self-trust and confidence might work in a client. We can compare the personality to a gigantic computing machine. Since the client is now more open to his experience, more data from his present situation as well as the extensive data from his past learnings are available to him. Since he is interacting more completely with his environment at any point he has more access to data from within and without. The client can more properly evaluate and select relevant data for the solution of his present problem. We feel that one reason people err in judgment is that they include data which do not belong to the present context and exclude data which do. Thus, people who exclude data from their present situation and react only in terms of memories and stereotypes from previous learnings, as if they were this reality, are in trouble. Prejudice functions this way. Or, conversely, people who react to present situations without the benefit of past experiences which may be locked, via repression, deep within the unconscious core system, may be in trouble as well. The present data may be "punched on the tape" in distorted form. All reliable data are needed to produce the most appropriate answers to life problems.

Operating in the spontaneous, self-trusting manner cited above does not mean the client will avoid errors. But it is hypothesized that such a client will correct errors due to omitted or distorted data without guilt or self-punishing defenses. Learning to trust one's feelings, as well as one's intelligence and experience, is a difficult state to achieve. Many people tend to want direction from without, to be dependent upon someone else to tell them what to do and how to do it.

Learning to express one's feelings—to live them—is stressed by many writers of psychological literature. Fromm (114) for example, emphasizes that the client "becomes alive" to his feelings. Knowing one's real feelings, expressing them in individually and socially satisfying ways is an extension of the psychotherapeutic process of uncensured emotional experiencing when the client *is* his anger, his fear, or his love. This experience of learning to like and trust one's self is one meaning of self-realization—of becoming a real person.

Creativity

Analytic psychotherapists, especially Jungian, place great stress upon the objective of the creative personality. The client is able to use more of his unconscious feelings which become his servant rather than his master. Many of the unconscious repressions have been lifted, faced, and understood. Having faced his weaknesses and inhibitions he can realize his creative potential. Much of the energy heretofore used to defend the unconscious impulses are now released to the ego system for the client to use more creatively. Maslow (197) postulates that all humans are given this creative potentiality at birth, but that they lose it through the process of acculturation. The creative impulses must not be thought of necessarily as being applied to the arts, as in writing, music, and art; but in more humble circumstances of everyday life. One can be a creative clerk, craftsman, teacher, or housewife.

Range of Feeling

After having experienced more of his innermost feelings over a long period of time, the client experiences a greater range and a finer differentiation of feelings. He finds that he does not live merely in terms of his ego system or intellect, but that he can experience some of his self-system feelings also. He can courageously and joyfully experience communication with more of his feelings. Again we quote Rogers' observations on this point:

> It seems to me that clients who have moved significantly in therapy live more intimately with their feelings of pain, but also more vividly with their feelings of ecstasy; that anger is more clearly felt, and so also is love, that fear is an experience they know more deeply, but so is courage. And the reason they can thus live fully in a wider range is that they have this underlying confidence in themselves as trustworthy instruments for encountering life (257, pp. 13–14).

Occasionally the phenomenon is called "freedom from emotional constriction." This means the capacity to experience a greater range of feelings without consequent threat.

Brown (43) expresses the experiencing of increased range of feeling in another way. He suggests that one goal of psychotherapy is to help the client to love more easily and to hate more wisely. Occasionally clients come who can express only positive feelings, having been forbidden to express hostile feelings at home. It has been our observation that the necessity to suppress expression of the negative feelings tends to have a constricting effect on the expression of positive feelings also.

Finally, the reduction of painful anxiety is a criterion of successful psychotherapy. The client is relieved of incapacitating guilt and anxiety so that the uncertainty and insecurity he felt formerly are replaced with more certainty and optimism.

Time-Binding Capacity

The mature client can postpone and modify decisions about others at this moment in this situation. The latter idea is often called a "time-binding" facility with which the client is better able to postpone pleasures and goals. For example, the graduate student undergoes much immediate sacrifice and strain to reach the satisfactions of a distant professional goal.

Living Existentially

Rogers' summary of his philosophical paper entitled *A Therapist's View of the Good Life* emphasizes the significance of a philosophy based on awareness and acceptance of one's own nature:

> I believe it will have become evident why, for me, adjectives such as happy, contented, blissful, enjoyable, do not seem quite appropriate to any general description of this process I have called the good life, even though the person in this process would experience each one of these feelings at appropriate times. But the adjectives which seem more generally fitting are adjectives such as enriching, exciting, rewarding, challenging, meaningful. This process of the good life is not, I am convinced, a life for the faint hearted. (It involves stretching and growing, of becoming more and more of one's potentialities. It involves the courage to be. It means launching oneself fully into the stream of life. Yet the deeply exciting thing about human beings is that when the individual is inwardly free, he chooses as the good life this process of becoming (257, pg. 13).

PLANNING A COURSE OF PSYCHOLOGICAL COUNSELING

From the preceding discussion the reader will note that the counselor or psychotherapist must make several judgments early in the process. The type and extent of help offered will depend upon the following factors.

Client Needs and Variables

The client has a problem to solve, such as choice of a mate, selection of an occupation, reaching a decision about divorce, or feeling more comfortable with anxiety. These expressions of client need may be construed by the counselor as problems to be solved in counseling and/or symptomatic expressions of deeper personality disturbances which must be worked through in this or some other relationship before the symptomatic problem can be resolved permanently.

Treatability is another client variable affecting therapeutic planning. Does the client really want help? Is he motivated and ready? Is he capable of profiting from the style of counseling or therapy I am able to offer? Is his character structure and defensive functioning such that he is not likely to change much? The therapist must realize that not every client can be helped. If most of the questions are answered negatively the only realistic recourse is to judge the client unready to undertake counseling at the present time. The counselor may be able to be of some limited service to such a client, however, in helping him think through the immediate choice he is forced to make.

Which persons should get the most time is often determined by the personal preferences and social values of the counselor. We feel that the main criteria of who should get counseling or therapy should be whether the prospective client can profit from the services offered and whether the counseling is going to help him more than some other person. In other words, the counselor should ask himself whether he thinks the client would be better off with or without the help he can offer. It should be recognized that other agencies operate on such criteria as the greatest good for the greatest number, younger rather than older people, mildly rather than severely disturbed, or those who can make the greatest social contribution.

Clients' knowledge of psychology and the principles of counseling may or may not be an asset. Our opinion is that psychological sophistication can accelerate progress if the knowledge has not been too inextricably tied up in the client's intellectualizing defenses.

Diagnostic formulations regarding the nature and severity of the emotional problems are factors also. These topics are covered in a later section and in the next chapter.

Counselor and Agency Variables

The counselor's or therapist's assessment of the client's needs, problems, and condition for help affect the planning. The counselor's competence determines the level or depth at which the counseling is to be pitched. The type of agency in which the counselor or therapist functions determines level also. For example, a counselor working in a high school situation has his limits set by the policies controlling psychotherapeutic functions in that agency. His level of counseling may be set at more surface and supportive levels no matter how competent he may be. A counselor functioning in a clinic setting where there are associates and specialists from other fields with whom he can discuss cases and share responsibility, can plan his counseling along broader and deeper lines.

After considering the client, agency, and counselor-therapist variables the counselor-therapist and client together must decide whether to proceed at all, the objectives or goals, length of time, and general style to be employed. The counselor-therapist takes the lead in this determination since he is the over-all guide of the process.

LENGTH OF PSYCHOLOGICAL COUNSELING AND THERAPY

The duration of counseling can be determined generally in the planning stage, whereas the length of psychotherapy is more difficult to predict. The amount of time available for any one client determines the level of involvement and influences the nature of the process goals. The extent to which the client wants to get deeply involved and to stay involved is a significant determinant of length also. It is assumed that to acquire many of the general goals mentioned in the earlier section on goals, however, psychotherapy must be many hours in length. Many immediate goals such as reduction of anxiety, vocational plans formulation, and decisions regarding further education or choice of a mate may involve just a few hours; whereas the achievement of a general level of insight necessary to act in a more personally satisfying manner may take many hours.

There is very little research on the relationship between length of therapy and outcome. Morton's study (212) of brief psychotherapy utilized a high degree of interpretation and emphasis on learning principles following Rotter's Social Learning Theory as a framework. Morton concluded that:

> We can assume with an extremely high degree of confidence that brief psychotherapy conducted in a rational manner, following a systematic theoretical orientation, and utilizing vehicles appropriate to the theory, will result in striking and lasting changes of adjustment in subjects who were seriously maladjusted (212, pg. 17).

Morton's study was quite restricted in scope and should not be overgeneralized. His study suggests, however, that means can be employed to shorten the process and still obtain some lasting beneficial outcomes.

Morton's process objectives in his experimental therapy sessions were to: (1) Test the limits of the resistance; (2) Ascertain the nature of the defenses; (3) Test the degree of insight in relation to the problems; (4) Establish the level of present adequacy in solutions to problems; (5) Determine the nature of the potential pathways for satisfaction of needs; (6) Determine the level and intensity of interpretation that should be used; (7) Establish a meaningful frame of reference in which the client could organize his approach to problems.

Generally speaking, the client should be kept in counseling only as long as he seems to be making satisfactory progress toward the general goals of the process and toward the solution of his immediate problems. The ethics of counseling make this viewpoint imperative, especially when there are fees involved.

DIFFERENCES IN PSYCHOTHERAPY WITH THE MILDLY AND SEVERELY DISTURBED

This book was designed for students in counseling and psychotherapy who deal primarily with clients classified as maladjusted normals, mildly disturbed, or neurotic. Some clinical psychologists in clinics and private practice, however, work also with clients having psychotic characteristics. Since the counselor or therapist never knows what kind of client will walk in the door, it is highly important that he be well fortified with information of two types: (1) An understanding of behavior disorders so that he can recognize severely disturbed or psychotic persons; and (2) a clear recognition of his own competence and limitations to deal with serious disorders both on an emergency and a referral basis.

The following figure after Klopfer suggests a continuum for normal, neurotic, and psychotic conditions (172, pg. 312, 174). It is noted in Figure 13 that the neurotic exhausts his defenses to the breaking point be-

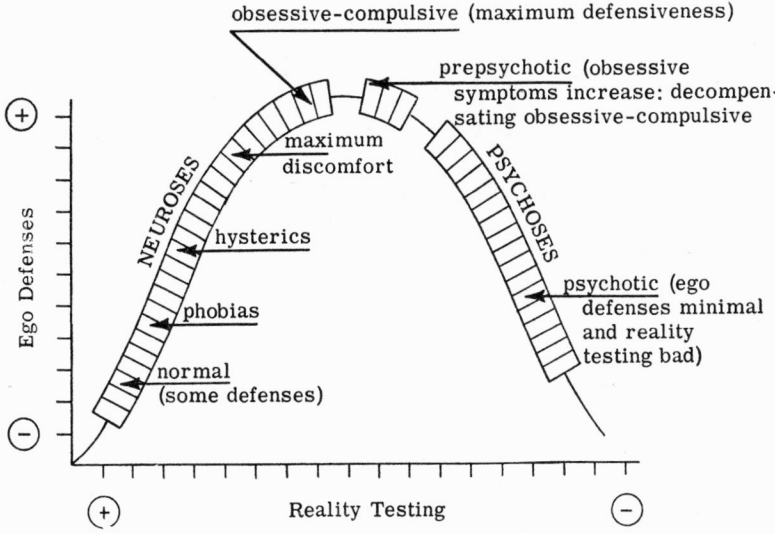

Fig. 13. Normal-Neurotic-Psychotic Ego-Defense Continuum. Adapted from Klopfer.

fore his reality-testing functions deteriorate. The average neurotic, before psychotherapy, has a heavy wall of defenses. The psychotic, on the other hand, has little defensive strength, little ego strength, and low reality contact.

The psychotic has a rich inner world of reality, but his perception of the meaning of his external reality is very distorted thus giving a delusional quality to his thinking. The neurotic, in contrast, experiences his outer world only photographically (filtered by his defenses) as Fromm (114) points out. The neurotic client is very sensitive to his outer stimuli; but is defended staunchly from perceiving the inner world of his self- and core systems. In Fromm's (114) conception of the healthy personality both poles are present; inner and outer perceptions are both accurate, thus enabling the client to see the world more objectively and to experience his own thoughts and feelings subjectively without distortion or over-reaction.

Some of these distinctions between "normal" and "pathological" are illustrated in terms of the multidimensional theory in Figure 14. The psychotic is pictured as having a loose defense system, a small ego system not too well differentiated from the "outside wall," and a loosely defined self-system. Core-system anxiety poses a potent mastery difficulty for the personality since the ego system handles it largely by dissociative mechanisms rather than directly in a problem-solving manner.

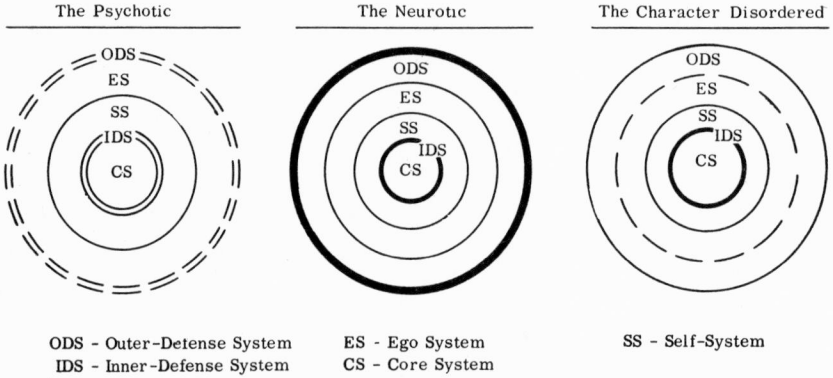

ODS - Outer-Defense System   ES - Ego System   SS - Self-System
IDS - Inner-Defense System   CS - Core System

FIG. 14. Personality Models of More Pathological Types.

The neurotic is seen as a personality model with rigid defensive systems which allow little interaction among elements in the personality, thus giving an impression of lack of integration, excessive inhibition, and an oversensitivity to demands of the outside world. The ego and self-systems of the neurotic generally may be similar to the non-neurotic normal, except that the ego system of the neurotic is more influenced by core-system feelings.

The client with a so-called character disorder has more "rubbery" defense systems. He has several facades which can be used to suit his advantage. His self-system is very constricted. He has very little of what we have defined in Chapter 2 as a sense of "self" or "individuality." The disordered character, or so-called psychopathic personality also has a very small ego system. He has difficulty profiting from experience, socially speaking, and has little in the way of close identification with the usual social groups—family, church, education, and society at large. This is the kind of personality which gravitates toward the prison rather than the clinic or hospital because of his anti-social acts.

The relationship has to be more patiently and carefully built with the psychotic than with normal and neurotic clients. More active encouragement and direction on the part of the psychotherapist is necessary in the treatment of psychotics. These differences are mentioned more as illustrations rather than as suggestions for psychotherapists.

Psychological counselors on the other hand do not work with psychotics except under clinical conditions, generally within the confines of a psychiatric team in the clinic or hospital. Even superficial manipulation of psychotics by poorly timed interpretations or too much catharsis by a counselor unskilled in psychotherapy with psychotics may make them even more acutely aware of conditions in their core system. The psychotic is already too sensitive to inner thoughts and feelings. Further attempts to help may deepen his preoccupation with himself and increase his deterioration and feelings of distress. Similarly, counselors need to be wary particularly of clients with severe obsessive-compulsive defenses. These individuals technically may not be psychotic, yet they may be moving toward a psychosis. This tends to be true especially if their obsessive defenses are stripped away.

The discussion may have given the impression that there are neat distinctions among normal, neurotic, and psychotic categories. The contrary seems to be true. There is a blending effect from one classification into another, yet there are widely recognized symptoms and signs which aid in classifying the severely disturbed. The student of counseling and psychotherapy needs to have a thorough grounding in abnormal psychology for this reason. The purpose here is to emphasize the necessity for the counselor to determine the extent of pathology present, and his capability of handling it, before he becomes too involved in the process.

EVALUATION

A significant part of the counselor's or therapist's thinking concerns his evaluation of progress toward goals. Some of the questions which go through his thinking are: Did the relationship help the client? In what respects did it help? If it did not help, why not? If the goals were not achieved entirely, what progress was made toward them?

One of the principal difficulties in evaluating counseling and psychotherapy is finding adequate criteria for judging progress. Some of the criteria which have been used in the past are: *Opinion* based upon observations of counselor or client that the goals were achieved; *performance* on a standardized test of personality, a projective technique, sociometric study, or a specially constructed test of information or attitude before and after counseling or therapy. Performance in the form of improved grades, occupational stability, job satisfaction, or decreasing numbers of dropouts have been used.

The literature on evaluation of counseling and psychotherapy is vast. The *Annual Review of Psychology* (290) lists the published evaluative studies for students interested in pursuing the details of this topic. One of the recent and, in our opinion, best of the studies of personality changes in psychotherapeutic counseling is Rogers and Dymond *Psychotherapy and Per-*

sonality Change (258) because of its thoroughness and variety of method. In general, counseling and therapy evaluation studies fall into four major categories: (1) follow-up studies of client attitudes toward their experiences by means of questionnaires or interviews; (2) the opinion of the counselor or therapist about changes which took place in the process and his estimate of the progress made toward the goals; (3) internal studies based upon close scrutiny of the verbal exchanges interview by interview. This method is best accomplished when the entire transcript is available from a tape. An example of client change would be the decrease in defensiveness exhibited in his remarks, or the signs of increasing client self-directedness manifested by comments such as, "I feel that I can really handle these feelings now," or, "I think I can make a decision about what I should do when I graduate." Other studies have used estimates of tension reduction based upon client statements of relief from disabling anxiety through a measure called the "discomfort-relief quotient" of Dollard and Mowrer (84); (4) External methods based upon objective measures of behavior changes. Examples are using personality tests such as the Minnesota Multiphasic before and after a course of counseling, or studying changes in Rorschach protocols obtained before and after counseling.

The first two methods of counselor and client opinion are based upon observations of the experience shortly afterward and are subject to the usual unreliabilities and biases of reporting. Though the third method, the internal, offers some significant ways of thinking about the changes taking place in counseling it has great limitations for evaluating counseling success. The criteria have a way of becoming the goals for the counseling and they become contaminated with many other changes. There is no effective way of knowing how permanent the changes are and what independent criteria might exist against which to match the internal criteria. The fourth method of using external devices has the limitation of not indicating what changes to attribute to the counseling and what to other life experiences. There is always the problem of the reliability of the instrument and the regression toward the mean phenomenon to consider in such studies using standardized instruments.

Although the field of evaluation criteria and methods at present is very inadequate for the needs of the practicing counselor, he still must strive to develop an attitude of criticizing his work. He must study the developments in the area of evaluating counseling and psychotherapy with the aim of developing his own research design for ascertaining the effectiveness of his own work.

SUMMARY

In this chapter a bird's-eye view of the process of psychological counseling and therapy was presented to serve as a guide for the student. Without attempting to oversimplify the process, the various stages in the more rationalistic styles of counseling psychotherapeutic types were discussed. The stages in the process of psychotherapeutic counseling were: developing the relationship, expression of feelings, and clarifying the problem, working through feelings, developing of insight, and planning and acting positively. Three critical points were identified in the middle stages of the process: (1) desire to leave after the first satisfying catharsis of feelings, (2) too fast and too deep expression of feelings, and (3) the tendency to leave counseling short of complete working through of the problem to the point of positive action. Counseling and psychotherapy have process goals, such as expression of feeling. There are general goals outlined in terms of a model personality with characteristics such as spontaneity, creativity, increased range of feeling, and reduction of uncomfortable feelings. Evaluation of such outcomes is a significant part of the counselor's and therapist's thinking.

II.

Techniques

5.

Preparation for Counseling
and Psychotherapy

This chapter covers three topics of concern to counselors and therapists as they begin the counseling process—building readiness for counseling, obtaining case histories, and psychodiagnostic evaluation. The first section of this chapter has more applications for the counseling level. The middle section applies equally to both and the last section has greater relevance to psychotherapy.

READINESS

Readiness for learning is a well-known educational concept. The child, for instance, is not "ready" to read until he has achieved a certain level of motivation, maturation, and basic skill development. Readiness for counseling and psychotherapy is similar in that certain conditions must be satisfied before the client can make full use of the relationship. One of the conclusions from Lipkin's study of client attitudes and therapeutic outcomes was:

> Our data strongly suggest that the client who is positively oriented to the counselor and the counseling experience, and who anticipates that his experience in counseling will be a successful and gratifying one, undergoes more change in personality structure than does the client who has reservations about the counseling experience (186, pg. 26).

The person himself may recognize that something is wrong in his life; but typically he has to have this pointed out to him by someone else. The suggestion that he needs help often aggravates a condition known as resistance which is a type of protective defense against change. In Chapter 8 the resistance phenomenon will be treated in detail; but it is significant for this discussion because the individual typically comes to counseling with some strong reservations even though he may come voluntarily.

Our culture places great emphasis upon the person's ability to solve his own problems and to stand on his own feet. Hence, the client frequently seems to perceive a counseling or psychotherapeutic relationship as threatening to his feeling of independence. Even when the client comes to counseling voluntarily he often has feelings of being different from his more "normal" or "adjusted" friends. People in our culture, furthermore, are taught that they should not need help, that they should be logical, and that they should depend on "common sense" to guide their actions. There is a feeling of shame if one cannot "master" his feelings and solve his own problems. Some of this feeling is a fear that the psychotherapeutic counselor, particularly, has methods for penetrating his innermost secrets and for getting him to do and say things against his better judgment. One concern of this chapter, therefore, will be over methods for getting clients interested in counseling and for working on their problems as expeditiously as possible.

The following discussion is oriented toward readiness principles and techniques, but we wish to stress that sound counseling practice and ethics demand that counseling be voluntary. It is a generally accepted principle that prospective clients should not be persuaded, cajoled, or tricked into a relationship. However, we feel that prospective clients should be given opportunities to learn about the potentialities and limitations of counseling so they can make, from their viewpoint, a sound decision about counseling.

Determining Factors in Readiness

Several factors determine the "readiness" of the client for a counseling or psychotherapeutic experience. His present motivation for help is perhaps the most important. Other factors are the knowledge the client has about counseling, his intellectual or conceptualizing ability, his present level of insight into his problem and himself, his expectations of the role the counselor will play, and the general rigidity or fluidity of his defense system. The difficulties in meeting these conditions are described below.

Obstacles to Readiness

Several factors militate against a client getting off to a good start. The first is the culturally based resistance mentioned above. A second obstacle is the physical setting. Often, privacy and comfort are lacking in the counselor's office, to such an extent that the client is ill at ease and quite suspicious that others may find out about his being there and what is discussed. Hence, privacy, comfort, and confidentiality are significant "musts" for good counseling readiness.

Previous unpleasant experiences with counselors, competent or incompetent, often start the interview with two strikes against it. The counselor's reputation is a related factor. The fact that he is known for his skill in helping people, or has some of the status symbols such as degrees, titles, certifications, and favorable references help considerably in the initial phase of counseling.

Lack of clear-cut understanding, on the part of the client, of the nature of counseling and psychotherapy is a widespread source of inadequate readiness to attack problems. It is important that the client know the limitations and possibilities of counseling as well as certain bits of information such as length of interviews, probable length of the process, or how he makes appointments. This element of readiness is handled under the term "structuring," to be discussed in Chapter 7. Intellectual inadequacy is a related readiness obstacle. In psychotherapeutic counseling, for example, Crider's study (72) indicated that the more intellectually able and the more psychologically sophisticated individual had the best chance of therapeutic success.

Lack of accessibility is another important obstacle to effective counseling readiness. A disturbed client, for example, may come in all set to go to work. He is told he will have to make an appointment for a later date because the counselor is booked up. Often he "cools off" to the point where he does not return. It would seem desirable to have an "intake" system to see each client, even if briefly, when he comes in the first time. This procedure would let him feel something is being done and would ascertain the degree of urgency for psychotherapy, counseling, referral to specialists, or other efforts.

A final obstacle in promoting effective readiness is the lack of an overall "climate" of acceptance of counseling within the institution. Some hospitals, schools, and colleges have an administrative policy or unfortunate history of rumors about counseling or psychotherapy which do not allow even the most skilled counselor to operate effectively. An example is having the counseling function tied in with disciplinary and regulatory activities of a school which tends to make the counseling function an administrative arm. Students are quick to sense this relationship. This does not mean, however, that counseling services cannot be used effectively as referral resources for a disciplinary officer; but it does mean that the physical proximity and emotional association of the disciplinary and counseling functions must be examined carefully and kept separate if at all possible.

The reputation of the service must be examined constantly. In a college or community service, for example, it is easy to get a reputation for being an "outpatient clinic" or a place where the "oddballs" are handled by the institution. To achieve and maintain adequate "readiness," there is constant need for interpretation of the philosophy of the service to its potential clientele.

Methods for Readying Clients

One way of reaching people with problems is through *talks*. Heads of agencies and counseling service directors report that every time they give a talk to a public group on mental health, family problems, study methods, or child behavior, for example, there are numerous requests for services. So, letting one's potential public know about the services and telling them the means of establishing contact is one sure means of readying a large number of clients.

A second method of motivating clients is through creating an *institutional climate conducive to seeking help*. In schools, for example, this is particularly important since very few student clients seek counseling voluntarily. Viewing counseling, especially psychotherapeutic counseling, as a usual and shameless means to help one's self to become a more mature person, a more proficient student, or a more effective spouse would go far to help clients make better use of counseling services.

A third method for stimulating weakly motivated clients and for building better readiness in those already seeking such services is that of *instructing referral sources*. Counselors constantly must work on sharpening the awareness of referral agents through conferences with physicians, teachers, advisers, ministers, lawyers, personnel directors, and others likely to make the first contact. Proper referral techniques are essential to readiness. There is considerable difference between shaming a potential client by saying, "You had better see a psychologist," and being interested enough to give him a referral in an unthreatening manner. An example is, "This is something which I feel is a little out of my area. I suggest you discuss this with Dr. Blank who may be able to help you work this out. He is a psychologist specializing in personal problems and he is located in the Plaza Building. His phone number is Pleasant 5554." Often the sophisticated person making a referral can supplement this statement by giving realistic, sincere, and reassuring statements about counseling so that the prospective client will act upon the suggestion.

A significant principle of referral is that of being honest and sincere about the problem observed. Evasion and embarrassment only complicate a referral. The person making the referral may call the prospective client in and say, "I've noted some things about which you might need or want help." Then he mentions the behavior and suggests the source from which he might obtain such assistance. Unless the client is ready to accept the suggestion, however, and has some awareness of the judgments others are making about him, this approach, too, could be very threatening.

Referral is more difficult when the counselor has worked some with the client and then feels obliged to refer him. Again, the sincerity with which the counselor approaches the matter is critical since it is so easy to imply judgment or to have the client feel rejected. The counselor attitude of, "I've taken you as far as *I* can go now" or, *"You* are too hot to handle" should be avoided. An attitude of: "Let's see what other possibilities there might be for help on this problem," would be better.

Referral techniques and resources are complicated and unique to a particular community. The counselor training staff at the Michigan State University has published a list of referral guides designed to help school and college counselors particularly, but the list has applicability to all workers and agencies which are faced with referral to another service.

(1) Check to see if the school has used all its own available resources in helping the student before looking outside the school for help.

(2) Try discussing an incipient problem with an agency or specialist before referral is urgent.

(3) Try to discover what persons have had contact with the parent or student in regard to the problem, and what results were obtained from these contacts before making a referral.

(4) Designate one person to be responsible in working with the parent and student in developing a referral.

(5) Learn whether a community agency is already working with the family, for a consultation with that agency is the proper first step in considering a referral in such cases.

(6) It is unwise and impractical to refer a student to community agencies without the knowledge, consent, and cooperation of his parents.

(7) Keep in mind when telling students or parents about available services in the school or in the community that the teacher should explain both the functions and the limitations of these services. Do not give the impression that any specialist or agency has all the answers and can work wonders.

(8) Do not coach a student or parent regarding how they might "wangle" hard-to-get services.

(9) Let the student or his parent make their own arrangements for service whenever possible. Do not "spoon feed" the student by being more "helpful" than necessary.

(10) Remember that in some cases, however, help may be needed by very immature, dependent, or ill students or parents in arranging an appointment or even in arranging transportation to the agency.

(11) Secure a signed consent from the student's parents before releasing information to a social agency.

(12) Help the agency or specialist by indicating which person should be the point of contact representing the school (205).

A fourth device for promoting readiness is to give the prospective client *information about himself*. This is quite easy in a school or college setting compared to private or clinic practice. Generally test batteries have been given, and personal records are completed routinely and cumulatively. The students are notified that they can come in to discuss the test results. Students in the highest quarter, for example, may be notified of this fact. They come in often expressing surprise at their high aptitude or lack of commensurate achievement.

Counselors can note items in personal records of students which indicate possible problems. If the climate of the institution as described above is favorable, the student often is relieved that someone has taken the initiative for him and brought matters to his attention. These may be items about which he has been vaguely aware, but from which he has been escaping for some time. There may be some question whether a counselor has the ethical right to precipitate a counseling relationship by this means; but it seems justified from the standpoint of an overall general educational mission of which counseling frequently is a significant part.

A fifth significant source of finding motivated clients is through the *educational process* itself. Robinson (246) who has studied the problem of readiness in student counseling mentions several such sources. The special courses in study methods: English, Reading Techniques, Orientation, Mental Hygiene, and Marriage, offer extraordinary opportunities to help people formulate their problems and to coordinate their desires for counseling help. This type of curricular experience helps the person with problems not only to come to grips with them, but also offers excellent opportunities to motivate the better student to achieve, what Robinson (246) describes as, "higher level adjustment skills." This achievement results in higher efficiency, more productivity, richer emotional experiences, and better health than would be attained by chance or whimsical living habits. Thus, counseling relationships can help the person who is already operating at a high level to improve himself even more.

Survey techniques are a sixth means of finding and motivating potential clients. Many problem checklists such as the Mooney Problems Checklist (210), SRA Youth Inventory (242), and Berdie's precounseling checklist (26), serve the useful purpose of making the person more aware of his problems and possibly motivating him to do something about them. Robinson (246) found that an average of twenty-five problems were generally checked during routine administrations to students. The following table is reproduced from Robinson's book on student counseling to illustrate the types and frequency of such problems in college-age youth.

Special *precounseling orientation* meetings are a seventh means of giving clients information about counseling and related functions such as testing, helping them formulate realistic expectations about counseling and the counselor's role, acquainting them with the philosophy of the particular counseling service, and reducing anxieties about the anticipated counseling experience. In another book (277) we describe a type of prevocational-counseling readiness meeting which attempted to describe counseling and related functions. Charts were used during the meeting to illustrate the nature of the process, the functions of the counselor, and the goals for vocational counseling. The general aim was to build a realistic "level of expectation" or perceptual "set" for counseling experiences and to establish initial rapport with the counselor who was often present at the precounseling sessions.

Precounseling orientation has the advantage of being economical. A counselor spends so much time in the simple educational function of structuring and explaining to each client the process of educational-vocational

Table 1†

DISTRIBUTION OF STUDENT PROBLEMS ON THE MOONEY PROBLEM CHECK LIST FOR THE CLASSES ON "EFFECTIVE STUDY AND INDIVIDUAL ADJUSTMENT" AND FOR "REGULAR" STUDENTS AT OHIO STATE UNIVERSITY AND AT ANOTHER COLLEGE*

Areas	Location: Composition of group	O.S.U. 231 M & W E.S. and I.A. Class	O.S.U. 171 W Dormitory	Colo. 190 M & W
		%	%	%
Adjustment to college work		28	20	21
Personal-psychological relations ...		15	15	15
Vocational and educational future .		10	11	9
Social and recreational activities...		9	10	12
Health and physical development ..		8	10	10
Curriculum and teaching procedures		8	9	3
Social-psychological relations		7	8	11
Courtship, sex, marriage		5	6	5
Finances, living conditions, and employment		4	3	7
Home and family		4	3	4
Morals and religion		2	5	3
		100	100	100

† F. P. Robinson, *Principles and Procedures of Student Counseling.* New York: Harpers, 1950, p. 8.
* N. A. Congdon, The perplexities of college freshmen. *Educ. and Psychol. Meas.,* 1943, *3,* pp. 367–376.
Source: R. L. Mooney, Personal problems of freshman girls. *J. Higher Educ.,* 1943, *14, pp.* 84–90.

counseling that the method seems justified on economy grounds alone. Evidence from studies made by Stone (289) and Richardson and Borow (245) corroborates the above-mentioned economy values of pre-vocational counseling orientation when coupled properly with individual counseling.

The orientation procedure would be limited in facilitating psychotherapeutic counseling, however, because a less cognitive and more individualistic approach is needed. Multiple counseling techniques are another effective means of readying the client for psychotherapy and counseling. These techniques will be described in Chapter 11.

Readiness Within the Interview

Most of the preceding methods of establishing readiness are concerned with locating and motivating clients. Once the client is in his office, the clinician has a special problem in readiness. Here attitude, setting, and technique are important factors. The clinician must be able to size up the situation to know if he should apply support techniques to ease the client's anxiety or whether to increase the client's discomfort, to get him more emotionally involved, and willing to work on his problem.

Therapists and counselors can be misled easily by the "facade" phenomenon. The client's unconscious resistance may cause him to open the relationship with the counselor by talking about such side issues as "no vocational goal," "poor name remembering," "stage fright," or "poor study habits," as the basic problem. We feel that the counselor should start at this level with the client and not jump to the conclusion immediately that this is a "facade" problem. Generally speaking, however, if the clinician's attitudes are appropriate, the client will come forth with a redefinition of his problem shortly. Attitudes which facilitate readiness to discuss problems are elaborated in the next chapter.

Criteria which the counselor can apply to ascertain the client's readiness to move forward are his positive attitudes toward the therapeutic process and a lowered defensiveness which gives an impression of spontaneity and eagerness to talk about his problems. Impressions that the client is ready to deal with the emotional implications of his problems, articulateness which enables him to express ideas and feelings directly, and a general acceptance of the therapist's or counselor's role, structure, and style of counseling are further indications of client readiness. The counselor should be alert also to the client who may not be able to articulate his problem or feelings directly, but by his attitude indicates a desire to go ahead. Similarly, he should be wary of the client who is too glib about going ahead.

THE CASE HISTORY

Nature and Problems in the Use of Case History Method

A case history is a systematic collection of facts about the client's current and past life. This history may take many forms depending upon the style and preference of the counselor or therapist and the type of problem situation. The psychoanalytically oriented therapist, for example, would stress the detailed facts of early emotional development through adolescence to his present status. The counselor trained in the social work tradition would place considerable emphasis upon the environmental circumstances of the client and would collect a detailed life history also. The vocational counselor would collect only those items which have a direct bearing upon the client's work of selecting life objectives. The self-theorist would tend to ignore a formal, systematic life history, letting the client select items which were important to him. The counselor in the Rogerian tradition would not ask specific questions to fill in gaps in the story as given by the client because this might tend to throw the responsibility too much on the counselor's shoulders. Nondirective counselors, in addition, feel that it is the client's present perception of his situation that is important, not the accurate systematic reconstruction of the past.

Limitations of Case History Methods

One of the key dangers of the case study method is the overemphasis upon counselor responsibility that is engendered by voluminous data-collecting. The client feels that the therapist is collecting information from which the therapist will later formulate an answer to his "case." Since making a case history generally demands much questioning, it has the frequently unfortunate effect of increasing the client's resistance to help and makes it more difficult for him to help himself later.

Although the method may be limited through the possible danger of using data inaccurately, the danger that a counselor may allow his bias or a priori assumptions to enter, in regard to a particular case, is especially potent when he is collecting case data. The counselor may find, furthermore, that he collects much irrelevant and unreliable data during a systematic review of the client's life. Clinicians know the subtle distortions which often characterize a client's reporting of past events. Preoccupation with case data has the additional disadvantage of being very time-consuming.

In addition to detracting from the job of building the relationship solidly, too much preoccupation with taking a case history may give the therapist a false sense of security that he has a meaningful diagnostic and prognostic answer to the client's problem. Mere data seem to have a morbid and powerful fascination for some counselors to the point that a neat collection of life facts gives the illusion that they understand the client.

Forms of Case Histories

Vocational Counseling Surveys: Case histories can be obtained in various ways. Vocational counseling generally requires a highly structured survey form designed to be completed by the client which covers areas most relevant to his planning. Such a form covers: (1) basic *identifying information* such as name, age, and sex; (2) *educational information* such as his school history, scholastic and activity record, subjects liked and disliked, and present educational status and plans; (3) *vocational history* such as part- and full-time jobs held, military experience, present and past occupational choices; (4) *personal data* including health history, disabilities, parental and marital status, family background with data on socioeconomic level, family aspirations, hobbies, personal problems, and the vocational plans of the client. To these basic data supplied by the client and often supplemented by the first interview are added the data from *school transcripts, work samples, test profiles* of interest, aptitude, personality, and achievement.

Psychotherapeutic counseling histories. In psychotherapeutic problems, the case history may focus more attention upon a systematic social record such as the family history, and the record of interpersonal relationships with parents, siblings, teachers, and peers. The data are often collected by means of the interview—often by a so-called "intake worker." This specialist, usually found in a clinic or agency, does not do the psychotherapy but collects the information, determines eligibility and suitability for help, and checks with the local social-service exchange for information on previous agency contacts. The method is used mostly by multidisciplinary clinics and agencies dealing especially with children.

In private practice and in school and college counseling agencies, the data generally are collected by the person doing the counseling. The writers have found that it serves the best interests of the client to collect information from him on a systematic form and to supplement this with data offered by the client in the course of his statement and elaboration of his problem. This procedure tends to avoid the pitfalls of the formal case history mentioned earlier in this section; yet it gives the counselor the basic data from which he must formulate his hypotheses and decisions about the course of future relationships with this client.

In compiling case data or presenting a report for a staff conference or review agent, it is preferable to start with broad general characteristics and move progressively to the specifics which give the "flavor" to his unique "life style." For example, case studies may start with the fact that the client is white, male, twenty-four years old, married, through more and more particular categories to unique characteristics, such as the fact that he has a deep-seated hostility toward dominant women.

The main justification for collecting facts by means of the systematic case history is to shed light on the present problems, their origins, past forms, and present meanings. The past has different meanings for clients. Some will enjoy preoccupation with details, even those events surrounding traumatic experiences, perhaps because this preoccupation enables them to escape responsibility for facing problems in the present. Other clients feel that the only way they are going to understand the present is to open the past; hence they become overly occupied with "family skeletons." To avoid these pitfalls, the counselor must de-emphasize the significance of collecting information in the interview and use the data only as tools to interpret material to the client or to use as a take-off point for discussion and for his diagnostic formulations.

Thorne (304, pg. 87) suggests the following outline as an aid to a systematic case study. The outline covers the major personality dimensions which describe the generality and uniqueness of the particular human being being studied.

(1) *Genetic.* Hereditary factors where demonstrable.
(2) *Constitutional.* The biologic calibre of the organism.
(3) *Psychophysiological-supporting functions.* Lower level supports of psychic functions.
(4) *Temperament, feelings and emotions.* The affective-impulsive basis for behavior.
(5) *Intelligence.* Factors of native ability.
(6) *Form of thought.* Perception, symbolic language functions and thinking.
(7) *Content of thought.* Ideological composition.

(8) *Consciousness and attention.* Orientation and sensorium.

(9) *Conditioning and habit formation.* The experiential context.

(10) *Self-control.* Voluntary functions in personality.

(11) *Attitudes, sentiments and complexes.* "Acting out" behaviors.

(12) *Group membership, role and situational determinants.*

(13) *Style of life.*

(14) *Self, self-concepts and ego development.*

(15) *Global dimensions of personality.* General factors.

Occasionally a more detailed study is needed when the existing data are sketchy or unreliable. Lewis' *Outlines for Psychiatric Examination* (184), for example, offers suggestions for a detailed study of the client's past and present life.

Cumulative records. Most schools and colleges have a cumulative record system wherein basic data about the development of the student are maintained. The first step which the counselor must take when a student becomes a client is to check on the recency and reliability of the data already collected.

The fragmentary data of the usual school cumulative record make hasty, superficial judgment a grave temptation. An example is jumping to conclusions about a client's mental ability from group test scores and course grades. Another problem relative to cumulative records involves the handling of confidential data. The general rule found most suitable to school and college situations is to keep confidential reports in a separate highly secure file with only a notation of the confidential file's existence in the cumulative record. Many school counselors, for example, can testify that a student can be a "marked" person because of entries made about earlier misconduct.

The cumulative record can be a useful counseling tool to aid in the readiness process. The counselor can formulate hypotheses about problems and can note discrepancies in data, such as the difference between John's test data and teachers' reports on his work. This preliminary exposure to brief case data saves valuable interview time. The counselor can spot possible "trouble" areas, noting that the parents have been divorced recently, that he lists two addresses, and that he is alternately with each parent.

However, some psychotherapeutic counselors prefer to start "with a clean slate" as it were. They feel they cannot trust the recorded data or even their own perceptions of data. They are afraid that their biases will affect their relationship with the client adversely. As in most other counseling issues, the value of records hinges on the individual preferences of the counselor and his care and skill in using them.

Case write-ups. Counselors and psychotherapists vary in their opinions about keeping notes on clients. Those who take elaborate notes feel they have more material for therapeutic planning, interpretations, and predictions; whereas the main arguments for not keeping notes are that the confidential material might fall into unauthorized hands and the fact that the relationship has been between the counselor and client only. We ourselves take the position that some notes are necessary. Certain identifying information and a brief outline of the topics and plans discussed are essential to note trends in the counseling process. With a heavy counseling load it is easy to get clients mixed up and to forget essential facts. The counselor may wish, or may be required, to put notations in the cumulative or agency records, but confidential material should be kept in the counselor's personal file only and destroyed after a period of time.

The autobiography. Client productions are other devices for getting information about the client and for starting him thinking about his current problems in light of his developmental history. Autobiographies may be of two types. In the systematic form, the client is given general instructions about covering topics such as family, friends, aspirations, and current feelings. The second type is a free response form where no specific topics are mentioned. The client is completely free to develop whatever style and content he wishes.

The essay. Here is another example of a personal document from which much rich material can be obtained about the client's self-perceptions and his readiness for psychotherapeutic counseling. In this method the client is assigned a specific topic to write about such as, "What I want to get out of life," "My family," "What I would do on a deserted island," "The most beautiful experience I have ever had." The following is a condensation of an essay voluntarily written by a client on the topic of "What I Want out of Life."

> I want to respect tradition such as carrying on the family name. Secondly I want success. I want people to know my name when they hear it. Then I think I want children—to follow the blood line through. I want to write, to travel, to learn. Next, I want to find myself. I want to understand why I do the things I do; why I think the way I do, why I am the way I am. Above all, I want to be happy. Is it perfection, or fulfillment, we sensitive ones are looking for? Is Joe the one I am best suited for, the one I'm better adjusted to? Ideas, talk, writing, thinking, planning, walking together. This is what I wonder about. Have I made a mistake in choosing my mate? or my life career? Just what have I done wrong all along through life? Why must I wait?
>
> Why can't I just dig into whatever I attain, desire, wish, and hope for. Basically what is the matter with me and my relationships with people? Do I really feel inadequate or is it just what I think I should be and feel that way.
>
> I want to make the name of Smith live in the minds of people. It did once and it can again. I am a living organism, I believe, with emotions, love, hate, sorrow, happiness. I do have ambition but I feel that my procrastination is tripping my ambition. I want to overcome it. I need direction. I come to you for it.

Such a document is full of meaning for the therapist and client. This twenty-year-old woman had difficulty getting involved in a psychotherapeutic relationship. It was hypothesized that this "lack of readiness" was due largely to ambivalent feelings about giving up her satisfying defenses and facing up to the pain she was experiencing with other people, academic failure, and feelings of inadequacy and guilt over letting the family down. This document gave both counselor and client an opportunity to talk about her diminishing resistance and apparent readiness to face up to her problems realistically.

The time graph. This device combines elements of the abbreviated autobiography with a strict time orientation. The client is instructed, for example, to outline his life by topics such as father, mother, home location, on the vertical dimension, with the decades or individual years clearly marked on the horizontal dimension. The values of this instrument lie in the perspective and contrasts it offers the client when he sees the significant people, places, and events of his life outlined in chronological order. It is believed that the autobiographical exposition process itself has therapeutic value. The counselor, too, can more easily pinpoint significant experiences for further elaboration when he has this panorama of his client's life before him.

PSYCHODIAGNOSIS

The Concepts and Issues

Diagnosis in the medical sense means a process of examining symptoms, inferring causes, integrating observations and fitting them into general categories, and, finally, pinning specific labels on disease entities. Psychiatric or psychological diagnosis is a similar process of ferreting out causation and of naming symptom clusters, schizophrenia for example, or reading deficiency, or anxiety state; but, there is no clear-cut psychological analogue to a medical concept like diphtheria or thrombosis, which have definite etiology. In these diseases it is mandatory that various types of medical diagnoses precede treatment.

In the psychological area, however, the diagnostic process takes on several meanings and is not as clear-cut as in medicine. Psychological diagnosis generally means a statement of the problems or present status of the client, probable causes of the difficulty, possible counseling techniques to solve the problems, and a prediction of counseling outcomes or future client behavior.

Psychodiagnosis may mean, first of all, a descriptive *classification* or taxonomy of problems similar to the psychiatric classifications for neuroses, psychoses, and character disorders. This process is often called "differential diagnosis" wherein the clinician attempts to differentiate one disease entity from another. Various differential classification schemes have been devised for different types of pathological behavior. The American Psychiatric Association's manual on types of psychoses, neuroses, and character disorders is the standard nosological reference for pathology (7).

In looking at nonpathological classifications used in counseling, Williamson (320) proposes a sociological type with five categories: Personality, Educational, Vocational, Financial, and Health Problems. Bordin (39) looked deeper, at the source, rather than at the kind of difficulty and developed five categories: No problem, lack of information, dependence, self-conflict, and choice anxiety. Pepinsky (231) has a similar set of categories for student problems including lack of assurance, lack of information, lack of skill, dependence, self-conflict (interpersonal, intrapersonal, cultural), and choice anxiety. Robinson (246) has a simple three-category system based on discussion topics: Adjustment problems (emotional and nonemotional), skill learning, and lack of maturity.

The value of diagnostic categorization of counseling clients is mainly for reporting and research purposes; although the lack of basic agreement on the dimensions of personality and personal problems makes reporting difficult. There has been little effort recently to classify clients or problems according to causes. Pepinsky (231) found that judges of case write-ups agreed with fair reliability on classifying clients' problems by his scheme; but they have not proved sufficiently useful in planning differential counseling.

Diagnostic categories may be useful in certain environmental manipulations and for offering specific treatment such as remedial help for slow reading problems; but in their oversimplifications they do not help the counselor very much in understanding the client.

Shorthand labels such as "neurotic" do little to help the counselor, or the client either, since they tend to make the client in a stereotype which may not fit the dynamics of the client in question. If this type of labelling seems necessary, a descriptive phrase rather than a single term is preferable. This type of understanding is merely one basis for applying the most appropriate counseling or therapeutic techniques.

One of the issues in diagnosis, involving diagnostic categories, is reliability of classification. The evidence is conflicting. One study by Ash (15) indicated that the reliability of diagnosing pathological categories was distressingly low, although this study has been severely criticized because of the inadequate categories involved. A later study by Schmidt and Fonda (266) on the reliability of psychiatric categorization revealed a high degree of reliability and met the usual standards of research design. The principal limitation of such studies is semantic in that more sound categories of pathology need to be developed before this issue of diagnostic reliability can be resolved.

A second meaning of the term diagnosis in counseling is that of *interpreting* case data, sometimes called "structural" diagnosis. Williamson (320) uses the term to mean the "pattern of consistency" which helps to explain or describe the client's behavior. Diagnosis is the step following analysis of the data wherein the counselor selects, from the mass of case data, the relevant facts which form the basis for a prognosis and a plan for later counseling or psychotherapy. By a process of inference the counselor is enabled to discover new meanings in the data which he can use in his therapeutic planning or which he can interpret directly to the client. This rationalistic view of diagnosis assumes a certain lawfulness and consistency of behavior, and was developed primarily for student personnel counseling which is heavily educational-vocational in character.

Klopfer (172) emphasizes the importance of collecting descriptive material on defense used, the strengths and ameliorative factors in personality, as well as the perceptual, conceptual, and affective pathological signs when making a diagnostic study. This practice is in line with the general trend to make psychodiagnosis a descriptive rather than a classification process.

Thorne (303), looking at the diagnostic problem even more clinically, asserts that an accurate diagnosis must be made before "rational treatment" can be planned and carried out. He gives, therefore, an elaborate rationale and procedure for accomplishing the "act of clinical judgment" in psychotherapy. Thorne, furthermore, depends heavily on tests for diagnostic aid in counseling and psychotherapy.

Thorne (304) builds his definition of personality diagnosis around the concept of personality integration, which is a dynamic process of organizing and unifying the behavioral field, as well as a phenomenological trait reflecting the organizational status of the person. The diagnostic process is partly one of understanding the various levels of organization existing at any given moment. In the diagnostic study, the person is examined to see if psychobiological substructures are intact and are supporting higher functions, to see if deep drives are being satisfied adequately and integrated with environmental demands, and if the person is able to use his personal resources to cope with life. In ascertaining the degree of integration, the diagnostician looks at the various levels of organization which the person uses to deal with his life situation. These levels vary from simple biological processes, such as digestion, all the way to complex learning, and the person's style of life.

Cautions in the Diagnostic Point of View

There are dangers in the interpretive point of view of diagnosis described above. The incompleteness or inaccuracy of data, or oversimplification of complex human problems, often cause the counselor to overextend himself on the diagnosing steps. The evidence cited later in this chapter indicates also that even the best clinical or statistical predictions are not reliable enough to base critical decisions upon.

The second major caution of this interpretive view is that it easily leads the counselor, especially the psychotherapeutic counselor, to become preoccupied with the history of the client, to neglect the present attitudes he might hold, or to ignore the client's current behavior. The diagnostic process must be rooted in the individual's current psychological milieu to be effective in understanding him.

A third caution is that the clinician is tempted to utilize tests too quickly to aid him in the diagnostic process. This act is likely to lead to a client expectancy of "answers" from the tests rather than from looking inside himself for the causes of his difficulties.

Losing sight of the client's individuality or unique self-system is a fourth difficulty in the diagnostic process. For example, the therapeutic psychologist may possess much comparative data on such things as intelligence measures and MMPI scores; but he may lose sight of the subtle distinctions which make his client an unique person responding in his own individual style to common social stimuli.

Since diagnosis has been associated historically with pathology, there is a further danger that the clinician will be preoccupied with morbidity rather than hygiology of behavior. As seen in Chapter 4, there are still too few terms to describe healthy creative personality states which would be comparable to the elaborate terminology of psychopathology. Therapeutic psychologists are devoted to a search for positive characteristics, asking such questions as, "What strengths does this client already possess?" "How much insight does he have now?" "What can we build upon?"

A final objection often cited for the heavily diagnostic approach to psychotherapy is that it leads to a judgmental attitude, a feeling that the therapist is going to "case" him, and then tell him what he ought to do. Responsibility is thus shifted too strongly to the psychotherapist who is put in the tempting position of pontificating to the client.

Therapists following the Rankian tradition, however, tend to eliminate the early formal diagnostic steps. Rogers (249) seems particularly adamant on the question of diagnosis. He claims that diagnosis, as understood in the preceding light, is an actual detriment to the psychotherapeutic type of counseling. Rogers does not ignore the significance of behavior causation; but he claims that the meaning of behavior lies within the particular way the client perceives his reality. The client, according to Rogers, is really the only one who can know fully the dynamics of his own perceptions and behavior. In order to change client behavior, therefore, a perceptual change must be experienced. Just getting more intellectual data about his problem isn't likely to help change his behavior very much.

Rogers feels also that a diagnostic point of view tends to pull the counselor away from the client's frame of reference and makes him preoccupied with intellectualizations about the client. Certain counselors would be prone to this overdiagnosing because of their particular judgmental attitudes. Rogers claims, further, that therapy is diagnosis in the sense that it is the client who is experiencing the process and really does the diagnosing in terms of formulating his own experience in meaningful terms.

Another more subtle social danger is seen by Rogers (249) in that too much emphasis upon diagnosis sets up the consequent temptation to make evaluative prescriptions. If clients rely on the "expertness" of the counselor, there is the potential danger of social control and influences where the counselor specifies the goals and makes the value judgments whether a behavior is appropriate or inappropriate, mature or immature.

Rogers is criticized for his extreme view of diagnosis because he seems to set up a "straw man," in that the understanding of the client in a diagnostic sense is imposing understanding on the client. There seems to be an assumption that if one takes a diagnostic viewpoint, one is automatically judgmental and cannot be accepting. Bordin (40) points out, also, that the client's perceptual awareness is only part of his experience, and that preoccupations with his own perceptions may lead the counselor to gain superficial rather than more penetrating understanding. He could achieve this deeper understanding by making more active contributions to the process.

Apart from Rogers' criticisms of the diagnostic position, there is another cogent reason for caution. Diagnoses are made partly for purposes of prognosis or prediction of clients' future behavior. Predictions based upon clinical judgment and clinical data are not what they should be, even for modest confidence. Clinical predictions, according to a recent review and critique by Meehl (202), are less valid than straight actuarial methods in which tests, for example, are used to predict behavior. One of the controversies in the psychological literature is the relative value of clinical and statistical methods for predicting client behavior. While some psychologists express confidence that, under the right experimental conditions, the clinical methods will show up better, the evidence to date is that statistical prediction is superior and that clinical prediction methods have many limitations for counseling.

Clinical prediction is based upon the assumption that the person is consistent within himself. The diagnostician is concerned with ascertaining the person's pattern of consistencies with which projections can be made about his behavior in the future. Meehl (202) concluded in his review of the problem of clinical and actuarial prediction that the problem can be resolved partly by specifying the conditions under which each method works best. He hopes clinicians will not be forced to think of clinical *versus* statistical methods much longer.

Resolving the Diagnostic Issue

It seems that there is still a third point of view which can be taken on the question of diagnosis. We find it difficult to escape the fact that the therapeutic psychologist must make some decisions, do some therapeutic planning, be alert for pathology to avoid serious mistakes, and be in the position to make some prognoses or predictions. It seems that the therapeutic psychologist is forced to play a delicate role between the Rogerian position of withholding judgment and attempting to stay within the client's frame of reference as much as possible, at the same time trying to understand the client diagnostically.

It is proposed that this simultaneous "understanding diagnostically" and "understanding therapeutically," to use Porter's (238) terms, be done by the view known as hypothesis or hunch-making. Although the counselor may decide to avoid some of the formal diagnostic steps, he is, nevertheless, allowing a series of hypotheses to formulate in his thinking about such questions as: "How serious is this matter from the standpoint of pathology?" "What would be the most appropriate approach to use at this time?" "How far should we attempt to go?" "What seem to be the basic dynamics operating (defenses, dominant needs, symptoms, environmental pressures)?" "What will the likely outcomes be?" The basic diagnostic question, however, should be: "What is going on?"

Hypotheses flowing from attempts to answer the preceding questions are constantly being revised until the pattern of this client's style of life, descriptions of the ego, self- and core systems, basic relationships with people, dominant values, principal defenses, main strengths, and limitations fall into a pattern. This pattern is the inference from observations we have just made. Viewed in this way, the counseling process itself is, according to Pepinsky, a process of ". . . hypothesis formulation and testing, a process of approximation and correction. . . ." (232, pg. 198). Pepinsky goes further to indicate that what a counselor does with his hypothesis-making is to formulate a hypothetical client with behavioral descriptions in terms of the counselor's basic constructs and assumptions. In other words, the clinician is thinking that if the client with whom he is interacting at the moment behaves like his model, then he can predict how he is likely to behave in the future. For example, we know from research and experience that depressed clients are potential suicide risks. We have a model of the suicidal person, and as the client tells us more about how he feels and what he has been thinking, we see the client conforming more and more to our model. This starts the prediction process going.

Action questions then come fast. Should I, as his counselor: (1) Refer him immediately to a specialist, a hospital, or contact his relatives; or (2) Would referral upset him even more and should I use some emergency support techniques? (3) Should I decelerate his rate of exploration of feelings, or cut discussion of them completely so he does not become more depressed? (4) Should I stop counseling with him as soon as I can conveniently shift responsibility to another therapist? (5) What other indications of pathology are present and what indications of personality strength does he manifest? (6) Is this a primary personality disorder or a secondary reaction to strong environmental stress? The answers to these questions will be indicated by the predictions made from our model. What the counselor is doing, in effect, is trying to verify his hunch that he has a likely suicide on his hands which requires a swift plan of action.

How the clinician thinks through this hypothesizing process is still quite mysterious and intuitive. Meehl (202) speculates that the process is somewhat as follows: (1) Collect data; (2) Have a set of assumptions and some general laws about behavior; (3) Generate a tentative specific hypothesis about behavior from comparing the case data and the assumptions; (4) Collect further facts and compare them to reduce the number of possible hypotheses; (5) Juggle the facts and the hypotheses until a meaningful pattern emerges; (6) Select through his best judgment the most specific tentative hypotheses, and then (7) make a specific prediction therefrom.

McArthur (191) reported some research and speculation on the clinical process also. He found that successful predictions were made from the model or "clinical construct" each clinician formulated, rather than from a single test, theory, or case datum. The clinicians seemed to be using an inductive method by which they fitted the case data to a model person. From this model they made their prediction as to how the client would likely behave. McArthur indicated that they seemed to be using such a phrase as, "He seems to be the sort of person who . . ." (191, pg. 204).

Koester (175) studied the diagnostic process by asking counselors to "think out loud" to a recorder while examining their case materials. He found that instead of a sudden insightful patterning of the data there was a more gradual buildup of the data into a more meaningful understanding of the case. Koester indicated that the steps which the clinicians seemed to follow were similar to a problem-solving procedure described earlier in this chapter: (1) Collection and comparison of the data; (2) Interpretation of the data; (3) Formulation of hypotheses; (4) Evaluation of the hypotheses.

Like McArthur, Koester found that the total formulations were more meaningful when approached openly without the rigidity of a single theory or set. Those counselors who failed to revise their hypotheses because of negative or contradictory data appeared to be the most rigid and single-theory-centered.

An illustration of the use of the clinical diagnosis-prediction process may be had from vocational counseling. Here, the need to formulate hypotheses about the client's abilities, interests, traits, and experiences in relation to the best model of a successful insurance salesman, home economics teacher, or architect, for example, is particularly important. Clinical prediction methods must be used in vocational counseling to supplement the actuarial methods which stress test scores and validity coefficients. Vocational counseling, therefore, illustrates the interplay of clinical and actuarial methods of prediction. It also illustrates the focus of the diagnostic process on prognosis or prediction, and the de-emphasis on some of the problems associated with other connotations of diagnosis.

A third illustration of the diagnostic process and of the utility of a separate diagnostic step can be found in the area of skill deficiencies. A client complaining of reading difficulties must go through a rational diagnostic procedure to determine the most likely combinations of causes such as visual, perceptual, emotional, experiential, or language deficiencies.

The clinical process in the illustrations from psychotherapeutic, vocational, and skill deficiency areas is going on continuously in the counseling process. Perhaps this is what writers like Rogers mean when they assert that diagnosis blends into the therapeutic process. A further observation on our part is that the further the client's complaint is removed from problems involving cognitive data such as vocational plans and learning difficulties, the less distinct the formal diagnostic steps seem to become.

Since the diagnostic problem in vocational counseling is a little more clear-cut, more might be said about it here. The function of vocational diagnosis is to achieve thorough understanding by both counselor and client of the client's interests, aptitudes, personality characteristics, aspirations, family history, and work background so that he can match these characteristics with job requirements. Although the preceding process is quite rational and logical there is a danger in ignoring the attitudes underlying the more cognitive features such as aptitudes. Just collecting information and collating it with vocational goals which seem to follow logically is oversimplifying a very complex process. In other words, diagnosis in the sense in which Williamson (320) uses it, as understanding of the meaningful pattern of data, is essential to educational-vocational counseling. The counselor cannot shift his responsibility as an expert in making this kind of prediction to the client or anyone else.

There is a principal objection to be stressed in this discussion if the diagnosis is made a separate and formal step. It is our conviction that this diagnostic thinking, though generally coming early in the process, tends to blend into the whole counseling process. Furthermore, this diagnostic process is not the precise definitive act which it is in medicine; in counseling it consists of forming and reforming hypotheses for the most appropriate choices. This formulation is then discussed with the client for assimilation and/or amendment. At this point, it generally becomes the client's hypothesis and all decisions and consequences are his.

As implied earlier in this discussion, the vocational counselor must make decisions about how emotionally involved he should allow the relationship to become. One of the most difficult things for him to decide is if, and when, he should cap off a persistent effort by the client to force the discussion into a psychotherapeutic relationship. Often, however, the counselor can help reduce anxieties over unsettled plans for the future or difficult relationships with people without implying deep psychotherapeutic assistance. But the diagnostic process comes to the counselor's aid in detecting pathology. This is the reason all counselors, regardless of their assignment or level, must be familiar with the signs of psychopathology.

The Psychodiagnostic Use of Tests

The nature and basic assumptions of psychodiagnostic tests. Tests are one of the therapeutic psychologist's main tools. The discussion to follow will be concerned with their diagnostic use mainly. There are other uses of tests—interpretive, information-giving, evaluative, and predictive— which will be described in later chapters.

The main purpose of all testing is to obtain samples of behavior in a standardized situation devoid of subjective judgment. Test results should represent objective factual material, whereas the subjective element enters into the interpretation of the factual results. Here, the therapeutic psychologist marshals his test data, case experience, and observations, into a series of diagnostic hypotheses about this particular client.

More specifically, psychodiagnostic testing is an endeavor to study "therapeutically relevant" aspects of personality. This means the therapeutic psychologist is interested primarily in the nature of the defense system, the qualities and strength of the ego system, the unique style characteristics of the self-system, and something of the anxieties and needs of the core system in light of how these characteristics can change or function more smoothly.

The aim of the testing phase of the diagnosis, here, is to arrive at the personality descriptions from tests alone without the laborious case history methods. For example, if tests would show a person to have strong aggressive needs which are expressed in an intrapunitive manner, thus explaining some of the client's self-defeating behaviors, it would be a useful shortcut; but, if the case material showed the same thing, all we have is the satisfaction of a neat, consistent case study. The tests haven't contributed any more to the understanding of this client than the case material had already indicated. It is the hope of clinicians and counselors that tests and their interpretive rationale will be sufficiently developed to accomplish the goals of confidence in the instrument. This is not to say that so-called "blind interpretation" without other case data is the goal; but if tests are going to be useful instruments they should give reliable and valid data in their own right on the structure and function of personality.

Personality characteristics, furthermore, must be studied in their dynamic form, that is, sampled frequently to assess changes. The personal characteristics should be studied, also, in their social context since personality is a product of social interaction. There is good evidence that even some of the difficulties in intellectual functioning, involving thinking, memory, concentration and perception, have their roots in impaired interpersonal relationships.

A further assumption underlying psychodiagnostic testing is that the unique patterns of thinking and feeling uncovered by the tests are indications of the client's basic character structure. This structure is presumed to be quite stable and consistent. The character structure refers to basic attributes of the inner- and outer-defense systems as well as characteristic ways of responding to social demands.

Uses of psychodiagnostic tests (1) screening. Although it is beyond the purpose and scope of this book to go into psychodiagnostic testing in detail, it seems important to the writers, however, to describe the diagnostic uses of tests briefly. One of the principal functions of tests for the therapeutic psychologist is as a rough "screen." Earlier in this chapter the questions of pathology, counseling strategy, and readiness were problems impinging on the counselor. By giving a brief test battery at an appropriate spot early in the process, the counselor can get a more clear picture of the road ahead.

Severe pathology often does not show up until later interviews. By giving a projective technique or a structured test such as the Minnesota Multiphasic Personality Inventory the counselor often can obtain a more clear understanding of the currently observed pathology, and occasionally he can detect hidden pathology trends earlier.

Similarly, on intellectual variables, the counselor often desires a quick estimate of the client's intellectual capacity and functioning in advance of more definitive data. A short vocabulary test such as the Stanford Binet or Wechsler Adult Scale vocabulary subtests can give these data. In addition, short tests like the Proverbs Test (127) give a quick, even though possibly unreliable, estimate of intellectual functioning. Oral reading tests such as the Gray Paragraphs (129) offer the counselor another quick estimate of intellectual skill-functioning.

Uses of psychodiagnostic tests (2) predicting success of counseling. Diagnostic screening tests can provide readiness-type information regarding ego-system strength, for example. There is evidence for the statement that the rapidity of achieving successful counseling hinges on ego-strength factors such as response adaptability, capacity to test demands of reality, and undistorted perception, therefore, the counselor can decide early in the process whether continued counseling with this client would be feasible or desirable.

Uses of psychodiagnostic tests (3) detailed information. There is no effective substitute for a diagnostic test in such skill areas as reading and arithmetic. Remedial help and concomitant counseling are often planned around information obtained in diagnostic achievement batteries.

Similarly, in personality trait or adjustment areas, such a test as the Minnesota Multiphasic Personality Inventory or the Bell Adjustment Inventory can give the counselor topics which could be profitably explored directly without the circuitous routes of client verbalization. For example, finding through tests that handling feelings of hostility is a problem helps to pinpoint sensitive areas early. This early detection may create less resistance to discussion of the problem later since the client tends to perceive the test results as "objective evidence."

Counselors working on vocational-planning problems find diagnostic information helpful; but the main focus in vocational planning is on prognosis. Detailed material on the important prognostic use of tests will be described later on the informational use of tests.

Uses of psychodiagnostic tests (4) diagnostic formulations. Pinpointing pathological types has been and continues to be a major forte of the clinical psychologist. The projective techniques such as the Rorschach and Thematic Apperception Tests have been used along with tests such as the Wechsler Adult Intelligence Scale to give a rounded picture of the perceptual, conceptual, and affective functioning of the client.

Clinic procedure often requires "pigeonholing" into nosological categories of neurosis, psychosis, and character disorders. Here, diagnostic testing is of some assistance, but the evidence for the accuracy of such diagnosing is not very convincing.

SUMMARY

Three preparatory concerns face the therapeutic psychologist. First of all, the therapeutic psychologist must face the problems of readiness or motivation for counseling as key difficulties in working with child, adolescent, or adult clients.

The case study is the second concern, expressed in the question: "What are the relevant data needed to help this client?" Various sources of data are available such as case histories, cumulative records, time graphs, autobiographies, and essays.

A third concern of the therapeutic psychologist, early in the process, is the form and extent of his diagnostic formulations. Diagnosis, as a method of classifying symptoms, has value in that it is a shorthand method of describing client problems; but as a procedure for determining causation, the diagnostic process has little utility. As a means of predicting future behavior, the diagnostic thinking process has great limitations also. Clinical and statistical predictions are still too limited in validity to be used with confidence. The clinician can, however, look at the diagnostic process as a procedure for formulating increasingly more tenable hypotheses regarding the nature of the client's difficulties. Examples of such questions are, "How much pathology is present?" "How far should I attempt to take this client along the road to mature living?" "In light of the best evidence available what seems to be the best answers to the client's search for a vocational or life objective?" Tests and case histories are valuable aids for the diagnostician in making preliminary estimates on the above questions, as well as in executing fine differential psychodiagnoses.

6.

The Nature of the Relationship
and Characteristics of the Therapeutic
Psychologist

The heart of the therapeutic process is the relationship established between the counselor and client. In the preceding chapter, the importance of client attitudes in approaching counseling was emphasized. In this chapter, further stress is placed upon the attitudes of the counselor as a variable in the relationship and how the relationship is used to help the client.

Before we can describe relationship techniques, which we shall do in Chapter 7, we shall analyze the significance of counselor traits and attitudes in this chapter. The relationship techniques will be presented later because we regard them as *implementations* of the therapist's basic attitudes toward the client and as generators of understanding.

The relationship is important in counseling and psychotherapy because it constitutes the principal medium for eliciting, recognizing, and handling significant feelings and ideas which are aimed at changing client behavior. Thus, the quality of the relationship determines not only the nature of the personal exchanges but whether counseling will continue at all.

We are becoming more and more convinced that the relationship in psychotherapy and counseling is a curative agent in its own right. Most neurotics do not have healthy, real interpersonal relationships. The psychotherapist's task, therefore, may be seen as establishing whatever relation the patient is able to make, solidifying it, gradually freeing it of irrealities and teaching the client the generality of the dynamisms thus disclosed. This is a positive picture of the therapist's role, as opposed to a more negative, analytic role. This role is also what makes the therapist's own relative freedom from neurotic distortion so centrally important.

Before proceeding further, the concept "relationship" should be defined. We prefer Pepinsky's definition of the relationship ". . . as a *hypothetical construct to designate the inferred affective character of the observable interaction* between two individuals" (232, pg. 171). It should be noted that in the definition, however, "relationship" refers to the *affective* or emotional elements of the interaction which can only be inferred from observation of client behavior. The writers feel that a description of the relationship should include additional dimensions which are surveyed in the next section.

CHARACTERISTICS AND DIMENSIONS OF THE RELATIONSHIP

Uniqueness-Commonality

Though certain general statements can be made about the therapeutic relationship, it is important to remember first that each client-counselor relationship is unique. The factors creating this uniqueness are as diverse as human differences. The unique factors include *counselor* attitudes, behaviors, and physical characteristics, in addition to the *client* attitudes, backgrounds, and behaviors discussed in the preceding chapter. This uniqueness makes generalizing about counseling difficult and makes reduction of relationship-building to a formula close to impossible. Each new counseling relationship is a fresh challenge to the counselor. The therapist cannot learn myriads of rules to cover all possible situations; yet we hold the view that he can function effectively in helping people if he knows clearly his own personality and goals, has certain basic attitudes toward people, and is conversant with a few fundamental techniques.

Another aspect of uniqueness in the therapeutic relationship is its distinction from other human relationships. While friends, relatives, and teachers have profound influence on behavior, one unique element of the counseling relationship is its structure, that is, its carefully planned and described psychotherapeutic framework. Another unique element distinguishing counseling relationships from others is the relatively complete acceptance of the client by the counselor. This is a rare experience in any other relationship.

Although counseling or psychotherapy is unique, compared to other human relationships, because of its intimate nature, structure, and attitudes, it also has similarities to other human situations, for example, family, friendships, teacher-pupil, doctor-patient, and pastor-parishioner. The acceptance, support, authority feelings, learning, and other phenomena common to these relationships are present in counseling also. In one sense, then, a counseling relationship is an extension of ordinary, yet healthy, living processes.

Objectivity-Subjectivity Balance

A second way to look at the relationship is in terms of its objectivity-subjectivity balance (226). This balance refers to the degree of emotional intensity of the relationship and the relative weighting of the intellectual and emotional elements. *Objectivity* refers to the more cognitive, scientific, generic aspects of the relationship wherein the client is regarded as an object of study or as a part of broad suffering humanity. In extreme objectivity, therefore, a counselor would not be emotionally involved with the client; he would remain psychologically very distant; and he would regard client views and values without personal judgment or criticism. In short, he would be the epitome of the scientist.

The meaning of the objective view for the client is that he feels the counselor will respect his views, will not force his ideas on the client, and will look at his problem rationally and analytically. It is observed so often, however, that the client seems to feel negatively about such an objective counselor attitude. He often wants the therapist to get emotionally involved and deeply concerned about him. This subjective feeling of involvement is one basis for his feeling "understood"; and seems to offer the reassurance that the counselor knows how he feels. Therefore, it is the writer's observation that clients tend to be ambivalent about counselor objectivity-subjectivity in the relationship.

Objectivity can have definite meanings and offer security for the counselor, also, since the essence of diagnosis is striving for an objective view of the client's situation. The therapist likes to feel that he is aware of his own feelings at all times and that he avoids forcing values and solutions on the client.

The *subjective* elements of the relationship include emotional involvement in the form of human "warmth" and psychological "closeness," as well as intense interest in the particular client and his problems. This element is often described as a feeling of "mutuality." The meaning which subjectivity has for the client is one of, "he understands me," and hence, of support. Conversely, some clients perceive counselor involvement as threatening, since they are "submitting" to another person. They experience anxiety, therefore, over feared loss of emotional control or over being overwhelmed. This anxiety is especially strong when the client sees the counselor allied with his externalized or rejected feelings. The client seeing the counselor, for example, as the loving mother becomes fearful of his own uncontrolled dependency needs.

The meaning of the subjective view for the counselor is that in some cases he might respond to the client's problem as if it were his own. Yet, the counselor must use his own generalized experiences and feelings as guides to experiencing the client's feelings. For example, how can a counselor really know how it feels to be loving and hostile to a parent simultaneously unless he has experienced this feeling himself and has been aware of the implications? This does not mean that the counselor must have experienced all feeling-complexes. He must have recognized in himself, however, those universal human experiences such as anxiety, ambivalence, and self-dismay. He must have worked them through enough to be able to tolerate recognizing and empathizing with them in his client.

The most reasonable goal seems to be that the counselor gets emotionally involved to the extent necessary to keep the client emotionally involved; but the counselor's keen interest in helping is tempered with a reserve and distance so that the counselor can accept attitudes and feelings expressed by the client without reacting personally to them. If the counselor gets too emotionally involved with the client, it is difficult to be objective about such attitudinal areas as religion, for example, or moral behaviors different from his own behaviors which may even disgust him personally. The counselor is objective, or "detached" in the sense that he regards these attitudes and behaviors as important manifestations of the client's personality. The difficulties in maintaining this position will be described later in the discussion of transference and countertransference phenomena.

Thus, it may be inferred that in counseling practice, objectivity and subjectivity are in a harmonic, yet paradoxical, relationship. This means that the counselor operates variously between the two positions and incorporates elements of both. For example, he is deeply and warmly interested in the client, but not in the same sense as lovers would be interested in each other or parents in children. Objectivity is needed in diagnosing, yet subjectivity is necessary to build the climate to use the diagnostic information to help the client. The term "participant-observer" is used in psychological circles to describe this dual relationship problem. The counselor participates fully in the intricate human interaction; yet, simultaneously, he maintains a detached observer role. It is as if part of his ego were at a distance observing the process.

Cognitive-Connotive Balance

Another dimension of the relationship is what Bordin (40) describes as the cognitive-connotive balance. Cognitive elements refer to intellectualizing, such as exchanging information, advising on courses of action, or interpreting; whereas the connotive elements refer to feeling expressions and exchanges. In understanding the client and in manipulating the relationship, the counselor must know when to encourage rational examination and interpretation of the client's problem and when to encourage more exploration of feelings and their ideational connections. Communication is going on at both levels all the time, so it behooves the counselor to be aware of the relative weight of these factors at any given moment. Techniques for handling the connotive aspects of the relationship are described in the following chapter, whereas those techniques for dealing with the more cognitive elements are described in the chapters on interpretation and information-giving.

Ambiguity-Clarity Balance

The notion of ambiguity and its therapeutic implications, as developed by Bordin (40), is a characteristic of a stimulus situation to which people respond differently and to which no clear-cut response is indicated. The counseling relationship is vague and ambiguous in many ways to the client. The counselor generally defines himself and the situation early by the process known as "structuring"; however, the degree of clarity or vagueness is a profound dimension of the relationship.

Ambiguity serves the functions of allowing the client to project his feelings into the ambiguous counseling situation. This is done easily since humans tend to handle ambiguity stimuli in terms of their own projected unique responses. This process of projecting feelings aids the client to become aware and concerned about his feelings, thus enabling the counselor to know and deal with them through counseling techniques.

Too much ambiguity for some clients can allow them to become filled with anxiety in their attempts to make something secure and structured out of the relationship. For example, being too permissive with clients early in the counseling process and encouraging too free exploration of feelings may make them panicky, or in extreme cases, send them over the psychotic brink.

There is some danger to the relationship if the counselor is too definite a personality to the client or he becomes too intimately known as a person by the client. This moderate personal ambiguity is necessary so that the client can project any role he wishes on the counselor. More of this idea will be explored later under "transference"; but it is necessary to point out that the less the client knows about the counselor's personal feelings and private life the easier it is for him to play an effective therapeutic role.

The problem is a *social distance* matter and should not be confused with the *emotional distance* discussion under the objectivity-subjectivity section of this chapter. If the counselor is too friendly with the client in the sense that he lets himself be known as a well-delineated personality, the counselor will find that he feels compelled to "act himself" too strongly in the interview situation. Thus, the interview might be pushed in the direction of social conversation and a *"kaffee klatch"* climate. This is a difficult matter to handle in the school situation, for instance, in which counselors frequently meet student clients on social and instructional as well as therapeutic levels.

In a clinical setting the problem of socializing with clients creates relationship problems. Most clinicians, therefore, consider it unwise to socialize with clients. The expectancies of the social relationship would tend to be quite different from the therapeutic relationship and would tend to interfere with a good counseling relationship.

Responsibility Balance

Accepting a client in a counseling relationship implies a willingness on the part of the counselor to assume some responsibility for the outcomes of counseling and some willingness to share in the client's troubles. Counseling is very serious business and must be matched by a seriousness of purpose on the counselor's part. It is the client's responsibility as well, which he must assume in great part since it is his problem and his behavior which is at stake.

Counselors differ in their interpretation of the proportion of responsibility which each participant must assume. We feel that the counselor does not take responsibility for running the client's life for him or of selecting goals for him. The acceptance of the relationship, nevertheless, places the counselor in a responsible leadership position where he must protect the client and assume certain liabilities for the outcomes because of the influence of his own personality on the relationship. The latter situation holds especially in psychotherapeutic relationships where the client is making such crucial decisions in his life as whether or not to get a divorce, leave home, commit suicide, change jobs, or drop out of school.

It is difficult to reduce the client's dilemma to a formula. The amount of proportional responsibility depends upon such factors as the age of the client, type of problem, type of agency setting, legally designated responsibilities, and professional expectations. Some counselors control the responsibility factors by discouraging clients from making crucial decisions, over such matters as divorce, while in the counseling relationship. Such counselors claim that the relationship offers them a vehicle for exploring the ramifications of divorce which puts the client in a better position to make a sound decision and to live with it. The writers believe that responsibility cannot be handled so neatly in most cases. The technique of structuring in the next chapter can help both counselor and client to face frankly the problems of allocating exclusive and mutual responsibilities.

If he is in an agency setting, the counselor has a further responsibility to be loyal to the institution for which he works. The preceding discussion emphasized the client's and counselor's responsibilities to each other. Mutual responsibilities of agencies and counselors are controlled somewhat by ethical considerations; but they involve the hard realities of agency responsibility to provide adequate facilities and legal protection, for example. Counselors have responsibilities to their agencies to carry out agency policy. Although this aspect of responsibility is not a dimension of the relationship it has a direct bearing upon it.

The counselor's responsibility to the broader society are covered in a later discussion on ethics.

PERSONAL CHARACTERISTICS OF THE THERAPEUTIC PSYCHOLOGIST

A principal consideration in the relationship is the counselor's personality. A counseling follow-up study by Forgy and Black (105) tends to confirm this assumption that the counselor's personality is important; although they found that it was the interaction of counselor personality and method which accounted for differences in counseling effectiveness. The changes could not be attributed to counselor personality only nor to methodology exclusively. Seeman (269), in a study of vocational counseling, concluded that methods are not as important in accounting for differing client reactions as are characteristics of "warmth, interest, and understanding." Fiedler (97) compared three differently oriented groups of experienced therapists with three groups of inexperienced therapists. Fiedler found that for experienced therapists, personalities and experience, rather than different methods, accounted for differences in therapeutic outcomes. Though serious questions have been raised about Fiedler's methodology and interpretation of findings, and though it would be dangerous to ascribe too much importance to the counselor personality at this time, there is sufficient evidence of its importance to warrant an extended discussion.

Many of the traits and attitudes to be discussed may seem idealistic and may evoke the picture of a "superman," nevertheless, they provide yardsticks against which the counselor can measure himself. What are the characteristics of the effective counselor or therapist? The APA Committee on Training in Clinical Psychology a few years ago compiled the following list of traits to answer this question:

(1) Superior intellectual ability and judgment.
(2) Originality, resourcefulness, and versatility.
(3) "Fresh and insatiable" curiosity; "self-learner."
(4) Interest in persons as individuals rather than as material for manipulation—a regard for the integrity of other persons.
(5) Insight into own personality characteristics; sense of humor.
(6) Sensitivity to the complexities of motivation.
(7) Tolerance: "unarrogance."
(8) Ability to adopt a "therapeutic" attitude; ability to establish warm and effective relationships with others.
(9) Industry; methodical work habits; ability to tolerate pressure.
(10) Acceptance of responsibility.
(11) Tact and cooperativeness.
(12) Integrity, self-control, and stability.
(13) Discriminating sense of ethical values.
(14) Breadth of cultural background—"educated man."
(15) Deep interest in psychology, especially in its clinical aspects. (12, pg. 541)

The following discussion of counselor characteristics affecting the relationship is derived from experimental and speculative studies on counselor characteristics, as well as from our own experience (70, 76, 128). A discussion of counselor characteristics suffers from the same difficulties as other areas of therapeutic psychology—that is, inadequate data from sound scientific study. As a recent attempt in this direction, Cottle and associates (68, 69) are publishing a series of articles on personality characteristics of counselors and how they differ from other defined groups, such as teachers. The methods used are largely standardized tests.

Counselor attitude studies have been another fruitful source of information about counselor personalities. Porter (237), for example, developed scales with which to measure counselor attitudes toward counseling with sufficient reliability to be useful in selecting counselors with distinct attitudinal orientations.

Before describing counselor characteristics, we wish to re-emphasize what we feel to be some focal points of this book:

(1) The counselor or therapist is engaged in helping others in a professional capacity. But, more importantly, he is a human being with personal weaknesses and problems of his own. This means that the therapist also has the capacity to grow. As teachers learn from students, so therapists learn daily from clients. He must take the responsibility for his own constant personal growth.

(2) The professional counselor or therapist is an expert in helping others, but he has no magic solutions. His technical training can be helpful, but only his continuous attempt to increase his own self-understanding and awareness of himself makes him believe in what he attempts to do with clients.

(3) Each client with whom he deals is a unique expression of human nature; hence, the textbook never applies completely. Also, he must respect himself as someone who is completely unique.

(4) Thus, counseling and therapy can be viewed as a workshop for the growth of both participants. Each client can help the counselor or therapist shed new light on his own personal integration.

(5) The central emphasis for any enlightened counselor or therapist must be, therefore, the development of a core of valid technique along with a flexibility for learning new ideas each day and for discarding old approaches which no longer seem to apply. Counseling and psychotherapy techniques thus develop for the client, and most of all for the therapist, acceptance of and permissiveness for change. Counseling and therapy, therefore, should not be guided primarily by a "school" of thought, but rather must be the dynamic interplay of a unique existential relationship between two unique personalities. As indicated in Chapter 2, this attitude is assumed within the framework of science, however, which enables counselors and therapists to develop sound generalizations to guide practice.

Intellectual Competence

To comprehend the enormous complexity of the human personality and to handle the involved abstractions of counseling theory demand that the counselor be considerably above average in general intelligence. Related to intellectual competence is the requirement of a vast knowledge of the culture acquired through general education and varied living. Intellectual breadth is significant also, since one basis for understanding the client and building rapport is to have some familiarity with the various cultural environments the client has experienced.

Ethical Behavior

A distinctive mark of the professional counselor and psychotherapist is his ethical handling of client relationships. The counselor's value system is an important determinant of ethical behavior. It is difficult to summarize ethical principles and to determine what is ethical behavior. There are typical questions, however, commonly arising in psychotherapy and counseling. The Committee on Ethical Standards of the American Psychological Association has published a *Summary of Ethical Principles* along with proposed modifications (9) to assist counselors and psychotherapists with their ethical decisions. The following are illustrations:

(1) How can I present my qualifications to my clients realistically and without misrepresentations? The psychological counselor is bound to maintain the highest standards of excellence and not to claim or imply qualifications which he does not possess. His publicity should be dignified and in the form of announcements to professional persons rather than commercial advertising or announcements directly to prospective clients (9, pg. 9).

(2) Should I tell the agency of my judgment that this person is potentially dangerous (as in the case of possible homicide or suicide)? Should I tell an instructor, for example, of a client's persistent use of notes in his examinations? The Ethical Code (pg. 4) indicates that, "A cardinal obligation of the psychologist is to respect the integrity and protect the welfare of the client. . . ," and "the psychologist should guard professional confidences as a trust" (pg. 5). Yet, the individual's welfare does not always take precedence.

In Section 1 (pg. 2) it is stated that "the psychologist's ultimate allegiance is to society, and his professional behavior should demonstrate an awareness of his social responsibilities." Another principle bearing on the question of suicide is stated as follows (Sec. 2c, pg. 5): "When information received in confidence reveals clear and imminent danger that the client may do serious harm to himself or to others, intervention by the psychologist may be required." The question of cheating is less clear. The counselor should indicate his intentions of mentioning the event to another person and seek the client's concurrence. "Otherwise, information obtained in professional work must be kept in confidence, recognizing that the clinical or consulting relationship can develop fully in an atmosphere of trust, and that the psychologist can serve society most effectively by not revealing confidences of antisocial events or intentions, but by helping the individual realize himself as a socially competent person" (pg. 5). If the counselor revealed this confidence in a school or college situation, for example, he would jeopardize the future effectiveness of his counseling with other students.

(3) If I refer a client, when is my responsibility ended? On this question the code is very explicit. Referral is mandatory when the counselor realizes that he is not competent to deal with the case in question. The following quotation answers the question. "In cases involving referral, the responsibility of the psychologist for the welfare of the client normally continues until this responsibility is assumed by the professional person to whom the client is referred, or until the relationship has been terminated by mutual agreement" (Sec. 2g, pg. 8).

(4) Are test scores confidential information? Whether test scores are confidential or not depends upon how they were collected. If the client took the tests as part of a college entrance requirement, he knows that the results will be seen by several persons, yet he realizes that the institution will protect them from becoming public knowledge. However, if the client were given a Wechsler-Bellevue, as a result of an interview, the information would be classified, generally, as confidential. The same principles as those cited in question 2 apply, namely, that the psychotherapeutic counselor must use his best discretion. If he appears to be too rigid about giving information on his student clients, his superiors or his colleagues perhaps might resent his "ethical purity." But, giving results in lunch rooms and hallways might be stretching the limits too far in the other direction, since this atmosphere invites a gossipy tone. It seems to be acceptable practice to convey clinical test information in professional case conferences only. Any further transmittal must be done with the client's permission. Other agencies requesting information usually ask the client to sign a statement authorizing release of clinical data.

(5) How can I answer this parent's inquiry regarding problems discussed in the interviews? Counselors in schools and colleges, for example, are plagued with this problem continuously. A teacher asks about a client's problems at lunch. What can the counselor say? In the case of young children who are brought to a psychotherapeutic counselor by the parent more latitude is allowed in transmitting information. This should be done in an interpretive and recommending manner, however, rather than in a narrative fashion. Thus, the relationship with the child is not jeopardized. With adolescents and adults, the counselor should acknowledge the interest of the parent and question the parent about behaviors they may have observed. Thus, the counselor can use information elicited from the parent

to interpret without resorting to interview data. This technique diverts the parent's attention away from the client interviews, yet enables him to gain the information he seeks. This method also avoids the unpleasantness of forcing the counselor to refuse flatly to discuss the client's interview material. This type of problem offers the psychotherapist an excellent opportunity to observe the parent, both for additional information to help the client and for the opportunity to determine whether it would be wise to suggest that the parent get help with the problem also.

(6) Should I tell my client I am recording his interviews? Recording information without the client's knowledge or permission is considered, generally, to be unethical. Clients assume that the interview will be recorded in some form such as notes or summaries. Some hesitate and would prefer not to have recordings made; but they rarely object. Taking a casual attitude towards the whole matter, and refraining from making a big point over permission to record, help immensely. An explanation that this is routine for purposes of later review and learning by the counselor, the reassurance that others will not have access to the record, and that no names will identify the record usually suffice.

(7) Can I mention my client's name in the case conferences with the staff? Whether names are mentioned in case conferences or not hinges largely on the make-up of the conference personnel and the mores of the particular institution. In a situation in which all participants are thoroughly infused with the ethical considerations in handling personal data, using names is considered permissible. The rationale for this view is that the ultimate welfare of the client is to be better served by this conference. Institutional policies, on the other hand, may lean to the side of strict interpretation in which no mention of names is made in discussing cases in staff conferences. The code states, "The psychologist should present his clinical findings in a manner most likely to serve the best interests of his client. . . . The psychologist should give clinical information about a client only to professional persons whom the client might reasonably expect to consider a party to the psychologist's efforts to help him, and the client's concurrence should be obtained before there is any communication exceeding these customary lines" (Sec. 2e, pg. 6).

The preceding questions cover only a small sample of the many which face the psychotherapeutic counselor in everyday practice. Since they involve elements of judgment as well as fact, it would be well if the psychotherapeutic counselor consulted his colleagues concerning questions of ethics in difficult cases. The counselor should look also into his own ethics and areas of bias to find possible sources of doubt and value conflict about the ethical implications of his behavior. Finally, one of the most important safeguards against unethical behavior is knowledge and experience.

There are other significant questions to be answered, such as, what causes unethical practice? Is damage or discomfort to the client as a result of ignorance or inadequate training unethical? Schwebel (267) asserts that unsound judgment and ignorance, though dangerous and having important selection and training implications, are not, strictly speaking, unethical. He hypothesizes further that generally it is self-interest which causes unethical practice. By "self-interest" Schwebel means seeking personal profit, self-enhancement, security, and status at the expense of others. Conflicts often arise, therefore, over the infusion of the counselor's values into the process. Wrenn (325) stressed the personal values of the counselor as a basis for counseling ethics. He states, in addition, that ethical behavior on the part of a counselor involves more than subscribing to a code of ethics; a feeling of responsibility to relate his behavior to his ethics is necessary as well.

Spontaneity

What was said about spontaneity as a characteristic of the mature personality in Chapter 4 applies doubly to the counselor. It has been mentioned several times that counseling is not a rigid mechanical application of formulas for producing behavior changes. The counselor's responses to client statements and feelings must be spontaneous outgrowths of his understanding of that client. The counselor must be free to move quickly and easily in his thinking and feeling in order to adapt to the subtle nuances of client behavior.

While no concrete suggestions can be offered concerning how this characteristic is acquired, it seems to be a by-product of both thorough preparation in counseling theory, attitudes, and methodology plus a non-rigid mature personality relatively free from threat.

Acceptance

It is well established in counseling theory that attitudes are changed very little by advice, persuasion, or threats. Client attitudes appear to change most effectively in the presence of other attitudes, for example, positive, tolerant attitudes on the part of the counselor. The client experiences acceptance as a feeling of being unconditionally understood, liked, and respected. Sometimes this positive attitude is described as a basic form of altruistic love (286). The evidence and logic presented by recent writers such as Fromm (113), Montague (209), May (200), and Sorokin (286) attest to the therapeutic power of altruistic love.

The counselor is in a position to handle love relationships in the interview which can have profound constructive or destructive effects on the client's security system and capacity to give and accept love. Observations seem to indicate that the person who has received sufficient love, particularly in early development, learns to be happy with himself and to love adults around him, which, in turn, enables him to direct considerable altruistic concern to all human beings later on.

Nygren (223) contrasts the eros and agape types of love in which eros refers to the ancient Greek term for a type of self-centered, erotic love which satisfies the organism's desires. Agape refers to a type of love in which a person seeks to assist other people to grow, contributes unequivocally to the welfare of the love object, and allows the loving person to be used for self-enhancement of the loved. Acceptance has many of the attributes of agape.

Another characteristic of this broad love, or acceptance attitude, is its *spontaneous motivation.* The presence of concern for the other person is a natural outgrowth of the basic attitudinal structure of the counselor or therapist personality. Acceptance is *altruistic* in the sense that the other person's welfare is sought, not exploited.

Acceptance attitudes are *nonjudgmental* in that the counselor holds a "neutral interest" in values held by the client. The counselor tries to say in effect, "I neither approve nor disapprove of your behavior and attitudes; but I deeply respect your right to feel as you please and your right to act or feel differently from me." The counselor makes the client feel that no matter how he feels toward the counselor it doesn't matter, and that he won't hold it against the client for coming for help.

In terms of the personality model of this book, the counselor has an element of "openness" of personality which permits the client to "use" the counselor's ego for building his own. Acceptance is a characteristic of the "relationship bridge" described in Chapter 2. Figure 15 illustrates the role

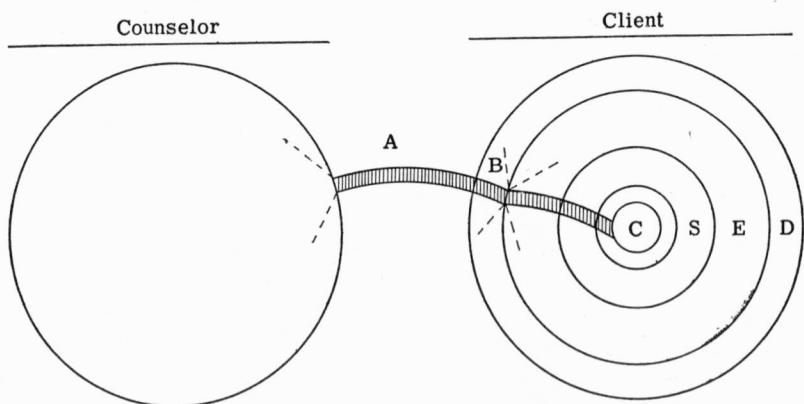

C – Unconscious   S – Self   E – Ego   D – Defense System

FIG. 15. Acceptance and the Relationship Bridge.

of acceptance in facilitating communication. Acceptance allows the bridge to widen at *A,* thereby allowing more free communication of feelings and ideas. Acceptance attitudes aid in reducing resistance at *B,* allowing more free access to the client's deeper feelings.

We feel that, at this point in the discussion of counselor characteristics, it must be mentioned that the counselor is not some sort of inert, bland agent to be manipulated at will by the client. In his attempts to accept the client wholeheartedly and to enter into a close relationship with him, the counselor or therapist *risks* himself as much as the client risks himself. The counselor, too, must open his defenses to make the relationship effective. The risk element involves the possibility of failure or rejection by the client and, if he does so, the counselor may lose part of himself.

Basic assumptions underlying acceptance. Holding an attitude of acceptance presupposes several basic assumptions. First, acceptance is based on the idea that the individual has *infinite worth and dignity*. In other words, human values are extremely high in the value hierarchy of the counselor. A second basic assumption is that it is the person's *right to make his own decisions* and lead his own life. This assumption is based upon a third even more basic assumption that the client has the capacity or *potential to choose wisely* and *to live a full, self-directed, socially useful life*. A fourth related assumption is that each person is *responsible for his own life*. The counselor's value system must be such that he will enhance this sense of self-respect and self-responsibility in his clients and in himself. As we indicated earlier in this chapter, while discussing responsibility, the counselor must realize that he cannot solve problems for the client.

The basic assumption of many counselors, particularly of those leaning toward the nondirective group, is that there exists within the individual creative growth forces which, when released by the counselor's acceptance, will allow the individual to grow toward the model of the well-functioning personality, and to recapture his mental health values. Rogers (249) cites evidence from several fields which appear to support this assumption of growth needs. Allport's concept of "propriate striving" as a positive, goal-directed, motivating force, deep within the personality, is related to this basic assumption (3).

The assumptions and attributes of acceptance mentioned above are rooted deeply in American democratic philosophy which in turn are based strongly in our Hebraic-Christian cultural traditions. The Leibnitzian philosophical position of viewing the human as an active, growth-motivated organism has contributed much also. The blend of eighteenth-century emphases on universal human rights and values with the nineteenth-century views on human uniqueness and individuality has created a rich background for counseling philosophy. Thus, the present cultural and educational climate in America appears to favor these assumptions and attitudes. This climate is making it easier for counselors to learn and apply basic attitudes.

A summary definition of acceptance has been stated by Rogers (249) as being a positive attitude toward the individual which views him as a person of worth and dignity with the right to make his own decisions. We have postulated that the major element of this positive attitude is a form of love. Being loved in this accepting sense makes the client capable of loving himself and others. Perhaps the following is the dynamic of acceptance: When the client has experienced an attitude of acceptance, he is able to take this attitude and experience it in the same way toward himself. Once he has accepted certain characteristics about himself, the client is able to accept those ideas, experiences, and drives which are a part of his basic self, but which, up to now, he has been denying or distorting.

Self-acceptance. There is some evidence for the twin ideas that acceptance of others is based on acceptance of one's self, and that self-acceptance is based largely on being accepted by others. Several studies (273, 329, 27, 234) point to the significance of self-acceptance and other positive self-regarding attitudes as basic for acceptance of others. The significance of these findings for a counselor is that he must accept himself before he can accept his clients sufficiently well to help them. The significance for a client is that acquisition of self-acceptance and understanding puts him in a position to accept others and to receive acceptance of social rewards from others. Fromm (113) points out that one great difficulty in this principle is that our culture frowns on self-love yet extols loving others. This difficulty seems to stem from our cultural inability to differentiate "selfishness" from "self-respect."

Values of acceptance. A point of great significance for the acceptance attitude is that *the client gets involved* in the counseling process when the client senses that the counselor really cares about what he thinks and feels, that the counselor can and wants to help him, and that he will not be judged. Counseling then begins in earnest and becomes meaningful to him.

A second value of the acceptance attitude is its effect on the *psychological climate* of the interview. By psychological climate is meant the emotional tone resulting from the personality interaction of the client and counselor. The climate may be described, in descriptive terms for emotions, as being warm, cold, serious, or frivolous. Conspicuous examples of emotional climates are those surrounding funerals or football games. Porter (237) defines psychological climate as those elements of a situation which have implications regarding the client's valuing himself as a person. In other words, the counselor's attitudes affect the interview climate which, in turn, influences the client's attitudes toward himself—attitudes of confidence, worth, and competence, for example.

The counselor, in addition, tries to keep a fairly consistent or stable attitudinal climate so that the client can express himself freely without expecting disapproval, criticism, argument, or other traditional responses he expects on the basis of his past experience. This accepting climate, and the fact the counselor does not react toward him as others have reacted, makes a favorable situation, we believe, for learning new responses and extinguishing old nonadaptive behaviors.

A third value of acceptance is its salutary effect on *defensive* attitudes. Feeling accepted is vastly different from feeling defensive. Why does the acceptance attitude have such power to counteract defensiveness in clients? A partial answer may be found in the description of personality presented in Chapter 2 which viewed the individual as being protected by a series of defenses, or protective mechanisms, which he employs to keep himself from being hurt psychologically. Rationalization, denial, justification, projection, and development of symptoms were a few examples.

What happens when the client feels threatened? The defenses, previously learned, are mobilized, as are gun emplacements and soldiers in a fort readied for action. He is like the old man in the fable who, when the wind began to blow, wrapped his coat around himself even tighter. You will remember that in the story it was the sun, with its warm rays, which created the atmosphere or climate which made the individual want to take off his coat. Acceptance, similarly, is that attitudinal set of the counselor which seems to create in the client a feeling of being so comfortable in his presence that he need no longer keep his guard or defenses up.

Acceptance—what it is not. Because we have endeavored to teach the meaning of acceptance, it has been our experience that many students misconstrue its real meaning. The following are some mistaken notions about acceptance; *Approval* or agreement is not acceptance. Accepting a person means neither approving nor disapproving of what he says or feels. It means simply taking him as a person with the right to feel and think differently from the way we think and feel, no matter how unfair, absurd, negativistic, wholesome, social, or pleasant his expressions may be. That the client, early in the counseling process, may misconceive of the counselor's acceptance attitudes as agreement with what he says and feels is a real counseling hazard.

A second misconception may occur over an attitude of *neutrality*. Acceptance is a *positive, active* attitude toward the client. It says in effect, "I *like* you even if I may not necessarily agree personally with all you think or feel." Another way of stating this idea might be, "I see, appreciate, and value these ideas and feelings along with you. You, the essential you, matters more to me than what you say or do."

A third distorted notion of acceptance is to equate it with *sympathy*. Sympathy goes much farther than acceptance, in that the counselor actually begins to feel in the way the client does—with a strong empathic response. The counselor actually feels sorry too as he becomes more emotionally involved. Acceptance, however, is more detached. The counselor says in effect, "I understand how badly you feel, although I do not personally feel that way." Sympathy, while intended as a supportive device, has the added disadvantage of tending to *minimize* the feeling of the client. A sympathy attitude says in effect, "You poor person, I feel so sorry for you since you cannot help yourself; let me give you encouragement and help." The client feels incapable of handling the feelings by himself and feels that he must look to outside support. The net effect is the creation of a psychological climate in which dependent and evasive behavior is learned. When the need in the counselor to offer sympathy is strong, it is suspected that this is an expression of his own dependency needs.

A fourth misinterpretation of acceptance is equating it with *tolerance*. Although tolerance may be a desirable social trait, in a counseling relationship it connotes "putting up with." It implies a negative acceptance rather than a positive one, as well as a more superficial kind of respect for personality. The tolerance attitude implies that there is a characteristic, such as race difference, of which the counselor is aware, and about which the client senses he is trying to be tolerant.

Permissiveness

This corollary attitude of acceptance characterizes the freedom and lack of authoritarian and judgmental attitudes in the counselor's personality. The freedom element concerns much of the nonjudgmental quality described under acceptance attitudes, and determines to what extent the client can accept the counselor. The counselor says in effect, "You may discuss anything you wish here without fear or judgment"; hence, he is neither offended nor shocked.

A completely *laissez faire* attitude, however, would operate to the disadvantage of the client since the relationship would be too ambiguous. If allowed too much free expression, the client may fear loss of emotional control and suffer anxiety. As indicated in the discussion of catharsis, too free an expression of feelings may serve to erode the client's defensive structure to the point where he is at the mercy of his feelings and may move toward a psychosis.

If he is too permissive, the counselor could be extremely cruel to the client who is vulnerable to anxiety. Such a client might flounder without direction. The counselor would abuse permissiveness if he were facetious. An extreme example would be the client who came into the office and announced, "I just killed my mother," to which the counselor replied, "Did you use an axe or a knife?" The client assumes that the counselor takes his professional responsibilities seriously and responses of the type made above tend to destroy respect for, and confidence in, the counselor.

The counselor's authority role often belies his attempts to acquire a permissive attitude. The counselor's personal prestige, his specialized knowledge, and professional "halos" make a permissive atmosphere difficult to achieve. The counselor often is tempted to use his authoritarian status to urge the client toward a definite goal, perhaps, or to select the content of the interview. The desirable amount of authority or direction to be given is the least amount consonant with the goals of the particular counseling case and the least amount which is comfortable for both. Techniques for implementing these attitudes will be clarified later under the subject of structuring.

When used appropriately, permissiveness allows the person more free expression of his feelings, thus allowing him to understand and dissipate them. A permissive counselor attitude puts the client in a favorable state to understand the defensiveness behind his feelings, and to accept his own and the counselor's interpretations.

Understanding

Counseling and therapeutic writings are replete with suggestions to "understand" the client; yet the term is seldom defined in behavioral terms. Effective counselors seem to be able to understand their clients more than ineffective counselors can, according to several studies (97, 98, 141). Porter (238) made a useful distinction between understanding diagnostically and understanding therapeutically. *Understanding diagnostically* refers to the intellectualized descriptions of the client's behavior. Examples are the information obtained through testing or observation for making diagnostic judgments for use in vocational planning. As one would expect, this aspect of understanding enables the counselor to make predictions about the client's overt behavior and of his self-descriptions. The test, then, of the degree of the counselor's diagnostic understanding would be the extent of his ability to describe, interpret, and predict the client's behavior.

Understanding therapeutically refers to feeling reactions on the part of the counselor which enable the client to feel understood, accepted, and empathized with. An attitude of therapeutic understanding emphasizes seeing the client as he sees himself.

Therapeutic understanding appears quite unrelated to the counselor's knowledge about the client (100). Effective therapists, although not able to predict their client's self-descriptions much better than the poor therapists (98, 190), were rated significantly better in their ability to establish and maintain a warm, accepting relationship. In this connection, one of Fiedler's significant findings was that there was substantial agreement among skilled therapists of three different schools of therapy as to what constituted an ideal therapeutic relationship. The skilled therapists of different schools agreed more with each other on definitions of the ideal relationship than with the unskilled members of their own school (48). If Fiedler's results can be interpreted at face value, it seems that understanding therapeutically is closely related to therapeutic competence.

Thus, "understanding" must be thought of both in the diagnostic-descriptive-predictive sense of Chapter 5 as well as in the therapeutic sense described in this chapter. The effective counselor apparently needs both types of understanding. Yet, the counselor may find that attempting to use both types of understanding is difficult indeed. There is a strong tendency to be preoccupied with the cognitive aspects of the client's difficulties and to overlook the connotive implications of his confusion and indecision. For example, while attempting to see the client's reasons for financial aid, why social work is more suitable than teaching, or which marital prospect appears most promising, the counselor might tend to ignore the threat to the client's independence involved in the financial aid, or the need to dominate children in the vocational choice, or the extreme dependency interfering with a marital choice.

However, with some orientations to counseling, the counselor might be tempted to ignore the more "here and now" cognitive aspects of the problem and be preoccupied with the feelings of the client. In some cases, perhaps, more emphasis needs to be placed on the reality level of the client's occupational choice rather than on the intricate feelings regarding his parents' wishes for success through him. This point is especially pertinent for many school counselors and advisers whose positions are structured around educational-vocational planning. We assume that the really effective therapeutic psychologist has the capacity to keep the understanding emphases in balance and to know when to stress one aspect of understanding over the other.

To accomplish this state of optimal judgment, it is presupposed that the counselor understands his own problems and weaknesses. The kinds of problems seen or ignored in clients, types of diagnoses made, or anxiety signs observed are all too often projections of the counselor's unrecognized and non-understood problems and anxieties. This condition implies a willingness of the counselor to evaluate himself continuously and thoroughly. If the counselor is struggling with a serious problem of his own, he should refrain from counseling until he has it worked out satisfactorily. This statement does not mean that the counselor would or should have no problems while engaged in counseling. He should recognize them, however, and be aware of the tendency of the relationship to intensify them. Further implications of this aspect of understanding in the counseling relationship will be treated under the topic of "countertransference" in Chapter 8.

The internal frame of reference. Another useful concept in understanding the client and in assisting the counselor or psychotherapist to assimilate basic attitudes is that of the internal frame of reference (250, 237). This concept is defined as the attempt by the counselor to perceive the client and his world as seen by the client. It means the attempt to think *with*, rather than *for* or *about* the client. By frame of reference is meant simply point of view or the observational vantage point. Rogers cites an example of the counselor's thoughts as he assumes this role:

> To be of assistance to you I will put aside myself—the self of ordinary interaction—and enter into your world of perception as completely as I am able. I will become, in a sense, another self for you—an alter ego of your own attitudes and feelings—a safe opportunity for you to discern

yourself more clearly, to experience yourself more truly and deeply, to choose more significantly (249, pg. 35).

An example of a counselor's thinking from the *external* frame of reference would be, "What is causing this difficulty, and why is he so preoccupied with marital problems?" The counselor thinks, "This fellow is in bad shape; I've got to find out what is wrong and try to help him save his marriage." An example of the *internal* frame-of-reference-thinking would be, "You see this as a very disturbing experience, and you want to do something about it." The counselor thinks, "I must try to understand how he looks at this problem and to help him clarify his own thinking about it so that he can make a decision in line with the best interests of all concerned."

To assist the reader in conceptualizing the problem of getting within the client's frame of reference, we reproduce an earlier diagram in Figure 16

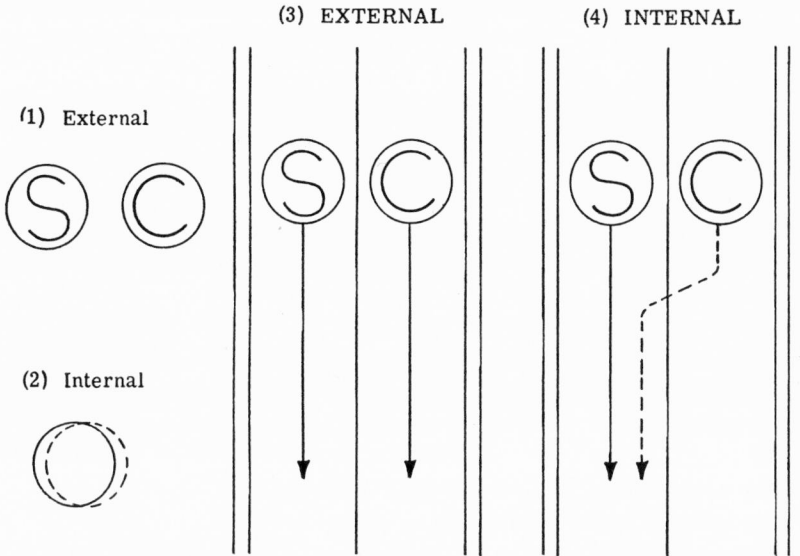

Fig. 16. The Internal and External Frames of Reference.

(277). In stage (1) the client and counselor are in an ordinary social interaction situation where *S* listens and *C* talks. The perceptions are formed largely on the basis of the unique past experience of each participant. Each moves down his respective experience lane as in stage (3). Often, the counselor who characteristically assumes the external frame of reference tried to get the client to come into his lane—to see things his way. Under certain circumstances this may be a legitimate objective; but it does not necessarily help in understanding the client.

When the counselor assumes the internal frame of reference however, he tries to make his perceptual framework match that of the client as in stage (2) of Figure 16. Stage (4) illustrates what happens when the counselor tries to get into the client's lane. At least temporarily, he attempts to think and feel the way the client does. We are assuming that this effort is necessary to understand how the client views his situation.

Learning to assume the internal frame of reference and to stay within it seem to be particularly difficult. As one contemplates the reasons for this difficulty, the following examples can be considered: *Language differences* constitute a major obstacle. As the adult tries to understand the adolescent or the child, or as the Easterner tries to fathom the particular lingo of the Westerner, it seems that the symbols used have different meaning to different people. This is a problem of semantics which has received much attention in the communications literature of recent years.

Biological differences are obviously another barrier. The difficulties experienced as a man tries to assume the feminine frame of reference, and vice versa, can be easily understood.

Socio-economic differences often cause client and counselor to be in different semantic worlds. Counselors, for example, having from five to eight years of college training, have difficulty assuming the frame of reference of those with little formal education. A thorough understanding of social class differences and their significance, therefore, should be part of every counselor's training. There is abundant evidence of the need for this type of understanding in studies by Havighurst (140), Warner (312), and Postman (239).

Related to cultural differences are *experience differentials*. Counselors, having life experiences different from their clients, can only see the client's world imperfectly in the light of his own frame of reference. Finally, *age differences* influence understanding in that one who has lived longer often finds it difficult to "see" the significance of the conflicts and frustrations of a much younger person. Teachers, for instance, often forget "how it feels" to be a student.

It was felt that a brief analysis of some of the obstacles to assuming the internal frame of reference would help to punctuate the necessity for striving very hard for broad life experiences as well as for asking ourselves the questions: "How does he look at this problem?" "How is he thinking and feeling about this matter?" "What is he trying to say?" This attempt at understanding the client by means of assuming the internal frame of reference pays heavy dividends in a better relationship and more appropriate counselor responses to the client's feeling and thinking.

Empathic response is another way of viewing understanding. Empathy is related to the German *einfulung* which means "feeling into." An illustration is the response of the crowd as the highjumper clears the bar. All vocalize "umm-mm" and lean forward as the jumper goes up. Bowlers often experience similar feelings when they "empathize" the ball. Similarly, counselors tend to "feel into" the attitudes of the client as they are being expressed. Although this capacity to empathize aids the counselor in maintaining the internal frame of reference, there is a tendency to get over-involved emotionally, the dangers of which have been described previously.

Warmth

Closely related to therapeutic understanding and acceptance attitudes is the oft-heard term "warmth" to describe an aspect of the relationship. Warmth appears to encompass the sensitive, friendly, considerate, and responsive elements of the counselor personality. "Relating easily to people" is a phrase often used to describe an aspect of warmth. Manifested "warmth" seems basic for rapport. The friendly conversation, preceding and interspersed in the process, however, adds little to the progress of counseling. It has been called "sawdust" by Rogers (250) meaning that it helps to maintain a friendly climate but doesn't result in much therapeutic progress.

Consideration for the client is rooted in respect for him as a person, and is another way of manifesting warmth. This counselor attitude conveys a feeling to the client that he is worthy of respect (a feeling which many clients do not have for themselves). Consideration is shown also in the ordinary courtesies of social communication, such as offering a chair and showing concern for the client's comfort. Consideration is shown through the intense interest exhibited in the client so that he feels he is an important, worthwhile person to the counselor, not just another research or practice "guinea pig."

Another external manifestation of warmth in a relationship is the smile. This behavior is the test of the genuineness of the counselor's attitudes. Clients can sense when the counselor is "just trying to be nice" and when he experiences genuine pleasure in knowing the client as a person and in spending time with him.

Honesty and Sincerity

The counselor must, above all, be honest and sincere in his attitudes. Counseling cannot be a masquerade. Honesty, as used here, is not perceived in moralistic terms but as a characteristic of "straight-forwardness." The beginning counselor, for example, learns quickly that if he tries to be accepting without truly feeling this way inside, the client does not take long to find it out. It is this quality of honesty which again distinguishes communication in the interview from ordinary social conversation. In much of social communication both parties keep up a "front," hence conversation is often a game of mild deceit. It seems that when the client experiences a relationship in which this deceit is not present and when he feels that

the counselor is serious and "on the level" with him, he realizes that he
can drop his own facade and that he can accomplish little by being deceitful
himself.

In order to be completely honest, it is necessary that the therapist or
counselor recognize frankly his own errors—that he makes errors of
judgment and technique. The therapist can more easily recognize and correct his errors when he can admit they are present. His perception and
humble acceptance of error, however, must be balanced by a mature
tolerance for the inevitable mistakes, especially the more trivial ones.
Clients seem to have a remarkable tolerance for counselor error providing
other aspects of the relationship are adequate. This attitude of alertness to
error serves as a useful antidote to counselor complacency, the "pedestal
syndrome," or the "Jehovah complex."

Flexibility

Carnes' (57) study of counselor flexibility points up the necessity for
this vital trait in the counselor's character. The counselor must move easily
and quickly from one role to another. For example, a role may be forced
upon him of father figure, teacher, or friend. Most of the time he must
represent a type of social reality to the client who, as Kelly expressed it,
"tries out psychological experiments of test-tube size in the laboratory of
the conference room" (165, pg. 619).

It is our viewpoint that the therapist must be flexible in the use of the
counseling techniques as he moves along all the dimensions defined at the
outset of this chapter. Sometimes he must be objective, and at other times
subjective. Often he utilizes techniques which are primarily connotive; at
other places they are primarily cognitive. For example, he explains a point
about client responsibility to create clarity; at other points he may promote
ambiguity deliberately, as will be explained in the next chapter. Sometimes
the counselor focuses on aspects of the client's problems which are common
to men and women in general. Then again, he may dwell upon the unique
problems of this particular client. The essence of the evolving eclecticism
view is flexibility in utilizing all approaches and methods as they seem appropriate.

THE SUPPORTIVE FUNCTION OF THE RELATIONSHIP

Nature of Support

The therapeutic relationship, in addition to being the vehicle for the
development of insights, serves a broad supportive role. As we have seen
earlier, an awareness of anxiety reduction and a feeling of security on the
part of the client are the principal results of a suitable emotional response
from the counselor. The essence of support, then, is this general feeling of

well-being, and satisfaction of "affect hunger," as Levy describes it, which the client experiences in the presence of certain counselor attitudes.

Support may be viewed in three ways. Its implicit form is the supporting nature of the relationship itself. The acceptance, warmth, and other characteristics of the counselor are construed by the client as security-provoking. The client experiences support when the relationship bridge is broadened so that feelings can flow freely from the unconscious core to the self- and ego systems as well as between counselor and client personalities. Rogers, for example, speaking of the counseling relationship says, "It is experienced as basically supporting, but it is in no way supportive. The client does not feel that someone is behind him, that someone approves of him. He does experience the fact that here is someone who respects him *as he is,* and is willing for him to take any direction which he chooses" (249, pg. 209). We agree with Rogers in principle, but there appear to be times when actual support techniques need to be applied. This effort to support a client also may seem contradictory to earlier statements about the use of anxiety and distress for motivating the search for insight. The principles of flexibility and timing, however, make it possible for the therapist to be accepting at times, more supportive at other times, and even threatening at appropriate times.

A second type of support experienced by the client is in the form of reassurance, change of environment, and various forms of help which remove environmental or internal pressures. There is a large group of counselors who feel this type of support is necessary with certain types of clients, especially in the early phases of counseling. Thus, whether support is offered explicitly through a medium such as reassurance, or only through the implicit support of the relationship itself, is one of the unresolved issues in psychological counseling. Reassurance techniques will be described in detail in the following chapter.

Support may be experienced by the client in a third manner when he feels the counselor assuming more responsibility for leading the interview, carrying the major verbalizing load, and making decisions. While this shift in responsibility may have a supporting effect, it should be viewed as a temporary expedient for reducing anxiety only. The danger of prolonged support of this type is primarily that of reinforced dependency and reduced capacity to assume responsibility.

Values of Support

A supportive relationship has four primary therapeutic values. One of its principal values is that it reduces excess anxiety and consequently develops security and comfort. The emotional presence of the therapist enables the client to feel worthy, loved, and respected. This aspect of support waxes and wanes according to the needs of the particular client at various points in the process. Those clients feeling inadequate, grief-stricken, unworthy, uncomfortable, lonely, or fearful about losing control of their feelings are given the specific relationship help they need. For example, the inadequate person is led to feel that here in the therapist is a pillar of strength on which he can lean temporarily while he develops confidence and strength.

He can feel also, that for the time being he does not have to be big and strong, mature, and capable. In other words, he feels he can walk before he is expected to run. This may seem, at first, to be promoting dependency, but its value lies in allowing the client to express his security and dependency needs, accepting them, and interpreting them later. It seems wise to go along with the client's dependency a short while so that he does not feel that the counselor is just another paternalistic adult anxious to push him into maturity.

The grief-stricken person can feel that here is someone who understands how he feels, with whom he can share his troubles, and with whom he can feel that he is not alone. A supportive relationship helps the client who is fearful of his impulses by enabling him to feel that it is all right to have the feelings, to express them, and to feel that they won't get him into trouble. In addition, the counselor may help the client to control his feelings by techniques designed to decrease the emotional intensity of the discussion.

A second value of support is the assurance that it gives to the client that he can be helped, for example, that he can make realistic plans, that he can improve his studies, or that he possibly will save his marriage. Clients in a state of anxiety often have a hopeless feeling about their problem or they feel theirs is an unique case. The counselor's calm, accepting, reassuring manner can be a powerful supporting medium for these clients.

A third value of support is the awareness it gives the client of his freedom to change his views or behaviors. By fully accepting him, the counselor says in effect that, though he may not agree with the client, he can be receptive to his views at the moment. Thus, the client is not given the reassurance that he is right about his present views. If the client feels overly reassured about having, for example, a picture of himself as a very shy person he may tend to feel guilty about changing this picture. In other words, he does not feel "caught" in his present attitudes and is able to try out new responses. Support enters again when he tries out the new response which may get him into even greater difficulties temporarily.

A fourth value of a supportive relationship is that it prevents the client from accepting abortive solutions to his problems. The client can feel that he does not have to take impulsive actions which may get him into even worse trouble. For example, he may see that becoming more settled in his feelings before going ahead with divorce proceedings might save him later regrets. Similarly, hospitalization may support the client until he is better able to work rationally on his problems.

Limitations of Support

Since a counselor is supportive when he helps the client to meet his emotional needs, it is obvious that this condition offers mixed blessings. One liability of over-support is the resentment or guilt a client may feel when he is aware of his dependence on the counselor. Some clients, in addition, are deeply threatened by too much "warmth" or emotional closeness, possibly because they have not yet learned how to handle a close human relationship. A second limitation is the strong dependency that may develop through prolonged support. This significant counseling condition is discussed in a later chapter under the topic of transference.

A third limitation or misinterpretation of support is that of sympathy. We have discussed the implication of sympathy earlier in this chapter. It should be emphasized again that liberal use of support may have a ring of insincerity or exaggeration.

Resentment against the apparent shallowness and stereotypy of liberal reassurance is a fourth limitation. The attitude that "everything will come out in the wash, so don't worry," has been offered many times by important people in his life. He knows that things don't always turn out all right; so, he is threatened by what appears to him to be insincere, stock techniques.

SUMMARY

Psychotherapeutic and counseling relationships have several basic dimensions, such as uniqueness-commonality, objectivity-subjectivity, cognitive-connotive, ambiguity-clarity, and responsibility. The counselor has the difficult task of recognizing and dealing appropriately with these seemingly paradoxical elements of the relationship.

Since therapeutic effectiveness hinges so much on the quality of the relationship between counselor and client, basic attitudes of the counselor are highly significant. The attitudes of acceptance and permissiveness have considerable consequences upon the psychological climate of the interview. This climate which these attitudes create holds important implications for the client's evaluation of his own personality. A key to an effective attitudinal climate is the counselor's assuming the internal frame of reference which is his attempt to understand the client by taking the client's view of his situation and himself as his frame of reference. The counselor must have additional characterictics of warmth, intelligence, flexibility, and a willingness to share the responsibility.

One of the principal functions of the relationship is to provide support for the client. Support is the promotion of comfort and security through the construction of optimal conditions of living. Support is considered generally to be an aim of psychological counseling and is often a condition necessary before more cognitive approaches can be made to solution of the client's broader problems.

7.

Relationship Techniques

In the last chapter, on counselor and psychotherapist attitudes, the underlying assumption was made that techniques are very limited unless there is full understanding of the therapeutic goals and fundamental counselor attitudes from which the techniques emerge. In other words, there is a danger in becoming too "technique-conscious" or "formula-centered." One characteristic of the charlatan is his blind adherence to pat techniques applied indiscriminately and invalidly to all clients.

Techniques, on the other hand, are somewhat personal in that counselors develop varying styles and techniques best suited to their own personalities and their estimates of client needs. Techniques are, after all, primarily media for defining and redefining relationships with people in many life situations. Useful techniques, in addition, have stood the test of time in empirical validation; and, in many cases, they have been experimentally validated.

In order to clarify our position, a word should be said about the applications of this chapter. The techniques described herein are fundamental to both counseling and psychotherapy. For the psychotherapist, Chapters 8 and 9 dealing with more intensive techniques are a vital core of therapeutic technique. However, a counselor in a school setting, for example, may find that the techniques described in this chapter are sufficient, or exceed his needs, in view of the level of his involvement with clients and the time limits of his job.

Considerable emphasis is placed on Rogers' contributions to the relationship techniques described in this chapter. Though we greatly respect Rogers' contribution to these techniques, we are at quite a variance with his basic theoretical position in the chapters which follow. We place more emphasis on variety of technique and spontaneity, along with greater acceptance and awareness of the counselor toward his own attitudes and feelings as he relates to the client. This emphasis tends to result in our more eclectic orientation. The techniques used are more a function of the natural, contemporaneous, existential relationship of client and counselor.

It was emphasized in Chapter 6 that the counselor or therapist is a human being with weaknesses, yet with a large capacity to grow. He is an authority in helping relationships, but has much to learn, also. The client with whom he works is a unique expression of human nature, but so is he, the counselor. Thus, counseling and psychotherapy tend to be workshops for the growth and development of both participants.

Keeping these cautions in mind, we offer the following discussion on technique to suggest the possible ways the basic attitudes and concepts of the counselor and psychotherapist might be manifested.

RAPPORT TECHNIQUES

By the establishment of rapport we mean the creation in the initial interview of a warm personal relationship with the client and an atmosphere of mutual trust. *En rapport* means a condition of mutual understanding and concern about common objectives. The principal purpose of rapport techniques is to build the relationship bridge. The counselor establishes rapport by revealing his attitudes of acceptance and his deep interest in the client and his problems.

The Greeting

In practice, the counselor's interest in a client is manifested by meeting him in the reception room with a firm hand clasp (if socially appropriate to his age level), greeting him by name, and escorting him courteously into the office. Ordinary human courtesy, therefore, goes far in building rapport.

The Topics

Before the first interview begins, a state of rapport may be expedited by opening the conversation on some topic such as a recent event known to both participants or a special interest of the client. Counselors vary, however, in their opinions on the necessity of beginning on conversational topics. Starting with an urbane or trite conversational topic might result in a more strained relationship than if the client were allowed to state his business frankly and immediately. This problem illustrates one of the areas of artful judgment required of a counselor.

Counseling generally deals with problems that are personal and intimate, hence, loaded with anxiety. It is often difficult to face these problems squarely and immediately, particularly in the presence of a strange person. The counselor must resolve the client's fear and restraint, which is natural in a new setting, by making him moderately comfortable. For this reason, most counselors have developed some common rapport-building topics. The following is an ilustrative list:

Reference to name of client
Reference to home town of client
Reference to mutual friends
Reference to "Conversation
   Piece,"
   (Picture, statue on
   desk, etc.)
Reference to appearance of
   client: (Style of
   dress, necktie,
   pins, or rings
   worn, etc.)

Reference to weather or common
   event
Reference to previous activity of
   counselor: for
   example, "I have
   just come from
   class."
Reference to status of client: for
   example, "You
   are a junior this
   year, aren't
   you?"

It should be emphasized, however, that these topics are merely "ice breakers" to enable the client to start perceiving the therapeutic attitudes of the counselor. Though varying with each client, opening conversation should take no longer than a few minutes. There is just as much danger that the relationship will get off on a conversational bent as on a "cold," resistive start lacking in rapport.

As an additional note of caution, rapport can be established just as easily on a non-verbal basis by a warm and friendly "waiting-for-you, my-time-is-yours" appearance on the counselor's part, and secondly, by competently meeting whatever lead the client gives for a starter. If a client is motivated to seek help, then engaging in "small talk," as suggested above, may tend to show a kind of disrespect for this need. Furthermore, too much "small talk" might imply that the counselor needs to protect the client from the reality of the situation. With such clients, a lead something like "would you like to tell me what brings you here" is most realistic and honest. In summary, the first remarks are largely matters of counselor preference or style.

The Physical Arrangements

One of the important determinants of rapport is the physical condition of the room, particularly the seating arrangement of counselor and client. For this reason, in the following Figure 17 the advantages and disadvantages of various types of seating are illustrated. In *Example A* the desk acts as a communications barrier, and is symbolic of authority. In general, the seating arrangement in example A is not recommended.

Some counselors prefer to get from behind their desks entirely and sit in a position which implies equality as in *Example B*. This causes embar-

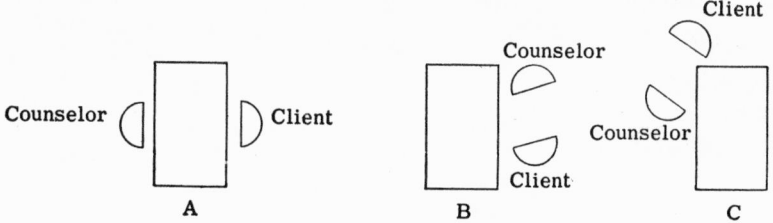

FIG. 17. Types of Seating Arrangements.

rassment for some clients who like to feel the security of being behind a desk. However, if both face somewhat to the side much of this embarrass-ment is overcome.

We prefer the arrangement shown in Example C in which the client is given the security of being partially behind the desk; but at the same time the desk need not be a relationship barrier. Example C allows for closer communication; yet it produces the necessary emotional security.

Other physical arrangements would seem to be taken for granted; but it is our experience that often they are overlooked by counselors. It is axio-matic, for example, that the client never is placed in a position where he must face the light. This means that if it is necessary to face the client toward the window that the venetian blinds or drapes be closed.

Another consideration is the nature of the client's chair. The counseling relationship seems to be improved through the installation of large com-fortable chairs of the same type for both counselor and client. This represents quite a change from the traditional arrangement whereby the counselor is afforded a comfortable swivel chair and the client is given any available straight chair.

The Attitudes

A degree of mysticism often surrounds the client-therapist relationship. Counselors sometimes give the client the impression that therapy is a form of magic and that the therapist is endowed with special powers which make him able to help people. In our experience a state of rapport and the re-lationship bridge are best built on a feeling of the natural human rela-tionship. It is assumed here that counseling is a natural, but unique, interpersonal process which differs only slightly from other human relation-ships. The counselor may explain that there is nothing mysterious about counseling or psychotherapy, for they are largely processes of re-investi-gating and re-learning.

As with all other techniques, building rapport is rather fruitless unless the counselor is warm, sincere, and non-judgmental in the sense described earlier, in Chapter 6. Above all, the confidential nature of the interview must be maintained. Counselors working in colleges and universities, often are tempted to use illustrations from their own counseling experiences in classes in counseling, mental hygiene, and abnormal psychology. Such procedure is unwise; yet counselors are apt to follow this procedure unless they are aware of the damaging effects this may have on rapport with future clients.

The four fundamental conditions for achieving a state of rapport are: a feeling of emotional warmth, realization of common objectives, assurance of confidentiality, and an awareness of naturalness. Initial rapport is facilitated by a set of techniques; but these procedures must be placed in an attitudinal frame of reference which is permissive and accepting if the condition of rapport is to remain in effect for the duration of counseling.

REFLECTION OF FEELING

The Significance of Reflection

One of Rogers' (250) significant contributions to counseling and therapy procedure has been to clarify the value of the technique of reflecting feeling. He presents it as one of the most important techniques in promoting a feeling of understanding. Since this technique is used so widely, we give it special prominence in this discussion of relationship techniques.

In the multidimensional approach to personality taken in Chapter 2, it was emphasized that much of the personality is beyond awareness. This technique helps the individual to go below the surface of consciousness and beyond the ego system in order to reach and become more aware of obscure feelings and to deal with them more effectively. What seems to happen is that the client talks of his feelings as "it" or "them"—something apart from himself. This tendency of the client to consider his feelings objectively at first serves a useful defensive function. The reflection technique, however, focuses on the subjective element of what the client says. Reflection emphasizes the pronoun "you" in the phrases, "you feel . . ." and "you think. . . ." Reflection serves a useful purpose in that it leads the client to think of the feelings and ideas he is expressing as part of his own personality and not outside of himself. Thus, reflection is a useful intermediate technique to be used after the initial relationship has been built and before the information-giving and interpretation stages in the process are begun.

We take the position that reflecting feelings is a skill, and as such, can be learned by understanding and practice. Phillips and Agnew (236) found from their data that reflection is definitely a learned clinical skill and that it is not commonly used in general interpersonal relationships by non-clinically trained, or even able and mature people.

The Nature of Reflection

Reflection of feeling is defined as the attempt by the counselor to express in *fresh* words, the essential *attitudes* (not so much the content) expressed by the client. The counselor attempts to mirror the client's attitudes for his better self-understanding and to show the client that he is being understood by the counselor. The word "fresh" is emphasized because, perhaps, the most glaring reflection error of the novice counselor is to express his reflection in words already used by the client. In a humorous anecdote, in which the counselor repeated almost verbatim the client's statement, the client's reply was, "What's wrong with the way I said it?" It is preferable to use sufficiently different words with an air of intense interest and effort to understand such as, "You seem to feel you want to make a decision; yet you find it so hard to do so."

The word "attitudes" is emphasized in the definition of reflection in order to make the counselor aware that he must be able to grasp the underlying feeling about what is being said, not just the content. Therapy is often likened to a river with the ripples on the surface corresponding to the content. But more important are the undercurrents—the feelings underlying the content. It takes considerable skill to develop the sensitivity necessary to identify these feelings immediately and to mirror them back as soon as the client has completed his statements.

A word of caution about client feelings is worth expressing. A common misconception arising from an emphasis on feeling is that the expression and identification of feelings have in themselves some great intrinsic merit. The conclusion often drawn is that feelings are more important than intellectualizations. Expression of feelings is encouraged by the reflection technique. Its effectiveness, however, seems to reside in the idea that the expression of feeling is a means and not an end in counseling. Expression of negative feeling, for example, keeps antisocial tendencies from being acted out.

Feelings are thought by the client to be subjective and not to be trusted. They tell him of danger when there is no danger, of presence of symptoms when he is tired and discouraged. The expression of feeling, therefore, is to make possible the discovery of the idea which underlies or is attached to the feelings. The client should be taught to *trust* the expression of his feelings. A person in a panic state, for example, is helped if he is allowed to express his feelings. The air is cleared of smog and, as a result of the clarification, he can examine and deal with the underlying basis of his insecurity.

The individual, through the aid of his ego system, is the evaluator of his experience. Feelings do not possess evaluational quality; they are not "right" or "wrong." Ideas, however, possess truth or falsity. But evaluation of thought is only possible after feelings have been clarified. This is why reflection of *content* is unwise in the early stages of therapy but appears to have real value in later stages. Thus, clarifying feelings leads to clarification of the *ideas* and *experience* underlying these feelings.

The counselor is interested in helping the individual to change his behavior or his undesirable ways of acting. The route to these changes, however, seems to be through the individual's feelings. The client's feelings, furthermore, are generated by his ideas or perceptions. This means that how he perceives and construes his world determines how he feels about his world. This process seems to work in a cyclical fashion also, since feelings, in turn, appear to influence perceptions and so determine what and how the client sees. His past experiences, feelings, and basic needs, therefore, are at the roots of his behavior. Feelings particularly can be described as the road to the deeper levels of ideas and experiences which constitute the individual's core system.

Identifying Feelings

In teaching the technique of reflection to new counselors, it has been found helpful to categorize the nature of human feeling so as to assist the novice in the immediate recognition of the feeling expressed. Reid and Snyder (241) found considerable variation among counselors in their ability to name feelings expressed by clients. There was high agreement among counselors rated as good, however. This implies that ability to reflect is partly a matter of general counseling skill and experience.

In general, it may be said that feelings fall into three broad categories: Positive, negative and ambivalent. Positive feelings are those which are ego constructive; while negative feelings are generally ego-destroying. Ambivalence refers to the presence of two or more contrasting or conflicting feelings expressed or implied at the same time toward the same object. In clinical counseling, it is found that such feelings underlie a great many interpersonal relationships; therefore, it is particularly important for the counselor to spot these apparent contradictions and to reflect them to the client. It is important for the client to see and to accept seemingly contradictory attitudes toward the same person, for this can be a source of great intrapersonal tension. One of the goals of psychotherapeutic counseling is to realize that we can both love and hate the same person at the same time.

The following table gives some examples of labels which fall into our two arbitrary categories of positive and negative feelings.

Positive		*Negative*	
Happiness	Self-worth	Guilt	Disgust
Security	Love	Resentment	Antagonism
Gratitude	Optimism	Fear	Rebellion
Self-confidence	Contentment	Depression	Rejection
	Warmth		Hostility

The beginning counselor who can observe and identify common feeling categories will find it easier to reflect feelings more quickly and confidently.

Difficulties in Reflecting

Stereotopy. A common error is made in reflection when the counselor uses a stereotyped introductory phrase, such as, "You feel . . ." This procedure, if it is not varied, will tend to arouse client feelings of resentment and attempts on his part to analyze the process hypercritically. The following variations are suggested:

> Use of the word that expresses the feeling; for example, "You were mad (sorry, confused, etc.) when that happened."
> "You think . . . ."
> "You believe . . . ."
> "It seems to you . . . ."
> "As I get it, you felt that . . . ."
> "In other words, ..."
> ". . . is that it?"
> "I gather that . . . ."
> Inflection—intonation of various words to express the reflection; for example,
>> Cl: "It really hurt me to hit her."
>> C: "It *really* hurt." (Note: This is an exception to the general rule of not reflecting content.)

Timing. Another error which the novice counselor seems to make is that of waiting for the client to stop his comments before reflecting. When much content and little feeling are expressed by the client, this is not serious. As counseling develops, however, a great many feelings may come rapidly. This condition often necessitates interrupting the client so as to focus on significant feelings that might have been overlooked.

Selection of feeling. When Rogers introduced this reflection technique it became associated with the Rogerian label, "nondirective." A cursory examination of the technique suggested that since the counselor was only repeating feelings which already had been expressed by the client, the counselor, therefore, was not "directive." A closer scrutiny of this technique reveals, however, that any reflection requires that the counselor *choose* from the verbalizations of the client those elements which he feels have greatest quality of feeling and are in greatest need of clarification. This means that the counselor, in a sense, is highly directive in using this technique, since every time he reflects he must choose from the variety of material presented to him by the client. This is a significant argument against the indiscriminate use of this technique by untrained people. In a sense, much damage can be done by failing to reflect accurately or by reflecting accurately and then not working through the feelings properly.

Porter (237) made a significant contribution to the use of reflection technique when he suggested that the counselor must learn to avoid the "four common errors of reflection." A paraphrased and illustrated summary is presented below:

Content. "Reflecting content" is an error in counseling which consists of reflecting back to the student his statement in essentially the same words that the student used. When the counselor does this, he does not convey understanding, but merely repeats blindly what has already been said. His reflection, moreover, is generally met with denial rather than acceptance.

> Cl: I've always just considered medicine because my father always dictated to all us boys what we should be.
> C: You've always sort of considered medicine because your father dictated to you and your brothers what you should be.

A counselor who uses these techniques is fortunate if the first interview lasts over five minutes. The counselor who has a "knowledge-of-acquaintance" in permissive techniques might reflect in the following manner:

> C: You just went along with him since you never thought of disagreeing with him?

This is an attempt by the counselor to get below the surface and to touch on the undercurrent of feeling expressed by the student. The counselor disregards the words of the student in favor of the feelings being expressed.

Depth. The counselor who fails to respond to the same degree of depth in feeling as expressed by the client is also not reflecting accurately. Some counselors are consistently too shallow in their reflections. Others are consistently too deep. An illustration follows:

> S: I want to be an engineer, but I just can't drive myself for four long years without her. . . . I just can't do it. . . .
> C: You'd like to be an engineer, but you'd also like to get married.

The reflection obviously is too shallow. A more accurate reflection might have been:

> C: It's just too long a grind without her.
> Or, the counselor might have reflected:
> C: You just wouldn't be able to live without her for four years.

This reflection perhaps is "too deep" and might be met with denial or by a change of subject on the part of the client.

Meaning. It is also important that the counselor does not *add to* or *take away from* the meaning of the client's statement. An illustration of such procedure is as follows:

> S: I just can't see myself as an accountant sitting at a desk all day.
> C: You don't think you'd like the idea of having to balance budgets, and making profit-and-loss statements, day in and day out.

It is obvious that the client did not say all that the counselor did. The counselor has read a great deal into his statement. The counselor might have taken away meaning also by a reflection of the nature of the following:

> C: You just don't like indoor work.

To be accurate in reflecting the proper meaning on the surface appears easy, but too often the counselor responds from his frame of reference rather than from the client's frame of reference.

Language. Experience by many trained counselors indicates that the counselor should always use the language most appropriate to the situation. Here is an example of a poor use of language:

> Cl: I just seem to be shy with girls. I just can't be friendly.
> C: This inferiority complex seems to be extremely active in these hetero-sexual relations.

The errors the counselor made in the reflection are mainly over-interpretation and pedantry as well as absence of feeling.

It should be emphasized that although reflections should be accurate, an inaccurate remark may still promote interview progress if the client perceives that the counselor is trying to understand him. For example, the counselor may say, "So you resent your father for doing this?" The client responds, "Oh no, I actually admire him for it." While inaccurate from the client's viewpoint, the remark may still be effective since the client feels compelled to clarify his feelings and correct the counselor. The net effect often is progress in the interview.

Types of Reflection

Immediate reflection. This type consists of reiterating a feeling immediately after it has been stated by the client.

Summary reflection. This involves "tying together" several feelings which have been expressed previously. This summary method is diagrammed in Figure 18. The summary reflection is a method of bringing together in one statement several feelings expressed previously. An illustra-

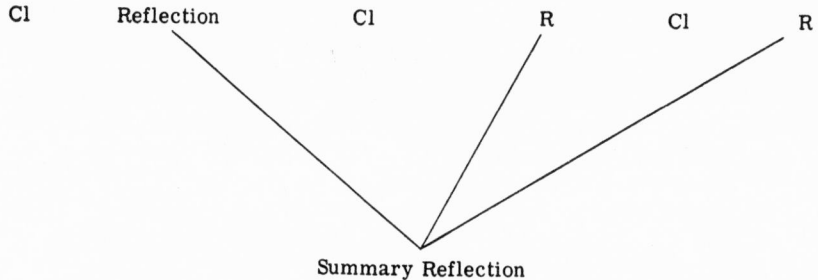

Summary Reflection

FIG. 18. The Summary Reflection.

tion is, "From your descriptions of your family relationships, school experiences, and now your new job, you seem to have strong feelings of personal failure in all of them."

Terminal reflection. This is a technique of summarizing the important aspects of the entire counseling hour. Terminal reflection may also include certain content material which summarizes the proceedings of the hour.

Reasons for Effectiveness of Reflection

It seems appropriate in the discussion of this technique to examine some of the possible reasons for its effectiveness in achieving the goals of counseling.

Reflection helps the individual to feel *deeply understood*. Most neurotics are defensive and feel misunderstood. When confronted with this technique their fear of feeling misunderstood is overcome. For the first time in the lives of many of them, the clarity with which the counselor reflects their deepest unverbalized feelings causes neurotics to feel deeply understood. Thus, reflection serves a supportive function and is used most effectively in the early and middle phases of counseling.

The reflection technique helps to break the so-called neurotic cycle, often manifested in marital counseling and expressed by such phrases as, "She won't understand me and therefore I won't understand her." The counselor, relying on the reflection technique, helps break this tenaciously held line of reasoning.

Reflection impresses clients with the inference that *feelings are causes of behavior*. Perhaps the most significant contribution that reflection of feeling makes to the counseling process is that it affords a vehicle for conveying deep understanding of causes. Feelings are elusive and often uncontrollable. Frequently we feel that we do not understand ourselves because of the emergence of strange or unwanted *feelings* from the unconscious self or core systems. When another human being tries so genuinely to understand us, and appears so capable of clarifying for us the elements of our own experience which are cloudy and fearful, this human being comes to be valued by us. Reflection serves, therefore, as a clarifying and simplifying function.

Reflection causes the *locus of evaluation* to be in the client. Another reason that reflection so effectively challenges the individual to take responsibility for himself is because it subtly suggests that a value system is not something inherent in any experience or object, but that the value is placed on it by the individual. The bombardment of the individual with such phrases as "you feel" and "you think" and "you believe" teaches the individual that he is the evaluator of his own experience and that values are alterable. The client sees that values are judgments made by the individual, based upon his experience. His values are also alterable if and when new experience gives new evidence. The term "locus of evaluation" is helpful here. In the early phases of therapy the client tends to put the locus of evaluation of his behavior *outside* of himself in his parents, his friends, his social groups. Toward the end of counseling, the individual finds that he can place and must place this evaluation of his behavior in himself.

Proper reflection gives him the feeling that he has the *power of choice*. A current tendency in our culture has been to shy away from personally responsible pursuits and to entrust our faith to the "expert." The specialist is expected to tell us how to rear our children, to advise us on marriage or divorce, to choose our vocation, to advise in matters of love-making, budgeting, *ad infinitum*. In matters of personal concern, the result is a continuous cycle of helplessness: The more the expert is consulted, the greater the feeling of helplessness, the greater the need for further advising. In counseling, the aim should be to create self-direction in the client. The reflection technique along with the lack of advice on these matters encourages the individual to achieve this end.

Reflection *clarifies the client's thinking* so that he can see the situation more objectively. The reflection technique by its very nature involves an attempt by the counselor to draw out the essential elements of the client's conversation for his reconsideration. The natural result of such a procedure is to present to the client the high points of his thinking, and to enable him to clarify his present situation and to see it in a more objective and focused fashion. Robinson (246) describes a special type of content reflection which he calls "clarification." Clarification, which summarizes the substance of the client's verbalization, is designed to accelerate insight development through simplification of his wandering and scattered responses without his feeling he is being "pushed."

Another reason why reflection seems to be such a useful technique is that it helps communicate to the client the idea that *the counselor does not regard him as unique* and different. The phrase, "you feel . . .", conveys the impression that the counselor is never shocked into inability to understand. Indirectly, therefore, the reflection technique serves a further supportive function in that it gives the client the feeling that he is "normal" and not weird or different.

Reflection helps the client to *examine his deep motives*. When the counselor concentrates on the individual's feelings rather than the ideational content of his remarks he is reaching the individual at a deep motivational level. This observation is illustrated by the question with which all of us have been faced, "Why did you do that?" The answer may have been, "Because I felt like it." People often do things just because they "feel like it." Feelings are manifestations of the needs and drives which compel us to act. Careful scrutiny of our feelings leads us to examine the motivating forces underlying these feelings. This process is illustrated by the comment, "Well I felt like it because . . ." The word "because" often leads us right to the core motive or experience.

ACCEPTANCE TECHNIQUES

Nature and Value of Acceptance Techniques

This is a simple technique of responding mainly with short phrases, such as, "mm-hm," "Yes, go on," which imply an attitude of acceptance. It is employed particularly in the early stages of counseling when much content or narrative material is produced, often without much associated feeling. Acceptance techniques are employed also in the later stages when the client is delving deeply into himself and is painfully bringing out significant material. It is simply a verbalization of the attitudes of permissiveness and acceptance of the counselor which say in effect: "Go on, it's safe, you needn't be ashamed of expressing how you really feel."

The value of expressions like, "I see," "Uh huh," are that they function as stimulators to continuing discussion along the same lines. Another value is the transitional bridging effect between ideas which gives a smooth forward-moving feeling to the discussion units.

Elements of Acceptance Technique

Simple acceptance technique has at least three major observable elements. First is the *facial expression* and nodding of the counselor. The counselor must convey genuine interest in his face. The counselor who puts on a feigned expression of interest will be discovered by the sensitive client.

Secondly, *tone of voice* and inflection tell the client whether the counselor is accepting, even if he uses conceptually meaningless vocalizations such as "mm" instead of words. Of course, the counselor who speaks so quietly that the client must strain to hear him hampers the process by conveying an impression of disinterest. But the counselor who speaks with an overbearing voice conveys an impression of dulled sensitivity to the expressions of the client.

Distance and posture make up a third consideration in acceptance. If the counselor leans over and sits comfortably close to the client, the client will infer a friendly attitude on his part. This conveying of an attitude of "towardness" as opposed to "away-from-ness" by posture is important, since the former attitude conveys the qualities of openness and sincerity of the counselor. Many clients are hypersensitive to cues like those mentioned above. They may interpret, therefore, the slightest negative gesture of the counselor as rejection or disinterest. Yawning, crossing and recrossing of legs, grasping the arms of the chair tightly are examples of negative cues which are easily discerned by the client and often interpreted as disinterest.

Ellis (90), in surveying the recent literature on couch and face-to-face therapy positions of clients, concluded that face-to-face therapy was preferable, partly because acceptance techniques could operate more effectively.

Nature and Value of Structuring

Structuring technique is the counselor's definition of the nature, limits, and goals of the general counseling process and the particular relationship at hand. In other words, structuring provides the client with a framework or orientation for therapy. He then feels that counseling has a rational plan. Structure provides him with a counseling road map and with a dossier of his responsibilities for using the road map, thus reducing the ambiguity of the relationship. The client should know *where* he is, *who* the interviewer is, and *why* he is there.

Rogers (249) and his students have de-emphasized attempts at formal structuring, although in his earlier writings (250) they felt this technique to be useful. They claim that verbal structuring or describing the relationship intellectually may distort the client's experiencing of the relationship. Rogers' work has been done primarily in a college counseling center where sophisticated students come by free choice and where counselors have no other significant roles with the students. Perhaps this fact along with the fact that the attitudes of the counselor are depended upon to carry the relationship help to explain why Rogers and others with similar views have not found it necessary to utilize structuring as much as is suggested in the eclectic position of therapeutic psychology.

The structure of counseling has two elements—the implicit element in which the very setting and known role of the counselor automatically set limits that are generally understood by the client. The second element, formal structuring, consists of the counselor's purposeful statements to explain and limit the counseling process.

The use of May's analogy (199) to illustrate the nature of implicit structuring may be helpful: Each person is traveling through life as though he were in a boat going down a river. Without the structure of the river bank the water would flow in all directions. The banks of the river provide the limiting factors which guide the boat and give it added power to go down stream. The individual, likewise, is free to make his own choices, but always there seems to be a frame of reference which limits and gives direction to choice. The client is thus aware of a plan of counseling.

Another illustration of the directional value of structuring is provided by a former client of one of us: "It was kind of like going down the highway on a foggy night. I drove my own car but the counselor provided the illuminated white line in the middle of the road for me."

Bixler's survey (32) on the therapeutic value of setting limits may be distilled to the following general principles: (1) limits should be *minimal,* consonant with the security of the client and therapist; (2) limits should be applied non-punitively; (3) limits should be *well defined* in regard to such things as action, time, and number of appointments; (4) limits should be structured *at the proper time*. Too early or too rigid structuring may destroy a relationship.

Dangers in Lack or Inadequacy of Structuring

It appears that the therapeutic process is a miniature social condition in which the individual should utilize his freedom, but in which he must simultaneously accept the limits imposed by that freedom. The counselor who fails to provide structure would be unfair to many of the clients who have no notion of what counseling is all about. Curran stresses this point:

> A confused person is likely to approach the first interview feeling a minimum of responsibility for himself and a maximum of fear, insecurity and defensiveness. Continued miscues on the part of the counselor in structuring the relationship seem to cause the client to depend on the counselor and to feel rejected and hostile if the counselor refuses to solve his problems, and finally in defensiveness and fear to flee the interviews and not keep subsequent appointments (75, pg. 189).

Structuring, therefore, has value in preventing early misconceptions about counseling such as, magical cures, fast help, single causes, advice-giving, smooth sailing, inevitability of cure, and counselor responsibility. By focusing on the positive learnings and roles of client and counselor, and the reasonable expectations of the process many misconceptions can be offset. This aspect of structuring, by the way, must be a continuous process, not a "one-shot hypo" in the first interview.

Rogers tends to feel that the structure of therapy can be provided for the individual at the nonverbal level; that is, the client will "get the idea" as he participates in the process. This may be true with highly sophisticated clients; but this does not seem to be adequate for the average clients.

Ingham and Love suggest that undesirable insecurity develops when structuring is not provided:

> The patient may at first feel that his task is unorganized and formless and that there are no rules. Then he experiences a strange feeling of helplessness and dissatisfaction. It is as though the therapist did not care what he talked about or how he spoke of it (152, pg. 81).

Lack of structuring might arouse anxiety in the client and perhaps account for a counseling failure. It is important, therefore, that the structure be made a *means* to enhance the security of the relationship and not an *end* in itself. Otherwise, the permissiveness and acceptance values are lost. Structuring in the beginning phases of counseling must be approached with caution since there is a danger of conveying a feeling that the counselor has a definite preconceived way of doing things which the client had better follow as an ultimatum. Another danger is that the counselor might convey an impression of how the client ought to feel rather than encouraging him to feel the way he *does* feel.

Sherman (273) found that failure to structure, so as to leave the client too much on his own resources early in the process, results in strong resistance. A feeling for the right amount of structure for each individual client is a paramount counseling skill.

It is important that the structuring technique not be imposed severely on the client. It should be blended skillfully with the attitudes of permissiveness and acceptance. As illustrated above, if structuring is done badly, it can be a relationship barrier. As well, if it is ignored in institutional settings, the results may be equally tragic since the client may build unreal expectations about the outcomes. Structuring has a positive value if it reduces the anxiety of the client who is not cognizant of the dual roles of his counselor or is not aware of situational limits which exist. An example is the counselor who has instructional or administrative relationships with a student. The counselor must point out that these relationships are different from his relationship as a counselor. Thus, authoritarian imputations will not spill into the counseling.

Robinson (247) cautions, however, that the counselor's compulsion to structure frequently, to set the client straight, may be a symptom of the inadequacy of his counseling technique.

Another caution in structuring is the tendency to imply that the relationship will continue with this particular client. It may turn out that the counselor will decide not to work with this client or that the client may not be suitable for this counselor. Hence, the client or the counselor may feel too committed to the relationship if it has been overstructured.

Types of Structure

In the earlier definitions the writers described structuring as the technique which defines the limits and the potentialities of the process. Paradoxical as it may seem, the provision of clear-cut limits provide the client with the power to move forward in therapy. The following discussion deals with some of these limits and potentialities.

Time limits. Perhaps the time limit is paramount in school counseling in which only a limited amount of time can be given for each interview. The counselor, therefore, must explain at the onset of the interview just how much time is available. We suggest that when time limits are presented, clients very often hasten the therapeutic process in an effort to accomplish as much as possible in the time available. This applies to short five- or ten-minute interviews as well as those lasting longer. An example is, "We have forty-five minutes; let's see what we can accomplish."

A second aspect of time limits concerns the time required for the process as a whole. It appears that one of the contributing factors to the success of psychoanalytic therapy, for example, is that the analyst emphasize very carefully to the patient that the process might take two to three years and will be costly. It is admitted that many clients cannot accept this, but at the same time, for the clients who can, the process seems to be facilitated. The counselor, in similar fashion, indicates that to reach the agreed goals, several sessions will be required. The counselor is careful to point out, however, that no commitments can be made as to outcome. For example, a counselor might say, "Ordinarily we get together a couple of times to go over the test data and other material collected, then we spend a session or two helping you plan a specific course of action. In all, it should take four or five hours."

In more emotional problems the counselor may feel that he does not want to become committed to a long-term therapeutic relationship. Structuring may help him prevent misunderstanding with the client as the following example shows:

> C: We have been talking about "first-aid" methods for a while. Perhaps we had better talk a bit about where we go from here. As you realize, we cannot become committed to a major personality overhaul job (pause).
>
> Cl: I see, more of a tune-up job then.

In structuring time limits the counselor must guard against being over-anxious for the client by making promises or raising false hope, even by stating that counseling "is a good investment." Promising success violates one of the ethics of psychotherapy. A positive attitude, however, on the part of the counselor, which creates confidence in himself, his client, and the process, can assist greatly an insecure and anxious client to begin working confidently.

Although it is difficult for the counselor to make definite long-range time commitments to a client, he should discuss fees very clearly early in the first interview. Phone calls and missed appointments, generally, are not charged for, though the counselor who does not charge for long phone calls and uncancelled missed appointments, plays into the manipulative client's hands. Also, it is not sound therapeutically because it does not take cognizance of the *reality* of the relationship.

Action limits. There are also what might be termed action limits. The counselor does not limit verbal expression, no matter how absurd, unfair, or foolish it sounds; but there are certain feelings which cannot be permitted direct expression in *action*. A younger client, for example, cannot break windows, or destroy furniture and equipment. He can say he does not like the therapist, but he cannot physically attack him. As Rogers (250) points out, hurting the therapist may arouse the child's deep guilt and anxiety in relation to the only person who can help him. Fear of retaliation and the threat of withdrawal of this unique kind of supporting relationship may destroy the possibility of therapy.

Role limits. In educational, industrial, religious, or medical settings we find that the counselor often has dual roles: Teacher-counselor, supervisor-counselor, administrator-counselor, minister-counselor, and physician-counselor. This means that these people also have a role of authority in the life of the client as well as the role of non-judgmental listener. This must be so structured. The teacher, after a permissive hearing, must ultimately point out for Johnny that he must take certain prescribed courses whether he wants to or not. Thus, one role of the adviser is to maintain the school structure. A foreman, counseling one of his men, cannot permit him to come and go on the job whenever he wishes. A teacher cannot permit a student client to avoid handing in class work. These are limits defined by the *role of authority* which these people have also.

In situations which make it necessary for the counselor to take dual roles, the use of the "coat analogy" is often helpful. The following is an example of how it may be used:

> C: Well, Jack, before we start I want to clarify my role with you. You might say I wear two coats around here—my teacher's coat and my counselor's coat. When I wear my teacher's coat, I have to be evaluating and judging to a certain degree in order to state your progress as a student. When I see you personally, however, in a relationship such as this, I am wearing my counselor's coat. This means that you can feel free to talk about anything you like and I won't hold it against you or make judgments about you. O.K.?

Procedural or process limits. If counseling is to be successful, the client must accept the nature of the process. In the first place, he must accept his *responsibility* for carrying on the major share of the interview. There are certain things he must know if he is to utilize the process most effectively. Ingham and Love (152, pg. 79–81) suggest six basic process values which must be conveyed to the client in the early structuring remarks and through basic attitudes.

(1) ". . . *that it is appropriate and good to investigate ourselves.*" This means facing his disturbing problems as much and as fast as he is comfortably able. This value suggests that there are causes of his difficulties which can be known and understood.

(2) ". . . *that it is better to investigate than to blame.*" This approach conveys the idea that there is a difference between a "bad" person and the "bad" act. The counselor stresses that he is trying to understand, not blame him. Thus, he will be better able to accept what he discovers within himself.

(3) *"to regard emotion as a real and important thing. . . ."* This value stresses the idea that emotions and their free expression are important realities and not signs of weakness.

(4) ". . . *that there must be relatively complete freedom of expression.*" The idea emphasized here is that the emotional importance of a topic, not its social acceptability, is the criterion of topic choice. This means that swearing, sex topics, and unconventional ideas are acceptable.

(5) *"the use of investigation of the past in developing an understanding of the present. . . ."* This is a common value among counselors and therapists, although they differ as to how much stress should be placed on past experiences and how much the client should be urged to explore them.

(6) A series of process *values centering about the client's present view of his world* are often mentioned in structuring. These are his capacity for human relationships, his own individual importance, and his own life values and morals as a basis for further changes through counseling.

Structuring process values. It should be emphasized that all of the aforementioned process values need not be made explicit. Clients have differing needs for explanations about how counseling proceeds. Generally, the counselor lets the client bring up his own topics and as it becomes apparent that he has misconceptions, or feels bewildered, helpless, or dissatisfied with this new experience, the counselor aids him through structuring. The counselor should start counseling on grounds familiar to the client and get him involved in the main job of counseling as quickly and comfortably as possible.

A second important use of structuring as a means of describing the process comes in the *handling of direct requests for advice.* In general, the authors recommend reflecting the feeling underlying this request first. This often allows the client to continue and to see his dependency needs as a problem. It is often necessary, however, actually to define this limit, as given by the following example:

> Cl: Can't we do something about this? The tension is really getting me. Can you tell me what to do? It might help both of us.
>
> C: I can understand how desperately you feel; but we have found that there are certain answers that only the individual can give himself. By working together I think that we can arrive at some answers for you.

Unfortunately, it is easy to give the client a feeling of getting the "brush-off" with a response like this. The anxious, dependent client tends to miss the structuring and reassuring intent of the counselor's response and may interpret it as, "So you are another one who doesn't want to help me."

A third use of process structuring is to present to the client the philosophy underlying the method of counseling. Porter (237, pg. 60) gives a good example of this method:

> *Counselor:* "I don't believe I know much about why you are here. The Dean mentioned you some time ago, but I know very little about it."
> *Frank:* "Well, the Dean and Professor R. wanted me to see you. They said you were a good psychologist, and that if you studied me you might be able to diagnose my adjustment. They think I'm not getting along very well and if you diagnosed what was the matter, you would be able to help me."
> *Counselor:* "They think you need some help, and you are trying to do what they wish?"

Frank: "Well, they say I'm not doing as well as I should, and if you studied me, you could say why."

Counselor: "Well, now I'll tell you, Frank, I really haven't had much luck helping students with problems that the Deans think they have. I don't know whether I can be of help to you along that line or not. When a student is concerned about some problem that *he* thinks he has, then frequently we can work out something together, but otherwise, I don't believe I get very far. I wonder, quite aside from what the Dean thinks about you, whether you feel there is anything about your situation that is causing you concern?"

Frank: "Well, I don't know—I suppose I don't live up to my ability."

Counselor: "That is something you feel a little concerned about?"

Frank: "Yes, I don't know, I guess I procrastinate; I just don't get things done on time. I don't see why. I've thought about that a lot and tried to analyze it but I don't seem to have helped it."

Counselor: "So you feel you really do procrastinate, and that you've been unable to do anything about it."

Timing of Structuring

A cardinal principle is that structuring is a continuous process; although the specific bits of content must be given at the right times. With some clients who demand more structure or seem to be confused, formal structuring of the process must necessarily come early. With others, the formal structuring must come later when attempts to shift the "locus of evaluation" to the counselor are made. With other clients who seem to take to the process easily, a very minimum of formal structuring is necessary in the beginning. In fact, if too many structuring remarks preface counseling, the client may interpret and resist them as ultimatums. Most sophisticated clients expect that the structure will grow out of the relationship rather than be dictated to them in a formal, instructional manner.

Additional structuring is done from time to time during the course of counseling when the client strays too far from the counselor's conception of the direction in which it should go or if the client seems confused about the goals or process.

From this presentation the reader may rightly infer that structuring is a controversial issue in counseling practice. Some writers emphasize the value of the technique while others minimize its value and stress its limitations. We have attempted to canvass and present sides of the current views so the counselor can develop the style most effective for him.

SILENCE AS A TECHNIQUE

It may seem strange, at first glance, to give prominence to silence as a technique of counseling. It is our conviction, however, that therapeutic silence is a technique which must be learned. Perhaps this is so, because the ethics of social conversation in our culture discourage silence. Hence, we have learned to become uncomfortable with silences and to regard long pauses as synonymous with a social vacuum. Beginning counselors, perhaps, often feel that when pauses are long they are not doing enough for the client.

The Meaning and Handling of Client Silence

In evaluating the significance of a pause, the time of its occurrence and whether it was initiated by client or counselor are significant. A long pause initiated by the client early in the initial interview conveys a different meaning to the counselor from one occurring later in the process. Pauses made by the client early in the interview may reflect embarrassment or resistance. As the counseling progresses, silence gradually comes to be a vibrant communicative medium for support, emotional expression, and thought.

In addition, it should be emphasized that counseling interviews are characterized by pauses of varying lengths from a few seconds to several minutes. It is difficult to assess the meaning of all pauses and no attempt is made here to catalog these possibilities. The following are offered merely as suggestions for interpreting and handling interview silences initiated by either counselor or client.

Any discussion of silence requires that recognition be given to two types: Negative or rejecting, and positive or accepting. Socially, we often use the "silent treatment" as a form of rejection, defiance, or condemnation. In social situations, when we argue with a person we are saying in effect that we respect him enough to want to change him. The negative silent treatment, however, says coldly in effect that the other person is not even worth talking to. Unfortunately, before a proper counseling relationship is established, it is possible for a client to interpret early silence in the interview as being this negative or rejecting type. This is true particularly when the client is still afraid of what the counselor is thinking about him. Appropriate discussion for building rapport and application of acceptance techniques frequently have a reassuring effect so that the client feels he does not have to impress the counselor.

A second meaning of silence is that the client or counselor has reached the end of an idea and is merely wondering what to say next. An extended pause may mean, also, that both have lost their way temporarily and that the interview has become confusing to both. The client may realize also that he has come to the end of the conversational period and must get down to work. Characteristically, there is an extended silence before getting down to serious work. The counselor can help the client over this hump by saying something like, "It is sort of hard to get down to serious business." The counselor's silence points up dramatically the transparency of small talk in later interviews. If the pause is of this "thought-collecting" type, it is considered wise not to interrupt. Tindall and Robinson (305) found in study-improvement interviews that this type of contemplative silence accounted for half the pauses.

A third meaning of silence is that of hostility-motivated resistance or anxiety-motivated embarrassment. This is true particularly when the client has been called for or sent in. At first, the client may be waiting cautiously for the counselor to make all the first moves and may answer or comment in short words or phrases followed by a long expectant pause.

The pause with a fourth meaning may be the signal that the client is experiencing some particularly painful feeling which he is not ready to verbalize; whereas consciously, he may want to express the feeling desperately. The counselor may say something like, "It is all right if you want to wait until words come along," or "It seems hard to say what you want at times, doesn't it?" Without pushing the client, the counselor might say, "Perhaps if you gave me some hint where your thoughts are moving, maybe I can help you put them into words." One of us has facilitated expression in this type of client by handing him a pencil and paper without comment so that he can write what he wants to say as a starter.

In the resistive or "foot-dragging" type of silence the participants may appear to be engaging in a contest to see who can outwait the other, like children trying to stare one another down. This may be due to a preconceived notion of counseling in which the client expects the counselor to ask questions, or has a cautious "wait and see" attitude. This silent response may indicate to the counselor that there is a need for structuring or for a brief exploration of some case history items to get the client talking. The counselor may provoke the hostility-motivated client to talk by making a disarming reflection, "You don't feel like talking just now, do you?" Another way is to ask him to interpret his silence, "What do you think has brought this about?" However, the client may consider that the counselor who takes the attitude of, "Well, I'll wait until you decide to talk," or, who pauses too long, is rejecting him.

If shyness seems to be the difficulty, it might be overcome if the counselor starts with some items from the client's life history, for example, "Here we've spent quite a bit of time together and you haven't mentioned your mother (pause)."

A fifth meaning of silence might be labelled as "anticipatory," wherein the client pauses expecting something from the counselor—some reassurance, information, or interpretation. Tindall and Robinson (305) found that counselors were quite sensitive in assessing and responding appropriately to this type of pause.

A sixth meaning of a client's pausing is that he may be thinking over what he has just said. In this case interruption of the pause may be inappropriate since it might destroy the client's train of thought and may throw the interview off the client's main theme.

Finally, a pause may mean that the client is merely recovering from the fatigue of a previous emotional expression. Here again, quiet acceptance of the silence is probably the best approach.

The problem for the counselor in the preceding illustrations might be simply stated as follows: Shall I interrupt the pause or shall I wait and let the client go on? In general, our view is to let the client assume responsibility for going on when he was responsible for pausing originally. This avoids interfering with a forward-moving activity. Yet, the counselor must be alert to those situations in which it seems best to support the client over rough places rather than to force him to face his problems, feelings, and responsibilities before he is ready. Problems of handling the negative silence are treated in the following chapter under "resistance" which will be defined and illustrated.

Values of Counselor Silence

It is one of our basic assumptions that silence of the positive and accepting type is a most promising counseling technique. The counselor's silence forces the client to talk. Similarly, being in the presence of another silent person often moves the client's attention to the task at hand—his problems. Silence on the part of the counselor then can have the value of focusing responsibility on the client.

A second value, emphasized from research with the Rorschach, indicates that introversive persons may be deeply creative individuals, with rich inner lives. They should not necessarily be seen as people inferior to the more socially-valued extroverted individual. In counseling, the client discovers that he can be a silent person and still be liked. Perhaps it is this acceptance of silence in the client which gives the less articulate person a feeling of worth and thereby helps the individual to accept himself for what he is. By feeling accepted as a shy and quiet person he is able then to experience this same attitude toward himself. The following case comments by Rogers suggest the therapeutic value of silence.

> I have just completed the strangest counseling case I've ever had. I think you might be interested in it.
>
> Joan was one of my very first clients when I started counseling one half-day each week at the local high school. She told the girls' adviser, "I feel so shy I couldn't even tell her what my problem is. Will you tell her for me?" So the adviser told me before I saw Joan that she worried about having no friends. The adviser added that she had noticed that Joan seemed always to be so alone.
>
> The first time I saw Joan she talked a little about her problem and quite a bit about her parents of whom she seemed to be quite fond. There were, however, long pauses. The next four interviews could be recorded verbatim on this small piece of paper. By the middle of November Joan remarked that "things are going pretty good." No elaboration on that. Meanwhile the adviser commented that the teachers had noticed that Joan was now smiling a friendly greeting when they met her in the halls. This was unheard of before. However, the adviser had seen little of Joan and could say nothing of her contacts with other students. In December there was one interview during which Joan talked freely; the others were characterized by silence while she sat, apparently in deep thought, occasionally looking

> up with a grin. More silence through the next two and one-half months. Then I received word that she had been elected "woman of the month" by the girls of the high school! The basis for that election is always sportsmanship and popularity with other girls. At the same time I got a message from Joan, "I don't think I need to see you any more." No, apparently she doesn't, but why? What happened in those hours of silence? My faith in the capacity of the client was sorely tested. I'm glad it did not waver (249, pp. 158–159).

Apparently the therapeutic value of spending time with someone who understood her and who had faith in her ability to solve her problem was helpful even though little was said.

A third value of the counselor pause or silence is that, after remaining silent for a long time, following a significant expression of feeling, allows the client to think and to come up with a profound insight. Had the counselor forced continued exploration, or verbalized too much, the insight might not have followed. The client often uses silence to delve deeply into his feelings, to struggle with alternative courses of action, or to weigh a decision. He wants to feel that the counselor approves of his doing this, and that he is not letting the counselor down by this behavior. In fact, one extreme style of therapy, called the silent interview method, consists almost entirely of this nonverbal type of communication wherein the therapist conveys to the client his understanding that he is struggling with deep, difficult feelings. Hence, one value of silence is that it forces depth of client penetration into his own feelings.

A fourth value of counselor silence is that it reduces the pace of the interview. Often the counselor senses that the client is rushing, or that he feels himself compelled to push too hard. He can reduce the intensity and pace to a more tolerable level for both participants by making the pauses longer. The counselor says in effect, "We are not in a hurry; take it easy." Thus, counselor silence in later interviews tends to have a beneficially calming effect on the client.

In the only available study of counselor use of pauses, Tindall and Robinson (305) classified the pauses of the counselor, giving educational skills counseling, into three types: deliberate (for emphasis), organizational (for transitions), and natural termination (to close counseling). Organizational pauses, in the vast majority of cases, helped most to clarify the subject discussed and prepared the way for information to be given by the counselor. Clients generally responded, only after a deliberate or natural terminal pause. It is, however, apparent from Tindall's and Robinson's study that pauses have many different meanings to clients.

Difficulties in Using Silence Techniques

In the training of counseling psychologists, we have found that it has been necessary to teach toleration of client silence without embarrassment.

To the untried therapist a minute of silence seems like an hour. He has, consequently, an overwhelming desire to interrupt the client's thought. Porter (237) suggests that one of the errors of reflection is that of completing sentences for the client. Many clients find it difficult to state what they mean precisely without fumbling for words. Therefore, a very common error that inexperienced counselors make is to put words into the client's mouth, or in some way to take the conversational initiative away from the client.

One of the most difficult aspects of using the silence technique is keeping silent when the client wants to talk. A greater proportion of client talk, however, is not necessarily an indicator of a more effective working relationship. Carnes and Robinson (58) analyzed 353 discussion units from four types of counseling interviews. They also concluded that ". . . a high talk ratio is not necessary to a good working relationship but it is good insurance" (58, 639).

The relationships between insight and talk ratio in the above study were inconclusive, although with study skill interviews, insight tended to be associated with low frequency of client talk. In other words, when the counselor explained things in study-skill interviews, the client apparently gained more insight than he did if he, himself, talked. For therapeutic problems, Carnes and Robinson found that it was not the amount of client talk per se which was related to insight; but it was the relative amount of client talk within the framework of a particular counseling style. In other words, keeping silent and just getting the client to talk more will not necessarily lead to more insight.

The most definitive relationship in the Carnes and Robinson study cited above was found between client talk and amount of client responsibility assumed for discussion unit progress. (The discussion unit is the verbal exchange between client and counselor on a discrete subject.) When clients felt primarily responsible for interview progress they talked more. It is interesting to note also that Carnes and Robinson found that the stronger the counselor's lead, the less the client talk. The general conclusions of Carnes and Robinson's study are that the causal relationships between desired interview outcomes and amount of client talk are not clear, and that it is not possible, therefore, to use the amount of client talk as a measure of counseling effectiveness.

LEADING TECHNIQUES

General Principles and Values of Leads

The term "lead" is used with two meanings. One usage refers to the extent to which the counselor is ahead or behind the client's thinking, and the extent to which the counselor directs the client's thinking or "pushes" the client into accepting the counselor's remark (57). Bugental (46) uses the term "impact" to describe the counselor's influence on the client and the interviewing process. Counselor questions, for example, would have a high impact compared to the accepting vocalization "mm." Silence would have a lower impact or lead.

Robinson (247) uses "lead" in a different, but related, sense. Robinson construes leading in counseling to mean "a teamlike working together in which the counselor's remarks seem to the client to state the next point he is ready to accept" (247, pg. 66). In addition, Robinson compares leading to the act of passing a football down the field so that the receiver's path passes the flight path of the ball at the same time. All techniques can be rated according to degree of lead involved; but in the present discussion the topic will be limited to general leading as a technique by itself.

The value of leading is that the counselor is enabled to retain or delegate varying amounts of responsibility for counselor-client talk and to generate client thought.

Using Leads

Three general usages of leading are recommended. One principle is to lead *only as much as the client can tolerate* at his present level of ability and understanding. Enough old material must be mentioned to form a bridge of understanding to the next new idea. Robinson (247) uses a ladder analogy to indicate that the counselor is not more than one rung ahead of the client, hence, close to his needs and interests. A lead too far ahead of the client generally pushes the outer-defense system severely and arouses resistance to counseling. Similarly, too little lead may annoy clients who feel that the counselor should carry more of the responsibility for the interview talk.

The second general principle of leading is to *vary the lead*. The amount of lead changes from topic to topic or within a discussion unit so as to match the pace and lead of the client.

A third principle is *to start the counseling process with little lead*. For example, begin the counseling process with relationship techniques which have little lead weighting until the relationship is well established. Then increase the lead as needed, with information and interpretation, which are useful in developing insight.

The *indirect lead* may be used to help the client elaborate upon a topic of his choice. Examples are, "Would you explain that a little more?" "How do you mean that?" This type of lead is used also in the form of general questions to start an exploration such as, "What would you like to talk about today?" "Is there anything more you would like to discuss?"

The *direct lead* indicates the area of discussion desired from the client and is akin to the probing techniques discussed in Chapter 5. Examples of the direct leads are: "Tell me more about your father"; "Suppose we explore more fully the idea of teaching"; "What do you think that means?" Asking the client a question, whether rhetorical or for information, is a means of shifting responsibility to the client. Conversely, if the client asks many questions of the counselor it may indicate more than a desire for information or interpretation; it may mean he is expressing his need to shift responsibility to the counselor.

Interpretive techniques which are described in Chapter 8 employ various degrees of lead. Leading utilizes Robinson's (247) principle of moving ahead of the client just enough to stimulate his therapeutic growth. The concept of lead is introduced in this chapter, however, to emphasize that some degree of lead is always present in the relationship techniques which the counselor uses. Even silence is a leading technique since lack of verbal response on the counselor's part causes the client to make a judgment about the significance of the material he has just presented. Thus the counselor, through his manipulation of the pauses, often is responsible for the direction of the interview.

REASSURANCE METHODS

Nature and Values of Reassurance

One relationship technique which has wide utility for conveying support is reassurance. In Chapter 6 the concept of support was introduced as a necessary ingredient of the counseling and psychotherapeutic relationship. The nature of reassurance is essentially a type of reward which has a reinforcing effect on behavior and builds expectancies for future rewards. The counselor says directly, or in effect, that, "You are a capable person; you can be consistent; you can be reasonable; you can be organized; you can feel better; you can solve this problem."

Reassurance also is a process of fitting counseling to the client's present belief system. Reassurance encourages exploration of new ideas or trying out different behaviors. In this capacity reassurance is a temporary expedient to keep the client in the relationship. Kelly (165) compares reassurance to the proverbial string and baling wire which is used to hold structures together until more solid or productive work can be done. Reassurance also prevents fragmentation of the client's ideas even though eventually he may want to change his maladaptive responses.

A second value of reassurance is the means it provides to reduce anxiety and insecurity directly. Although anxiety in the proper amount is a positive motivating force to keep the person in counseling, and is a useful guide to indicate where the trouble lies, excess amounts interfere with the therapeutic process. Reassurance tends to keep the anxiety generated by the counseling process itself under control by assuring the client that he doesn't have to explore his feelings too fast. This use of reassurance is particularly valuable in controlling anxiety outside the relationship, for example, over weekends and vacations.

A third value of reassurance is the reinforcing effect it has on new patterns of behavior. It is often difficult to launch a new course of action, even after significant insights have been achieved. The client often feels discouragement, leading to loss of confidence, which arises from small failures to make his planned adjustments. An example is the student who is attempting to improve his failing grades. Reassurance in the form of praise for his attempts, assurances that he will pull through the temporary setbacks, and the encouragement of confident attitudes generally help him to retain or regain his new behaviors.

Reassurance is thus a form of expressing implied counselor value, a form of promising improvement which we feel is wholly consistent with a eclectic frame of reference that places value on the counselor's honest expression of his own feelings as well as those of the client. This expression of counselor feelings must be consonant with client welfare, however. It may be seen from this point of view that permissiveness must be double-tracked, for client and counselor. We feel that the counselor's failure to express reassurance when he honestly feels it is a form of therapeutic dishonesty. A counseling relationship which does not allow any expression of his feeling puts the counselor in a form of emotional straight-jacket which may be harmful to the relationship.

Use of Reassurance

The *approval or acquiescence remark* is one means of reassurance. Its purpose is to give the client some feeling of security about the ideas or feelings he is expressing. Expressing approval of the client's remarks tends to have a reinforcing effect also. An example is:

> Cl: It seems that people resent being critized or told they are wrong.
> C: That's right; a very interesting observation and a good rule about personality.

This technique goes beyond acceptance; it is actual agreement with the client. Though generally reassuring, it may be hazardous, because the client may feel he cannot change his position without admitting error. Thus, the approval technique tends to have the unfortunate effect of rigidifying the client's thinking.

The counselor who suggests that there are other ways of thinking and acting builds expectations of success in his client. For example, the counselor assures his client that he can change himself and that counseling can be an effective means to help him change.

Prediction of outcomes is a phrase used by Kelly (165) to describe the consequences of counseling or psychotherapy over the following few days.

Avoiding sweeping predictions, the counselor makes a limited forecast about how the client is likely to feel between conferences. An example is, "We've been talking about your problems in a more intensive fashion. You will probably find that you will be more uncomfortable and moody the next few days. Don't be alarmed, because this is part of the process. You will be able to handle it all right."

Postdiction of outcomes is a related reassuring technique, also described by Kelly. An example is, "It is my guess that during the last few days things have been tougher for you to handle. We opened up many sensitive areas last time which may have upset you during the week. Is this correct?" Another example is, "Perhaps you were disturbed by our session last time; but this is a normal part of the process." The reassuring value of such comments comes from the impression the client gets that his behavior makes sense to the counselor and is predictable.

The *interview conditions* tend to be reassuring. As we pointed out in our earlier discussion of support, it is the acceptance, structured limits, attention, affectional warmth, and outward signs of friendship in the counselor which have a powerful reassuring effect. This is true particularly with children whose behaviors can often be drastically changed through the reassuring effect of emotional support. Thus, meeting specific emotional needs of the client is one of the key uses of reassurance.

Factual reassurance can be given to the client who feels his problem is unique. When he knows that many other people suffer from the same feelings his fearful bewilderment may subside. Related to this point is the reassurance that his problem has a solution and that the cause of his difficulty is known. Thus, a person can tolerate anxiety and annoying symptoms when he knows that they are, very likely, temporary reactions to his basic problem. He can also feel reassured that he can reach specific objectives, such as achieving an educational goal, formulating a vocational plan, getting better grades, or saving his marriage.

Often, the counselor's reassurance of his client that he does not have to feel ashamed, guilty, or alarmed about his problem helps. He can feel that the problem does not have to be viewed moralistically, but as a personal problem to be solved in an objective way.

Reassurance that the best of help available to science will be given to him is an often successful means that the counselor can employ to reduce his client's anxiety about the efficacy of treatment. Sharing diagnostic and prognostic formulations with the client when they are favorable is a very convincing type of reassurance.

Reinstating defenses is another psychotherapeutic "first-aid" method. The client may be using a defense, such as vigorous sarcasm, to handle his hostilities. In the course of counseling the client sees the inappropriateness of his extra-punitive tendencies; but he has not worked them through sufficiently. So, he develops incapacitating migraine headaches which appear to be manifestations of intrapunitive hostility. The client is better off if he is "given back" his former defensive mechanisms through being encouraged to express his hostilities more outwardly—the social consequences of which are less severe than the personal consequences of repressed hostility.

Limitations and Cautions

This section is not intended to discourage the student from utilizing reassurance techniques. However, these limitations are mentioned in the following paragraphs in order to acquaint the student with the fact that reassurance is a two-edged sword in many ways. It can be most helpful when utilized properly in the situations described, and most detrimental when used indiscriminately.

Reassurance is a technique which is particularly vulnerable to misfiring. Reassurance is so easy to use that there is a temptation to be over-liberal. It is so common a vehicle in everyday human relationships that it may be stated fairly that reassurance is much overused in counseling. A frequent misuse of reassurance is in the false concealment of the true nature of a serious situation. This is an ethical problem as well as a procedural concern.

Reassurance is used crudely in the approach that "everything will come out in the wash." The "just relax, everything will come out all right" attitude and the old aphorisms, such as "every cloud has a silver lining" serve only to create resentment in clients.

Reassurance might be interpreted by a very disturbed person as artificial and insincere sympathy. Reassurance, at best, is a temporary expedient and the counselor must be reconciled to the slowing of progress if he uses it. There is the obvious limitation that the whole relationship can be put in jeopardy because subsequent events did not bear out the optimistic predictions of the counselor.

Reassurance has the additional liability of promoting a dependency relationship between client and counselor. The periodic need for reassurance is a type of substitute satisfaction for real accomplishment. The responses reinforced by the reassurance tend to become fixed learnings and the client feels a strong need to get his reassurance from this particular person. Some clients use the reassurance as an excuse not to change their behavior.

If the client interprets reassurance as agreement, he may limit himself in the sense that he will feel guilty about changing his behavior or experimenting with new methods of viewing his problem. In other words, he may feel trapped in his present efforts and may think that he can't find any solutions to his problems.

It has been stated earlier that reassurance is most valuable in supporting the anxious, distressed client. It can be grossly misused if given to the client who is already overly aggressive or self-confident. This type of client needs discouragement of his often insensitive, rigid, ego-centric behavior rather than support for it.

The effective termination of counseling is as important for counseling success as is the establishment of rapport in the initial phase. How neatly the counselor "settles his dust" or "ties up his package" determines the ease with which the client can assume complete responsibility for himself and the extent to which his progress can be consolidated.

Since the problems and procedures for closing interviews and changing discussion units during the counseling process are related to techniques for terminating the process, these are considered together in the following discussion. We have grouped them under the general category of termination techniques.

Terminating a Discussion Unit

A discussion unit can be closed by the summary reflection described earlier wherein the counselor ties together the loose ends of several related ideas. The net effect of this summary is to give a feeling of closure and progress to the client, whereupon he generally proceeds to another topic. The counselor must sense when the client is ready for such a summary, knowing that its application will result in a change of topic.

A second device for ending the discussion unit is the *capping technique*.[1] This consists of shutting off the flow of talk or feeling in such a way that the client does not stop talking altogether, delay over-all progress too much or feel rejected. Frequently, the counselor senses that the more the person delves into his feelings the more uncomfortable he becomes, or the more dissociated he seems to get. When the counselor feels that the client's defenses are not sufficiently functional to protect himself he helps the client regain his defensive armor through capping techniques. He does this with the hope that it is a temporary expedient, and that the client will be more ready to attack the conflict at a later time.

Capping techniques consist of *changing the subject* to something less intense yet still propelling the interview forward. The subject can be changed back to a topic previously discussed, the original symptoms, or a new and less-loaded topic. Reducing the *length of counselor lead* and the general *pace* of the interview often reduces the client's discomfort, resistance, or undesired feelings toward the counselor. The counselor can help to decelerate the pace by *pausing* longer and more frequently. In order to cap exploration which has become too intense, he can reduce the frequency of the interviews. It is well known in counseling and psychotherapeutic prac-

---

[1] A term used by Professor Robert A. Good in comparing emotional expression to an oil gusher. The consequent tightening of expression is described as "capping."

tice that the intensity of the relationship varies directly with the frequency of interviews per week. The counselor, for example, may suggest meeting every two weeks instead of once a week. Sometimes reassurance that there is plenty of time to work through the problems helps to take feelings of pressure off the client. Increasing the amount of *counselor talk* has a "shutting off" effect on client communication, thus preventing his delving deeper into his problems.

There may be times, also, when the quality of the relationship is such that the counselor can use *direct interpretation* to terminate a topic. An example is, "You are getting quite disturbed about this. Suppose we drop it for a while and go on about your plans after graduation." The client may need further explanation for changing the subject and reassurance that he can come back to this topic at a later time.

Terminating an Interview

The counseling literature contains very little information about the nature of skills for terminating an interview. Yet most counselors would agree that it is important that the interview be drawn to a definite close and not be left hanging in mid-air, with the client feeling that nothing has been accomplished. Beginning counselors report that ending an interview is one of the most difficult tasks they face.

Reference to time limits is one natural way to remind the client that the hour is up. No matter what the length of the interview, it is important that the counselor inform the client at the beginning of the interview that he has a fixed length of time. In a clinical setting a forty-five- or fifty-minute period is usually standard. In other settings, such as public schools, a much shorter time may be more appropriate. Interview time is a matter of agency policy, case load, and the purpose of the interview.

Generally, it is felt that a minimum of forty-five minutes is needed to deal with a client's most pressing problems. This allows the client a few minutes for "warmup" wherein he moves slowly into the main content of the interview and picks up the loose threads from the preceding session and gives him a few minutes at the end of the hour to "pull himself together." This is especially necessary after a therapeutic counseling session which delved deeply into feelings. It is desirable to help the client leave in a comfortable emotional state.

In school counseling, however, time and case load pressures often force the problem to be stated and analyzed in interviews of ten or fifteen minutes. In any case, as long as the time limit is set, the successful conclusion of the interview can be more assured. At the end of the interview, for example, the time limit can again be brought up by such a statement as, "Our time is nearly up; when would you like to come back again?" or "Well, that does it for today" or "It seems we've reached the end of the hour." This provides an easy transition to the calendar, the door, or the receptionist.

Summarizing is a second means of terminating the interview. This can be done by the counselor, the client, or as a collaborative act. When the counselor sees that the interview is drawing short he can summarize the essential factors of the interview himself. Again, the terminal reflection technique can be used if the counselor is disposed to summarizing the essential feelings which have been expressed by the client during the interview. A topical summary to reflect the major content of the interview would be in order also.

From the counseling literature it appears that client summaries are used widely. The counselor asks the client for a summarization of key feelings and ideas as follows: "Tell me how you think the situation looks now," or "Now suppose you tell me what you think you have accomplished in this interview."

The counselor usually precedes the collaborative summary with such a phrase as, "Suppose now we take a look at what we have done today. As I see it, we have said. . . . Perhaps you could state how you have seen it."

Reference to the future is a third and graceful way for the counselor to terminate an interview; but at the same time, an indication of his desire to maintain the relationship is made by the use of a statement which would refer to subsequent meetings with the client. Such a statement would be as follows: "I am sorry our time is about up today. When would you like to come in again?" or "Would you like to make it at the same time next week?" or "I have Thursday at three and Friday at two open. Which would you prefer?" It is important to end with a warm positive tone following the setting of the exact date and time with a parting phrase such as, "Fine, I'll be expecting you then at two next Friday," rather than a doubtful, "Then you'll come next week at two?"

Fourthly, *standing up* is frequently a persuasive technique for ending the interview. With particularly difficult clients, such as obsessive-compulsive people who do not wish to terminate the contact, it may be necessary for the counselor to stand up as a more blunt means of indicating that the interview is finished. This can be done gracefully at a "low point" before the client has a chance to delve into another topic of conversation. In more formal situations, especially with adults and at the end of first interviews, the offering of the hand as a parting gesture is helpful too.

Subtle gestures are a fifth category of cues to close the interview. While most counseling contacts close naturally at the fixed time, some clients continue to chat on. The counselor should feel free to utilize certain gestures to indicate that the interview is to be terminated and that it is time for the client to depart. For example the counselor might put his hands on his knees as if to rise, glance at his watch or desk clock, and lean forward. It should be mentioned that the counselor should not use the common devices of fidgeting, distractibility, irritability, and shuffling desk papers to cue clients that the hour is up.

Ushering the client to the door and opening it for him aids a graceful and prompt departure. Ordinary courtesy demands that the counselor rise with the client and walk to the door with him. This makes it much easier for the client to leave than it would be if the counselor left the whole burden for terminating the interview upon the client.

Summary notes are a sixth useful aid to terminating interviews. In certain types of counseling where decisions are being made, some counselors find it useful to jot down notes while the interview is in process. They may have another sheet with carbon between so that at the end of the interview the client is handed the carbon of the counselor's notes. This is especially important in vocational planning where data are profuse and significant. Many counselors feel that the client will remember the interview if they make a concrete summary of the salient features of the interview. Other counselors encourage the client to make his own notes, thus encouraging independent action in the client.

The *"homework"* or *"prescription" method* can be utilized as a terminating device. Herzberg (143) suggests the use of the "social task"—doing something like joining a folk-dance group before the next interview. Sullivan (295) also suggests giving the client something to do between interviews. Examples would be, "Before you leave I'd like to suggest a little 'homework' . . ." or "I wonder if you could give some thought to these questions which have arisen in our conversation today (mention items)."

Related to the activity approach is the *arrangement for tests* or *occupational reading* if the problem is primarily educational or vocational. This is another natural way to end the interview. It should be stressed that endings are arrived at cooperatively and by counselor suggestion; they are not coerced.

It is important that the interview end on a note of positive planning in that the client knows exactly what he is going to do. If the counselor is ambiguous about plans or expectations concerning the client, he may arouse insecurity and consequent anxiety in him.

One of the rules in terminating an interview is to start *tapering off* in intensity a few minutes before the scheduled end. A counselor should never let a client leave without allowing him to pull himself together again and to reduce the feelings stirred up by the interview. Yet, this very condition makes it difficult for the client to leave. He tends to relax when he feels the pressure is off. The client often becomes very spontaneous and he will try to detain the counselor with new and interesting material. The counselor can hold to his structure or he can use the "five-minutes-more" technique. This technique is ushered in as follows: "I have a few minutes between interviews. I'll share them with you. You may have five minutes more if you wish. Then we will have to close for today."

The counselor may decide that the material coming out is so significant that he may decide to use the "extra hour" device if he by chance has the

next hour free. He says, "I have this next hour free; I gather this is a significant area for you. Suppose we take more time, then, while the matter is
still hot." This hour may be extremely productive since the usual defenses
may not be prepared for it. The client is likely, therefore, to be exceedingly
spontaneous. It is our experience that material often comes out in this hour
which very likely would not arise in interviews for which the client is more
"set."

One danger of the "extra hour" technique should be mentioned. Once an
extra hour has been given to a manipulative client, he may try to get extra
hours again and again. His approach would be "You helped me then—why
don't you again?" It may also result in the client remaining superficial in
the first hours as his defenses get reset. In any case, this technique is useful
if used with discretion.

Regardless of the device used to end the interview and to get the client
out the door, the interview should end on a positive and friendly note. The
counselor should not adopt a cold, neutral attitude, in an effort, perhaps, to
avoid deciding for the client whether he will continue and when he will
return.

Techniques for terminating interviews, in summary, should be planned in
advance, and should be friendly, definite, and collaborative. These characteristics are necessary in order to help the client feel wanted, to know what
he has accomplished, to know what to do next, and to realize that he participated cooperatively with the counselor in solving his problems.

Case Termination

The problems. Practically speaking, no case is ever closed in the sense
that the problem is "solved." Effective counseling opens possibilities of
client growth which are never finished. Yet, there comes a time in the
process where either client or counselor feels that the client should be
placed completely on his own resources. How does the counselor tell when
closure has been reached? The client often gives cues that his expectations
of counseling have been satisfied or that he has hopes of reaching his goals
on his own efforts such as, "Well, I guess this answers my questions," or
"I feel much better about it now."

Generally, the counseling process tends to terminate spontaneously. A
series of elaborate studies of the counseling process indicate that client
responses tend to become more positive and self-directive toward the end of
counseling (269).

There are other cues which the counselor can use to effect closure. He
can watch for indices that the general goals of counseling have been accomplished. The client's goals might be insight and understanding of himself and his problems, an intellectual awareness of solution and direction to
the problem, diminution of such symptoms as anxiety, and most importantly

behavior improvement. The counselor must be wary, however, of the "hello-goodbye" or "flight into health" phenomena. Clients often experience feelings of euphoria and completion after an interview or two. They may feel that their problem is solved when their symptoms subside after a cathartic interview. They feel better and frequently wish to terminate counseling. Yet, the counselor realizes that no lasting insight has been achieved and that the client will be back as soon as another little decision or crisis upsets him.

A distinction must be made between termination of the process by the client and by the counselor. Clients terminate counseling for many reasons. There may be completion according to a structure and plan. They might stop because of a disruption caused by resistance, ignorance about counseling, trauma, impasse, time, finances, or a feeling that the counselor is no longer needed.

The question naturally arises as to why clients leave therapy rather than become addicted to it. In addition to the cost in time, and generally in money also, the client may experience pain and humiliation at having to face further aspects of his self-system. Or, in the successful case, the functions which were once located in the counselor are now the client's property. He no longer has a "need" for counseling since what he has learned in the process has now become part of himself and his way of life.

The counselor terminates counseling, in contrast, when he feels that the goals of counseling have been achieved, or when lack of progress does not warrant, in his opinion, the continuation of the relationship. Many counselors, once the problem is delimited, structure the time limits of the process in such a way that when this limit is reached closure proceedings are begun. For example, the counselor starts the closure by saying something like, "Well, here we are nearing the end of the term when we said we would try to finish off our counseling. Suppose we examine where we have been, where we are now, and our next steps." This method of terminating at fixed limits has great drawbacks and some danger in that the person may not be ready to terminate, or may be ready long before the structured limit. However, it is felt that the client's anxiety, which often accompanies lengthy counseling, is alleviated when he can anticipate the approximate time of closure.

Often the counselor's skill and patience are tried by the dependent client who resists assuming personal responsibility for his life. The counselor can only have faith in the client's capacity for and interest in personal growth. It is assumed here that lingering feelings of dependence upon, affection for, or resentment against the counselor, (to be defined as "transference" in the next chapter) have been resolved. These feelings may show in relatively short informational or supportive types of counseling too, if a client, lonely or dependent, simply cannot face the deprivation of the counseling relationship, even though his most pressing problems have been resolved. A useful procedure with this type of client is to space interviews in increasingly longer intervals prior to final closure.

Steps and methods of closure. The first step taken to close the interviews is called *verbal preparation*. The client is reminded of the time limits agreed upon in the initial interview. For example, "Well, this is our fourth and last interview. . . ." Statements of client growth as a lead to termination of contacts may be expressed as follows: "You seem to have achieved some important insights and some realistic plans; do you think you can go it alone from here?" Other examples are: "It seems we have come to a point where you can work this out by yourself," or "You seem to feel that you can carry on from here without further help from me. . . ."

The counselor should then work out a *final summary statement* with the counselee. This may be a general review of accomplishments, arrangements for referral or follow-up, or preparation of a brochure or written summary. An example of written summaries made during counseling on vocations is the "Life Planning" booklet described by Shostrom and Brammer (277). This brochure contains the client's tentative objectives with educational plans to match. Supporting data from occupational research, test results, and interview conclusions are often included. This step corresponds to Sullivan's "prescription of action" in his terminating technique (295). We prefer not to use the term "prescription" in this context; it is important, nevertheless, that the client knows what he is going to do next and that he leaves with clear notions about the goals, results, possible courses of action, and limitations of the interviews.

Another step the counselor may take is to leave the door open for possible *follow-ups*. This is especially necessary in short-term, highly structured interview series. Abruptness is avoided when the counselor can say something like, "Drop in to see me when you are around campus," or "When you try it alone for a while you may wish to drop in to review how things are going." It is debatable how much this type of "open-door" policy should be encouraged since it has possibilities of renewing the dependency of the client and of laying the counselor wide open for attempts to reconstitute the relationship. However, with a younger client in a school situation, the counselor may wish to establish a "standby" contact to observe his development or to give him further information. An interest inventory may be used in the case for example, "It is a good idea to take inventory of your developing interests occasionally. . . ." This type of statement generally has a reassuring effect on clients and permits continuous observation without an intensive relationship.

A variation on the third step is possible *referral*. If the counselor has gone as far as he felt capable of going, or if another type of therapist or agency is going to take responsibility for the relationship, referral technique is used. Here it is important that the counselor structure the nature of the referral in order to pave the way for easy transition to the new relationship without revealing the nature of that new relationship in advance. As indicated in Chapter 5, reasons for the referral should be discussed carefully with the client so he does not get the "run-around" feeling. The client must convince himself that the referral is necessary or helpful. If the counselor were to say, "I think you ought to see a psychiatrist about this," the client would be likely to be resistive or frightened. To avoid these possible negative responses the counselor might say, "Our psychiatrist might be able to help us on this problem. Would you care to make an appointment?" These same principles apply whether referral is to the school librarian, a social agency, the speech therapist, employment agency, or physician.

Another consideration the counselor should keep in mind in making referrals to outside persons is the desirability of mentioning two or three names, say of physicians, from which the client may choose. It is assumed, of course, that the counselor is familiar with the intake and eligibility policies and conditions of the agencies to which he refers clients, as well as the policies of his own institution regarding referral channels and procedures. Schools, for example, have definite channels established for handling relationships with social agencies, courts, and professional persons in private practice.

The fourth step is the *formal leave taking*. What was said about concluding the final phase of the individual interview applies here with emphasis upon parting with a cordial and confident tone. It should be recognized by the counselor that the steps just cited do not always unfold smoothly. The client may make several abortive attempts to operate alone with his newly discovered insights, only to be forced to return to the same or another counselor.

Before leaving this topic of termination the writers would like to examine Thorne's concepts of overtreatment and undertreatment (303). Thorne places the responsibility for determining the safety and appropriateness of termination squarely with the counselor. Some of the attitudes counselors have which tend, according to Thorne, to result in undertreatment are: "Therapeutic nihilism," in which the counselor has a pessimistic attitude that his counseling will not work with this client as a result of which he gives up; "diagnostic failures," wherein the counselor fails to find or deal adequately with pathological processes and so terminates counseling prematurely; "passive methods," with which a counselor fails to deal actively enough with client problems; "lack of confidence" in attempting to counsel difficult cases; "lenience" in not following up clients persistently, and "overwork" of the counselor from taking too many cases, which results in his rushing through appointments, or becoming stale in his therapeutic attitudes.

Though these dangers may be valid for certain cases, Thorne cautions that the counselor may err on the side of "overtreating" also. By this, he means that a counselor might carry the client beyond the point of ethical treatment, or beyond the point of his competence. Some overtreatment may result from the overconscientious attempt to be thorough, thus, perhaps, reinforcing the dependent client's need for constant support. However, a loose type of relationship over an extended period may have a prophylactic effect which would prevent further deterioration of the client's problem-solving ability. As in so many other areas of counseling methodology, the counselor must assess the situation, weigh the advantages and disadvantages of a course of action, and then use his best judgment.

SUMMARY

The techniques for implementing the basic principles of relationship in the preceding chapter have been classified into eight categories—rapport-building, reflecting feeling, accepting, structuring, pausing, leading, re-assuring, and terminating. Each method has its unique values as well as limitations for creating the optimal kind of relationship necessary for the development of insight and appropriate actions. In the next chapter some of the conditions which create difficulties in building and maintaining an optimum relationship and applying relationship techniques will be explored.

8.

Special Relationship Problems

The counselor may apply counseling techniques with all the wisdom and skill at his command, but he must recognize that certain phenomena indigenous to the counseling process occasionally limit his efforts. Transference, countertransference, and resistance are three conditions which may help or hinder the process, depending on how they are expressed and handled. These three terms are central to psychoanalytic technique. Since these concepts are so vitally significant for psychotherapy and of such considerable consequence for counseling, they will be elaborated in this chapter.

TRANSFERENCE

Nature and Origin of Transference

After examining the original writings of Freud and the elaborations of Fenichel, Fromm-Reichmann, Alexander, French, and others, it appears there are several meanings of the term "transference." In a broad sense, the term refers to any feelings expressed or felt by the client toward the therapist, whether a rational reaction to the personality of the therapist or the unconscious projection of earlier attitudes and stereotypes.

We favor the view of the existential therapists (198). The neurotic client does not really "transfer" his feelings about family members to the therapist. Instead, as May says, ". . . the neurotic is one who in certain areas never developed beyond the limited and restricted forms of experience characteristic of the infant. Hence in later years he perceives wife or therapist through the same restricted, distorted 'spectacles' as he perceived father or mother" (198, pg. 79). Hence, the problem of transference for the neurotic client is primarily one of relationship to events of the present and his perception of his present situation through the colored glasses of his past experience.

Psychoanalytically, transference means the process whereby client at-

209

titudes formerly expressed or felt toward another person important to the client are unconsciously "transferred" or projected to the counselor. For example, feelings of love, hate, ambivalence, or dependence at one time directed toward a parent are now irrationally repeated with the psychotherapist as the object.

The intensive conception of the transference process is called the "transference neurosis" by the psychoanalysts. Transference is a necessary component of the analytic process wherein the person transfers his intrapsychic conflicts into the interpersonal relationship between the therapist and client in such a way that it replicates the other neurotic relationship past and present. The analyst then uses the transference as a vehicle of therapy.

In the therapeutic use of the transference neurosis, the therapist does not view transference as a *problem,* but rather as a fortunate circumstance making the neurosis available in miniature. In existential terms, the transference feelings expressed by the client give the therapist valuable information on how he perceives and manipulates his world.

Sometimes the term transference is used as a synonym for relationship as in the phrase, "The transference was established early. . . ." We feel that this usage is too loose. In this sense, the psychotherapeutic relationship described in earlier chapters could be considered as a type of transference because of the mutual acceptance feelings which are present. An equally vague usage is to regard transference as any expression of feeling toward another person.

Rogers (249) states that transference feelings develop when the client perceives that the other person understands him better than he understands himself. The way of viewing transference, whether hostility or dependency, depends largely on the degree of threat involved.

We prefer to view transference as a concept midway between the classical Freudian view with emphasis on the past and the position that all feelings currently expressed toward the counselor are transference. In other words, transference is viewed as a type of projection of the client's past or present unresolved and unrecognized attitudes toward authority figures and love objects, toward the therapist, for example. This projection is done in such a way that the client responds to the therapist in a manner similar to the way he responds to other love objects. Clients build certain expectations of therapists and their roles through this transference process. The client may expect the therapist, for example, to be succorable and supporting; or he may expect him to be a punishing or controlling agent. In other words, transference is a term describing how the client construes the therapist and how the client behaves toward the therapist.

Intensive transference, commonly found in psychotherapy, is regarded as a type of relationship which goes beyond that considered desirable or optimal for counseling. A concept of degrees of transference relationship is illustrated in Figure 19. The client, in Figure 19, enters the counselor's

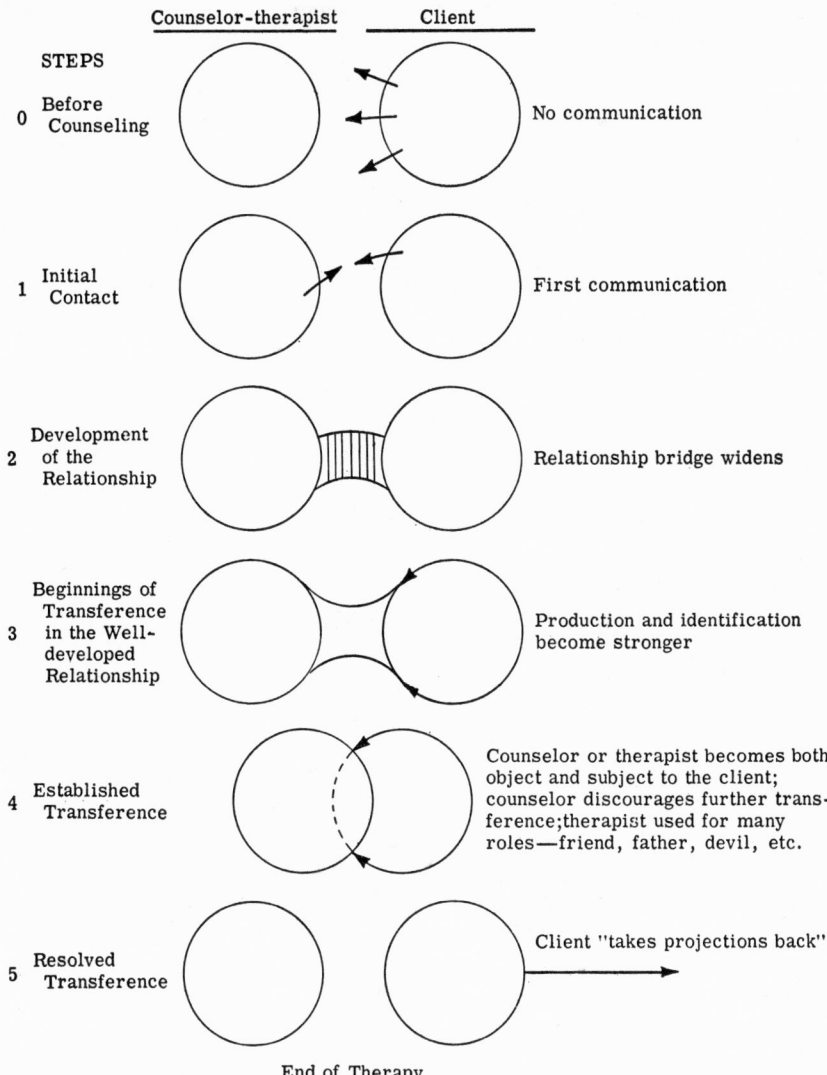

FIG. 19. Development and Resolution of the Transference Relationship.

presence with the usual mixed feelings people have as they meet strangers. Since counselors and therapists generally are cordial and emotionally warm, the relationship bridge begins to widen and client feeling flows more freely toward the counselor. At this point, the transference relationship begins. Clients with strong affection or dependency needs may project these so intensively at times that the client's perception of the counselor is grossly distorted. An extreme example of this idea is the unusual client who literally hugs or throws himself upon the psychotherapist. Often, clients with weak ego systems must "use" the therapist's ego and partake of his strength. In this sense, transference may be a necessary prelude to building the client's own ego strength.

Parenthetically, we believe that Step 4 of Figure 19 illustrates a fundamental distinction between counseling and psychotherapy. The counselor develops a close personal relationship with his client, but he does not encourage or allow strong transference feelings as does the psychotherapist.

The resolved or broken transference relationship is conceptualized in Figure 19 as a complete emotional detachment with the vectors of the client's feeling moving away from the counselor as a person and in the direction of investing feeling in other mature human relationships.

Transferences may be designated as positive or negative. A positive transference would be made by the client when he projected his feelings of affection or dependency to the counselor, perhaps perceiving him as a loving, helpful father. A negative transference would be made by the client when he projected his feelings of hostility and aggression. These transference feelings change form, sometimes quite suddenly. For example, a client may experience warm feelings toward the counselor while describing his problem, yet feel fearful and resentful for having told "all" or for having exposed his perceived "weaknessess." Often, the client's positive transference will change to negative feelings when the counselor doesn't give him all the reassurance or advice he expects. Sometimes a client responds to the counselor in a manner similar to that he used during his childhood "confessions" to his real parents.

Origins of transference feelings. As we explained in the preceding material, transference feelings have their roots in the client's life experiences. The counselor's personal reactions to the client or his institutional role (minister, dean, or physician, for example) arouse selective feelings in the client. The counselor should be aware also of feelings which he might elicit from the client. These feelings might be very normal social reactions to what the counselor is, says, or does. As illustrated in Chapter 7 on the nature of the relationship, the more ambiguous the counselor personality, the more opportunity the client has of projecting his inner needs and attitudes rather than of responding socially and rationally to the situation. The nature of the physical setting of the counselor's office seems to have a pronounced effect on the client's emotional responses to the counselor also, although little is known about this phenomenon.

Implications of Transference for Counseling and Psychotherapy

Since the counselor depends primarily upon a relationship of mutual trust and acceptance, a strong transference, especially of the negative or hostile type, tends to interfere with his counseling effectiveness.

The psychotherapist, on the other hand, does not view transference as an interference. He uses transference-type feelings to help his client recognize what he is trying to do with the relationship to the therapist, that is, how he may be trying to manipulate the therapist. The clients' demands help the therapist to understand what sort of person the client is trying to be or wants to be. The transference relationship, therefore, provides valuable clues for later interpretations to the client on how his interpersonal relationship mechanisms are functioning.

The counselor recognizes also that, though he does not depend upon a transference relationship for effective therapy, transference feelings are present in varying amounts. For example, there are the clients who fear the counselor, depend on him, love him, or expect varying roles of him. These responses may be projected self-regarding attitudes and may be related to earlier experiences with parents; nevertheless, they must be recognized and handled therapeutically even though they are not dealt with as directly as in psychotherapy.

Clients are often aware of these feelings and express them openly. Wood (324) analyzed five completely recorded client-centered counseling cases. He found only 61 out of the total of 1,900 client responses dealing directly with a discussion of the relationship. Qualitatively, however, there were a number of responses which indicated a deep emotional involvement with the counselor. The following excerpts are illustrations:

> (Second interview) ". . . it seemed to me that as we were talking along, that you, not only as a counselor, but you as an individual, were getting sort of excited about this thing too, just as I was. And that, well, at times, you were no longer a counselor to me, but you were just another person that I was talking over this problem with" (324, pg. 74).

> (Fourth interview) "As a matter of fact, a peculiar thing,—I hate to admit it — (laughs) is that, except in the last two interviews, I don't believe I've been much concerned with your reflections. You probably realize I've been moving pretty fast, and somewhat running up the middle of your spine at times without, uh, knowing it, desiring to go ahead. A sort of manic euphoria (laughs). But I guess I've done enough to you today" (324, pg. 74).

It seems to us that the examples are transference-laden and probably indicate the early phases of a true "transference neuroses" situation. Counselors, in briefer forms of psychological counseling, rarely attempt to analyze such "transference neuroses." Client-centered counselors, in particular, do not regard this situation as a significant therapeutic problem. The result is that persons using the client-centered or non-directive style of counseling rarely confront intensive transferences, and they reflect it as they would any other feeling. Rogers' writings suggest this procedure:

> In client-centered therapy, however, this involved and persistent dependent transference relationship does not tend to develop. Thousands of clients

have been dealt with by counselors with whom the writer has had personal contact. In only a small minority of cases handled in a client-centered fashion has the client developed a relationship which could in any way be matched to Freud's terms. In most instances the description of the relationship would be quite different (249, pg. 201).

Another cause of low-intensity transference phenomena in counseling might be the counselor's approach to a transference feeling. He does not usually try to analyze deeply the manifold ways in which his client manipulates his life relationships. Instead, the counselor utilizes reflection of feelings and acceptance techniques which aid the client to see that the transference feelings reside within his own inadequate perception and not within the counselor.

The counselor tends to regard the expressions of negativism, hostility, and guilt more as manifestations of resistance in an incomplete growing up process. The psychotherapist generally handles transference feelings with interpretation of the unconscious impulsive nature of the feelings; whereas, the counselor, dealing with the same feelings at a more superficial level, tends to use a variety of responses, including a more oblique approach through reflection of feelings. The counselor, furthermore, looks upon his task as a continuation of the maturation process which has been incompletely guided by the client's natural parents. The counselor tries to help the client to understand and accept his feelings and to see what he has been trying to accomplish with his attitude. After gaining a more rational understanding, he can take his projections on the counselor back to himself, so that, for example, he can be less dependent. The client also is helped to understand in which ways his former behavior was ineffective in reaching his goals of emotional satisfaction.

Often, the client persistently tests the counselor's or therapist's sincerity through repeated criticisms, unrealistic expectations, aggressiveness, resistance, and irritability. Gradually, however, the client feels "safe" in dropping his defensiveness and changing his perception of himself and the counselor. The client, for example, finds himself able to reconstruct satisfactory relationships with others as well as with the counselor, since he learns he may not always expect counteraggressive acts when he is hostile to others.

Negative transferences often follow positive transferences. When the client suddenly realizes he has been idealizing or has been depending upon the counselor or therapist, he begins to perceive the counselor as he really is rather than in the client's "God-like" image. This is the counselor's and therapist's welcomed cue of client growth. The therapist must help the client work through these feelings of disillusionment, however, by "giving him back" his projections. The situation is analogous to "falling out of love." The lover, in fairness to his former beloved, for example, returns her projections of idealized images (romantic love) so that her ego system is restored to its former state.

Not all negative feelings expressed in the interview are transference feelings. Instead of being projected to the counselor, they may be directed inward. Intrapunitive hostility or guilt, for example, can lead to depression. Though the counselor must be alert to pathological forms of depression which should have more extensive treatment, he can interpret anxious and mildly depressed feelings as a sign that the client is struggling with important feelings. For example, the counselor says in effect, "If we stick together, we can make use of these feelings because they show us that we are very close to something which is important."

Therapeutic functions of transference feelings for counselors. While strong transferences toward the counselor often complicate his task, it should be recognized that this process serves significant functions for clients. The awareness of freedom to express previously repressed irrational feelings is a unique experience which often reduces his anxiety.

Transference serves to build the relationship by allowing the client to express distorted feelings without the usual counterdefensive responses. For example, a client with a "chip on his shoulder" expects his irritability to arouse counterhostility from others. When the counselor does not react as expected (by getting irritated), the client can safely reduce his defensiveness and, hence, has less need to feel guilty because of hostile impulses, and less need to project his hostility on others. This refusal of the counselor to respond according to the client's projections is one of the main vehicles for accomplishing therapeutic goals. For example, if the client's former human relationships have been characterized by rejection or devaluation, the counselor is very accepting and warm. If the client has felt exploited and abused, the counselor is careful in making demands upon the client. The general principle here is that the counselor should not fit himself into the client's projections so as to satisfy the client's neurotic needs. If the counselor fulfills the client's expectations, there is the possibility they will be perpetuated by virtue of having been reinforced.

A second function of transference, implied above, is to promote the client's confidence in the counselor through his wise handling of the transference feelings. Such feelings also have the net effect of amplifying the client's emotional involvement with his problem, thereby enabling him to stay in counseling.

A third function of transference is to enable the client to get insight into the origin and significance of these feelings in his present life through interpretation of his feelings. The transferred feelings, along with their maladaptive behaviors, tend to disappear with insight so that he can establish more satisfying and mature relationships with people.

Working through transference feelings and preventing deep transference relationships. The counselor's main task in this regard is to encourage the free expression of feelings while simultaneously keeping the transference attitudes from developing into a deep transference relationship.

In psychotherapy a deep transference relationship often develops, and the therapist is faced with a long and arduous task of working through the transference feelings. Several general suggestions for handling and resolving transference feelings are presented sequentially in terms of depth involved.

(1) A primary technique for resolving transference feeling is by means of *simple acceptance* as one would handle any type of client feeling. This procedure enables the client to "live out" his feelings, "take back" his projected feelings, or continue to express them more freely in the interview. The client recognizes, then, that the transference feelings reside in himself and not in the counselor.

(2) The therapist (and sometimes the counselor) may ask *clarifying questions* regarding the forms of anxiety which the client seems to be manifesting. An example would be, "You seem to be unloading on me today. Why do you suppose this is happening?" This statement is a prelude to the interpretation likely to follow; but it explores the client's attitude first and gives him the opportunity to do his own interpreting.

(3) The transference feeling in the client's statement may be *reflected*. For example the therapist might state, "You feel that we shouldn't discuss this because it may make *me* uncomfortable."

(4) The therapist may *interpret* the transference feelings directly. For example, "Sometimes when people feel they have been telling too much, they get insecure about their relationship with that person. Do you suppose this is happening here?" You will note that, even with the use of interpretation, the therapist seeks the feeling response of the client since it is his distortion of human relationships and feelings which very likely are at the root of his difficulties. The main goal of transference interpretation, then, is to clarify the relationship between the client's earlier interpersonal experiences and his present behavior. A second goal is to reassure the client that these feelings and their resolution are a normal part of the process.

The interpretations generally emphasize present problems and crises and do not dwell on earlier experiences. Interpretations also come relatively late in the process so as to allow the therapist to accumulate data from which to make valid interpretations. Sometimes interpretations come as "shock treatment" where the therapist says in effect, "Congratulations; you are now able to take these projections and see them as existing in yourself." (The counselor then may go on to explain the nature and function of transferences.)

(5) The following suggestion by May that the counselor or therapist focuses on the *what* rather than the *why* provides a most fruitful technique for the handling of the difficult problem of transference.

> In existential therapy "transference" gets placed in the new context of *an event occurring in a real relationship between two people.* . . . the only thing that will grasp the patient, and in the long run make it possible for

her to change, is to experience fully and deeply that she is doing precisely this to a real person, myself, in this real moment . . . Part of this *sense of timing* . . . consists of letting the patient experience *what* he or she is doing until the experience really grasps him. Then and only then will the explanation of *why* help.

This is a point the phenomenologists make consistently, namely, that to know fully *what* we are doing, to feel it, to experience it all through our being, is much more important than to know *why*. For, they hold, if we fully know the *what,* the *why* will come along by itself (198, pp. 83–84).

(6) In general, calling attention to the transference causes the client to react in the opposite manner. Therefore, therapists usually adhere to the principle of calling attention to negative transference feelings, but not calling attention to the positive transference unless it has reached a level where it is interfering with therapeutic movement.

(7) The counselor may *refer* the client to a therapist qualified to give more extensive psychotherapy if the relationship develops to an intensity which is beyond the competence and responsibility of the counselor.

The following discussion covers more problems on transference and illustrates the use of the principles discussed above.

Ambivalent *authority* feelings are commonly transferred to the counselor. In American middle class society, which provides the bulk of the psychological counselor's clientele, authority feelings are exceedingly mixed. The client, in addition to having possibly both dependent and hostile feelings about authority figures, becomes anxious when he divulges personal information to the counselor. The emotional material may come up too fast for him to handle, resulting in anxiety and a possible breakdown of control mechanisms. His feelings may change suddenly to hostility directed toward the counselor for allowing him to tell so much.

The following excerpt illustrates an authority-type of feeling transfer: (The client is a nineteen-year-old single woman who has spent two previous interviews describing her feelings of inadequacy and hostility toward her father.)

Cl: I just can't talk any more.

C: You feel run down like a clock spring?

Cl: No, I'm just finding it harder and harder to talk to *you*.

C: You feel that I as a person am making it harder for you?

Cl: Well, yes, I mean (long pause and signs of distress).

C: You mean that somehow I remind you of someone—like your father perhaps?

Cl: Yes, I never thought of it that way; but I guess most men do; but you just sitting there looking at me (pause) bothers me.

C: When you think of me as a man, you get the same mixed up feelings as you do when you think of your father. Is that it?

Cl: When I really think about it, I know I haven't any real reason to (pause) well, to think of you as my father. It seems silly, but it makes me feel better to know why I feel this way.

(Followed by further discussion of relationships with father.) The counselor in the excerpt tried to maintain an attitude of understanding and acceptance. He had listened to her outpouring of feelings for two sessions. Mild interpretation from the counselor led her to see that her growing difficulties in expressing herself were not due to the counselor's austere paternalistic attitude, but were more the projections of her own feelings. She realized that she could be secure and that she had no palpable reason for feeling that the counselor was censuring her or that he represented father to her. This reperceiving experience, as well as the intellectual awareness of projection tended to reduce her defensiveness. Thus, she could perceive of the counselor as he really tried to be—a personality which understands and accepts rather than evaluates. Rogers emphasizes the value of the above perceptual change in clients:

> The whole relationship is composed of the self of the client, the counselor being depersonalized for purpose of therapy into being "the client's other self." It is this warm willingness on the part of the counselor to lay his own self temporarily aside, in order to enter into the experience of the client, which makes the experience a completely unique one, unlike anything in the client's previous experience (249, pg. 208).

The following example illustrates a type of transference feeling involving *dependency:* (This is a first interview with a nineteen-year-old woman)

Cl: I'm not doing so well in school.
C: Mm-hm.
Cl: I thought you could help me by telling me what I'm doing wrong.
C: You are confident that I can help you improve your school work possibly by analyzing your procedures?
Cl: Well, yes; I've heard you have tests and things.
(After further structuring the role of the counselor and client and further elaboration of the problem, the client is still thinking along dependent lines.)
Cl: I certainly hope these tests give me the answers. I know they aren't very accurate; but with your experience with them, you should be able to tell me what I should do.
C: While you recognize the limitations of tests, you still feel I will be able to suggest a definite course of action. However, I will interpret the results to you and discuss them with you in such a way that you will be better able to decide.
Cl: Well, I guess that is what you are here for, aren't you?

In the preceding example, it became clear that the client was depending on the counselor to solve her problem. In spite of the counselor's patient acceptance and later interpretation of her dependency, the client continued to look for further support without much evidence of insight. The counselor's effort to shift responsibility gently back to her was met with a negative transference remark. The counselor, realizing that his own personality or technique might be arousing this aggressive transference, finally decided that continuation of this relationship would merely reinforce the client's dependency and would very likely arouse some counter-transference feelings. He utilized the "capping" technique to ease out of the counseling relationship and to refer her to a psychotherapist more able to work with this type of client.

While hostile or affectional transference feelings seem to be more adequately resolved by counselors, it is this persistent form of dependency which gives them most difficulty. The dependent client insists that the counselor take over his decisions and self-management. This dependent attitude generally shows up early in counseling so that the counselor can decide whether his skills can cope with the alternating apathy and aggression often accompanying the dependency. The client frequently does not obtain the solutions and support he seeks; hence, he becomes defensive. The resulting aggression severely tests the counselor's ability to inhibit his own negative feelings and to maintain an attitude of acceptance and understanding until such time as client insight is achieved. The psychotherapist, in contrast, generally reacts more openly with his feelings since he has the time and confidence to think through the unconscious aspects of the relationship.

Another danger in dependency transference is that the client's desires to solve his problem may be outweighed by his wishes to prolong the counseling. It is often necessary to put a "brake" on the regressive-dependent type of transference feeling early in the process before it becomes a persistent response.

Rogers (249) offers the hypothesis that a dependent transference arises when the client feels he is being evaluated and when he feels that the evaluation has more accuracy than his own estimate of himself. The net effect is to decrease self-confidence and to increase dependency. Use of techniques, such as interpreting a test score, or reassuring expressions such as, "It is normal to feel that way," or interpretive remarks such as, "Maybe you do not resent her as much as you thought you did," convey the idea that the counselor has a high degree of omniscience; hence, the client feels relieved to place responsibility for his decisions on the counselor. Again; in psychotherapy situations, the therapist is not afraid of assuming responsibility toward the client for a prolonged period before working through the unconscious emotional aspects of the transference.

In amplifying the hypothesis in the preceding paragraph, Rogers (249) suggests that as the client explores his feelings more deeply, he becomes more threatened. Then there generally is a tendency to displace or project these threatening feelings to the counselor. This feeling of threat and its accompanying anxiety often result in more dependence, which only the psychotherapist is willing to deal with on a long-term basis.

A third common type of transference attitude is that of *affection*. This feeling is elicited largely as a function of the understanding and accepting attitude of the counselor. A client with strong needs for love and attention will often respond to the counselor's or therapist's "warmth" with feelings ranging from friendly interest to intense erotic love.

Since this interview may be the first relationship in which the client has experienced genuine acceptance and in which he shares his deepest feelings, it is easy to understand how intense positive feelings, even of intimacy, may develop. This development of feeling, unless recognized, becomes increasingly more difficult to handle by both client and counselor. It was this type of situation which, in the early days of formal psychotherapy, produced so many rumors of irregularities in the conduct of therapists. This is another reason for counselors to limit the build-up of strong transferences. However, these positive feelings elicited by a therapist's accepting attitude can be utilized to create understanding of unconscious need deprivations.

Three classes of feelings—hostility, dependency, and affection—were utilized here for expository purposes. You, however, are reminded that feelings exist in a vast array of types and combinations. The basic techniques for all, however, are similar.

In the concluding phases of counseling or therapy, it is necessary that any strong residual transference feelings be discussed frankly with the client and broadly interpreted. He must be made aware, for example, that he must become less dependent on the counseling or therapy relationship as well as on the counselor since the present relationship is about to terminate. The affection felt toward the counselor or therapist, in addition, must be generalized to include all human beings. Any resentments lingering toward the counselor must be completely understood by the client in light of the total psychotherapeutic discussion of parents, siblings, etc. Thus, the client is not left struggling with unresolved feelings dredged up during the counseling.

In counseling, the diminution of transference feelings is due to increased client awareness of previously unaccepted, distorted or partially known experiences. In psychotherapy, there is usually a more pronounced personality change and the decreases in transference problems run parallel to personality changes.

The preceding discussion on resolving transference feeling is not intended to be adequate in dealing with the deep transferences which severe neurotics and psychotics often make. Since counselors rarely undertake therapy with these individuals, deep therapy techniques for treating transference have not been included here. The psychotherapist who finds these problems increasing as he undertakes deeper therapy should read such sources as Alexander (2), Fromm-Reichmann (118), and Wolberg (323).

Summary of Transference Discussion

In this section, transference was described as a largely irrational part of the counseling process wherein the client projects to the counselor self-regarding attitudes and unresolved feelings from earlier human relationships. Intensity of transference seems to be a function of the type of client involved, setting, length of counseling, extent of emotional involvement, counselor personality, and counselor technique. Although the expression and working through of transference feelings has therapeutic values, it is the intense feelings or involved relationships that create counseling problems. In psychotherapy, however, the development and working through of transferences is considered to be a significant part of long-term personality change.

The resolution or working through of transference feelings is accomplished if the counselor maintains an attitude of acceptance and understanding and also if he applies reflection, questioning, and interpretive techniques as the counseling becomes more psychotherapeutic in nature.

COUNTERTRANSFERENCE

The Nature of Countertransference

The following section applies to counseling and therapy; so, the more general term, counselor, will be utilized for both.

The reader may have deduced from the previous discussion that countertransference refers to the emotional reactions and projections of the counselor toward the client. In an extensive review of the writings on countertransference, Cohen (64) concluded that, although the term transference has fairly standard meaning, countertransference has not. Winnicott's (322) "objective countertransference," wherein the counselor's resentment of the client, for example, is based upon some objective antisocial or psychotic behavior which would be objectionable to any human being, is on one end of the continuum. Fromm-Reichmann (118) separates the type Winnicott mentions from the more subtle unconscious forms—especially the counselor reactions to client transference feelings. Alexander and French (2) include all attitudes of the counselor toward the client. Other writers include only affectionate or libidinous feelings under countertransference.

We view countertransference broadly to include conscious and unconscious attitudes of the counselor toward real or imagined client attitudes or overt behavior.

One of the qualifications mentioned in Chapter 6 was that the counselor have insight into his own immaturities, prejudices, objects of disgust, anxieties, and punitive tendencies. No counselor is free of these feelings. Unless he has an awareness of his attitudes, however, his responses to client statements will all too frequently be tainted with his own feelings. These negative attitudes tend to have a deleterious effect on the relationship by arousing negative transference feelings in the client. Positive countertransferences, made by the counselor, can be even more deleterious since he is less apt to recognize them and the client is more upset when they are withdrawn.

There are positive and helpful countertransference attitudes, as described in Chapter 6. Attitudes of acceptance are essential in building a therapeutic relationship. In the counselor's attempts to understand the client there seems to be a type of identification or empathic process with the client's ego system. The counselor, furthermore, must decide how much of a "real person" he must be to the client. In Chapter 6, the question of ambiguity was discussed with the general conclusion that the more surface or ego-centered the counseling is, the more distinct the counselor can be as a person. This means that in surface types of counseling with limited goals, the counselor can react with more feelings and behaviors which are part of the usual everyday social world. There is also the consideration that the counselor must be flexible enough to play roles of varying ambiguity to suit the therapeutic needs of the client at different stages in the process.

Since handling client feelings is reported to be one of their principal difficulties, countertransference complicates the problems of beginning counselors. These counselors are relieved to know that it is commonplace to have some mixed feelings about the client. In addition, the client is an overvalued person in the beginning counselor's life because of his own strong desires to succeed in counseling.

There are few studies with implications for the subject of countertransference; but Chance (61) studied the attitudes of therapists toward their clients and found that, as therapy progresses, the clients become more alike in the therapist's eyes. The results of this study suggest that as psychotherapists anticipate client progress, the clients become more like the therapist's projected "generalized client," rather than more sharply differentiated people.

Sources of Countertransference Feelings

Cohen (64) hypothesizes that anxiety, either felt or defended by the counselor, is the prime source of countertransference behaviors. The counseling relationship mobilizes anxiety from former relationships in a manner similar to transference. The anxiety patterns in the counselor may be classified into three types: unresolved personal problems of the counselor, situational pressures, and communication of the client's feeling to the counselor by empathic means.

The first category, the counselor's unresolved personal problems as a source of interview difficulties, needs little explanation. The main solution here is counseling for the counselor. Even after having had personal therapy, counselors and therapists must increase self-awareness so as to avoid countertransferences.

The category of situational pressures is tied in with the counselor's problems but may aggravate latent feelings. An illustration follows. The counselor had just come from a fatiguing meeting. He had to wait a few minutes for a late client who, noting the austere facial expressions of the counselor, apologized profusely. He felt that the counselor was provoked with him, when in reality it was the emotional exhaustion and frustration experienced by the counselor in a previous hour which caused him to respond so severely to the client.

Situational pressures exist for the counselor in the form of his feeling responsibility to see that the client improves, or feeling that his professional reputation is at stake if he fails with this client. As a result, the counselor "tries too hard," by pushing the client; and thereby he may defeat his own purposes. The counselor must be on guard so that his anxious feelings of frustration when a client does not improve are not transmitted to the client.

The third category of countertransference sources is the communication of client feelings to the counselor. When the counselor tends to be overly sympathetic, is it because he has unwittingly responded to a strong bid for sympathy and attention? When the counselor feels himself becoming anxious or resentful, is it due to the contagion of the client's anxious feelings? That this happens frequently is due possibly to the counselor's special training in alertness to client feelings. The counselor then responds empathically to minimal cues, such as changes in posture, voice, and manner. The counselor may not be aware that the stiff jerky walk from the reception room to the office, the grating voice, or the loud aggressive talk of the client generate tensions in him.

It should not be overlooked, perhaps, that in addition to the empathic explanation, the preceding behaviors are related also to the counselor's past personal problems. One of the ways the counselor manifests his anxiety is to emit impulsively a verbalization of his own—a question, comment, or change of subject which may not technically be relevant to the counseling process at the moment. The net effect is often disastrous from the standpoint of stopping or diverting the flow of client feelings, throwing him off the loaded topic, or creating more transference feelings.

In addition, the counselor may reveal his anxiety by feelings of uneasiness. Reusch and Prestwood (243) studied the transmission of feelings in an experiment which involved psychiatrists listening to recordings of therapeutic interviews. The investigators found that the emotional tone of the listeners varied significantly with the rate of speech, use of personal pronouns, and frequency of expression of feeling. A relaxed client resulted in a relaxed listener. Those interviews heavily laden with anxiety resulted in listener reports varying from being ill at ease to being angry or disturbed.

Any discussion of the source of countertransference attitudes would not be complete without mentioning the counselor's value structure again. As was indicated in earlier chapters, the very nature of the relationship puts the counselor in a position of influencing the client. This happens even though he claims to be objective, non-judgmental, and permissive. It is difficult for the counselor to avoid conveying the feeling that he regards emotional maturity, for example, as an important goal for counseling. It is quite easy for the client to guess by emotional implication, if not verbally, the values which the counselor holds after a discussion of moral problems.

The counselor conveys two types of values to the client—those relating to how he should live, and those concerned with how he should behave in counseling. There is no question professionally that the counselor can convey counseling process values which facilitate counseling. Examples are: "It is important to express how you really feel here." "It is all right to tell me how much you resent your aunt."

There is considerable question how far a counselor should go in promoting his own moral concepts or styles of life in the interview. On the one hand, it may be desirable to help a racially prejudiced client to perceive others in a less-rigid manner consonant with his capacity for insight; but, on the other hand, it might lead to unfortunate consequences to specify a particular type of religious faith.

There are two reasons for restricting value projection. One is that the counselor might succeed. We cannot safely trust even a sophisticated counselor to be a type of "cultural high priest" where he poses as the best judge about right and wrong or appropriate or inappropriate beliefs. If it is felt that the client needs more information and clarification in the area of religious values, for example, it is preferable in our opinion to refer him to a reliable minister from whom there is clear understanding that he will receive instruction in values.

Another reason for restricting this activity is that the counselor's deliberate efforts to influence the client's values might fail. The unsuccessful attempt might interfere with a good therapeutic relationship by promoting unwanted negative transference attitudes. Yet, a counselor is an expert in the process of living. There are so many commonly accepted behaviors in the area of legal conformity, marriage, and generally mature behavior which the counselor can feel justified in espousing. He cannot use his own or society's frame of reference on value completely, however. The counselor constantly must be aware of the client's personal standards and beliefs. He must try to see these values as the client sees them and help the client utilize them for his own benefit.

Ingham and Love suggest a technique for handling the instances where the client is aware of the counselor's values. The counselor explains the situation by saying, for example, "You've picked up something of my feeling about marriage. I don't mind your knowing what I think about it, but it doesn't mean that you should follow my ideas" (152, pg. 78). Here the counselor admits he has given his values and allows the client to accept or reject them; yet he does not refute his own feelings about the values.

Signs of Countertransference Feelings

The following checklist of signs is offered to the counselor to test himself regarding anxious or defensive countertransference involvement with his clients.

(1) Finds himself getting sleepy, or not listening or paying attention as well as he might.

(2) Sees himself denying the presence of anxiety and thinks to himself, "I feel all right about this topic and should feel upset; but I don't." (If there were no anxiety present, why would the counselor even think about it?)

(3) Finds it difficult to shift positions or feels himself "tighten up."

(4) Feels himself becoming sympathetic rather than empathic or becoming overemotional in face of client's troubles.

(5) Selects certain material to reflect or interpret and wonders afterward why he selected this material rather than some other material.

(6) Finds himself consistently reflecting or interpreting too soon or incorrectly (and the result cannot be accounted for on client resistance grounds only).

(7) Finds that he underestimates or misses the client's depth of feeling consistently.

(8) Has unreasoning dislike or attraction for the client. He gets angry at the "unappreciative" client.

(9) Finds he cannot identify with the client. For example, when the client feels upset, the counselor feels no emotional response.

(10) Overidentifies himself with the client, as in becoming aggressively sympathetic when the client cites maltreatment by an authority figure.

(11) Discovers a tendency to argue with the client, becomes defensive, or is otherwise vulnerable to client criticism.

(12) Feels that this is his "best" or "worst" client.

(13) Finds himself preoccupied with the client in fantasy between sessions, even to the extent of thinking of responses to be made.

(14) Realizes that he is habitually late in starting interviews or runs over the hour with certain clients.

(15) Attempts to elicit some strong affect from the client by making dramatic statements.

(16) Finds himself overconcerned about confidential nature of work with the client.

(17) Feels the compulsion to do something active; hence, makes too strong an impact with "shotgun" interpretations and suggestions.

(18) Dreams about the client.

(19) Is too "busy" to see the client or may complain of "administrative duties."

An insidious form of countertransference is compulsive advice-giving. This "if I were you" approach is so exceedingly common in everyday human relations that it tends to spill into counseling relationships also. The counselor may feel the need to convince the client that the course of action discussed is best for him; yet the advice, persuasion, or reassurance is motivated more by the counselor's personal needs. A possible motive for advice-giving is extrapunitive hostility. It is a way of controlling others, depreciating them, and elevating one's self to a dominating role. There are conditions, however, where *information* and *opinions* can be offered. These conditions are discussed in Chapter 10 on information techniques.

A common form of countertransference feeling is the idea that the client must somehow like the counselor and that the counselor must please the client. Though the relationship is built upon mutual trust and cordiality, there are times when the counselor must risk this client admiration. For example, sometimes the therapist must help the client see that he must give up important things and that removal of pleasant symptoms is sometimes painful.

Fiedler (99) found in his studies of the factors in the counseling relationships that the poor, or nonexpert, counselors had the tendency to "not hear," "ignore," or communicate poorly with clients. The expert counselors had them significantly less often. This study suggests that such countertransference signs, as Fiedler found, are not a great problem for experienced therapists.

For the counselor who feels that he is not vulnerable to countertransference tendencies, a revealing and sobering exploratory study of Fiedler is cited. He found that there was a high relationship between therapeutic competence and lack of negative countertransference attitudes. Fiedler's method consisted of comparing the similarity of the counselor's and the client's self-descriptions. The counselor's "ideal" description, then, was used to determine the nature and intensity of countertransference feelings. An implication of this study is that, as the counselor grows in counseling experience and personal understanding, his harmful countertransference attitudes diminish.

Resolving Countertransference Feelings

Although little research has been done in the area of resolving a countertransference, there is a body of clinical experience which may be useful to the counselor in handling his feelings toward the client.

(1) *Locating Sources of Feelings:* The first step consists of the therapist asking himself, "I wonder why this is so?" This question is precipitated by the feeling that the counselor is not communicating with his client. The following list of questions should give every counselor additional reasons to ponder his countertransference attitudes.

> *A Counselor's Guide to Self-Criticism*[1]
> Why did I make this particular response to this student's remark? What was behind it?
> What was I reacting to when making this remark?
> What was I endeavoring to convey to the client?

---
[1] Adapted from Johnson (158).

Why did I ask that question?

Was it really asked for purposes related to helping the client?

Was I merely curious?

Was I really being judgmental by asking that question?

Why did I feel impelled at this point to give advice?

Was it because I felt that the client expected me to have all the answers? And did I respond by being all-wise?

Why did I become so emotionally involved with the client who felt so unloved and insecure?

Could it be that basically I too still feel unloved and unlovable?

Why did I want (or did I not want) to bring the parent, husband, or wife of this client into counseling?

Can it be that I have overidentified with the client and have already rejected the spouse? (or the parent?)

Why in this first interview did I talk so much instead of letting the client tell his story?

Was it because I felt I had to impress the client with my own knowledge so he would return?

Why does it upset me when appointments are broken?

Is it because I am really insecure and uncertain concerning my skill?

Why am I so reluctant to "let go" when the counseling with a client has reached a good termination point, or when I know the client should be referred for a different kind of help?

Am I using the client for my needs or am I letting him use me?

Each counselor must accept the fact that he has varied feelings about the client and that he will be changed somewhat by the counseling experience. The counselor must be aware also that he has anxieties coming from insecurity in the counseling role and the client's expression of anxiety.

The counselor must control his tendencies to give reassurance to the client because of his own needs for reassurance. For example:

Cl: Sometimes I feel like screaming out loud in a quiet place like the library. In fact, I feel so tensed up at times I feel like wringing somebody's neck till he dies.

C: It is all right to feel that way. After all, thinking of killing isn't the same as murder.

This counselor response is likely to arouse more anxiety in the client, whereas, the following response would recognize his feeling, would tend to tone down the reassurance, and yet would not show the counselor's anxiety (even if the counselor realistically pictures himself as a possible object of the client's homicidal feelings).

C: Sometimes these feelings do seem hard to control and we feel an urge to let them go at times. Perhaps you would like to mention some experiences with other people or situations which make you feel this way.

The counselor controls his anxiety through the knowledge that nonpsychotic clients rarely assault counselors, and that the hostile threatening language is often a clever device used by disturbed clients to frighten counselors and therapists.

(2) *Supervisory Assistance:* There are times in the professional life of every counselor when he must admit that certain types of personalities make him defensive or are beyond his level of competence. He can handle this problem by assessing the client as a case "too hot to handle" and referring him to another therapist. An additional recourse is the supervisor or a colleague with whom he can discuss, with considerable candor, the feelings involved without breaching the confidences of the relationship. For example, a counselor may recognize that he has trouble with hostile aggressive women; hence, he might suggest that such a client change counselors. Again, discussing this problem in a counseling relationship with a supervisor helps the counselor resolve his own feelings.

(3) *Discussion With the Client:* Though there is no objective evidence to indicate that it is expedient to discuss countertransference feelings with the client, we have found a mild reassuring and interpretive reference occasionally helpful in allaying anxiety, for exampe:

(This is a second interview with a thirty-three-year-old married woman, after a discussion about an involved marital problem.)

> Cl: Well, there it is—straight from the shoulder.
> C: You feel you have told the story quite frankly. Perhaps you have noticed that there are times when things you say may seem to disturb me a bit. I trust though that you will not hold back any feelings for fear of disturbing me.
> Cl: I appreciate your telling me this. It might make it easier to talk to you.

Another example wherein the counselor rationalizes his unwarranted intrusion follows. The counselor has just interrupted the client and says, "I'm sorry; I didn't intend to stop you. Sometimes we are so eager to help we interrupt your train of thought."

(4) *Counselor Growth:* The counselor can use his own awareness of himself as reflected through the therapeutic process to enhance his own growth and resolve his difficulties. Cohen (63) cites an example of a psychotherapist who doubted his own intellectual adequacy and habitually overrated and competed with his more intellectual clients. This situation made it difficult for the counselor to help the clients who use intellectualized defenses against their own anxieties.

(5) *Referral to Group Counseling or Therapy:* Another technique for handling a countertransference is to require that the patient discuss his problem in group therapy. For example, if it is obvious that a woman client has strong affectionate feelings toward the therapist, he can ask that she talk about this matter in a group-therapy situation. This procedure depersonalizes the problem and removes much of the possibility of any undesirable countertransference reaction.

Summary of the Countertransference Section

The purpose of this section is to impress upon the reader the significance of the counselor's irrational attitudinal responses. Another purpose is to suggest ways of resolving these feelings. We support the hypothesis that the counselor's attitudes are one of the most important determinants of interview climate. A counselor can resolve his feelings toward the client by recognizing that he has countertransference feelings, by examining himself concerning why the feelings exist, possibly admitting that he should not work with this client, and using the recognition of countertransference feelings as information to enhance his own personal growth outside the interviews.

The next section contains a consideration of the phenomenon of resistance which draws upon elements of the transference and countertransference discussion; yet, the resistance phenomenon has unique characteristics of its own.

RESISTANCE

The Nature of Resistance

One of the principal realities of building and maintaining an effective counseling relationship which must be dealt with, is resistance. Resistance may be viewed as a special defensive form of transference. The term resistance, as we use it, refers to a characteristic of the client's defense system which opposes the purposes of counseling or therapy. This conscious or unconscious thwarting of the interview goals is a product either of the outer-defense system, protecting the client from situational threats, or of the inner-defense system, protecting the client from unconscious coresystem impulses.

The term resistance was introduced by the psychoanalysts to indicate the unconscious opposition toward bringing unconscious material into consciousness as well as the mobilization of the repressive and protective functions of the ego (111).

The Existentialists' view of resistance is stated by May as follows:

> . . . this is an outworking of the tendency of the patient to . . . renounce the particular unique and original potentiality which is his. This "social conformity" is a general form of resistance to life; and even the patient's acceptance of the doctrines and interpretations of the therapist may itself be an expression of resistance (198, pg. 79).

Resistance, like transference, has different implications for counseling as opposed to psychotherapy. In general, counselors see resistance as something which opposes progress in problem-solving and therefore is something which the counselor tries to reduce as much as possible. The therapist, in contrast, sees resistance as an important phenomenon for intensive analysis. If he can understand the client's unique form of resistance, then he will more likely be able to help him understand and change his personality. The aim of psychotherapy, therefore, is not just to ascertain the client's defensive system or to "find out his secret." Rather, it is the significant question, "How does the client hide his secret?" A significant part of psychotherapy, therefore, involves the intensive analyses of resistances and transferences.

Resistance exists in varying amounts in all interviews and may be viewed as being at the opposite end of a continuum from free emotional expression. Daulton's (78) and Sherman's (170) data appear to support this thesis of a continuum relationship. Haigh (137) found a significant inverse relationship between defensiveness in early interviews and later expressions of positive attitude.

Resistance may vary from rejection of counseling and overt antagonism, on the one hand, to subtle forms, such as hesitation and inattention, on the other. Clients may say: "I know what I want to say, but I can't say it"; "I'll have to leave early today since I want to study for a test"; "I don't think that applies in my case"; "I'm sorry I'm late, but I almost forgot about our interviews"; "I thought you were supposed to be the expert."

Although resistance is present in some degree in all interviews, it is seldom recognized by the client. Hence, resistance exists largely as an unconscious phenomenon and is manifested by an ambivalent attitude toward counseling. He wants help, yet he resists the very help he seeks. This ambivalent client attitude is one of the most baffling situations confronting the inexperienced counselor. Even experienced counselors occasionally cite resistance as an excuse for not establishing an effective relationship.

Freud emphasized that the ambivalent and paradoxical attitude is a normal state of affairs in therapy. Many psychotherapists typically regard resistance as a normal mechanism which functions independently of therapy, also, to prevent disturbing unconscious impulses from coming to conscious levels of the personality.

The degree to which it is necessary to focus upon resistance to reach the goals of therapy illustrates, further, the differences between counseling and psychotherapy, as indicated in the following examples:

(1) *Counseling:*
Cl: I can't seem to be successful as a salesman—I just can't get along with other people.
C: You've pretty well ruled out selling then? Have you considered some of the other occupations on which you score high on the Strong Test?
Psychotherapy:
Cl: Why do you find it necessary to keep people distant from you?
(2) *Counseling:*
Cl: I can't seem to get along with my supervisor.

C: Since this seems such an obstacle, let's look at some techniques for getting along with such people.
Psychotherapy:
Cl: You seem to have much resistance to working with persons in authority.

Sources of Resistance

There appears to be general agreement among counselors that resistance arises when the client perceives the counselor, topic, or situation as threatening. Since anxiety is present in response to threat, the client is compelled to defend himself further against the anxiety through behaviors which are resistive in nature.

Resistance can be classified conveniently as "internal" or "external" in origin. Internal resistance comes from within the personality structure of the client and is a generalized response to threat; whereas external resistance is provoked as a result of the counseling setting, the impact of counselor technique or countertransference attitudes.

Internal resistance. One common source of internal resistance, for example, is the tendency of anxious clients to retreat from usually painful attempts to explore or alter patterns of behavior or of personality structure.

There seems to be anxiety associated with change in life status or attitude. Clients fear the expression of anxious or hostile feelings because they have learned to anticipate judgmental labels such as "immature," "lazy," "neurotic." These feelings seem to be most manifest when the client is expressing feelings too fast, in which case he feels that he is exposing himself to the anxiety of ego-relevant stimuli faster than he can judge the safety of these stimuli. Crider (72) in his study of the hostile personality found repressed hostility, especially in persons fearing expression of aggressive feelings, to be a prominent source of resistance.

Margolies (196) uses the term "facade" to describe another form of *internal* resistance. Facade refers to the initial statement made by a student client; for example, to explain his poor showing in college. Examples are: "I guess I hang around with the gang too much"; "I must be in the wrong major"; or "The Army is going to get me soon"; "My study habits are no good." Although these statements serve a useful function as reference points for further discussion, they are very often rationalizations and expressions of resistance. The client seems so captivated by the simple logic of his statements that he often finds little motivation to overcome his resistance and explore the situation further.

Another phenomenon creating resistance is "Reification anxiety"; that is, the client's fear that to put his feelings into words will make the condition real. An example of this basis for resistance is reluctance to express anxieties about having cancer, of death or of losing love.

External resistance. Some counselors are convinced that external resistance grows out of poor technique. Rogers, in his earlier work on counseling, offers the hypothesis that resistance is not necessarily ". . . an inevitable part of psychotherapy, nor a desirable part . . . ," and that what resistance is present appears to come from attempts to accelerate or to cut the process of therapy short (250, pg. 151).

An illustration of *external* resistance is the case where the counselor has made modest suggestions about improving study efficiency. The client may be anxious about carrying them out because of a supposed feeling of closeness or obligation to the counselor. He may resent being "drawn in" to this type of relationship at this stage of development, or he may have experienced a family relationship where children were obligated to return helpful favors in kind. The counselor's suggestions here create a negative transference which interferes with counseling effectiveness.

Another illustration of counselor technique which arouses resistance is a situation where the counselor gets too far ahead of the client, and reveals it by reflecting an implied feeling or offering a premature interpretation.

> Cl: "My parents are always criticizing me and threaten to stop giving me money for school."
> C: "You resent your parents for these things they say and threaten to do."
> Cl: "No, not exactly, I don't dislike my parents for it, I think they are right in lots of ways; I'm wasting my time here at college, really . . . I shouldn't be talking about them like this."

Here, reflection and interpretation, although very likely accurate, pinpointed feelings which could not be recognized and accepted at this stage.

Another cause of external resistance is related to lack of proper readiness. The client may misunderstand the counselor's role or he may not have faith in the value of verbalization. The client may not realize that counseling takes time; therefore, he may resent spending the time which he could devote to other less threatening activities. The client may be embarrassed to admit that he has a problem which he is unable to solve by himself.

The counseling relationship itself presents a paradoxical situation to the client. The accepting atmosphere encourages free expression of feeling; yet the client often is neither ready to express nor accept his own feelings. The relationship tends to force the premature examination of his own feelings, thus creating a source of considerable resistance. A common device clients use for manifesting this type of resistance is to talk about someone else's problems. An example is the case of a mother who worried about her four-teen-year-old daughter's behavior. The mother felt guilty, in addition to having intense feelings of failure. When the counselor encouraged the mother to talk about her own feelings, she felt compelled to continue discussing her daughter's difficulties.

English (92) cites further examples of situational anxiety as an obstacle to an optimal therapeutic relationship. He found that using lead techniques low in intensity early in the interview left the client dominated by his anxieties. English indicated that he found it necessary very often to reduce some of the anxiety temporarily by taking a greater lead and giving more support.

Mixed sources of resistance. In addition to the client's perception of threat in the interview or anxiety concerning his own impulses, other conditions exist as causes of resistance. Such conditions as fatigue, disease, mental deficiency, foreign language barriers, and psychoses cause resistance. The schizophrenic, from one point of view, exemplifies his resistance through withdrawal into hallucinations, muteness, or general negativism and projection. The neurotic may manifest his resistance defensively through rigidity, concern over details, irritation, and argumentation.

Knowing the sources of resistance, particularly the internal type, should be reassuring to the counselor who tends to feel personally responsible for the resistance he encounters. On the other hand, since the counselor's manner is the trigger for so much resistance, he must study continually his techniques and professional setting to reduce external resistance cues.

Positive Functions of Resistance

In addition to the protective or defensive functions of resistance for the client, there are valuable clues which the phenomenon provides for the counselor. A principal value of resistance for the counselor is that it gives an indication of general interview progress and the basis for diagnostic and prognostic formulations. Noting resistance symptoms is the first step toward taking appropriate measures to ignore, reduce, or utilize them.

A second function of resistance is the glimpse into the client's defensive structure which it affords the counselor. The presence of resistance tells the counselor that the client does not wish to explore these particular feelings further at this moment. Areas involving morals and deeply held beliefs are usually defended rigidly. Hence, resistance symptoms inform the counselor when he is treading temporarily in taboo territory. When these areas of threat become known, therefore, they offer the counselor much valuable interpretive information. Resistance is the counselor's cue that perhaps his usefulness has ended as a therapeutic agent and that the counseling should be formally terminated. Rogers (251) comments that the client often changes his feelings of warmth and acceptance toward the counselor to resentment when he no longer feels the need of the relationship. This manifestation, therefore, may be a healthy indication for terminating the relationship.

Resistance acts as a protective mechanism for the client through keeping acute anxiety under control, and through avoiding the disintegration of his defensive structure prior to establishment of new constructive behaviors. In this sense, resistance often serves a useful decelerating function for the early stages in the counseling process.

Manifestations and Classifications of Resistance

Although it is futile to attempt to list the myriad forms of resistance, it may be helpful to indicate some of the subtle as well as glaring examples of resistance. We feel that a distinguishing mark of the experienced counselor is his ability to recognize resistance and deal with it appropriately.

Resistance may manifest itself in a number of negativistic ways. For example, the client criticizes the counselor, expresses dissatisfaction with the results of counseling, fails to hear or to understand the counselor, comes late or fails to keep appointments, remains silent, forgets the fee, engages in intellectual discussion using complex psychological terms especially, expresses negative attitudes toward psychology, desires to end counseling prematurely, is unproductive in associations or with unfamiliar material, introduces irrelevant topics, makes unreasonable demands on the counselor, is pessimistic about counseling, or expresses skepticism about interpretations.

The client's resistance may take less aggressive forms as, for example, agreeing unequivocally with everything the counselor says, refusing to get emotionally involved, being overly cooperative, prolonging a dependency transference, maintaining persistent facetiousness, forcing the process into a semantic wilderness of abstractions and philosophical notions, pressing the limits of the relationship by asking for overtime, perhaps, and expressing strong interest in the counselor's personal life.

Two scales for organizing signs of resistance, and one study on scaling signs in order of intensity, have been reported in the counseling literature. From a hypothetical base line of ideal free expression, Bugental (46) postulates five levels of symptom intensity varying from *lagging* through *inertia, tentative resistance, (true) resistance,* to *rejection.* The headings used by Bugental are illustrative of the behavior he is describing.

At the *lagging* level, the client shunts responsibility to the counselor, is sluggish in response, distractible, and concerned with intellectualization rather than emotional content. Understanding is difficult for the client who must ask for frequent clarification from the counselor.

The *inertia* level contains more pronounced disinterest manifested by short answers, disregard of counselor leads, and fatigue.

Tentative resistance includes indications that the client is unwilling to continue the interview. Some indications are: arguing, excessive qualifying, showing physical tension, and inhibiting expression of hostility, anxiety, and guilt feelings. Bugental regards this type as temporary, but of crucial importance in the interview, since it is while he is manifesting tentative resistance that the client vacillates between more active resistance and co-operation.

True resistance is described as an intensification of the tentative type with more open and direct attack or withdrawal behaviors, such as making vague or diffuse answers to counselor questions, remaining silent, assuming a hostile attitude to counselor leads, questioning the competence of the counselor, or using vituperative language.

The most extreme form of resistance in Bugental's framework is described as *rejection*. The forms are generally extreme, such as terminating the interview by flat request, making hostile remarks about the counselor or institution, or refusing to communicate sufficiently.

Sherman developed a similar five-point scale on which interview units may be rated for amount of resistance.

(1) Definitely resistive—rejects counselor point of view or manner of structuring interview in a somewhat belligerent manner, refuses to talk about a real problem, or attempts to close interview.

(2) Somewhat resistive—rejects counselor point of view or suggestions but in a polite manner, does not talk freely, or may show a tendency to contradict counselor.

(3) Apathetic—takes no initiative, but accepts counselor suggestions usually in a noncommittal fashion.

(4) Counselor and client work together fairly well—talk together rather freely, although there may be some friendly parrying to advance points.

(5) Counselor and client work together on a real problem—talk very freely, feeling of mutual respect is marked (273, pp. 57–61).

Daulton (78), extending the work of Sherman, studied forty-eight interviews of twenty counselors. She found that the most frequent and intense forms of resistance were rejection of counselor suggestions and denial of counselor statements. Reticence in expressing feelings was rated as frequent but not intense. It seems that these findings would indict counselor technique as a potent source of resistance.

The counselor must evaluate the significance of resistance signs in light of the individual client's expressed feelings. Some clients exhibit many verbal symptoms of resistance because of a less inhibited personality and a strong verbal fluency; in contrast, others are excessively cautious or suffer acute distress before they actually verbalize their resistance. In other words, the signs and symptoms cited above do not have the same meaning for all clients. The "life style" of the client and apparent voluntary control over resistance determine the significance to be attached. As Thorne has stated, for example, "Many clients, particularly in the higher intelligence groups, conduct their human relations as they would a game of chess. Every move is more or less deliberately calculated" (303, pg. 238).

Research on resistance phenomena is meager. In addition to the studies cited above, Mowrer (218) produced a series of studies on the relationship between two parameters of the therapeutic process—psychological and physiological tension. Hypotheses that increases and decreases in resistance are associated with measurable tension changes have been studied. The principal techniques used to prove these hypotheses have been subjective ratings by subjects on "tension" and "happiness," palmar sweating, and discomfort-relief quotients derived from analysis of interview recordings. The tentative results indicate these approaches to be valuable means of studying observable changes in tension as a result of therapy. The interested reader is referred to the extended reports of Mowrer and his co-workers (218).

Techniques for Handling Resistance

In one sense, all of the readiness and relationship techniques mentioned in preceding chapters are designed to build a relationship and, consequently, to reduce or to prevent resistance. How this is accomplished is an intensely practical problem for the counselor because the resistance variable determines to a considerable extent whether a client will leave counseling or continue. We assume at this point that the main aim for the moment is to keep the client in counseling and to prevent his loss of confidence in the counselor.

Davis and Robinson (79) studied the resistance-handling techniques of experienced counselors and found great variation in frequency of use and type. Those techniques used most often by counselors, according to the study, were questions, personal reference, approval, reassurance, nonpersonal illustration, and humor. Davis and Robinson had little to offer on the evaluation of the differential effectiveness of these techniques and indicated that frequency was not necessarily a measure of effectiveness. These authors found frequent use of personal reference techniques, such as, "I think . . . ," and "I would do this . . ." However, the frequency finding should not be construed as endorsement of this dubious device.

In the same study, Davis and Robinson found that counselors were strongly tempted, when encountering resistance or decreasing rapport, to use techniques of sympathy, reassurance, approval, humor, research citations, personal experience, anecdotes, and rhetorical questions. The investigators concluded that these techniques alone were not sufficiently effective to close discussion units with good rapport. The only exception was approval technique (a support device) which was associated with high rapport in discussion units on vocational problems. A discussion unit is a discrete interview topic in Robinson's (246) research designs.

The counselor's first step in dealing with resistance is to make himself aware of possible external causes in himself and the influence of the amount of lead in his techniques. The counselor then can take judicious steps according to the following suggestions.

(1) The *noting-but-disregarding technique* consists largely of ignoring the symptoms; but it includes alertness to increased resistance. Mere presence of mild resistance does not mean the counselor should do something about it. The content of the discussion unit which arouses resistance is examined for possible adjustments in lead. The counselor realizes that this type of resistance is a normal artifact of counseling. Instead of blaming himself or the client, the counselor concentrates on understanding the unique defensive style or security operations of the client. Resistance indicates to the counselor that the psychic balance in the client is in favor of repression and anxiety control rather than expression.

(2) *Minor adaptations technique* is applied by the counselor when he feels that he must do something actively to reduce the client's resistance if it has reached the second level in Bugental's and Sherman's systems (pronounced inertia, with an outward appearance of cooperation). Obviously, there are no rigid rules about the most efficacious thing to do. The main goal is to reduce the client's defensiveness and to keep him exploring his problem further. Generally, at this level, no attempt is made to change the topic.

One of the minor adaptations which counselors use is *lessening the emotional impact* of the discussion by moving to a more intellectually loaded aspect of the topic which has aroused the resistance. This tends to reduce the pressure felt by the client. Examples are referring to test results, using a nonpersonal illustration, or asking a question which can be answered in a matter-of-fact, casual way. Rhetorical questions can be especially useful when anticipating resistance during the interpretation of personality-appraisal results.

A second minor adaptation technique is a *change of pace* effected by lessening the length of counselor lead, pausing, shifting posture to a more relaxed state, and busy work, such as lighting a cigaret.

A third minor adaptation technique counselors can rely upon is the *judicious use of mild humor* which often eases the tension felt by the client. This must be a natural and spontaneous act, however, since a strained or awkward use of humor, or use with an implication which makes the client appear ridiculous, will "backfire" on the counselor in the form of increased resistance.

Supportive and accepting techniques, as described in the preceding chapter, are often the keys to reduction of resistance, particularly when the client can accept the counselor.

(3) The *temporary diversion technique* involves redirection of interview content to less threatening areas when it appears that the client cannot protect himself adequately by his own defenses. The strategy is to return to the painful subject at a later time. This technique is used with resistance which is hindering, but not yet obstructing interview progress.

The principal element of diversion technique is changing the subject gently. Secondly, the counselor limits his own ego involvement in the process by assuming a more detached and disinterested attitude. This device has the effect of taking pressure off the client by reducing the speed and intensity of the interview. Korner (177) speaks of a "disengagement" technique wherein the counselor examines his own ego involvement in the interview and personal threat in the presence of resistance. In applying this technique, the counselor changes the tone of the feeling of the interview rather than the topic; hence, it is difficult to cite illustrations. The counselor assumes a more reserved and cautious bearing, limits interpretation, or reduces the speed and intensity of the interview.

A third diversion technique is the citation of related research findings, illustrations, a suggested test, or bibliotherapeutic reading matter. These devices often provide the needed change of pace without straying too far from the subject.

(4) *Direct manipulation techniques* are used when the client appears to be aware of his feelings of resistance. Their use assumes a fairly effective working relationship and a well-structured interview. Because these conditions take time to build, direct manipulation techniques are more useful in later interviews. The counselor says, for example, "You have been spending a great deal of time talking about things you wanted to talk about; now let's talk about those things you don't want to talk about."

Interpretation of the resistance, a principal direct technique, involves an explanation of what the client is doing to resist. This technique helps the client develop a tolerance and acceptance for his own resistance as well as an intellectual understanding of its uses and the difficulties caused when resistance gets out of hand. The counselor expresses his own acceptance of the resistance along with the interpretation. This acceptance helps to decrease the likelihood that the client will take offense at the interpretation. Examples are:

> Cl: I just can't talk about it.
> C: You feel that sex is a topic to be avoided. Perhaps you can see that this tendency is serving some useful purpose which we cannot yet understand.
> Cl: Yes, that makes me feel a little better about it.

An example of interpretation of a transference-type problem follows:

> C: (replying after the client has made a series of skeptical comments about the counselor and after a preminary exploration of family relalationships) Do you see that your feelings toward this relationship of ours are possibly related to your feelings about your father? You felt you couldn't trust him and now you unconsciously see your father in me.
> Cl: I never looked at it quite that way before. I'll have to think about that.

Reflection of the feelings of resistance often is effective as a direct technique when the client appears to have an intense feeling, such as guilt, about resisting. It is an effective technique in the earlier interviews where interpretation might be premature.

Referral techniques are needed occasionally when intensive resistance is encountered. The counselor should assess his own therapeutic competence carefully before penetrating the defenses of a highly resistant client. Sometimes, if he shifts the client to another counselor he can remove the source of external resistance which has been inhibiting therapeutic progress.

Threats in veiled form, though a last resort, are useful occasionally in a high-risk attempt to motivate a resistive client to change his behavior. This situation would be apparent where the counselor's role included, in addition, that of Dean, Personnel Manager, or other authoritarian position. For example, a student client having academic difficulties has been resisting discussion of his problem. The counselor may say, "If you don't want to work this out, I suggest we stop getting together."

Summary of resistance: Since one of the counselor's key professional problems is helping clients to overcome resistance, this section was devoted to a discussion of the nature of resistance, illustrating and classifying its manifestations, and suggesting appropriate methods of handling the resistance. Resistance was regarded as a normal part of the counseling process.

SUMMARY

Although transference, countertransference, and resistance are ever-present phenomena in the counseling process, the counselor must deal judiciously with these conditions to keep the process moving toward satisfactory termination. Transference feelings, the projections of stereotypes from the past to a counselor, have an ambiguous status in counseling. Transference feelings can be useful psychological data. They also can hinder counseling progress. Countertransference, the transference feelings of the counselor, is a tendency which must be recognized and resolved by a counselor before counseling can progress satisfactorily. Resistance is the natural blocking of interview progress and must be resolved by a number of counseling techniques—from ignoring the resistance to direct interpretation. Resistance signs serve as useful cues concerning sensitive personality areas, general interview progress, and the nature of the client's defensive structure.

9.

Interpretation Techniques

Techniques which are used primarily to establish and maintain a working relationship between client and counselor have been discussed in Chapter 7. These techniques are fundamentally attitudinal and have the immediate goal of establishing a climate favorable to giving the client security and confidence in the relationship. This is a necessary preface to the important task of assisting the client to develop insight through the medium of interpretation. In contrast to the relationship techniques which establish the counseling climate, the insight-priming, "working-through" techniques with which this chapter is concerned are more intellectualized and laden with content.

Interpretation, like so many psychotherapeutic terms, is construed differently by therapists. The so-called classical psychoanalyst, for example, would label many of the techniques described in the previous chapter interpretation. Remarks intended to confront the client with the nature of his resistance would be considered interpretation as well. Mention is made of this so that the reader will not be led to conclude that only the techniques mentioned in this chapter are categorized universally as interpretation.

NATURE OF INTERPRETATION

The kinds of data which may be interpreted to a client are usually classified by psychologists into two broad categories. Some of the data, in one category, derived from external data which include the wide variety of test results which can be presented and explained to the client in terms of statistical expectancies or, as in the case of projective techniques, as hypotheses for further consideration. Interpretation of such objective data will be discussed in Chapter 10.

The data in the second category are derived from interpersonal data revealed during the counseling process. Interpretations of these data has the purpose of making the client more aware of the relationships among his personal experiences and of enabling his feelings and actions to become more meaningful at a conscious level.

Definition of Interpretation

Interpretation has been defined as an attempt by the counselor to impart meaning to the client. The counselor implies in some way what the client might or ought to think. We prefer a less valuative and directive definition as follows: Interpretation means presenting the client with an *hypothesis* about *relationships* or *meanings* of attitude behaviors for the client's consideration. Interpretation from this viewpoint gives the client more freedom in the resolution of his problems.

Interpretation techniques are used by psychotherapists of most "schools." Nondirective or "client-centered" therapists, however, generally do not favor such techniques as they are defined above. Such psychotherapists appear to restrict their techniques primarily to clarification and reflection of feeling. The Nondirective view holds that interpretation fosters resistance and puts too much therapeutic responsibility on the counselor. We believe, however, that most reflections of feelings are really mild or conservative interpretations. Whenever the psychotherapeutic counselor reflects feeling, he must always *select* from the material which the client has presented to him. These feelings are emotionally toned ideas which the counselor judges to be the most significant of all that have been expressed. Therefore, reflection of feeling is interpretive in the sense that the counselor's judgment of significance is involved. The counselor, through his additional efforts to clarify feeling, generally adds more meaning than the client did originally. On this issue, the nondirective counselor claims that he is not interpreting because he tries to remain completely within the client's meaning framework.

It is posited, therefore, that there is a continuum of differences between reflection of feeling and interpretation with much blending of the two into what we have chosen to call "reflectation." It seems, furthermore, that the alternatives are not either interpretation or reflection, but rather *what kind* and *degree* of interpretive-reflective response the therapist chooses to use. This interpretive continuum concept has been described earlier by Bordin (40) and Collier (66).

The Process of Interpretation through Kelly's Construct System

The psychologist who has described most recently the basic processes of interpretation is George Kelly (165). He considers the material of interpretation to be the personal construct, which he defines as an anticipatory concept or predictive idea which the individual utilizes in dealing with the events or experiences of his life. Kelly, therefore, sees interpretation as a process in which events of life are compared and contrasted with one's constructs. In order to make this process clear, Kelly suggests the utilization of a "Repertory Grid" as illustrated in Figure 19.

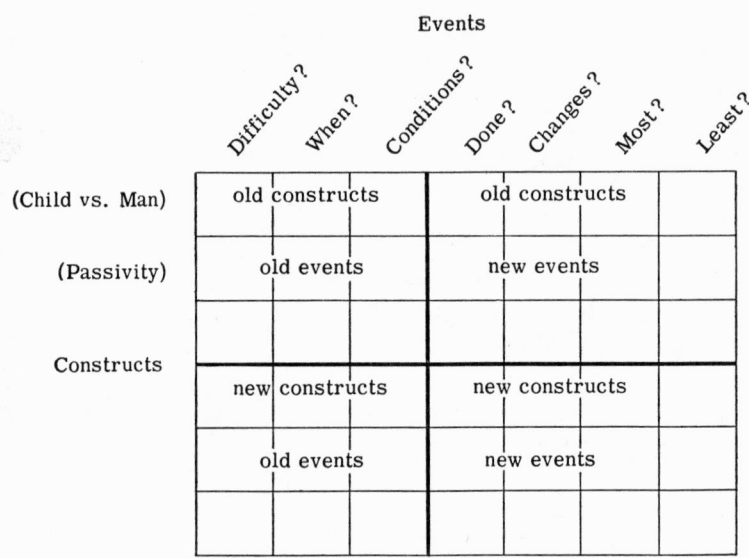

FIG. 19. Kelly's Repertory Grid. Adapted from G. A. Kelly (166a, pg. 28).

It should be noted in Figure 19 that the constructs are arranged as rows and the events as columns. Four quadrants eventually emerge; the upper left-hand quadrant consists of old constructs and old events; the upper right-hand quadrant consists of new experiences applied to old constructs; the lower left-hand quadrant consists of new constructs seen in terms of old events; finally, the lower right-hand quadrant involves new events interpreted in the light of new ideas or constructs. Kelly believes interpretation technique is most effective in this last-mentioned quadrant. The process of interpretation in Kelly's system has five basic steps:

(1) *Seven Basic Questions:* A client makes a generalization about himself which he utilizes as a construct to predict his life events and behavior. For example, he might have feelings of inadequacy which would result in his predicting failure at a task. Unless this construct is related to the events of life, it is meaningless. Kelly proposed seven basic questions by which the therapist can get an elaboration of the client's construct or complaint:

(1) What is the difficulty?
(2) When was it first noticed?
(3) Under what conditions was it first noticed?
(4) What has been done about it?
(5) What changes have come with treatment or the passing of time?

(6) Under what conditions is it most noticeable?

(7) Under what conditions is it least noticeable? (166, pg. 2).

In terms of the Repertory Grid, these seven questions become the vertical columns of Figure 19.

These seven questions are used to elicit statements from the client about significant events in his life. These and other events are then schematically represented in the Repertory Grid by vertical columns. The columns are in turn related to each other by means of constructs with which they are interwoven to give them psychological meaning. Kelly cites the following example:

> Suppose we sketch a simple one-sentence answer to each of the seven questions. A client says he feels inadequate—his answer to the "difficulty" question. He first noticed it when he was in the ninth grade—his answer to the second question. Next, that was the year his companions started having dates. From time to time he sought the solace of his teachers. He became increasingly discouraged about the prospects for his career. As long as someone took a special interest in him things were not so bad. But when he was expected to make it on his own, it became clear how inadequate he really was (166, pg. 3).

(2) *Relating Columns:* Kelly proceeds to his second step in interpretation:

> With the initial answers to our seven basic questions we now have something to construe along with the complaint; that is to say, we have six columns in our Repertory Grid, in addition to the complaint column, and we can start asking in what ways the columns can be related. What are the similarities and contrasts between his companions' having dates and the solace of considerate teachers? What are some of the similarities and contrasts between having a career and having someone take a special interest in him? How do these constructs relate to the feeling of inadequacy (166, pg. 3)?

It should be noted that Kelly's system of contrasting various events could employ the technique which we have labeled reflectation. In setting up the client's statement in different columns, he also enables the client to look at his complaints at different points in time, thus utilizing the contiguity-reflection technique introduced earlier in this Chapter as well.

(3) *Construct Elaboration:* The third step in Kelly's system requires that the therapist focus on constructs which relate to events in the client's life. This process adds to the vertical dimension of the Grid in Figure 19a. Kelly views constructs as dichotomous, black-and-white evaluations about life, since every behavioral act expresses both an affirmation and a denial. Kelly uses the example, "He sought comfort from his teachers from time to time, and that this seems like something quite different from running as a child to his mother, much more like playing the part of a man companion

to his female peers" (166, pg. 7). Here the therapist uses the construct *"frightened child versus man companion"* to see how it applies to other events. With each additional construct developed a new row is added.

(4) *Interpretive Extension:* The fourth step is to construe the columns in terms of construct rows. In this frame of reference, interpretation is defined as applying ideas or constructs to new events, and thus getting over into the right-hand quadrants of Figure 19. Eventually, as the client interweaves constructs and events, *new* constructs are extended to *fresh* events. Kelly illustrates this process as follows:

> Aha, we have been talking all this time about *passivity*, and I understood, of course, that this and that and the other things I have done have really been what we call "passive." But last night, let me tell you, I started to say something to my friends and there it was, just as clear as sin— passivity! . . . Not only that, but "passivity" isn't just a term to describe my behavior with; it is what I, myself, do. It's the game I play whenever I get in a tight spot (166, pg. 11).

(5) *Validation:* Finally, the fifth step in Kelly's system is that of validation which means testing constructs by using them as wagers on the future:

> When they fail, one must go back to his lower left-hand quadrant and reconstrue the events that clutter up his life with confusion. Our client with a burst of insight may find that his notion of passivity still does not point as sharply to subsequent events as it should (166, pg. 12).

We feel that Kelly's system of interpretation is noteworthy as a process of presenting working hypothetical constructs about which facts can be assembled and from which predictions can be made and tested. We feel that Kelly's Repertory Grid System should not be followed rigidly, but it can provide a directional model for the therapist in his therapeutic journey with his client. The interested reader will find Kelly's system of constructs elaborated in his two-volume work (165). His model fits our personality model, presented in Chapter 2, quite well. Kelly's constructs, for example, can be peripheral (those which can be altered without serious modification) or they can be core constructs (which govern the client's maintenance and evaluational processes) (165, pg. 565).

The Rational Approach

A prominent feature of the interpretive phase of counseling and psychotherapy is the emphasis on rational processes. In this tradition Ellis has evolved a point of view for psychotherapy which he calls "rational psychotherapy."[1] We believe that this system has value for certain types of clients, particularly for those who are bright and flexible in their thinking. Because the Ellis approach has implications for our discussion of interpretive techniques, we are including a summary of his views.

---

[1] Albert Ellis, "Rational Psychotherapy," *J. Gen. Psych.* (1958), *59*, 35–49.

Rational psychotherapy "is based on the assumption that human beings normally become emotionally disturbed through acquiring irrational and illogical thoughts, philosophies, or attitudes" (pg. 3).[2] The therapist analyzes the client's feelings of hurt, anger, fear, and guilt, and shows ". . . him that these emotions arise not from past events or external situations but from his present irrational attitudes or illogical fears about these events or situations" (pg. 3).[2] To Ellis, therefore, "Emotion itself is conceived of as *largely being a certain kind, a biased, prejudiced kind, of thought"* (pg. 3).[2]

Some of the major illogical ideas or philosophies which have been learned and believed by troubled individuals in western culture are described by Ellis in the following excerpts. We quote them in full so the reader can get a more complete picture of the kinds of values and ideas which Ellis suggests as replacements for what is often regarded as irrational thinking. The reader is referred to our earlier discussion of values in Chapter 6 and of semantics, later, in Chapter 10. The following excerpts illustrate the problem of broadening the client's value possibilities and perceptions of his world so as to find the most effective means of construing his life circumstances.

1. The idea that it is a dire necessity for an adult to be loved or approved by everyone for everything he does—instead of his concentrating on his own self-respect, on winning approval for necessary purposes (such as job advancement), and on loving rather than being loved.

2. The idea that certain acts are wrong, or wicked, or villainous, and that people who perform such acts should be severely punished—instead of the idea that certain acts are inappropriate or antisocial, and that people who perform such acts are invariably stupid, ignorant, or emotionally disturbed.

3. The idea that it is terrible, horrible, and catastrophic when things are not the way one would like them to be—instead of the idea that it is too bad when things are not the way one would like them to be, and one should certainly try to change or control conditions so that they become more satisfactory, but that if changing or controlling uncomfortable situations is impossible, one had better become resigned to their existence and stop telling oneself how awful they are.

4. The idea that much human unhappiness is externally caused and is forced on one by outside people and events—instead of the idea that virtually all human unhappiness is caused or sustained by the view one takes of things rather than the things themselves.

5. The idea that if something is or may be dangerous or fearsome one should be terribly concerned about it—instead of the idea that if something is or may be dangerous or fearsome one should frankly face it and try to render it non-dangerous and, when that is impossible, think of other things and stop telling oneself what a terrible situation one is or may be in.

---

[2] Albert Ellis, "The Treatment of a Psychopath with Rational Psychotherapy," published in Italian, *Quaderni di Criminologia Clinica* (1949), 2, 1–11.

6. The idea that it is easier to avoid than to face life difficulties and self-responsibilities—instead of the idea that the so-called easy way is invariably the much harder way in the long run and that the only way to solve difficult problems is to face them squarely.

7. The idea that one needs something other or stronger or greater than oneself on which to rely—instead of the idea that it is usually far better to stand on one's own feet and gain faith in oneself and one's ability to meet difficult circumstances of living.

8. The idea that one should be thoroughly competent, adequate, intelligent, and achieving in all possible respects—instead of the idea that one should *do* rather than always try to do *well* and that one should accept oneself as a quite imperfect creature, who has general human limitations and specific fallibilities.

9. The idea that because something once strongly affected one's life, it should indefinitely affect it—instead of the idea that one should learn from one's past experiences but not be overly attached to our prejudiced by them.

10. The idea that it is vitally important to our existence what other people do, and that we should make great efforts to change them in the direction we would like them to be—instead of the idea that other people's deficiencies are largely *their* problems and that putting pressure on them to change is usually least likely to help them do so.

11. The idea that human happiness can be achieved by inertia and in-action—instead of the idea that humans tend to be happiest when they are actively and vitally absorbed in creative pursuits, or when they are devoting themselves to people or projects outside themselves.

12. The idea that one has virtually no control over one's emotions and that one cannot help feeling certain things—instead of the idea that one has enormous control over one's emotions if one chooses to work at controlling them and to practice saying the right kinds of sentences to oneself (pp. 40–41).[1]

Ellis adds that there is more to therapy than changing some beliefs, but Ellis does not seem to believe that it is necessary, as in psychoanalysis, to focus on historical events to show the patient how he *became* disturbed. Rather, he feels that after any necessary support or ventilation of feelings, emphasis should be placed on *attacking* his irrational beliefs and on showing how he is *sustaining* his neurosis by still believeing them. He then teaches him how to *re-verbalize* and *re-think* these ideas in a more logical, self-helping way. Finally, he encourages the client to engage in *activity* which will prove the validity of his newly formed and valid assumptions about life.

THE INTERPRETIVE CONTINUUM

In the chapter on relationship techniques, great emphasis was placed upon reflection of feeling. There are additional therapeutic techniques which may be placed on an interpretive continuum between reflection of feeling and interpretation.

The key idea underlying reflection of feeling is that the therapist goes no further than the client has already *explicitly* gone in his verbal productions. A technique which goes beyond this just slightly is called "clarification" which means clarifying to the client what is *implicit* in what he has just said. Clarification, therefore, reflects relationships or meanings for the client which are *suggested* or *implied* in the feelings or ideas brought out by the client's actual responses.

A third point on the interpretive continuum is expressed by the term, "reflectation" we have described earlier. Reflectation goes beyond clarification in that it deals with material which, in the judgment of the counselor, is just beyond the *consciousness* of the client. Both deal, however, with material which is *implicit*.

Reflectation requires knowledge of psychodynamics and mechanisms of which the client is not aware, usually. In using reflectation, the counselor adds strong cognitive elements to his reflection of feelings. It gives the client a feeling of forward movement in that it verbalizes material which the client may have felt only vaguely. It is analogous to the pacing of a young race horse by a more mature one. The counselor goes far enough beyond the client's conscious verbalizations to stimulate further thinking, but not so far that he loses him.

A fourth point on the interpretive continuum is the technique called "confrontation." Here the counselor brings to the attention of the client ideas and feelings which are *implicit* but *unconscious*. In using this technique, the therapist confronts the client with his own words, but relates past to present, pointing out similarities, differences, and discrepancies of which the client is unaware.

Finally, in depth interpretation, the therapist introduces new concepts, relationships, and associations which are rooted in the client's experience, but which are taught at a fairly deep unconscious level. It is as if the therapist were grafting ideas to some of the client's deep roots, giving him suggestions for new directions of growth which are felt necessary for his developing maturity.

Some examples of the above levels of interpretation follow:

> Cl: Last night I was really bothered by a wet dream I had which involved a little seven-year-old girl who looked partly like my baby sister and partly like my little daughter.
> (1) Reflection:
> "It was really disturbing to have such a dream."
> (2) Clarification:
> "It bothered you to have an experience which suggested erotic impulses toward your daughter or sister."
> (3) Reflectation:
> "It concerns you that you may be having the same impulses toward your daughter that you have had toward your sister."
> (4) Confrontation:

"You apparently have similar erotic impulses toward your daughter as you reported you had toward your little sister.

(5) Interpretation:

"You are becoming more free to admit your past and present impulses toward those whom you love, even though it is disturbing to express feelings that are so strictly forbidden in our society."

The foregoing discussion is summarized in Figure 20.

TECHNIQUE

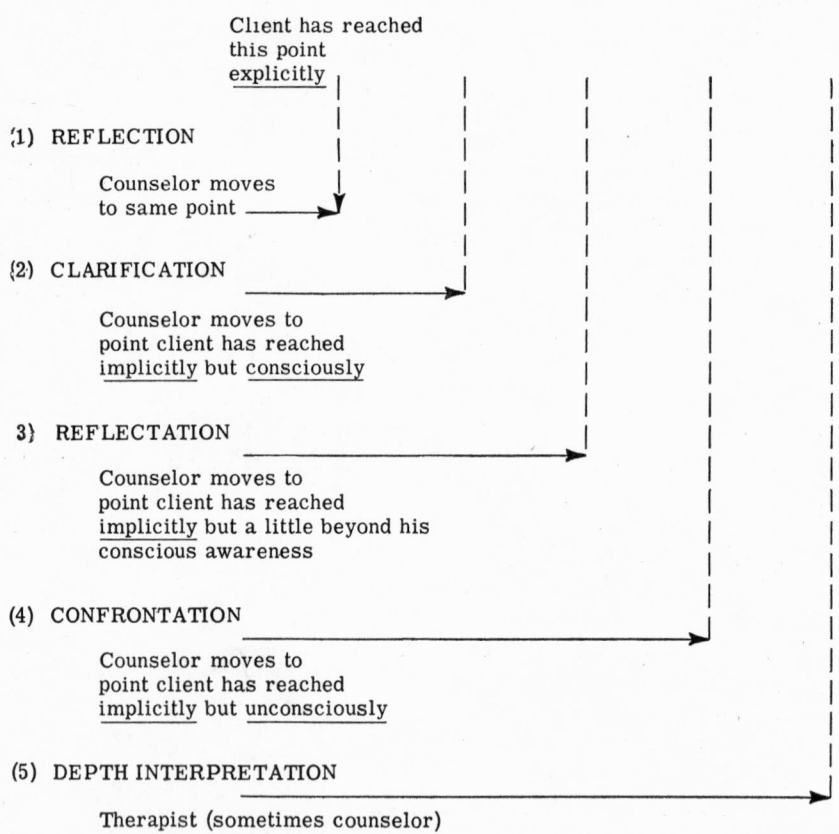

FIG. 20. The Interpretive Continuum.

In the following discussion, the technique of reflectation is expanded. Reflectation has two major forms which are described as *associative* and *suggestive*.

Associative Reflectation

In this type of reflectation the counselor presents an hypothesis which draws together or makes associations between the client's explicit or implicit thoughts or feelings. Four major forms of association can be distinguished.

(1) *Similarity:* The counselor may draw together two ideas with similar content as follows: "What you are saying now about your wife appears to be very closely related to the feelings which you expressed about your mother a few weeks ago. Would you say that is a fair statement?" (2) *Contrast:* The counselor may associate two dissimilar ideas. An example of this form would be: "I gather, from what you said, your feelings about your father are almost the opposite of those you have about your mother." (3) *Contiguity:* The counselor may associate ideas which are close in space and time. For example, "You seem to get these feelings of tension whenever you come into the biology laboratory?" (4) *Distance:* The counselor may associate ideas or feelings which are far apart in space and time. For instance, "You seem to have many of the feelings toward this person that you had toward your mother several years ago under similar circumstances."

In all associative reflectations the counselor may relate feelings or ideas to each other which have been evident in prior sessions and which seem to have some relevance to the client's present expressions. The counselor may thus be said to reduce the distance in time and space between the client's feelings and thoughts in order to make them more comprehensible, to stimulate finer differentiations, or to promote integration of feelings and ideas.

Suggestive Reflectations

A second type of reflectation is that of the suggestive reflectation. In this type, the counselor suggests to the client certain ideas and feelings which are related to material already presented. It is hypothesized that these ideas and feelings are "unconsciously suggested" by the client's presentation, although not consciously verbalized. Suggestive reflectation verbalizes this connection. An example is, "You seem to understand that your feelings of hostility might be at the root of your social difficulties."

Suggestive reflectation differs from general interpretation in that nothing new is brought out in the interview except that which is "unconsciously," or by remote implication, suggested by the client's comments. In contrast, by the general interpretation method, hypotheses or meanings are imparted to the client which may or may not be thought by the counselor to be suggested by the client.

Curran (75) uses the term "forking response" to describe a situation where it is important, in the counselor's opinion, to bridge superficial problems in order to reach deeper concerns. The counselor accepts the client's feeling that perhaps the problem goes beyond the one he has just stated, and he broadens his reflective response to include references to the deeper problem. For example, a client is describing at length his scholastic difficulties and has included a few references to girl problems implying a lack of information on sex. The counselor responds, "School work has been difficult for you and it seems to have been complicated by problems with girls. I gather that sex is part of the difficulty. You seem to feel that all of these things are tied together." This response opens the way for the client to talk about his more emotionally involved concerns and is an open invitation to move away from the topic of scholastic difficulties to the underlying problems. The "forking response" is a further illustration of the use of suggestive reflection.

Suggestive reflections can be classified into five general categories:

(1) *Pacing Reflectation:* Here, the counselor words his reflection in a manner which will pace the client. In other words, the counselor moves out just a little ahead of the client's thinking, but in the direction which he believes the client is unconsciously going. An example follows:

Cl: It's difficult to talk about these things.
C: They are painful to you. (Implying that growth is often painful.)
Cl: You might put it that way—and yet I need to face them.
C: It's painful, and you feel it necessary to discuss it; yet would you say it is a relief too? After you talk about them you feel better? (Introduces a clinical principle.)
Cl: Yeah. Once I get it out it doesn't seem so strong any more.
C: It's like an internal cleansing process.

(2) *Selective Reflectation:* Using this form, the counselor selectively emphasizes feelings or ideas expressed by the client which the counselor judges to be of therapeutic significance even though these feelings or ideas have not yet been given this weight by the client. An example follows:

Cl: I just feel so all alone. I have no one. I guess I'm just weak. You don't like me either, do you?
C: You don't think much of yourself? (Relates to self-concepts.)
Cl: No I don't. Oh, I guess I'm not all bad—there are some things about me which I like.
C: Not all black; some lighter shades of grey? (Reflects ambivalent self-regard.)

It may be noted here that material relative to the client's self-concept is suggested to him directly.

Should the counselor select the most important feeling to comment on, or should he reflect all those that have been stated? Though it may be desirable to give summary reflections in later interviews, it is our opinion that responses should be short in the first interviews because of the client's need to get release. The clarification and insight value of more complete counselor reflectations is likely to be overshadowed by the frustrations of emotional-release needs.

(3) *Labeling Reflectation:* Here, the counselor utilizes some of the common psychological labels which may assist the client in understanding his situation more concisely.

> Cl: I just can't seem to get to the things which really bother me. I keep talking about all kinds of irrelevant things.
> C: Let's learn a new word today. Would you say that you are kind of "resisting" the process?
> Cl: Yes, that's it.

One danger of this method is that the discussion may become too abstract and may sound like the table of contents from a textbook.

(4) *Reflectation of Unhealthy or Untenable Attitudes:* Many adjustment problems of normal people relate to unhealthy or untenable attitudes which are acquired in experience. Sometimes this takes the form of "canned thinking" where people act or believe certain assumptions about human behavior which they have learned from people without psychological sophistication. Bugental suggests other ways in which clients have crystallized their attitudes in unhealthy neurotic thinking. Many of these perceptions have come from general cultural attitudes and not from the personal experience of the client. He gives the following as examples:

> Something is wrong with a person who feels both love and hate toward the opposite sex; you should be devoted to your spouse, and if anyone else interests you, it shows you are fickle or over-sexed. It is childish to want something you can't have. If you've once given up a habit, you should never feel any desire to practice it again. If one doesn't try to be the best in whatever he does, he's giving up, a quitter. The easy way is, *ipso facto,* the wrong way. If you have to *learn* how to get along better with people, it isn't natural. Normal people (or, other people) know why they do anything and want to do whatever they do. If I were only in the right field, I would want to work hard and wouldn't have to force myself (45, pg. 5).

The counselor should be sensitive to ideas, beliefs, or attitudes such as those given in the examples and suggest their fallaciousness through reflectation. The following is an example:

> Cl: I hate my father. And there's no reason for it. It makes me feel awful because it's a sin to hate your father—especially if there's no reason for it.
> C: You feel that a person just shouldn't hate his parents, especially if there is no reason for it?
> Cl: Yes, don't you think so?
> C: Many people do have such feelings; we call them ambivalent feelings—

feeling both ways about the same person. I gather, however, that this is objectionable to you.

(5) *Humorous Reflectation:* This type of reflection employs the use of humor by the counselor to help the client to regard his situation more light-heartedly. Crying and laughing seem to be fraternal twins. Adlai Stevenson's comment upon losing the election in 1952 is an illustration: "It hurts too much to laugh and I'm too old to cry." Psychotherapy is not a laughing matter, but there are times when the introduction of humor may facilitate the growth process. Humor seems to help the client gain perspective and makes bearable the anxiety which often destroys decision-making powers.

> Cl: I hate this place, and everybody in it; including you. You make me so damn mad just sitting there.
> C: Boy, you're really giving me both barrels today, eh?
> Cl: Yes, damn it; real shotgun barrels, too.
> C: I guess this is the season for counselors. Why do you think you feel this way?

Humor in this instance implies the acceptance of the client's feelings and may serve to reduce guilt feelings. The counselor can also use it to reduce or put in perspective a client's strong feelings. It can also be a kind of "capping off" effect.

It should be mentioned that the use of humor in therapy, although many times effective, should be used with caution. It certainly should not be overused, nor should it be used with anxious, guilt-ridden clients. Generally humor should not be used until the relationship is well established.

TYPES OF INTERPRETATION

Karl Menninger (204) presents an interesting scheme for identifying various types of interpretation in terms of the time sequence in psychotherapy. It is presented here according to the logic of the present volume.

(1) *Preparation for interpretation:*

> Having identified some connections, or certain common elements, in a considerable number of events in the patient's life, . . . the next step is to further the preparation for real interpretation (204, pg. 136).

Our system for presenting reflection and reflectation techniques early in the interview seems to fit here. Essentially, reflection or reflectation techniques are viewed as those methods which help the client to perceive connections or common elements in his life.

(2) *Real (content) interpretation:*

> Sooner or later, the therapist is in a position to say something like this: "This thing, then—(this trick, this experience, this defense, this defeat)—

happens to you repeatedly; it seems to happen especially to you. You seem to have something to do with its happening. Perhaps it doesn't just *happen,* possibly you actually do it. You have done it before. Perhaps you have some hidden purpose behind it, a purpose which was once valid but which is no longer valid. This can be seen as what Fate does to you; but let us look at what you do with your Fate!" (204, pp. 136–137).

As Menninger recognizes too, such interpretations tend to be hard blows to the client. He will attempt to justify, to "not get it," to theorize, to digress, to dawdle at some of these interpretations.

(3) *Interpretation of resistance:*

Instead of rubbing his nose in it, so to speak, one proceeds to the interpretation of the resistance. One says in substance "You do not want to see this for certain reasons." First, one points out that such resistance exists, then one points out how it manifests itself; then one points out its obvious purpose (and, of course, if one doesn't know what its obvious purpose is, then the patient's cooperation has to be enlisted in that search). In general, of course, the purpose is to avoid seeing the unpleasant truth (204, pg. 137).

(4) *Transference interpretation:*

It (the real interpretation) may be further obscured by various transference patterns and purposes; the patient may be bribing, defying, or seducing the analyst (204, pg. 137).

It may be seen, above, that transference, as we have already mentioned, is a form of resistance to real interpretation which is yet too painful to accept.

(5) *"Working through" or repeat interpretations:*

. . . Resistance will often cover with the same obliviousness the repetition of the same old pattern, so that all that was won by painstaking labor seems to be forgotten. . . . We have to begin (over and over) again from the beginning (204, pg. 138).

This necessity for "working through," for the analyst to repeat interpretations until they are taken hold of is a reflection of the extension of the neurosis into many different aspects of or events of the patient's life. His defensive structure isolates these events from one another, so that he is not aware of the common tendency running through them. In the language of some learned theorists, the "transfer" or "spread of effect" of the insight from one situation to other situations is limited or blocked. In Freud's words "One must allow the patient to get to know his resistance. . . ." Hence the necessity of repeating the interpretations as the patient repeats his neurotic behavior in different contexts (204, pg. 138).

The discussion emphasizes our view that "resistance" in the interview can be perceived as a reflection of the style of life or manner of approach to life which the client has developed. This resistance pattern generally must be made clear repeatedly to the client before he comes to understand its significance.

In connection with the earlier discussion on the differences between counseling and psychotherapy, you may have seen that when the counselor makes the therapeutic plunge into a "real interpretation," he has become, by definition, a psychotherapist. He must be prepared to handle the resistance, transference, and "working through" problems which follow. A counselor usually does not attempt to work at this deeper interpretive level because of time, training, and experience limitations.

USING INTERPRETATION

Although there are no universally valid rules for interpretation, there are some guidelines which, if individualized, and applied judiciously by the counselor can help the client in his insight-seeking venture. The following discussion leans heavily on Fromm-Reichmann (118).

Knowing What to Interpret

The content of interpretation is determined by the particular stage in the counseling process. In the early interviews it may be necessary for the counselor to interpret attitudes toward counseling and the meaning of resistance. He keeps interpretations very general and tentative at first, the main purposes being to explain the process to the client and to open up new areas for consideration.

Later, the interpretations take the form of explanations of how defense mechanisms develop and function in reference to the client's unconscious drives. Here, in the middle of the process, the counselor makes interpretations more specific. At the end of the working-through phase, he makes the interpretations more general and vague to encourage the client to do his own interpreting. He also has the goal of closing issues, rather than stirring up new problems. So, interpretations become fewer and more general toward the end of the process.

Knowing When to Interpret

Perhaps the most important consideration in the use of interpretation is that of timing. In general, interpretations are made very cautiously and, in the counselor's judgment, not until the client is ready to accept them. Freud has stated many times that an interpretation should be given only when the client is at the point where he can almost formulate it himself.

It is wise for the counselor to interpret, or to elicit interpretations from the client, after he has gained some awareness of the subject area of the proposed interpretation. In other words, interpretations should rarely be offered "blindly." There are occasions, however, when clients may be accelerated by a thoughtful "shot in the dark"; but this should be regarded as a high-risk technique.

As a general rule, reflection of feeling dominates the early phase of counseling, followed by the tentative formulations of reflections. In the later stages when insight must be consolidated, general interpretation is appropriate. Figure 21 illustrates the time relationships of technique to the counseling process.

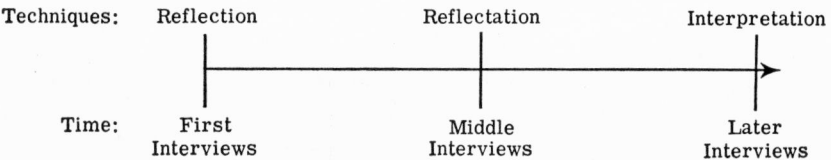

FIG. 21. Process Timing of Interpretations.

Interpretation is usually reserved for later interviews when the relationship is well established and when the client is in a less resistive state. The counselor's interpretations must be based upon and verified by the information obtained in earlier interviews. This avoids making the client feel that he is being treated as a stereotype rather than as an individual. He may feel, rightly, that the counselor is way off base when he gives him explanations with little supportive evidence.

The counselor, generally, should not offer interpretations unless he has an extensive picture of his client's personality and an evaluation of any pathology. The client should be able to handle the additional anxiety expected to be generated by the interpretation without regressing or developing other symptoms.

It should be made explicit that many times an interpretation may be appropriate because the client's fear is operating to keep a threatening emotional linkage unconscious. For the counselor to interpret without assessing the client's readiness and ability to cope with the interpretation is to risk breaking a dam that has served the psychic economy and may flood the client with truly destructive anxiety.

Often the counselor will make interpretations early in the interview so there will be sufficient time for him to work through the client's reactions. This is especially true when deep or potentially threatening interpretations have to be made. When such interpretations are made late in the interview, the client may become panicky before the next counseling session or may build up resistances to facing this issue in later sessions so that there is a step backward instead of forward.

There is an occasion when interpretations are given more appropriately toward the end of the interview, when it is necessary to prepare the client carefully for the interpretation and to collect current documentation to support the interpretation. There are also occasions when the counselor should plant interpretations in the form of suggestions at the end of the interview to stimulate the client's thinking between sessions.

When the counselor offers an interpretation, however, the elaboration should come from the client. This takes time. A useful technique, in this connection, is to let the client describe his problem and then encourage him to get off and look at it. For example, the client has just given a long description of a family problem. The counselor responds, "Now that you have described your feelings about your parents, what do you think this means? How does it seem to you?"

The greatest danger to the counselor in the use of this important technique is in giving interpretations which as yet are too painful or intolerable for the client to face. A client can be thrown into a panic state or even stimulated to suicidal attempts if interpretations are forcibly presented before he is ready. The counselor must be able to sense when the client has sufficient ego strength to accept and to assimilate constructively the new ideas. The more extensive the counselor's background and understanding of abnormal psychology and human psychodynamics, and the more he knows and understands the individual client, the better prepared he will be to time interpretive techniques.

Authoritative Interpretation

Although the principles of interpretation presented so far in this chapter are based on the idea of tentativeness and hypothesizing, there are certain occasions when tentative interpretations have little impact. Here, a bold authoritative interpretation may, in the words of Wolberg, "upset the balance between the repressed and repressing forces" (323, pg. 442). Even if the client denies the authoritative interpretation he may later work through to its acceptance. The fact that the client vehemently denies the authoritarian interpretation, is often a sign that he accepts it as valid. The following interview excerpt is an illustration of this form of interpretation:

    C: Does this fear of being critical relate to other people? (Exploring a neurotic pattern.)
    Cl: Not everybody.
    C: How about me? (This is an attempt to see if her critical feeling applies to me.)
    Cl: (Pause, patient's eyes tear.) This is silly. I'm afraid you'll think me silly. (Cries) (The fact that this emotional reaction is evoked shows that transference may be operating.)
    C: You are afraid to be critical of me. (Authoritative interpretation of her reaction to the expression of criticism toward me.)

> Cl: (Continues crying) There have been several things you said that hurt my feelings. (Cries) (323, pg. 443).

It is generally true that interpretation is given when the client is "ready." However, there may be situations when an interpretation, such as the one given above, is given for a type of "shock" effect to establish a new train of thought. The counselor, however, should be prepared for the resistance likely to follow. If an interpretation is not accepted immediately it is not necessarily an indication that the interpretation was ill-timed or inaccurate. Occasionally clients will mention hours later an interpretation which started them thinking seriously along a certain line, but which was met with resistance at the time it was given.

Criteria for Judging the Adequacy of Interpretations

Schafer (265) suggests that in using projective techniques, the counselor must distinguish between thoroughness and recklessness in giving test interpretations. We feel that the same principle holds for psychotherapeutic interpretations. Schafer presents six criteria for judging the adequacy of a test interpretation which are modifed below to apply to therapeutic interpretation:

(1) *There should be sufficient evidence for the interpretation.* Usually it is unwise to interpret until a definite trend becomes evident in the client's discussions. There should be several expressions which confirm the hypothesis underlying the interpretation. An example is: "You have said a number of things now which suggest that you are trying to prove something. Could it be that . . . ?"

(2) *The depth of the interpretation should be appropriate.* By depth is meant the degree to which an interpretation is historical, or the extent to which the interpretation reveals deeply unconscious core material. Depth interpretations usually are not given until the latter half of psychotherapy when there is enough material to justify the interpretation and the relationship between therapist and client is good enough to withstand the trauma which a deep interpretation may cause. Deep interpretation is not generally made in counseling relationships, but is a significant part of deep psychotherapy. An example is: "Your dreams and the experiences you have had in the past as well as recently all point to the idea that you have refused to recognize the feminine elements in your personality."

(3) *Whenever possible, the manifest behavior of the interpreted tendency should be specified.* To give, simply, an interpretation without evidence which the client can see in his own behavior is not helpful. When the counselor can point out evidence to his client which he cannot deny, it is much more likely that the validity of the interpretation will be apparent to him. The deeper an interpretation, the greater is the difficulty to make it. The counselor can interpret a defensive tendency and can give

many examples of this difficulty to the patient. To interpret a drive or motive, however, is more difficult. An example from early in the psychotherapy process might be: "You seem to handle things in your situation with a certain compulsion—that is, by keeping a very tight schedule for yourself. Is this true?" An example from later in the therapy process might be: "Can you see how your mother's need to toilet train you so early might have given you a tendency to be 'just so' and overconscientious?"

(4) *The intensity of the interpreted trend should be estimated.* Schafer (265) suggests a five-point rating scale to describe the intensity of the counselor's interpretation: (1) extreme (intense), (2) strong (marked, conspicuous), (3) moderate, (4) weak (slight), and (5) negligible. This scheme may seem to contradict earlier statements in which it was suggested that interpretations should always be tentative. But, there is always the question of "How tentative?" If sufficient evidence warrants the interpretation, it seems that the psychotherapist is unfair to himself if he does not express a certain degree of confidence in his interpretation. Furthermore, the counselor must distinguish between the *data* which suggest a logical interpretation and his own intuitive feelings which involve being authoritative about his interpretation. The former, it seems, is more justified to mention in the interpretation. An example follows: "You have mentioned a number of times, now, some actions toward your father which indicate that you dislike him intensely even though you haven't said you feel this way."

(5) *The interpreted tendency should be given a hierarchic position in the total personality picture.* Schafer distinguishes between "chain-like interpretations" and "hierarchic interpretations." The former are given without attempts to tie them together dynamically, as can be seen in the following example: "You seem to be a hostile sort of guy. You are at the same time very anxious and you do a lot of things which are inefficient."

The hierarchic type of interpretation attempts to synthesize the data into a well-established clinical pattern, such as: "You have strong feelings of hostility which you are trying to defend yourself against by a compulsive need to stay close to home. Because you cannot completely contain these hostile feelings this way you are expressing them by appearing anxious." As Schafer points out, assigning hierarchic positions to the data presupposes a hierarchic personality theory, such as has been suggested in Chapter 2. The interpretation then may start peripherally and move centrally, or *vice versa,* as in the following paradigm:

> Drive (Unconscious) Defense—Adaptation (Conscious)
> Attitudes (Conscious) Values—Identity (Self-Concept)

(6) *The adaptive and pathological aspects of the interpreted tendency should be distinguished.* Interpretations should emphasize the adaptive strengths as well as the pathological tendencies of the client. As Schafer

points out, the same trend can have both adaptive and pathological aspects. Examples are: "Your inability to admit your hostility makes you outwardly gentle and kind, but on the other hand, it keeps you from being self-assertive and gives you a saintly approach which makes others mad at you." "Your withdrawal tendencies have helped you to cultivate your artistic talent, but on the other hand, they have maintained your distrust of others."

General Methods of Interpretation

Tentative approach. Nondirective counselors frequently are critical of directive counselors because they feel that their interpretations are given dogmatically and without finesse. This is a gross misconception because even the highly directive counselor generally suggests interpretations rather than states them harshly. He does not say, "This is the way it is"; but rather, "This appears to be this," or "This seems to be this way with you." This method is similar to Robinson's "tentative analysis" technique (246) wherein the counselor suggests a fresh approach to the problem.

Free association. Especially in the early stages of interpretations, it is important for the counselor to stay *with* the client and not to get too far ahead. The counselor should not give the impression he is a detective trying stealthily to observe, diagnose, and influence the client. One of his main goals is to help the client do his own interpreting. This is done through a process of loosening his thinking so that new relationships become more apparent to him. Loosening is facilitated by encouraging more free associ- ation. For example, the counselor reminds the client to "say whatever comes into your mind"; "Let yourself go"; "Don't try to be consistent and logical"; "Just give me parts of ideas"; "Say it, even if it seems vague or unimportant to you."

Free association is a fundamental technique of psychoanalysis which was introduced by Freud. As Sullivan suggests, however, "trying to tell patients what is meant by free association, and trying to get them to do it, can be quite a problem" (295, pg. 83). He recommends that the best way to handle this problem is for the counselor to demonstrate it to the client by having him associate to a particular question which may arise in the in- terview, for which he has no answer. For the counselor to ask him at that time to talk at random about the question often gives a convincing demon- stration of the effectiveness of this technique. An example might be:

C: You seem to be stuck on this question of the importance of your mother's influence on you. Suppose you try stating the word "Mother" and then follow it with as many words as come to your mind in rapid-fire order. Get it?

Cl: I think so . . . Mother—nice—soft—does things—silly—mad—stu- pid—damn her.

C: You really resent her doing so many things for you, and yet you like it too?

This fragmentation and association of ideas often leads to relationships which the client might never have discovered. When the free association leads to significant areas the counselor may then accelerate the reintegration process again by using short-lead interpretations, such as questions. An example would be, "This discussion reminds you, then, of how your past ways of looking at your parents and your present feelings are similar?" One of the goals of the counselor here is to move among the different levels of client thinking, pointing out parallels and contrasts as described in the section on reflectation technique.

A cardinal goal of all counselors for clients is assisting them toward *self-interpretation*. The client must get the insight, not the counselor.

Karpman (162) developed a self-interpretation method which he has labeled "objective psychotherapy." Here, the client gives the counselor the preliminary case data from which the counselor formulates questions. The client takes the questions home to write out answers and weave in materials from his reading. When the client returns, he and the counselor discuss the written materials and do further interpretation. From this discussion, an additional set of questions is formulated. At certain places in the process the psychotherapist gives the client interpretive memoranda which the client comments upon in writing.

Because so much written material is involved, the Karpman technique appears to require more than average intelligence, cooperation, and persistence from the client. It is offered here as an additional device to encourage client participation in the interpretation process. The ultimate usefulness of this device, however, must depend upon the adequacy of interpretations made both by the client and counselor, and upon an evaluation of whether this intellectualized approach reinforces defensive intellectualization.

Phrasing interpretations. Phrasing is a significant element of interpretation. It is suggested that counselors should use "soft" words which imply tentativeness rather than certainty such as,

> "perhaps; will you; it's possible; do you suppose; I wonder if; would you buy this; does this seem to fit." These carefully chosen words tend to minimize resistance.

Thorne (303, pg. 301), furthermore, suggests some more acceptable phrasing for interpretations and suggestions.

"Would you buy this idea . . ."
"Is this a fair statement . . ."
"What would you think of . . ."
"For what it's worth . . ."
"You feel this is the only solution . . ."
"Ben Franklin had a saying . . ."

The best interpretations are phrased in the client's own terms and constructions. The counselor does not have to use the exact words of the client, but he should maintain the same general style and concept level.

Thorne (303, pg. 302) suggests some *unacceptable* phrases which are often cited in criticisms of interpretation.

"I think you should . . ."
"The only thing for you to do is . . ."
"If I were you I would . . ."
"I'm going to tell you what to do . . ."
"There's only one right way to do it . . ."
"I want you to do this . . ."
"There is a better way to do it . . ."
"You must try to do this . . ."
"If you don't do this you may be sorry . . ."

Counselor Insecurity and Hostility. Interpretations should not be made on the basis of projected personal experience of the counselor. Neither should the counselor reason that "this worked in another case; so it should apply here." If the counselor feels insecure about an interpretation, he would do well to avoid it.

Hostility from clients is encountered frequently and should not disturb the counselor or tempt him into an argument with the client. Interpretive techniques occasionally provoke client hostility and the fact that this feeling is aroused and that the interpretation is not accepted gives the counselor valuable data. Perhaps it would be better if the interpretation were dropped and raised again at a more opportune time.

Repetition. Repetition is an important interpretive principle. Since a useful and valid interpretation may be resisted, it may be necessary for the counselor to repeat the interpretation at appropriate times, in different forms, and with additional supporting evidence. The client often achieves understanding after this concerted effort which he might not after one early interpretation.

Although repetition is an important learning principle, it should be mentioned that the counselor would do well to re-examine his interpretive hypothesis and try to understand the evidence pro and con on it rather than blindly pushing it again and again on his client. One of the best checks in therapeutic work is to test whether the therapist's hypothesized model of the client's dynamics can explain the *resistance* to the interpretation as well as the interpretation itself.

Interpretive questions. Interpretations are hunches or hypotheses based upon client observation more than they are declarative statements of fact. The question, therefore, is a common format for interpretation. These questions vary from general leads such as, "Would you care to discuss this idea a little further?" through moderately structured questions such as, "How do you mean that?" "What does this mean?" "Would you like to talk about it?" "How did that make you feel?" to highly structured interpretive questions such as, "Do you think, then, that perhaps you distrust men because your father did not treat you well?"

In a special approach to questioning, Boileau (38) suggests that often the client is endeavoring through some behavior to satisfy a certain basic need. His mode of expression or way of satisfying this need may be inappropriate. The problem, therefore, is not the need, but is more the manner of expression. He recommends that the counselor simply ask the client, "What's wrong with that?" This starts the client to explore his behavior to determine the root need. The client typically reacts with all of the social moralizing which prohibits such behavior. The implication of the question, however, is that he can go on with this type of "acting out" if he so desires. However, continued questioning of this type usually leads him to an evaluation wherein he determines whether or not this behavior is to his greatest interest and advantage. The main limitation of this technique is the danger of incurring client resistance. The following example illustrates Boileau's method:

> Cl: I just have to buy new clothes all the time.
> C: What's wrong with that?
> Cl: Well, you just can't spend all your money that way.
> C: Why not?
> Cl: You wouldn't have any money left.
> C: So——
> Cl: You'd starve!
> C: Oh?
> Cl: I know, there are other needs that we have to satisfy, besides being pretty.

Another approach to the utilization of questions in psychotherapy is the idea that therapy is not so much a process of giving quick and easy answers as it is a process of assisting the client to ask himself appropriate questions. An example of a basic question that needs to be faced squarely by any client is: "Shouldn't you be concerned about yourself too?" As several writers, notably Rogers (249), and Snygg and Combs (285) have suggested, the preservation and enhancement of the self is a most important need. Fromm (113) suggests the importance of recognizing the significance of self-love and respect. As indicated in Chapter 7, each client, from our experience, must cope with this basic problem of self-love. By the use of appropriate questions, the counselor can assist the client to ask himself some of the basic questions which lead to answers needed for self-acceptance and a healthy personality.

Limitations of Interpretation

Although much has been written about the value of interpretation for promoting insight, there have been strong arguments and some data advanced against the overuse of the technique. The principal limitations cited are that interpretation is threatening; hence, resistance is aroused which blocks spontaneous new perceptions and understandings. Interpretation may have the effect of reducing client self-explorations. Bergman (29), for example, in studying recorded interviews, found that when counselors interpreted at the client's request for evaluation there was a significant drop in further self-exploratory responses.

Interpretation technique may tend to overintellectualize the client's problems prematurely, thus encouraging the use of interpretation as a type of defense mechanism. This happens because the client is searching for all means possible to keep his feelings from awareness. He isn't ready to invest responsibility for control of feelings in the counselor.

Utilizing Interpretation to Facilitate Emotional Involvement

On the other side of the above argument, it should be emphasized that there is a tendency on the part of many counselors, particularly among the nondirectivist types, to think that interpretation is simply intellectual. This is not so, because many counselors and therapists are most effective in utilizing interpretation to get *emotional involvement.* The following responses are examples:

> C: "You've told me about your family as though you were a disinterested observer; what do you feel when you are with them?"

Another example:

> C: "You've several times lost the train of thought as you got around to the topic of your mother's death; I wonder if you're hesitant to show how deeply it still affects you?"

Client Reactions to Interpretation

If reflection of feeling is performed accurately it is usually accepted by the client. Thus, the criterion of client acceptance as an indication of successful reflection is easy to apply. With reflection and interpretation, however, the problem of evaluation is more difficult. Client reactions to interpretations and evaluation of the reactions may be categorized as follows:

Acceptance. The client may ostensibly accept the interpretation, and go on. If genuine insight has been achieved the client will spontaneously see its application in additional ways. "All of a sudden I realized. . . ."

If there is merely acceptance of the ideas, but no evidence of insight, then one may assume that the counselor and not the client had the insight. The counselor should be alert to the "oversold" client who seems to be overly rigid in trying out the new ideas or who oversimplifies the insight. Similarly, the counselor should be alert to the dependent client who will "over-accept" interpretations to please the counselor.

In addition, there are the clients who are so elated with superficial insights after brief work that they take what has been earlier labeled as a "flight into health." Such "flights into health" tendencies usually are regarded as forms of resistance in which the psyche yields up the symptoms to avoid the exposure of anxiety-laden areas through further therapeutic inquiry.

When the client readily accepts an interpretation without resistance, the interpretation may not have been necessary. This probably doesn't do any harm, but it is superfluous for helping the client. Verbalizing these interpretations may help the counselor become better oriented to the client's problem, however.

Indifference. The client's resistance to the idea that an interpretation applies to him may take the form of facetious glibness or blandness about the matter. However, lack of immediate acceptance does not mean that the interpretation is a failure. Beneath his indifference, the client may be struggling with the idea as a prelude to insight.

Rejection. The client may react with hostility to an interpretation without verbalizing or showing his aggression. He may initially accept the ideas offered by the counselor and then reject them. Sometimes this is a temporary relapse following the achievement of a profound new insight. Some clients show their resistance by going back over the problem again, emphasizing the lack of progress, and perhaps verbalizing dissatisfaction with counseling. In this situation, reflection of feeling becomes useful again to help the client work through his temporary regressive reactions to the interpretation. Rejection can serve as a warning signal to the counselor that: he has hit an area of resistance; the client is not ready; the interpretation is not appropriate.

Vehement protest. The client rejects the interpretation and shows it through vigorous protests. As mentioned in the introductory illustration, the fact that the client gets upset about the interpretation may mean that it is correct or is approaching correctness. In any case, it is futile for the counselor to pursue the matter further with the client at the time without jeopardizing the entire relationship.

TECHNIQUES FOR MAINTAINING TENSION

Therapists agree generally that a most difficult problem is that of maintaining sufficient tension in the client so that he continues to work through his problems. Simply providing an opportunity for catharsis, alone, often produces a pseudo-relaxation which the client may interpret to mean that all is well and that he has achieved the goals of psychotherapy. Therefore, in order to use interpretive techniques in the working-through stage of the process there must be optimum anxiety to motivate continued search. Symonds points out that though it is the goal of psychotherapy to reduce anxiety and guilt, anxiety arousal is, paradoxically, a necessary part of the process:

> . . . therapy cannot take place until symptoms are transformed into anxiety. Symptoms, in general, represent a substitute for anxiety—they take the place of anxiety (301, Vol. II, pg. 387).

The process thus seems to be one of temporary arousal of anxiety so that symptoms can be eliminated; then therapy is applied consisting of reducing this anxiety to enable the individual to make a new adjustment without the old symptoms.

Several methods are used for creating tension in the client. The counselor may:

(1) Focus on topics or symptoms which provoke tension.
(2) Ask challenging questions on painful subjects.
(3) Give interpretations of attitudes or behavior.
(4) Use counselor silence, thereby forcing client verbalization.
(5) Decrease support.

Ingham suggests some additional techniques for provoking anxiety in the client when it seems therapeutically expedient to do so (152, pg. 93). Some examples are:

(1) Explaining the significance of symptoms
(2) Decreasing support
(3) Suggesting the end of treatment
(4) Interpreting transference feelings
(5) Giving a provocative new interpretation
(6) Implying that he should be making more progress
(7) Decreasing emotional outlets as in reducing amount of smoking

These techniques, of course, must be used with extreme care. As with medicine, a too heavy dose at the wrong time can kill. Wolberg points out that tension should not "be permitted to grow to a point where it overwhelms the coping resources of the individual, producing destructive or infantile reactions. . . . In the event such contingencies occur, the therapist will have to step in with supportive measures" (323, pg. 178).

SPECIAL INTERPRETIVE ADJUNCTS

The scope of therapeutic psychology, as outlined in Chapter 1, includes major techniques of counseling and psychotherapy, but it does not include a detailed focus on such specialized psychotherapeutic techniques as dream interpretation and hypno-therapy, or the use of drugs such as sodium pentothal or lysurgic acid in collaboration with medical specialists. The student who specializes in long-term psychotherapy will want to explore these techniques further.

Dreams, for example, can be regarded as coded messages from the unconscious. Special study and training are required to become an effective dream analyst. A similar statement can be made for hypnosis as a therapeutic technique. Fromm's work, *The Forgotten Language,* is recommended as an introduction to dream interpretation. LeCron and Bordeaux present an informative introduction to hypnosis in *Hypnotism Today.* Wolberg's *Hypnoanalysis* is a fruitful source also. Psychologists who work with drug-induced therapy always work in collaboration with a medical specialist, and the procedures utilized are beyond the scope of this volume. It is interesting to note, however, that an increasing number of psychologists in private practice are utilizing collaborative drug therapy.

RELATIONSHIP OF INTERPRETATION TO PERSONALITY THEORY AND PROCESS

In the early phases of counseling and psychotherapy, when the relationship between client and counselor is being built, the counselor's role is a less-direct one in which he conveys his attitudes of acceptance and permissiveness through reflection of feeling and other techniques. As the client continues through the process, however, he delves more deeply into himself. The counselor assists him at this later stage in the process largely by using the techniques of reflectation and interpretation.

Employing the personality model we developed in Chapter 2, it may be seen that psychotherapy consists of assisting the client to "take back" much of what he has defensively projected into the outside world. Much of what he talks about as "it," external to himself, is really "it" within his self- and core systems; but he is unable to make this admission. This process is illustrated in Figure 22.

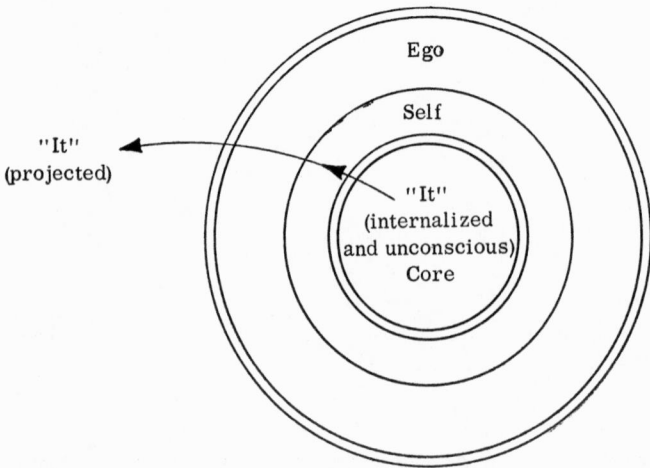

FIG. 22. The Projection Process.

It seems that a requirement which must be imposed upon the client early in therapy is that he must sense and accept "it" material which he has rejected as being "I." In order to facilitate this step, the counselor at first utilizes reflective phraseology such as *"you* feel," *"you* think," etc. This assists the client to accept into his ego and self-systems that which he has formerly rejected. After the client has accepted the material as part of himself he can again reject and *consciously* abandon it as unworthy of the personality. The material thus traces a course from "it" to "I" to "it."[1]

Another way of expressing the mechanism is to say that psychotherapy consists of the draining of pathologically projected material from the unconscious levels of personality to the external world. This material is, first, considered as the external object ("it"-projected), then, the internal subject ("I") and finally, the external object ("it"-rejected to the external world and vanished). Figure 23 illustrates this process. The client experiences the process in the following manner:

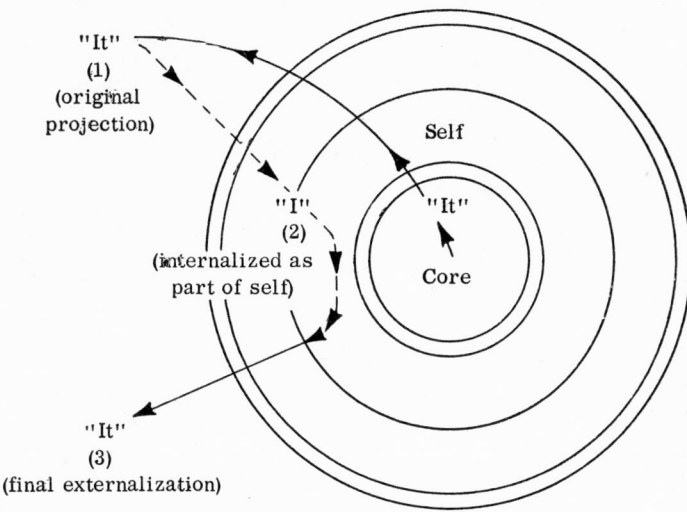

FIG. 23. Interpretation and the Projection Cycle.

(1) "It"-projected: "I have nothing to do with this—it doesn't belong to me . . . it would hurt badly to feel like this . . . could I really be like this . . . ?"

(2) "I": "My gosh, I really *am* like this . . . this is just a part of me . . . this affects me."

(3) "It"-rejected: "It still affects me somewhat . . . it doesn't mean much to me."

---

[1] The writers are indebted to Dr. John Watkins for stimulating conversations on topics in this section.

These theoretical considerations suggest that reflection and then interpretation should be utilized in psychotherapy when the client makes his transition from Stage 2 to 3. When he has been able to move from Stage 1 to 2 and really accept his projections, he then needs to *reject* them *consciously* or accept them so thoroughly into his personality that they have little subjective meaning. This process, it seems, can be facilitated by the counselor if he makes interpretations which begin to talk of the client's material as "it" again. This method involves the proper timing of interpretation. The therapist must not interpret more "you" material than the client's ego and self-systems can tolerate as "I." The interpretations which follow must be balanced with "you" and "it." Then, the counselor moves gradually from the "you" to "it" so that the client is not traumatized as he faces and then rejects disruptive and painful revelations about himself.

SUMMARY

Interpretation is the principal technique the counselor uses during the phase of the counseling process when the client is working through to insight. Often, reflection and interpretive techniques are mixed in, in varying degrees, to form a technique described as reflection. The major goal of interpretive techniques is to promote client understanding and self-interpretation.

10.

Use of Advice, Information, and Tests

The use of data and test devices for the purpose of diagnostic evaluation was discussed in Chapter 5 with emphasis on the values and limitations of their application for the counselor. This chapter is concerned primarily with the use of data as a therapeutic agent or an interaction medium between client and counselor. From this viewpoint, the use of advice, tests, information, and semantics will be examined.

ADVICE IN COUNSELING

In the thinking of the man in the street, counseling and psychotherapy are almost synonymous with giving advice. Offering "common-sense advice" is probably the oldest form of psychotherapeutic counseling, the aim being to offer substitute attitudes and behaviors for those the client holds. It is an appeal to the client's intellectual powers through logical reasoning and evaluation of his experience.

Generally, the advice-giving is accompanied by a heavy dose of persuasion because the counselor, in giving the advice, often has a personal interest in seeing that the client follows the advice. This point is valid, particularly when a teacher-counselor's value to his colleagues or superiors, for example, is judged by the behavior changes he effects in student clients. Although professional counselors give valid information when it seems appropriate, they do not use advice of the bold, "here is what I think you ought to do" variety.

Use of Advice and Suggestion

Persuasive advice-giving is a standard technique used by unsophisticated persons. Nevertheless, there are occasions when advice in the form of suggested alternate courses of action might be indicated for the client to follow. The word "suggested" should be emphasized so as to leave the evaluation and decision about the course of action with the client. Examples are those situations when a parent is exploring possible ways in which she has been mishandling her young child, or when a client feels caught on the horns of a dilemma about which occupation to select, and for which the counselor suggests additional possibilities.

Sullivan (295) distinguishes between "prescriptions for action" (suggestions) which he advocates, and outright "advice" which he condemns. He claims that good advice is usually an elaboration of the obvious and an insult to most clients; but advice based on incomplete or faulty data is often completely dangerous.

The use of suggestion and opinion is most appropriate when it is known in advance that the contact will be short and where a relatively inconsequential life decision must be made quickly. The counselor recognizes that this is a superficial, intellectualized approach which generally does not affect basic attitudes. If used sparingly and cautiously on normal people with situational problems and with minor decisions to be made, little risk is involved. Normal people generally are capable of evaluating suggestions and rejecting them when not acceptable.

Thorne (303) suggests the use of persuasive advice in crisis situations where cooperative action of several people must be secured to prepare clients for major readjustments and to prevent emotional trauma. Examples are situations where reorganization of families is undertaken in cases of hospitalization, divorce, imprisonment, loss of job, or financial crisis. Complex classroom changes in school situations, for example, usually require the concerted efforts of several people, obtained through the medium of persuasive recommendations.

Experiments in short-term counseling have been made from time to time. These studies often involve persuasive informational techniques. An example is given by Herzberg (143) who uses persuasion and intellectual appeals to change behavior by manipulating the inhibitory powers of the personality. Much research is needed on the rationale and techniques of persuasion, suggestion, and advice-giving before these methods can be advocated unequivocally as effective short-term counseling techniques.

Limitations of Advice and Opinion

One of the greatest limitations of advice-giving is the temptation it arouses for the counselor to use it indiscriminately and profusely. If he gives advice excessively it may court strong resistance from the client even to the point of causing him to terminate the relationship. Strong dependency relationships may be built up when the counselor meets the demanding overtures for solutions to a dependent client's problems.

A chief danger, however, is that the counselor may be tempted to give advice which is not in the client's best interests because it is a projection of the counselor's needs, problems, and values. This is known as the "If I were you . . ." approach. The client may take the counselor's advice and suggestions, then, later, find that they are not valid. Bach (18) observed that in group therapy, advice-giving originated when the person giving the advice perceived the problems brought up by another as consciously or unconsciously his own. In other words, interest in giving advice is aroused when we identify with the person having problems which are similar to our own. Bach asserts that objective advice-giving is rare except when it is attempted in professional psychotherapy, where, he claims, that it has limited utility only.

Even if his values permitted direct advice-giving, a counselor cannot know enough about a person or his situation to decide what that person should do concerning such questions as, "Should I get a divorce?" or "What occupation should I enter?" If the client follows the counselor's advice, the client's situation may change so that the original opinion is obsolete, perhaps even dangerous. There is also the danger that the counselor will be blamed if things do not work out right. In any case, the jeopardy to the relationship hardly warrants the risks involved in the counselor choosing sides in the client's conflicts.

Counselors, using the client-centered approach to counseling, are critical of advice-giving on the grounds that its use shifts the responsibility for solutions to the client's problems upon the counselor and limits the client's opportunities to make his own changes in fundamental self-evaluative attitudes.

The issue on the use of suggestive advice boils down to the old problem of good judgment on the psychotherapist's part. The weight of counselor opinion, however, seems to be against the use of straight, opinionated advice. It certainly has gross limitations for extended psychotherapeutic types of counseling. A distinction must be made, furthermore, between giving valid information and offering opinionated advice. The methods for presenting information to a client are offered in the following sections.

Case Management

The management of cases often involves suggestions which might be classed as advice. Occasionally the counselor must advise referral, hospitalization, or some other significant move, which, in his professional judgment, would be in the best interests of the client. The counselor or therapist constantly must evaluate himself in terms of what he can do with this client. He must, also, assess the client's life circumstances in light of his ability to profit from the counselor's services. Finally, the institutional setting must be appraised in terms of what kinds of services can be safely and legitimately offered. Often, the conclusions drawn from the appraisal of these factors must be communicated to the client in the form of suggestions of steps to be taken next.

TESTS AND OBSERVATIONS IN COUNSELING

It is assumed that students and practitioners reading this volume are familiar with the basic principles of measurement and are acquainted, also, with the most commonly used tests. This section will cover some of the questions involved in the functions and choice of tests as well as in the use of tests in the interview. Tests are viewed in this chapter as tools to be used in the therapeutic process and not as central emphases. We feel that tests have been used too profusely in counseling in the past, largely because they have been a convenient "screen" to hide a lack of counseling knowledge and an "escape" from facing the real problems of growth.

However, one of the key contributions to clinical practice is the use of tests to help clients make their own decisions and plans. There seems to be a continuing trend in the therapeutic use of tests in counseling in addition to the improvement of their traditional diagnostic use where they are used to help the counselor formulate his hypotheses about the client.

Functions of Tests

Tests help the counselor in surveying and diagnosing personality characteristics and problems with the aim of giving the client useful information about his own personality. The counselor who locates problem areas by means of personality inventories, problem checklists, and temperament tests often accelerates his client's exploration of problems and economizes exploratory interview time.

Clients come to psychotherapeutic and vocational counselors expecting to take tests to find out more about themselves; hence, they expect direct and useful answers from the tests. For the psychologist in a clinic setting, in contrast, the survey function of testing may be important for helping the counselor obtain hypotheses or to verify some of his hunches about the functioning of the client's personality. Here, the client takes tests without necessarily expecting to have the results given to him. In fact, some of the interpretations under clinical conditions frequently would prove very mystifying and threatening to the client.

The diagnostic function of tests is well recognized. Counselors rely extensively upon tests for assaying reading and learning difficulties, for example, where several hours of interviewing would be needed to get the same information.

Bordin (40) proposes that an important area the counselor may analyze with tests is the client's sense of reality, by having the client try out his self-expectations through his own behavior samples on tests. Just as one tests his abilities in athletics through tryout experiences, the client can test his perceptions of his abilities and traits through the medium of testing. A by-product for the client of this reality-testing experience is the development of a desire to explore his motivations and capacities further.

Discovery of interest and value clusters is another use of tests and inventories in counseling. Clients generally know their manifest interests well. For example, they have little idea of how they compare with individuals in known groups such as men in general or college women. It is the relative standing on definitive norm tables which gives tests their value for appraising the client's interests, aptitudes, achievement, and other personality variables. Thus, an important question which tests help to answer for the client is, "How do I compare to others with whom I will be competing?"

A third significant function of tests is the prediction of behavior. Aptitude tests are examples of instruments which take behavior samples from which the counselor can make inferences about the client's ability to pursue a particular educational or vocational plan. Predictions are made in terms of probabilities of success in a given program. The probabilities are directly related to the specific validities of the tests used.

Selection of Tests

In many clinical situations, standard batteries of tests are administered: Wechsler, Stanford Binet, Rorschach, MMPI, and sentence completion. Yet, for many clients, the test batteries must be selected to bear more appropriately upon age and unique problems. In problems of vocational planning, selection of tests is especially important because of the special needs for accurate prediction.

Most often the counselor selects the tests which he thinks would be most useful from a standard checklist much in the same fashion that a physician writes a prescription. This method puts the responsibility upon the counselor. The counselor being, of course, the expert in the matter of appraisal, should have the prerogative of determining the tests to be used. In private-practice settings, for example, therapists often test each new client routinely with the MMPI and/or the Rorschach to determine suitability for therapeutic help. Yet, client responsibility can often be enhanced if the counselor allows the client to participate in the selection of tests.

The counselor should suggest tests when the client reaches the point where he feels he needs more data about himself for the decision at hand. The client may wish to know, for example, whether he has enough scholastic aptitude to succeed in college. He also may desire an interest inventory to help him ascertain the major most likely to give him satisfaction. This principle of timing in test selection is especially important in psychotherapeutic counseling. If the counselor proposes personality tests at the outset of therapy, the client may come to overvalue them as a means for suggesting solutions to his personal problems rather than to depend upon the relationship to accomplish this act of understanding. If the counselor suggests them too far along in the process, it is very likely that the client may tend to feel that the counselor is baffled by his case or that it is more serious than was thought at first. The counselor must sense the most appropriate point early in the process when tests can be given and when it can be explained to the client that this procedure is routine.

When the client expresses a desire for more data, the counselor may then bring up the topic of tests and suggest specific types which would give the kind of answers sought. At this point, the counselor would do well to explain that sometimes tests can give helpful data on the problem and sometimes not. It should be stressed, however, that the client should have a genuine desire to take the tests which have been suggested as an outgrowth of his feeling the need for more data. There is some evidence from studies by Bordin and Bixler (41), Seeman (268), and Shostrom and Brammer (278) that client participation in test selection tends to facilitate the client's development of self-direction or self-actualization more than when the counselor alone prescribes tests.

The client-participation method of test selection presupposes some readiness of the type described in Chapter 5. Before the counselor allows the client to participate in the selection of tests, he should inform him about the values and limitations of tests as well as the various types available. Thus, the process to be described assumes that the client has some test sophistication plus the verbal ability to comprehend the fundamental principles of testing. Generally, the selection of tests proceeds as follows (277): (1) The client and counselor decide from their discussion what types of data are needed to help solve his problem. (2) The counselor describes the various categories into which tests are classified. (3) The counselor recommends those specific tests which will give the kinds of data sought by the client and recommends against testing in areas where there are already sufficient data or where tests would not help much. (4) The counselor allows the client to react to the selections so that any doubts or negative feelings about tests can be worked through. (5) Arrangements are made for the tests to be administered.

The degree of client participation would depend largely upon his maturity and sophistication. We participated in a study (277) in which it was found that superior college freshmen could do an adequate job of selecting their own test batteries with the technical assistance of the counselor. It was felt that this tended to get the client more involved in the process and to reduce, somewhat, the tendency to view test assignment as a prescription. This tendency to lean on the expert judgment of the counselor could lead the client to gain an exaggerated confidence that tests somehow would give him the answers he needed, hence, to remove responsibility for choices he made.

Counselors who oppose giving clients responsibility in the test-selection process use the analogy that physicians as technical experts do not ask their patient's opinions about taking laboratory tests to help in the diagnosis of the problem. One difference between a physician and a psychological counselor in this situation is that the physician assumes a large share of the medical responsibility for the patient's recovery, whereas, the counselor does not assume similar responsibility for the choices made by the client. The psychological counselor, though assuming some professional responsibility for what the client does in his relationship, does not attempt to make a definitive diagnosis on the basis of his fallible tests. He does not attempt to make final prognoses or prescriptions about the course of the client's behavior since he recognizes the unreliability of his instruments. The counselor, then, takes responsibility only for giving the most reliable information he can, with interpretations and explanations to the client commensurate with the known reliability and validity of the instruments. In our opinion, the counselor must leave responsibility for decisions to the client. As part of the preparation for these decisions, furthermore, the counselor should keep the client involved in all phases of the process including the selection of any tests.

At this point it should be emphasized, however, that tests given in clinical or hospital settings by a clinical psychologist largely for the purposes of diagnostic evaluation involve considerations different from those required in counseling. The data generally are gathered for a psychotherapist who evaluates the psychometric data along with much other case material and assumes responsibility for the use of the data.

Principles of Using Tests in Counseling

(1) The first rule of test use is to *know the test thoroughly*. This means more than knowing just the manual. The test should have been taken by the counselor himself and should have been investigated in the journals and in such collections of critiques as Buros' *Mental Measurement Yearbooks* (52). The weaknesses and limitations as well as the strengths of the test should be known to the counselor.

(2) *Exploration* of the client's reasons for wanting tests and past experience with tests is undertaken. The client's expectations are important data to be considered, since he may be expecting much more than tests can reasonably be expected to perform. Some clients have been to several counselors and have taken tests with each; yet they are still searching for the magic answer which they hope tests will reveal. Further testing adds little to these situations and more of a psychotherapeutic approach is needed to help them understand their compulsive searching.

Often clients have been traumatized by tests made earlier in school. They may regard them with deep suspicion, skepticism, or outright hostility. As a first step, the counselor should determine the client's feelings about the threatening aspects of testing to avoid distortion of the results of the interpretation and possibly failure of the counseling itself. Adults, especially, seem to feel threatened by any kind of testing, whereas, adolescents have had so many tests in school that most of them seem to take tests without emotional difficulty.

(3) *Structuring* of the test-interpretation session is especially important to prepare the client for meaningful, undistorted information. The counselor must ascertain the client's knowledge of the limitations of testing as well as the values for giving various self-information. An example is a discussion of the fact that tests do not give answers to problems. This is done in a casual manner to allow the client to ask questions and react to the counselor's introduction to the test interpretations. Test interpretation should grow out of the general discussion of the client's problem with the counselor stressing how tests add to the pool of data about the client's personality.

(4) The *meaning* of the scores should be established early in the discussion. That is, the client should know clearly what type of measure is being discussed—interest, aptitude, achievement, or personality. Most counselors probably could cite instances when they have been annoyed or embarrassed later by having a client interpret his Kuder Preference Record scores to a parent or friend as abilities.

(5) The *frame of reference* of the test results should be specified clearly. That is, the client must know at all times which norm group is being used so that he has some yardstick for judging how high a high score really is. In helping a client to estimate his chances of success in a liberal arts college program, for example, it makes a tremendous difference whether he is being compared to high school seniors or college freshmen at the institution of his choice.

(6) *Test results,* not scores, should be given to clients. If tests are given to a client with his expectation that he will be informed of the results, he is entitled to know the outcomes. Numerical scores are merely technical symbols for use by the counselor. Clients generally have just enough information about the meaning of numbers, such as I.Q.'s and percentile scores, that they tend to fix on the single score as "their score." Numbers are thus subject to the distortions which reflect the client's stereotyped meanings. Perception is focused, then, on the score symbol instead of on the meaning behind the symbol.

The counselor would do well to use trait terms and descriptive phrases such as, "Your high capacity to use language and to do verbal reasoning . . . ," instead of, "Your high scores on the scholastic aptitude test. . . ."

A corollary to this rule is to avoid using exact scores in interpretation. The lack of sufficiently high reliability in most tests indicates that the score symbol reported by the psychometrist represents a range or band of possible scores about the reported score. Brief mention of this phenomenon to clients often dispels their tendency to repeat requests to be told their reported scores.

Although counselors and psychotherapists are familiar with standard errors of measurement, it would be well for every counselor to pause periodically to examine data, such as that in Table 2, which point out the wide band of possible scores which exist around a "true" score when the reliability coefficient is known. The percentage of error reduction and the accountable variance are given for representative correlation coefficients. It should be noted that a typical correlation of .50 between scholastic aptitude tests and grades reduces the error of prediction over chance by only 13 per cent. A correlation must be around .70 before error reduction reaches 30 per cent and half the variance can be accounted for. The correlation must be almost .90 before the per cent of error reduction is 50 per cent.

Table 2

SIGNIFICANCE OF A CORRELATION COEFFICIENT
IN MAKING PREDICTIONS

Correlation Between Variables X and Y	Percentage of Error Reduction in Prediction of Y from X	Percentage of Variance Accounted for
.10	.5	1.00
.20	2.0	4.00
.30	4.6	9.00
.40	8.3	16.00
.50	13.4	25.00
.60	20.0	36.00
.70	28.6	49.00
.80	40.0	64.00
.90	56.4	81.00

Source: Adapted from J. Guilford. *Fundamental Statistics in Psychology and Education.* New York: McGraw-Hill 1942, pg. 221.

A third important point, relative to interpretation, concerns the language used to convey the relative significance of his test results. In light of a lack of research on the matter, there seems to be a consensus that the counselor should use broad categories in presenting the client's relative rank. For example, if the client's rank is in the middle range of the distribution, the terms "average," "high average," "low average," or "middle range" are meaningful. If around the 70th to 85th percentile range, the phrase "high" or "upper quarter," or "upper 15 per cent" is descriptive, although the term "high" has unfortunate value connotations for many clients. The terms "low" and "below average" certainly have negative associations for many clients. Phrases implying rankings for low scores such as "lowest ten per cent of machinist apprentices" are meaningful without stirring negative self-regard feelings.

(7) Test results should always be *verified*. Another way of stating this principle is that test results should be presented with an air of tentativeness. This cautiousness is especially important until further data are collected to verify the test results. Again, knowledge of all the various sources of unreliability in test administration and reporting leads the counselor to the position that he should never accept a test score at face value.

There are many ways to check the reliability of a test score. Comparison of the score with past academic achievement gives a rough check on scholastic aptitude scores, although grades themselves are notoriously unreliable. Giving an additional test, especially an individually administered form, is desirable when the results are suspect. Interest inventory scores can be checked from case data on hobbies, reading, and activity interests.

As a corollary to the principle of verification, the counselor should never use a score in *isolation*. Test results should be woven in with other case data to check on the validity as well as the reliabilty of the test score. Decisions which people make as a result of counseling interviews are most often too consequential for the counselor to risk making predictions on skimpy and unconfirmed data.

(8) *Counselor neutrality* in imparting test results is important since it is so easy to slip into evaluative phraseology. Examples of evaluative phraseology are, "You did extremely well on this test." "The results look pretty good; I think you will be pleased." "I think this test means that . . ."

The test results should speak for themselves without the counselor's personal value projections. The client, in addition, should formulate the evaluations for himself. It would be preferable for the counselor to avoid overpersonalizing scores by indicating something like, "Adults with results like these seem to find college work quite easy," or "People with results like these would very likely find engineering training very difficult."

(9) *Meaningful and clear* interpretations should be the counselor's constant aim. The client should make his own evaluations, as indicated in the previous principle. However, he should not have raw data thrust at him for his own interpretation. Neither should the counselor explain the meaning of test results in technical language. Ambiguous reporting of test results invites distortion of the interpretations since the client can more easily project his own meaning into the results.

If the counselor is overcautious in making his interpretations, however, he encourages the client to become overanxious, and, consequently, to distort them. Though the counselor should not go beyond his data, he should be willing to state his predictions with forthrightness when he is reasonably certain that the client would be able to accomplish a planned course of action, such as attending college.

Diagrams and profiles aid the counselor in giving meaningful interpretations. Counselors vary in their opinions on the appropriateness of showing a profile to a client because the client tends to look for identifying labels and specifics. Unless used properly, the profile may be very misleading as in the case where several tests are reported on one graph; yet each has differing standardization groups. Tests having comparable scores because of a common standardization population, such as some of the recently developed aptitude batteries or standard interest test profiles, can be presented on a single graph so that comparisons among tests in the battery would have meaning relative to each other.

Shostrom and Brammer (277) report a procedure for presenting test results to clients in vocational counseling interviews. A normal curve was used with one hundred schematic figures drawn on it. A few reference points, in percentile terms, were indicated to give the client some idea of how he compared to the norm group. The counselor proceeded somewhat as follows, "Your scores fall approximately above the point indicated by the red arrow," whereupon the counselor drew a small arrow under the diagram to indicate the approximate range of all scores.

We usually sketch a diagram to indicate the idea of a distribution of scores and what it means to fall in a certain area under the curve. Since most college student clients have been exposed to the idea of the normal curve and score distributions in their school work, this is an easy concept to grasp. With high school students and adult clients, who do not have this specialized knowledge, it is doubtful how wise it would be to make a long discussion of scores, distributions, and normal curves.

(10) Accurate *prediction* is the principal aim of testing. Test results should be stated in terms of statistical predictions. This rule hits at the heart of the testing problem—that of validity. So few test batteries have been developed sufficiently or standardized according to the local population, that the counselor has the principal difficulty of giving probability figures to his clients. It would be fine if the counselor could say, "Three out of four students with results like these succeed in law," "A person with results like these has a 60 per cent chance of succeeding in engineering." In spite of the general absence of these more exact probability figures, the counselor can still rely on probability language in which to couch his interpretations. He may say for example, "With results like these the chances are very high that one could succeed in a liberal arts program."

(11) *Client participation and evaluation* is another aim in the test interpretation phase. Interaction between client and counselor is valuable because it gives the counselor constant information regarding how the client is receiving the interpretation. In a study by Dressel (87) it was

found that more self-understanding and satisfaction was associated with high client participation. Asking the client an occasional question, or asking if he has questions, often prevent the counselor from going off into long didactic soliloquies concerning test data. Pausing occasionally to allow the client to react serves to increase his assimilation of the results. Perceptual research by Kelly (164), interpretation studies by the Bixlers (33), and studies of memory by Bartlett (20) point out clearly the tendencies of clients to hear selectively and to distort and forget what they hear. So much of the research growing out of the Gestalt psychology approach, such as Wulf's studies (327), bears out the tendencies to reproduce figures more in line with the "good gestalt." Clients, then, unconsciously distort their perceptions in ways which make their sensory data more understandable and meaningful. There is the presumption here that this perceptual distortion phenomenon takes place also in test scores which are laden with threat potential. The counselor must be alert to these tendencies so he can help the client perceive the results as accurately as possible and to see the distorting effects of his own motivational structure.

(12) The interpretation of *low scores* to normal clients is one of the most difficult problems the counselor must face. We have found from experience that it is best to start the interpretation period with the client's high scores. This tends to build the confidence which is so helpful to acceptance, later, of low scores.

A second helpful device the counselor may use is to test the client's readiness to accept low scores by asking him to predict what he thinks his relative ranking might be on the trait in question. Clients often have a good hunch of how they rank. The counselor then makes a statement confirming the hunch with the test results. However, if the client does not have a clear idea of how he ranks, and if he is emotionally ready for the results, the counselor should present the results factually and wait for the reaction. The counselor should be ready for whatever feelings may be elicited— surprise, disappointment, pleasure—and be prepared to reflect these and help the client work them through.

The counselor should be especially cautious and tentative in giving low scores since they may be fallible. The client who achieves scores which do not seem to be confirmed by other case data should be questioned to discover the cause. That is, the counselor should determine if his client suffered from excessive fatigue, test anxiety, misunderstood directions, or improper test readiness. The counselor should entertain the possibility that unreliability due to the test itself might be a factor.

(13) *The appropriate conceptual level* for phrasing test interpretations is very significant if the client is to understand test results. If the counselor uses phrases such as "scholastic aptitude," "linguistic aptitude" with many clients, for example, he conjures up a stereotype of foreign language ability. It would be much more appropriate for him to use the client's symbols and

to speak in terms of "ability to use words." Asking questions to test the client's understanding of the interpretation is one technique to help the counselor stay on the most appropriate conceptual level.

Specific Informational Uses of Tests

Paper-and-pencil personality inventories. These inventories are divided into three general categories—those which propose to measure presence and strength of such traits as dominance or submission, presence and strength of emotional problems, and, finally, the extent to which the client has feelings and problems similar to a standard diagnostic category such as hysteria.

Paper-and-pencil tests of the trait-measurement type have little utility in counseling because they do not give the counselor clear information with which to assess discrete traits or trait clusters. In our opinion, the tests have a second limitation because the counselor could not relate the tenuous traits to anything meaningful, even if he could find them. Few useful validity coefficients have been worked out using trait-type inventories.

So-called "adjustment inventories," as The Bell Adjustment Inventory (24), which purport to inventory personal problems are useful in providing an opening wedge for discussion of the client's problem. Adolescent clients, especially, have resistance mechanisms which can be modified by personality test results because they are so curious about their own personalities. However, the questionnaire type of adjustment inventory often is unreliable, and its use tends to divert the client from his real problems to a preoccupation with test results.

The third type of personality inventory, which measures the degree to which a client has symptoms, judged similar to psychiatric categories, is mainly useful in rough-screening. This adjustment inventory, of which the Minnesota Multiphasic Personality Inventory (139) is an example, has a "can opener" function, also, to help clients get to the descriptive level of their adjustment problems more quickly. The MMPI, as it is called, helps the counselor make his diagnostic formulations, although he must exercise great caution in using the diagnostic categories of the instrument literally.

Projective techniques. Another category of personality appraisal devices is the projective technique group which allows the client to project his own unique perceptions upon ambiguous stimuli in the form of ink blots, pictures, and three-dimensional objects.

Projective techniques are useful to help the psychotherapeutic counselor make his diagnostic formulations as well as to give him leads for counseling. There are some indications that projective techniques are useful in making predictions for vocational counseling also.

A picture-story type of instrument, such as the Thematic Apperception Test, is used in counseling or therapy principally for client self-interpretation. Several studies by Bettleheim (30), Deabler (80), Jacques (154), and Morton (213) indicate the usefulness of having the client interpret his own stories. Morton found the TAT an especially useful device to expedite brief psychotherapy since the themes and their interpretations tended to center the client's attention upon immediately pressing problems and their solution. One of the strategies of short-term psychotherapeutic counseling is for the counselor to get the client to talk about his present perceptions of his problems, the nature of his defenses, and his goals rather than to dwell at length upon past events.

Deabler (80) uses the TAT as a device to reflect back important client attitudes so that further expression of feeling is facilitated. The client then suggests his own interpretations, thereby generating insights more quickly than he would if the counselor were to use direct methods of interpretation.

Rorschach protocols can be used to get immediate data for therapeutic purposes also. Although the Rorschach cannot be used by clients in self-interpretation, as can the TAT, the findings from the content and the psychogram can be used to stimulate much therapeutically valuable material from the client in the early phases of counseling or to get him off a resistance "plateau" later. For example, the counselor may interpret the life-style elements of the Rorschach psychogram as follows: "As this instrument is interpreted, you give the picture of a person who has difficulties establishing satisfactory interpersonal relationships, or as we say, relating to others. Does this fit with your estimates of yourself?" Often, if the counselor makes this type of interpretation, early in the interview, he can pinpoint the defensive areas faster than he could if he allowed the client, himself, to approach them through the often tortuous channels and shoals of free conversation and resistances.

Pepinsky (230) describes more informal projective methods for counseling through use of common objects, such as room furnishings. For example, Pepinsky, referring to a landscape picture on the wall, would casually ask clients how they felt about it. One typical response was given, as follows, when a bright freshman girl was describing her disturbances over her failing midterm reports:

> C: You would like to relax. Would it help you to look at my picture here? (Points to picture on wall)
> Cl: (After a brief pause): I'm looking at it, but I don't like it.
> C: Can you tell me more about that?
> Cl: (Clenching her fists): The branches of that tree—they seem to be clutching for something they never reach—just like me. (Bursts into tears)

Pepinsky summarized the values of the picture device as allowing the client to feel at ease in dealing with a stimulus which seemed external, thus enabling the counselor to get more verifying data with which to firm up his diagnostic formulation. A further value was that of keeping the responsibility for analyzing the problems directly on the client.

There seem to be many implications and many promising leads in the use of projective devices in counseling. A few examples are given here, of some of the possible uses. Serious clinical students have access to many books on projective techniques which will enable them to go far beyond the brief introduction made here. The whole area of the use of projective tests in psychotherapy, however, needs more study before definite statements can be made of the utility of the methods.

Expressive movement. Observation of the posture, speech, artistic productions, and gestures of clients has always been a rich source of data for counselors to make inferences about their internal world. Fidgeting and sweating are especially valuable indicators of the general state of tension in the client.

Interest and value inventories. Inventories, in this category, have utility primarily in educational and vocational counseling situations. They help the client to compare his casually stated or manifest interests with his solicited opinions on an inventory. According to his measured interests, the client is compared to other groups having known interest patterns, such as boys in general or engineers. By helping the client to see that the various approaches to interests corroborate each other and that his interest patterns are consistent, the inventories serve a supportive function in counseling. Conversely, inventories help to point out indeterminate or immature interest patterns. If a counselor should find that one of his adult clients has no dominant interests, it may have much clinical significance, suggesting that the dynamics of his personality should be investigated. A lack of interests may mean, for example, that the client is incapable of identifying with a group, that he has general emotional immaturity, or that he is inexperienced. Patterson (229) indicates that the emotionally disturbed client tends to be more interested in creative talent and social-service types of occupations which may be interpreted as escape into the arts, or self-help efforts.

A second value of interest and value inventories in counseling is that they shed light on the client's self-concepts. What he likes to do, what he values are important clues to the characteristics of his self-system.

As a third use, interest inventories may be used by the counselor to predict the amount of satisfaction the client will derive from a given occupational area. Strong's research (292) on the value of interest inventories in predicting later vocational choices and work satisfaction is illustrative of this function. Inventories of interest are limited largely to mature adolescents and older clients who have more stable interest patterns than younger clients. Sometimes, however, a general inventory made early in adolescence can give the client a general idea of the relative strengths of his interests, according to such broad areas as mechanical and clerical.

The problem of the use of specific tests in counseling is a vast topic and beyond the scope of this volume. It is assumed that the general reader is familiar with the tests commonly used. If not, we recommend Super's *Appraising Vocational Fitness* (296) as a good source.

Aptitude and achievement tests. There is extensive literature on aptitude and achievement testing. The purpose of this section is only to point out some of the principal informational uses of this type of test in the counseling relationship.

One function of aptitude and achievement tests is to give the client support. So frequently clients feel "stupid" or "inadequate" without factual basis for such feelings. If used along with psychotherapeutic techniques, a test of aptitude for scholastic work, for example, can help to give the client a more realistic indication of approximately where he would stand relative to the group in which he would compete. This group may be the general population, college freshmen, engineering freshmen, art students, or other groups for which the test is normed. It is often reassuring to clients to have more accurate knowledge of where they stand so that more realistic planning can be undertaken.

A second function of aptitude and achievement tests in counseling is to give the counselor a basis upon which to make predictions of the possible success of a client in a given general or specific effort. Examples are predicting success for a client in engineering training, a college liberal arts program, or a teacher-selection program. Validities of tests and prediction tables are not as useful as counselors would like, though such tests are better than choices based upon whimsy.

Aptitude testing often serves a third, but oblique, function in counseling. If the client is threatened easily by judgmental situations, doubts his ability, or has discrepancies between his ability and his ambition, the testing program catapults these anxieties forcefully into the relationship where the counselor can deal with them psychotherapeutically.

The main purpose of all testing in counseling is to provide the client with reliable and valid information about himself so he will be able to make wise choices.

SEMANTICS

Semantic analysis in counseling is more an approach to problems of communication than a series of techniques. The basic postulate of the semantics approach is that emotional disturbances arise largely from misuse of words, lack of clear understandings, and distorted meanings caused by malfunctioning of the client's symbolic processes. Through the use of clarification, restatement, and interpretive techniques the client is helped to correct his faulty language habits.

By using the semantic approach in discussions with the client, the counselor can correct faulty thinking he may have concerning unrealistic ideals. The counselor, thereby, can prevent the frustration and disappointment which result from the client's efforts to achieve "success." Johnson (158) called the tendency to set unrealistic goals the "IFD disease"—idealization, frustration, and demoralization. Helping the client to define his goals more accurately helps him to avoid the above semantic pitfall.

Clients who have difficulty in assigning accurate symbols to feelings and ideas present another type of problem in communication. One of the principal values of counseling is that it provides a verbal structure for emotions. The client becomes able to verbalize ambivalent feelings, for example, and to see that it is possible to construe one's self as having two opposing feelings toward the same person at the same time.

Counselors may use semantic analysis to correct loose thinking—another problem in communication. Loose thinking is generally accompanied with "ovoverbalization" and characterized by a frantic search for meaning. The individual who ovoverbalizes is really avoiding thinking. The counselor can encourage tighter thinking by asking the client frequently what he means by his statements, or by attempting to restate and clarify the ideas just stated by the client, or by encouraging longer pauses.

Sometimes rigid thinking, along with underverbalization, is symptomatic of semantic difficulties. The use of stereotypes, prejudice, dogmatism, single causes, absolutism, and "either-or" are examples of thinking difficulties of this type. The counselor can help clients to see, for example, that human traits are not dichotomous, but exist in all shades and combinations.

Semantics, then, is an approach to the problem of expressing feelings by describing them accurately in order that the client can handle them in a problem-solving manner, and so he can see the relationship between his feelings and his thoughts. Semantics also helps the counselor clarify meaning, tighten thinking, and to make the client aware of his tendency to abstract and to confuse symbols with reality. The counselor can overcome emotional difficulties when the client stops asking vague questions and stops accepting ambiguous answers.

INFORMATIONAL READING AND BIBLIOTHERAPY

The use of literature to help people with problems is a very old practice. Reading is used for two purposes in counseling—information and psychotherapy (commonly called bibliotherapy).

The Informational Use of Reading

The informational use of library materials covers such situations as educational and occupational study in vocational counseling, sex and marital education in marriage counseling, and religious instruction in pastoral counseling. Reading materials are used in these situations mainly to economize time in the counseling hour. The client is given responsibility, for example, to look up material on training institutions for law or to read occupational pamphlets related to law as a vocation.

The informational approaches are useful mainly in surface types of counseling problems when ego-system levels of personality are involved. The counselor's suggestions for occupational reading are generally accepted without question by clients although he must include some motivational factors to stimulate the client's independent exploration of the materials. The suggestions for reading are introduced at a time when the client seems to exhibit a need for information. Principles for using specific types of informational material will be covered in Part III on their applications to various human problems. It should be noted that many of the principles in using bibliotherapeutic materials apply to general informational reading matter.

The Bibliotherapeutic Function of Reading

In his review of the literature on bibliotherapy, Brower (42) indicated that there is little data bearing on the usefulness of bibliotherapeutic techniques. Many psychotherapeutic counselors, however, attest to its usefulness with certain types of clients. The intelligent client seems to make most use of this device.

There are two types of bibliotherapeutic literature. One type, fiction, biography, and inspirational literature, offers much in the way of varied expressions of human experience. Shrodes (278), for example, edited a volume entitled *Psychology Through Literature* which is a compilation of excerpts from well known literary works. The materials are classified into sections devoted to family life, economic pressures, and emotional conflicts, for example. This approach to reading about human problems through literature helps the client to broaden his understanding of human motivation and culture conflicts. It is claimed also that literature offers the client the opportunity to share experience, which can be therapeutic. Many clients find that reading the Bible and other religious literature provides them with much emotional support.

The other type of bibliotherapeutic literature, on mental hygiene, is designed to give useful information for solving human problems and covers practical principles and facts on adjustment problems. Examples of pamphlets are the SRA Life-Adjustment Booklets and the Public Affairs pamphlet series.

One of the values claimed for bibliotherapy in counseling is the time-saving feature. Reading materials, appropriate to the problem, serve as a device to start the client thinking about related features of his feelings. Often clients are so eager for information that the counselor may resist giving it to prevent the relationship from starting on a too highly intellectualized basis. Suggesting some special reading satisfies the client and protects the rapport, yet enables the counselor to avoid the tendency to get involved in a question-answer sequence. Such efforts are frequently resistance devices of the client.

A second value of therapeutic reading is that it provides the client with more familiarity with the terminology of testing, mental hygiene, defenses, and emotions in general. The semantics values for the client of finding more exact language to express his ideas and feelings seem to be encouraged by proper reading.

A third value of therapeutic reading is that it stimulates thinking. The client runs across ideas which may start him on a new track toward insight. A mother, for example, finds that while she has been telling her child that she loves him, she has not been accepting many of his characteristics. The child, in turn, interprets the mother's behavior not as loving but as rejecting. Reading about such ideas often encourages the individual to apply to his problems more than the interpretations of the psychological counselor.

Bibliotherapy, as a final value, enables the counselor to give support. When a client is anxious about his problems it may help to have him read about such problems. He finds that others have the same feelings and same problems. He discovers that his marital difficulties, for example, are not as unique as he thought.

Limitations of Bibliotherapy

We have pointed out some of the functions of bibliotherapy which are cited by psychotherapists as being helpful for some clients. Bibliotherapy has apparent limitations as well. One of the foremost is based on the fact that people tend to rationalize their problems when they read about them. Hence, any readiness for counseling which they may have had is reduced, and their neurotic defenses would tend to become aggravated rather than diminished. Reading would become a type of resistance to going ahead with a plan of psychotherapeutic counseling.

A second limitation of bibliotherapy is that it encourages the client to think that the reading is helping him to solve his problems. Unless the reading is carefully described as being an aid to counseling, the client may substitute the vicarious and pseudo-insight he gains from the reading for the painful experience of genuine growth to be gained from the counseling relationship itself. It is estimated that few behaviors are changed through reading. It is feared also that too many of the so-called insights achieved through reading turn out to be as ineffective and elusive as the New Year's resolution.

There are, in addition, the clients whose anxieties are reinforced by reading about mental hygiene problems. They see themselves in every case and, if suggestible, acquire more symptoms for their defense repertoire. This personalizing tendency is particularly acute in paranoid individuals and in clients with weak defenses.

Principles in Using Bibliotherapy

Knowledge of the books the counselor recommends is a first principle. The counselor who refers clients to books with which he is not familiar runs the risk of misleading them and might fail to meet their needs or their level of sophistication. Missing the client's level of understanding could have deleterious effects on rapport. This principle puts a severe burden on the counselor to keep abreast of the literature and to keep the titles in his immediate memory. This familiarity, however, enables him to suggest books not only appropriate from a content standpoint but also for age, experience, and language level.

The counselor should *evidence confidence* in the suggested reading to interest the client in it and to make sure that he accepts the ideas presented in it. Readings are *suggested* rather than prescribed.

Timing is a third significant principle the counselor must consider to insure that his client properly understands and accepts the idea of reading. The counselor does not want to convey the idea that the client's problem is so simple it can be solved by reading a book rather than working it out through the counseling process. Neither does the counselor want to convey by poorly timed suggestions that he can no longer help the client and that reading might be a way out of the therapeutic impasse. A significant timing principle is to make the suggestions during a period of low resistance. The counselor who suggests readings at a time when the client is struggling with a feeling or when he is rolling toward insight will annoy him and be considered as lacking understanding.

Discussion of the results of the client's reading is important to ascertain the effect the reading had upon him. The client can ask questions and point out ideas which were especially valuable. Often, related passages can be read aloud for clarity. It is very important that distortions and misunderstandings are corrected at this point and that a realistic evaluation of the ideas is made. Some significant questions are: How authoritative was the writer? How recent is the material? Some books written in the twenties and thirties do not reflect current psychological thought. Are opinion and fact clearly differentiated? So many popular writers are not scrupulous about the factual bases of their opinions.

Lists of suggested readings and mimeographed tables of contents can be used to stimulate reading. Books and pamphlets, often with passages underlined, can be left in the waiting room for clients to browse through and to borrow. Often the browsing itself directs a client's thought process which produces significant material for the counseling hour. The following is an example:

> Cl: I was reading an article in one of the journals in the waiting room. It discussed reasons why people are apt to create marital problems for themselves. I don't believe that writer had all the answers. I could think of some reasons that the author didn't mention.

Smaller doses of reading seem to be more helpful than larger amounts. A pithy article or pamphlet is often more helpful than a book. It is easier for the counselor to pinpoint his suggestion in a short work since so much material extraneous to the client's immediate concern may distract him and dilute the emphasis desired.

SUMMARY

Giving information and suggesting materials for client reading are important counseling functions. The use of advice and suggestion is appropriate under some counseling conditions. The principal danger in advice-giving is that it often becomes a projection of the counselor's needs and values. Tests of personality, interest, aptitude, and achievement are widely used informational tools designed to give the client information about himself with which he can make wiser decisions. Tests are highly technical devices necessitating special training in their careful selection and use. Semantics principles help the client to sharpen his ability to think about his problems and to communicate more clearly. Informational reading and bibliotherapy are techniques designed to give the client valid ideas for use in planning his future and solving his present problems.

11.

Group Dynamics, Multiple Counseling, and Group Psychotherapy

One of the recent trends in the field of counseling and psychotherapy is employing group techniques in collaboration with individual approaches. Most of the same distinctions between counseling and psychotherapy cited in Chapter 1 hold for multiple counseling and group psychotherapy. The term "multiple counseling" seems to have wider usage than group counseling. "Group psychotherapy," conversely, has been a standard term for many years.

The most significant difference between the two terms is on depth of emotional involvement. Multiple counseling groups generally work on a common theme, interest, or problem area, such as academic achievement or getting along with parents. Depth of feeling is more controlled during multiple counseling than in group psychotherapy which not only permits, but encourages, members to express deep core feelings. For example, during group therapy the member would elaborate on such feelings as his intense hatred of women or his deep anxieties about being alone in a hostile world.

The reader will find the material in the second half of this chapter more suited to psychotherapeutic purposes rather than counseling aims. The techniques described, though not limited to a particular setting, are those which facilitate deeper involvement in the psychotherapeutic process. Even with this restricted coverage, the present discussion is not intended to be a definitive overview of the field. It is presented primarily to illustrate some similarities and differences between individual and group approaches, and to introduce the student to some of the techniques, problems, and issues in group methods.

Various combinations of individual and group methods have been utilized. Buhler (49) suggests four basic alternatives: (1) Primary emphasis on individual methods with group methods secondary or supplemental; (2) Primary emphasis on group methods with individual methods secondary or supplemental; (3) Group methods, only, as the primary technique; (4) A balanced approach utilizing both individual and group approaches with equal emphasis.[1]

GROUP DYNAMICS

Counselors, industrial supervisors, and social workers are some of the people whose work focuses more on group dynamics, that body of knowledge in which the emphasis is on understanding *inter*-personal relationships and group processes. Group therapy, and to some extent multiple counseling, in contrast, tend to focus on *intra*-personal factors involved in personality change. In the material to follow, a brief summary of some of the considerations involved in the field of group dynamics is presented.[2] The techniques and illustrations have particuar relevance for multiple counseling.

The principles which underlie the leader's understanding of groups at work may be classified into three categories: leader behaviors, discussant behaviors, and content analysis. Students of group dynamics can utilize the following outline for analyzing group behavior in terms of the three categories.

Typical Leader Behaviors

Problem setting. The leader states the issue or question to which the group is to address itself. This may occur at the outset or at various points in the discussion. The statement is made without indication of what solution should be reached or which side the leader favors.

Moderating. The leader calls on some members or asks others to withhold comment; he asks for order or attention. This category has nothing to do with content of the discussion but only with who shall or shall not participate at any given point.

Sentiment testing. The leader seeks to learn the balance of opinion in the group. He may call for a show of hands of other votes or he may simply state his impression of the trend of opinion and ask for confirmation.

Idea developing. The leader seeks to aid in the clarification and development of ideas before the group by restating, summarizing, or contrasting them. He does not inject new material, but, by his handling of what has been said, seeks to make issues more clear or to insure more general understanding.

---

[1] The reader is referred to George R. Bach, *Intensive Group Psychotherapy* for a more comprehensive survey of organizing group therapy.

[2] We are indebted to Dr. James F. T. Bugental for the main ideas of this section.

Monitoring. The leader reminds the group of limits and constraints under which it is operating (for example, time limits, authority bounds, ground rules).

Energizing. The leader seeks to motivate the group to its task. He may cite reasons for its work or simply enjoin the group to greater activity or chide it for inactivity.

Group serving. The leader performs service functions for the group (for example, keeping notes, recording on a blackboard, distributing paper, adjusting lighting). There may be no verbal aspect to this function.

Content participating. The leader takes part in the discussion, as another member and without exercising his leadership functions in any way.

Leaders also utilize certain *progress facilitation techniques* with a view toward carrying forward the discussion of his group. The following list is a compilation of such techniques.

Initiating. He proposes new ideas, procedures, or orientation. Major content is not derived from previous work of the group but mainly from "within" the current speakers.

Amending. He develops ideas already before the group. He may add new "twists," but basically he modifies more than he initiates.

Supporting. The leader lends emphasis, reason, or other aid to ideas already before the group. He does not seek to change them, but only to accelerate their acceptance.

Opposing. He may question, challenge, or detract from ideas before the group. He may seek to change them and to influence the group to reject them.

Summarizing. The leader brings out common or contrasting ideas before the group, reduces issues to essentials, and focuses or clarifies points.

Questioning. He seeks information, opinion, or similar material. (Some other forms are disguised as questions. The test is whether the answer is more valued than the question.)

Digressing. The leader generally leaves the topic before the group (not in the sense of developing another aspect). He may joke, socialize, or make personal comments.

Controlling. The leader may seek to regulate who will talk, when, or how much; he may intercede for less vocal members.

Informing. He provides information to the group (sometimes in response to a question), often simply to supply data, but he may have a secondary intent to influence the group. However, the main aspect of this device is to transmit facts or what are offered as facts.

Discussant Behaviors

Although discussants often utilize some of the foregoing techniques also, it is possible to identify certain unique techniques and characteristics of discussant behavior.

Frequency and volume. Participant frequency of each group member can be made simply by tallying each of the group member's responses. When a member speaks for a longer than average period, the tally can be underlined. When the volume is particularly loud, the tally can be blackened so as to indicate the strength of the response.

Types of appeal. In any discussion, the speaker's appeals and group influence can be determined. Sometimes this influence will be grossly explicit and sometimes more subtle. Some examples follow:

Appeal to reason and logic.................."it seems only reasonable"
Appeal to interest........................."should be interesting"
Appeal to sanity..........................."don't be foolish"
Appeal to decorum and good taste..........."not in mixed company"
Appeal to enjoyment ...."might be fun to. . ."
Appeal to a need, such as dependence ...."would help us to . . ."

Indirect influences. Many influences on group members are implicit and indirect, since they are not a part of the topic or discussion content. Some examples are: personal characteristics (sex differences, age differences, physical-size differences); status characteristics (vocation, position, community or civic activity, educational background, experience); and, non-verbal "signalling" techniques (contrasting voice volume, pounding the table, sex appeal, fidgeting and restlessness, silence followed by strong activity, staring). In making these observations, it is useful to watch for those individuals whose behaviors are at a variance with that of the group as a whole, for example, those who make a soft-spoken response when everybody else has been shouting. Thus, though one may watch a particular individual, it is well to be aware of the whole group as a frame of reference.

"Addressed to" patterns. Certain persons in the group seem to have the power to be "addressed to" more than others. Sometimes group members address the total group. At other times, however, certain group members seem to draw and often monopolize the attention and expressions of the group.

Content Analysis

Topical development. In listening to a discussion, particular attention can be given to the "life history" of the topics. Though it is not possible nor necessarily desirable to be highly precise about this historical analysis, nevertheless, the following scheme can help: How does the topic arise— from one individual, from the interactions of several members, from some other topic? How does the group work with the topic—by arguing contrasting aspects of it, by illustrations and examples, by emotional appeals, by responding to the influence of particular members? What changes occur in the topic as the group works on it—a part gradually displaces the topic as a whole, it is expanded and generalized, it is gradually lost sight of, it is thoroughly examined and concluded? What is the eventual fate of the topic —it is dropped, it becomes a part of the group's product, it is blended with other topics?

Topical concurrence. By concurrence is meant the degree to which a second speaker seems to understand, accept, and extend the subject matter of the first speaker. The second speaker does not necessarily agree with the first, but he stays with the same general ideas. Following is a scale demonstrating four types of concurrence:

1. *Concurring:* (No new content areas are opened; direct agreement or disagreement; repetition)

> Speaker A: "I think we should try to get more time to do the job."
> Speaker B: "I agree"; or "I don't think we need any more time"; or "Yeah, we don't have enough time."

2. *Expanding:* The same basic content area is covered, but it is expanded, developed, amplified, or illustrated. The next logical step is taken, or a direct challenge to the preceding remarks is made without bringing in a new focus of attention.

> Speaker A: "I think we should try to get more time to do the job."
> Speaker B: "If they want more than a hasty piece of work, we certainly need more time"; or "There's no use seeking more time until we've seen what we can do as it is"; or "Look, if we've got to plan the next meeting, arrange for the speaker, and do all those other things, then we've got to have more time."

3. *Altering:* The topic as covered by the first speaker is only generally the same as that covered by the new speaker; a major change of emphasis or application is made; the ideas previously expressed are given quite a different turn.

> Speaker A: "I think we should try to get more time to do the job."
> Speaker B: "Yeah, we certainly need it to settle this question about whether to have a lecture or a film. If we're going to use a film, we have to decide which one. I think it should be . . ."; or "No, it isn't more time we need; it's more good ideas; Time won't help us until we start really producing. . . ."

4. *Changing:* The previously expressed ideas are ignored or given only a perfunctory recognition in what is essentially a new topical development.

> Speaker A: "I think we should try to get more time to do the job."
> Speaker B: "Yes, that's a good idea. Now about those films we were talking about. It seems to me that . . ."; or "What's the name of that film we saw last week?"

GENERAL CONSIDERATIONS IN GROUP THERAPY PROCEDURE

Usually when the client comes for therapy he is seen individually by the psychotherapist first, so that he knows the client well before he places him in a group. A group is selected which seems to meet the needs of the client as well as of the group. The client may then continue to meet his therapist individually once a week and also work in his group once a week. He may reduce the number of individual visits, depending on the setting and problem.

Selection of Group Members

Background. One of the first questions that usually arises is, "Who should be in the group?" For a long time, counselors and therapists suggested that members be selected according to diagnostic problem categories. Joel (156) contends that problems and dynamics should be relatively similar, but that diagnostic categories should be forgotten. Winder (321) holds that, whenever possible, the members should be chosen so as to have fairly homogeneous backgrounds. This opinion is shared by Coffey (62). Cohen (64), however, feels that a calculated attempt should be made to include varied personality types in the composition of each group, namely, one or two outspoken or aggressive individuals, several mature and stable personalities, and several depressed, anxious members, for example. From experiments with grouping of individuals for therapy, Glatzer (125) found that judicious grouping of varied personalities was important for optimum therapeutic movement. Powdermaker and Frank (240) concluded from their research that, except for alcoholism, none of the attributes usually considered in grouping—age, intelligence, education, marital status, clinical diagnosis—are significant in themselves, either in determining which clients are suitable for group therapy or in selecting those to be treated in the same group. Similarities or differences in any one of these factors may be important in a particular group under special circumstances, but their effects can be understood only in terms of their importance to the issue with which the clients were concerned at the time. Bach (18) states that the selection of an individual client is really meaningful only in relation to the factors of group dynamics in the particular group for which membership is being considered.

Bach has introduced a theory of grouping which he calls the "Nuclear Expansion Theory." Here, the group is started with two or three members and the expansion is made according to the identification and similarity needs of these particular individuals. We tend to subscribe to Bach's point of view on selection of members.

Type of role in group therapy. Fundamental to the decision of placement, is the concept of "role" vacancies in a group. It is felt by most group therapists that groups should have a balance of roles represented. Some of the many possible role needs for a mixed group are as follows:

1. Father figure or "critical parent."
2. Mother figure or "mother hen."
3. Sex object or "sweetheart."
4. The prodder or facilitator of discussion.
5. The "warm understanding" member.
6. The adolescent or "delinquent" member.
7. The referee or "compromisor."
8. The religious, "self-righteous," or moralizing member.
9. The "devil," Don Juan, or "wolf."
10. The "snob."
11. The "good wife."
12. The "bad wife."
13. The "good husband."
14. The "bad husband."
15. The "executive" or "very important person."
16. The "woman hater."
17. The "man hater."
18. The "masculine" woman.
19. The "feminine" man.
20. The "learned scholar" or "professor."
21. The "working man."
22. The "castrating female."

Placement in a particular group, therefore, would be determined partly by role vacancies which exist in a group.

A further consideration in role placement is that of the individual needs of the client. Placement is often made when the new member is expected to identify with, or will feel close to, other members. Predicted hostility to other members can be a criterion for placement also.

Sex and age composition. The most common group is composed of mixed sexes, unless there is a definite reason for like-sex grouping. Like-sexed groups are sometimes found in schools or hospitals where there is a sex segregation policy. If one assumes, however, that the group therapy or multiple counseling situation must be viewed as a part of the transference phenomena, then as Slavson indicates (283), a mixed group may favor the tendency to act out problems in a therapeutic fashion. Slavson states that during certain stages in the treatment process clients develop libidinal desires directed toward the psychotherapist as a parent surrogate. These can be displaced or retransferred upon fellow group members who resemble parental images.

When considering the age composition of a group, Joel (156) feels that mixed groups are best. Older persons offer more significant transference and identification opportunities for younger members and vice versa. Bach

(18), who uses the principle of heterogeneity in the selection of his clients, contends that it is desirable not to mix very young adults having had little sexual and social experience with more experienced adults. Conversely, in educational institutions, the older experienced persons would tend to be excluded because of their scarcity in the school and college populations.

Criteria for exclusion of members from groups. When selecting certain members for groups Hobbs (145) has found that there are several types of persons who tend to disrupt or hinder group progress. They are: (1) psychologically sophisticated persons who use knowledge of psychodynamics cruelly on others; (2) extremely aggressive or hostile people who destroy the atmosphere of acceptance and freedom essential to the success of the group; (3) people who are continuously in close contact with each other outside of the group.

Bach (18) uses four personality criteria for exclusion of members from groups: (1) insufficient reality contact; (2) extremes of culturally tabooed or illegal behavior; (3) the dominant character who would be a chronic monopolist of discussion; and (4) those with psychopathic defenses and impulsiveness (pp. 18–22).

Size of groups. In organizing a therapeutic group for counseling or psychotherapy, the question usually arises as to how many persons should be included. Size is important because it can be a barrier to effectiveness of communication. A suggested minimum number for an effective social unit is three to five. Ten to twelve would be the maximum. It is generally agreed by group therapists, however, that eight is an optimum number. Loeser, for example, has several properties which he feels are characteristic of therapy groups with four to eight members:

1. It is large enough to dilute libidinal drives to safe and easily handled quanta.
2. It is large enough to provide a variety of intragroup transference potentialities to suit the needs of each patient at any given time.
3. It is large enough to avoid the strong positive and negative polarity of reaction of the dyad (two member group) and triad (three member group) and hence is more enduring. It cannot be destroyed by one or even two people.
4. It is large enough to permit heterogeneity and diversification of psychodynamic types and thus implement the group interaction process.
5. It is large enough to permit acting out in a diluted and workable manner.
6. On the other hand it is small enough to be handled by a therapist with a minimum of leadership and control. The therapist can maintain his uncritical, permissive and passive role, all of which are necessary for effective therapy.
7. It is small enough to operate without strong or numerous rules or regulations. Beyond a few simple rules such as hours, meeting places, etc., very few regulations need to be introduced.
8. It is small enough to permit each member a reasonable amount of attention and time, but large enough to remove the tensions of face-to-

face talking. The passive individual can remain inconspicuous until his confidence is built up before he need take on an active role (187, pp. 11–12).

Hobbs (145) and Joel (156) contend that more interaction is obtained if the group is not large since discussions led from within the group can operate more effectively. Such discussions are desirable because leadership from within the group seems to be more preferable than therapist leadership for controlling monopolists and for drawing out shy members. The "Post Session Technique," described later, is essentially such a discussion which operates most effectively when the number of members is small.

Seating and Physical Setting

The group is arranged in such a way that all can participate in an easy and informal manner. For effective participation the group members must be able to see and hear each other easily. The circle arrangement seems to facilitate participation better than rectangular table arrangements. The use of a table should be avoided for it can serve as a psychological barrier to free interaction. If there is a co-therapist in the group, he should sit several seats away from the therapist in order to avoid having the focus of leadership in one area. Another factor of importance is that each client should have the opportunity to choose his own chair.

The physical settings in the room must be conducive to group processes. It is suggested that the room be furnished to some degree like a comfortable living room.

Session Length and Time Interval

The length of the sessions and the time interval between them have been found to be as important in group therapy as in individual therapy. The number of sessions and the length of each vary according to the particular therapist. Some counselors and psychotherapists contend that as many as three meetings a week are preferable because continuity and intensity of personal interaction are facilitated by the greater frequency of meetings. If three meetings are held they generally continue for one hour (Joel 156). Still other groups will agree to have only one or two meetings a week, with one-and-a-half to two hours of actual group work (18, 145). Generally, multiple counseling sessions are held once a week for an hour to an hour-and-a-half to keep the emotional involvement factor under control.

Hinckley (144) found that the majority of group members from the Student Mental Hygiene Clinic at Minnesota preferred meeting one hour a week. Sessions longer than one hour were tried but were found to be unsatisfactory. Usually the first hour was very active and productive; but the succeeding hour was much less productive. In general, it may be said that therapists differ in their opinions about length of session; but group-therapy meetings usually last from one to two hours in length, depending on the number of sessions held during the week.

Role of the Co-Therapist in Group Therapy

It is not uncommon for groups to employ the services of two therapists. The second therapist acts as an interpreter-observer in many instances or he may remain quite passive. The question often arises whether or not two therapists in the same group setting are conducive to group progress. In our experience it is most helpful to have co-therapists. The facilitative role is then performed by one therapist, the interpreter-summarizer role by the other.

From psychoanalytic theory one might hold that the co-therapist is better played by a female, so that both "mother" and "father" roles are played by the therapists. In terms of Fromm's theory, however, one therapist can play the mother role of being accepting and permissive, while the interpreter-summarizer role is more akin to Fromm's idea of father love, that is, love with expectations and demands (113). Joel and Shapiro (156) contend from their experience that the presence of two therapists, especially if they are of the opposite sex, more readily revives the family situation. We have observed that clients appear to be flattered to have their proceedings recorded and summarized by a special observer.

Closed and Continuous Groups

There are two kinds of groups—closed and continuous. In the closed group, the same members are maintained throughout the life span of the group. This is often the case in educational settings where groups run the length of the academic semester. In the continuous group, replacements are made when a member leaves.

There is some degree of speculation among certain therapists whether closed groups offer more advantages than continuous groups. Some think that the closed group has more advantages because data can be accumulated and the group composition kept constant. If members drop out, however, because of an unavoidable circumstance, it may make the group unduly small. An advantage of an open group is that a new member, who has just come to the group, sometimes fosters a reworking of rivalries and competition in the group. Also, a new member may help therapeutic movement through a consolidation of group feeling. New members may reduce their defensiveness by identifying with other members who have already overcome theirs. The presence of less-advanced group members appears to have some ego-strengthening effects on the older members. The old members gain therapeutically through the experience of sharing and helping new clients adjust to the group.

TECHNIQUES OF GROUP THERAPY AND MULTIPLE COUNSELING

The leader should be, first of all, competent in individual counseling and therapy techniques. He uses all of the relationship, interpretive, and informational techniques discussed earlier in this volume in group therapy. In addition, he must use other techniques which are unique to, or which must be adapted to, group work. These techniques are presented in the following sections.

Structuring

Although there are many theories of group psychotherapy and multiple counseling, most practitioners agree with Frank and Asher (107) that the group provides support, stimulation, and reality-testing opportunities. In the group setting, clients have an opportunity to express themselves freely. Support is provided for the member by the reassuring social climate of the group in which each member feels safe in saying what he wants to say. The therapist, however, often initiates group discussion by some type of structuring in the first session. Hinckley (144) gives examples of this method, as follows: One therapist explains, "We are here to learn about ourselves and to help each other manage our natural feelings in more comfortable ways. Now, my name is ——————, as most of you already know. Perhaps the simplest way of beginning is for each of us to introduce ourselves and to say something of our symptoms." Another therapist comments, "In group sessions we come together to talk over some of the feelings we have which may be causing us discomfort. By finding out how much we are like other people, we sometimes feel better. Also, we may learn how other people handle some of their worries." A third therapist states, ". . . and there will be times in our meetings when it will be very hard to talk about our feelings because they may be painful to us. No one need talk of his troubles, though, until he is ready." A fourth therapist says, "Most of us can feel a little better when we learn to share, that is, talk out some of our troubles. This is possible in here. When we are able to get along comfortably in a small section of society like this group, perhaps later we will feel comfortable in larger groups. Shall we introduce ourselves now and begin by telling a little about ourselves? We don't have to speak of painful matters immediately."

In the structuring process the therapist should make it clear why the clients have come together. The members should be aware of the fact that conflicting feelings and attitudes are the basic reason for the formation of the group. It is also appropriate to state some advantages of group therapy so that clients can anticipate realistic results. It should also be stressed that what goes on in the group is strictly confidential.

The reassurance of structure is needed because group therapy is generally a new experience for clients. Further reasons and techniques of structuring are covered in Chapter 7.

Bach (18, pp. 29–30) has prepared a mimeographed preparation sheet on which six procedural principles are structured for the new group member.[3] The new member is given this sheet when he accepts group membership. We have modified this preparation sheet for use in our practice and present it below:

PREPARATION SHEET FOR NEW GROUP MEMBERS

(1) *Size of group:*
The group's size is limited to a minimum number of six and a maximum number of ten clients.

(2) *Admission of new members:*
When an old member leaves the group his or her place in the group will be filled by a new member. The selection is made on two bases: (a) which group is best for the prospective member, and (b) which prospective member is best for the group.

(3) *Extraoffice meetings:*
The regular office meetings of the group with the therapist, while of central therapeutic importance, are only part of the total program. Experiences during the post session between members of the group, provide important material for self-observation and analysis. No extraoffice meetings other than post-session meetings are allowed.

(4) *Sharing of mutual experiences:*
Group members usually adhere to the principle that everything anybody says, thinks or does, which involves another member of the group, is subject to open discussion in the group. In other words, the emotionally important experiences of any member are shared by all members. There are no secrets *inside* the group.

(5) *Ethical confidence:*
In contrast to Principle No. 4, everything that goes on within the group—everything!—must remain an absolute secret as far as any outsider (nonmember) is concerned. Anyone participating in group therapy automatically assumes the same professional ethics of absolute discretion which bind professional therapists.

(6) *The group's goal:*
The group goal is free communication on a nondefensive, personal and emotional level. This goal can be reached only by the group effort. Experience shows that the official therapists cannot "push" the group; the group has to progress by its own efforts. Each member will get out of the group what he puts into it. As every member communicates to the group his feelings and perceptions and associations of the moment as openly as he can and as often as he can, the group will become a therapeutically

---

[3] George R. Bach, *Intensive Group Psychotherapy,* copyright 1954 (New York: The Ronald Press Company), pp. 29–30.

effective medium. The goal of free communication is freedom to be one-self most fully and comfortably.

I have read the above and agree to cooperate fully.

Signed:_____

The "Going-Around" Technique

The going-around technique is often used as a warm-up device by the therapist to pitch the communication at a more emotional and less intel-lectual level. Each member describes his feelings about how every other member in the group affects him emotionally. This is usually done from neighbor to neighbor, "going around" the group circle. This technique is particularly useful in situations involving "newcomers." Older group mem-bers give their first impression to the newcomer in a casual manner. Then the newcomer has an opportunity to do likewise with the group members.

The Communication-Training Technique

This method is used by the group therapist to promote communication among group members. The therapist presents at appropriate times the following communication rules:

(1) The principle of *direct communication* is stated to the group as follows: "We never withhold feelings that we have about another person in the group. When we communicate these feelings we look directly at the person to whom we are talking, and we use his name or the pronoun, you." A poor example would be: (Talking to group in general) "I think Bill is not facing this problem with his wife." A better example would be: (Talk-ing directly to Bill) "Bill, I think you are not facing this problem with your wife."

(2) The principle of *question analysis* is stated as follows: "Whenever we ask a question, we must state the hypothesis behind our question." A poor example is: "What was your wife's reaction?" A better example is: "I was curious about your wife's reaction because I wondered if she reacts like my wife does."

(3) The principle of *advice analysis* proceeds as follows: "Whenever we give advice we must speculate on what it was in our own life experience which has made us so alert to this particular advice." A poor example is: "Why don't you leave your wife?" A better example is: "I think you ought to leave your wife, since you have the same situation which caused me to leave my first wife."

The Psychodramatic or Role-Playing Technique

The role-playing technique permits the client to apply playful acting-out of his problems as a serious attempt to understand his conflicts. The value of this method lies in the fact that participants reveal feelings and tensions without the burden of shame. It facilitates presenting a situation with fewer words and with greater clarity than can be achieved with the ordinary discussion methods. Driver (88) claims that role-playing is an effective alternative for talks and is an excellent warm-up device for discussion.

Role-playing as a counseling technique often helps a client to gain a better perspective of himself and others. It can be used, for example, to practice social situations which are difficult for the client. Even when it is used in a group situation by qualified workers, emphasis should be placed on the fact that many complications can arise if it is not used properly. Bach (18) warns of the possible traumatic effect of premature externalizing of threatening materials through role-playing.

Some of the major types of psychodramatic procedures in a group-therapy setting are described below.[4]

(1) *Role reversal* is a procedure which allows two individuals to exchange roles. Role reversal is used in the following example. A mother and daughter figure might be discussing what would be a reasonable hour for the latter to come home from a date. The daughter could exchange roles with the mother to see her side. Conversely, the parent could be afforded the frame of reference of the daughter.

(2) *The double technique* allows a second individual to assume the identity of the subject. This is a technique whereby two identities may seem merged into one. Functions of the double are illustrated in a situation in which one individual has to make a decision. For example, when meditating over whether or not to buy a new car, one might be in doubt about its being a good buy. A double ego, in this situation, would function as the subject's conscience and desire, and would verbalize the conflict in a low tone of voice at the same time the subject was verbalizing his dilemma.

(3) *The soliloquy* is a technique to make known "hidden" thoughts of role-playing participants. Another purpose of the soliloquy is to clarify and fix newly gained insights. For example, in a conference, each individual is allowed to speak his piece. Then, as the scene is "frozen," each is asked to soliloquize or to speak out what feelings are going on in his mind which he is not expressing. For example he is asked, "What thought occurred? How do you really feel about the other person?"

(4) *The mirror technique* is an attempt to allow the subject to see himself. It is used when it is thought to be helpful in seeing himself in action. For example, a subject may wish to observe himself at a given task, such as a job interview. The person serving as the substitute ego is placed across from the subject and mimics his behavior.

(5) *Periodic stimuli technique* is a method used to test the client's range

---

[4] Adapted from Del Torto and Cornyetz (81).

of expansiveness within the role. It is designed also to test his spontaneous adaptation to surprise elements. For example, a situation might be created where the subject is an artist working in his studio. At periodic intervals the director may send in a landlord demanding rent, his complaining sponsor, or a cantankerous model. The basic situation is not changed; only the stimuli are varied.

(6) *The hidden theme technique* brings out the subject's ability to perceive a behavioral theme in a social situation and to create an appropriate role to deal with it. For example, a subject is sent out of the room. He is told beforehand that when he returns, a social situation will be in progress and that he should relate himself meaningfully to the situation.

(7) *The mute technique* is used to reveal nonverbal resources for communication and expression. A theme is given to the subject and other clients with instructions that they communicate by gestures and bodily movements. An example would be a card game involving four people who are allowed to communicate only by gestures.

The Summary Interpretation Technique

Usually after forty or forty-five minutes of the therapeutic hour have elapsed, the group therapist or co-therapist, if there is one, finds it propitious to make a summary interpretation of what has happened in the hour. We feel that this summary task is best performed by a co-therapist rather than by the therapist himself. The latter usually has a facilitative or management role, and would find it difficult psychologically to perform both the summary interpretation and the facilitative role.

The interpretation technique has been found helpful in giving the group a picture of what has happened during the hour. We have found the following types of summaries to be useful:

(1) *"Theme" summaries:* Hobbs (145) suggests that group therapy is much like a musical composition, in that there are certain "themes" which run through group conversation. The co-therapist identifies these themes in the summary. An example is: "Tonight we have been talking about competition. Sally and Jack see themselves as always running away from it. In the area of romance, Bill says he just gives up, or disposes of the possibility of winning. In interpersonal competition, we have decided that we have to define the problem clearly. This means defining the assets and liabilities of our competitors and then defining our own assets and liabilities. We can then decide on which techniques we ought to work. Doreen is competing now with another woman for her husband. One thing she can do better than this other woman is to be a good mother to her children and a good wife to her husband. She has decided this is one of her chief assets which she can develop. We have also discussed the idea of 'shooting against our own par'—that is, competition with oneself is one of the best ways for

improvement. This method doesn't hurt anybody in the process. Jim does this in his golf game—and we can do it here too."

(2) *Individual analysis summaries:* Sometimes the discussions of a group do not center on a particular theme, but the individual group members discuss their own unique problems. The co-therapist then summarizes more individually, as for example: "Our discussion tonight has focused on four people, and I'd like to say something about each of them. We might call these people by certain pseudonyms.

"Alex here is Accepting Alex. He wants to be so accepting of everybody, because he has learned that this is what good psychologists do. But this is only half the story. Before we can really accept others, we first must learn to accept ourselves—both the negative and positive parts of ourselves. When Alex is able to do this completely, he'll not have trouble accepting others' positive and negative sides too.

"Doreen we might call Doormat Doreen. She has spent seventeen years being a doormat for her husband, and now she wants to change. She has been thinking that one way to do that is to take off from teaching this year so that her husband will not have the money she makes to depend on. But Les and Sam are in agreement that a better way would be to continue teaching, since just sitting around might make her more depressed and tired than before. Les found that out in his own experience. Furthermore, we know that most of us get more tired from underwork than overwork. If Doreen then continued to teach, she could keep her own money and really be selfish for once in her life.

"Will we might call 'Un-Warm Uncle Will.' He just doesn't want to admit he is warm, and yet Doreen has shown us that he really is. He doesn't want to be this way, and for the first time tonight has asked us to pull him down from his stand-offish position. He has humbled himself to do this, and I think we can help him."

(3) *Interpersonal dynamic summaries:* Instead of focusing on the individual problems of clients, the therapist can describe the interpersonal dynamics of feelings which have been taking place in the hour. An example is: "We have had many feelings shown here tonight. Some of them have been obvious, others not so obvious. Pete and Ted have both openly expressed their warm feelings toward Connie. Jack has expressed hostility by saying that he doesn't like her because she is so pretty, that everyone likes her, and that rejection is good for such a person. But after analyzing this feeling we find that Jack is saying this because he fears that if he were to express his real feelings of warmth to Connie, she might reject him, so he takes the offensive instead by rejecting her first. But he finds that this isn't very satisfying, because it leaves him feeling, as he says, lousy."

These methods of interpretation may be combined in summarizing the session; but they are presented separately above for purposes of clarity in exposition.

The Post-Session Technique

One of the techniques recommended by Bach (18) is the post-session technique. This is a procedure of allowing the group to remain after the therapeutic hour for the purposes of integrating the accomplishments of the hour and for the purpose of preparing one another for further therapeutic work. Bach sees the following goals for post-session work: (1) therapeutic reinforcement of insight gained in the work session of the group; (2) preparation to deal with difficult and resistance-evoking material through the development of social alliances; (3) opportunity to release pent-up tensions that were instigated but remained unleashed in the clinical work session; and (4) provision of experiential data on neurotic set-up (acted out transference) behavior for later working through.

There are several basic rules which must be observed with the post-session technique. First, the group members must stay together as a group. There must be no post-session pairing off and departing from the group. Group members are told that, other than in the post-session, they must not socialize outside the group. Furthermore, all material discussed in the post-session should be brought out ultimately in the regular session. Clients are encouraged in their individual sessions with their counselors to discuss what happened in the post-session.

SUMMARY AND CONCLUSIONS

In this chapter, some group-therapy techniques to supplement the individual counseling methods described elsewhere in this book have been presented. General considerations for development of groups such as selection problems, composition, size, seating and physical setting, time and interval, role of the co-therapist, and closed versus continuous groups have been outlined.

It was suggested that the effective group therapist must be familiar with all the individual techniques presented in this book. In addition, certain supplementary group techniques were considered important. These techniques are: structuring, "going-around technique," communication-training technique, psychodramatic methods, group-summary and interpretation technique, and post-session technique.

III.

Special Areas of Application

12.

Marriage Counseling and Psychotherapy

Marital counseling is tied in closely with therapeutic psychology; yet, it has a unique history. In the past, marriage counseling was performed, for the most part, by clergymen and social workers in public-welfare agencies and in family-service organizations.

At present, *additional* helping professions, such as psychology and psychiatry, are involved extensively in marriage counseling because marriage difficulties are seen by these groups primarily as another variation of human relationship problems rather than as a special area needing unique methods and training. These specialists recognize, however, that people with marriage problems often need the services of lawyers, clergymen, or physicians.

Social workers analyze the total family situation. Historically, they have worked mainly in agencies with low-income clients who have not been able to seek professional help on a private basis. More recently, however, social agencies have begun to develop services designed for the middle-income group (104).

The development of marriage guidance as a specialty dates back to such pioneer work as that of Stone, who established the first marriage consultation center in New York in 1929, and of Popenoe, who established the Institute of Family Relations in 1930. Much pioneer work has been done by Emily Mudd since 1932, when she established the Philadelphia Marriage Council. These people established marriage counseling as a specialty separate from family casework. Two organizations dedicated to professionalizing this field are the American Association of Marriage Counselors (311) and the National Council on Family Relations.

The clergy is another profession which has been associated with marital counseling and particularly pre-marital counseling of individuals who come to them to be married.

The family physician, also, has played a particular role in pre-marital counseling, since professional medical men are necessarily involved in the establishment of healthful attitudes toward sex and contraception.

Lawyers, because of their special role in relation to divorce, find themselves doing marital counseling by the very act of accepting or refusing a client. In any case, the highly specialized area of legal information and rules makes the lawyer an important partner in marital counseling.

The courts are paying increasing attention to the part they can play in bringing about reconciliation rather than granting divorce. Judge Louis Burke founded the Conciliation Court of Los Angeles, in which psychologists and social workers give reconciliation counseling. This development emphasizes the need for, and effectiveness of, interdisciplinary approaches to marriage problems. More recently, with the advent of clinical and counseling psychology established on a private practice basis, psychologists are applying their psychotherapeutic techniques and are making special applications to the field of marriage and legal problems.

SIGNIFICANCE AND COMPLEXITY OF MARRIAGE PROBLEMS

It is recognized, generally, that divorce is a major social problem today. It is estimated that, presently, one out of every three marriages in the United States ends in disruption, although areas differ in this respect. Mary Ann Callan in the *Los Angeles Times* (54) cites the County Clerk's Office of Los Angeles County to the effect that in 1957 the number of marriages for the entire county totaled 38,333, while the number of suits for divorce, separate maintenance, and annulment tallied 32,563. Thus, in Los Angeles County the number of divorces and marriages approaches a one-to-one ratio.

A Philosophy for Marriage Counseling

We take the position that the counselor or therapist does not have the right to decide whether or not divorce is the best solution for those who seek marital counseling. Marital counseling can assist in healthful adjustment for each of the parties concerned, whether or not divorce is a part of the solution.

The counselor should recognize that there are probably some couples whose emotional separation has been of such long duration, with so much bitterness, that no reconciliation is possible. Where great personality damage has been done to one or both individuals, reconciliation may be a dubious answer. This does not mean that divorce is the only solution. A couple may be helped to live together in relative harmony and security even though the goal of a close marriage tie is impossible.

In some instances a separation is the only means by which a marriage can be saved. Frequently, of course, this leads to final dissolution of the marriage. However, separation often may serve to help individuals face the realities of living instead of blaming one another for their problems. If the counselor can make the couple stop quarreling over petty issues, he may make it possible for one or both of them to do some basic growing. Later, they may be able to cope with marital interactions on a more constructive basis.

Separation is seldom instigated by the counselor. Usually it is a reality factor to be considered in the particular counseling situation. But the counselor who is aware that separation can serve constructive purposes can help his clients more effectively.

Effects of Disruptions on Children

Sometimes a separation is a necessary transition to final divorce. It can facilitate reasonably amicable post-divorce relations and minimize unnecessary bitterness which likely will react unfavorably upon the children caught in the middle. Thus, one of the most common considerations in divorce is the effect it will have on the children involved. Despert, in an analysis of the effects of divorce on children says, "Divorce is not the costliest experience possible to a child. Unhappy marriage without divorce— what we shall call emotional divorce—can be far more destructive to him than divorce" (82, pg. 18).

Mahler and Rabinovitch, among others, list ways in which marital conflict may affect a child's development adversely. The following list is an adaptation of their discussion of marital conflict and children:

(1) The child is made a buffer between parents; either or both turn to the child for satisfactions not obtained from the partner.
(2) The child is made a pawn, something planned for, conceived, and used to cement a marriage already in jeopardy.
(3) The child is made a confidant to either or both parents who are hostile to each other, thus burdening him emotionally beyond his capacity.
(4) The child is hurt by impulsive actions, such as confronting him with major decisions or changes.
(5) The child is subjected to recurrent or violent scenes, sometimes alternating with periods of false peace.
(6) The child is exposed to protracted subtle discord, such as "the pre-divorce uncertainty."
(7) The resolution of the oedipal phase is made difficult since it is accomplished through identification with the parent of the same sex.
(8) The child's period of dependency on mother is prolonged, since his dependency phase has been arrested at this level (194, pp. 50–54).

When divorce takes place, the counselor frequently can help clients assist their children through the difficult period. Despert (82, pg. 42) thinks that the child of estranged parents needs to know: (1) he is not to blame; (2) his parents still love him; (3) something is wrong—but not, as he fears, everything; (4) parents are not gods but human beings who have made mistakes.

Unfortunately, bickering families not only develop maladjusted personalities, but they also tend to perpetuate their unhealthy patterns in the marriages of the next generation. Marital counseling, in many instances, is the most direct and suitable approach to breaking this "vicious circle." The conclusion which seems warranted here is that there is no "one best way" to solve marital difficulties.

The discussion above has suggested the complexity and consequences of the problem and that it is frequently impossible that any solution will be absolutely constructive for everyone concerned. The discussion which follows can only outline some of the major problems in the complex area of marital counseling and suggest some techniques for handling them.

THERAPEUTIC PSYCHOLOGY AND MARRIAGE COUNSELING

Marital counseling differs from other types of counseling in that one or both of the marriage partners seek help because they believe their marriage is in difficulty. It is this emphasis on the problems of the marriage relationship itself, at least in the early stages of the counseling process, which makes marital counseling a specialty.

Foster (106, pg. 213) has contrasted individual psychotherapy and marriage counseling in the two figures which follow. In Figure 24, illustrating

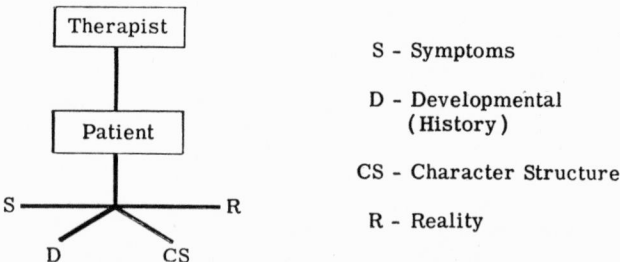

FIG. 24. The Individual Psychotherapy Model.
Adapted from Foster.

psychotherapy, the therapist is directly connected with the client, who, in turn, is concerned directly with his symptoms, developmental history, character structure, and reality.

In Figure 25 Foster (106, pg. 214) shows a direct, individual connection between the separate entities of marital counselor, husband, wife, and the marriage. In addition to the symptoms, developmental history, and reality with which husband and wife are individually concerned, the marriage substitutes its own conflict patterns for the individual character structures. Thus, it is important to note that individual psychotherapy is very much a

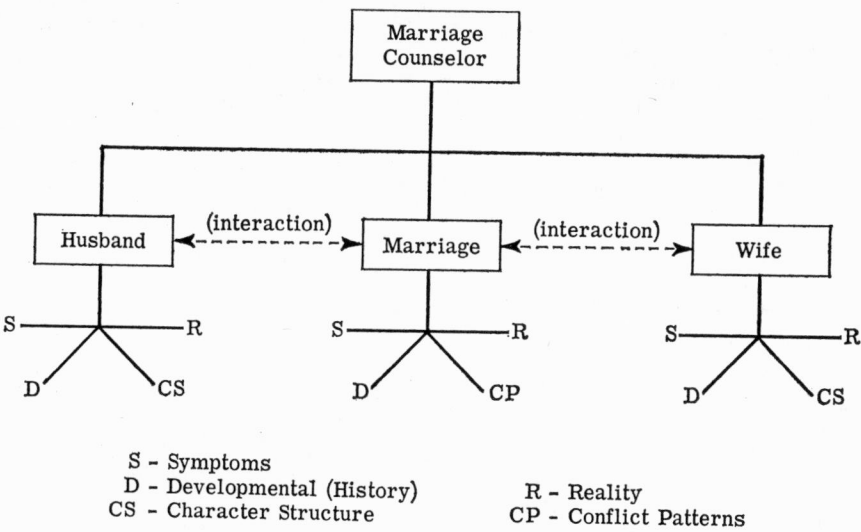

S - Symptoms
D - Developmental (History)   R - Reality
CS - Character Structure   CP - Conflict Patterns

FIG. 25. The Marriage Counseling Model.
Adapted from Foster.

part of marriage counseling; but to this is added the emphasis upon conflict patterns within the marriage, as well as the marriage symptoms and developmental histories.

Foster distinguishes marriage counseling from psychotherapy in that the former must deal with a third element, the marriage relationship, as well as with the individual histories and conflicts of husband and wife. However, he did not make clear the dynamic relationships among these three elements. The naive or inexperienced marriage counselor tends to focus on the *relationship* in marriage counseling only, concentrating on such problems or symptoms as bickering and unkindness. Consequently, he attempts to smooth out the relationship between husband and wife. The result, generally, is superficial. Marital psychotherapy usually requires that the therapist begin with the individual spouses themselves and their unique problems. The marriage therapist works with the individual first and then with the relationship. Marriage counseling does both but tends to focus on relationship problems.

Infidelity Problems

An analysis of many marital conflicts leads to the conclusion that the basic problem is lack of a healthy self-regard in one or both partners. Infidelity is often a symptom of not having achieved this major therapeutic goal of personal worth. The typical spouse, not feeling a sense of personal worth or love from husband or wife, seeks to prove that he is lovable by engaging in an extra-marital affair. Counselors find, however, that simply to eliminate the third person in the triangle does not help. What is required is a type of therapy which helps the individual to determine the causes of his lack of self-love and to develop feelings of worth and adequacy. Once this is achieved, he will be able to see the neurotic need which is being met by the affair and be able to express his hostility to his spouse for not having been loved. The spouse responds typically by recognizing his dependence on the errant spouse. Finally, having worked through the unexpressed and unrecognized dependencies, the relationship improves. The improvement, however, comes about after the therapist has concentrated on the ego and self-systems of the client.

Horney describes the multiple factors involved in reactions to infidelity. The counselor often must deal with the spouse not involved in the infidelity. Her discussion illustrates the meaning of such problems from the viewpoint of the "innocent party."

> There are a number of reasons that might explain why she feels and acts in this way, quite apart from a genuine hurt about the breach of confidence. (1) It may have hurt her pride that the husband could be attached to anyone but herself. (2) It may be intolerable to her that her husband could slip out from her control and domination. (3) The incident may have touched off a dread of desertion. (4) She may be discontented with the marriage for reasons of which she is not aware, and she may use this conspicuous occurrence as an excuse for expressing all her repressed grievances, thus engaging merely in an unconscious campaign of revenge. (5) She may have felt attracted toward another man and resent the fact that her husband indulged in a freedom that she had not allowed herself (150, pp. 283–84).

Reconciliation Processes

The course of reconciliation in marital therapy may be diagrammed as in Figure 26. What is suggested here is that, initially, marital therapy causes the marital relationship to get worse rather than better. Thus, the idea developed in Chapter 4 that "you get worse before you get better" holds true here also. In Figure 26 the course of marital therapy suggests that, at first, the spouses seem to separate psychologically. For this reason, it is unwise in the initial phases of therapy to focus on reconciliation, as indicated at Point 2. To do this would be to limit the necessary expression of hostile feelings toward one's spouse. Therapy brings to consciousness these hostile feelings, many of which have remained dormant for years. The expression of such negative feelings enables the client to reach Point 1 in Figure 26. Here he comes to regard himself as a person of worth and dignity who does not need to stay with the marriage at any cost. This is the "brink of disaster" point, psychologically speaking.

Conscious recognition of these facts, however, leads the client to make a choice. He can be free of the marriage; but he is free also to *choose* mar-

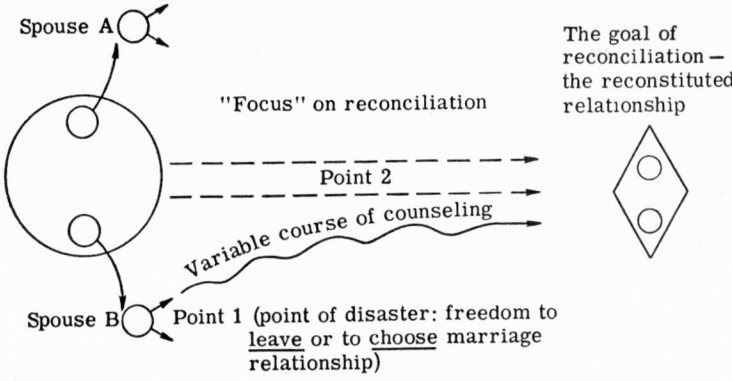

Spouse A

"Focus" on reconciliation

The goal of reconciliation — the reconstituted relationship

Point 2

Variable course of counseling

Spouse B Point 1 (point of disaster: freedom to leave or to choose marriage relationship)

FIG. 26. The Process of Marital Counseling.

riage and not be neurotically bound to it. When he makes the latter choice, he is able to relate effectively to his partner for the first time. Parenthetically, this means that it may be unwise for the client or the therapist to consciously focus on "saving the marriage at all costs" if therapy is to run its course. If the attitude is to "save or reconcile at all costs," it may prevent the spouse from reaching the "brink of disaster" point which seems to us such a fruitful therapeutic condition in successful marital therapy.

In light of the above discussion it is asserted, therefore, that the special area of marriage counseling is but a special application of the broad area of therapeutic psychology. Marriage counseling is more extensive in scope, however, since it deals with the elements of a sick marriage as well as the personalities of the parties involved. All of the techniques described thus far are applicable to the counseling of people *individually* who happen to be married. The balance of this chapter deals with the specialized considerations necessary in dealing with individuals as they anticipate, or are involved in, a marital *relationship*.

PRE-MARITAL COUNSELING

Skidmore and Garrett indicate that the "basic aim of pre-marital counseling is to assist the prospective mates to gain a better understanding of themselves, of each other, and of what marriage entails." (281, pg. 323) It is most difficult to categorize certain problem areas as being unique to *pre-marital* counseling. However, there are a number of considerations which are basic to this area. The following comments relate to the counseling of young people, anticipating and coping with the many problems that arise in courtship and young marriage.

The Problem of Mate Choice

A basic consideration in pre-marital counseling is the obvious question of mate choice. Psychologists have pointed out that many mate choices are based on some form of neurotic attraction. Mittleman, for example, lists some common types of neurotic attraction of which the following is a summary:

(1) One aggressive and sadistic versus one dependent and submissive.
(2) One self-sufficient through emotional detachment versus one demanding love.
(3) Mutual attempts at domination.
(4) One neurotically ill versus one extremely considerate.
(5) One with fluctuating helplessness and assertiveness versus one fluctuating in responsibility and disappointed desire for love (208, pp. 82–83).

One of the major jobs in pre-marital counseling is to help young people determine the extent to which their choice of a mate is healthy and the degree to which it is neurotic. Fromm (113) suggests the criterion that to love someone because you "need" him is neurotic; to need him because you love him is healthy. Fromm points out also that love in this sense is both an emotional feeling and a decision. It must not be regarded as solely one or the other.

Maslow (197) suggests also that marriage between healthy, self-actualizing people is a merging of feelings and intellectual choices. The choice is *felt* to be right. Their cognitive acts confirm their feelings, or vice versa. This reciprocal confirmation and convergence process takes place in varied ways with the individuals involved. Either approach is suitable as long as the two are balanced.

The Nature of Love

A second area of prime concern in pre-marital counseling is the meaning of love. Unfortunately, too few people who are preparing for marriage have ever taken time to develop any rational definition of love, let alone to evaluate what love means to them as individuals. When asked, most people are likely to say they married for love; but they cannot, if asked, verbalize what they meant then or what they mean in the present when they say they love or do not love their mates. Fromm's *The Art of Loving* should be read by all those seriously considering marriage, since it might help such couples evaluate the true bases of their love. The discussion on love which follows draws heavily from Fromm.

Frequently a person's concept of love does not distinguish between "romantic love" and "mature love" between man and woman. Romantic love has cultural roots in the past; but it survives unfortunately in the present, nurtured by an endless barrage of fairy tales told in myriads of slightly different forms in movies, magazines, novels, and TV. They cater to the susceptible day-dreams of the immature and tend to make them addicts of romantic emotionalism. This happens because in their immaturity they appear unable to understand, let alone grow into, mature love relationships without assistance.

A counselor needs to be familiar with the common psychological interpretations of the forms of love and the processes of loving. Although a thorough analysis cannot be made here, certain generally accepted ideas concerning love will be described as they affect the problem of pre-marital counseling.

Romantic love is defined as the projection of an individual's emotional needs onto a love object. Romantic love is the search for the ideal mate. This ideal mate personifies all the perfection and divine attributes that the individual feels he himself lacks or needs. Mature love, by contrast, comes only after a knowledge of and experience with the loved partner. It may follow a "period of disillusionment" associated with romantic love. "Falling out of romantic love" results from a shattering of the idealized, romantic, love illusion. One "falls out of love" because one does not work through the period of disillusionment to a new conception of love based not on projected needs, but on a realistic appraisal of one another and a deep valuing of each other as unique persons.

"Counterfeit" or "profane love" are terms referring to a symptom not uncommon in marriage conflict. Counterfeit love can be recognized when the relationship is degrading, exploitive, possessive, violent, antisocial, irresponsible, sadistic, or masochistic. These are the symptoms that point to a neurotic personality which must be helped to maturity before a normal love relationship can be developed.

Fromm lists the following distorted ideas that many people have in regard to love: (1) They ". . . see the problem of love primarily as that of *being loved* rather than that of loving. . . ." (2) They ". . . think that to *love* is simple," whereas to find the correct love object is difficult. (3) They feel that love is beyond understanding, and they cannot learn how to love (113, pp. 1–4).

Fromm states, furthermore, that mature love includes four basic elements: (1) ". . . the *active concern for the life and growth of that which we love.*" (2) *Responsibility* for the needs, physical and psychic, of the other. (3) *Respect* for the other, the ability to see a person as he is, to be aware of his unique individuality. (4) *Knowledge* of self, of the other, and of the nature of love (113, pg. 26).

Many other psychologists and philosophers emphasize that love involves learning to give and receive love, and that the needs of the other must be at least as important as your own; otherwise love, mature love, does not exist. Maslow, for example, expresses it as follows: "One person feels another's needs as if they were his own and for that matter also feels his own needs to some extent as if they belonged to the other" (197, pg. 249).

Gibran emphasized that mature love requires ". . . spaces in your togetherness." "Stand together yet not too near together: For the pillars of the temple stand apart, and the oak tree and the cypress grow not in each other's shadow" (122, pp. 16–17). The idea that love is not possession, incorporation, or destruction is further described by Gibran when he said, "Love gives naught but itself and takes naught but from itself. Love possesses not nor would be possessed. For love is sufficient unto love" (pg. 14). "Love between man and woman may be defined," Blanton writes, "as a relationship in which each helps the other to preserve and enlarge the life of the other" (35, pg. 83). According to Overstreet, "Love of a person implies not the possession of that person, but the affirmation of that person. It means granting him, gladly, the full right to his unique manhood" (227, pg. 103).

The concept of a mature love relationship as a long process of growth and not something which comes and goes as if by magic, is a fundamental concept running through much philosophical literature.

There is no blueprint for telling how a counselor can help a client understand and feel the meaning of these concepts. Each individual must discover what love means and how he can become lovable and loving in his own way. But an awareness and a willingness on the part of the counselor or therapist to interpret these formulations on the meanings of love can greatly assist the client in his search for understanding and expressing love.

Sex

Fromm suggests that the neurotic individual often seeks to establish intimacy with another by sexual contact rather than through a gradual association. "Such experiences of sudden intimacy are usually short-lived and unsatisfying" (113, pg. 53). Sexual desire often is mistaken for love, and frequently sexual desire is motivated by other neurotic needs. Fromm suggests four: (1) the anxiety of aloneness; (2) the wish to conquer or be conquered; (3) vanity; (4) the wish to hurt or even to destroy (113, pg. 54).

Faulty sex education or unhealthy sex attitudes learned in childhood are, of course, frequent sources of trouble. The client often is helped by facing the feelings which these early experiences developed within him. Frequently, if the counselor gives specific sex information, he can rectify problems based on misinformation or a lack of knowledge. In the process of sex education, the counselor can be reassuring and helpful by giving specific information, although it is important that he make the client realize that it is not faulty information but distorted attitudes which are the seat of the real trouble. If not carefully used, the "sex manual" approach can be grossly misleading.

It is important that, during pre-marital counseling, the counselor impart an understanding of the relationship of sex to love. In order to complete a human relationship, it may be said that biological desire must be joined with love as it has been described heretofore. A common social value we have inherited through our Hebraic-Christian tradition is that sex is one means of expressing love. This means that unless both elements are present, there is a "psychic prostitution." Parenthetically, this interpretation suggests that there is often much of this type of prostitution in many marriage relationships. When present it tends to have a destructive effect on the personalities involved.

Differences Between Men and Women

Closely related to understanding the love relationship in marriage is understanding that the differences between men and women are more than physiological. Again, the client may need help in understanding how he developed his attitudes toward his own sex role and that of the opposite sex. His early lack of proper sex-role identification or his early resentments relating to sibling rivalries may be the source of much hostility in marriage. He may need considerable assistance in learning to understand, on an emotional level, just what his responsibilities and privileges are in regard to marriage.

Jung is a great exponent of psychic sex differences. He points out that women operate in terms of the "Eros Principle" and are basically feeling or intuitive in their approach to life. Men operate on the "Logos Principle" and tend to be more intellectual, systematic, and power-centered in their approach (161). Fromm, too, suggests some basic character differences in men and women. The masculine character he describes by such terms as "penetration, guidance, activity, discipline, and adventurousness." The feminine character he describes in terms of "productive receptiveness, protection, realism, endurance, and motherliness" (113, pp. 36–37).

The main therapeutic implication of the preceding opinions is that each individual needs to recognize that his mate has different needs, has had different experiences, and, of necessity, looks at life differently, and reacts to life's demands, in a different manner. This area of psychological sex differences illustrates why a counselor probably will have little success in helping the client develop new attitudes if he relies solely upon authority. Actually, the conflict between a man and a woman needs to be understood in terms of the two unique personalities. What is *this* woman like? What is the personality pattern of *this* man?

A further counseling implication is that an understanding of cultural and physiological forces at work can take some of the sting out of the conflict between the sexes; but essentially each human being must learn to accept and develop his own sex role in relation to his past experiences, his present situation, and his future goals. In practice, it is noted that once the client has been helped to understand, accept, and enjoy his own role he can then be helped to accept the fact that the differences of his mate need not be a source of hostility. He can see that they are an important basis for enriching his marriage and his personal life. He sees that learning to value differences is a measure of personal and marital maturity.

Empathy

Although the subject of empathy was discussed at length in Chapter 6, its relevance for marriage counseling will be elaborated here. Murphy makes the following distinction between empathy and sympathy: "Empathy is 'direct' apprehension of the state of mind of another person, without, as in sympathy, feeling as that other person does. In sympathy shared attitude is the chief matter" (220, pg. 985). Building upon an understanding of the differences between men and women as well as the basic concept that each personality is unique, it is important that the counselor helps the marital client to develop insight into the personality, feelings, and behavior of his mate, that is, to have *empathy* for his mate.

Too frequently an individual's background has not prepared him for any further stage in human relationships than a sympathetic role. When empathy is not experienced, such an individual often feels there is no basis for the relationship. Consequently, the marriage appears doomed, unless mutual empathy can be developed. Skidmore (280, pg. 69) lists empathy as one of the four major bases for building confidence and security in a marriage.

"I would never do that," "How can he feel that," "I can't understand why she would ever say such a thing," are all attitudes which may be approached from the viewpoint of developing empathy. Of course, the counselor's own ability to empathize with the client frequently can be used as a meaningful starting point for the client. The client knows, or can be helped to realize, that the counselor's acceptance is not the same as approval or sympathy. Having received an empathic response, the client then may be more ready to show empathy for others.

Experiencing empathic responses from a counselor in itself sometimes suffices to stimulate the client's potential growth. In other cases, the counselor can demonstrate to the client his stubborn resistance to empathy and can use the demonstration as an interpretive stepping stone to give him a deeper understanding of his defense mechanisms and personality development. Without empathy there can be little basic acceptance between human beings. Growing empathy between husband and wife can be a measure of improvement in the marriage relationship.

Communication

In some marriages, one or both of the individuals have such distorted means of communication, that, even in casual conversation, they misinterpret simple facts. Poor communication, then, becomes a focal point of many quarrels. The individual may reduce exaggerated expressions of hostility which may be standing in the way of his understanding the more basic causes of his conflict, first, by learning to recognize precisely what others mean or feel.

The counselor's emphasis upon using principles of good semantics can be an important learning experience for the client. When the counselor makes a point of being sure he understands what it is the client is telling him, he can demonstrate further how accurate communication takes place.

Accurate communication in a marriage not only can reduce hostility based upon misunderstanding, but also it can be a basis for developing a feeling of closeness or oneness within the marriage. It is a practical means for alleviating the loneliness which so many people feel in our society. Practical steps to improve communication do not obviate the need for emotional insight, but they are ways in which the client can consolidate the progress he is making and can encourage him toward further growth. Following are some practical suggestions to be used cautiously for improving communication:

(1) Repeat what the first person says. Try to rephrase it in your own words and try to get into the other person's frame of reference. (See Chapter 7 on reflection techniques.)

    (a) Ask, "When you say so and so, do you mean this and that?"
      Example: "When you say I am too strict with the children you mean I shouldn't have punished Bobby for taking the cookie?"

    (b) Ask, "What do you mean by such and such?"
      Example: "In what ways do you mean I am uncooperative with you?"

(2) Learn to recognize that people express themselves differently.

    (a) Some people express affection or any other emotion by words —some by behavior.
      Example: Some people say, "I love you," others bring a bunch of violets, and others keep the house in tip-top repair without being asked.

    (b) Just because something isn't expressed verbally doesn't mean it isn't felt.
      Example: The individual who is "never" hostile outwardly may express it by illness, sarcastic jokes, or sly innuendoes.

(3) Reduce generalities to a minimum.

      Examples: "You *never* smile when I come home." "*All* men make life miserable for their wives."

(4) State your own feelings clearly first before expecting your partner to express his feelings.

      Negative Example: "Do you think we ought to move now?"

Positive Example: "I think we ought to move . . . for the following reasons . . ."

(5) Distinguish the *situation* from the *person:*

Example: "I would like to talk to you longer, but I have someone in the office and I can't *now*."

(6) Set aside time for communication *regularly,* even when there is no particular problem to resolve. Get the "communication habit." Let good communication be a preventive measure to head off incipient problems.

Hyakawa's[1] theorem is pertinent here: "Misinformation breeds in an information vacuum." An example follows. If communication between persons A and B is bad, A then makes guesses. The longer the time that elapses, the less A's "information vacuum" resembles reality. For example, John is expected home at seven o'clock. As the time elapses past this hour his wife begins to make more and more false assumptions: "Has he been in an accident, or is he drunk, or has he been killed?"

Before concluding this section, it is pertinent that Terman's significant research on *Psychological Factors in Marital Happiness* (302) be considered as an example of the many prediction studies of marital happiness. Terman found ten important background factors which have been found to be highly related to happiness in marriage. Young people contemplating marriage often find these factors valuable for analyzing a prospective partner as well as for giving him a better understanding of what kind of marriage partner the client might be. The factors are stated in the form of questions which can be asked of the client. Each "yes" indicates a better chance for happiness in marriage.

(1) Have your parents been happy?

(2) Have you had a happy childhood?

(3) Have you gotten along well with your mother?

(4) Has there been firm, but not harsh, discipline in your home?

(5) Do you have a strong love for your mother?

(6) Do you have a strong love for your father?

(7) Have you gotten along well with your father?

(8) Have your parents been frank about sex?

(9) As a child was your punishment mild and infrequent?

(10) Do you have an attitude toward sex that is free from disgust and aversion? (302, pg. 372).

It must be re-emphasized that much of the foregoing material in the various forms of background information, philosophy, and techniques will be of importance to clients in marital as well as in pre-marital counseling. The discussions of problems which follow, however, have greater applicability to marital counseling.

---

[1] From personal communication with Dr. Don Hyakawa.

MARRIAGE PROBLEMS

Once the marriage has been consummated, two basic types of problems may arise: (1) Those involving the individual personality adjustment of the married partners, and (2) those more related to the marriage itself.

Special Personality Adjustment Problems In Marriage

There are several deep characterological problems which often are seriously aggravated by marriage. These problems include alcoholism, gambling, extreme jealousy, compulsive nagging, chronic complaining, and violent temper. Moralistic admonitions to do the "right thing" will not help these individuals. In most instances they need considerable individual psychotherapy.

In addition, the mate of a client with these types of problems frequently can be a deciding factor in the outcome of therapy. The "innocent" mate needs help in understanding the reasons for his original marital choice, the underlying dynamics of his reactions to his mate's present symptoms, how he has aggravated the problem, and finally how he can realistically help his mate.

Special Areas of Conflict in the Marriage Relationship

It would be presumptuous and unwise to suggest specific answers to problems which commonly arise in the marriage relationship. Nevertheless, the practicing counselor must be aware of these problems; and, as has been suggested earlier, he must know the right questions to ask. The following list concerns problems in which there must be some consensus in marriage. It must be remembered, however, that disagreement is only symptomatic of a poor relationship, and that before the relationship is dealt with, individual therapy on pertinent personal conflicts generally must be handled by the therapist.

(1) *Finances.* Is an inability to agree on finances a cover-up for more basic disagreements? Which partner (or is it both) is immature in handling finances? Are financial difficulties a symptom of over-all immaturity? What significance does money have for this individual and his mate?

(2) *Social Life.* Do these individuals actually have different social aims? Are they temperamentally different in terms of sociability? Is each lacking in understanding of the other's social needs? Why is one of them placing great emphasis upon social life? Is there basic dissatisfaction with the demands of family living generally or of this marriage specifically?

(3) *Parent-Child Relationships.* Is there basic disagreement in regard to discipline? Has either of these individuals a distorted idea of discipline? Is there overidentification with a child or the children by either parent? Is

there jealousy of one parent's closeness to a child? Is the parent-child difficulty a displacement of hostility? Is there a resentment of the responsibilities of marriage expressing itself through parent-child difficulties?

(4) *Religious and Life Values.* Are differences in religion being used as a cover-up for other differences? Why did this couple marry in the first place? Why is this couple now having difficulty with a difference they evidently felt could be resolved before marriage? What does religion mean to each of these individuals? How much real effort have they made to resolve this difference? How important were religion and other general life values to these clients while they were growing up?

(5) *In-Laws.* Are the in-laws the problem or is it the client's attitude toward them? If there is not unity in handling this problem how much unity is there on other problems? Is jealousy a major issue? Is one client complaining about his in-laws because his own parents are his problem? How mature is this individual in terms of maintaining his own independence?

(6) *In-Family Triangle.* Why is this individual alarmed by his mate having close ties with someone else in the family? Was this ever a close marriage? Is this client basically possessive? Is the mate expressing hostility by over-devotion to some other family member?

(7) *Extra-Marital Relationship.* How has this client failed to build a marriage which meets the needs of his mate? Is he overly hostile or overly forgiving in his attitude? Is this client really interested in re-establishing the marriage? Or is this client playing the martyr role? If this be the client who has "strayed," is he overly repentive or overly defiant? What was he trying to accomplish, in terms of his own needs, by extra-marital entanglement? What kind of individual did he pick to make the triangle and why?

(8) *Job pressures.* Why are job pressures impinging upon the marriage? Is the individual really in a dead-end job or the wrong type of work? Does one or both have resentment or shame in regard to the job's prestige or income level? Are the hours of work really excessively long or is the job used as an escape from the home? What goals did this couple have originally in regard to economic status? Is the wife jealous of the husband's career?

(9) *Inadequate Self-Actualization.* Is this individual really bogged down with too much responsibility and too many pressures? Does he really want to help himself or does he want some magic solution? Is this client unprepared for the responsibilities of family living? Are there practical things which could be done to give this individual some opportunity for creative activity which he has not tried? Is this client really trying to pull away from the marriage?

(10) *Different Cultural Background.* What part did defiance of family play in the original choice of each other? Is one enjoying basically what he considers a superior role? What do this couple have in common? Is one using cultural differences to cover up more basic dissatisfactions?

It should be emphasized, of course, that the counselor must not ask the client these questions directly. Rather, he should use them to develop his own insight into what is behind the client's problems. It might be well, here, to re-emphasize, also, the importance of the counselor's periodic analysis of his own reactions to the client's problems. He must remember that his own standards will not necessarily serve as a solution for this particular client's problems.

Going one step further, it should be understood that these questions about cultural backgrounds may be a means whereby the counselor can lead the client from a superficial approach to consideration of deeper problems. The goal is to make the client understand how the problem developed, what underlying attitude is reflected, and what it symbolizes in the marriage. Knowing the client's cultural background will help the counselor to decide which of the client's remarks he will choose for reflection.

(11) *Sexual conflict*. Though mentioned in the introductory paragraphs as a problem in marital relationships, sexual conflict is considered again here to emphasize its importance as being an especially difficult problem. Clients eventually report sexual adjustment problems, although, at first, they obscure them by many resistive types of rationalizations. Marriage counselors generally work on the underlying psychological problems of the couples rather than directly on the sexual problems, since the sexual maladjustment is so often merely symptomatic. There are situations, however, where problems of inadequate knowledge and technique contribute to the difficulty, or where physiological problems are present. The latter problems should be investigated and dealt with first by specialists competent to diagnose and treat them.

There is considerable variation in clients' willingness to go beneath the surface of the problem confronting him. The client should be the main person to determine the length of marital therapy and the depth of insight to be achieved. Frequently, the manner in which the counselor helps the client to think about the problem, even on a superficial level, will make the client seek deeper counseling. It is not a matter of forcing the client against his desires, but of planting ideas which can come to fruition later when the client is more ready. For this reason, the counselor's understanding of the broad implications of presenting symptoms is an important facet of his proficiency.

THERAPEUTIC TECHNIQUES ESPECIALLY APPLICABLE TO MARITAL COUNSELING

Therapeutic techniques which have particular application to marital counseling are:

(1) *Structuring:* In the beginning phases of marital therapy this tech-

nique is frequently very important, particularly with unsophisticated clients who know very little about the process.

There are several basic attitudes which are important for the counselor to structure to the client early. Following are some of the basic counselor attitudes which must be communicated verbally to the couple. The therapist does not tell the couple how to run their lives. He does not function as an arbitrator, telling the couple who is right and who is wrong. He does not act like a "top sergeant" or parent substitute, telling them what to do. He is not a "tattle-tale" who carries stories back and forth. He does not place blame, nor is his goal to give approval. He plays no favorites, but is equally interested in helping each client to realize more satisfaction from the marriage.

However, the therapist may structure the process by telling the couple that he has had training and experience in helping people to understand themselves and their mates. His purpose is to help them to understand how others have solved similar problems. The counselor hopes that by helping his clients understand how their problems originated they will develop insight and techniques for handling present and future difficulties.

Frequently, only one marriage partner is willing to be counseled and he may really work hard at counseling. The other may come to the counselor but he usually does not participate beyond the most superficial discussion. In such cases, the counselor can structure the relationship by suggesting that marriages often have been helped when one partner takes the initiative. The cooperative client can learn to build a better life for himself within the marriage as well as to improve the marriage itself. It is not unusual for the noncooperative client to change as a result of the observable changes actuated by the cooperative client.

(2) *Fee Problems:* With the low-income family, finances are likely to be one facet of the family's problems. For this reason the low-income group traditionally has received counseling in a social agency where a casework approach and financial aid were most appropriate.

In the middle-income group, high fees can aggravate a marginal problem. In many instances, this condition shortens the counseling process to a few sessions, thus jeopardizing the effectiveness of the work.

The best generalization that can be made concerning fees seems to be that it is desirable for the client to pay a fee reasonable for his income level. A broad definition of a reasonable fee is one which does not substantially increase the client's problems. The fee does, however, put enough pressure upon him to work at his problems conscientiously.

(3) *Handling information:* In the third element of marital counseling, concerning the marriage itself, information is more important than some other types of counseling. The counselor must exercise as much skill when giving information as when performing other forms of counseling, and is often the crucial factor in improvement.

Basic to successful information-giving is the attitude with which the counselor presents data. When information is given suggestively as a basis for the exploration of ideas, and not pontifically or as reinforcement for preconceived ways of thinking, the client can be helped to grow.

Referrals in Marital Counseling: The marital counselor frequently finds it necessary to make special referrals. Ideally, he should be well informed about, and have direct contact with, the available resources in his community.

Some clients may, in the counselor's opinion, need a complete referral. The individual may be so seriously damaged that medical care may be indicated. Finance or other broad family problems may suggest a social-casework approach; hence, referral to a social agency would be preferable.

At times the counselor may continue to work with the client under a partial referral arrangement. If there are physical symptoms such as headaches or stomach ailments, it is essential that a physician decide if they require medical care, or at least that counseling and medical care can be carried on simultaneously.

The establishment of a working relationship between the psychologist and an attorney makes for the facilitation of cross referral between psychologist and attorney. In marital counseling, it is often necessary for the psychologist to refer clients to an attorney for pertinent information concerning marital laws, adoption, and annulment, for example. If it were necessary to refer the client to an attorney, located some distance from the counselor's office, the client might not accept referral readily. However, if the attorney can be summoned into the psychologist's office at the critical time, or if the psychologist can be brought into the attorney's office at a time when psychological help is suggested, referral is easily facilitated.

Clients with a marriage problem are often in trouble legally as well as psychologically. One client, for example, revealed that she had completely repressed a former marriage. Skillful legal help assisted her to dissolve the first marriage without social incident or involved legal maneuvers. Another young man was assisted immeasurably during pre-marital counseling by the attorney when the legal problems surrounding a pre-marital pregnancy came up in the therapy.

Similar arrangements are made for collaboration with ministers and physicians where close office association is made for purposes of easy cross referral. In institutions, such as schools and colleges, this collaboration is made quite easily except for legal services which generally are nonexistent.

Multiple-Counseling Techniques

Whether one or two counselors should handle one marriage is a question which cannot be answered definitely at the present time. It depends upon the couple, the counselor, and the setting in which the counseling is done.

We have used both methods; although research is needed on this point to help decide upon the most efficacious procedure.

The following material explores the arguments for and against relying upon more than one therapist. A general rule seems to hold that, if the problem involves intensive psychotherapy for each partner, two therapists would probably be indicated. If the problem were primarily one of marital counseling on relationship problems, one therapist or counselor would probably be sufficient and satisfactory.

The counselor who sees both partners in a marital dispute has the advantage of participating in a relationship with both and seeing the likely reality or distortion of the material each presents to him. Mittelman (208, pg. 93) feels that the advantages of one counselor working with a married couple are as follows: (1) The counselor secures information which makes him more able to perceive accurately the problems of both partners. (2) The counselor can see the distortions or omissions in the material from one or both of the mates. (3) During times of stress for one of the mates, the counselor can modify the behavior of the other which was complicating the problems of the partner.

Even in cases where one counselor is definitely indicated, the counselor has a difficult role to play. Mace (193, pg. 136) thinks that, "As a rule the relationship between the two individuals with whom he is counseling is initiated by conflict. In the presence of mutual hostility and recrimination, the marriage counselor must remain impartial and maintain the confidence of both husband and wife." In many instances, this is not an easy task.

Mittelman (208) points out that special transference problems may develop where one counselor sees both husband and wife. This transference is expressed by one mate in the form of concern over whether or not the therapist agrees with his evaluation of his mate, fear that the therapist is siding with the other partner, and wish-fulfillment fantasies that the therapist will change his mate by magic, thus saving the need for working out his own conflicts.

Mittelman (208) states, furthermore, that the counselor who handles both marital partners needs a reliable memory to know from which mate he got what information, the capacity to withstand the usually sustained rivalry and attack of both mates, the ability to be impartial but not neutral, and the courage to take a clear-cut stand in critical situations concerning who contributed what to a dispute. In other words, the therapist should behave like a benevolent, impartial, and firm parent to keep quarrels from getting out of hand.

Sometimes the counselor may find that what he says (or doesn't say) is so distorted or misinterpreted by one or both that the marital conflicts become exaggerated beyond repair. Under these circumstances two counselors, particularly if they can work in close collaboration, can do more effective counseling than one.

Mittelman (208) suggests two reasons against using one counselor with both parties: If one of the partners seems paranoidal in the sense of blaming everyone for his problems, and who therefore would probably blame the therapist for the termination of his marriage, it would seem more wise to have two therapists work with the partners. Secondly, if one spouse objects to working with the same therapist as the other, or, if such a client were advised to go to the same therapist, he might refuse to be treated at all and might hide all resistance to help behind the cloak of his objections to concurrent therapy.

One of the advantages of having separate counselors for each of the parties in a marital conflict is that the transference and memory problems suggested by Mittelman above are avoided. Each partner perceives his problems in a unique way; and to get into the frame of reference of just one of the perceivers of a marital dispute often is much easier. Furthermore, since the counselor does not have to remember who said what, he does not have the problem of keeping confidences.

If each partner has his own therapist, the therapists should confer at regular intervals, in order that they might cooperate in the therapy. It is important for each of them to remember that he received the information from the conference. Martin and Bird (311) suggest the importance and value of this cross-communication approach. By this they mean that therapists should meet regularly for the purpose of comparing their ideas on the problems of their respective, concurrently counseled clients. They may approach the problem by having one therapist present the picture of some event which took place in the life of the married couple in the frame of reference of his own client. The other therapist would then report on the same incident as he reconstructed it from his client's presentation. The two perceptions would finally be placed side by side, leading to the fusion effect of a stereopticon, hence the term "stereoscopic technique." The ability to discover distortions of reality on the part of one or both partners is most valuable. We feel, also, that this method leads to the recognition of ego defenses and impulses.

Some advantages of the dual approach are that it frees the therapist from distortions due to his single observation; it saves time in a quicker recognition of the client's distortion of reality; it cuts through the therapist's and his colleague's counter-transference.

Some disadvantages of the dual-counselor approach are that it is more time-consuming since it demands regularly planned conferences between therapists, and it is more complicated.

In the later stages of counseling, separate therapists and "joint sessions" or multiple counseling can be introduced. As counseling continues, husbands' and wives' perceptions of their relationship become more congruent. Then counseling of both partners at the same time by two counselors may be helpful. The two counselors may rely upon a profitable technique, at this time, of appearing particularly understanding of their respective client's mate.

Another technique is that of requiring one spouse to interpret what the other has just said to his satisfaction before he is allowed to state his own views.

Group therapy, as an adjunct to individual psychotherapy, can be of immeasurable help in overcoming marital problems. We have developed two principles for utilizing supplementary group methods: Husbands and wives are always placed in different groups; communication between them on what happens in their own groups is not allowed.

Eitzen[2] has developed a unique therapy technique for marital counseling. The program is arranged on a twelve-week-series basis. During the first four weeks, only spouses of the same sex are placed together. During the second four weeks, they participate in a mixed group, but not with their own spouses. Finally, husband and wife are assigned to the same group. After the first eight weeks, they are more ready to understand each other.

Vincent (311) suggests some ways in which group therapy can be helpful: Loss of the feeling of being isolated, different, or inadequate; catharsis and reassurance from talking without disapproval or condemnation; development of communicative skills and their transference to husband-wife discussions at home; awareness of the roots of sexual maladjustment in early experiences; insight into the many factors which militate against a complete sexual response; and breaking down of previously unrealistic sexual expectations.

Appraisal Devices

The specialist in marital counseling applies all the appraisal devices available for individual psychotherapy, such as the MMPI, TAT, and Rorschach. If the marital partners are not seriously ill and they permit its use, a comparison of personality profiles can be a useful therapeutic technique.

The Sex Knowledge Inventory (192) is the result of many years of research on the most pertinent sex information for marriage preparation as well as for successful marital relationships. The client may take the test, consisting of eighty multiple-choice questions, and then review the answers with the counselor. In the process, he may learn much about his problems beyond the simple recognition of their existence.

Bugental suggests having each partner take a test such as the Allport-Vernon *Study of Values*. In addition to completing a blank on how he responds to the questions, each partner completes a blank on how he would predict the responses of the spouse. Comparative profiles can then be drawn which could be very instructive for all concerned.[3]

[2] Dr. David Eitzen, from personal conversation.

[3] Dr. J. Bugental, from personal conversation.

SUMMARY

Marriage counseling is the term applied to efforts to help both husband and wife in their marital relationships. Marital therapy, in contrast, focuses on intensive efforts to help the individual partners in the marriage. Inter-disciplinary cooperation is especially important in this type of counseling and psychotherapy. For example, attorneys and psychologists can collabo-rate profitably in the solution of client marital problems. As well, the gynecologist-psychologist, counuselor-minister, or psychiatrist-counselor specialists team up for a total approach to marriage problems. Counselors help clients with premarital problems involving mate selection, developing a mature outlook on love and sexual attitudes, and preparing themselves psychologically for marriage.

13.

Counseling of Children
and Parents

The developmental aspects of personality were discussed in Chapter 3 for two purposes. One purpose was to remind the counselor of the kinds of problems which characterize individuals from birth to old age. A second purpose was to assist the counselor in understanding the child in the adult, because many of the frustrations experienced by the troubled adult have their origins in an earlier developmental stage and can be more readily understood through historical perspective. The techniques of counseling and psychotherapy have, thus far, been discussed in a framework where the client is usually an adult.

When the therapist is working with children, rather than adults, it becomes necessary to modify the techniques of counseling to meet their particular problems of youth and immaturity. The first part of the chapter is devoted to problems of counseling young children and their parents. The second section discusses the problems of counseling adolescents and their parents. Finally, and because of its central importance to working with children and adolescents, disciplinary techniques are considered.

THE COUNSELING OF CHILDREN

Special Counseling Problems

The goals of counseling are similar for children and adults, but because of the child's immaturity and dependence on others, modifications of technique are necessary. The most apparent difference between child and adult is in the level of communication they use. The dependence of the child on adults forces the counselor to consider the needs of these close adults along with those of the child. Because the child is pliable, and because his defenses are not as entrenched as are the adult's, there seems to be less stability in therapy. This condition contributes to a fluidity of progression that makes it impossible to predict any permanency in the changes which take place. Because of these difficulties, the counselor must accept more responsibility for directing and protecting the client (313).

Communication. Some form of communication is a requisite to an effective therapeutic relationship. Poor communication is a difficult obstacle for the therapist to overcome when he is counseling a child. He is restricted in his ability to communicate for two reasons. For one reason, the child's capacities to differentiate and integrate his outer world with his inner feelings are incompletely developed. His conceptual thinking and verbalizing abilities are at a relatively primitive level with many gaps, inaccuracies, and elements of magical thinking present. The second reason is that the child has had so little practice communicating that his conversation is not a reliable or even intelligible bridge between himself and the therapist.

Because of the child's limitations, the counselor must rely upon a behavioral rather than a verbal medium for a solution to the difficult problem of achieving adequate communication between himself and the child. For this reason, the use of play therapy as a communication medium and a therapeutic technique has been given impetus.

Dependency. Because of the child's dependency, some adult is always involved in a child's therapy. The importance of the role of the adult depends on the age of the child and the adult's sense of responsibility toward the child. A close adult, usually the mother, is frequently the *informant* through whom the therapist is able to obtain a preliminary history of the child and to obtain assistance in the therapeutic planning. The conference with the mother also gives the counselor an opportunity to evaluate the mother's role in the child's problems, her own emotional disturbances, and some idea of the family relationship. Also, it is an opportunity to establish a good working relationship with the mother which is especially important if the child is to remain in the home. Without the assistance of the parents, the child is not likely either to progress or to be kept in therapy.

Help for parents. Since the child's difficulties are tied up with those of the adults who created his problems, it is often wise for the counselor to insist that one or both parents cooperate to the extent of entering therapy themselves. There is increasing evidence from therapeutic experience, especially that of psychoanalysts, that disordered behavior in the child has frequently been taught unconsciously as a result of observing the parents act out their own forbidden repressed feelings and impulses.

Parental attitudes and behaviors are decisive in determining the developmental progress of their children. Thus, therapy for a parent can play a decisive role in changing the child's environment from one of unmanageable threat to one of security and love. Beverly (31) implies that parents often see things in their children which are not there and try to force attitudes upon the child which are impossible to accept. Occasionally it will be impossible to get the adult to participate in any form of therapy. When this happens, the counselor may gain some measure of reassurance from Axline (17) who reports several instances of successful child therapy in which no adult was counseled.

We have evolved the following time arrangements when scheduling parents and children for therapy. If the child is under six, it seems advisable that the parent be seen two hours for each hour the child is in therapy. Between ages six and twelve, therapy may progress satisfactorily when the parent and child are seen for an equal number of hours. When the child is over twelve, seeing the parent once every two sessions with the child is adequate.

Therapist responsibility. Since the child is less able to absorb stress than the adult and has very little control over his environment, the therapist must often assume a greater responsibility for the welfare of the child by giving direct help. Strang (291) maintains that the first step in treating an emotionally disturbed child is to change his environment so he can handle it more comfortably. As he experiences success where he had formerly only experienced failure, he will begin to realize that the world is not as hostile and defeating as he thought. Sometimes a summer camp experience or a new school will provide this change. The therapist may act specifically in the interests of the child by arranging a transfer to a new school or by reporting maltreatment of a child to the proper authorities.

Awareness of need for help. In contrast with the adult, the child is less aware of a need for help because his limited experience tells him "this is the way things are." He seldom refers himself for therapy; instead, he is usually brought or sent in because he has displeased some adult. Consequently, he seldom comes to the therapist with a conscious desire for self-exploration as do most adults. The child will usually say that he "has no problem," but that his parent or teacher thinks he has. Axline reports the case of a disobedient twelve-year-old boy who enters the playroom and says, "Well, here I am. I just came because . . . I can't understand what mother was talking about. She said that you would help me with my problems, but I don't have any problems" (17, pg. 30). In spite of this beginning, the boy had told the counselor of his troubles with his stepfather, the substitute teacher, and his peers at school before the end of the first session. He had also selected a medium (puppets) through which he could act out his problem. After this first session, the child usually looked forward to returning to the playroom.

It is often more difficult for the therapist to establish a common purpose with a child than an adult. The child is less able to understand the role of the therapist. His past experience conditions him to think of adults as authority figures who deal out rewards and punishments. The child's expectation of reward may make him try to please the therapist by acting the way he thinks a good boy should and by avoiding expressions of hostility.

Fear of punishment may increase his anxiety so that his emotions become even more diffused.

Immaturity. The child's immaturity leads to greater fluidity in therapy than does the adult's comparatively greater maturity. One reason for this is that the child often mixes fantasy with reality. He has difficulty distinguishing the real from the imagined and may often relate a mixture of fantasy material with real events. Fluidity may also have a longitudinal dimension. For example, a child who at one session may be working through a deep emotional conflict may at the next session merely wish to act out something from TV or play a game of checkers. Because of this fluidity there is greater unpredictability in working with children than with adults.

Voluntariness. The child cannot discontinue therapy when he wishes. Even though the therapist maintains that it should be up to the child to decide to continue or to quit therapy, in reality, a parent or teacher may insist that the child continue until certain unacceptable behaviors are changed.

Group therapy with children. Axline (17) and Moustakas (215) found it helpful for the child to experience peer relationships within group therapy. Slavson (282) found also that many children can be helped toward insight in a group situation. He reported that children substitute the therapist for their parents rather than develop a transference relationship in the adult sense. Their ties to their parents are still primary and intense, so that other adults are subsidiary. More detailed group techniques which can be applied to child therapy are discussed in Chapter 12.

Play Therapy

The techniques of play therapy evolved because the child is unable to express himself adequately on a verbal level. Play seems to help the child develop more elaborate and effective techniques for controlling his environment and appears to give him an opportunity to interact with an adult who takes a different attitude toward his person (313).

History of play therapy. The use of play therapy as a technique dates back to the analytic movement, when Anna Freud (314) used play to win children's friendship and when Klein (170) developed a "Play Analysis" which in principle was true to the psychoanalytic tradition. Taft and Allen contributed to the movement with a modification on Rank's theories on relationship to the therapist. Rogers, although not the first to state it, hypothesized that the individual had a strong capacity for self-direction and growth. Axline (17) then applied Rogers' client-centered philosophy to children at play. Axline cites examples which imply that immature and dependent children have the capacity for self-direction and growth. The parents of some of her children would not enter therapy. Other of her children came from public institutions and the adult supervisors were not directly concerned with them. Despite these limitations, the children apparently were able to overcome traumatizing experiences. This is possible because as a child undergoes a personality change, however slight, his environment is no longer quite the same. The child's stimulus value to others changes, and, as a consequence, he is perceived and reacted to in a different way.

Room and materials. Play therapy requires a playroom and some kind of materials. The room should be brightly colored, cheerful, and soundproof if possible. The walls and floors should be of a type easily cleaned and of a material that will withstand clay, paint, and mallet attacks. A washroom with hot and cold water should be accessible. For research and teaching purposes, the therapy room can be wired for phonographic recordings. Also, if the room is provided with a one-way mirror and is wired for sound, observations can be made without the child being aware of the observer. If observations and recordings are made, it is assumed that the ethical requirements have been met.

The list of materials used successfully in play therapy grows each year. Klein (170) used only a few primitive toys laid out on a low table. Axline (17) suggests a long list of "acceptable toys." Since then, many other toys have been used with success. The success of Lebo (181) in using toys that had not been recommended by any other therapists suggests that there are no apparent limitations with respect to play devices that may assist the child in working out his problems. It seems wise to select a wide variety so that the child may find a personally convenient medium for expressing his particular feelings.

Some techniques. Many experiments have been reported in which dolls provided a highly adequate means for working through problems. Dolls, generally appealing to young children, are simple as well as suitable for exploring many different problem areas. Since the child's problems stem frequently from family relationships, a complete family of dolls: father, mother, brother, sister, and baby are essential. Dolls can help the child to work through sex anxieties and to accept sex differences. Dolls and a bottle with a nipple are a must for the small child who is working through his dependency needs.

Toys that are used often by children in expressing aggression are: guns, trucks, soldiers, masks, and inflated plastic figures. Axline found it convenient to use a sand box placed flat on the floor as a background for the doll house, furniture, and family. She found that sand was a good medium for expressing aggressive feelings. The child buries toys in it or uses it to represent rain, snow, bombs, or any number of other imaginative symbols. Puppets are very popular with older children between the ages of six and twelve. They provide a helpful means for role playing with readily identifiable figures such as, hero, villain, mischievous monkey, horrible alligator, or giants (315).

Finger and easel painting are very popular with some therapists. Shaw (271) and Alschuler (5) have had success with these media and hypothesize that color offers many clues to the nature and degree of emotional life of the child. Messing materials, such as finger paints and clay or sand and water, are popular with children who are having difficulty working through early training conflicts.

Controlled versus free play. There is a difference of opinion as to whether play should be controlled or free. Levy (315) controls the play by selecting definite toys which he feels the child can use to work out his particular conflicts. Levy seems to make no attempt to point out feelings to the child, to develop transference, or to promote changes in behavior; yet he has been highly successful in therapy with children between the ages of two and ten.

From the child's history, Levy decides the probable cause of the child's present problem. For example, a boy of seven had nightmares of being bound and tortured. He would awaken with cries of pain. Levy learned that two weeks previously some of his classmates had tied him to a tree and pretended to torture him. A little later a story had been read in school about two knights who nailed an innkeeper to the door of the inn. These two experiences were highly threatening because of their strong similarity to a traumatic experience the boy had a few years earlier when he had been wrapped in blankets for the puncture of his ear drums without anaesthesia. Levy set up the playroom with dolls to represent a knight, doctor, and boys. There were toys to represent the inn, rope, tree, and blankets. Using the toys, the boy worked through his experiences and the symptoms were removed in four sessions (315). This illustration does not imply that a rapid solution is usual. Most problems require many more sessions for satisfactory resolution.

Levy finds that children under six are helped, apparently without their knowing why they were sent to the clinic and without perceiving any relationship between their play and their behavior at home. There is a possibility that Levy's success reflects the fact that fantasy and reality are not strictly differentiated at the younger age levels (315). The success of Mann using a similar process supports this hypothesis (195).

Axline (17) and Moustakas (215) insist upon a free choice of materials. They set the playroom up in the same way for all children and with all equipment available for the child to use as he pleases. Spontaneous choice of materials is less artificial; the child selects his own media and proceeds at his own speed. The therapist may not even know the problem which the child is working through. Axline reports a little girl who would make a limping clay man, punch holes in him, tear him to pieces, and finally bury him. She continued to make and destroy the clay man at each session for several weeks. Not until after the girl was dismissed did the therapist learn that the mother was considering marriage to a crippled man.

Special play techniques for dealing with child frustration have been presented in films such as those produced by Vassar and Sarah Lawrence colleges. These techniques, developed by the late Eugene Lerner, suggest that an individual may react in many different ways to a frustrating situation according to his present needs. It is suggested that as a child learns to overcome these obstacles in play, he gains insight into the solving of other frustrations in his life.

In the film, several children in succession play with an adult who presents a series of play obstacles. The child is first presented with a situation in which the adult's and the child's car meet on a narrow track. The adult says, "We meet in the middle. How can my car pass?" The child's verbal or action response gives the counselor an idea as to the child's dependency, aggressiveness or fear of authority. Ruch suggests three responses the child may make to this question (261, pp. 474–475). The child may turn his car around and go back so the adult's car may proceed; he may poke at the adult's car or hit the adult's hand; or he may coyly answer the adult's question in the negative and then slowly ease the adult's car back out of the way of his own car.

The adult had his doll stop the child's car. What happens? Is the adult's doll run over or asked to ride? In play with the cars, the adult says, "Let's see who can get there first." The therapist observes if the child must always be first or if he must never win. Does the child permit the cars to crash and, if so, does he seem to enjoy the crash or does he appear frightened?

When playing house, the adult asks, "May my doll come into your house?" After a short time the role is reversed. When the child's doll wishes to enter the house, the therapist says "no" and notes the child's reactions. A wide variety of situations similar to Lerner's may be used to explore the child's feelings and reactions.

Both free and controlled play seem to have merits in assisting the child to work out his problems. The success of the various methods, as used by different therapists, suggests that the counselor can be versatile and use discretion, either selecting the media himself or allowing the chid to do it. It should be pointed out that there does not appear to be an adequate rationale for explaining the success of play therapy. Just as in adult therapy, there are many hypotheses springing from the various theoretical positions.

Limits of play therapy. It is important that the child be permitted great latitude of self-expression in the playroom with fewer restrictions than he experiences outside. However, it appears equally important that the child observe certain limits if therapy is to progress. These limits must be well defined and concrete, but need not be mentioned to the child until he threatens to break them. In this way he learns what he is permitted to do as he explores the relationship with the therapist.

Well-defined limits within the therapeutic framework have as their purpose the preservation of reality, the psychological security of the child, and his health and safety.

The first element of reality to be considered is time. There must be a definite time to begin and to end the session, regardless of how interesting the play may be. Besides being a necessary consideration for the counselor who works on a schedule, the child learns that freedom is not unlimited and is encouraged to focus his activities within a definite time limit. Another element to be considered is the rule that materials may only be used inside the playroom and cannot be taken home. However, the counselor may permit the child to take home the pictures he paints or simple toys that he constructs of paper or clay if this seems important to increase his feelings of worth. In such situations, it is wise for the counselor to instruct the parents regarding how they should react. Parents can demonstrate interest by asking the child to tell them about his handiwork and taking time to listen to his story.

The child should not be permitted to destroy irreplaceable items or to throw a toy through the window. Giving the child unlimited freedom with property does nothing to teach him the reality value of possessions or help him channel his feelings into less aggressive and destructive behaviors. Too much freedom very likely will increase his anxiety.

Most therapists follow the general rule of forbidding the child to hit the therapist since striking an important person in his life may create guilt feelings or reinforce openly destructive behaviors.

Health and safety considerations rule out any behavior that will harm the child. For example, should he wish to break a glass bottle against the wall, drink the paint water, or throw sand in someone's face, the therapist would stop him.

Bixler (32) suggests three mechanics for enforcing limits. (1) The therapist may reflect the child's desire or attitude, for example, "You are very angry—you would like to hit me." (2) The therapist may verbally express the limitation, for example, "You can't hit me but you may hit Bobo." (3) The therapist may control the child by physical means, perhaps holding his hands or sitting him firmly in a chair and saying, "You may pound with this mallet." If the child continues to try to fight, the therapist must put him outside the playroom for the remainder of the session. The therapist must not be punitive in his attitude, but must carry out, exactly, everything he says he will. If he does not, he invites more aggressive behavior. However, in his firmness he must make the child understand that his actions are being rejected and not he himself. Bixler suggests that limits in the playroom may be as important for progress as acceptance of the attitudes that provoke the behavior. This is similar to the idea on acceptance discussed in Chapters 6 and 7 on permissiveness and structuring in adult counseling.

The playroom with its equipment is but an aid to the attainment of a primary goal of child therapy—helping the child establish a working relationship with a permissive adult. When the therapist can act as a permissive parent, he creates an emotional climate that stimulates the child to verbalize and dramatize his conflicts in play. This helps the child to extend himself, to expect warmth from an adult, and thus learn that all adults are not punitive.

COUNSELING TECHNIQUES WITH CHILDREN

In developing a relationship with children, the counselor must be aware of the techniques mentioned in Chapters 6 and 7, but he must adapt these methods to the maturity level of the child. He must respond to the child's feelings just as he does to an adult's. Because of the very real communication barrier imposed by the child's immaturity, the therapist frequently has to develop other means of understanding and interpreting feelings and behaviors to the child.

In the counseling of adults, the therapist is frequently assisted in his understanding of the client by inferences drawn from observing facial expressions, mannerisms, gestures and other body movements. In children, such behavioral expressions are frequently the principal conveyance of the child's feelings. Therefore, the success of the therapist depends in large degree on his ability to observe, understand and interpret the child in action. Since children use gestures as a means of expression to a much greater degree than adults and in turn give personalized meanings to the gestures of others, the counselor must be mindful of his own facial and body movements and the interpretation the child might give to them. For example, if he should suddenly raise his hand in an explanatory gesture, he might frighten the child. Likewise, raising his voice, or even prolonging silence might be interpreted as anger. From such reactions, the counselor may infer some of the principal learnings of the child as well as how he, the therapist, may best convey accepting, loving attitudes to the child.

Some counselors suggest using the same words the very small child uses to avoid talking over his head. Axline mentions the value of reflecting the gestures of the small child. For example, if the child stamps his foot, the counselor stamps his foot, or if the child shakes his head, the counselor does likewise. Other therapists feel that what one says is not important as long as the reflection conveys an honest empathy of feeling.

However, there are a few general suggestions that apply to all children. The therapist's responses should be brief, relaxed, and natural. Care must be taken, also, to avoid talking down to the child, acting like an authority figure, or engaging in baby talk.

It is often helpful for the counselor to sit on a low chair or flat on the floor so that he is on an eye level with the child. This seems to help create a "we" feeling which adds to the rapport of the counseling session.

The counselor must at all times be aware of the sensitivity of the child to the sincerity of adults. One often hears the comment, "You can't fool a child or a dog," with the implication that they are able to sense the true intentions of adults through their pretended intentions. The aphorism, "What you are speaks so loudly I can't hear what you say," is a strong reminder to the counselor.

In summary, the counselor can help to overcome communication barriers by paying attention to the expressive movements of the child and himself. His verbal responses should reflect the attitudes and feelings of the child in simple, relaxed, natural phrases and gestures. By keeping his responses simple and sincere, he helps to build the understanding and the relationship bridge that will permit the child to change his attitudes and behavior.

Goals of Child Therapy

A primary goal of child therapy is to help the child attain inner strength so that he can cope more successfully with his environment. An hypothesis here is that this goal comes about naturally when the child is exposed to a good therapeutic relationship. As he gains insight, he learns to grow emotionally and to gain faith in himself as a responsible individual. Moustakas (215) suggests that there are three basic attitudes inherent in this good relationship; they are faith, acceptance, and self-respect.

The attitude of faith is intangible. It is reflected when a child considers himself to be an important person—one having something important to offer himself and others. If he comes from a home in which the emotional climate is negative and critical, however, he isn't as likely to have such faith in himself. Jourard and Remy (160) suggest that a person's self-appraisal is closely related to his perception of his parents' appraisal of him. To overcome the often negative effects of parental judgments, the therapist must believe sincerely in the child's ability for self-growth and self-realization. This belief can be expressed to the child with such remarks as "What do you think?" or, "I'm sure you know more about that," or, "How you feel is the important thing."

Acceptance is a popular term in counseling, as noted by the frequency with which it has been used in the preceding chapters. Because the concept is so easily misunderstood, it is well to emphasize again that it is not a passive, noncommittal attitude. To accept implies a positive action in which there is non-judgmental recognition of the child's feelings, symbolisms, and perceptions.

If the counselor is able to build a relationship of faith and acceptance, self-respect is not difficult to achieve. When the child thinks that his feelings and interests are understood by the counselor, he believes that the counselor is sincerely interested in him. For example, the counselor's attitude might be as Moustakas has stated it: "These are your feelings and you have a right to them. I shall not try to take them away from you, to divert you from them, or to deny them to you, for they are a part of you, and I shall honor them as I do all aspects of yourself" (Moustakas, 215, pg. 5). The counselor should accept the fact that the child feels that his parents have mistreated him, without making him feel guilty or ashamed for not "honoring" his parents. The child must believe that he is still a person of worth, even though he has many feelings that society considers "bad." The respect of the counselor thus goes a step beyond acceptance because he implies, through his respect, that the child has the freedom to express negative feelings. He is also implying that the child does not become an inferior person because he holds "bad" feelings (21).

The therapeutic process in play therapy seems to pass through three definite stages, similar to the process discussed in Chapter 4. At first the emotions of disturbed children are diffused, undifferentiated, and very negative in expression. They are angry and afraid of everyone because they have lost contact with the source of their frustrations and fears. In the playroom, they either want to destroy everything indiscriminately, or they wish to retreat in silence and be left alone.

As the relationship between the therapist and the child grows, the child is able to express his anger more specifically. Pounding, smashing, and the desire to kill may still be present, but it is likely to be directed toward a particular person such as a parent or sibling. In this second stage, the child releases and expresses his negative feelings directly toward the people in his environment who have made him feel inadequate. It is assumed, of course, that the parent has been prepared for these events. As the child releases negative feelings and as they are accepted, he begins to feel himself a more worthy person. Hence, he is able to express more constructive feelings (21).

The child shows a great deal of ambivalence in the third stage. He still expresses specific anger, yet at the same time, he shows kindness. He will love and fondle the doll one moment, and spank it harshly the next moment. These ambivalent reactions are often intense in the beginning; but gradually, as the more positive feelings emerge, the child enters the final stage of the therapeutic process. Now, he sees himself and his environment more realistically. For example, a seven-year-old boy said of his five-year-old sister, "She's pretty cute sometimes, even if she *is* a spoiled brat."

During the therapeutic process, then, the child's anger and fear move from a diffused feeling to a focused and specific feeling, which he is able to express verbally or in play. As the child learns to express these negative feelings specifically, he begins to express positive attitudes occasionally. Finally he is able to separate more realistically his positive and negative attitudes toward his environment.

Even though insight is limited to the maturity level of the child, it is conceded that insight can be gained by the small child without verbalization

(16). The behavior of the child changes as a result of his experiences in play therapy. The bully becomes a helper without explanation. Just as a chimpanzee can learn to solve his problem of reaching food by putting two sticks together, so the small child is able to bring together different ideas from his experience that help him solve his problem. This therapeutic process does not occur automatically in a play situation. It is made possible by the counselor's responding with constant sensitivity to the child's feelings, accepting his attitudes, and conveying a consistent and sincere belief in the child's worth as an individual.

COUNSELING PARENTS OF YOUNG CHILDREN

Since parents are often responsible for the unhappiness of their children, one way of changing the child's environment is to change the parent or parents responsible. For this reason, the child counselor often insists that the parent enter therapy as well.

The kinds of problems which parents have are of two broad and overlapping kinds. First, the parent may have anxieties and problems not strictly related to the child, but which are passed on to the child through attitudes of tension, emotional inconsistency, strictness, thoughtlessness, and the like. In such cases, the procedures are the same as for adult counseling, but with efforts to help the parent understand the effects of his or her behavior on the child.

Secondly, the parent may be well-intentioned enough but be inadequate through ignorance of the developmental perspective to understand that everyone passes through certain physical, mental, and emotional phases in growing from infancy to adulthood. This knowledge, summarized in Chapter 3, is usually very reassuring to parents and helps them anticipate and meet problems of development with more confidence. Children's behavior must be evaluated in terms of the norms for particular age levels. Reference to a work, such as Gesell has written (120), is helpful in this regard, although parents need to be cautioned about the atypical samples and overgeneralization. The developmental approach gives parents a framework in which limits can be set. Parental guilt, anxiety, and primitive attitudes then can be reduced or eliminated.

Some of the persistent developmental problems encountered by the counselor in working with parents of young children are presented below with pertinent information which will facilitate therapy with the child.

Sexual Tensions

The management of sexual tensions in the young child is often difficult for parents because of their own problems in this area or their ignorance concerning psychosexual development. The counselor can recapitulate for the parents how, in the first months of infancy, the strongest feelings of pleasure center around the mouth. When the baby begins to sit up, the lower part of the body becomes more activated and feelings are centered around the anus. Betwen the ages of four and five, this concentration shifts to the sexual organs. Knowing this, parents can accept more readily the child's normal exhibitionistic and exploring activities. When the parent understands that sex play is normal in the small child, he is more able to react to the behavior in an accepting manner. He can accept his child's questions and his playfulness with his body in such a way as to avert further stimulation. When the parent shouts, "Don't touch! Shame!", the child's curiosity is often stimulated to experiment in erotic activity (244). This judgmental approach also may lay the foundation for guilty feelings and sexual fears later in life.

The young mother can be encouraged to explore her own attitudes toward sex. She can observe her feelings as she bathes the baby. Most mothers are amazed at their rejection of certain areas of the baby's body; but with insight, the mother can accept the fact that consciously or unconsciously, she is teaching her baby attitudes toward his body through the manner she handles him.

Though many parents are unduly prohibitive with respect to the small child's erotic activities, there are also those unfortunate parents who tend consciously or unconsciously to sexualize relationships with their children.

Because of age-old taboos about sex, however, the average parent finds it difficult to accept the fact that all healthy children are endowed from birth with erotic impulses which are normal and valuable for psychological maturing. In order to guide the growing child, it is necessary for the parent to accept the expression of primary pleasure feelings without embarrassment, disapproval, or undue enhancement.

Bowel and Bladder Problems

Bowel and bladder training usually present problems for parents. There is no set time for this training because every child is different. There are some suggestions from research in growth and development that there is a relationship between walking, muscular control of the body and sphincter control of the bladder and bowels (244). About this time, erotic feelings around the anus are experienced by the child. Consequently, bowel movements become a pleasurable activity. Often, because a small potty chair is placed conveniently, and elimination is as accepted as any other activity, the small child trains himself (244).

Enuresis is a common problem which can sometimes be traced to unconscious feelings of jealousy and/or resentment toward parents or siblings. Axline (16) gives examples of this symptom in children who feel rejected by their parents. Carmichael (56) reports that there is sometimes a relapse of bladder training due to jealousy of a new sibling. When such feelings of jealousy or rejection seem to be the basis for the bladder problems, assurance of love from the parent helps the child regain his control.

Ribble reports that enuresis frequently represents a breakdown of too early training (244). When a child is trained before his sphincter muscles have developed, the training is merely a conditioning to the pressure of the parent and may lose strength as the child grows older. Carmichael reported studies in treating enuresis by further conditioning. The children in the study were required to sleep on mats which, when urination began, short circuited and rang a bell. Each child was instructed to arise immediately, disconnect the circuit, go to the bathroom and finish urinating. The authors reported success in thirty cases between the ages of three and thirteen. The children learned to anticipate the bell, so arose before the bladder tension became great enough to cause reflex urination (56). This experimental device is now produced commercially and is often prescribed for discouraging enuresis when other possible underlying causes have been eliminated.

Aggressiveness

Most parents of young children are concerned with the handling of aggression. Permissiveness without direction can be as harmful as neglect or undue prohibition. The child's aggression needs to be channeled so that it will not be postponed, disguised, or displaced (22). This attitude requires understanding and self-control on the part of the parent. If the mother is worried about what the relatives say or think of her as a parent, she may try to force the child into some ideal model which restricts the child's range and spontaneity of feeling. When she begins to think of the child's behavior as a release of tensions due to his feelings of frustration, she is more likely to sense the causes and take constructive measures toward temper tantrums. When she learns that biting, grabbing, and hitting are normal symptoms of the two-year-old's development, she is better able to direct his behavior into more acceptable channels by providing opportunities for the child to exercise his natural functions of sucking, biting, climbing, and messing.

Parents need to be more aware of the importance of verbalization for the young child. Anxious parents are constantly asking for specific things to do to facilitate the child's progress in therapy. The counselor can encourage parents to talk with the child and to help him talk out his feelings with them—including his angry feelings. When parents realize that it is normal and healthy to "talk back," they can begin to accept the child's full range of feelings—his hate as well as his love—without being threatened. Verbalizing with the child helps him to understand his feelings and prevents the accumulation of resentment. The parent in turn gains understanding of the child. When parents can accept negative feelings, yet remain firm about required behavior, the child can adopt socially acceptable modes of expression with fewer tensions (22).

Mechanical remedies, however, for handling problems relative to the child's sexual activities, toilet training, and aggressive feelings are no substitute for genuine love and respect for the child by the parents. If the child senses the sincerity of parental interest, he can tolerate many frustrations; and if parents have true loving consideration for their children, they have the most basic ingredient for meeting and coping with problems as they arise. There are unconsciously rejecting and guilty parents who, having followed the dictates of the "best" books and formulas, feel relieved of guilt concerning parental responsibility. They have, in fact, given their children a poor substitute for genuine warm feelings.

COUNSELING THE ADOLESCENT

The adolescent is usually too mature for play-therapy techniques, but since he is still a dependent with special developmental problems, some techniques additional to those used with adults are often applicable. The developmental outlook assists adults in understanding the adolescent as well as other age groups. At the same time, the counselor should believe in the adolescent's potential to solve his own problems when he understands himself and his particular problem. The following are illustrations of suggested ways in which the counselor may be of help with certain typical adolescent concerns.

A characteristic difficulty in working with adolescents, and one which makes it difficult to keep them in therapy, is their impatience. They want the answers right now. Impatience is part of their problem and must be accepted by the counselor. Since adolescence is a transition stage from childhood to adulthood, it is usual to find conflicts and confusion relative to long-term satisfactions versus immediate pleasures. The counselor can assist the adolescent to realize that his impatience is part of this conflict and help him make realistic choices.

Vocational Choices

Many national surveys indicate that adolescents regard finding a suitable job as their principal problem (65). The techniques of vocational counseling, described in Chapter 14, are appropriate for this age group. Adolescents, however, may change their interests, markedly, between the ages of fifteen and twenty-five as a result of the resolution of their conflicts and because they have gained more knowledge and experience. For this reason, vocational tests should be given every few years to children in this age group.

Peer Relationships

Counseling adolescents requires that the therapist appreciate the importance of peer-group pressures and at the same time be able to help the individual to recognize and respect the *limits* which must be imposed on inappropriate behavior. Satisfactory *peer relationships* are very important for the development of personal and social maturity. There is no time in an individual's life when he does not wish to be popular with his peers, but the desire is much stronger in adolescence. Preadolescents and adolescents like to imitate their peers or those slightly older. In the preadolescent or conformity period, the "gang," a small group of the same sex, is formed. Preadolescents have a great need to belong and conform, as shown in their dress and their jargon. They have their own standards, values, purposes and methods of protecting themselves from too much adult interference (119). The "gangs" are usually small and their objectives are adventure and excitement (65). This drive for adventure and excitement causes the child to experiment with dangerous activities. If he is allowed too much freedom at this period, there is danger that he will become involved in delinquent activities.

Sexual Problems

The age of adolescence brings unique sexual problems. When dating begins, usually in the early teens, the first dates are usually arranged by the respective gangs of the boy or girl. There is often much embarrassment involved for the dating couple because of the interest of peers and uneasy feelings of parents, especially if the couple start "going steady." Herman (142) suggests that going steady is a phenomenon which results from the need of the adolescent to belong. Mead (201) comments interestingly that "going steady" at this stage is a kind of game, with popularity as the reward.

Sexual behavior may be used for releasing tensions of hostility as well as for an expression of love (21). Sometimes, boys and girls go the limit in an effort to find a closeness of human understanding that is lacking in their lives. Others gain a sense of achievement and prowess through sexual exploits. Some try to prove that their fears of being hurt and punished are unfounded. For these reasons, Baruch suggests that adults should take a firm stand with adolescents and tell them, "It is better for you to wait to have intercourse until you are old enough to marry. And it's best to be married before you do." She lists the following three reasons for this:

1. Sexual compatibility is important in marriage. Because of feelings we do not fully comprehend, it often takes a while to work out a sexual relationship so that it is satisfying. Full, mutual enjoyment may not be reached for a period of time.
2. To enjoy sex fully, one must be able to be oneself fully. One must be able to be free and vital in many aspects of the mutual relationship.

But where fear of desertion enters, constriction enters also. This ties a person up and defeats sexual adjustment.

3. Among the conditions that facilitate compatibility is the intimate tie of living and working together. Sharing a home and mutual endeavors backed by the feeling of steadiness that comes from marriage—this is more conducive to sexual adjustment than the fly-by-night arrangements. For the latter cause anxiety and unrest to enter during a time in which making adaptation to one another calls for stability and peace (21, pp. 152–3).

During adolescence, the youth usually starts to masturbate again or continues with stronger force. He tries to stop but often can't, so he is filled with fears and self-condemnation. Adolescents can divert sexual feelings into nonsexual channels. They throw themselves with wholehearted enthusiasm into activities: satisfying achievements, sports and hobbies, outgoing friendly relationships, and active group participation in social and church activities. Occasionally, fanaticism of one sort or another is the result of the adolescent's attempt at sublimation.

The counselor must help the adolescent verbalize his fears so he can accept his natural urges with self-respect. The counselor should supply specific sex information if desired. Counselors can help parents to talk of important life situations in a natural, relaxed manner, so that the child can accept his body sensations as being natural, rather than something to fear.

Relationships with Parents

Several additional concerns of adolescents include smoking, drinking, automobiles and money. These problems often are the foci of conflict between parents and their adolescents. The counselor may wish to explore the social and physical implications of smoking and drinking. His family attitudes, his own feelings and his particular group's "code" must be considered in helping the adolescent to evaluate his own opinions concerning these problems.

The automobile is a source of many conflicts between parents and their adolescents. Today, the ability to drive a car, and the permission to do so, are strong factors in teenage prestige. Many sixteen-year-olds are physically and mentally competent to drive a car, but it is doubtful if they are sufficiently self-controlled to be allowed unlimited freedom.

With all of his problems, the adolescent often needs help from adults to evaluate the importance of long-term satisfactions versus immediate satisfactions.

COUNSELING PARENTS OF ADOLESCENTS

The primary goal of counseling parents of adolescents is to help the child channel his feelings into constructive activities. The parent is often reassured to learn that rebellious behavior is a necessary part of growth. As we mentioned in Chapter 3, this phase of development can be less painful for the parents and the adolescents if insight into the process is gained before serious misunderstanding develops. Parents should understand that the adolescent is trying to adapt in his own individual way. Consequently, it is unwise to force patterns of adulthood on young people; rather, they should be permitted to grow at their own individual rate. Parents should have a concept of growth from within, instead of a forced growth from without, in order to understand their children.

Baruch (21) suggests that parents need to give their adolescents three things—*understanding, practical sex information,* and *help in becoming an independent person.* Understanding is difficult without acceptance, as defined in Chapter 6. The youth should be permitted to express his feelings without fear and the parent should attempt to accept his right to talk back. This view may be very threatening to the parent, which suggests that the parent can't understand the child's feelings unless he understands his own feelings. This parental lack of insight is one of the reasons why it is so necessary that parents enter therapy with the adolescent. As the parent learns to talk out his true feelings with his child, he learns to understand himself and his child better.

The parents can be assured that the youth needs their help in learning to express feelings and to control actions. Baruch (21, pg. 69) suggests five ways of channeling these negative feelings into socially acceptable actions: (1) verbalizing the grievance; (2) writing out the bad feelings; (3) drawing pictures of the hated person; (4) painting, modeling, and dramatizing; and (5), playing games, such as tennis, golf, checkers, or chess in order to work out family or peer battles.

To understand the adolescent, parents must realize that their child's present and past feelings cause him to act the way he does. Behind unacceptable actions are negative feelings which may have had their origins in early childhood. These feelings not only result from what actually happened, but also are tied up with the child's fantasy of what happened. This imagined fantasy also plays a part in the imagined attitude of the parent toward the youth (21). If a child felt a lack of love, trust, or a sense of belonging in his early life, he will tend to find it difficult in adolescence to feel at home with his peers. Therapy with the adolescent must uncover basic feelings from childhood which are causing unwholesome actions in adolescence.

The parent needs assistance in learning to help his child avoid dangerous behavior. This may be accomplished in two ways. First, the parent may anticipate certain interests and provide opportunities for the needed activity with a structured environment. Ball leagues, hot-rod clubs, camping, fishing and hunting trips are examples. Secondly, the parent can be taught to accept the youth's negative feelings and verbalize them back to him. If the parent can accept the negative feelings, it is easier for the adolescent to accept them and thus eliminate his guilt feelings.

Parents often complain, "What about me? I have feelings too." They need assurance that it is sometimes necessary for them to express feelings also. They should express anger, and then if they have regrets, say so in sincere humility. Usually, the parent is surprised at his adolescent's understanding and acceptance when he, as a parent, admits a problem too. This de-idolization goes a long way toward building rapport between a parent and his child and building teenager respect for parents' feelings.

Parents need assurance that limits on adolescent behavior are still necessary. Youth must accept the necessity of following certain customs and rules. Baruch suggests three reasons for limits that can be understood by the adolescent: "This is important for health and safety. This is important to protect property. This is important because of law and order and social acceptability" (21, pg. 11).

Dynamics of Parent-Adolescent Relationships

The problem, from the therapist's point of view, is to help the adolescent secure as much freedom as he is able to handle. There are certain difficulties which make it hard to achieve this goal even if the therapist tried. The following devices, derived largely from Wickes (318), are suggestive of the neurotic ways parents use or control adolescents.

(1) Utilizing love as a dominating and holding force to satisfy personal needs in the parent which "may happen when the parent is disappointed in other human relations and, pouring out all the pent-up emotion on the child, also feeds himself upon the child's love" (318, pg. 90).

(2) "Placing the youth under a burden of gratitude and sense of duty because of values received" (318, pg. 90).

(3) Treating youth as emotional toys; thus, not allowing the child to reach for greater maturity.

(4) Prolonging one's own youth beyond its rightful time. "Daughters are kept the little girls; the son begins to assume the place of the youthful lover" (318, pg. 96).

(5) Being overstern and authoritarian, on the parents' part, and refusing to allow the child to break the submissive role.

(6) Being too weak and too ready to yield, on the part of the father, and being unable to accept his responsibilities. "This may inspire only contempt in the son; thus the adolescent problem of freeing himself becomes too easy, and his contemptuous attitude is carried over toward all the struggles of life. A weak and acquiescent son, having a similar identification, may gravitate toward failure—even as his father has done. He is inclined to present his father-identification as an excuse for his own failure to meet life" (318, pg. 99).

(7) If mother is the stronger parent, she represents not only love but authority, thus making it more difficult for the son to break away and establish independence. He may now fear the power of women, as he may

acquiesce and lose his masculine attitude. Furthermore, he may break the bond completely and consistently undervalue women in an effort to deny their power.

(8) Being suspicious and unreasonable, on the part of the mother, toward the father may create a similar unconscious attitude toward men on the part of the daughter.

(9) Holding inappropriate attitudes, on the part of the father, may furnish the daughter similarly inappropriate expectations toward men in general. For example, if he is too fond of her, there is a danger that the daughter will find herself unable to break the close bond for marriage. She goes through life looking for her father's image in a prospective husband. If he is too dominantly devoted, the daughter may repudiate his overinsistent demands and repudiate him. "She is frequently suspicious of men and their demands upon her. She senses sexual motives where none really exist, or if they do exist she refuses to see their normal aspect in adult life" (318, pg. 106).

Conversely, indifference and neglect on the part of the father may cause feelings of inferiority, and may motivate the daughter to go about looking for a father surrogate who will give her the fatherly devotion she has missed. Other girls may feel only hatred and resentment toward such a father. Lacking the proper discipline which is a part of development, she is torn by a conflict between rebellious aggressiveness and a desire for submissiveness.

It is the counselor's job to become thoroughly acquainted with dynamic patterns such as those above and to place them in the perspective of the child's and parent's lives so that both can see more clearly what is operating. All the counseling skills described in earlier sections of this book are needed to do this job well.

DISCIPLINARY TECHNIQUES

To conclude this chapter, a discussion of disciplinary techniques, as they may be applied to children, is presented. This section is included because the counselor often must present a workable philosophy of discipline to the parents (or teachers). Working through conflict situations where disciplinary problems are involved is such a common task of parents and teachers.

Methods of Discipline

Disciplinary techniques fall into two broad categories. One is characterized as an external, authoritative, or control type. The other is characterized by being internal, self-imposed, and more positive. The latter type is spoken about most often as self-discipline, where the child's internalized values are the guiding principles.

Action-centered discipline embodies the ideas of reward and punishment and is still the accepted method practiced by many parents. "Spare the rod and spoil the child" and "Children should be seen and not heard" are typical household phrases that reflect this attitude. Many different techniques are involved in action-control methods. Verbal punishment, unfavorable comparison, isolation, deprivation of privileges, and physical punishment are used to achieve control of behavior.

The real effect of punishment is to inhibit behavior or repress feelings. Punishment causes anxiety and tends to produce nervous manifestations characteristic of repression. Punishment often arouses hatred for the punisher and along with displaced counter-aggression frequently arouses guilt feelings which result in need for further punishment. Finally, punishment often arouses feelings of insecurity and inadequacy. The punished child perceives himself as fallen from the good graces of the punisher and, as a result, he tends to feel more insecure. The child is made to think of himself as bad, incompetent, and worthless; as a result, he often acts in terms of these self-pictures.

The action-control method of discipline assumes that punishment leads to reform. Actually, however, studies of criminals lead to the conclusion that punishment does *not* prevent or deter antisocial behavior; it may actually encourage that which it sets out to destroy. Ellis (90) points out that punishment as discipline really focuses on the *past* and neglects the fact that the all-important question for people who err is "How am I going to correct my ways and make fewer mistakes in the *future?*" He points out that all antisocial acts are caused, basically, by the perpetrator's stupidity, ignorance, or emotional disturbance. There is a long accumulation of human experience to indicate that blaming or punishing such people does not help them to improve; it actually aggravates their unfortunate conditions. Often, the history of the person who is emotionally disturbed is likely to show that he got that way, in the first place, by criticism, rejection, blame, or punishment. Heaping more of the same on him after he has committed an offense will hardly make him *less* disturbed.

Because of the increasingly widespread knowledge of basic psychological principles, many parents find that they are no longer comfortable with the foregoing disciplinary methods. They know that they want their children to behave in ways which are socially acceptable and which are best for their physical and mental health. Yet, they are unsure how to achieve such behavior. They fail to recognize that their demands for respect and obedience often are results of their own insecurity. They do not have the ego strength to recognize that hostility expressed by children within reasonable limits is actually necessary for emotional growth.

Feeling-centered discipline has for its goal self-control rather than obedience to others. In order to achieve discipline from within, an attitudinal approach is proposed. This method incorporates three basic principles.

Needs or feelings existing in the unconscious levels of the personality are *causes* of inappropriate actions. The actions are simply the *results* of such feelings. If a child feels secure, adequate, and worthy, there is less chance that he will be a discipline problem. A reflection of feelings and acceptance meets the need of the child for understanding.

The feeling approach to discipline cannot be reduced to a set of rules which must be followed and which, if broken, require punishment. Discipline is more a matter of attitude and feeling. The individual who is being disciplined must be accepted as a human being with feelings and rights of his own, not as an automaton. The teacher or parent who can handle attitudes and feelings well will handle discipline problems skilfully also. If the emotional climate is warm and accepting, the child will still feel secure when *firmness* is used and when appropriate limits are set in accord with the child's developmental level.

The feeling-centered approach to discipline requires the separation of attitudes from actions and the separation of the individual from his actions. One may be displeased with what a child has done (his actions); but one's feelings toward him as a person (friendliness, acceptance, love, approval) need not change. The theoretical discussion which follows enlarges on the preceding idea.

A Theory of Disciplinary Counseling

Whenever one disciplines a child, he can do it either in terms of *actions* or in terms of *feelings*. The counselor (or parent) and student (or child) operate on a continuum existing between these two behaviors. This concept is presented in Figure 27. The center line which extends downward from

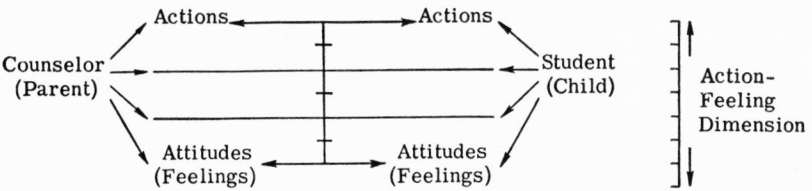

Fig. 27. A Model of Disciplinary Counseling.

actions to attitudes may be described as a continuum from outer observable actions at the top to the more obscure underlying feelings at the bottom. The child being disciplined will exhibit to the counselor or teacher behavior which falls somewhere on this attitude-action continuum. The underlying principle is that the counselor or parent reacts to the child at the point on the action-feeling continuum at which the child is himself behaving. For example, if the child is discussing feelings, the counselor reflects feelings (the same level); but if the child moves into the action field, the counselor then must often deal with him at this level. Some examples of how this principle might work in disciplinary counseling situations in a school setting are given below.

Situation 1 (attitude only): A student comes for counseling and begins complaining about his teachers and the principal. This activity is in the *field of force* of the student's feeling and represents only student feelings or attitudes on this subject. Therefore, the counselor responds according to the *field of force* of his own feelings.

> C: We've found through experience that it isn't good to go around talking about others in the outside world; on the other hand, we all need a place where we can blow off some steam once in a while—so that's what you can do here if you want to.
> Cl: Sometimes I feel mad enough at this school that I'd just like to blow the whole darn place sky-high. They let a guy work and slave, and where does it get him? Another guy comes along and gets all the A's because he apple-polishes the teacher (pure feeling).

Note that attitude is met with attitude here. As long as the client stays in the attitudinal field, psychotherapy can continue satisfactorily.

Situation 2 (before the act is committed):

> Cl: I feel so mad at this school that I think I'm going to wait until school is out, and then I'll break all the windows in the darn place (expressing feeling and contemplating action).
> C: Well, I can see you feel very sharply about this. Let's see what would happen if you did break the windows . . .

Now the student is moving from the feeling field to the action field. That is, in addition to expressing feeling, he is actually discussing acting out his feelings. At this point, the counselor also has the right to enter the action field. The action he chose at this point was to structure the consequences of the contemplated action. After structuring, it might have been wise for him to have continued reflecting feeling to see if growth changed his stated desires.

Situation 3 (action has been committed and punishment is questionable): If a student tells of an argument in which he "told off" a teacher, this is in the action field. However, in this case it would do no harm to respond to the student's feelings, since the "good" or "bad" of his actions is itself debatable without a large amount of knowledge about the situation. It is more important that no injury results to the student or to others. Permissiveness at this point may enable the student to go ahead with his "catharsis" which he needs before he can look at the situation intelligently:

> S: I was sent to you because I sassed Mr. Jones.
> C: Well, now, suppose you tell me about it. You feel you were justified in doing so?

Situation 4 (act has been committed and punishment is required): If the counselor has been designated by the institution as the disciplinarian who must impose punishment for actions which have been committed, it is still possible for him to remain personally non-judgmental. If students have committed a misdemeanor, the counselor can refrain from expressing his own moral indignation:

> C: Fellows, I called you in here because I wanted to discuss the broken windows in the school gym with you. Is there anything you'd like to say about them? I might not be able to help you; but would you like to talk about it? (Here he gives the boys a chance to express their feelings.)
> C: Well, fellows, from what you say, I gather that you feel you are not entirely responsible. On the other hand, the rules apply here, just as in a basketball game when the referee blows the whistle on a foul. What do you think would be a fair penalty in this case?

In this kind of situation, the students could discuss their attitudes toward the punishment, administered not by the counselor but by the institution, until it becomes a real growth experience toward self-responsibility. In other words, the punishment should be made *external* to the relationship of student and counselor.

The following principles are suggested as a summary of the foregoing theory of discipline:

(1) Separate feelings from actions. Be non-judgmental of the individual himself, even if his actions must be judged. In disciplinary counseling, the foregoing principle is one of the most important. Separation of the child from his actions permits the counselor to accept him on a genuine friendly basis. The child knows he is liked for himself but that his actions are not accepted and need to be improved. Actions are the result of feelings (of rejection and/or of hostility). In order to change actions, the feelings must be understood and handled first.

(2) Study the child to determine whether you are dealing with a normal or neurotic child. In the disturbed child, the action must be considered as a symptom of a much deeper emotional difficulty, probably caused originally by criticism, rejection, blame, or punishment. To impose punishment arbitrarily in such a case simply would cause such a child to become more disturbed.

(3) Accept and reflect the child's feelings. Arrange conditions so the child can let off "steam," "blow up," or safely release his hostile feelings which he has been trying to suppress.

(4) If punishment is required, allow the child to suggest what he thinks would be a fair and reasonable punishment for his actions. Experienced counselors report that the child usually will recommend more severe punishment for himself than that which ordinarily would be imposed by the authority figure.

(5) If punishment must be imposed, differentiate between the counselor's role and the institutional or family role. Be sure the child realizes that it is his action of breaking a rule that results in punishment. Help him to see that rules have been established for group conduct and must be obeyed, just as the rules of a basketball game must be binding upon all of the players.

(6) Work with the child on discipline as a "mutual problem." Let him know that you feel it is a mutual problem—not just his own problem. This technique suggests the idea of separating the problem from both the student and the counselor, figuratively setting the problem out at a distance where both counselor and client can examine it and work on it together. Suggesting that the problem has an external reference point enables the child to refrain from making the discipline situation an interpersonal conflict.

(7) Limits must be placed on dangerous and destructive actions. Permit expression of feeling; then assist the child to rechannel actions which cannot be allowed. This is the basic formula for a dynamic approach to discipline.

SUMMARY

Some of the basic problems in counseling and psychotherapy with children, young adolescents, and parents revolve around achieving accurate communication, handling dependency feelings, working with the whole family, and helping clients to become aware of their need for help, while still keeping the relationship voluntary. Play has been found to be one of the best media for therapy with children. The principal goal of individual and group therapy with children is to help them achieve strong egos so they can cope with their environmental demands and their own inner pressures. Counseling with parents involves many problems common to the development of young children such as sexual and elimination problems, excessive aggressiveness, and unresolved dependency. Adolescents have their unique problems, also, in the form of vocational choices, sexual adjustment, and relationships with parents and peers. Disciplinary problems often become mixed with the counseling role. The main problem is to center the discussion on feelings rather than actions and to help the child develop self-discipline instead of a reliance on external controls.

14.

Educational, Vocational, and Rehabilitation Counseling

The choice of a satisfying and productive life work is one of the principal objectives of human development. Work days consume such a vast proportion of the individual's life and have such great potential either for giving personal satisfaction and life fulfillment or for causing frustration and personality deterioration that serious attention needs to be given to vocational problems.

The social consequences of vocational choices are considerable also. One criterion of a profession proposed in Chapter 1 was that individuals as clients are provided with socially useful services which they cannot render to themselves. The principal values of professional vocational-counseling services to society are the discovery, utilization, and conservation of human talent. In the present era of rapid technological change and competition with other nations for supremacy and possibly even survival, the development and utilization of all talent become of monumental social importance.

Counseling, and the collateral area of appraisal, cannot become manipulative tools or instruments of national policy, however, since this would violate our highly valued freedom. Therapeutic psychology seeks to help the client become aware of his assets, limitations, and opportunities in all possible areas so that he will make wise choices and will use his unique talents if he cares to do so. We believe that when individuals know their talents and use them in ways of their own choosing, the effects ultimately will be best for the society in which they live. In addition, counseling serves broad social purposes through helping individuals overcome obstacles to effective learning and achievement by means of remedial and rehabilitative planning and action. This chapter principally gives an overview of the problems and methods of counseling clients who have manifest vocational, educational-planning, remediation, or rehabilitation problems. Selective elaboration will be made in this overview to illustrate the growing complexities and trends in educational-vocational counseling.

VOCATIONAL COUNSELING

Our Point of View

Vocational choice has been regarded historically as vocational guidance —a process of helping the client to choose, prepare for, and succeed in a given occupation. This process was centered around counseling, which consisted largely of examining data from the client and looking over the occupational possibilities to find a specific occupational goal, whereupon, an educational plan was formulated to reach the occupational goal. Although this rationale is still basic in educational-vocational counseling, there have been recent changes in the perception of the significance and scope of vocational counseling.

One of the principal changes is the perception of vocational counseling as part of general clinical counseling, or in our terminology, a task of therapeutic psychology. Vocational problems cannot be singled out as a special branch of counseling and psychotherapy, largely because vocational counseling must be accomplished in the context of the individual's total personality and in relationship to the client's culture. Optimally effective vocational counseling cannot be an isolated and mechanical process of matching people and jobs. Vocational choice pervades the client's entire personality structure —his ego, self-, and core systems—and calls upon the best of clinical and actuarial procedures.

Vocational counseling goals can be construed in several ways. First, and most commonly, vocational counseling is a process of confirming the choice already made by the client. Many clients have done a fair job of sizing up themselves and their opportunities and of making tentative choices, as a result of other life experiences with parents and teachers. Secondly, vocational counseling is a process of clarifying vocational objectives. People are collecting information about vocations and their personalities all the time; but they have difficulty interpreting the meaning of the data and stating the vocational-choice problem precisely. Counselors can help this type of client perceive his problem in more clear terms. The third manner in which vocational counseling is helpful to clients is that it allows them to discover facts about themselves and the working world which they had not known before. Although this is the most spectacular, it is also the most rare type of counseling, since the findings of counseling seldom come as a great surprise to clients. The most revelatory aspects are those in which occupational choice limits are broadened to include many which the client had not considered in his original formulations.

Therapeutic psychology is uniquely suited to accomplish this broad goal of effective vocational planning as part of life-planning. The techniques described in earlier chapters, plus some special tools uniquely suited to educational-vocational planning, are the principal requirements for effective vocational planning. It was pointed out in Chapter 4 on the counseling process that vocational-planning problems differed somewhat from other types of personal problems because there is more emphasis upon rational problem-solving methods and more involvement of the ego-system functions. It should be emphasized, however, that any vocational counseling worth its salt includes considerations of the client's self-regarding attitudes, aspirations, and deep feelings, as well as psychological needs for dependence-independence, security, and fundamental values. Vocational choice, from the research results reported to date, is not a strictly rational process. Neither is it a process of choice-making on the basis of a few interviews with a counselor. Vocational choices are the product of a long series of life experiences and learnings which come to a focus in the interviews with the counselor, or some other life experience, wherein the client understands and accepts facts about himself and relates these facts to his occupational environment.

Theories of Vocational Choice

Prior to examining some of the problems and procedures in helping clients to make vocational choices, some of the principal theories on how such choices are made will be presented.

Psychoanalysts view the origin of interests as a response to an ego need for recognition and status satisfactions. Explanations are made along the lines of expression of unconscious needs, as illustrated by the person with aggressive, sadistic tendencies wanting to be a policeman. There is little research evidence to support this point of view.

Roe (247) has formulated a series of hypotheses to account for the early determinants of interest. These determinants are basic human needs and early family experiences of acceptance, avoidance, and emotional concentration. These early experiences influence the general orientation of the child toward things or people. Roe has classified occupations according to eight clusters, each with six levels. She hypothesizes that the clusters can be identified in terms of major orientations toward people and objects, and that the early life experiences of the child predispose him toward certain major occupational groups.

Ginzberg (124) viewed vocational choice as a process covering three developmental periods—the fantasy (six-eleven), the tentative (twelve-seventeen), and the realistic choice (eighteen up). Ginsberg indicated that he thought the process was largely irreversible, a result of many compromises of values and opportunities, and a function of the person's perception of the job rather than a realistic view of work. Criticisms of Ginsberg's study center around the inadequate design, lack of description of the compromise process, and the fact that he ignored the phenomenon of occupational mobility.

Carter (59) claimed that the individual's vocational attitudes develop from efforts to adapt to direct family and social pressures and to his own perceptions of his needs and capacities. His interests develop from identification with an occupation and are confirmed through try-outs in that vocation. Eventually, the individual incorporates the occupational demands into his self-concepts and the occupational interest becomes relatively stabilized. Others, such as Bordin (40), feel that occupational interests are by-products of personality traits and self-concepts in particular. Interests shift when the self changes or when the individual's stereotype of the particular occupation changes.

One of the most comprehensive and data-supported theories of occupational choice was formulated by Super (299). The gist of his theory is that occupational choices are implementations of the self-concept. According to his theory, a person is qualified for many occupations; each occupation requires a characteristic pattern of abilities and traits (with wide tolerances); since individual self-concepts and social situations change, the process of choice is continuous due to growth, exploration, establishment, maintenance, and decline; the career pattern (level, sequence, and duration of occupations) hinges on parental socio-economic level, ability, personality, and opportunity; vocational development is mainly that of developing and implementing a self-concept which is the product of interacting heredity, physical factors, opportunity for various roles, and the extent of approval from superiors and peers; compromises between individual and environmental variables, between self-concepts and reality demands, are made through role-playing opportunities in fantasy, counseling, school, or work; satisfaction depends upon the extent of adequate outlets for personality needs, a work situation in which a congenial and appropriate role can be played. Super is verifying his theories through his Career-Pattern Study (297) consisting of longitudinal and horizontal research on how children and adolescents make their career choices. Super is using actuarial, life-history, and career-pattern-analysis methods to study the career choices of youth.

Appraisal and Diagnosis

For didactic purposes, the vocational-counseling process will be divided into three elements: appraisal and diagnosis, information methods, and counseling techniques. The methods and areas of vocational appraisal are summarized in Figure 28. The various methods of appraisal in vocational counseling are listed in the outer circle, and the matching areas to be appraised are indicated in the inner circle.

Most of the methods listed in Figure 28 are designed for the purpose of

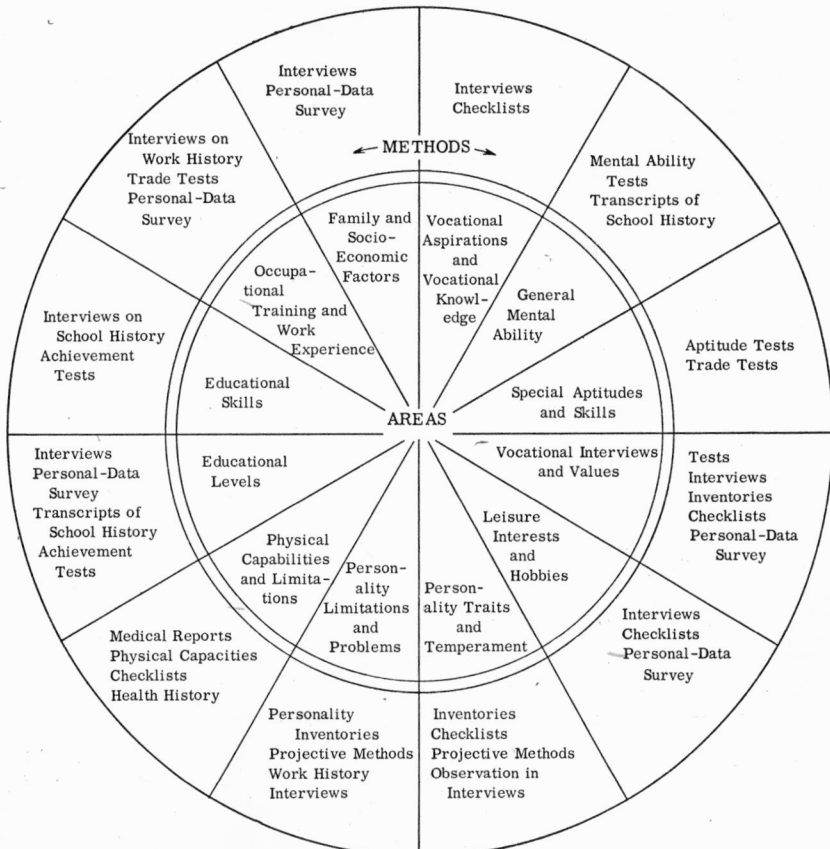

FIG. 28. Areas and Methods of Appraisal in Vocational Counseling.

appraising the personality characteristics which are close to the surface and to aid in the diagnosis of the more manifest vocational problems. Hence, this discussion will focus on those personality levels the counselor must deal with, which are related to the problem of vocational adjustment.

The diagnostic process in vocational counseling follows the principles of diagnostic thinking cited in Chapter 5. The following material illustrates some of the diagnostic formulations built upon appraisal instruments. Detailed use of specific tests will not be discussed since there is so much material available elsewhere.

Aptitude appraisal. One of the counselor's first diagnostic tasks is to note the congruence or discrepancy between the client's vocational aspirations and his aptitudes. The first step he should take to accomplish this goal is to ascertain the client's vocational aspirations and knowledge. General mental-ability tests, along with special aptitude measures, then, are made to infer the client's relative capacity to perform job functions or his potential to succeed in specified tasks or curricula. This procedure may be applied to many individuals, such as the seventeen-year-old boy who wants to be a lawyer, but for whom reliable and valid aptitude measures indicate that he is in the lowest 10 per cent of the college freshman population on scholastic aptitude.

Aptitude measures may be applied, as well, to the student who is performing beyond a comfortable level of achievement. This type of student is called, in school terms, an "overachiever." Although it is desirable, perhaps, to emphasize high achievement, experienced teachers note that many clients of this type achieve above their rated aptitudes even though it is not emphasized to them. Many of these clients experience much anxiety about status and failure. Some even pay the heavy price of mental illness later as a result of allowing their inordinate ambition to outstrip their capacities.

Aptitude tests may be applied to a third type of client—the so-called "underachiever." This client has aptitudes which are known, which it is also known, he is not using to the fullest. He may not be using his aptitude to the utmost because of a deep-seated motivational difficulty, educational-skill deficiency, or health problem. For this type of client, a more refined diagnostic process must be initiated.

Aptitude discovery is a further problem in appraisal. A client, for example, finds that as a result of the aptitude survey he has potentialities in the area of numerical reasoning and arithmetic problem-solving which he did not know existed.

Two additional types of clients the vocational counselor is frequently confronted with are those without tangible aptitudes and those with many high, aptitudes. For the former, vocational counseling is difficult because training and placement of such clients is a problem. The problem is made even more difficult if the client or his parents have unrealistic aspirations for a certain occupational pursuit. For the latter type, with multiple aptitudes, the counselor's difficulty often boils down to his determining which of the high aptitudes fits other factors of the client's interests and opportunities.

Interests, Attitudes, and Values. Although aptitude appraisal is a matter of capacity and vocational performance, interest and value measurement are concerned with vocational satisfaction. Various measures purporting to appraise interest are correlated closely with measures of job satisfaction. Aptitude is not so related.

The client with a conflict between his interests and values and his measured aptitudes, that is, with a diagnostic problem in the interest and value area, is often met with in counseling. Such a client, for example, may have much interest in science, but have little aptitude necessary for work in that area. The counselor may note, however, that he has artistic talents. The counselor may reconcile the discrepancy by suggesting that the client, perhaps, become a scientific illustrator.

Another type of client, presenting a diagnostic problem to the counselor, has measured interests which are not related to stated interests or ambitions. For example, the client says he wants to be an engineer because he likes to manipulate and repair mechanical objects. However, the pattern which he gives on a standard interest test is that of social service with no measured interests in common with persons in engineering.

The client who lacks well-defined interest patterns is another type the counselor encounters. He may not have interest maturity, as a cause of his condition, especially if he is an adolescent. There may be no dominant pattern or even an above-average interest area. His life experiences, out of which interests develop, may have been constricted. The solution may lie mainly in waiting a few years until a crystallized pattern develops. Strong (293), for example, found considerable instability of interests in men younger than twenty-five. This lack of significant vocational interests may have some clinical meaning in that the client cannot get interested in anything, or identify with a particular family of occupations because of some deeper personality problems.

Counselors occasionally meet clients who have unused or undiscovered interest patterns which are revealed by inventories. This condition creates counseling problems since the discovered interest pattern may be related to a field which the client cannot enter because of limited finances, family, religion, or some other socially constricting circumstance.

Part of the diagnostic picture in vocational counseling is the relationship between interests and values. Values are prime motivating characteristics which should be explored in any vocational counseling process. Their importance for vocational planning is contained in fundamental questions such as, "What is my philosophy of life?" "How do I feel I want to use my life?" "What is important to me?" These questions are closely bound up with occupational choice; but there is little research to indicate the ways in which material related to these fundamental questions can be used effectively in vocational counseling. The counselor must depend upon his skill in helping the client clarify his attitudes about these important questions and in helping him find activities which fulfill the demands of his philosophy. Some instruments such as the Allport-Vernon study of values are useful to the counselor to help clients identify their dominant value clusters.

Physical and Emotional Adjustment. Counselors make attempts to appraise emotional factors related to vocational predictions; but, not very much is known concerning the influence of these factors. There are few validity studies of personality traits or styles of life which are related to specific occupations. Apparently, there is considerable intra-occupational variability on such personality traits. Emotional problems, however, have a direct bearing on occupational success, in that attitudes toward authority, hypochondriacal tendencies, and other emotional adjustment problems, involving neurotic and psychotic characteristics, affect the client's ability to obtain and hold employment.

Physical factors play an important part in the counselor's diagnosis of occupational problems. These factors will be considered later under rehabilitation problems. As noted in Figure 28, there are many other considerations which must be made in vocational planning—finances, family situation, opportunities, and pressures from teachers, relatives, and friends.

Special Information Techniques

Although we covered the general topic of using information in counseling in Chapter 10, there are several types and sources of information especially useful in counseling on vocational problems.

Types of occupational information. Occupational information covers quantitative data, such as the number of people employed in certain occupations, and qualitative data, such as the structure and description of occupations. The several types of information which a vocational counselor must know are occupational structures, facts, and trends. These data serve two general purposes in counseling—exploration and verification (262). The exploratory function is performed in the early phases of vocational counseling before the client makes a career decision. Browsing through occupational readings, seeing occupational films, evaluating part-time jobs, and watching selected television programs offer direct or vicarious tryout experiences. Rusalem (262) points out how these exploratory experiences are emotionally toned and how they become part of the self-concept. Clients, during this exploratory phase, must get "the feel" of an occupation.

The verification function of occupational information comes late in the process when the client observes or reads about occupational material to verify his tentative choices. He may actually try out the occupation to test the congruence of work reality with his expectations and self-concepts. For example, a prospective medical student obtains summer work as an orderly to check upon the reality of his perceptions of medical environments.

Approximately half the U. S. population is in the labor force. There are various schemes for classifying these workers, such as that used by the *Dictionary of Occupational Titles* Part II (308). This volume contains roughly 40,000 jobs classified into nine major groupings, as indicated in Table 3. *The U.S. Census Occupational Classification* is somewhat similar,

Table 3

OCCUPATIONAL GROUPINGS BASED UPON THE
Dictionary of Occupational Titles OF THE U.S. EMPLOYMENT SERVICES

    0– Professional and managerial occupations
        0–0 through 0–3: Professional occupations
        0–4 through 0–6: Semiprofessional occupations
        0–7 through 0–9: Managerial and official occupations

    1– Clerical and sales occupations

1–0 through 1–4: Clerical and kindred occupations
1–5 through 1–9: Sales and kindred occupations

2– Service occupations
    2–0: Domestic service occupations
    2–2 through 2–5: Personal service occupations
    2–6: Protective service occupations
    2–8 and 2–9: Building service workers and porters

3– Agricultural, fishery, forestry, and kindred occupations
    3–0 through 3–4: Agricultural, horticultural, and kindred occupations
    3–8: Fishery occupations
    3–9: Forestry (except logging), and hunting and trapping occupations

4– and 5– Skilled occupations
6– and 7– Semiskilled occupations
8– and 9– Unskilled occupations

with eleven major groupings. The classification of jobs is based on the skill and training each job requires. The Dictionary is useful for the purpose of acquainting clients with a large variety of occupations, their interrelationships, the work performed in each, and their relationship to an industry.

The *Minnesota Occupational Rating Scales* (228) rate 432 occupations according to seven abilities. There are 214 types of jobs under this classification to which the counselor may refer to find occupations for persons with various weightings of aptitude. Although the application of such a scheme as the *Minnesota Occupational Rating Scales* to vocational counseling may make it appear that the counselors are slotting people according to a formula, they have utility for expanding occupational horizons of clients if the scales are used with extreme care. The same cautions apply to using Part IV of the *Dictionary of Occupational Titles* on entry levels. Part IV can be very useful to find areas for entry-level occupations based upon hobbies, part-time jobs, and interests.

One of the most promising newer schemes for classifying occupations is Roe's (247) two-way classification by eight groups. The groups indicate primary focus of activity and six levels of skill, training, and degree of autonomy. Table 4 is based upon Roe's original work and on modifications by Mosier, Dublin, and Shelsky (214). Table 4 indicates the titles of occupational groups, levels of function, and illustrations of occupations.

The United States Employment Service is conducting occupational research designed to produce a unitary occupational structure (101). Classification is based upon the assumption that workers are involved to varying degrees with things, data, and people. It is focused, therefore, on what the worker does on the job. Jobs are broken down into eight components, some of which are: interest, aptitude, temperament, educational development, and work performed. Twenty-six worker functions, such as computing,

Table 4

A CLASSIFICATION OF OCCUPATIONS (REVISED FROM ROE)

Level	I Service	II Business Contact	III Business Organization	IV Technology	V Outdoor	VI Science	VII General Cultural	VIII Arts and Entertainment
1. Professional and Managerial (Higher)	Research Scientist (Social)	Sales Manager (Large corporation)	Cabinet Member (Large Corporation) President (Large Corporation)	Inventor (Industrial Research) Research Scientist (Engineering)	Research Engineer, Mining	Dentist Doctor Research Scientist (Physics, Chemistry)	Judge Professor (History, Math., etc.)	Orchestra Conductor T.V. Director
2. Professional and Managerial (Regular)	Administrator (Social welfare) Manager (Penal institution) Probation Officer Social Worker	Personnel Manager Sales Engineer	Banker Broker CPA Hotel Manager	Air Force (Pilot) Engineer Flight Analyst Superintendent (Factory)	Conservation Officer Fish and Wild Life Specialist Geologist Petroleum Engineer	Chemist Geneticist Pharmacist Veterinarian Physicist	Clergyman Editor News Commentator Teacher (high school, primary)	Architect Baseball Player (Major league) Critic Sculptor
3. Semi-Professional and Managerial	Employment Interviewer Nurse (Registered) Physical Director (YMCA) Recreational Therapist	Freight Traffic Agent Salesman, auto, insurance, bond, real estate Wholesaler	Accountant Owner (Small grocery) Postmaster Private Secretary	Aviator Brine Foreman (DOT Foreman II) Contractor (General, Carpentry, etc.) Engineer (Locomotive)	Apiarist County Agent Farmer (Small independent owner) Forest Ranger	Chiropodist Embalmer Physical Therapist	Justice of the Peace Law Clerk Librarian Reporter	Ad Artist Athletic Coach Interior Decorator Photographer
4. Skilled	Army Sergeant Barber Chef Headwaiter Policeman Practical Nurse	Auctioneer Canvasser Survey Worker Salesman (House to House)	Compiler Morse Operator Statistical Clerk Stenographer	Blacksmith Carpenter Dressmaker Paperhanger Plasterer Foreman (DOT Foreman I) Shiprigger	Landscape Gardener Miner Rotary Driller (Oil Well)	Medical Technician		Chorine Illustrator (Greeting Cards) Window Decorator
5. Semi-Skilled	Chauffeur Cook Elevator Operator Fireman (City) Fortune Teller Navy, Seaman	Peddler Salesclerk Ticket Agent	Cashier Clerk (File) Mail Carrier Telephone Operator Typist	Carpenter (Apprentice) Crane Operator (Portable) Meat Curer Railroad Switchman Truck Driver	Farm Tenant Fisherman Gardener Hostler Nursery Worker Trapper		Library Attendant	Clothes Model Lead Pony Boy
6. Unskilled	Bellhop Janitor Streetsweeper Watchman	Newspaper Boy	Messenger Boy	Carpenter's Helper Deckhand Laborer (Foundry)	Animal Tender Ditcher Farm Laborer Nursery Laborer		Copy Boy	Stagehand

analyzing, serving, and copying, are weighted and organized into a hierarchy according to requirements for each job and not according to skill level. For example, a plumber is given a weighting of 6 on precision working, 3 on computing, and 1 on taking instructions (101). This line of research shows great promise in vocational counseling, particularly for those occupations requiring specific on-the-job training rather than broad general types of advanced education.

Occupational classification schemes are useful to the counselor as a means of orienting the client concerning his occupational objectives, on a level which the client can understand. They are valuable, in addition, because they suggest occupational goals which might otherwise have been overlooked in a systematic search for suitable occupations.

The counselor needs all the facts on various occupations his client is considering in order to describe to the client what demands each occupation will make on him. It is apparent from Ginzberg's (124) and Super's (299) research that it is not the external objective reality of the occupation which enters into vocational choice as much as the client's subjective perception or idealization of that occupation. Hence, there is much need for transmitting accurate and comprehensive job facts to clients. Most of this information is obtained in job analysis surveys performed primarily by the U. S. Bureau of Labor Statistics. The specific kinds of career information needed in vocational counseling are as follows: Opportunities (current and long-range), compensation (salary or wages and supplemental benefits), hours (number and regularity), entry levels, and related jobs, qualifications and restrictions (sex, physical characteristics, marital status, race, memberships, licenses, certifications, examinations, and special personal qualities, and training requirements).

Sources of Occupational Facts

Occupational facts found in thousands of occupational books and pamphlets are usually classified according to characteristics considered important for persons entering the occupation, or characteristics and duties of the jobs. There are three main sources of such information: Federal Agencies, commercial publishers, and trade associations. The Bureau of Labor Statistics and the Bureau of the Census generally do the basic research. This is published in a variety of government pamphlets. Many of these occupational data are written up in attractive format and style by commercial publishing firms. Trade associations publish a plethora of occupational information, mainly of the recruitment type.

The counselor should note the *source* of the data in estimating the reliability and usefulness of the information for his client. He should note also the *date* of the publication and of the underlying basic research since out-of-date occupational data can be very misleading. Data on salaries, which have changed very rapidly, become out-of-date quickly as well. However, most descriptive information remains valid over a long period of time.

Agencies in which vocational counseling is performed compile the occupational data in a library. The data are classified by an alphabetical or numerical scheme such as that of the *Dictionary of Occupational Titles*. Often a specialist librarian is employed to locate information for clients and to perform the monumental chore of keeping the information current. Several bibliographic sources contain compilations of current publications of value in vocational counseling. State departments of education often have special services for counselors in the location and dissemination of occupational literature. Useful references on sources and uses of occupational information may be found in Baer and Roeber (19) and in Greenleaf (131).

The study of occupational trends is another source of useful data to indicate future prospects of occupations. The numbers of farmers and laborers, for example, have declined considerably and clerks and semiskilled workers have increased greatly. As in the case of occupational-structure information, these quantitative data are useful mainly for the general orientation of counselor and client. A client, for example, would not desist from choosing farming as an occupation merely because the national trend for employment of farmers was way down. Local occupational trends, however, might influence very much the choice of an occupation if the client were planning to stay in the local community. The principal problem here is that local data are most often nonexistent or outdated. School guidance directors sometimes take leadership in conducting a community survey of local economic, population, and job trends with the aim of predicting employment opportunities for young workers entering the labor market. For the structure and method of conducting community surveys see Shostrom and Brammer (278).

The Occupational Outlook Service of the Department of Labor is one of the best sources of information on national occupational trends. A significant tool for the counselor is the *Occupational Outlook Handbook* (310) and its supplements which contain trends and other pertinent data on the occupations.

National economic trends are useful data for counselors, also, since they give clues to areas of potential employment. An example is the increased need for atomic energy for power purposes and rocket propulsion for transportation, which, in turn, requires the reorganization and building of entire communities around atomic and rocket industries. These industries call for new skills and training in the research, development, manufacture, and operation of novel machines and processes. The phenomenon of population mobility demands that the counselor keep up with national, state, and regional occupational trends as well as those in his local community.

In the preceding paragraphs it was emphasized that the counselor working with vocational planning problems must have a vast array of occupational data at his fingertips. In Figure 29 we have summarized the types and major sources of occupational data for use in counseling. The source of the occupational facts are listed in the outer ring, and information from those sources is located in the inner ring.

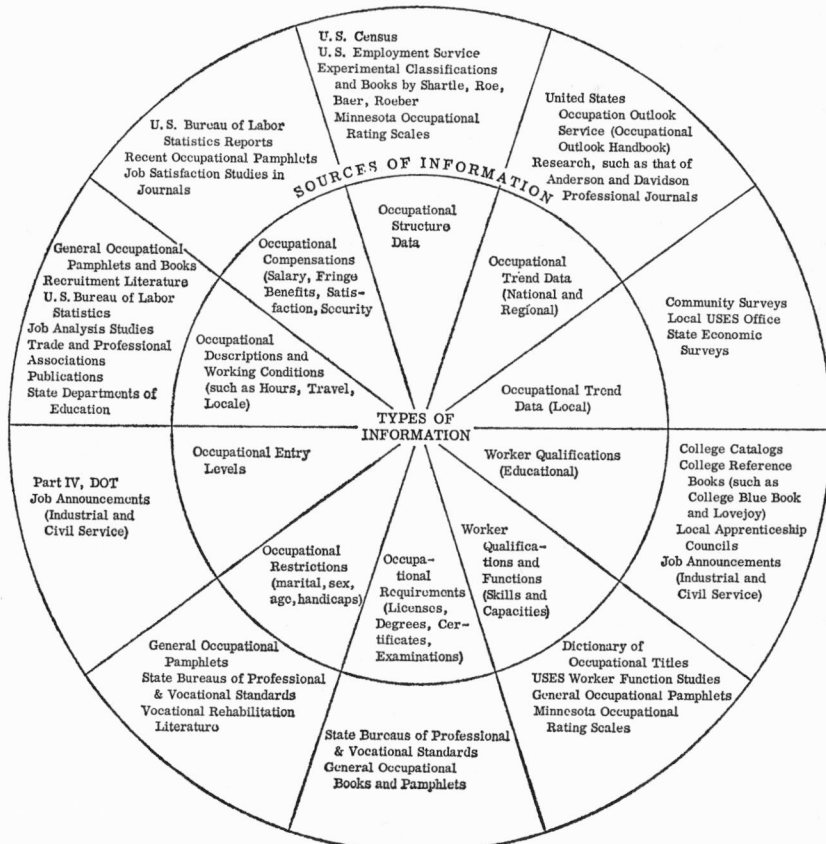

FIG. 29. A Summary of Types and Sources of Occupational Data Needed in Vocational Counseling.

Counseling Methods for Career Planning

Vocational counseling is more than a rational process of matching an appraisal of the individual and appropriate occupational information into a career plan. Vocational counseling is largely the implementation of the client's self-concept (299). This means that the client perceives himself as behaving in a certain manner with status, pleasures, social contacts, and other values satisfied through his occupation. This is why vocational counseling cannot be a simple process of fitting "a square peg to a square hole."

The counselor must be familiar with many facets of the client's self-pictures to help him choose a satisfying and productive vocational area. The following material illustrates this process.

Survey and evaluation interviews. Early in the vocational-counseling process, the counselor collects data on the client from which he makes predictions about probabilities of the client's success in training or work. Data are collected largely from the interview, the personal-data summary blank, case records, and test instruments. The data are weighted informally by the counselor from his experience and are then put in a type of multiple regression equation by means of which he makes his predictions. This process was described in the diagnosis discussion of Chapter 5.

Newer methods of thinking about prediction problems, such as Information Theory (73), include the application of logic and mathematics to the interaction of predictor variables and their relation to the final decision to be made. Much information and more useful theories are needed on how vocational predictions are made. It seems that the best that can be done at present is for the counselor to make the most accurate hypotheses possible on the basis of the most valid and reliable clinical data and utilize the best of the present statistical prediction methods with tests.

The early interviews in vocational counseling are marked by this preoccupation with the reliability and validity of data from interviews, surveys, records, and tests. The counselor is asking himself constantly what kinds of criteria (successful educational plans and vocational pursuits) are related to all the data being collected. The counselor also should ask himself how he can bring the client more closely into this predicting, decision-making process. Gustad (133) points out eloquently how research of the future must take into account the interactive process between counselor and client in the prediction process.

The synthesis interview. The counselor reviews material from the first interviews, examines the personal data summary, reviews the test data, and studies relevant occupational information. The client considers the interpreted test data, reviews his own values and feelings, and collates the findings with the results of his independent occupational study. The client and counselor discuss these data in the synthesis or decision-making phase of the vocational counseling process. The synthesis interview ordinarily consists of the test interpretation, a discussion of occupational data, and then a synthesis discussion of these data plus information and predictions from the personal histories and earlier interviews. Counseling techniques mentioned in earlier chapters are used throughout the process.

Establishing the occupational objective. Prior to the synthesis interview the client has done his own occupational study. This study may have been performed as part of a class, or it may have been accomplished specifically for this interview. The client is aided greatly, of course, if there is an occupational library file which concentrates occupational literature in one place. A guide or outline of relevant facts that he should observe about occupations is a great aid also. Such a guide should cover the facts listed under an earlier section describing the content of occupational pamphlets.

From the synthesis process the career plan is formulated. Generally, this takes the form of specifying the general areas of greatest promise, such as science, service, or business. Then, depending upon the client's age and need to be specific, occupational goals of a more exact nature, such as machinist, typist, engineer, or elementary teacher are specified. This more specific selection usually is the culmination of a long process of vocational exploration and study, so that the choice naturally evolves out of the data. Often, however, the choice must be made in a short time to prepare for a training program or immediate employment. Such was the case with many veterans seeking vocational counseling after World War II where the counselor had seen the client twice, had given him several tests, had made his "shotgun" predictions, and then had come up with several specific objectives in preferential order in order to formulate an immediate training plan. This "short-circuiting" of the vocational-choice process is to be regarded strictly as an expedient. Vocational counseling should have built-in arrangements for follow-ups. Furthermore, there should be a thorough understanding with the client that a specific choice made in such a short time is strictly tentative.

The process of formulating an occupational objective is characterized by the counselor suggesting vocational ideas for further exploration. The client makes his own decisions on the objective. The counselor may give specific occupational data from his knowledge and experience; but it behooves him to be right. It is preferable, therefore, that he use the source of the data verbatim to avoid distortion. There is evidence, such as that of Speer and Jasper (287), which indicates that it is the counselor's presentation of occupational data which is most effective in selecting suitable goals. Independent reading on the part of the client, in itself, was not of much value in selecting suitable occupational goals. Counselors, therefore, must take a more active role in presenting occupational facts and guiding client readings. Counselors should point out that occupational information is more than just facts about jobs. It should be presented in terms of a way of life, of a relationship between worker and job, and relationships among workers. Fine (101), for example, points out how persons planning careers "fit in" to the jobs performed. In family and school a person can be creative, be himself, be expansive and spontaneous. Most jobs, however, require that he conform to expectations, that he be a team member. Fine emphasizes how lack of understanding of this fundamental principle leads to frustration, hostility, and general job dissatisfaction. In other words, the counselor must consider career planning in terms of the values, life experiences, and expectations of the client. It is for these reasons that the vocational counselor must have a thorough understanding of therapeutic psychology also.

The counselor has an additional responsibility to show the client how an occupational objective of his choice does or does not fit the data. The counselor then must let the client come to his own conclusions. The counselor can show the client how his tentative objective fits into organizational patterns and job families. The counselor may have organizational charts of typical industries, related to the client's interest, to show how a geologist, for example, fits into the organizational structure, or how a school psychologist fits into a public school administration organization.

An important principle in presenting occupational information is timing. The client should be ready. Generally, he is ready when he is aware of his personality characteristics, from the appraisal phases, and is wondering what relationship they have to career choices. The counselor judges that the client is ready, for the most part, when he begins to ask for information. The counselor may make an exception to the principle if he feels that it is desirable to give the client a broad orientation to the world of work by going over job charts or Part II of the *Dictionary of Occupational Titles* to broaden the client's occupational outlook.

The educational plan. After the client has selected the general occupational area and made some specific occupational choices in preferential order, a plan is made for obtaining the necessary education to achieve the objective. This education may take the form of college, trade school, or on-the-job training. Methods and tools for accomplishing this plan are discussed in the next section under educational counseling.

Many counselors prefer to have the client leave with some kind of plan on paper. Hence, various career and life-plan brochures can be made which list the client's principal vocational choices, educational plans, and general profiles of test results. An example of such a life-plan brochure is described in Shostrom and Brammer (277). In a process as complicated as vocational and educational planning, distortions of the life plan take place over a period of time; hence, a summary of the results would tend to reduce distortion, at least in the factual elements of the program.

Try-outs and follow-ups. It is necessary to convey to clients the idea that general-area choices, specific objectives, and training plans are tentative until confirmed by try-out. This can be done without undermining the client's security. It is deemed unwise and unethical for the counselor to imply that, after taking some tests and talking things over for a few hours, he has found the answers to his life plans.

Because of the process nature of vocational counseling it is necessary to try the plan and re-evaluate the objectives in light of the educational or occupational try-out. Follow-up interviews are arranged to check on the adequacy of the objectives and the preceding counseling.

EDUCATIONAL COUNSELING

Educational counseling consists of two distinct types of counseling assistance: educational planning and remedial help. Educational counseling has acquired special social significance in light of talent searches and encouragement of the academically able student.

Educational Planning

Selecting a training institution. This type of counseling is aimed essentially at helping the client select the most suitable educational goal and the best type of educational institution for him. Several factors must be considered in helping a client select an educational institution: scholastic aptitude sufficient for admission and retention, financial capacity, and suitability of the college program to the client's interests, general educational needs, and vocational goals. There are several characteristics about an educational institution which a client must consider also. Does it have suitable living facilities? What is the reputation of its faculty? What is the placement record for its graduates? Is it accredited by the regional accrediting agencies and by the professional associations for the particular curriculum being considered? Other factors, varying in significance from person to person, must be considered, such as the size of the institution, and extracurricular programs.

Some of the standard references the client may rely upon to make a thorough study of educational institutions are: the *College Blue Book* (51), *American Universities and Colleges* (154), *American Junior Colleges* (37), *Lovejoy's College Guide* (188), and *Junior Colleges, Specialized Schools and Colleges* (264). These references are used to supplement information from the catalogues of the individual colleges. All students planning to take educational counseling must be familiar with them.

References for other types of educational institutions are *American Trade Schools Directory* (74) and *Lovejoy's Vocational School Guide* (189) for trade schools, the *Home Study Blue Book* (211) for correspondence schools, and *Private Independent Schools* (50), *Handbook of Private Schools* (263) for the numerous private pre-college educational institutions.

Predicting success in training and education. One of the principal problems the counselor must face in educational planning is making predictions of probable success in a given college. Many institutions have predictive indices, or, at least, a validity coefficient based upon a correlation between a standard aptitude measure and grades in that college or curriculum. These validity coefficients generally fall in the low fifties for Pearson correlations. For the counselor making predictions about training success, the previous grades of the client in high school are still the best reference since grades generally have higher validity than a standard scholastic-aptitude test. For example, the counselor can fairly accurately predict success in the first year of engineering training in college relying on high school grades, mathematics achievement tests, and general scholastic-aptitude tests (Layton, 180).

So far, studies in the area of predictions indicate it is much easier to predict success in training for an occupation than in predicting success in that occupation. There are more definite criteria of success in training, such as grades and completion of the program. Obtaining criteria of success in many professional occupations is very difficult.

Financing training. An important consideration in college planning is finance. Major sources of tuition, besides parental subsidies and savings, are scholarships, fellowships, and loans. Private and governmental sources of such aids are becoming more plentiful. Counselors working in areas of educational planning should have financial-aid bulletins of the major colleges and should have access to such reference volumes as Feingold's *Scholarships, Fellowships, and Loans* (94).

Remedial Assistance

Although overcoming educational deficiencies is more an instructional rather than a counseling responsibility, the counselor practicing in an educational institution comes face to face with this problem frequently. We take the position that the counselor must be able to diagnose remediation problems in order to recommend steps to remedy deficiencies, or to make suitable referrals to remedial specialists. The availability of diagnostic-testing instruments for assessing the achievement level and the precise areas of difficulty, as well as a dearth of experts in remedial assistance, make such diagnostic studies by counselors feasible and necessary. Appraisal instruments, along with supplementary diagnostic interviewing, often can be used to indicate to a client where the causes of his difficulties lie.

Diagnostic skills. Knowledge of diagnostic procedures in basic skills is of value to both the counselor working in educational institutions and to the private practitioner. Achievement problems are a key reason for referral in a school or college. In private practice the psychologist spends much of his time with clients having difficulties in school. The psychologist is in a key position to work with problems of educational achievement also because of the complex psychological factors usually operating in cases of low achievement. There may be combinations of emotional problems, educational-skill deficiency, low motivation, physiological handicaps, or lack of practice in the basic skill. A thorough diagnostic and remedial program, therefore, calls upon the skills of many specialists. The psychologist often is selected to coordinate the various specialists' diagnostic studies and to make recommendations to the tutors, teachers, or remedial specialists.

Although it is beyond the scope of this book to describe educational diagnostic methods in detail, some of the areas to be investigated are mentioned to give the counselor without orientation in these skills some background. There are two areas of investigation—general study methods and reading. Several inventories exist for diagnosing study difficulties. Examples are the Wrenn "Study Habits Inventory" (326) and the Brown-Holtzman "Survey of Study Habits and Attitudes" (44). Though inventories identify problem areas, they do not differentiate between habits of good and poor students. A well-conducted study at Ohio State University revealed that even superior students used widely variable and unrecommended study procedures. The students apparently were superior in spite of their study methods (77).

Diagnosis of educational problems should start with a good *physical examination* with particular attention put upon sensory and metabolic factors. Secondly, a close look at *motivational factors,* with special emphasis upon personal problems, should be taken. There are generally many complicating factors in achievement deficiencies; however, attitudinal difficulties are often at the root of the problem. One should not overlook the possibility that emotional problems are the result as much as the cause of educational achievement problems. Often, achievement problems reveal some deep-seated hostility toward parents or confusion of values. These problems indicate therapeutic counseling perhaps more than remedial educational techniques.

The counselor should examine *basic skills* and *knowledge* which underlie achievement. Some of these are rate and flexibility of reading, level of comprehension and vocabulary, interest, quantity of reading, and interfering habits such as finger tracing, word reading, regression, and vocalization. These diagnostic data enable the educational counselor to formulate the client's problem more accurately than the usual "I can't concentrate" or "I can't read fast" type of offhand symptomatic statement of the client. This diagnostic survey enables the counselor either to make a referral to a remedial specialist or to offer some suggestions from his general knowledge in the field of remediation.

Remediation. Generally speaking, counselors do not perform remedial instruction since individual tutoring is so time consuming. Counselors can spend their time so much more profitably in other types of services. Most agencies offer remedial-type courses which give the client an opportunity to learn basic skills over a fixed period of time in a group or clinic setting. Though there are many books and pamphlets available for self-help on educational problems, there is no evidence to indicate that a person improves his skills substantially by reading a pamphlet. The educational counselor may use the pamphlet-reading technique on a prescription basis, however, to give the client some background for later conferences on specific learning and study skills. The pamphlets and time-study schedules are useful as diagnostic devices to help the client find areas of weakness. Pamphlets are useful when a lack of learning techniques is not at the core of the achievement problem, but, something more basic in attitude and approach to learning tasks.[1]

Counseling on problems of academic deficiency. There seems to be considerable folklore among educational counselors about the efficacy of short counseling interviews with poor students. Klingelhofer (171) performed one of the few studies indicating that short-term, direct-suggestion counseling with such clients has value in raising course grades. His study suggested that organized counseling was associated with improved scholastic performance, although the differential amounts of counseling given the groups did not seem to effect similar differences in grades. The same achievement level was attained whether the student received one or four hours of directive counseling.

Margolies (196) points out the heavy resistance encountered from poor scholarship students who are called by the counselor for discussion of their achievement. He points out the necessity for looking behind the "facade" of the student's resistance and logic-tight rationalizations. The purpose is to look for dynamic factors and points where the insight process might be started.

REHABILITATION COUNSELING

Basic Concepts

Vocational rehabilitation has become one of the most significant social services of our time. Rehabilitation is a process of restoring the client with handicaps to the fullest possible usefulness to himself and society. It is estimated that there are approximately three million disabled or severely handicapped persons in the productive years between fourteen and sixty-four (307). Of these, two million come within the scope of services offered by vocational rehabilitation programs. Most of these two million could achieve happy and productive lives through suitable work. Vocational rehabilitation services offered through the states and assisted by the United States Government have been working with this group since 1918. These programs have been able to help clients overcome their dependency and contribute to their society. The programs, furthermore, have enabled clients to achieve personal satisfactions which come from engaging in productive work and to avoid the stigma of social and economic liability.

The various categories of disability suffered by applicants for vocational rehabilitation services are indicated in Figure 30. The occupations most frequently entered by rehabilitants are indicated in Figure 30 also. Occupa-

---

[1] For a detailed coverage of diagnostic and remedial methods for study and reading problems, see H. Bamman, and L. Brammer, *How to Study Successfully* (Palo Alto, Calif.: Pacific Books, 1959).

tional distribution of the handicapped is roughly similar to that of those who are not disabled.

Counseling plays a vital part in the rehabilitation process. Counseling techniques for handicapped persons are little different from counseling for the able-bodied. State bureaus of vocational rehabilitation employ special counselors called vocational rehabilitation officers who are specially trained in the rehabilitation process. The US Veterans Administration employs counseling psychologists to perform similar rehabilitative functions in veterans hospitals with more stress, however, placed upon the counseling function. Quite often the state office of vocational rehabilitation takes over from the counseling psychologist when the client is released from the hospital.

Per cent of rehabilitants, by types of disability at acceptance and by major occuptional group at closure, fiscal year 1957

DISABILITIES   MAJOR OCCUPATIONS

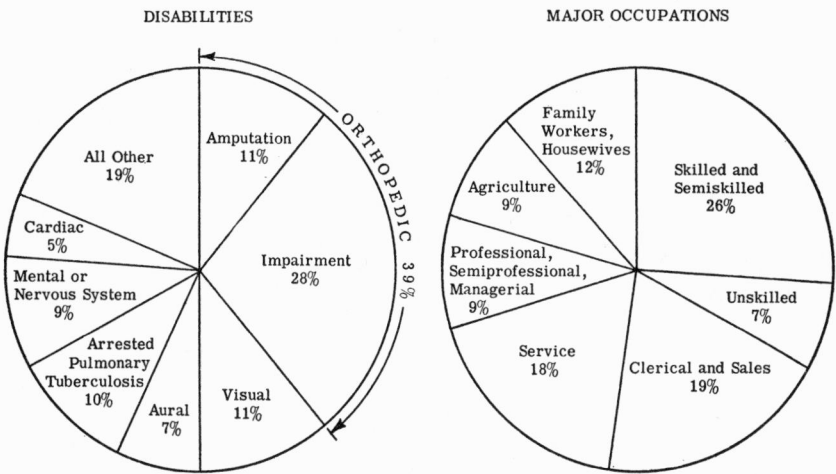

FIG. 30. Disabilities and Major Occupational Groups. Per Cent of Rehabilitants, by Types of Disability at Acceptance and by Major Occupational Group at the Closure of the Fiscal Year 1957. *Annual Report* (1957). U.S. Department of Health, Education and Welfare.

Interest in professional counseling organizations has grown rapidly in rehabilitation circles during the past few years. In 1957, the Division of Rehabilitation Counselors was organized as a division in the American Personnel and Guidance Association. Division 17, Counseling Psychology, of the American Psychological Association has increased rapidly the number of psychologists working primarily in vocational rehabilitation.

Rehabilitation Services

The vocational rehabilitation counselor must have the same skills and knowledge that others in other helping professions must have. He is a professional case worker since he usually handles the client's problems from the first interview to satisfactory placement and follow-up. His counseling functions are very much like those described in this book, with special emphasis upon psychometrics and vocational counseling. He must be conversant with medical and psychiatric terminology and must be familiar with community service agencies. In state agencies he is an expediter and a coordinator of many services to clients.

The vocational-rehabilitation process covers many services to the handicapped client. In addition to the diagnostic and vocational counseling techniques described in this book, there are orderly sequences of services, such as physical restoration, training, psychiatric treatment, provision of training materials, maintenance while training, placement, license acquisition, and furnishing of equipment such as vending stands to establish a business under the supervision of the agency.

Generally the process proceeds according to well-established steps, beginning with the *intake interview* which includes orientation to the service and determination of eligibility, assignment to a counselor and the *initial interview,* the *case study, psychological evaluation, counseling,* formulating the *rehabilitation plan, training* and/or *placement,* and *follow-up* (307). These steps are aimed at promoting maximum vocational usefulness as soon as possible.

The Rehabilitation Counselor

As indicated above, the vocational-rehabilitation counselor must be a versatile person. Many lists have been drawn up to indicate what he should know to do his job well. Cantrell (55) studied the matter of training rehabilitation counselors by asking a large number of counselors in the Veterans Administration, officials of state vocational rehabilitation centers and counselors in private practice what they felt was important in training and how they would rank the material in usefulness. Though there were some disagreements in rankings among the three groups of practitioners, the average rankings, from first to last choice in significance for their work as vocational rehabilitation counselors were as follows:

(1) Counseling theory, principles, and practice
(2) Professional activities including ethics, duties, interprofessional teamwork, professional growth, and public relations
(3) Supervised field work, including visits to agencies
(4) Psychological information including developmental, abnormal, personality theory, and effect of disability on personality
(5) Testing principles and practice
(6) Occupational information
(7) Casework history, principles, and method
(8) Rehabilitation, including history, philosophy, legal, and administrative aspects

(9) Social and community resource information

(10) Medical and related information, including knowledge of physical restoration resources

(11) Research and statistics methods

It was noteworthy in Cantrell's study that the practicing counselors considered counseling the very center of the process of rehabilitation and that the major emphasis in training should be upon counseling. The other areas, such as medical information and case methods, were considered necessary supportive elements to the counseling relationship.

SUMMARY

Therapeutic psychologists often specialize, or become involved at some point, in problems of vocational choice, educational planning, diagnosis on remediation problems, and rehabilitation counseling of the handicapped. Though there are various theories on how vocational choices are made, there is much agreement among counselors that suitable vocational choices have profound consequences for the individual client and society. Educational and vocational counseling draw heavily upon appraisal and diagnosis functions, yet, retain counseling techniques as the core of the process. The principal sources of data used in educational-vocational-rehabilitation counseling are tests, case histories, client self-evaluations, clinical observations, occupational information materials, training directories, and tryout work experience.

15.

Counseling on Problems
of Values

Psychology as a science and a profession has become more concerned about values—the value assumptions underlying science itself as well as the values people hold as an object of study. The term "value" in this context is defined as a firm, conscious or unconscious belief in the worth of an idea or feeling. For the purpose of this chapter, the philosophical problem of the origin of values and the question of the absoluteness or relativity of values will be treated only incidentally.

The Problem in Therapeutic Psychology

The purpose of this chapter is to examine some of the relationships between therapeutic psychology and religious counseling. We shall use Wrenn's description of the two approaches ". . . religion and psychology complement each other. Psychology contributes to an understanding of the *nature* of self and of one's relationships with others, religion to an understanding of the meaning and purpose in life, and the *significance* of these same relationships. Both may contribute to more effective living" (325, pg. 331).

In the psychological literature there appears to be an awakening interest in philosophical problems underlying the psychological study of man. Mowrer, for example, states that psychology, perhaps, ought to examine its long-fostered assumption that the nonphysical elements of personality (conceived popularly as man's mind or spirit) serve the body (219). Although the personality grows out of needs to serve the body, Mowrer wonders whether the "mind" has its peculiar needs, characteristics, and survival demands also. He realizes that this is a disturbing question since the topic moves from the traditional pale of naturalistic observation to the area of the "spirit"—a traditionally religious subject. Yet, psychologists are becoming concerned, increasingly, about the subject of "psychological survival" and the "human situation." Human problems, especially those in the mental-health areas mentioned earlier, have become such an acute social concern that practicing psychologists are willing to examine all available means for helping clients to survive psychologically. Apparently, they are willing to do this even if it means going beyond the traditional laboratory and strictly behavioristic methods of studying and helping man.

It is a truism that psychotherapists and personal counselors deal with the fundamental problems of life, namely, loving, becoming an independent person, handling normal guilt, and gaining a mature perspective on the frustrating and tragic incidents of everyday living. The writers are aware of the difficulties in approaching the topic of values in the context of therapeutic psychology. This chapter is offered as a starting point for the student who may not have done much previous reading or thinking about the numerous value problems confronting client and therapist.

Psychological counselors have been reluctant to face the possibility that they might have functions and responsibilities which might be termed broadly as "religious." This reluctance has been due to the empirical tradition, basic philosophical differences between social science and theology, alleged emotional extremes and hypocrisy in much of organized religious behavior, and the counselor's own spiritual ignorance or conflict. More psychological counselors are recognizing, however, that religious sentiments and feelings become powerful positive or negative motives in their client's lives.

Traditionally, psychology is biologically oriented. The early models and scientific procedures of the late nineteenth century were based upon physiology and physics. Darwinian philosophy had considerable influence on psychologists' view of man as a continuation of the animal world and subject to the same natural laws. Early American psychology added a functional note to the biological models imported from Germany. There was a very strong effort to divorce psychology from its earlier philosophical roots and to make the understanding of behavior a strictly scientific venture.

We do not advocate a return to rationalistic and other philosophical methods as a substitute for careful observation and rigorous experimentation. Psychology as a science must remain firmly planted in scientific methods and critical thinking. We are in accord, however, with the trend in psychological services to examine the methods and assumptions of psychology in regard to their adequacy for understanding man's basic problems and helping him to deal with them more effectively. Part of the difficulty is that the hunger for knowledge about man and efforts to assist him with his problems is making premature and unrealistic demands upon such an infant endeavor as scientific psychology. Nevertheless, the therapeutic psychologist is faced with the practical reality (or at least the pressure) for looking beyond his scientific methods and psychological techniques to help his clients with values beyond the process itself.

The assumption that it is necessary to go beyond strictly psychological techniques in helping clients with value problems puts the therapeutic psychologist squarely in the area of traditional religious concern. Here again, the history of psychology at some points has run counter to formal religion. Freud, for example, is well known for his indictment of organized religious endeavors in his provocative *The Future of an Illusion* (110) wherein he asserts that so much of religious dogma and behavior are projections of unconscious wishes. In addition to the maligning of, or indifference toward, formal religious belief there has been an attitude of suspicion toward a professional psychologist who had any strong personal religious beliefs. He was automatically suspect because of the assumed interference these beliefs had with the attitude of objectivity so necessary for his psychology.

Jung's attitude toward religion was that the client's present belief system should be used in such a way that it would hasten his recovery of healthy attitudes. This view was a radical departure from the Freudian position which, as described above, tended to regard much of formal religion as a form of illness itself. Jung is reputed to have advocated finding God within experience as part of the individuation process (126). The "God within" the racial unconscious of the Jungian system is then equated by many persons with a transcendental "God without." Jung admits that it is not the business of the psychologist to establish or even investigate objective truth regarding the existence of God. He states, furthermore, that neither is it the psychologist's business to construct a pseudo religion out of primitive yearnings or myths. Jung tries to stay close to empirical facts in this realm and to concentrate on the oak rather than on the acorn (317).

White (317), a priest as well as a psychologist, approached the problem of God and the psychology of the unconscious in a spirit of compromise. He attempted to tie together the idea of an external reality, called God, with the inner nature and psychological realities of man. Kunkel (179), a psychiatrist, also made efforts toward reconciliation of the two realms into a "religious psychology." The elements of this collaborative relationship are naturalistic observation and depth psychology. They are used to help understand behavior on the one hand, and religion is needed to give purpose and direction to behavior on the other. Kunkel feels that a human helping relationship such as therapy and the goals of maturity need both approaches working together.

Efforts were made even earlier to tie more closely psychotherapeutic methods and assumptions to those of religion. Putnam, a New England physician of the early twentieth century, tried very hard to encourage his psychoanalytic colleagues to join him in efforts to broaden the base of psychoanalysis so as to include problems of the larger community and the cosmos. There was strong resistance and some outright rejection in Europe and America of his proposals to tie a religiously oriented metaphysics to psychoanalysis. This resistance persisted until such contemporary writers as Fromm (117), Mowrer (219), and White (317) reopened the question without suggesting that psychology compromise on its scientific bases.

A Point of View

We are discussing values in this book because clients often confront the counselor with their problems concerned with such as resolving value conflicts, handling guilt over immoral behavior, meeting crises, overcoming deep-seated anxieties, feeling worthwhile, and relating to something significant. The counselor is often put in a difficult position when the client expects more of him than help in gaining insight into himself. Many clients, in effect, beg the counselor to tell them how to live, what kind of person they should be, how they can meet the vicissitudes and seeming meaninglessness of life. Frequently, clients expect the counselor to relieve them of basic anxieties such as fear of nonbeing, or death.

We are not proposing that the counselor set himself up as an authority on such questions, nor that he should yield to the client's demands for answers to basic questions by giving his own personal philosophy. What is being suggested, though, is that the counselor be very much aware of this problem and be cognizant of the temptations to pontificate on philosophical and religious questions. The therapist should note that his role is to make positive suggestions to the client concerning where he might find "answers" or "grist for his religious and philosophical mill."

Interdisciplinary Relationships

It seems that one must recognize that religious and psychological concepts are not mutually exclusive. One must not assume that either religious concern or psychological interpretation is the total solution to, or explanation of, man's problems. Many people put this proposition into the form of an uncomfortable dichotomy. They feel inclined either to reject psychological interpretations and explanations of behavior or to reject their religious belief system. There seems to be a third position for clients to take which we would like to explore. This is that there is considerable overlap and congruence as well as conflict between the psychological and theological views of man. One should recognize these points of overlap and conflict and then look assiduously for areas where the meanings are congruent and seem to give greater combined insight into man's existence and the solution of his human problems.

We think that it is important to encourage colleagues to ponder questions on the relationships between scientific psychology, philosophy and religion. If such an endeavor is successful, a "breakthrough" might be achieved which would be of great benefit to counselors and clients struggling with these interdisciplinary problems, many of which are presently outside the scope of scientific and professional psychology.

There are some compelling social reasons why such a breakthrough is needed. As we mentioned earlier in this chapter, the problem of mental health is bound to questions of life philosophy or *weltanschauung*. Mowrer (219) thinks that we need a type of mental hygiene for twentieth-century man which will have genuine psychological survival value, something over and above the concern for mastery of his natural environment. Such an approach appears to be needed to prevent mass psychoses and neuroses. A means must be found, in addition to formal religion, to help clients with feelings of disillusionment, depersonalization, being unloved and abandoned, and of being a "thing" unscrupulously manipulated by other people. Development of such a philosophy may help the client to cope with his gnawing free-floating anxiety, guilt over real or imagined misdeeds, and feelings of helplessness and resentment during periods of crisis. These are questions with which the average psychological counselor feels quite inadequate to cope, other than to use the general techniques of psychological support and relatedness offered through a warm therapeutic relationship.

Several groups are searching for interrelationships between psychology and religion. The Academy of Religion and Mental Health is an example of such a group. The Society for the Scientific Study of Religion is another group designed to facilitate intercommunication between students of religion and social science.

Professional meetings of psychological and counseling groups have an increasing number of sections devoted to value concerns. There are committees within the American Psychological Association and the American Psychiatric Association devoted to this problem of relationship to values and formal religion. The pastoral-counseling movement has grown rapidly also and is being accelerated through the clinical training of student clergymen.

Pastoral Psychology

Counseling pastors are ordained clergymen trained in psychological counseling to deal with problems of belief, morals, guilt, and life crises. Such counselors assist parishioners with a wide range of human problems from marital conflicts through child-rearing. The family clergyman and the family physician, as the only sources of help, traditionally have been turned to in most communities.

The minister of today has manifold leadership responsibility in his parish and in his community. Therefore, it is imperative that he be reliably oriented in dynamic psychology so that he can make wise professional referrals.

The average minister has had three years of general professional education leading to the B.D. degree. In pursuit of this degree, he is given general classes in personality and counseling theory as well as supervised clinical experience in a hospital setting for six weeks to a year in residence.

The term "Pastoral Psychology" refers to a more extensive graduate specialization. Such leaders as Hiltner, Wise, Johnson, and Eitzen have developed curricula leading to a Doctor's degree in this speciality. These graduates usually serve as therapeutic counselors in pastoral counseling centers as part of a group effort of various churches in a city, or as teachers on the college or seminary level.

To assist in establishing a frame of reference for pastoral counseling, the various levels described by Oates (224) are cited. Most of the pastoral functions listed below have some counseling aspects:

(1) Level of friendship (rapport)
(2) Level of comfort (support)
(3) Level of confession (cathartic)
(4) Level of teaching (informational)
(5) Level of pastoral counseling (psychotherapeutic)
(6) Level of referral

The act of affirmation or loving, in the broad "agape" sense, is involved in pastoral counseling too. Pastoral counselors generally subscribe to the view that man's love for man is rooted in God's love for man. The religious counselor ties in this client acceptance of himself and his fellow man with God's love for man as the principal source of his attaining insight, freedom, security, maturity, and similar therapeutic goals. The counseling relationship is often construed as a quest for the "kingdom of God" in man. These positions do not necessarily militate against an optimal counseling relationship unless they are accompanied by a judgmental and authoritarian attitude.

The religious counselor, particularly one in the Christian tradition, begins with a different set of assumptions about anthropology and psychology from that of the professional psychologist. The central values of the pastoral counselor reside in what is called divine law. It is difficult to generalize or be categorical about the teleological assumptions of theologians since they seem to hold many views depending upon their unique perceptual vantage points and training. For example, some theologians do not see the traditional dichotomy between God and man since they view God and man in a common relationship. In any event, the view one holds about the nature, purpose, and origin of man influences his approach to counseling problems.

The psychologist, in contrast, generally operates on the more humanistic assumption that ultimate values are rationally determined and are found in man himself. Herein lies, in our opinion, the central issue between pastoral counseling and nontheologically oriented counseling. It is possible, however, to resolve this issue, somewhat, at the technique level, since both are concerned with helping suffering humanity. Psychologists can evaluate the techniques they use on the criterion of effectiveness in reaching limited goals quite apart from the basic philosophical assumptions and basic purposes involved.

For an extensive and fair analysis of the comparative assumptions underlying psychological science and Christianity the reader is referred to the volume *What, Then, Is Man* (203) which is a symposium report on the unique and interrelated features of two basic ways of construing man.

There are many things which clergymen can do to promote the same mental-health goals as therapeutic psychology. It must be recognized that the religious leader is concerned about many more aspects of his parishioners' lives than their mental health and that mental health is defined variously; but this is one area for which people look to him for leadership, albeit under a variety of guises. The pastoral counselor should recognize that the recent surge of religious interest and church attendance is probably more than a simple desire to renew the ties of childhood to a community institution, or to escape from tension. It may be viewed also as a deep expression of man's search for a moral and spiritual framework for life, a foundation upon which to build a rich and satisfying life for himself and his family. It should be recognized that throughout history social crises have produced such great surges of religious interest.

Attempting to provide answers to the quests of his parishioners presents a tremendous challenge and responsibility to a religious leader. The counseling relationship is only one of the media for achieving his goals. Therefore, we feel it would be a mistake for a minister to become too involved in therapeutic counseling with clients unless the question involved discovering answers to deep-seated, but rather clear-cut, moral and spiritual problems.

So often the client's deep psychological problems come in the guise of moral or spiritual problems. The clergyman must have the skill with which to distinguish the basically spiritual problem from one involving pathology in the personality. He must know, also, his own limitations in dealing with problems construed by the client as "spiritual," since one can put this type of interpretation upon almost all human difficuties.

The pastoral counselor's role in relation to other specialists. The pastoral counselor's principal role, as far as psychological counseling is concerned, would seem to be to explore the client's initial problem to see where it touches upon areas of spiritual concern and knowledge, and where emotional conditions would warrant the services of a therapeutic psychologist, psychiatrist, or social worker. The principal techniques employed would be supportive and informational. Delving into unconscious motives could lead to a relationship fraught with deep transference and countertransference feelings, expectations of unrealistic accomplishments, or aggravation of a developing mental illness.

Personal problems may be approached from an interdisciplinary point of view in which the pastoral counselor and the psychologist or psychiatrist work together and where cross referral can be accomplished easily. Practically, however, this is difficult to achieve because remnants of mutual suspicion exist among the practitioners, and clients often become confused when working with two similar types of specialists, which complicates the method. This type of cross referral among pastors and psychologists can work satisfactorily, but, only under conditions where the primary responsibility is invested in one of the two specialists.

Contributions of therapeutic psychology to pastoral counseling. The tools of therapeutic psychology are useful to the pastoral counselor in many ways. The application of relationship techniques, such as listening, accepting, and reflecting, for example, can go far in overcoming the traditional authoritarian advice-giving role into which the clergyman is so often cast. The understanding of unconscious motivation in behavior and human culture can go a long way to gaining an understanding of defensiveness and emotional problems as a type of sickness or ignorance rather than thinking of these behaviors in traditional moralistic terms so destructive to a good counseling relationship. Greater knowledge of human motivation should help the clergyman deal with his concepts of freedom of the will, moral responsibility, guilt, and responsible action more understandingly.

Possibilities and limitations of the ministerial role in counseling. The clergyman can take advantage of a strategic helping relationship with his clients which is based on a traditional "pastor" perception of the clergy. He has an advantage over other helping professionals in that he is known and perceived of by the family as a helper. He can deal with the whole family, as a case-work problem, which is often as important as dealing with a selected individual. However, he suffers from the client's aforementioned perception of him as an authoritarian figure, a teacher, or as the symbol of moralistic judgment. Yet, in counseling it is imperative that the counselor be perceived quickly as a permissive, nonjudgmental, understanding person. The traditional exhortational or advice-giving role is inimical to the general goals of present-day counseling.

The pastoral counselor is in a unique position to assist clients in confronting profound life problems, such as developing a philosophy of life. He is in a strategic position to discuss moral problems also. Even here, the cultural anthropology frame of reference is helpful in ascertaining more clearly the areas of right, wrong, and neutral. When the religious dogma is not clearly interpretable in a given case, it is useful to know the mores of the culture and how these are distinguished from clearly delineated religious codes or conduct. For example, a behavior which a client may regard as "sinful" and from which he suffers considerable anxiety and guilt may be more a deviation from the cultural norms than a violation of the moral code of his religion or denomination.

VALUE PROBLEMS CONFRONTED BY THERAPEUTIC PSYCHOLOGISTS

Although pastoral counselors were cautioned regarding the dangers of exceeding their role as spiritual counselors, so, the therapeutic psychologist in his counseling and psychotherapeutic role must be aware of the same danger. The therapeutic psychologist generally does not consciously give a client answers on values. His principal role is to help the client to clarify his thinking and to discover feelings and thoughts regarding questions of values in his own personality. When such values are lacking, considered by the client to be inadequate, or are not discoverable with the usual therapeutic techniques, then the psychologist may present various cultural viewpoints and trends on the problem in question or refer him to religious specialists for more detailed information. There, he can obtain ideas in a type of setting characterized by teaching. These ideas can be discussed further in the psychotherapeutic interviews where he can scrutinize his belief system and religious experiences. Finally, through counseling, the client can integrate his new discoveries smoothly into his self- and core personality systems.

The therapeutic psychologist generally does not attempt consciously to influence a client's basic life values. Yet, it would be pure sophistry to presume that in the deeply human relationship of counseling the counselor does not influence the client's values. It is often quite apparent how the counselor feels about marriage and divorce, extramarital sex, existence of God, and similar values without his expressing himself directly on the questions. For the manifold problems in this area the reader is referred to the countertransference discussion in Chapter 8.

Perhaps the transmission of personal values is unavoidable in the close human relationship of psychotherapeutic counseling. Sullivan (295) even went so far as to claim that the therapist's personal values and attitudes toward life influence his professional work as much as his skills and training. If this statement is as valid as it seems on the surface, then there are many implications here for the selection and training of therapeutic psychologists and for referrals to psychological specialists.

However, there are counselors working in therapeutic psychology, or related areas, whose own personal problems are so well worked through in the value area that they are in a strategic position to help clients work through their value problems. Some therapists and counselors have particular interests and skills in working with basic value problems just as they might have interests and abilities in marriage or vocational problems. For counselors with such interests the following sections are included as samples of some counseling problems on value questions.

Our position on the question of transmitting counselor values is that, if the counselor's own problems in the value areas are worked out to his satisfaction, if he does not feel a conscious need to "clear up" or "reform" the client's thinking, and if he is aware of his unconscious needs to do the same, then he could work with clients having basic value problems. If such help, however, involves information or interpretation of dogma, this should be done by a reliable minister on referral or through bibliotherapeutic references. If these conditions still do not allow a comfortable relationship, or they are doing violence to his own belief system, the counselor then must face the issue frankly with the client and refer him to another counselor.

Developing a Philosophy of Life

An assumption of this section is that each individual has a life philosophy, a life style, a set of religious beliefs, even though they are implicit and not consciously known or felt by the person. A companion assumption is that behavior is an expression of his basic philosophy. When the behavior and the basic philosophy of life are at odds, the personality usually is in trouble. A person's philosophy of life usually includes his beliefs about the origin and nature of truth, the purpose and significance of his particular life, the nature of reality, including the possibility of a personal God. Further elements of his philosophy would include the nature and the hierarchy of values he holds, the origin and destiny of man, and the relative functions of reason and faith in the knowing process. His beliefs are sets of assumptions about these philosophical areas.

The process of learning, projecting, and incorporating values into a mature belief system or philosophy of life, as we see it, is diagrammed in Figure 31. The unconscious beliefs in the core system (a) are learned during the growing-up process from values held by parents and others close to the person. These internalized external values (b) are reperceived later as external to the person since they are projections of previously learned values.

During this projection process (c) the core and ego systems modify the projected values so that there is no one-to-one relationship between the core values and the projected values. For example, the person may project his security value system to external objects in such a way that he builds his security around a bank account, a family member, or an ideology such as communism.

The therapeutic task seems to consist of helping the client examine his implicit beliefs, know how he is projecting these core values, and then see how he is perceiving external values. This phase of counseling leads him to reinvest, so to speak, these projected perceptions of external values into his self-system as in (d) of Figure 31. He can see how his unconscious core-system values are influencing his self-system also. Armed with this rationally derived knowledge and insight he can proceed to the development of a trustworthy and unified self-system value structure which is no longer focused on external values. As a result, he should be no longer a blind slave to his core needs and values, nor a victim of an externally imposed value system. He need not, for example, depend as heavily upon the ideas,

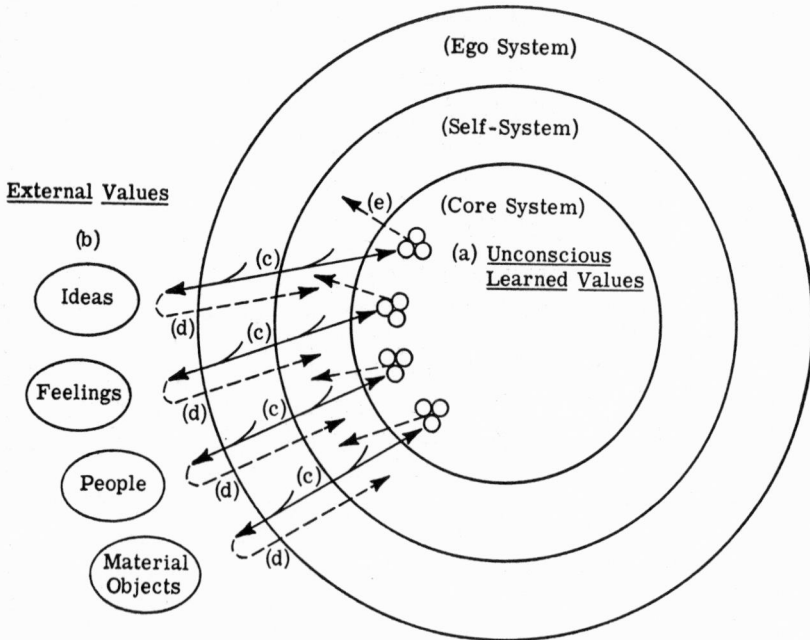

FIG. 31. The Process of Developing a Philosophy of Life.

feelings, people, and objects about him since he now has a cohesive independent value structure uniquely his own.

The role of the counselor in helping the client achieve a mature philosophy of life appears to us as diagrammed in Figure 32. At the beginning of counseling (*a*) the main task is to become aware of and to clarify the client's current value system—to bring it more to the self- and ego-system levels.

The second task is to accomplish the phases associated with the previous discussion of Figure 31 covering the process of developing a mature philosophy. These phases take place during the working-through stage of the total counseling process. Here the client evaluates the effectiveness of his beliefs and explores ways of implementing them. Out of this effort often comes a more mature, expanded, unified, and effective world and life view.

If the preceding steps do not seem effective, it may be that the client needs more specialized information or help which the counselor either cannot provide or declines to give. This condition may necessitate referral (*c*) for information and interpretation through resources such as bibliotherapy or pastoral counseling.

Finally, if all goes well in the process, the client reaches a point (*d*) where he works out a tested personal philosophy adequate for his times and circumstances.

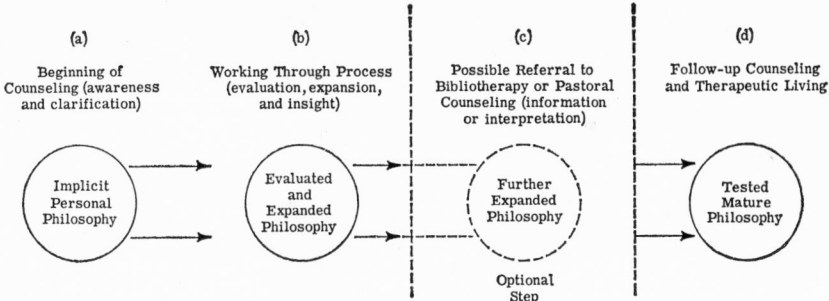

FIG. 32. The Role of Therapeutic Counseling in Value Problems.

Though it is not the purpose of this section to set up a philosophy of life, we consider it to be important to point out some of the problems clients face in developing or changing a philosophy of life. There seems to be evidence of a need for each person to work out a philosophy to fit his times and circumstances. If he does not have such a philosophy, he generally suffers from feelings of drifting, pessimism, loneliness, disillusionment, and possibly even disintegration. Having a satisfying philosophy appears to build self-system strength and to make more possible the goals of mature growth outlined in Chapter 4.

Meaning problems. It is common knowledge that one's personal beliefs about the fundamental questions cited in the introduction to this section are personal and vary widely according to cultural backgrounds and denominational dogma. As recommended earlier, this type of problem is considered from a therapeutic standpoint to be primarily one of instruction and clarification by a specialist in theological matters.

Belief conflicts, however, are at the root of so many client anxieties. Most counselors, for example, are familiar with the typical late-adolescent problem of discovering that one's familial beliefs brought along from childhood suddenly seem to deteriorate into a morass of confusion and disillusionment. An example is the student who comes to college from the sheltered life of a small community with a cohesive theistic world-view and is thrust suddenly into an intellectual atmosphere of naturalism, rationalism, scientism, humanism, and many other "isms" which pose threats to his neat childhood belief structure. This conflict and disillusionment may result in an even more rigid adherence to his childhood beliefs; or the conflicts may lead to a type of agnosticism where he refuses to take a position on the significant questions. As a third possibility he may reject his former beliefs as revealed by violent emotional and educational upheavals. Out of these upheavals often comes an allegiance to a different system offering similar satisfactions, such as political movements, science, or philosophy.

If the client chooses one of the theistic views of life, he bases his search for meaning on faith in God and builds his world-view about the central idea of God's existence. One way of viewing the so-called "human quandary" is man's estrangement from, and later efforts toward, reconciliation to God. He would take the position that man has a transcendental self to be associated ultimately with God. He would feel that man is not alone in a universe which is not indifferent to his fate. He believes he is a creature of God, responsible to God, and with the hope of reconciliation and reunion with God. A significant problem for him is how to be his true self within the tragic framework and disorder of his society.

The Christian view emphasizes man's alienation from God, and man's realization of this estrangement results in much basic anxiety. Klann in a symposium on psychology and Christianity stated the view as follows:

> Man's anxiety is the product of his sinfulness, that state af alienation or contradiction which exists between him and God, between man's will (taken as the expression of his being) and God's will. Because man's being is derived from God, as had been stated before, man in contradiction to God has good reason to feel himself threatened in his existence. It is the consequence of the threat upon his disobedience: "Thou shalt surely die" (Genesis 2:17) (203, pg. 55).

The redemptive and conversion doctrines of Christianity provide the means whereby man is reconciled to God. The interested reader is referred to Klann's summary in *What, Then, Is Man* (203).

Basic to a theistic view of life, then, is the existence of a personal God. Some clinicians, such as the Viennese neurologist Viktor Frankl, postulate a strong need for God, similar to the biologically-based needs of hunger and thirst (108). He postulates this need because of man's striving to attach meaning to his life. Frankl asserts that the human personality (*Das Geistige*) has laws which go beyond psychological laws and are concerned with man's ideals and responsible behaviors. He calls the methods of helping man to become more aware of his ideals and to focus on the awareness of his responsibilities "logotherapy." This is a form of therapy devoted to discovering the central purpose and meaning of life. The "existential analysis" methods of logotherapy do not determine which values the client will choose; but they impress upon him the fact that he must make a choice. The methods of logotherapy are claimed to be especially suitable for conditions which an individual must accept, such as invalidism and suffering.

Mowrer[1] is representative of a slowly expanding group of psychologists who are becoming alarmed about the notion (spreading rapidly during the past four decades) that neuroses and psychoses are fundamentally illnesses. The sickness concept of emotional disorders, and troubles of normal persons also, implies that the states of irresponsibility, narcissism, dependency, and extreme aggression, for example, are not one's own fault. The sickness

---

[1] O. H. Mowrer, *Sin, The Lesser of Two Evils.* Unpublished manuscript.

view indicates that the person can hardly be "blamed" for his condition. He can place the blame conveniently on parental behaviors, environmental deprivation, or other factors outside of his control or personal responsibility. Mowrer indicates that we need to examine this sickness concept of emotional problems very carefully, even to the point of exploring the theological doctrine of sin as an explanatory concept for personality disorder. Emotional disorder, then, according to this latter view, is a type of moral problem emphasizing *personal responsibility* for behavior.

Mowrer proffers the idea that perhaps clergymen also are becoming too bedazzled by the sickness concept of personality disorder and with psychoanalytic explanations of human problems. At this writing we are not prepared to comment on this trend except to say that this moral construction of the human predicament bears serious study and close watching during the next few years.

A second major philosophical choice, or focus of belief is that position broadly described as humanism. The basic value of this view is man's own existence. Two fundamental postulates are that man is alone in a morally neutral universe and that man is his own moral referent. His troubles are believed to be of his own making. He is limited in his achievements only by his nature. Man's quandary is solved within himself by a process of reason and the methods of self-discovery involved in psychotherapeutic methods such as psychoanalysis. There is a strong belief in man's powers of growth and positive motivation to solve his own and society's problems. Conditions like death, for example, must be accepted as human fact with no necessary implications for further life.

Erich Fromm is selected as an example of an "existential humanist" who attempts to bridge the chasm between these divergent views. The humanist position has its roots in the philosophical upheavals which took place during the enlightenment period of the seventeenth century. Fromm's view of the human problem, which we trust is fair and typical of his ideas, is summarized in the following excerpts:

> Humanistic religion . . . is centered around man and his strength. Man must develop his power of reason in order to understand himself, his relationship to his fellow men and his position in the universe. He must recognize the truth, both with regard to his limitations and his potentialities. He must develop his powers of love for others as well as for himself and experience the solidarity of all living beings. He must have principles and norms to guide him in this aim. Religious experience in this kind of religion is the experience of oneness with the All, based on one's relatedness to the world as it is grasped with thought and with love. Man's aim in humanistic religion is to achieve the greatest strength, not the greatest powerlessness; virtue is self-realization, not obedience. Faith is certainty of conviction based on one's experience of thought and feeling, not assent to propositions on credit of the proposer. The prevailing mood is that of joy, while the prevailing mood in authoritarian religion is that of sorrow and guilt.

> Inasmuch as humanistic religions are theistic, God is a symbol of *man's own powers* which he tries to realize in his life, and is not a symbol of force and domination, having *power over man* (Italics ours) (117, pg. 37).

Fromm indicates in another source that:

> There is only one solution to his problem: to face the truth, to acknowledge his fundamental aloneness and solitude in a universe indifferent to his fate, to recognize that there is no power transcending him which can solve his problems for him. . . . If he faces the truth without panic he will recognize that there is no meaning to life except the meaning man gives his life by the unfolding of his powers, by living productively (115, pp. 44–45).

An essential point in the humanistic position is that man lives in a confused human situation. He must face up to the incongruities in this human situation through his own powers. He must discover his own values within himself and lean heavily on consensus and cultural norms. His possibilities and troubles are largely of his own making.

There are many individuals who are trying to construct a "bridge" between these two basic views of man's situation in this universe. Clients often express anxieties about such problems, and it behooves the therapeutic psychologist to be aware of the basic philosophical assumptions underlying various belief systems. The counselor can aid the client to see discrepancies and contradictions in his system and can help him to a more clear definition of his life values. Lifton, for example, applies three criteria of counselor effectiveness in helping clients to more clear ideas in the area of religious belief:

> (1) The client's feelings of achieving a satisfactory solution to his problem; (2) the counselor's feeling that the client is doing what the counselor believes is most appropriate; and (3) the degree to which the client's solution coincides with the approved answer in terms of mores of his society (185, pg. 367).

We agree most closely with criterion one. There is much potential danger in the counselor projecting too many of his own values into the discussion as in criterion two. Criterion three in Lifton's list again is primarily the client's own concern, provided the implications of his religious beliefs do not threaten the welfare of others. The religious counselor probably would feel obliged to take a view different from these criteria because of his particular sectarian commitments.

Existentialist views are having an increasing influence on American counseling and psychotherapy. These views, imported from Europe, grew rather spontaneously and simultaneously in several centers. Existential views do not constitute a new school or new set of theories, but rather a fresh way of looking at human existence. The two basic problems in understanding the Existential movement are the variety of ideas, some contradictory, which have come under its semantic cloak, and the difficulties in finding English language for the experiences and concepts developed within the existential framework.

Essentially, the existential approach seeks to avoid the usual subject-object approaches of studying human behavior wherein man is broken into segmental "essences" by looking beneath these characteristics (May, 197a). It is an effort to understand the essential nature of a particular man in addition to the usual objective approaches of science. In psychotherapy, for example, attempts are made to help the client experience his essential being or humanness. Counseling and psychotherapy experiences are especially appropriate to this task because one finds this essential being in periods of crisis and distress which often characterize clients in the course of a therapeutic relationship. In fact, Existentialism is a view of man as being in a perpetual process of becoming through continuous crisis.

Since Existentialism is not a philosophy or a way of life with palpable goals and identifiable axioms, but an effort to grasp reality, the reader is enjoined to investigate some of the original sources through writings of Kierkegaard, Jaspers, Heidegger, Tillich, Binswanger, and Buber, for example. May (198) has written a summary and edited a collection of papers on Existentialism and therapy which will serve the reader as an introduction.

The Counselor's and Therapist's Role in Belief Problems. What can the counselor, *as a counselor,* do with client questions of religious belief? First, he can recognize the significance of religious sentiments and beliefs in personality development in general and in the life of this particular client. Secondly, the counselor should know how to handle his own religious problems which are precipitated by the client's problems. He should work them through to the point where he does not project them and where they do not interfere with an optimal relationship. Also, he should know his own faith well enough so that he can be accepting without jeopardizing his own faith through the empathy process. Thirdly, he can regard problems of religious belief in much the same manner as he would treat any other affect-laden problem concerning marriage, job, children, or sex.

The counselor should have certain knowledge about the client, such as the origin of his beliefs. Were they derived from Sunday school, movies, or family instruction? It would be well to note the client's social background, such as parental beliefs and church background, and their effects on his religious beliefs and practice. Finally, if the counselor finds his techniques and relationship are not meeting the client's needs, then something else, in the form of religious counseling by a specialist, may be needed after a thorough discussion of relevant philosophical viewpoints.

Problems of Relatedness

To feel at home in the universe, to be valued as a person, and to feel close to someone are deep personal needs. Counselors are impressed by this overpowering need for relatedness, or more broadly speaking—love. The problems of giving and receiving love have been discussed at length elsewhere in this volume. The purpose of including the topic at this juncture, however, is to consider the gyroscopic effect of relatedness and love on a human life.

One of the appeals of membership in and identification with broad social, political, and religious movements is the feeling of close belonging and of being important to a significant cause. One's group affiliations, then, play a significant part in developing feelings of relatedness. It should be stressed that the relatedness must involve a high degree of intimacy—close friendships, comradeship, work organization, or marriage. Of these, marriage provides opportunity for the greatest satisfaction of the relatedness need because in marriage there is at least one other person who cares deeply about one's self.

Work provides further outlets for such feelings; but work is a paradox in several respects. Though work offers relatedness satisfactions, it often gives the individual the feeling that he is being manipulated and of being regarded as a "marketable product." The specter of the "company man," for example, frightens many thoughtful people.

A second problem in connection with work relatedness is the common picture of the business executive or professional man who derives most of the satisfaction for his feelings of relatedness in his work. Frequently, he obtains little satisfaction from, or contributes little of himself to, the familial situation. Counselors and therapists often observe the phenomenon of the "vicious circle" of the individual gaining decreasing satisfactions from family life and increasing his searches for satisfaction from work. This cycle can lead to other signs of personality deterioration such as alcoholism or infidelity. Shoben (276) has analyzed the problem neatly in the less severe cases where the client's feelings of self-worth are sought increasingly in his occupational pursuits or in tangential social or sexual activities.

Many men and women feel they must choose between their families and their work. The balance of these two features in a person's life is again a personal affair not to be dictated by the counselor. There seems to be, however, an optimally proportionate emphasis upon work and home which leads to maximum satisfaction and productivity for all concerned. Freud is reputed to have answered the query on what a person must do to be mature with the reply, *"Lieben und arbeiten."* The mature, well-functioning person in our society must be able to both love and work in the proper balance.

The main therapeutic implication here is that often client symptoms appear in the form of a basic management problem—such as finding the optimal balance among work, family, play, and civic participation. Such clients, furthermore, tend not to find their need satisfactions for relatedness and self-worth in the activities they currently employ. The counselor may be requested by the client to help him find some person or group to which he might relate. This bid needs to be assessed and interpreted in light of possible dependency reinforcement, and the extent to which the counselor feels he can afford to be maneuvered into the role of an "agent" for the client. The therapist very definitely can help the client to understand his deep-seated needs for security and self-worth which might be attainable through a more satisfying human relationship.

There are conditions where the counselor may need to help the client accept the limitations of his current situation through insight methods and support. Examples of such situations would be the low probability of marriage for a chronic invalid or the loneliness felt by new widows and divorcees where such individuals may need to develop inner resources to cope with the lack of intimate relationships. Sometimes such clients can find compensations through small group relationships in church, school, or community.

Closely related to the relatedness-loneliness problem is that of depersonalization. We are not speaking so much of the type of detachment or splitting of affect and cognition which occurs in the psychotic as much as the normal person's feelings of being an "object" to be manipulated, bought and sold, traded, seduced, or used. Fromm (116) warns of the damage which may result in personalities when they are led to feel like a "thing," a marketable commodity, rather than a person.

The counselor can help such clients through helping them to establish points of relatedness to people. The principal vehicle is the therapeutic relationship where the client can see his defenses more clearly, especially those which alienate him from other people. He will be less likely also to regard other people as "things" to be manipulated, used, or exploited when he discovers the defensive distortions in his own personality.

Meeting Life Crises

Medical and pastoral counselors generally confront clients in severe life crises more than psychological counselors. There are occasions, however, where working through problems associated with losing a job, death, divorce, disability, or financial disaster are brought to the psychologist for the purpose of working through the feelings associated with the crisis. Kunkel (178) has developed a point of view on handling real or projected crises which seems to be valuable for the therapeutic psychologist.

Often the crisis is due to a misperception of a situation, although the experience of anxiety or dread from the projected problem can be just as intense as the more objective kinds of crises. An example is the individual who had taken an examination for entry into a much-coveted position. A clerk made a remark to the candidate which was interpreted by the man that he had failed. He brooded at length and finally moved into a mild depression and headaches for the next three days prior to receiving word of his standing. He was even blaming his God for letting him down. He heard that he passed the examination and that he would very likely be appointed in the near future. The clerk's remark was then reperceived as being a warning that passing the examination did not necessarily mean employment in the desired position. The emotional effect, however, persisted for several days.

Kunkel's thesis is that people learn to face large crises later in life by a process of meeting minor life crises from early childhood on through development. He sees human life as one "unending chain of crises" (178, pg. 150). Old behavior patterns are disrupted and discarded for the new patterns required by the crises. The feelings of creativity and confidence which come out of a crisis solution constitute, according to Kunkel, an important part of personality growth. He feels that the client's experience of desperation and helplessness is the prelude to critical examination and transformation of his defenses. Suffering is regarded as a facilitative force in the growth process.

Crises require judgments. The process of making judgments which propel the person forward in his mastery of life draws upon many elements of personality and demands a high level of functioning. Each life crisis, according to Kunkel, has rich potentiality for building spiritual strength in the mature personality. Therefore, we feel that counseling on matters of life crises is within the province and skills of the therapeutic psychologist.

What can be said about the person with feelings of inadequacy, failure, and incapacity to meet crises? If this problem is construed as being in the realm of therapeutic psychology, then surely more must be considered than the aforementioned feelings. The whole problem of the client's life style, creative potential, life philosophy, and religious outlook must be considered. In addition, the therapeutic psychologist must allow the client to explore his deeper feelings and relationships to parents in early life experiences. This is done to throw further light on why he lacks the personal resources to meet life crises. Through counseling, clients may obtain insight into their defense mechanisms and their problems of developing spiritual strength for meeting life crises. An example is the case where a client projected certain expectations of the help provided by his mother to God. When the crisis came and mother was not nearby to nurse his hurts, he blamed God who had become equated psychologically with mother. He began to see that his inadequacies in meeting life demands and crises were not failures of his God, but of his own immaturity and fear of psychological and spiritual creativity. The therapeutic psychologist, in short, utilizes the life crisis problem to help the client gain insight and to make progress along the road to maturity.

A critical factor in achieving these objectives, as indicated so many times in this volume, is the therapeutic relationship itself. The opportunity to face his feelings of doubt, inadequacy, insecurity, and defeat in the presence of a warm and accepting counselor is what seems to us to be the primary factor in drawing from the client new powers to meet life's challenges. This phenomenon of discovering either within or without his person, this feeling of confidence and creative power is what Kunkel has called the ". . . miraculous center of every constructive crisis" (178, pg. 163). The alternatives to this creative experience are continued feelings of discouragement, defeat, and emptiness, often leading to personality deterioration.

Moral Problems

Moral problems are related to religious concerns in that formal religions incorporate an ethical and moral code and use the weight of religious authority to enforce the code. Moral problems, defined broadly as behavior contradictory to the established mores of the social order, can exist apart from problems of religious belief. The therapeutic psychologist's principal concern in the moral area is over the feeling of guilt associated with immoral behavior and the defensive function which immoral behavior performs for the personality. The psychologist is concerned also about the enhancing or damaging effects of moral and immoral behavior on clients and others affected by their behavior.

As background for the discussion of therapeutic counseling on moral problems, some conceptions of morality are described briefly. One viewpoint stresses the dual and simultaneous presence of the "good" and the "bad" in man. For example, he is said to be sinful and destructive, yet potentially virtuous and loving too. The problem then becomes how to help the individual seek victory of the "good" over the "evil." This view may presuppose either an inherent knowledge of good and evil or a learned series of attitudes and behaviors. A contrary view is held also that "good" and "bad," used as nouns, are social artifacts and that man is neither by nature. When used as adjectives, they imply an arbitrary standard to be meaningful.

The view that man is by nature a sinful being (hence, by definition bad and reprehensible) is commonly held by the Hebraic-Christian world. This sinful-nature conception of man's moral condition is accompanied by a belief that there is potential good in man expressed in such terms as man's capacity to be kind, loving, conscientious, and to hold similar virtues. The "sinful nature" and "total depravity" concepts refer to man's condition from God's viewpoint. From a human standpoint classical Judaism and Christianity both hold that man has great potential for either goodness or evil.

Certainly not all persons in the Hebraic-Christian moral framework subscribe strictly to this fundamental position; however, it is representative of the majority. To some extent, this view of innate evil is common to the Freudian group also. The main implication here is that this innate evil conception of moral behavior leads to the attitude that human nature cannot be trusted, must be restrained by external forces, or transformed by a mystical process.

That man has basically a heredity of socially constructive forces in his nature is a third view of the moral nature of man. This is a faith in the basic "goodness" of man. The main implication is that man's principal moral problem is to create conditions where the "good" can be brought out and the "bad" learnings extinguished.

Horney holds a growth and personal responsibility view of morality described briefly as follows:

> . . . the problem of morality is again different when we believe that inherent in man are evolutionary constructive forces, which urge him to realize his given potentialities. This belief does not mean that man is essentially good—which would presuppose a given knowledge of what is good or bad. It means that man, by his very nature and of his own accord, strives toward self-realization, and that his set of values evolves from such striving. Apparently he cannot, for example, develop his full human potentialities unless he is truthful to himself; unless he is active and productive; unless he relates himself to others in the spirit of mutuality. Apparently he cannot grow if he . . . consistently attributes all his own shortcomings to the deficiencies of others. He can grow, in the true sense, only if he assumes responsibility for himself (147, pp. 14–15).

Kirkendall presents the hypothesis that immoral behavior is that which destroys self-respect and heightens difficulties in interpersonal relationships:

> The obvious concern of students in classes in marriage and family life for values and principles of moral living has led me to the formulation of a concept useful in making decisions on right and wrong. The concept is that moral decision and conduct are those which result in improving the capacity of people to work together with trust and understanding. The outreach of individuals and groups toward others should be constantly furthered, and individual self-respect should be heightened by moral living. Immoral or wrong conduct is that which creates distrust and suspicion, produces withdrawal, and a decline in self-respect (169, pg. 5).

We are indebted to Hugh Bell for many illustrations in this discussion on moral behavior and counseling (25). Bell illustrates the variety of forms through which moral problems are brought to the psychological counselor. The most common problems are sexual ones which take the form of anxieties about promiscuity, homosexuality, infidelity, masturbation, and exhibitionism. A second type concerns accuracy of reporting which involves occasional dishonesty and lying all the way to gross and habitual deception and cheating.

Disturbing the property and personal rights of others is another area of morals which involves the occasional client. Disturbing others' rights often creates guilt and anxiety when the acts are committed impulsively or under the influence of a narcotic.

There is another category of moral behavior surrounding the classification of psychopathic or inadequate personality. This group includes the delinquents, alcoholics, vagrants, truants, and drug addicts. Their acts of hostility though directed against themselves, sometimes, are mainly expressed against others. Their feelings, rather than their acts, however, are the principal concern of the therapeutic psychologists.

Most of the problems of the psychopath involve some legal action against him. In this discussion we will not cover the legal, moralistic, or disciplinary implications of these behaviors, but will attempt to suggest therapeutic roles and techniques for dealing with the feelings associated with problems which are judged by the client or society to be moral problems. The therapeutic psychologist is not concerned, then, with the concept of the "goodness"-"badness" dichotomy so commonly thrust on human behavior. He is interested primarily in a rehabilitative approach, although he is interested also in the diagnostic problem of the meaning which the immoral behavior has for the client and what some of the causes leading to this behavior might be. The therapeutic psychologist is interested also in the ethical problem of protecting the client and others who might be influenced by his behavior.

The problem of guilt. A striking characteristic of a client coming for help on a moral problem is the feeling described as guilt. The term guilt has two meanings in the present discussion. The first is a broad pervasive feeling of "wrongness." The client often feels a vague sense of "something is wrong with me; I'm not really doing what I should be doing; I should be something better." This feeling is closely related to feelings of inadequacy and fears of failure. Even persons successful by the usual social standards often have such feelings which seem to come from early experiences and learned ways of handling hostile and dependent feelings, especially toward parents. The child experiences, very early, strong love and hostility feelings toward parents. Such ambivalent feelings may be distorted and experienced later as guilt. It seems that this type of normal guilt is an intimate condition of human life and may even perform protective functions for the individual and his society. Therefore, it may not necessarily be a personal liability.

A second type of guilt feeling is that experienced as an acute emotional reaction to a specific behavior. For example, breaking rules against lying, cheating an associate, or stealing property may arouse strong subjective feelings of having done something reprehensible which can be described as guilt. One is very much aware of having broken a social rule, a religious injunction, or a moral "law." These feelings seem to be characteristic of most cultures in the forms of awareness that one is being watched and will be held accountable for his acts. Fromm summarizes the origin and consequences of the preceding type of guilt feeling as follows:

> The problem of guilt plays no less a role in psychoanalytic procedure than it does in religion. Sometimes it is presented by the patient as one of his main symptoms. He feels guilty for not loving his parents as he should, for failing to do his work satisfactorily, for having hurt somebody's feelings. The feeling of guilt has overpowered some patients' minds and they react with a sense of inferiority, of depravity, and often with a conscious or unconscious desire for punishment. It is usually not difficult to discover that this all-pervasive guilt reaction stems from an authoritarian orientation. They would give a more correct expression to their feeling if instead of saying that they feel guilty they said that they are afraid—afraid of punishment, or more often, of not being loved any more by those authorities whom they have disobeyed. In the analytic process such a patient will slowly recognize that behind his authoritarian sense of guilt is another feeling of guilt which stems from his own voice, from his conscience in the humanistic sense. Assume that a patient feels guilty for leading a promiscuous life. The first step in analyzing this guilt feeling will be to discover that he really feels afraid of being found out and criticized by his parents, by his wife, by public opinion, by the church—briefly, by anyone who represents authority to him. Only then will he be able to recognize that behind this authoritarian feeling of guilt is another feeling. He will recognize that his "love" affairs are in reality expressions of his fear of love, of his inability to love anyone, to commit himself to any close and responsible relationship. He will recognize that his sin is against himself, the sin of letting his power to love go to waste (117, pp. 90–91).

It seems to us that Fromm, in the quotation, is pointing out the distinction between normal and neurotic guilt which is developed later in this section.

Meehl and his symposium coworkers presented a distinction between valid and displaced guilt. Valid guilt is claimed to be present when man realizes that his relationship with God is not proper. His feeling is manifested by an awareness of anxiety, or even dread. The symposium described valid guilt as follows:

> . . . we have been suggesting that man's objective sinful and alienated relation to God, with its attendant effects upon his relation to his fellows, gives rise to a psychological state of valid guilt (203, pg. 221).

Displaced guilt, however, is that feeling of guilt which is detached from the original idea (the alienation phenomenon described above) and appears in the individual's awareness as a different idea such as remorse over some small act or a haunting fear that he has done something reprehensible like injuring someone with his automobile.

Conscience. There is considerable difference of opinion concerning the validity and origin of the concept "conscience." In common usage, the term "conscience" connotes three quite different things: (1) involuntary submission to external authorities with the concomitant fear of discovery and punishment; (2) condemnatory self-accusations; and (3) discontent with self in a constructive sense (148).

The classical religious conception of conscience from the western Christian point of view is that man is born with a rudimentary, though very imperfect, knowledge of right and wrong. This rudimentary conscience is sharpened through religious training by means of the following rationale: God created man with a certain nature; man is obligated to live according to that nature; God revealed how he wants man to behave; if man disobeys, he has made an offense against God and, hence, is estranged from God. The result is that he feels guilty; this feeling of guilt creates a need for God's forgiveness and ultimately brings him back to God. This is an oversimplification, of course, but it points out the basic rationale for the development of conscience and guilt feelings from a religious point of view.

The Freudian view of the superego development, in contrast, is typical of the psychological viewpoints on conscience. It is considered a learned concept arising largely out of internalization, or "introjection," as Freud called it, of parental prohibitions, threats, and values. These internalized values are picked up through the process of incidental learning during early childhood. Punishments rather than rewards seem to be the decisive determinants. The child learns to "hear" the parental voice of authority whenever he comes against similar circumstances, and he suffers painful feelings when he transgresses.

In the Freudian framework, personality problems are caused, to a great extent, by a severe superego overwhelming the ego and forcing it to repress the biologically based primitive impulses of the id. Mowrer (216) feels that a more correct view of the Freudian model would be that disturbances in personality are caused by the id and the ego joining forces against the superego. The latter is a type of guilt theory where the ego functions are immature, and, under the influence of the id, have done things of which the superego disapproves. In this sense, the person with a diminutive superego and an immature ego would tend toward antisocial, criminal acts; whereas, the person with the overdeveloped superego would lead to oversocialization and rigidity which would place severe demands on the ego and restraint on the id. According to Mowrer (216), a dual task of the counselor is to help the client develop a stronger ego that is able to escape control by the id and to develop a working relationship with the superego.

The preceding elaboration of Freudian superego or conscience theory, and its implications for counseling and psychotherapy, is an oversimplification of a very complex metaphorical system. We sketched it here because it is such a commonly held point of view in therapeutic psychology. We prefer to think of conscience and guilt in terms of our own self-system theory which follows.

If the child grows up feeling that this conscience is somehow absolute and synonymous with divine or cosmic law, the child may go through life trying to live up to these expectations, justifying his actions, and forever feeling guilty that he should be doing something he isn't doing or not doing something he is doing. The psychological viewpoint (largely psychoanalytic in origin) is that the client must be helped to recognize the relativity of value systems and must be helped to develop his own frame of value reference suited to his times, unique circumstances, and needs. This is the aforementioned basic humanistic view which sees man as his own moral referent.

Allport (3) asserts that the preceding explanation helps to account for childhood conscience; but it does not explain the adult conscience adequately. He postulates a shift from *ad hoc* habits of obedience built up through conditioning and punishments to broader permeation of the personality (in our model—the self-system). The shift is from fear of punishment to feelings of obligation. In other words, the person has incorporated his former learnings into a value structure in the self-system. He changes his view from must to ought and from compulsion to obligation. He behaves, then, more in keeping with his self-system image.

Normal or healthy guilt, in the mature adult, becomes a feeling of having violated the integrity of the self-system, a feeling of self-hostility for not achieving the ideal of the self-image. Thus, a more voluntary and seemingly purposeful ethical act is substituted for the conditioned habit and fear of punishment. The habit of obedience in the adult, according to Allport, gives way to self-guidance based upon a ". . . broad schemata of values that confer direction upon conduct." (3, pg. 73) The child, in developing this mature schemata of values, sees that restraint and ideals have purposes other than merely pleasing one's parents. Horney emphasizes this approach to normal guilt or the mature conscience, too, in her term "constructive discontent with self" (147).

We believe that the preceding theory of conscience results in more permanence and flexibility than the views stressing internalization of parental authority or the theories of genetic origins. We feel, also, that conscience can be a positive creative force in interpersonal relationships, as well as an inhibiting, guilt-provoking force. According to May's (200) view of conscience, learnings from past experience become blended with present experiences so that one's ethical sensitivity is sharpened and one's level of insight is deepened. The healthy conscience then becomes a device for tapping one's enlarged experience and for developing mature ego and self-systems.

In Figure 33, the writers present their views on the development of a mature conscience beginning with the rudimentary awareness of social values resulting from demands and punishments of parents. As the child grows, parental demands become internalized into feelings of "rightness" and "wrongness." Conditioning plays a significant part here also, since rewards and punishments are important. As the child grows into adolescence, he acquires a self-picture as a moral person, with the mores a part

DEVELOPMENT OF A MATURE CONSCIENCE

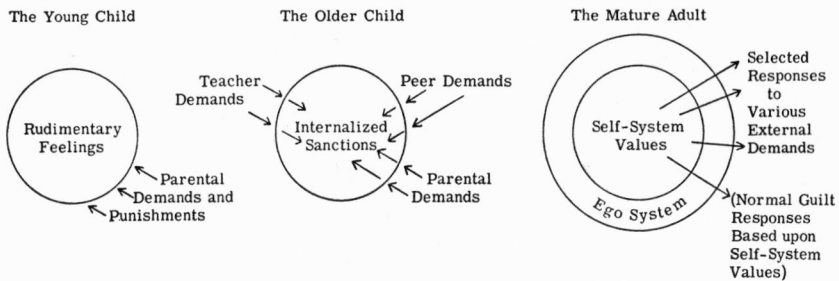

FIG. 33.

of his basic value system. This value system is based upon earlier learned values, a growing self-awareness, and a rationally determined view of the mores. As a mature adult he makes more selective and rational responses to environmental demands according to his growing self-regarding attitudes. He still feels guilt, but it is *normal* guilt, which helps him to reduce the gap between healthy self-values and inappropriate behavior.

Regardless of the position taken on the nature and origin of conscience, psychologists tend to agree that the phenomenon of conscience is a profound factor in the control of impulsive behavior and opportunism. They believe that it has a significant long-range influence on goals and values also. A key therapeutic implication here is that one of the roles of counseling is facilitating the transformation of the blind, impulsive, infantile conscience into a mature value structure in the self-system. A second implication is the possibility of helping the client whose childhood conscience is overly severe or fixated at a childhood level. The counselor may help to modify the compulsive demands and consequent neurotic guilt feelings of such conscience while the mature value system is developing.

Therapeutic Handling of Guilt and Conscience Problems

The handling of guilt in therapy is a most critical problem. A summary of methods for dealing with this significant problem in the therapeutic interview follows.[2]

The counselor's first step is to release his client's tensions within a relationship characterized by acceptance on the counselor's part. The nonjudgmental attitude of the counselor is especially important to encourage free expression of guilt feelings. When the working-through phase of the process is reached, the client can be helped to see and understand the origins of his guilt and conscience problems.

---

[2] The ideas expressed here represent a compilation of ideas, many of which come from Dr. Rollo May from a workshop with the Los Angeles Society of Clinical Psychologists in Private Practice, Los Angeles, March 6 & 7, 1959. Many of these ideas are also to be found in Chapter II of *Existence* (198).

Guilt is best understood if a differentiation is made between normal and neurotic guilt. Normal guilt is universal and is of three basic types: guilt against one's self for not fulfilling one's potentialities; guilt against one's fellow man for not meeting his needs; and guilt against nature or God and a feeling of separateness or alienation therefrom. Neurotic guilt is defined as unaccepted and repressed normal guilt. Therapy, therefore, consists of assisting the client to accept and face his neurotic guilt and to turn it into normal guilt. This is in sharp contrast with the view that therapy should water down, expunge, or neutralize guilt entirely. The following steps are suggested for changing neurotic to normal guilt. The counselor should:

(1) Help the client to *admit* what he has done to feel guilty.

(2) Help him to face the *motives* underlying his guilt feelings, especially those of destruction and hatred.

(3) Cut through the *rationalizations*. This implies taking responsibility for what one does.

(4) Transform neurotic (unfaced, repressed) guilt to normal guilt by assisting the client to see that it can be tolerated and constructive. When the client is able to experience normal guilt, he can utilize the gap between his self-image and what he actually is for further growth.

Traumatic incidents can be desensitized so that the intense suffering associated with neurotic guilt can be minimized and understood. Neurotic suffering, for example, can be understood as a kind of atonement which the severe conscience is exacting for real or imagined misdeeds. Suffering from normal guilt can be used as a springboard to extensive insight as indicated in the earlier discussion on crises.

The client can be helped to understand the defenses he has used to handle his guilt feelings. Sometimes this takes the form of physical symptoms and requires the collaboration of a physician. Often, the defense takes the form of projection where others are blamed for the very behaviors for which the client feels guilty. This development comes later in the working-through process, however, since it presupposes considerable ego strength to tolerate the loss of defensive strength. Another illustrative projective mechanism is that of the overdeveloped conscience which expresses itself in a paranoid delusion. This type of client projects his guilt feelings to others whom he accuses of criticizing or blaming him. This projection may involve the belief that his deity is constantly condemning and punishing him also.

A related defense often seen in guilt cases is the pharisaically self-righteous client who defends his guilt feelings stoutly by means of a superior demeanor and condemnation of others.

Counseling or therapy on guilt might involve referral. If the traditional rituals and methods of formal religious experiences are meaningful and acceptable to the client, perhaps referral to a church group or pastoral counselor would assist in both the emergency reduction and in the long-term resolution of his guilt feelings. This is especially true for clients who are preoccupied with religiously oriented perceptions of their own sinfulness in cases of sex conduct or feelings of "letting someone down," for example.

When it comes to the action phase of the process, the counselor frequently is in a dilemma. If the client has acquired some insight, but his ego system is still quite weak, he may not follow through with responsible behavior. Should the therapist assume a very authoritarian role and use shock techniques to assist the client to feel personally responsible for his behavior? An example is the case of a married man with family dating a young girl. Should the counselor depend upon the relationship and the client's maturation potential to develop a conventional solution to the problem? The answers would depend greatly on the counselor's basic orientation to therapy as well as the degree of confidence he feels in his own value system. We feel that with some types of clients, direct methods can often effect drastic behavior changes. The limitations, however, are that without deep insight the changes will be temporary at best. In any case, it is very important for the counselor to assist the client to feel a sense of decision and responsibility for his own behavior. Therapy consists of assisting the client to make a decision even if it turns out to be a wrong decision.

The over-all goal of counseling on moral problems is to help the client to develop greater feelings of responsibility to his deeper self, especially if his problem is one of too little anxiety about his behavior. The counselor also may suggest that the client, having too much neurotic anxiety about his moral behavior, develop a more stable and mature value structure which consequently can lead to a greater degree of internal direction for his behavior. A positive self-regard appears to us to be the most dependable route to moral behavior.

As the client learns to trust his innermost feelings about himself, he learns that such trust will help him to make the more wise decisions. As he learns to listen to *all* these feelings, both positive and negative, his internal "computing machine" will be found to be trustworthy for making decisions which will be beneficial not only to society but to himself as well.

SUMMARY

In the science and profession of psychology keen interest is being exhibited in problems of value. This chapter included some of the implications of value problems, such as developing an effective philosophy of life and working out feelings associated with moral problems. The therapeutic psychologist has a role to perform in each of these areas which is different from, but overlapping with, that of the pastoral counselor. The pastoral counselor has a unique role; yet, in many ways, it is similar to that of the therapeutic psychologist. A principal task of the therapeutic psychologist is helping the client to transform neurotic guilt into normal guilt.

16.

Human Relations Counseling in Industry and Government

Psychologists have traditionally contributed to management training with personnel selection and placement techniques, job analyses, fatigue studies, and market research. There have been trends, since World War II, toward assisting executives to become more sensitive to the requirements of their subordinates and to become more aware of their own limitations and personality needs.[1]

Sensitivity training for managers is a program designed to help executives develop counseling skills in their professional human relations. Training is carried out in a small group of from ten to fifteen members, each group having an experienced trainer with a background in the various social sciences and applied human relations. These small groups are designed to encourage a high level of individual involvement and participation. In addition to small weekly group meetings, which last approximately an hour, general sessions, offering a variety of theoretical experiences, are provided. Sensitivity training attempts to provide opportunities for each participant to: (1) learn more about himself and his impact on others; (2) understand his own feelings and how they affect his behavior toward others; (3) become more sensitive to the ways people communicate with each other; (4) learn active listening for subtle meanings and for feelings; (5) learn how people affect groups and groups affect people; (6) learn how to function more effectively in face-to-face situations; and, (7) learn how to help groups function more effectively.

Essentially, therefore, sensitivity training attempts to teach management personnel in industry some of the basic skills and understanding described in this volume. The purpose of this chapter is to describe how the principles

---

[1] An example of such an approach for executives is called "Sensitivity Training," conducted by the Institute of Industrial Relations, University of California at Los Angeles.

and techniques of this book can be utilized by men and women in responsible leadership positions of business, industrial, governmental, and civic organizations. There are a number of barriers, however, which executives and supervisors, in business and government, must overcome in order to counsel subordinates effectively. In this chapter some of these problems and the modifications of technique required to deal with them are described.

HUMAN RELATIONS COUNSELING[2]

The relationship techniques, described in Chapter 7, are of fundamental importance to the supervisor-counselor. Thomas Gordon of the Institute of Industrial Relations at UCLA has suggested that a modified approach to these techniques be utilized by the supervisor-counselor, since his position is as much one of being a "coach" to his workers as it is of being a "counselor." This chapter covers the nature of this "coaching and counseling interview." The terms "supervisor" and "manager" will be used interchangeably and in most instances substituted for the term "counselor," because of the broader connotations implied in the managerial function.

TWO PSYCHOLOGICAL PROBLEMS FOR THE SUPERVISOR

The supervisor or executive who tries seriously to utilize counseling in a business or industrial organization eventually runs into two basic problems —*dependence* and *evaluation*. Although there are no clear-cut answers to these problems, a brief look at them may help supervisors begin to think about how they will face them on the job.

Dependence

The dependency problems arising out of the supervisor-subordinate relationship in industry have been described by Douglas McGregor[3] as follows:

> The outstanding characteristic of the relationship between the subordinate and his superiors is his dependence upon them for the satisfaction of his needs. Industry in our civilization is organized along authoritative lines. In a fundamental and pervasive sense, the subordinate is dependent upon his superiors for his job, for the continuity of his employment, for promotion with its accompanying satisfactions in the form of increased

---

[2] The authors are indebted to Dr. Thomas Gordon, a training colleague of one of the writers in the Institute of Industrial Relations, for the major portion of this chapter.

[3] Douglas McGregor, "Conditions of Effective Leadership in the Industrial Organization," in S. D. Hoslett, *Human Factors in Management* New York: Harper, 1946, pp, 40–41.

pay, responsibility, and prestige and for a host of other personal and social satisfactions to be obtained in the work situation. . . .

. . . Psychologically the dependence of the subordinate upon his superiors is a fact of extraordinary significance, in part because of its emotional similarity to the dependence characteristic of another earlier relationship: that between the child and his parents. The similarity is more than an analogy. The adult subordinate's dependence upon his superiors actually reawakens certain emotions and attitudes which were part of his childhood relationship with his parents, and which apparently have long since been outgrown. The adult is usually unaware of the similarity because most of this complex of childhood has been repressed. Although the emotions influence his behavior, they are not accessible to consciousness under ordinary circumstances.

What this dependency characteristic means for the counseling situation is that dependent people tend to want others to take responsibility for solving their problems. Thus, the supervisor who attempts to utilize counseling as a managerial tool often will find it difficult to help subordinates learn to solve their own problems and to become motivated for self-directed development. This will be especially true when the supervisor is attempting counseling for the first time. His subordinates will find it difficult to change, especially if they have been in the habit of relying heavily on him as their supervisor.

At first, the supervisor must expect some employees to ask him frequently what *he* would do, to toss problems in *his* lap rather than try to solve them on their own, and to exhibit other symptoms of dependency and fear of responsibility. Since one of the ways to help people become responsible is to give them responsibility, counseling supervisors must guard against the tendency to give glib answers, suggestions, and advice, even when requested. He must learn to communicate such growth-producing attitudes as: "What do you think?" "What solutions have you considered?" "I don't have the answer, but let's see if we can find one together." "What is your reaction to this?" "I'm not sure I understand how you see this thing with your own eyes." "I understand your problem; now would you like me to help you think through different alternative solutions?" Of course, this principle does not mean that supervisors should never give information, since, very often, specific information is all that is asked. But, giving factual information is quite different from solving an employee's problem for him, giving opinionated answers, or jumping in quickly with advice.

Evaluation

In most organizations, the supervisor is expected to evaluate the performance of his subordinates. Because evaluation threatens people, it often increases their dependence and blocks self-responsible behavior. The fear of evaluation causes them to try to limit themselves to what they expect will be accepted or approved—and this is the enemy of creative, independent behavior.

How can you, as a supervisor, foster creative thinking, independence, and self-responsibility despite the problems raised by evaluation? Here are some suggestions:

(1) Reduce the evaluative function to periodic, systematic evaluation interviews (every six months or a year, depending on needs of the organization). Between these performance reviews, think of your main job as that of helping employees develop and improve performance.

(2) Try to avoid evaluating subordinates unless you can take the time to get their side of the story. Remember, your evaluation of another is only the way *you* perceive things. *He* also is a perceiver of things.

(3) Let employees know the standards or criteria against which their performance is being measured. Better yet, as some companies have done, get all the employees' participation in setting these standards for themselves.

(4) Let employees know that you actually believe that creativeness, responsibility and independent thinking *are* important criteria of effective performance—in other words, that they will be *rewarded* for this kind of behavior. To convince them of this possibility, however, you must demonstrate these beliefs every day and by your behavior in your counseling interviews with them.

(5) Make evaluation interviews more like problem-solving sessions, a discussion between you and the employees in which all of you are seeking solutions to a problem—in this case, the problem of improving the employees' performance.

The problems of dependency and evaluation lead to a number of barriers to genuine understanding in a counseling interview. The effective supervisor must realize they exist and must learn ways to remove them. Some of these barriers are:

(1) The subordinate may not feel his job would be safe if he expressed his true thoughts or feelings.

(2) The subordinate may fear he will be judged negatively by the supervisor.

(3) The subordinate may not want to accept any responsibility for solving a problem, preferring to depend upon the supervisor.

(4) The supervisor may not listen carefully, feeling that he already has the answer to the problem.

(5) The supervisor may be under too much pressure to take the time required to fully understand how the subordinate sees things.

(6) The subordinate may have trouble expressing himself clearly.

(7) The supervisor may be sensitive to criticism himself and so feels a need to argue with the subordinate and defend himself.

The following suggestions constitute techniques for dealing with the barriers by an approach described as the "coaching and counseling interview."

THE COACHING AND COUNSELING INTERVIEW

The coaching and counseling interview is a basic managerial tool used by the supervisor to help employees to develop and to help them solve personal or on-the-job problems. More importantly, however, it is a tool for the supervisor to use to help the individual to help himself, as opposed to the supervisor's using it to do something *for* him. The supervisor's job becomes one of creating the conditions or facilitating the process whereby his subordinate assumes greater responsibility for his own development and for solving his own problems.

The differences between the manager's coaching and counseling goals and other types of counseling assistance are illustrated in the following examples:

(1) He tries to convey "What do you think should be done?" as opposed to "Why don't you try this?"

(2) He asks "How do you see it?" instead of saying "Look at it this way."

(3) He says "Let me better understand how you actually feel," instead of "Don't feel that way about it."

(4) He asks "What can be done to make your job easier?" rather than comment "You should be doing things differently."

(5) He says "I have confidence that you can do an effective job," not "Here's what your job requires."

In other words, the idea behind the "coaching and counseling" approach is based on two assumptions: (1) that an individual cannot be changed from the outside, any significant change that takes place in him must be self-directed; and (2) given the proper atmosphere and encouragement, that the worker has the power to help himself and, in the process of doing so, to become more independent, fully-functioning, and creative. The supervisor-counselor's main function, therefore, is to get the employee actively involved and participating in solving his own problems and developing his own potentialities. This is accomplished only partially by the interview itself.

NECESSARY CONDITIONS FOR EFFECTIVE MANAGERIAL COACHING-COUNSELING

Before effective coaching and counseling is possible, the management must create the appropriate psychological atmosphere throughout the organization. Moreover, the supervisors cannot learn effective interviewing techniques unless they themselves develop certain basic attitudes toward people and toward themselves which we described in Chapter 6 and which are expanded in the next section.

Management Attitudes

Effective coaching and counseling is difficult to apply in an organization where the cards are stacked against the supervisor's efforts to foster self-improvement, self-learning, self-responsibility and effective problem-solving behavior on the part of his subordinates. To make coaching and counseling effective, management must fulfill the following conditions:

(1) Recognize that the economic motive alone will not make employees more productive, more creative or satisfied.

(2) Sincerely want to tap the creative resources lying dormant in the employee group.

(3) Learn to trust all levels of supervision as well as the employees and to delegate authority and responsibility commensurate with this trust.

(4) Appreciate the vitalizing effects of participative, or joint, decision-making at all levels of the organization.

(5) Recognize that the participation of lower levels of the organization in goal-setting and policy-formation will pay off in terms of increased morale, motivation, productivity—and better decisions.

Some of the conditions required if the employee is to feel secure and develop his own potentialities have been pointed out by Douglas McGregor[4] as: approval, knowing what is expected of him, knowing where he stands, being forewarned of changes, working under a consistent discipline, sensing security with supervisors, having the opportunity for participation, opportunity for responsibility, and the right of appeal over immediate supervisors. Whether or not one agrees entirely with each of these "conditions," the total list conveys something of the kind of organizational atmosphere that must prevail. If an organization falls far short of providing such an atmosphere, coaching and counseling will be looked upon by employees as simply another management gimmick for increasing production or fostering employee loyalty and dependence.

THE SUPERVISOR'S ATTITUDES

If the supervisor is to be successful as a coach and counselor, his attitudes toward people must be consistent with the objectives of the coaching and counseling interview. He must have, within himself, a certain degree of personal security and self-acceptance. If his own energies are being dissipated in a continuous struggle to prove himself or seek reaffirmation of his own importance, it will be difficult for him to devote energy to facilitating the development, or alleviating the problems, of others.

To utilize coaching and counseling as a managerial tool and conduct successful counseling interviews, he needs to have the basic attitudes described in Chapter 6, primarily, a belief that the worth of a person lies in the fact

[4] *Ibid.*, pg. 51,

that he is a unique, complex developing person, and is quite unrelated to his social class, occupational status, personal traits and abilities, appearance, race, and religion.

Another attitude which needs restressing, as a prerequisite for the effective counselor, is a basic trust in the capacity of people to act responsibly, constructively and creatively. A supervisor who feels that employees have little to contribute in the way of good ideas or feels that employees cannot be trusted with responsibility will not be very effective in trying to help his subordinates solve problems or develop their potentialities. The supervisor who knows definitely that employees have a wealth of resources that have not yet been tapped is the one who can give them confidence to utilize their potentialities and can help them find constructive solutions to their problems.

The value of certain other attitudes—open-mindedness, or the willingness to listen to other people's ideas, a genuine liking for people, the ability to put one's self in the other person's shoes—is more obvious and well known to supervisors.

All attitudes toward others, however, are conditioned by the supervisor's own inner security and self-confidence. He cannot be an effective counselor for his subordinates if he himself is not relatively secure in his job and happy with himself. It is difficult for the supervisor to be other-centered when his attention is centered upon himself and his own problems.

PLANNING AND PREPARING FOR THE INTERVIEW

A successful coaching and counseling interview depends to a great extent upon how adequately the supervisor plans for it and prepares himself for the role of counselor. Of course, since some interviews will be arranged on the spot, planning for them will be minimal. In most instances, interviews are arranged far enough ahead of time to permit adequate planning.

Choosing the Setting

Privacy is the first essential for a supervisory interview. An employee may want to discuss highly personal problems or he may feel the need to explore some of his deeper feelings. It is not unusual, if a supervisor is skilled in creating a safe and permissive atmosphere, for an employee to shed tears as he works through an emotional problem or openly express feelings of anger or hostility toward the supervisor. Obviously, privacy is a *must,* if the expression of such feelings and attitudes is to be encouraged or facilitated.

A quiet setting is important, too, since ordinary communication is difficult enough without the addition of factory or office noise.

The typical "boss's office" is not conducive to the necessary permissive atmosphere. The various symbols of the boss's power and status, such as the large desk and carpeting, are usually all too apparent. The desk, as mentioned in Chapter 6, may act as a psychological barrier to effective communication if the supervisor sits behind it during the interview. Some supervisors and executives prefer to come out from behind the desk and seat themselves closer to the employee. One executive has installed in his office a large work table around which subordinates gather for group meetings or for individual conferences with him. Getting out from behind the big desk adds to the informality of the interview and also helps break down the employee's idea of the supervisor as "the boss."

One thing supervisors and executives frequently overlook is to have all telephone calls intercepted during a counseling interview. It can be very disconcerting to the employee to have to wait while the supervisor answers several phone calls or is interrupted by secretaries.

The Initial Contact

Whether it is requested by the supervisor or the employee, the tone of the interview is often set by the way in which the first definite arrangements are made.

Any interview is usually initiated either by a written request or by a personal phone call. The phone call is preferable to the written request because it gives the employee an opportunity to react and ask questions, and because it gives him an opportunity to participate in setting the time. It is also considered good practice to indicate the purpose of the interview so that the employee is not left to worry, fret, or wonder what the boss wants now or what he himself has done to be called in for such an interview.

One executive, who has been unusually successful in using the coaching and counseling interview, when phoning an employee for an interview, makes a practice of: (1) asking first if he is free to talk; (2) stating the problem—"Such and such has come up and I think we should talk together about it"; (3) asking him if he would be interested and willing to discuss the problem with him; (4) giving him a choice of times and asking when it would be most convenient.

Many effective coaching and counseling interviews take place when the employee himself initiates a request for a discussion with his supervisor. One of the most frequently encountered problems in this connection arises when the supervisor is too busy to arrange an interview at the moment. Too many executives and supervisors leave it up to their secretaries to handle this problem and, as a result, the employee is told simply, "Mr. Jones cannot be disturbed now." Even if the executive asks the employee to come back later, it means he has to leave his job to come back and then not being sure of a hearing. A better way of handling this incident would be for the executive to make a note of the request and say that *he* will phone the employee when he is free. The principle underlying this method is that once the employee has taken the trouble to request a conference and has to be turned away, the responsibilty for fulfilling his request is then assumed by the supervisor.

Another effective way of handling such requests is to ask the employee how urgent the problem is. His answer will guide the supervisor in case he has other requests for conferences and needs to juggle his schedule to take care of more urgent requests.

Structuring the Interview

This important technique, described in Chapter 7, is especially important when applied to business or government employee interviews. It is particularly necessary to discuss how much time is to be available and what the purpose of the conference is to be. How much planning is needed depends upon the circumstances in each particular case. It is often helpful, however, if the employee has some ideas to how much time he will have to discuss his problem. When the employee has requested the interview, especially, a structuring discussion will help him to decide how much detail he can go into. It is better for the supervisor to explain, "I have a half-hour free now. Will that be enough time, do you think?" than for the employee to be worried about whether he is taking too much of the boss's time.

It is also best for the supervisor to know and to explain clearly and honestly the purpose of the interview. One of the frequent failings of supervisors is to be vague and to beat around the bush about the purpose. There appears to be an almost universal myth in government, business, and industry to the effect that, in dealing with people, one has to be tactful, careful, indirect, subtle, guarded, evasive, and ambiguous. In a recent survey of employee attitudes toward an unusually effective plant superintendent, who based his methods almost entirely upon coaching and counseling interviews, it was found that one of the main reasons he was highly respected by the foremen under him was because they felt they could rely on him "to tell them the plain, unvarnished truth." If a foreman calls in an employee to discuss poor work, for example, although it may sound blunt to describe his work as such, it is still better to say so at the beginning so that both foreman and employee can tackle the problem directly and constructively.

Another point that may have to be considered early is the question of confidentiality. The supervisor must know in his own mind how confidential he is prepared to keep the interview, that is, whether or not he can guarantee that all things said in the course of the interview can be kept in confidence.

This problem may not arise if the supervisor has already conveyed to employees the idea that he does not reveal personal problems to others. In some instances, however, supervisors are not prepared to promise full secrecy because they feel they have an obligation to top management to report anything that might be detrimental to the organization. Some supervisors resolve this problem by assuring confidentiality with the stipulation that, should they feel obligated to report something to top management, they would talk this over first with the employee.

Working into the Interview

It's a good idea, at the beginning of the interview, to have the one who initiated it carry the brunt of the conversation. The supervisor is too often tempted, even in interviews initiated by the employee, to take the initiative away from him right at the start by saying, for example, "While I have you in my office, I might as well take up this matter with you," or "Before we begin, how many units did Department A produce yesterday?" By doing this, the supervisor is showing lack of respect and conveying the idea that he really isn't interested in the employee's present problems.

However, the supervisor must recognize that the employee might be having difficulty in beginning. Because of his lower status, he may feel that he needs the supervisor's permission to begin. The supervisor can smooth this over by asking: "What's on your mind?" or "Would you like to tell me why you wanted to see me?"

The good supervisor-counselor also has to recognize that people often have difficulty communicating their ideas clearly—especially if their emotions are involved. Therefore, he tries to allow enough time to wait out the client, allowing him to develop his problem at his own pace. Aside from gaining a better understanding himself, the counselor thus gives the client a chance to see through to his basic problem. Often the client's initial statement of his problem is not quite the real issue. For example, an employee states, at first, that his problem is how to change "that so-and-so foreman." A more complete exploration, however, leads him to define his problem as one involving not only the foreman's behavior but his own behavior in relation to the foreman.

CONDUCTING THE COACHING-COUNSELING INTERVIEW

The Counselor's Attitudes

Attitudes have a way of showing through all relationships, especially in counseling situations involving supervisors and employees. Experienced counselors have found that it is difficult to hide antagonistic feelings, for example, even with conscious effort. People somehow have a sixth sense about how others feel toward them. Suppose, for example, a supervisor is dissatisfied with an employee's performance and feels that he is lazy and uncooperative. He seeks an interview with the man in the hopes of changing him. Analyzing his underlying feelings more closely, he comes to the conclusion that these attitudes will not help him to help the employee. Having pre-judged the person, he will find it harder to listen to the employee's side;

having decided the employee must change, he is less likely to see possibilities of changing himself or the work situation.

When the supervisor-counselor recognizes these negative attitudes, however, he can try either to conceal them or to admit them. Many counselors have found that they might as well admit them. In this case, for example, the supervisor might openly and honestly express his dissatisfaction with the employee's work, then sit back and help him express his own attitudes, trying hard to be openminded as to the causes and the ultimate solution.

More important than the supervisor's attitude toward the specific situation, however, is his attitude toward employees in general. He cannot do an effective job of helping employees solve problems or to develop their capacities unless he feels that they are capable of constructive and creative ideas and good decisions.

Listening and Feedback

The supervisor-counselor's main technique is quite simply *listening.* People want more than anything else to be listened to and understood. When the supervisor is successful in showing that he has *heard, understood,* and *accepted,* changes in the employee generally take place.

It is necessary to indicate that most people don't believe that they are really being understood and accepted when someone just listens to them. They have had too many previous experiences with people who only pretend to listen while they are actually thinking thoughts of their own. That is why the supervisor-counselor employs the feedback principle. Much as a complex electronic computer feeds back information which tells whether its computations are being accurately performed, the supervisor-counselor feeds back to the client feelings and information which tell him that he actually has been understood accurately. Some feedback methods are the reflection of feeling technique described in Chapter 7, and the reflectation technique described in Chapter 9. The following interview illustrates the use of the techniques described above in a recorded coaching and counseling interview:

Supervisor-Employee Interview

> *Supervisor:* Joe, it's real good to see you again. I understand you have something on your mind.
> *Employee:* Oh Boy! have I got something on my mind! I'm burned up! There's a reason why I'm upset! I wouldn't be sitting here if I wasn't upset! Believe me I'm upset—burned up—mad—angry. It was a real bad trick you guys pulled last week.
> *S:* You want to tell me about it?
> *E:* Well, I don't think it will do much good. I've had this happen before. Put that other engineer in over my head and he failed to see that I've been here twenty-five years. This guy came right out of college, is

single, and he gets it. I just wonder why it pays to work your head off. I really mean it.

S: This really hurts you?

E: Of course it hurts me—burns me up inside. I'm emotionally upset. I'm taking it out on my people, and look at the way I'm twisting around in my chair and everything else. I'm real——this has got me! I just don't know what you are up to—I can't get a feel for it—no help from you at all—none!

S: There's the feeling that somehow we're doing something here to you, or just kind of——

E: Sure, that's what I'm looking for, and do I get it. No! Not a bit! I don't say it's all your fault. It might be your boss's—like, you know, you're just taking what he says and bringing it back to me.

S: In other words, as you think it through, then it might not just be me that you're griping at, but you can see—it's the system.

E: Yeah, that's what it is! It's the system that's wrong. I've told you that before—you just didn't choose to see it.

S: I should have seen it then and I didn't.

E: I kind of felt that you should have at least paid attention to what I was saying, instead of making me feel like I was just talking into a barrel, and you'd carry it off like you might do something about it and I'd never see nothin! No results!

S: You've been disappointed in me then, in the past?

E: How would you feel? Let me ask you that! How would you feel? Twenty-five years on the job, and what do I get out of it? That young guy out of college—he gets the job! You know I was bucking for that.

S: It's been a long time you've been working for this and now it makes you feel like the bottom has kind of dropped out.

E: Not entirely! Look, I still have a job—I don't say the bottom has dropped out exactly, but I feel like I would like to have had this plum. I think I've done a good job in my work here. Stop to think about it a little bit—I'm making a nice salary. But it's just that this was a special one.

S: Yes.

E: Why the new fellow coming in? This is what I asked myself.

S: This was kind of the frosting on the cake that you've been hoping for?

E: Exactly, that's it! That's the whole thing. That's it exactly—the Ford-Cadillac business.

S: Mm-Hm. And now it seems like it's kind of lost?

E: Well, I don't say it's lost. I think there's going to be other opportunities, but I guess I'm just temporarily a little upset over this—like this is the particular one I didn't get and that's the one I wanted.

S: Mm-Hm.

E: Now I realize that there are areas where I could—like putting out the same kind of effort I've done before, I might get another opportunity—but it's the top brass that worries me. I just don't know whether they are looking at me the way I look at myself. You know what I mean? Am I getting across to you? This experience—this thing that has happened——

S: This has started you to wonder about a lot of things and now you are wondering if somebody up there is viewing you in the wrong way?

E: Well, I think they're thinking "Little John—he'll always be here." You know what I mean? Did you ever have that feeling? That's what I think they're doing.

S: You think that they're thinking that you're just an old shoe anyhow and no matter how much they kick you around, you'll be here anyhow.

E: Well, I sometimes feel that this is it, and then I get to thinking about it—I was talking to the wife the other night, you know—talking about this same problem, and she said, "Aren't you guilty of being just a little bit premature?" And then she mentioned the trip to Albuquerque and a few other things that these other fellows wanted, and I got— and when you look at it in that light, I guess maybe I've had a few things here that maybe a few other fellows would like to have had, but I think I see a point. Now let me go back over this—see why this particular fellow got this particular job. Now, this is where I may need your help.

S: Mm-Hm.

E: What he did! What he put into this thing that I could not, or did not— maybe then—but on the other hand, look—you don't voice your opinions in these cases—I have this feeling you don't.

S: You think that I've let you down—that I really haven't supported you enough?

E: Well, on that last trip to Frisco—I wanted that in the worst way. Did I get it? You were the one who could have supported this, and you didn't do it. Why didn't you do it? I've been working for you for most of these years.

S: This particular thing—you felt I let you down on this?

E: On this particular item—I think you did. I honestly felt you did.

S: That's the one where I really knifed you?

E: Well, I know you had other problems at the time you had this decision. Maybe you had a problem there that I just didn't understand. It's so hard to see the other fellow's viewpoint, isn't it? Maybe that's the worst problem I have.

S: In other words, maybe this is really the hardest one of the problems that you really have. That you've never been able to put yourself in the other guy's shoes—see how he might feel about it.

E: I think so. I seem to feel that I lose faith occasionally and I don't know whether that's a product of getting old or what, but I just don't have that feeling like——

S: You get anxious and you want to move things faster than they can move.

E: Right!

S: You're wondering whether this is another thing that might contribute here to this decision not to give you the chance.

E: Well, I think this is probably true—sometimes I get kind of confused, I must admit. I don't know just exactly—sometimes I view it this way —I know what is expected of me—just elementarily, you expect a certain output. I try to put this out. I've been doing this for twenty-five years, haven't I? Then I see this younger fellow with some new philosophy, such as this philosophy that seems to be the rage now days. They come in here and your people seem to feel that this is a new genius—the fair-haired boy—you know? Good old John over there in the corner—he'll be there, when I'm on my way—he'll be there.

S: The "boy wonder"—and we had to use him.

E: But you know something—I've got a feeling that the basic problem is—maybe rather than worrying about that guy, I should be learning some of these new trends myself.

S: You've been holding on too long to this stuff here that hasn't any use.

E: Yeah, that's probably it.

S: Gee, I'm real glad you say this because I felt this way too and to have you really feel that this would be a good direction for you makes me feel real good about you.

E: Well, it's a thought I had and I don't say I developed it all by myself. My wife happened to mention it too and of course you know the reason I didn't do it before was that I felt I was just too damn old.

S: That's another one of the things that keeps cropping up here.

E: You can say this—you're a lot younger.

S: In other words, I can't really understand how you feel when you get to be your age. How old are you?

E: Forty-five.

S: You kind of feel like you're crossing over the bridge, huh? Critical time for you?

E: Right! This is a basic problem. But my wife convinced me that some guys go to college when they're forty-four. If they can do it, maybe I can do it.

S: Your wife seems to help you a lot in these things.

E: Yes, she has—well, she's sometimes a little bit on the hard-nosed side —but she has a pretty straight-forward way of looking at things and she doesn't view things emotionally as I do—I admit. But I can't be like her.

S: You can't be like her? You have to be yourself and she has to be herself.

E: Right!

S: Joe, you've said a number of things here that really interest me. You've suggested some things about yourself that maybe do need working on —this business of really seeing the other person's point of view, the fact that maybe you have pushed too hard with your own ideas, and maybe some of your ideas seem to be outdated, and I'm real pleased that you can see this. It may be true what you said about me. I get kind of upset sometimes that people don't really tell me what they feel about me and I've always been pleased that you can sit down with me and say what you feel. I'll kind of watch this too, and it may be, that as you work on your part of it, and I work on my part of it, why, maybe when the next opportunity comes, things might be different.

E: I hope they will be—I'd just like to know in advance of anything coming up—so I have an "in."

S: Well, I can prepare you for anything new that's coming so that you can sort of think through.

E: That's it—let me feel that I am at least being considered—that's my problem. I won't feel that everything is marching right on past me.

S: Since you're concerned about your age here and you're kind of stuck here in this situation, you just want to be informed on what is happening and if you are informed, why you'll be able to kind of get in step, hm?

E: Well, don't you feel that you'd like to have the same thing done for you? Isn't it natural to feel this way?

S: I think that is true.

E: The feeling of belonging, security, chance for advancement, and all that?

S: And if you don't feel this with me, I certainly want you to tell me about it.

E: Well, to be honest with you, I didn't feel it until tonight—just sitting here talking like this makes me feel like you can see inside of me— see how I am thinking.

S: You feel closer to me?

E: Well I feel a lot more relaxed—a little bit more like I belong, I must admit that.

S: Well, I know that we are all kind of erratic in these things and perhaps I haven't told you about how much I do appreciate you and I want you to know how much you mean to our department and how much you have helped me as we have worked on these various projects.

E: Thanks.

S: Well, Joe, it's been real good to see you and our time is up and I'll have to leave, but I do want you to feel free to come and see me any-time and to talk about this or anything else that comes up. O.K.?

E: Thanks a lot. I really do appreciate that.

SUMMARY

Counseling attitudes and techniques are valuable management tools to promote the mutual interests of employee and supervisor. Proper coun-seling attitudes can reduce communication barriers, enhance employee growth, and help the supervisor to deal with two key supervisory problems —employee dependency and the threats of performance evaluation. Proper employee counseling in industrial and government settings is not much different from that of the formal counseling and psychotherapy consultation. Relationship techniques of structuring, silence, and reflection of feeling are of special value in supervisory counseling. An essential element in sensitivity training of management personnel is to help them to become fully aware of their own and their employees' feelings so that they can respond genuinely, warmly, and acceptingly to employees who come to them with problems.

References

1. Adams, D. K., *et al. Learning Theory, Personality Theory, and Clinical Research: The Kentucky Symposium.* New York: Wiley, 1954.
2. Alexander, F., and French, T. M. *Psychoanalytic Therapy.* New York: Ronald, 1946.
3. Allport, G. W. *Becoming: Basic Considerations for a Psychology of Personality.* New Haven: Yale University Press, 1955.
4. Allport, G. W. *Personality: A Psychological Interpretation.* New York: Holt, 1937.
5. Alschuler, Rose H., and Hattwick, La Berta W. *Painting and Personality: Study of Young Children.* Chicago: University of Chicago Press, 1947.
6. American Board of Examiners in Professional Psychology. Annual report. *Amer. Psychologist,* 1954, *9*, pp. 766–770.
7. American Psychiatric Association. *Diagnostic and Statistical Manual of Mental Disorders.* Washington, D.C.: American Psychological Association, 1952.
8. American Psychological Association. Bylaws for the American Psychological Association. *Directory American Psychological Association.* Washington, D.C.: American Psychological Association, 1954.
9. American Psychological Association. *Ethical Standards of Psychologists.* Washington, D.C.: American Psychological Association, 1953 (Proposal for modification: Standards of ethical behavior for psychologists. *Amer. Psychologists,* 1958, *13*, pp. 266–271.)
10. American Psychological Association. *Psychology and Its Relations with Other Professions.* Washington, D.C.: American Psychological Association, 1954.
11. American Psychological Association Committee on Counselor Training. Recommended standards for training counseling psychologists at the doctorate level. *Amer. Psychologist,* 1952, *7*, pp. 175–181.
12. American Psychological Association Committee on Training in Clinical Psychology. Recommended graduate training program in clinical psychology. *Amer. Psychologist,* 1947, *2*, pp. 539–558.
13. American Psychological Association Subcommittee on Counselor Trainee Selection. Annual Report. *Counseling News and Views,* 1953–1954, *6.*
14. Ansbacher, Rowena. *The Individual Psychology of Alfred Adler.* New York: Basic Books, 1956.

15. Ash, P. The reliability of psychiatric diagnosis. *J. abnorm. soc. Psychol.*, 1949, *44*, pp. 272–276.

16. Axline, Virginia. Mental deficiency: Symptom or disease. *J. consult. Psychol.*, 1949, *13*, pp. 313–327.

17. Axline, Virginia. *Play Therapy*. New York: Houghton, 1947.

18. Bach, G. *Intensive Group Psychotherapy*. New York: Ronald, 1954.

19. Baer, M. F., and Roeber, E. C. *Occupational Information: Its Nature and Use*. Chicago: Science Research Associates, 1951.

20. Bartlett, F. C. *Remembering*. Cambridge: Cambridge University Press, 1932.

21. Baruch, Dorothy. *How to Live with Your Teenager*. New York: McGraw, 1953.

22. Baruch, Dorothy. *New Ways in Discipline*. New York: McGraw, 1949.

23. Baruch, Dorothy. *One Little Boy*. New York: Julian, 1952.

24. Bell, H. M. *The Adjustment Inventory*. Stanford: Stanford University Press, 1938.

25. Bell, H. M. Counseling Students with Moral and Religious Problems. Chico, Calif.: Chico State General Lectures, 1952.

26. Berdie, R. F. An aid to student counselors. *Educ. psychol. Measmt.*, 1952, *2*, pp. 281–290.

27. Berger, E. M. The relation between expressed acceptance of self and expressed acceptance of others. *J. Abnorm. soc. Psychol.*, 1952, *47*, pp. 778–782.

28. Bergler, E. *The Revolt of the Middle-Aged Man*. New York: A. A. Wyn, 1954.

29. Bergman, D. V. Counseling method and client responses. *J. consult. Psychol.*, 1951, *15*, pp. 216–224.

30. Bettleheim, B. Self-interpretation of fantasy: The thematic apperception test as an educational and therapeutic device. *Amer. J. Orthopsychiat.*, 1947, *17*, pp. 80–100.

31. Beverly, B. *In Defense of Children*. New York: Day, 1941.

32. Bixler, R. H. Limits are Therapy. *J. consult. Psychol.*, 1949, *13*, pp. 1–11.

33. Bixler, R. H., and Bixler, V. H. Test interpretation in vocational counseling. *Educ. psychol. Measmt.*, 1946, *6*, pp. 145–155.

34. Black, J. D. Common factors of the patient-therapist relationship in diverse psychotherapies. *J. clin. Psychol.*, 1952, *8*, pp. 302–306.

35. Blanton, S. *Love or Perish*. New York: Simon & Schuster, 1956.

36. Blos, P. Psychological counseling of college students. *Amer. J. Orthopsychiat.*, 1946, *16*, pp. 571–580.

37. Bogue, Jesse P. (ed.) *American Junior Colleges*, 4th ed. Washington, D.C.: American Council on Education, 1956.

38. Boileau, V. New techniques in brief psychotherapy. Psychological Reports, Monogr. Suppl. #7, 1958.

39. Bordin, E. S. Diagnosis in counseling and psychotherapy. *Educ. psychol. Measmt.*, 1946, *6*, pp. 169–184.

40. Bordin, E. S. *Psychological Counseling*. New York: Appleton-Century-Crofts, Inc., 1955.

41. Bordin, E. S., and Bixler, R. H. Test selection: A process of counseling. *Educ. psychol. Measmt.,* 1946, *6,* pp. 361–374.

42. Brower, D. *Progress in Clinical Psychology,* Vol. VI. New York: Grune and Stratton, 1952.

43. Brown, J. F. *Psychodynamics of Abnormal Behavior.* New York: McGraw, 1940.

44. Brown, W. F., and Holtzman, W. H. *Survey of Study Habits and Attitudes.* New York: Psychological Corporation, 1955.

45. Bugental, J. F. T. *A Phenomenological Hypothesis of Neurotic Determinants and Their Therapy* (Unpublished paper). Los Angeles: Psychological Service Associates.

46. Bugental, J. F. T. Psychological Interviewing. Unpublished manuscript, 1952.

47. Buhler, Charlotte. Maturation and motivation. *J. Pers.,* 1951, *1,* pp. 184–211.

48. Buhler, Charlotte. Personal communication with the authors.

49. Buhler, Charlotte. Unpublished paper presented before Group Psychotherapy Association of Southern California, June, 1958.

50. Bunting, J. E. (ed.) *Private Independent Schools,* 10th ed. Wallingford, Conn.: Editor, 1957.

51. Burckel, C. E. *The College Blue Book,* 8th ed. New York: Author, 1956.

52. Buros, O. K. *The Third Mental Measurements Yearbook.* New Brunswick: Rutgers University Press, 1949.

53. California State Department of Education. *The preparation and training of pupil personnel workers.* Bulletin Series, 1952, No. 5, Volume 21, Chapter 1, pg. 15.

54. Callan, Mary Ann. Family court urged to cut down divorces. *Los Angeles Times,* January 16, 1958, Part II, pg. 1.

55. Cantrell, Dorothy. Training the rehabilitation counselor. *Personnel Guidance J.,* 1958, *36,* pp. 382–387.

56. Carmichael, L. *Child Psychology.* New York: Wiley, 1954.

57. Carnes, E. F. Counselor flexibility: Its extent, and its relationship to other factors in the interview. Unpublished doctor's dissertation, Ohio State University, 1949.

58. Carnes, E. F., and Robinson, F. P. The role of client talk in the counseling interview. *Educ. psychol. Measmt.,* 1948, *8,* pp. 635–644.

59. Carter, H. D. Vocational interests and job orientation. *Appl. Psychol. Monogr.,* 1944, *2.*

60. Cattell, R. B. *Personality.* New York: McGraw, 1950.

61. Chance, Erika. Measuring the anticipations of therapists about their patients. Unpublished paper, 1958.

62. Coffey, H. S. Group Psychotherapy, in Berg, I. A., and Pennington, L. A. (eds.), *An Introduction to Clinical Psychology.* New York: Ronald, 1948.

63. Cohen, Mabel B. Countertransference and anxiety. *Psychiatry,* 1952, *15,* pp. 231–243.

64. Cohen, R. C. Military group psychotherapy. *Mental hygiene,* 1947, *31,* pp. 94–103.

65. Cole, L. *Psychology of Adolescence.* New York: Rinehart, 1956.

66. Collier, R. M. A basis for integration rather than fragmentation in psychotherapy. *J. consult. Psychol.,* 1950, *14,* pp. 199–205.

67. Combs, A. W. Counseling as a learning process. *J. clin. Psychol.,* 1954, *1,* pp. 31–36.

68. Cottle, W. C. Personal characteristics of counselors: I. *Personnel Guidance J.,* 1953, *31,* pp. 445–450.

69. Cottle, W. C., and Lewis, W. W., Jr. Personality characteristics of counselors: II. Male counselor responses to the MMPI and GZTS. *J. counsel. Psychol.,* 1954, *1,* pp. 27–30.

70. Cox, Rachel D. *Counselors and Their Work.* Philadelphia: University of Pennsylvania Press, 1945.

71. Crampton, W. How U.S. Men Can Live Longer. *This Week,* Feb. 20, 1955, pp. 7–26. Also printed in Solomon, C., and Brooks, R. (eds.), *How to Enjoy Good Health.* New York: Random House, Inc., 1955.

72. Crider, Blake. The hostility pattern. *J. clin. Psychol.,* 1946, *2,* pp. 267–273.

73. Cronbach, L. J. Counselor's problems from the perspective of communication theory, in Hewer, V. H. (ed.), New Perspectives in Counseling. *Minnesota Studies in Student Personnel Work, No. 7.* Minneapolis: University of Minnesota Press, 1955.

74. Croner, U. *American Trade Schools Directory.* New York: Croner, 1953.

75. Curran, C. A. Structuring the counseling relationship: A case report. *J. abnorm. soc. Psychol.,* 1944, *39,* pp. 189–216.

76. Cutler, R. L. The relationship between the therapist's personality and certain aspects of psychotherapy. Ph.D. thesis, University of Michigan, 1954.

77. Danskin, D. G., and Burnett, C. W. Those superior students. *Personnel & Guidance J.,* 1952, *31,* pp. 181–186.

78. Daulton, Joan. A study of factors relating to resistance in the interview. M.A. thesis, Ohio State University, 1947.

79. Davis, S. E., and Robinson, F. P. A study of the use of certain techniques for reducing resistance during the counseling interview. *Educ. psychol. Measmt.,* 1949, *9,* pp. 297–306.

80. Deabler, H. L. The psychotherapeutic use of the thematic apperception test. *J. clin. Psychol.,* 1947, *8,* pp. 246–252.

81. Del Torto, J., and Cornyetz, P. Psychodrama as an Expressive and Projection Technique, in Moreno, J. L. (ed.), *Psychodrama Monograph #14,* New York: Beacon House, 1945.

82. Despert, J. L. *Children of Divorce.* Garden City, N. Y.: Doubleday, 1953.

83. Dollard, J., and Miller, N. E. *Personality and Psychotherapy.* New York: McGraw, 1950.

84. Dollard, J., and Mowrer, O. H. A method of measuring tension in written documents. *J. abnorm. soc. Psychol.,* 1947, *42,* pp. 3–33.

85. Dorfman, E. Chapter 6, in Rogers, C. R. (ed.), *Client Centered Therapy.* Boston: Houghton, 1951.

86. Dressel, P. L. Implications of recent research for counseling. *J. counsel. Psychol.,* 1954, *1,* pp. 100–105.

87. Dressel, P. L., and Matteson, R. W. The effect of client participation on test interpretation. *Educ. psychol. Measmt.*, 1950, *10*, pp. 693–706.

88. Driver, Helen I. *Multiple Counseling: A Small Group Discussion Method for Personal Growth.* Madison, Wis.: Monona, 1954.

89. Durnall, E. J., Moynihan, J. F., and Wrenn, C. G. Symposium: The counselor and his religion. *Personnel & Guidance J.*, 1958, *36*, pp. 326–334.

90. Ellis, A. New approaches to psychotherapy. *J. clin. Psychol.*, Monogr. Suppl., 1955, *11*.

91. Ellis, A. The sexual element in non-sexual crimes. *Psychological Newsletter*, 1957, *8*, pp. 122–125.

92. English, H. B. The counseling situation as an obstacle to non-directive therapy. *J. consult. Psychol.*, 1948. *12*, pp. 217–222.

93. Erikson, E. H. *Childhood and Society.* New York: Norton, 1950.

94. Feingold, S. N. *Scholarships, Fellowships, and Loans.* Boston: Bellman, 1955.

95. Fenichel, O. *The Psychoanalytic Theory of Neurosis.* New York: Norton, 1945.

96. Fensterheim, H., and Tresselt, M. E. The influence of value systems on the perception of people. *J. abnorm. soc. Psychol.*, 1953, *48*, pp. 93–98.

97. Fiedler, F. E. A comparison of psychoanalytic, nondirective, and Adlerian therapeutic relationships. *J. consult. Psychol.*, 1950, *14*, pp. 436–445.

98. Fiedler, F. E. The concept of an ideal therapeutic relationship. *J. consult. Psychol.*, 1950, *14*, pp. 339–345.

99. Fiedler, F. E. Method of objective quantification of certain countertransference attitudes. *J. clin. Psychol.*, 1951, *7*, pp. 101–107.

100. Fiedler, F. E., and Senior, Kate. An exploratory study of unconscious feeling reactions in fifteen patient-therapist pairs. *J. abnorm. soc. Psychol.*, 1952, *47*, pp. 446–453.

101. Fine, S. A. A structure of worker function. *Personnel & Guidance J.*, 1955, *34*, pp. 66–73.

102. Fine, S. A. What is occupational information? *Personnel & Guidance J.*, 1955, *33*, pp. 504–509.

103. Fisher, J. *A Few Buttons Missing.* Philadelphia: Lippincott, 1951.

104. Fizdale, Ruth. A new look at fee charging. *Social casework*, 1957, *38*, pp. 60–65.

105. Forgy, E. W., and Black, J. D. A follow-up after three years of clients counseled by two methods. *J. counsel. Psychol.*, 1954, *1*, pp. 1–8.

106. Foster, R. G. A point of view in marriage counseling. *J. counsel. Psychol.*, 1956, *3*, pp. 210–216.

107. Frank, J. D., and Asher, E. Corrective emotional experiences in group therapy. *Amer. J. Psychiat.*, 1951, *108*, pp. 126–131.

108. Frankl, V. E. *Ärtzliche Seelsorge.* Vienna: Franz Deuticke Verlog, 1946.

109. Freud, S. *The Basic Writing of Sigmund Freud.* A. A. Brill (trans. and ed.). New York: Modern Library, 1938.

110. Freud, S. *The Future of an Illusion.* New York: Liveright, 1928.

111. Freud, S. *A General Introduction to Psychoanalysis.* New York: Liveright, 1935.

112. Freud, S. *An Outline of Psychoanalysis*. New York: Norton, 1949.

113. Fromm, E. *The Art of Loving*. New York: Harper, 1956.

114. Fromm, E. *Escape from Freedom*. New York: Farrar and Rinehart, 1941.

115. Fromm, E. *Man for Himself*. New York: Farrar and Rinehart, 1947.

116. Fromm, E. Man is not a thing. *Sat. Rev.*, March, 1957, pp. 9–11.

117. Fromm, E. *Psychoanalysis and Religion*. New Haven: Yale University Press, 1950.

118. Fromm-Reichmann, Frieda. *Principles of Intensive Psychotherapy*. Chicago: The University of Chicago Press, 1950.

119. Garrison, K. C. *Psychology of Adolescence*. Englewood Cliffs, N.J.: Prentice-Hall, Inc., 1956.

120. Gesell, A. *Child Development*. New York: Harper, 1949.

121. Gesell, A., Ilg, F. L., and Ames, L. B. *Youth: The Years from 10 to 16*. New York: Harper, 1956.

122. Gibran, Kahlil. *The Prophet*. New York: Knopf, 1923.

123. Gilbert, Jeanne G. *Understanding Old Age*. New York: Ronald, 1952.

124. Ginzberg, E. *Occupational Choice, an Approach to General Theory*. New York: Columbia University Press, 1951.

125. Glatzer, H. The relative effectiveness of clinically homogenous and heterogenous psychotherapy groups. *Int. J. group Psychother.*, 1956, *6*, pp. 258.

126. Glover, E. *Freud or Jung*. New York: Norton, 1950.

127. Gorham, D. R. Proverbs test. Missoula, Montana: Psychological Test Specialists, 1954.

128. Graver, P. A. A study of counselors in selected industrial, education, and social service institutes. Unpublished doctor's dissertation, Northwestern University, 1948.

129. Gray, W. S. Gray oral reading paragraphs test. Bloomington, Ill.: Public School Publishing Company, 1923.

130. Green, A. W. Social values and psychotherapy. *J. Pers.*, 1946, *14*, pp. 199–228.

131. Greenleaf, W. J. *Occupations and Careers*. New York: McGraw, 1955.

132. Gustad, J. W. The Definition of Counseling, in Berdie, R. F. (ed.), *Roles and Relationships in Counseling*. Minneapolis: University of Minnesota Press, 1953.

133. Gustad, J. W. The evaluation interview in vocational counseling. *Personnel & Guidance J.*, 1957, *36*, pp. 242–250.

134. Hadley, J. M., and Asher, E. J. Clinical counseling and school clinical psychology at Purdue University. *Amer. Psychologist*, 1955, *10*, pp. 71–73.

135. Hahn, M. E. The training of rehabilitation counselors. *J. counsel. Psychol.*, 1954, *1*, pp. 246–248.

136. Hahn, M. E., and McLean, M. S. *General Clinical Counseling*. New York: McGraw, 1950.

137. Haigh, G. Defensive behavior in client-centered therapy. *J. consult Psychol.*, 1949, *13*, pp. 181–189.

138. Harlow, H. F. The formation of learning sets. *Psychol. Rev.*, 1949, *56*, pp. 51–65.

139. Hathaway, S. R., and McKinley, J. C. *The Minnesota Multiphasic Personality Inventory*. New York: Psychological Corporation, 1942.

140. Havighurst, R. J. *Human Development and Education*. New York: Longmans, 1953.

141. Heine, R. W. An investigation of the relationship between change in personality from psychotherapy as reported by patients and the factors seen by patients as producing change. Unpublished doctoral dissertation, University of Chicago, 1950.

142. Herman, R. The "going steady" complex. *Marriage and Family*, 1955, *17*, pp. 26–40.

143. Herzberg, A. *Active Psychotherapy*. New York: Grune and Stratton, 1945.

144. Hinckley, G. and Hermann, Lydia. *Group Treatment in Psychotherapy*. Minneapolis: University of Minnesota Press, 1951.

145. Hobbs, N. Group-Centered Psychotherapy, in Rogers, C. R. (ed.), *Client-Centered Therapy*. Boston: Houghton, 1951.

146. Hogan, R. A. Theory of threat and defense. *J. consult. Psychol.*, 1952, *16*, pp. 417–424.

147. Horney, Karen. *Neurosis and Human Growth*. New York: Norton, 1950.

148. Horney, Karen. *The Neurotic Personality of Our Time*. New York: Norton, 1937.

149. Horney, Karen. *New Ways in Psychoanalysis*. New York: Norton, 1939.

150. Horney, Karen. *Self-Analysis*. New York: Norton, 1942.

151. Hughes, E. C. Psychology: Science and/or profession. *Amer. Psychologist*, 1952, *7*, pp. 441–443.

152. Ingham, H. V., and Love, Lemore R. *The Process of Psychotherapy*. New York: McGraw, 1954.

153. Irwin, Mary (ed.) *American Universities and Colleges,* 7th ed. Washington: American Council on Education, 1956.

154. Jacques, E. The clinical use of the TAT with soldiers. *J. abnorm. soc. Psychol.*, 1945, *4*, pp. 363–375.

155. Janowitz, M. Some observations on the ideology of professional psychologists. *Amer. Psychologist*, 1954, *9*, pp. 528–532.

156. Joel, W., and Shapiro, D. Some principles and procedures for group psychotherapy. *J. Psychol.*, 1950, *29*, pp. 77–88.

157. Johnson, D. Understanding and use of the self in counseling. *Bulletin of the Menninger Clinic*, 1953, *17*, pp. 29–35.

158. Johnson, W. *People in Quandaries*. New York: Harper, 1946.

159. Jourard, S. M. *Personal Adjustment*. New York: Macmillan, 1958.

160. Jourard, S. M., and Remy, R. Perceived parental attitudes, the self and security. *J. consult. Psychol.*, 1955, *19*, pp. 364–366.

161. Jung, C. G. *Modern Man in Search of a Soul*. New York: Harcourt, 1933.

162. Karpman, B. Objective psychotherapy. Clinical Psychology Monographs, No. 6. *J. clin. Psychol.*, pg. 195.

163. Keet, C. D. Two verbal techniques in a miniature counseling situation. *Psychol. Monogr.*, 1948, *7*.

164. Kelly, E. C. *Education for What is Real*. New York: Harper, 1947.

165. Kelly, G. A. *The Psychology of Personal Constructs,* Vols. 1 and 2. New York: Norton, 1955.

166. Kelly, G. A. Verbal Communication in Psychotherapy. Unpublished manuscript of lectures presented to a post-doctoral institute of the Los Angeles Society of Clinical Psychologists in Private Practice, January 17–18, 1959.

167. Kinsey, A. C., Pomeroy, W. B., and Martin, C. E. *Sexual Behavior in the Human Female.* Philadelphia: Saunders, 1953.

168. Kinsey, A. C., Pomeroy, W. B., and Martin, C. E. *Sexual Behavior in the Human Male.* Philadelphia: Saunders, 1948.

169. Kirkendall, L. A. Implications for college teaching of a concept of morality. Unpublished paper, Oregon State College.

170. Klein, M. *The Psychoanalysis of Children.* New York: Hogarth, 1949.

171. Klingelhofer, E. L. The relationship between academic advisement to the scholastic performance of failing college students. *J. counsel. Psychol.,* 1954, *1,* pp. 125–131.

172. Klopfer, B. *Developments in the Rorschach Technique.* Vol. 2. Yonkers, N.Y.: World Book, 1956.

173. Klopfer, B. Personal communication.

174. Klopfer, B. Rorschach clinical diagnosis. Unpublished mimeographed paper, pg. 4.

175. Koester, G. A. A study of the diagnostic process. *Educ. psychol. Measmt.,* 1954, *14,* pp. 473–486.

176. Kohler, W. *The Mentality of Apes* (Trans. E. Winter). New York: Harcourt, 1925.

177. Korner, Ija N. Ego involvement and the process of disengagement. *J. consult. Psychol.,* 1950, *14,* pp. 206–209.

178. Kunkel, F. Growth through Crises, in Doniger, S. (ed.), *Religion and Human Behavior.* New York: Association Press, 1954.

179. Kunkel, F. *In Search of Maturity.* New York: Scribner, 1955.

180. Layton, W. L. Selection and counseling of students in engineering. *Minnesota Studies in Personnel Work No. 4.* Minneapolis: University of Minnesota Press, 1954.

181. Lebo, D. The expressive value of toys recommended for nondirective play therapy. *J. clin. Psychol.,* 1955, *11,* pp. 144–148.

182. Lee, A. M. Social pressures and the values of psychologists. *Amer. Psychologist,* 1954, *9,* pp. 516–522.

183. Lewin, K. *Principles of Topological Psychology.* New York: McGraw, 1936.

184. Lewis, N. D. C. *Outlines for Psychiatric Examinations.* Albany, New York: New York State Department of Mental Hygiene, 1943.

185. Lifton, W. M. Counseling and the religious view of man. *Personnel & Guidance J.,* 1953, *31,* pp. 366–367.

186. Lipkin, S. Clients' feelings and attitudes in relation to the outcomes on client-centered therapy. *Psychol. Monogr.,* 1954, *68,* pg. 372.

187. Loeser, L. H. Some aspects of group dynamics. *Int. J. Group Psychother.,* 1957, *7,* pp. 5–19.

188. Lovejoy, C. E. *Lovejoy's College Guide.* New York: Simon & Schuster, 1956–57.

189. Lovejoy, C. E. *Lovejoy's Vocational School Guide.* New York: Simon & Schuster, 1955.

190. Luft, J. Implicit hypotheses and clinical predictions. *J. abnorm. soc. Psychol.,* 1950, *45,* pp. 756–759.

191. McArthur, C. C. Analyzing the clinical process. *J. counsel. Psychol.,* 1954, *1,* pp. 203–208.

192. McHugh, G. *The Sex Knowledge Inventory.* College Station, North Carolina: Duke University Press, 1950.

193. Mace, D. Your marriage today. *Women's Home Companion,* April, 1956, pp. 29–33.

194. Mahler, Margaret, and Rabinovitch, Ruth. The Effects of Marital Conflict on Child Development, in Eisenstein, V. (ed.), *Neurotic Interaction in Marriage.* New York: Basic Books, 1956.

195. Mann, L. Persuasive doll play: A technique of directive psychotherapy for use with children. *J. clin. Psychol.,* 1957, *13,* pp. 14–19.

196. Margolis, B. D. The problem of "facade" in the counseling of low scholarship students. *J. consult. Psychol.,* 1945, *9,* pp. 138–141.

197. Maslow, A. H. *Motivation and personality.* New York: Harper, 1954.

198. May, R., Angel, E., and Ellenberger, H. *Existence.* New York: Basic Books, 1958.

199. May, R. *The Art of Counseling.* New York: Abingdon-Cokesbury, 1939.

200. May, R. *Man's Search for Himself.* New York: Norton, 1953.

201. Mead, Margaret. *Ladies Home Journal Treasury.* New York: Simon & Shuster, 1956.

202. Meehl, P. E. *Clinical Versus Statistical Prediction.* Minneapolis: University of Minnesota Press, 1954.

203. Meehl, P. E., *et al. What, Then, is Man?* St. Louis: Concordia, 1958.

204. Menninger, K. *The Theory of Psychoanalytic Technique,* Menninger Clinical Monograph Series 12. New York: Basic Books, 1958.

205. Michigan State University. *How to Make Referrals.* East Lansing, Michigan: Guidance and Counselor Training, College of Education, Michigan State University, 1956.

206. Miller, J. G. General behavior systems theory and summary (Part 3, Behavior theories and a counseling case: A symposium). *J. counsel. Psychol.,* 1956, *3,* pp. 120–124.

207. Miller, J. G. Toward a general theory for the behavioral sciences. *Amer. Psychologist,* 1955, *10,* pp. 513, 531.

208. Mittelmann, Beta. Analysis of Reciprocal Neurotic Patterns in Family Relationships, in Eisenstein, V. W. (ed.), *Neurotic Interaction in Marriage.* New York: Basic Books, 1956.

209. Montague, A. *On Being Human.* New York: H. Schuman, 1950.

210. Mooney, R. L. *Mooney Problem Checklist.* New York: Psychological Corporation, 1950.

211. Moore, B. V., and Bouthilet, Lorraine. The V.A. program for counseling psychologists. *Amer. Psychologist,* 1952, *7,* pp. 684–685.

212. Morton, R. B. A controlled experiment in psychotherapy based on Rotter's social learning theory of personality. Doctor's dissertation, Ohio State University, 1949.

213. Morton, R. B. An experiment in social psychotherapy. *Psychol. Monogr.*, 1955, *69*, pp. 1–17.

214. Mosier, Helen P., Dublin, W., and Shelsky, I. M. A proposed modification of the Roe Occupational Classification. *J. consult. Psychol.*, 1956, *3*, pp. 27–31.

215. Moustakas, C. E. *Children in Play Therapy*. New York: McGraw, 1953.

216. Mowrer, O. H. Anxiety Theory as a Basis for Distinguishing between Counseling and Psychotherapy, in Berdie, R. (ed.), *Concepts and Programs of Counseling*. Minneapolis: University of Minnesota Press, 1951.

217. Mowrer, O. H. *Learning Theory and Personality Dynamics*. New York: Ronald, 1950.

218. Mowrer, O. H. Tension Changes During Psychotherapy with Special Reference to Resistance, in *Psychotherapy: Theory and Research*. New York: Ronald, 1953.

219. Mowrer, O. H. Some philosophical problems in psychological counseling. *J. counsel. Psychol.*, 1957, *4*, pp. 103–111.

220. Murphy, G. *Personality: A Biosocial Approach to Origins and Structure*. New York: Harper, 1947.

221. National Home Study Council. *Home Study Blue Book*. Washington, D.C.: National Home Study Council, 1956.

222. National Vocational Guidance Association. *Counselor Preparation*. Washington: National Vocational Guidance Association, 1949.

223. Nygren, A. *Agape and Eros*. London: SPCK, 1953.

224. Oates, W. E. *The Christian Pastor*. Philadelphia: Westminster, 1951.

225. O'Kelly, L. I., and Muckler, F. A. *Introduction to Psychopathology*, 2nd ed. Englewood Cliffs, N.J.: Prentice-Hall, Inc., 1955.

226. Oppenheimer, O. Some counseling theory: Objectivity and subjectivity. *J. counsel. Psychol.*, 1954, *1*, pp. 184–187.

227. Overstreet, H. *The Mature Mind*. New York: Norton, 1949.

228. Paterson, D. G., Gerken, C. d'A., and Hahn, M. E. Revised Minnesota Occupational Rating Scales, in Williamson, E. G. (ed.), *Minnesota Studies in Student Personnel Work, No. 2*. Minneapolis: University of Minnesota Press, 1953.

229. Patterson, C. H. Interest tests and the emotionally disturbed client. *Educ. psychol. Measmt.*, 1957, *17*, pp. 264–280.

230. Pepinsky, H. B. Application of informal projective methods in the counseling interview. *Educ. psychol. Measmt.*, 1947, *7*, pp. 135–140.

231. Pepinsky, H. B. The selection and use of diagnostic categories in clinical counseling. *Appl. Psychol. Monogr.*, 1948, No. 15.

232. Pepinsky, H. B., and Pepinsky, Pauline N. *Counseling Theory and Practice*. New York: Ronald, 1954.

233. Perls, Laura P., Goodman, P., and Hefferline, H. *Gestalt Therapy—Excitement and Growth in Human Personality*. New York: Julian, 1951.

234. Phillips, E. L. Attitudes toward self and others; a brief questionnaire report. *J. consult. Psychol.*, 1951, *15*, pp. 79–81.

235. Phillips, E. L. *Psychotherapy; a Modern Theory and Practice.* Englewood Cliffs, N.J.: Prentice-Hall, Inc., 1956.

236. Phillips, E. L., and Agnew, J. W., Jr. A study of Rogers' "reflection" hypothesis. *J. clin. Psychol.*, 1953, *9*, pp. 281–284.

237. Porter, E. H., Jr. *An Introduction to Therapeutic Counseling.* Boston: Houghton, 1950.

238. Porter, E. H., Jr. Understanding Diagnostically and Understanding Therapeutically, in Williamson, E. G. (ed.), *Trends in Student Personnel Work.* Minneapolis: University of Minnesota Press, 1949, pp. 113–119.

239. Postman, L., Bruner, J. S., and McGinnies, E. Personal values as selective factors in perception. *J. abnorm. soc. Psychol.*, 1948, *43*, pp. 142–154.

240. Powdermaker, Florence, and Frank, J. *Group Psychotherapy.* Cambridge: Harvard University Press, 1953.

241. Reid, Dorothy K., and Snyder, W. U. Experiment on "recognition of feeling" in non-directive psychotherapy. *J. clin. Psychol.*, 1947, *3*, pp. 128–135.

242. Remmers, H. H., Drucker, A. J., and Shimberg, B. *SRA Youth Inventory.* Chicago: Science Research Associates, 1948.

243. Reusch, J., and Prestwood, A. R. Anxiety. *Arch. Neural Psychiat.*, 1949, *62*, pp. 1–24.

244. Ribble, M. *The Personality of the Young Child.* New York: Columbia University Press, 1955.

245. Richardson, H., and Borow, H. Evaluation of a technique of group orientation for vocational counseling. *Educ. psychol. Measmt.*, 1952, *12*, pp. 587–597.

246. Robinson, F. P. *Principles and Procedures in Student Counseling.* New York: Harper, 1950.

247. Roe, Anna. *The Psychology of Occupations.* New York: Wiley, 1956.

248. Rogers, C. R. *Becoming a Person.* Oberlin College, Ohio: Board of Trustees, Oberlin College, 1954.

249. Rogers, C. R. *Client-Centered Therapy.* Boston: Houghton, 1951.

250. Rogers, C. R. *Counseling and Psychotherapy.* Boston: Houghton, 1942.

251. Rogers, C. R. *Counseling with Returned Service Men.* New York: McGraw, 1946.

252. Rogers, C. R. The fully functioning personality. Unpublished paper.

253. Rogers, C. R. A personal view of some issues facing psychologists. *Amer. Psychologist,* 1955, *10*, pp. 247–249.

254. Rogers, C. R. Persons or science? A philosophical question. *Amer. Psychologist,* 1955, *10*, pp. 267–278.

255. Rogers, C. R. A process conception of psychotherapy. *Amer. Psychologist,* 1958, *13*, pp. 142–149.

256. Rogers, C. R. Some Directions and End Points in Therapy, in Mowrer, O. H. (ed.), *Psychotherapy: Theory and Research.* New York: Ronald, 1953.

257. Rogers, C. R. A therapist's view of the good life. *The Humanist,* 1957, *5*, pp. 291–300, American Humanist Association, Yellow Springs, Ohio.

258. Rogers, C. R., and Diamond, Rosalind F. *Psychotherapy and Personality Change.* Chicago: University of Chicago Press, 1954.

259. Rosensweig, S. An Outline of Frustration Theory, Chapter 11, in Hunt, J. McV. (ed.), *Personality and the Behavior Disorders*. New York: Ronald, 1944.

260. Rotter, J. B. *Social Learning and Clinical Psychology*. Englewood Cliffs, N.J.: Prentice-Hall, Inc., 1954.

261. Ruch, F. L. *Psychology and Life*. Chicago: Scott, Foresman & Co., 1948.

262. Rusalem, H. New insights on the role of occupational information in counseling. *J. counsel. Psychol.*, 1954, *1*, pp. 84–88.

263. Sargent, P. *The Handbook of Private Schools*, 35th ed. Boston: Porter Sargent, 1954.

264. Sargent, P. *Junior Colleges and Specialized Schools and Colleges*, 2nd ed. Boston: Porter Sargent, 1955.

265. Schafer, R. *Psychoanalytic Interpretation in Rorschach Testing*. New York: Grune and Stratton, 1954.

266. Schmidt, H. O., and Fonda, C. P. The reliability of psychiatric diagnosis: a new look. *J. Abnorm. and Soc. Psychol.*, 1956, *52*, pp. 262–267.

267. Schwebel, M. Why unethical practice? *J. counsel. Psychol.*, 1955, *2*, pp. 122–127.

268. Seeman, J. A. A study of client self-selection of tests in vocational counseling. *Educ. psychol. Measmt.*, 1948, *8*, pp. 327–346.

269. Seeman, J. A., *et al*. A coordinated research in psychotherapy. *J. consult. Psychol.*, 1949, *13*, pp. 154–195.

270. Shaw, F. J. Some postulates concerning psychotherapy. *J. consult. Psychol.*, 1939, *12*, pp. 426–432.

271. Shaw, R. *Finger Painting*. Boston: Little, 1934.

272. Sheerer, Elizabeth T. An analysis of the relationship between acceptance of and respect for self and acceptance of and respect for others in ten counseling cases. *Amer. Psychologist*, 1948, *3*, pg. 285.

273. Sherman, Dorothy. An analysis of the dynamic relationships between counselor techniques and outcomes in larger units of the interview situation. Unpublished doctor's dissertation, Ohio State University, 1945.

274. Shoben, E. J. Psychotherapy as a problem in learning theory. *Psychol. Bull.*, 1949, *46*, pp. 366–392.

275. Shoben, E. J. Special review: Some recent books on counseling and adjustment. *Psychol. Bull.*, 1955, *52*, pp. 251–262.

276. Shoben, E. J. Work, love and maturity. *Personnel & Guidance J.*, 1956, *34*, pp. 326–332.

277. Shostrom, E. L., and Brammer, L. M. *The Dynamics of the Counseling Process*. New York: McGraw, 1952.

278. Shrodes, Carolina (ed.) *Psychology through Literature, an Anthology*. New York: Oxford, 1943.

279. Shuttleworth, F. K. *The physical and mental growth of Girls and Boys age six to nineteen in relation to age at maximum growth*. Washington: National Research Council, 1939.

280. Skidmore, R. A., *et al*. *Marriage Consulting*. New York: Harper, 1956.

281. Skidmore, R. A., and Garrett, Hulda. Joint interview in marriage counseling. *Marriage and Family Living*, 1955, *17*, pp. 320–324.

282. Slavson, S. R. *Analytic Group Psychotherapy with Children, Adolescents and Adults.* New York: Columbia University Press, 1950.

283. Slavson, S. R. *The Practice of Group Psychotherapy.* New York: International Universities Press, 1947.

284. Smith, H. L. The value context of psychology. *Amer. Psychologist,* 1954, *9,* pp. 532–535.

285. Snygg, D., and Combs, A. W. *Individual Behavior: A New Frame of Reference for Psychology.* New York: Harper, 1949.

286. Sorokin, P. A. *Explorations in Altruistic Love and Behavior.* Boston: Beacon, 1950.

287. Speer, G. S., and Jasper, L. The influence of occupational information on occupational goals. *Occupations,* 1949, *28,* pp. 15–17.

288. Steiner, L. R. *Where Do People Take Their Troubles?* Boston: Houghton, 1954.

289. Stone, C. H. Are vocational orientation courses worth their salt? *Educ. psychol. Measmt.,* 1948, *8,* pp. 161–181.

290. Stone, C. P. (ed.) *Annual reviews of psychology,* Vol. 1–9. Stanford, Calif.: Annual Reviews, 1950–1958.

291. Strang, Ruth. *Child Study.* New York: Macmillan, 1954.

292. Strong, E. K. *Vocational Interests Eighteen Years After College.* Minneapolis: University of Minnesota Press, 1955.

293. Strong, E. K. *Vocational Interests of Men and Women.* Stanford: Stanford University Press, 1943.

294. Sullivan, H. S. *The Interpersonal Theory of Psychiatry.* New York: Norton, 1953.

295. Sullivan, H. S. *The Psychiatric Interview.* New York: Norton, 1954.

296. Super, D. E. *Appraising Vocational Fitness.* New York: Harper, 1949.

297. Super, D. E. Career patterns as a basis for vocational counseling. *J. counsel. Psychol.,* 1954, *1,* pp. 12–19.

298. Super, D. E. Transition from vocational guidance to counseling psychology. *J. counsel. Psychol.,* 1955, *2,* pp. 3–9.

299. Super, D. E. Vocational adjustment: Implementing a self concept. *Occupations,* 1951, *30,* pp. 88–92.

300. Symonds, P. M. *Dynamics of Psychotherapy,* Vol. I. New York: Grune and Stratton, 1956.

301. Symonds, P. M. *Dynamics of Psychotherapy,* Vol. II. New York: Grune and Stratton, 1957.

302. Terman, L. M. *Psychological Factors in Marital Happiness.* New York: McGraw, 1938.

303. Thorne, F. C. Principles of Personality Counseling. *J. of clin. Psychol.,* 1950, pp. 301–302.

304. Thorne, F. C. Principles of psychological examining. *J. of clin. Psychol.,* 1955, pg. 87.

305. Tindall, R. H., and Robinson, F. P. The use of silence as a technique in counseling. *J. clin. Psychol.,* 1947, *3,* pp. 136–141.

306. Tyler, Leona E. *The Work of the Counselor.* New York: Appleton-Century-Crofts, Inc., 1953.

307. U. S. Department of Health, Education, and Welfare. *Annual Report.* Washington, D.C.: U. S. Government Printing Office, 1957.

308. U. S. Department of Health, Education, and Welfare. *Orientation Training for Vocational Rehabilitation Counselors.* (Mimeo) Rehabilitation Service Lives #332. Washington, D.C., 1955.

309. U. S. Employment Service. *Dictionary of Occupational Titles,* 2nd ed. Washington, D.C.: U. S. Government Printing Office, 1949.

310. U. S. Government Occupational Outlook Service. *Occupational Outlook Handbook.* Washington, D.C.: U. S. Government Printing Office, 1951.

311. Vincent, C. E. (ed.) *Readings in marriage counseling.* New York: Crowell, 1957.

312. Warner, W. L., Meeker, Marchia, and Ells, K. *Social Class in America.* Chicago: Science Research Associates, 1949.

313. Watson, R. I. *The Clinical Method in Psychology.* New York: Harper, 1951.

314. Watson, R. I. *Psychology as a Profession.* New York: Random House, Inc., 1954.

315. White, R. W. *The Abnormal Personality.* New York: Ronald, 1948.

316. White, R. W. *The Abnormal Personality,* 2nd ed. New York: Ronald, 1956.

317. White, V. *God and the Unconscious.* Chicago: Henry Regnery, 1953.

318. Wickes, F. *The Inner World of Childhood.* New York: Appleton-Century-Crofts, Inc., 1927.

319. Williamson, E. G. Counseling and the Minnesota point of view. *Educ. psychol. Measmt.,* 1947, *7,* pp. 141–156.

320. Williamson, E. G. *How to Counsel Students.* New York: McGraw, 1939.

321. Winder, L. Group Psychotherapy, in Moreno, J. L. (ed.), *Group Psychotherapy—A Symposium.* New York: Beacon, 1945.

322. Winnicott, D. W. Hate in the countertransference. *Int. J. Psychoanal.,* 1949, *30,* pp. 69–74.

323. Wolberg, L. R. *The Technique of Psychotherapy.* New York: Grune and Stratton, 1954.

324. Wood, A. B. Transference in client-centered therapy and in psychoanalysis. *J. consult. Psychol.,* 1951, *15,* pp. 72–75.

325. Wrenn, C. G. Psychology, religion, and values for the counselor, Part III, in the symposium, the counselor and his religion. *Pers. and Guid. J.,* 1958, *36,* pp. 326–334.

326. Wrenn, C. G. The ethics of counseling. *Educ. psychol. Measmt.,* 1952, *12,* pp. 161–177.

327. Wrenn, C. G. *Wrenn Study Habits Inventory.* Stanford, Calif.: Stanford University Press, 1931.

328. Wulf, F. Uber die Veränderung van Vorstellangen. *Psychol. Forsch.,* 1922, *1,* pp. 333–373.

329. Zelen, S. L. Acceptance and acceptability. *J. consult. Psychol.,* 1954, *18,* pg. 316.

Index

Index